PRIMATES
Studies in Adaptation
and Variability

Contributors

C. K. Brain
Transvaal Museum,
Pretoria, South Africa

I. Eibl-Eibesfeldt
Max Planck-Institut für
Verhaltensphysiologie, Germany

John O. Ellefson
Stanford University, Calif.

John Frisch, S.J.
Sophia University, Tokyo

J. Stephen Gartlan
University of Bristol, England

David A. Hamburg
Stanford University, Calif.

Phyllis C. Jay
University of California, Berkeley

K. R. L. Hall
Formerly at University of Bristol,
England

Hans J. Kummer
Delta Regional Primate Center,
Covington, Louisiana

Jane B. Lancaster
University of California, Berkeley

Peter M. Marler
The Rockefeller University, New York

William A. Mason
Delta Regional Primate Center,
Covington, Louisiana

Jane Van Lawick-Goodall
Nairobi, Kenya

Sherwood L. Washburn
University of California, Berkeley

Kenji Yoshiba
Japan Monkey Centre, Japan

PHYLLIS C. JAY, Editor

University of California, Berkeley

PRIMATES

Studies in Adaptation

and Variability

HOLT, RINEHART AND WINSTON

New York • Chicago • San Francisco • Atlanta

Dallas • Montreal • Toronto • London

Dedication

This volume, based on a symposium of primate social behavior, is dedicated to the memory of the late K. R. L. Hall. The first part of the volume is an account of his life, his bibliography, and five of his most important papers. These serve both as a tribute to his memory and as a partial substitute for what he would have contributed to the Primate Social Behavior Conference. Yet we know that nothing could really take the place of the contributions he would have made. Many of us attended previous meetings with K. R. L. Hall and had the pleasure of his support, the advantage of his criticism, and the value of his experience. It is with a keen sense of loss that we recognize how much better this volume would have been if, rather than being a tribute, it might have drawn upon his organizational ability and scientific insight.

Phyllis C. Jay, Editor

Lita Osmundsen, *Director of Research*
David P. Boynton
C. K. Brain
Alice Davis
B. Irven DeVore
I. Eibl-Eibesfeldt
John O. Ellefson
John Frisch
J. Stephen Gartlan

David A. Hamburg
Hans J. Kummer
Jane B. Lancaster
Peter R. Marler
William A. Mason
Hugo Van Lawick
Jane Van Lawick-Goodall
Sherwood L. Washburn
Kenji Yoshiba

Preface

This book is based on the results of a symposium on primate social behavior sponsored by the Wenner-Gren Foundation for Anthropological Research and held at the European conference headquarters of the Foundation, Burg Wartenstein, Austria.

There are three major parts in this volume: first, a tribute to the late K. R. L. Hall and a reprinting of five of his most important papers; second, seven studies demonstrating the variability of primate behavior; and third, seven chapters on problems of the analysis of primate behavior. It is the central theme of this book that there is now enough information to enable us to see behavior as responsive to varying local conditions. We hope to start the analysis of major topics such as learning, communication, and aggression, and to consider the implications of field studies for anthropologists, psychologists, and zoologists.

The emphasis in this book is on field studies. Contributions represent research by individuals from many disciplines—those that traditionally include the study of animals in natural situations, and those that do not normally encompass observations or analyses of broad patterns of behavior, much less entire social systems of animals living freely. Individual field studies tend to reflect the major differences in method and attitude that characterize the orientation of the investigator's parent discipline. The traditional experimental psychologist, for example, has not considered behavior in the same way as have the anthropologist and the zoologist. Predictably, the kinds of studies undertaken vary with the disciplinary backgrounds of the investigators.

This volume demonstrates that our analysis has been enriched by the participants' various dimensions of interest and differences in focus. If social relationships are to be understood, it will be only as a result of the coordinated efforts of many different specialists. Many areas of research are involved because social behavior is multidimensional. It has a biological basis; animals act and interact as they are predisposed by factors that include anatomy and physiology. The sum of these factors is the outcome of interactional processes between evolutionary heritage and environment. In few areas of research has it become clearer than it is in primate behavior studies that properly framed questions and valid answers will require the crossing of traditional academic boundaries. It is fitting that this volume is a tribute to a man who helped make us aware of the importance of combining observation and experimentation on nonhuman primates in free-living and in more controlled conditions, as well as the implications of such work for the study of man.

Among the most exciting aspects of our study are the ways these joint efforts increase our understanding of modern man. His behavior and attitudes are the results of a long process of evolution and reflect the conditions of his past existence. Several aspects of the biological basis of our behavior and some of the pressures that produced modern man are explored in the following chapters. The emergence of human language and the phenomenon of aggression are only two of many possible topics that are important in understanding why we behave as we do.

Man has long had difficulty in seeing his own nature; as the pages of anthropology testify, he has been slow to discard ideas that have shaped his notions of himself as special and somehow different from other primates. Although a portion of this image (particularly his aggressive capabilities) may be unattractive to those who desire a more peaceful world, only by recognizing this can we ever hope to cope realistically with the serious problems in adjustment posed by modern living. We may never be able to understand certain aspects of human behavior without comparative information on how nonhuman primates behave.

Several of the following chapters demonstrate the effective use of information on monkey and ape behavior to increase understanding of our own behavior and of its evolution to present form. If all nonhuman primates behaved the same way it would be a hopeless task to try to reconstruct ancestral conditions. Differences, subtle and gross, among living primates are crucial for the reconstruction of the evolution of man's behavior, and of how he came to be what he is. The further investigation and elucidation of these differences emerged from our conference as a clear and important goal.

Many of the results of the conference on which this volume was based will become apparent only in the coming years. Hours of informal discussion during the symposium stimulated new projects and new ideas. What appears in this book is but a small measure of them. Complex questions concerning populations of fossils, predation, diet, and behavior were discussed and many of us left the conference with decades of research ahead of us. Hopefully, this clarification of controversial issues will result in the resolution of these problems with an ensuing increase in our collection of knowledge.

We have selected for reprinting five of Hall's outstanding and most representative papers, and these appear as Part I of this volume. "Social Organization of the Old-World Monkeys and Apes" (Chapter 1) was chosen because it is Hall's last major statement on the interpretation of the behavior of monkeys and apes. "Behavior and Ecology of the Wild Patas Monkey in Uganda" (Chapter 2) is included because ecology was one of Hall's major interests, and his were the first of the studies on free-ranging primates to stress the great importance of ecology in the interpretation of behavior. "Experiment and Quantification in the Study of Baboon Behavior in its Natural Habitat" (Chapter 3) represents another of Hall's major interests, the working interrelationship between laboratory and field research. He used these two kinds of knowledge, so frequently regarded as conflicting, to supplement each other. His field research carried on the ethological tradition of his earlier work on birds. In "Tool-Using Performances as Indicators of Behavioral Adaptability" (Chapter 4) Hall brought new pespective to an old problem. In "Aggression in Monkey and Ape Societies" (Chapter 5) he was concerned with the application to human problems of the understanding gained from field studies of monkeys and apes. These five articles represent major trends in Hall's thinking; they stand as a monument to what he accomplished.

The following people attended the symposium at Burg Wartenstein: David P. Boynton, C. K. Brain, Alice Davis, B. Irven DeVore, I. Eibl-Eibesfeldt, John O. Ellefson, John Frisch, J. Stephen Gartlan, David A. Hamburg, Phyllis C. Jay, Hans J. Kummer, Jane B. Lancaster, Hugo Van Lawick, Jane Van Lawick-Goodall, Peter R. Marler, William A. Mason, Sherwood L. Washburn, and Kenji Yoshiba.

Participants in the symposium wrote preliminary chapters before the meeting, but these have been so modified as a result of our discussions at Burg Wartenstein that the present versions are essentially new. Chapters 12, 18, and 19 are completely new; other contributions have been substantially altered; and several chapters have developed as joint efforts between two participants.

At the conference, papers were presented in a somewhat different order from the order in which they now appear. As discussions progressed and as much revised versions developed, an order became apparent making clear the direction of future research. The great loss in the death of Hall has implications for future primate studies; his own potential contributions will never be made, but we hope this volume will call attention to the significance of his work for further research. Then we note that many new species have been reported upon since the earlier *Primate Behavior* volume was published in 1965. But it is also clear that many more detailed and extended field studies are needed.

In February 1966 a small group of those who had been in Austria the previous summer met and discussed the manuscripts and the ultimate form of this volume. Present at this working meeting were David P. Boynton, Anne Brower, Alice Davis, John O. Ellefson, David A. Hamburg, Hans J. Kummer, Phyllis C. Jay, Jane B. Lancaster, and Sherwood L. Washburn.

This volume is in no sense a complete survey of fieldwork on the non-human primates—such a survey would not be possible in one book—nor is it a complete perspectus for future research. Much excellent data closely related to topics dealt with here are not presented, and there are excellent studies of species other than those discussed in detail here. Although the field is small, there are many more researchers whom I, as organizer, would like to have invited to participate in this effort.

All of the participants wish to thank the Wenner-Gren Foundation for Anthropological Research for making this symposium possible and for graciously hosting us at the European headquarters. I would like to thank Lita Osmundsen for her encouragement and assistance. I wish to thank Stephen Gartlan for his statement on Hall's life.

Without the participants this volume would not exist, and I want to thank all those who contributed for their time and effort. The discussions at the symposium are not reported as such here, but where relevant they have been incorporated in the various chapters. It would be impossible to cite the origin of many ideas included in these pages since all the participants shared their knowledge so liberally.

There are several people to whom I offer special gratitude. Sherwood L. Washburn provided constant support and encouragement; without his contributions, his unique insights into primate behavior, and his broad understanding of primate evolution and its biological base this volume could not have taken its present form. Alice Davis, *rapporteur* at the symposium, assisted in countless ways to make this volume a reality. Anne Brower, a veteran editor of primate behavior manuscripts, helped to make this a more unified and readable volume than it would otherwise have been, and considerably lightened my editorial task.

Irven DeVore was present at the symposium and contributed to our discussions. No volume could ever be produced without the suggestions and help of people who generously read and commented upon manuscripts; to Jane B. Lancaster, Lewis L. Klein, Judith Shirek-Ellefson, Thomas T. Shruhsaker, and Carol Carson, and to Barbara MacRoberts, who assisted with the bibliographies, I express my thanks.

P. C. J.

BERKELEY, CALIFORNIA
FEBRUARY 1968

Contents

PRIMATES
Studies in Adaptation
and Variability

K. R. L. Hall. (*Photograph by Stephen Peet*)

PART ONE

K. R. L. HALL
A Memoir

Stephen Gartlan

Ronald Hall was not a conventional academic. His boundless enthusiasm, physical energy, and strong personality were traits associated more usually with the great naturalist-explorers of the nineteenth century than with contemporary scientists. Hall was physically and temperamentally suited for the particular demands of primate field studies; during his undergraduate days at Oxford he played many sports and excelled in several, at one time representing the University in boxing. He retained his physical fitness and preferred to carry out his fieldwork on foot rather than by vehicle. His was a very characteristic figure, stocky and muscular, marching across the open country in khaki shorts and shirt and a battered felt hat, accompanied by his African ranger. Hall believed that fieldwork should begin at dawn and continue as long as there was sufficient light to make observation possible. Africa was a challenge he enjoyed, and his fascination with the country and outdoor life never waned. As a child he had an early exposure to the continent when his father was Acting Governor and Commander in Chief of Nyasaland.

He was educated in England at Cheltenham College, and then went on to Oxford University to read law. His interests at that time paralleled his later interests in lan-

1

guage, communication, and logic, and foreshadowed the development of his characteristically lucid prose style, and possibly his long-standing interest in experimental method.

Hall's university career was interrupted by the outbreak of World War II. Having obtained his degree in law, he left the University for the Army, and began his military service as a captain in the Royal Artillery. During the war he served in both the Middle East and Germany. In 1941, he married Pauline Assinder, a psychologist he had met at Oxford. After the end of the war he returned to Oxford to carry out research, but his main interest then was psychology rather than law. His research topic was the relationship between words and perception, and his first published work (1950) was on perceiving and naming a series of figures. He was awarded the degree of Doctor of Philosophy, the first to be given by Oxford for a research thesis in psychology. In the same year, 1949, he was appointed as head of the Department of Experimental and Clinical Psychology in Bristol Mental Hospitals. This was a post that carried with it a part-time lectureship in the Department of Psychology at Bristol University.

His interests at this time, reflected in the list of his published work, were mainly concerned with the problems of intellectual deterioration and the question of cutaneous pain. He came to be more and more involved throughout this period with the role of the experimental method in clinical psychology, a role that he considered vital, but often applied inadequately within the field.

In 1955, on being appointed to the Chair of Psychology at the University of Cape Town, he returned to Africa. The main research interests of his Bristol days were continued, and he began to extend the range of his interests. He gave a series of talks on social influences on human behavior which were broadcast over the South African radio service. His interest in ornithology, which had been strongly influenced by the Oxford ethologist Niko Tinbergen, began to be reflected in a series of papers on bird behavior. He was especially interested in plovers. His own expanding interests and conversations with other people (especially Professor Monica Wilson of the Department of Anthropology of the University of Cape Town), convinced him of the importance of studying the social behavior of the baboons in South Africa. The first papers resulting from this work appeared in 1960, and in the subsequent five years he attained a world reputation for careful and systematic studies of baboons and patas monkeys.

In 1959 he returned to Bristol to take the Chair of Psychology at the University, a post that carried with it a great deal of administrative responsibility. He was one of the few persons appointed to such a chair, who was able to succeed in maintaining an efficient administration and simultaneously continuing his research and actually increasing its volume. At Bristol he established a program of research on the terrestrial monkey species of Africa —a program that included studies of baboons, patas monkeys, gelada baboons, and vervet monkeys. He was also interested in the arboreal blue monkeys.

I knew him during the last three years of his life, and we spent part of this time together in the field. We spent a month together on an isolated and uninhabited island, a situation that necessitates a close relationship, engendering strong emotional reactions. Ronald Hall's personality was such that after this period of isolation my respect and admiration for him were only increased. Although a man of strong personal opinions, he rarely talked about himself. He had a fine critical mind and never generalized his dislike of an opinion to the person putting forward the point of view. He was a very humane and approachable person, one who had the air of being pleasantly surprised at his success; he was scrupulously fair and extremely loyal. His courage is well illustrated by an incident that occurred in South Africa when a colleague was being attacked and gored by a normally harmless wildebeest. Hall jumped down from the tree in which he had taken refuge, slipped off his jacket, and approached the angry animal; slipping one arm of the jacket over each of the animal's horns, he very effectively blinded it. Thus distracted, the animal dashed off into the bush taking Hall's jacket with it. The victim was rushed to the hospital, and did survive the attack.

His fieldwork was careful and detailed. He drew upon anthropology, ethology, and ecology, and used a conceptual framework and techniques derived from psychology. His special contribution to the study of primate behavior was in using fieldwork as a source of hypotheses that were then tested in the laboratory; in this way very complete pictures of the social organization and behavior of species were built up. For example, in the Bristol laboratory he had set up groups of captive patas monkeys for longitudinal studies of social changes.

Ronald Hall died on July 14th, 1965. The world has lost a great scientist; those who knew him have lost a great friend.

K. R. L. Hall Bibliography

Hall, K. R. L., 1950, "Perceiving and Naming a Series of Figures," *Quart. J. Exp. Psychol.*, 2:153–162.

———, 1950, "The Effect of Names and Titles upon the Serial Reproduction of Pictorial and Verbal Material," *Brit. J. Psychol.*, 41:109–121.

———, and R. C. Oldfield, 1950, "An Experimental Study on the Fitness of Signs to Words," *Quart. J. Exp. Psychol.*, 2:60–70.

———, 1951, "The Fitness of Signs to Words," *Brit. J. Psychol.*, 42:21–33.

———, 1951, "The Testing of Abstraction, with Special Reference to Impairment in Schizophrenia," *Brit. J. Med. Psychol.*, 24:118–131.

———, and T. G. Crookes, 1951, "Studies in Learning Impairment I: Schizophrenic and Organic Patients," *J. Ment. Sci.*, 97:725–737.

———, 1952, "Conceptual Impairment in Depressive and Organic Patients of the Pre-senile Age Group," *J. Ment. Sci.*, 98:256–264.

———, 1952, "Experimental Method in Clinical Psychology," *Brit. J. Med. Psychol.*, 25:26–30.

———, 1952, "The Experimental Study of Pain and Fatigue Tolerance in Mental Patients," *Quart. Bull. Brit. Psychol. Sociol.*, 3:36.

———, and T. G. Crookes, 1952, "Studies in Learning Impairment II: Psychoneurotic Patients," *J. Ment. Sci.*, 98:273–279.

———, A. E. Earle, and T. G. Crookes, 1952, "A Pendulum Phenomenon in the Visual Perception of Apparent Movement," *Quart. J. Exp. Psychol.*, 4:109–120.

———, 1953, "Studies of Cutaneous Pain: A Survey of Research since 1940," *Brit. J. Psychol.*, 44:279–294.

———, and A. E. Earle, 1954, "A Further Study of the Pendulum Phenomenon," *Quart. J. Exp. Psychol.*, 6:112–124.

———, and E. Stride, 1954, "Some Factors Affecting Reaction Times to Auditory Stimuli in Mental Patients," *J. Ment. Sci.*, 100:462–477.

———, and ———, 1954, "The Varying Response to Pain in Psychiatric Disorders: A Study in Abnormal Psychology," *Brit. J. Med. Psychol.*, 27:48–60.

———, 1955, "Relation of Skin Temperature to Pain Threshold," *Quart. J. Exp. Psychol.*, 7:74–81.

———, 1956, "The Study of Mind in Relation to Brain Function," *University of Cape Town Lecture Series* 8. Cape Town, South Africa: Oxford.

————, 1957, "Conditioning and Learning Techniques," *Experimental Abnormal Psychology,* J. Zubin, ed. New York: Wiley.

————, 1957, "Pain and Suffering," *S. African Med. J.,* 31:1227–1231.

————, 1957, "Pavlov's Contribution to Psychological Medicine," *Med. Proc.,* 3:629–636.

————, 1958, "Conceptual Thinking and Its Impairment through Injury or Operation," *Proc. S. African Psych. Assoc.,* 7–8:8–9.

————, 1958, "Observations on the Nesting Sites and Nesting Behaviour of the Kittlitz's Sandplover *Charadrius pecuarius,*" *Ostrich,* 29:113–125.

————, 1958, "Perception of Heat-stimulation as Painful in the Absence of Heat Sensitivity," *S. African J. Sci.,* 54:327–333.

————, 1958, "Record of Black-winged Praticole *Glareola nordmanni* near Cape Town," *Ostrich,* 29:91.

————, 1958, "Social Influences on Human Behaviour," *S. African Broadcasting Corp. Public.* P57/10E.

————, 1958, "Spatial Summation for Heat-pain," *Nature,* 182:307–309.

————, 1959, "A Study of the Blacksmith Plover *Hoplopterus armatus* in the Cape Town Area: I. Distribution and Breeding Data," *Ostrich,* 30:117–126.

————, 1959, "Nest Records and Additional Behaviour for Kittlitz's Sandplover *Charadrius pecuarius,* in the S. W. Cape Province," *Ostrich,* 30:33–38.

————, 1959, "Observations on the Nest-sites and Nesting Behaviour of the Black Oystercatcher *Haematopus moquini* in the Cape Peninsula," Ostrich, 30:143–154.

————, 1960, "Egg-covering by the White-fronted Sandplover *Charadrius marginatus,*" *Ibis,* 102:545–553.

————, 1960, "Pavlov, Ivan P.," *Encyclopedia Britannica.*

————, 1960, "Social Vigilance Behaviour in the Chacma Baboon, *Papio ursinus,*" *Behaviour,* 16:261–294.

————, 1960, "The Social Behaviour of Wild Baboons," *New Scientist,* 7:601–603.

————, 1961, "Feeding Habits of the Chacma Baboon," *Adv. Sci.,* 17:559–567.

————, 1962, "Behaviour of Monkeys Towards Mirror-images," *Nature,* 196:1258–1261.

————, 1962, "Numerical Data, Maintenance Activities, and Locomotion of the Wild Chacma Baboon, *Papio ursinus,*" *Proc. Zool. Soc. London,* 139:181–220.

————, 1962, "The Sexual, Agonistic and Derived Social Behaviour Patterns of the Wild Chacma Baboon, *Papio ursinus,*" *Proc. Zool. Soc. Lond.,* 139:283–327.

————, 1963, "Observational Learning in Monkeys and Apes," *Brit. J. Psychol.,* 54:201–226.

————, 1963, "Some Problems in the Analysis and Comparison of Monkey and Ape Behavior," *Classification and Human Evolution,* S. L. Washburn, ed. New York: Wenner-Gren Foundation, pp. 273–300.

————, 1963, "Tool-using Performances as Indicators of Behavioral Adaptability," *Current Anthrop.,* 4:479–494.

————, 1963, "Variations in the Ecology of the Chacma Baboon, *Papio ursinus,*" *Symp. Zool. Soc. London* 10:1–28.

————, 1964, "Aggression in Monkey and Ape Societies," *The Natural History of Aggression,* J. D. Carthy and J. F. Ebling, eds. New York: Academic Press, pp. 51–64.

————, 1964, "A Study of the Blacksmith Plover *Hoplopterus armatus* in the Cape Town Area:II. Behaviour," *Ostrich,* 35:3–16.

————, and M. J. Goswell, 1964, "Aspects of Social Learning in Captive Patas Monkeys," *Primates* 5:59–70.

————, and G. B. Schaller, 1964, "Tool-using Behavior of the California Sea-otter," *J. Mammal.,* 45:287–298.

————, 1965, "Behaviour and Ecology of the Wild Patas Monkey, *Erythrocebus patas,* in Uganda," *J. Zoology,* 148:15–87.

————, 1965, "Breeding Record for the Pratincole, *Glareola pratincola,* in Uganda," *Ostrich,* 36:107.

————, 1965, "Ecology and Behavior of Baboons, Patas and Vervet Monkeys in Uganda," *The Baboon in Medical Research,* H. Vagtborg, ed. San Antonio: University of Texas Press, pp. 43–61.

————, 1965, "Experiment and Quantification in the Study of Baboon Behavior in its Natural Habitat," *The Baboon in Medical Research,* H. Vagtborg, ed. San Antonio: University of Texas Press, pp. 29–42.

————, 1965, "Nest Records and Behaviour Notes for Three Species of Plover in Uganda," *Ostrich,* 36:107.

————, 1965, "Review of G. B. Schaller *The Mountain Gorilla,*" *Current Anthrop.,* 6:298.

————, 1965, "Social Organisation of the Old World Monkeys and Apes," *Symp. Zool. Soc. London* 14:265–289.

————, 1965, "Tool-using Behaviour of the Californian Sea-otter," *Med. Biol. Illustr.,* 15(4):216:217.

————, R. C. Boelkins, and M. J. Goswell, 1965, "Behaviour of Patas, *Erythrocebus patas,* in Captivity, with Notes on the Natural Habitat," *Folia Primat.,* 3:22–49.

————, and I. DeVore, 1965, "Baboon Social Behavior," *Primate Behavior: Field Studies of Monkeys and Apes,* I. DeVore, ed. New York: Holt, Rinehart and Winston, Inc., pp. 53–110.

————, and J. S. Gartlan, 1965, "Ecology and Behaviour of the Vervet Monkey, *Cercopithecus aethiops,* Lolui Island, Lake Victoria," *Proc. Zool. Soc. London.* 145:37–56.

————, and B. Mayer, 1966, "Hand Preferences and Dexterities of Captive Patas Monkeys," *Folia Primat.,* 4(3):169–185.

————, and ————, 1967, Social Interactions in a Group of Captive Patas Monkeys (*Erythrocebus patas*)," *Folia Primat.,* 5:213–236.

————, (in press) "Social Interactions of the Adult Male and Adult Females of a Patas Monkey Group," *Social Communication in Primates,* S. A. Altmann, ed. Chicago: University of Chicago Press.

DeVore, I, and K. R. L. Hall, 1965, "Baboon Ecology," *Primate Behavior: Field Studies of Monkeys and Apes,* I. DeVore, ed. New York: Holt, Rinehart and Winston, Inc., pp. 20–52.

Hemphill, R. E., K. R. L. Hall, and T. G. Crookes, 1952, "A Preliminary Report on Fatigue and Pain Tolerance in Depressive and Psychoneurotic Patients," *J. Ment. Sci.,* 98:433–440.

1

SOCIAL ORGANIZATION

OF THE OLD-WORLD

MONKEYS AND APES*

K. R. L. Hall

INTRODUCTION

Periodically, in the short history of naturalistic observational study of the old-world monkeys and apes review articles and books have summarized the evidence and attempted certain generalizations from it. When Yerkes and Yerkes (1929) reviewed the literature on the great apes, not a single field study, either of apes or monkeys or Prosimiae had, in the modern definition of such a study, been carried out. The same was true when Zuckerman's (1932, 1933) remarkable syntheses of physiological and behavioural data appeared. These, even to this date, have not been superseded by any comparable standard works, and contain in their pages many object lessons in critical thinking and method. The classic studies of Köhler (1925) and Yerkes (1943) on the chimpanzee in captivity were known mainly for the demonstrations of "intelligence" displayed by these animals, and even the most commonly used of laboratory monkeys, the rhesus macaque, has only recently been comprehensively studied in its natural setting as a group-living animal. It was primarily through the inspiration of Yerkes that the first field studies of the anthropoid apes (Nissen 1931; Bingham 1932; Carpenter 1940) were set going, although these, as viewed against recent, much longer,

*Reprinted with permission from the *Symposium of the Zoological Society of London*, 1965, 14:265–289.

TABLE 1–1   MAJOR FIELD STUDIES OF ECOLOGY AND BEHAVIOUR OF MONKEYS AND APES (DURATION OF THREE MONTHS OR MORE)

Scientific Name	Common Name	Investigator	Location	Years of Study	Duration of Study
			AFRICA		
Papio cynocephalus	Olive	De Vore	Kenya	1959–1960; 1963	10 months; continuing
		Altmann	Kenya	1963–1964	12 months
hamadrayas	Chacma	Hall	Southern Africa	1958–1961	12 months
	Sacred	Kummer	Ethiopia	1963–1964	12 months; continuing
Cercopithecus ascanius	Redtail	Haddow and others	Uganda	1940–1950	10 years; intermittent
aethiops	Vervet,	Gartlan	Uganda	1963–1964	18 months
	grivet	Struhsacker	Kenya	1963–1964	18 months
Colobus abyssinicus	Black and white	Ullrich	Kenya	1955–1957	? 6 months
Erythrocebus patas	Red hussar	Hall	Uganda	1963–1964	7 months; continuing
Gorilla gorilla	Mountain gorilla	Schaller	Congo	1959–1960	13 months
Pan troglodytes	Chimpanzee	Goodall	Tanganyika	1960–1964	28 months; continuing
		Reynolds	Uganda	1962	9 months
		Kortlandt	Congo	1960–1963	?
			ASIA		
Macaca fuscata	Japanese	Imanishi, Itani and others	Japan	1950–1964	14 years; continuing
mulatta	Rhesus	Southwick	N. India	1959–1962	12 months
		Carpenter, Altmann, Koford and others	Puerto Rico (island colony)		25 years, with some long interruptions; continuing
radiata	Bonnet	Simonds	S. India	1961–1962	6 months
Presbytis entellus	Common langur	Jay	N. India	1958–1960	18 months; continuing
	Ceylon langur	Ripley	Ceylon	1962–1963	10 months
Hylobates lar	Gibbon	Carpenter	N.W. Thailand	1937	3 months

Notes: (1) Duration of study: where a period of fieldwork has been completed, as for DeVore, "10 months; continuing" means that further periods of study of the same species are in progress or planned for the near future.

(2) The list, adapted partly from DeVore and Lee (1963), is as known to the author up to the end of 1963, and includes no studies which had not, to his knowledge, been started by then.

studies can be classed as only pilot studies. Under the same inspiration, Carpenter's other field studies of South American species were initiated and what might have been a gathering impetus for such work was interrupted by the Second World War. Carpenter's (1942*b*, 1942*c*, 1945, 1952, 1954, 1958*a*) various reviews had, of necessity, to confine themselves to a very small sample of evidence, mostly from his own work. Recent reviews (Imanishi 1960; Bourlière 1961; Altmann 1962*b*; Southwick 1962) have concentrated on particular aspects of non-human primate social organization. From 1958, more major field studies have been completed than in the whole of the preceding period, and several are now in progress or planned for continuation (Table 1–1).

SURVEY OF FIELD STUDIES

In attempting to do justice to the wealth of material now available, it has been decided to confine the present review to work on the monkeys and apes of the old world. Much important work is becoming available on the Prosimiae (Petter, 1962*a*, 1962*b*), while major studies of South American species, other than those of Carpenter (1934, 1953, 1962), Collias and Southwick (1952) and Altmann (1959), on the howler monkeys and a short study by Carpenter (1935) of the red spider monkey, are still not available for review. It seemed, therefore, appropriate to leave review of these two important classes of non-human primates until a later occasion.

The studies listed in Table 1–1 are only those arbitrarily defined as "major," in that at least three months were spent, continuously or intermittently, by one or more observers in working on the same species. This is not to discount the value of other shorter studies, or studies of more than one species in the same period of field work, such as those of Bolwig (1959) and Booth (1957). The "major" studies vary enormously in their objective and in their comprehensiveness. Of the many publications from the Japanese Monkey Centre, only a few are available in English translation (for example, Miyadi 1959; Imanishi 1957; Kawamura 1959), with two general reviews of the work by Frisch (1959) and Simonds (1962). Because of the "provisioning" technique used, it has not always been possible to evaluate the comparability of the data with that obtainable on unprovisioned groups. Nevertheless, this body of work is, to date, the most comprehensive that has been carried out on any single species. The studies of the Cayo Santiago rhesus colony begun by Carpenter (1942*a*) are also outstanding because they represent a continuing research programme, even though in an "artificial" natural situation, and because, for the first time (Altmann 1962*a*), exact techniques of social interaction analysis have been applied to free-ranging groups, and year-by-year data on the sexual reproductive cycle (Koford

1963a, 1965) of groups has been analysed. What is, perhaps, of even greater significance and urgency is that these data can now be compared with field studies of the same species in the natural habitat (Southwick *et al.* 1961, 1965).

Studies of the baboon genus are to be distinguished; firstly because studies of two races of the same species (*Papio cynocephalus*) were carried out independently in widely different habitat regions, and subsequently analysed and directly compared by the investigators (DeVore and Hall 1965, Hall and DeVore 1965); secondly because the preliminary report by Kummer and Kurt (1963) on *P. hamadryas* reveals a remarkable difference in the social organization typical of the two species.

Studies of the anthropoid apes are inevitably of a special fascination. Schaller's (1963, 1965) work on the mountain gorilla is likely to remain a classic for many years to come, not only for the intrinsic interest of his data on an animal whose habitat in that region may be threatened, but because he successfully adapted his techniques of field observation to enable him to get within very close range of an animal reputedly "dangerous" and living in a very difficult terrain. Goodall's (1962, 1963, 1965) work on a chimpanzee population in a savannah habitat is a remarkable achievement. Not only has she already spent a longer period of field observation than has ever before been concentrated on a single species of monkey or ape by one observer under fully natural conditions, but she has, by an admirable combination of persistence, enterprise and careful observation, achieved a record of data of tremendous significance for comparative animal ecology and behaviour, and for students of human evolution.

Selection of these field studies for special comment in no way minimizes the achievement of other notable field researches, such as those of Jay (1963, 1965) on the common Indian langur, and Gartlan (1965)* on an island population of vervet monkeys. Each species offers its own especial observational problems. Each study location has its special difficulties and advantages. All such studies require of the field worker an unusual combination of intellectual and temperamental characteristics, which will enable him or her to persevere, often in harsh climatic conditions, in recording observations day after day, often for ten or twelve hours a day, with few, if any, social or scientific amenities.

While the record of achievement from these studies is outstanding scientifically and personally, it can readily be seen that this is only the important beginning. The "easier," more widely distributed, and primarily terrestrial species, are those which inevitably have so far received greatest attention. The supposedly more difficult arboreal species have scarcely been sampled. The more localized forest dwellers, such as the mandrill and drill, have

---

*As with other studies cited when this review was written, some of the material is now in press.

never been studied, nor has the gorilla in its lowland forest habitat, and it will be necessary to reconnoitre the habitats of such species prior to launching full-scale field work, in order to find suitable study areas. Whole genera, such as the mangabeys, are unstudied, and even the commonest monkeys such as the baboons and vervets, require a much wider range of sampling, for comparative purposes, than has yet been achieved. Further, continuing research programmes on one species, comparable to those undertaken at the field research centres in Japan and Puerto Rico, need to be initiated before the presently available opportunities are too greatly attenuated (Bourlière, 1962).

The combination of field with laboratory or zoo group study and with field experiments on behaviour has been all too rarely attempted. The species on which social behaviour has or is being studied under both types of condition (Table 1–2) are seven in all. The list is not exhaustive, including only

TABLE 1–2   SPECIES ON WHICH MAJOR FIELD AND CAPTIVITY STUDIES RELATING TO GROUP BEHAVIOUR AND ORGANIZATION ARE AVAILABLE OR ARE IN PROGRESS

Species	Field Investigators	Free Ranging (transported colony)	Captivity Investigators
Pan troglodytes	NISSEN; Goodall; Kortlandt; Reynolds		Yerkes, NISSEN and others; Köhler
Gorilla gorilla	Bingham; Schaller		Yerkes and others
Papio hamadryas	KUMMER and Kurt		Zuckerman; KUMMER
Macaca mulatta	Southwick *et al.*	Carpenter, Altmann, Koford and others	Hinde and Rowell; Harlow; Bernstein, Mason and others; Chance; Wingfield
M. fuscata	Japanese Monkey Centre workers	Island colonies off Japanese coast (see Simonds 1962)	Japanese Monkey Centre workers
Erythrocebus patas	HALL		HALL, Goswell, Boelkins
Cercopithecus aethiops	Gartlan; Struhsacker		Brain; C. Booth

Notes: (1) Many experimental and observational studies are not included under the "Captivity" column because they have not been primarily concerned with group behaviour.

(2) Others, such as those of Andrew (1962–1964) and van Hooff (1962), are not included because they deal with particular aspects of the behaviour of several different species.

(3) Names in small capitals (for example, NISSEN) indicate where the same investigator has carried out both types of study on the same species.

major undertakings. Many other short captivity observations have been reported, for example, Carpenter (1937) and Schaller (1963) on gorillas, Bolwig (1963) on the rearing of one infant patas monkey. Only Kummer (1956, 1957) has the distinction of having made a thorough ethological study of a species as well as a major field study. Captivity observations on the patas are still in progress, with the same objective as Kummer's (Hall 1962*a;* Hall, Boelkins, and Goswell 1965). The orang-utan is being thoroughly studied in excellent conditions of a semi-natural kind (Harrisson 1960, 1962, 1963), but has so far not been the subject of any studies beyond surveys (Schaller 1961) in its free-ranging wild condition.

COMPARISONS OF SOCIAL ORGANIZATION

Certain key concepts and classes of data relating to them feature in almost all surveys of the non-human primate literature. The methodological problems arising from attempts at comparative analysis between species have been reviewed elsewhere (Hall 1963*b*). The problem of terminology is still one of great difficulty. Adequate areal sampling, within a species, before inductive generalizations are attempted, is of considerable importance in these animals, because of accumulating evidence of significant regional differences in the widely distributed species. Time sampling of field data from a particular population area has only been sufficiently adequate in the Japanese macaque studies and in the Cayo Santiago rhesus studies, to provide an account of crucial long-term problems, such as seasonal variations in mating and births, population dynamics, and behaviour ontogeny within the group. Concepts directly relating to social organization, such as dominance and territorial behaviour, have to be used with critical awareness that these are, at present, only descriptive terms whose reference is very limited. When their original reference has been to a particular, limited class of social behaviour in birds or other nonprimate animals, it may be misleading to extend them to quite different types of social organization.

Social organization in the old world monkeys and apes can be viewed in many different facets, which receive a somewhat different prominence in the field studies according to the training and interests of the investigator. At one stage, it was adjudged by Zuckerman (1932) that a primary determinant of the forms of social organization of these animals might be the all-the-year-round sexuality of males and females, this creating the bonds of attraction that maintained the group in its coherent form. This group coherence is contrasted with the seasonally varying social organization of rut mammals. On the other hand, those primarily interested in the determining influences of the ecological setting in relation to which a species has achieved its physical and social adaptations, are more likely to emphasize the survival value to the group structure (for example, Washburn and De Vore 1961*a,* 1961*b*) of pronounced sexual dimorphism of the adults, the correlative aggressive primacy of the large males and the numerical discrepancy in the adult male to adult female sex ratio. Both types of emphasis may be seen to require some elaboration and qualification in terms of the studies now available. In the following sections, the abundant ecological data on feeding, day ranging, predation, etc., will be only considered *passim*. Species primarily, partly, or regionally terrestrial, such as baboons and vervets, can be regarded as omnivorous (Hall 1962; De Vore and Washburn 1963; Wingfield 1963), as also are the savannah habitat chimpanzees (Goodall 1965). The gorilla in its mountain habitat is a vegetarian (Schaller 1963), as also is the arboreal *Colobus abyssinicus* (Ullrich 1961), and the common langur (Jay 1963, 1965). Significant correlations may eventually be made between such obvious adaptations as area of distribution, variety of diet, and form of social organization, but the sampling of species is still too small for such relationships to be meaningful. We can say that the most aggressively organized species (baboons and rhesus macaques, for example) are successful in utilizing very varied habitats, obtaining their food in open and in forested country, on the ground and from trees and bushes. But the common langur and the vervet are also widely distributed, and the former has a relatively placid kind of social organization (Jay 1965), while it is still too early to classify that of the latter, pending the results of Struhsacker's and Gartlan's investigations. Chimpanzees, in Goodall's area, have a much looser form of social organization than that of the monkey groups studied, and the adult males are not always present to protect the family parties. Yet these animals utilize their habitat for food in much the same way as do the compact baboon groups. The more data accumulated, the greater the apparent diversity between the social adaptations and ecological patterning. While the physical adaptations of sheer size, and of sexual dimorphism with well developed canines in the adult males, have obvious relevance as to whether or not a species relies on threat display, aggressiveness, or concealment and dispersal in dealing with carnivorous predators, other factors seem to enter into the comparative accounts such as the general adaptability of the species, in terms of social and traditional learning, which may enable it to modify its social organization to meet its local needs.

With such points as these in mind, we can now consider some of the interrelated classes of data that bear upon the whole picture of social organization in relation to species.

Sexual Behaviour and the Annual Reproductive Cycle

The field data now available are reviewed by Lancaster and Lee (1965), while Wingfield (1963) has attempted a thorough analysis of data from zoo birth records, with some additional field observations of his own. The distinction has to be drawn between a discrete birth season, a yearly cycle with a peak of births over a limited period with a few births in any other month, and one in which there is no evidence of significant seasonal variation. There is evidence for all three types of cycle in the species we are here reviewing, although far more data are still required. For the macaque genus, the best data come from the Japanese birth records for the wild *M. fuscata* population over a period of five years. These show a discrete season for births, covering a few months, with only slight variations year by year. For *mulatta,* the best data are Koford's (1963*a,* 1965) for the Cayo Santiago population. Again, there is a discrete birth period of a few months. Field observations on the species (Southwick *et al.* 1965) support this pattern. Similar data are quoted by Wingfield (1963) from Zeuner on the *M. sylvana* colony at Gibraltar, but there is no evidence for this species in the wild.

Less certain results are available for two *Cercopithecus* species. Haddow's (1952) analysis of samples of *C. ascanius* taken in the wild indicates a discrete season, but requires confirmation from a year-round field study. Wingfield's own observations of *C. aethiops* in the wild cannot substantiate whether the data would fit the discrete or birth peak kind of pattern. Gartlan's (personal communication) field data on the same species likewise indicate a distinct peaking of births, and with none occurring in some months of the year. For patas groups in Uganda, Hall (1965*b*), from analysis of the age structure of the groups and from captive birth records, infers that there is certainly a peaking of births, but cannot yet determine whether the spread is only within a discrete season.

A similar kind of field evidence is available for the two *Papio* spp., *cynocephalus* and *hamadryas*. A birth peak is reported in the Kenya habitat of the former species (De Vore and Hall 1965), and is to be inferred from the age structure of groups in Uganda (Hall 1965*c*) and in Southern Rhodesia (Wingfield 1963). Hall's (1962*c*) data for the groups in the Cape and Zuckerman's (1932) sample collected near Grahamstown, while indicating that births occur in every month of the year, are insufficient to show whether or not there are birth peaks at particular seasons. Kummer's observations (quoted by Lancaster and Lee 1965) show a seasonal birth peak but with some births occurring at any time of year.

For the chimpanzee and mountain gorilla, the samples of births in the wild are too small to show a clear trend, though it is possible that there is a slight birth peak for the latter species (Schaller 1963). The problem of getting reliable data for these two species is accentuated by their comparatively slower birth rates, and by the small numerical size of the populations so far studied.

The annual distribution of copulations shows a close but not exact correspondence with the distribution of births in a population (Lancaster and Lee 1965). This correlation is best in evidence in the Japanese macaque data and in that for the Cayo Santiago rhesus. Seasonal differences in copulation frequency were noted for the Cape baboons by Hall (1962c) and for *hamadryas* by Kummer. In the other baboon studies, and in the common langurs (Jay 1965), copulations were observed in all months of the study periods, but no differential frequencies were recorded which might reliably indicate whether or not there were significant seasonal variations in this respect. In the ape studies, copulations were so rarely observed as to provide no clue as to seasonality or otherwise. Schaller (1963) recorded only two copulations in thirteen months for the mountain gorilla, and Goodall (1965) only twenty-three in twenty-five months, all during a three-month period, in her chimpanzee study. The difficulty of making observations may partly account for the paucity of evidence on sexual behaviour in these two species, as also for the negative evidence available for the arboreal *C. ascanius* (Haddow 1952), and for forest-living langurs (Jay 1965).

By comparison with similar evidence on nonprimate mammals, typical species or population differences in the annual reproductive cycle as manifested by birth occurrences and mating frequencies, may be related to seasonal variations in food availability or other ecological variants. We are not here concerned with appraising what these relationships may be in our sample of field studies, but only with demonstrating some of the factors other than primary sexual motivation which may contribute to the year-round coherence of monkey and ape groups. Those species with the clearest evidence for mating seasonality, the macaques, show no more indication of seasonal changes in the grouping pattern than do those, such as the baboons, where mating occurs at any time of year. Another important group-cohering factor may well be the tendency of mothers with young infants to seek the protection of adult males, and thus stay near to them, and the adult males of *cynocephalus* groups are notably attentive in protecting such mothers from being harassed, even by other members of the group. There can be little doubt that an important bond making for group coherence is initiated in the mother-infant and adult male relationship in some species, and it is known that "family" attachments of mother and recent infant, together with her offspring from previous seasons, may form strong affectional nuclei within groups of, for example, rhesus, and probably baboons of both species. Laboratory studies such as those of Harlow (1960) have already done much to clarify the nature of the basic affectional systems in the rhesus monkey, and similar studies are required, closely linked with field observations, of other species. However, even when the primary affectional variables are worked out observationally and experimentally for a species, a significant residual has still to be accounted for, namely, why it is that, for all the species so far systematically studied, only the mountain gorilla and the patas go about typically in groups small enough to be defined as family parties. A variation of this form of social organization is to be seen in the *hamadryas* one-male-unit (Kummer and Kurt 1963), but in some of the other species group sizes are to be found that must comprise a coherent entity of several families. The factors that may account for these larger groupings will now be examined.

Numerical Data

If primary affectional factors, together with primary sexual motivation and protection-seeking and protection-giving, were the only ones determining the size, structure and existence of relatively constant groups, we should expect to find in all species, either the hamadryas social pattern, or the existence of rather small groups with a maximum of about twenty animals each. In considering the actual evidence available to us, a sample of which is given in Table 1–3, we find several examples that are far in excess of such a limit, and it is necessary to examine to what extent such large groupings owe their existence to a conditioned or habitual extension of the basic social relationship and to what extent external, ecological factors determine the sizes. For *P. cynocephalus,* in particular, we find enormous regional varia-

TABLE 1–3   CENTRAL TENDENCY AND RANGE OF VARIATION IN GROUP SIZES FOR SPECIES OF OLD-WORLD MONKEY AND APE

Species	Source of Data	Central Tendency	Range of Variation	No. of Groups	Comment
Presbytis entellus	Jay: N. India	25	5–120	29	
Gorilla gorilla	Schaller: Congo	17	5–30	10	
Macaca mulatta	Southwick *et al.*:				
	India temples	42	16–78	15	Groups in other
	Forest	50+	32–68	7	habitats subject
Macaca radiata	Nolte: India	32	32–33	2	to frequent trap-
		} 38	} 6–58	} 0	ping.
	Simonds: India	41	6–58	4	
Papio cynocephalus	DeVore:				
	Nairobi Park	42	12–87	9	
	Amboseli	80	13–185	15	
	Hall:				
	Murchison	27	14–48	8	
	S. Rhodesia	46	12–109	18	
	S.W. Africa	27	8–65	20	
	S. Africa	34	15–80	15	
Cercopithecus aethiops	Hall and Gartlan:				
	Lolui	12	6–20	46	
	Hall: Murchison	13	4–22	10	
Erythrocebus patas	Hall: Murchison	15	5–22	7	

tions in group size (Hall 1963*d*, 1965*c*; DeVore and Hall 1965) which seem to be related to habitat differences, perhaps mainly in food density. The largest group so far reliably counted is 185 and Altmann (personal communication) has recently seen a group in the same area numbering 200, while several others of over 100 are also recorded. The upper limit in other regions is only about 60. For rhesus groups, Southwick *et al.* (1965) also noted variations in modal tendency in different habitat regions, while the upper limit with artificial feeding is very much larger than any so far recorded in the wild—about 120 in the largest group in Cayo Santiago. Likewise, we find that *M. fuscata* groups may become very large indeed under "provisioning," the Takasakiyama population recently being formed into two groups, one of about 620 animals, the other of about 120. Unfortunately, no adequate information seems to be available for the Japanese species under fully natural conditions, but this is perhaps less important for our purpose than the simple demonstration that free-ranging groups of this species can maintain an apparently coherent social organization when far in numerical excess of any groups of any species ever recorded in the wild. Common langurs, bonnet macaques, vervets, and patas are so far recorded as having a much lower group size, but it must be noted that the sampling range is less comprehensive than that of *P. cynocephalus*. Nevertheless, the trends look as though they will be significantly lower for these species, and the range of variation may be less, although it will be seen that the upper limit for the common langur is 120.

In terms of the possible ecological factors that may relate to these differences, it is perhaps notable, first, that the patas, which are as terrestrial as the baboons in the same habitat region, have a mean group size of about half that of the Murchison Falls Park baboons; second, that the vervet population of Lolui Island, where food appears to be abundant and ground predators non-existent, is formed into groups of almost exactly the same numerical distribution as that of mainland groups at Murchison where the predator situation may be markedly different, and where food availability is probably less consistent.

At present, it is only possible to present the evidence as it has been gathered by competent field workers, but we have to allow for the likelihood that there may be highly significant differences in the intergroup relationships in the various populations where spacing between groups is markedly different. This likelihood we can examine more closely in the following section.

The gorilla groups, in Schaller's (1963) study, were as constant in their composition as those of the monkey species cited, but the upper limit is only about the same as that for the patas, with an average of about the same order as patas and vervets. For both the latter species, larger groups than those shown in Table 1–3 have been reported (Wingfield 1963), but with no indication of a central tendency, the samples being far too small.

Chimpanzee groupings are quite different from the gorilla-monkey pattern,

Goodall (1965) observing no consistency in the composition of the 498 temporary groups that she observed. The largest temporary grouping, seen only once, numbered twenty-three, and both Kortlandt (1962) and Reynolds (1963) and Reynolds and Reynolds (1965) report occasional aggregations, during feeding, of this numerical order, but these dispersed into much smaller parties later.

As already noted, Kummer and Kurt (1963) find a different grouping pattern in *hamadryas,* the social units being described as comprising one adult male with one to nine adult females and their young. At the sleeping cliffs, however, "unstable associations" of groups numbering from 12 to 750 baboons may be seen, these being unstable in the sense that the social units go their own separate ways when moving off to feed during the day, and different social units may assemble at the cliffs at night.

In terms of the composition of groups, the sample of data for some of these species relating to the ratio of adult males to adult females (Table 1–4) shows a considerable degree of variation between species, and even a quite marked regional variation within the *P. cynocephalus* species. The most extreme discrepancy so far recorded is for the Uganda patas, for, in each of seven groups, only a single fully grown male was to be seen. At the point of near-equality in proportion are the chimpanzees (within the study population), the Murchison baboons, the vervets of Lolui Island, and the bonnet macaques (very small sample only). All ratios, except that for the chimpanzees, include only those males defined as belonging to a group, or peripheral to it but remaining consistently within its orbit. Truly isolated males are *not* within a group's orbit. No reliable estimate of the occurrences of such animals is known for any species, but such males have been reported for several species, though only in the common langur are male parties known to occur. Simonds (1965) records that, on reaching near-adult size, males do not leave bonnet macaque groups, nor do they become peripheral in the social structure as in rhesus or baboon groups.

If we now take into consideration both the size trends in the groups and the evidence for differential ratios between adult males and adult females, it seems probable that two interdependent kinds of social adaptation are responsible for the species social organizations. Cohesive forces, as DeVore (1963) has emphasized, may be derived from the ecological pattern in, for example, the savannah-ranging baboon groups. It is thought to be advantageous for such groups, when ranging (often widely spread out, it should be noted) over the savannah away from the refuge of trees or rocks, to consist of several large males so spaced as to offer maximal protection to the mothers and infants that tend to move in the spatial centre. From the point of view of day time predation, however, it would seem to be of greatest advantage to the group to have as high a proportion as the birth rate would permit of fully-grown males to females, instead of a ratio of about one to two only. This, rather than absolute size, would seem to constitute the most important

TABLE 1–4   ADULT MALE : ADULT FEMALE RATIOS IN GROUPS OF OLD-WORLD MONKEYS AND APES

Species	Grouping Pattern	Adult ♂	:	Adult ♀	Extragroup Individuals
Pan troglodytes	Highly variable	1 (in population)	:	1	More adult ♂♂ than adult ♀♀
Gorilla gorilla	Consistent	1	:	1.8	Occasional adult ♂
Papio cynocephalus	Consistent	1 (Hall, Murchison)	:	1.3	Occasional adult ♂
		1 (Hall, Southern Africa)	:	3.3	
		1 (DeVore, Kenya)	:	2.3	
Papio hamadryas	Consistent for units, variable for larger groupings	1 (Kummer and Kurt, Ethiopia)	:	2	?
Macaca mulatta	Consistent	1 (Southwick, Temple areas, 15 groups)	:	2	
		1 (Southwick, forest areas, 7 groups)	:	3	
Macaca radiata	Consistent	1.2 (Simonds, N. India) (including adults and sub-adults)	:	1	
Ceropithecus aethiops	? Intermediate	1 (Hall and Gartlan, Lolui Island)	:	1.4	
Presbytis entellus	Consistent	1 (Jay, N. India)	:	2	Occasional single adult ♂♂ and small parties of 2–10 ♂♂
Erythrocebus patas	? Consistent	1 (Hall, Uganda)	:	6.3	Occasional adult ♂ and one all-♂ party

advantage, and this, in fact, seems to be nearer the case in the Murchison Falls Park groups where the ratio is one to one point three, and the average group size is only twenty-seven. The very fact of the wide spacing out during savannah feeding would seem to indicate that the predator situation has very little to do with group size differences, and that food-density is more likely to be a primary determinant as to the point at which a group divides into two that then take up adjacent, overlapping home ranges, rather than building up to a huge aggregation whose feeding area would have to be proportionately great. The facts also indicate that some of the largest groups occur in wooded areas, at least in Southern Rhodesia, but the mean for groups in the arid thornveld of S.W. Africa was only twenty-seven, the same as for the Murchison groups.

Thus, while there can be no doubt of the effectiveness of the combined aggressive-defensive potential of several fully-grown male baboons in the face of, say, cheetahs or perhaps hunting dogs or hyenas, it would seem that the determinants of regional variations in group size are primarily to be found in food density as averaged over a year. It is, however, much too soon to be sure about this, simply because no long-term surveys in the same area, over several years, have yet been completed. From the Cayo Santiago and Japanese data, in habitats where no large predators exist, it is clear that food availability is the major factor permitting of greater than normal extensions of group size. Thus the primary affectional factors and sexual motivation, with their habitual derivatives, might allow of enormous groups of monkeys to occur in unnaturally favourable food environments, but the structure of such a group, on detailed analysis, might be far looser, might be much more readily described in terms of sub-groups or even units comparable to those in the hamadryas assemblies. The fact that such sub-groups co-exist without major conflict is perhaps no more remarkable than that several groups, as we shall see in the next section, tolerate each other's close presence at frequent intervals when drinking or when at an abundant seasonal food source. We seem to be dealing here with gradations from sub-group, to group, to aggregation or assembly, the limits of which are far from easy to define on present evidence. The fact that such gradations occur at all may be an indication of the social flexibility of the species, and of the social learning skills in which this is manifest.

So far, the patas groups seem to differ very clearly from those of the baboons, in both numerical aspects of size and adult composition. The way of life of this species is notably different from that of the baboons. Their small groups are essentially silent, they disperse with individuals far apart on separate trees or bushes on the savannah towards dusk, and the one large male, conspicuous in appearance and in his positioning high on trees, is continually watchful and cautious. The aggressive-defensive potential of this one male in relation to any likely ground predators is negligible, and field observations clearly indicate that his function is to watch for and locate a potential danger, then divert the danger towards himself and away from the group which may remain concealed and completely silent in the long grass. This survival pattern, combined with the typical habitat utilization for food, water and resting, could scarcely go along with much larger groups, nor would there appear to be any advantage in there being several large males, which would only serve to make the group far too conspicuous, and would probably add to the difficulty of the other individuals maintaining contact.

Vervets and common langurs, although certainly ranging on the ground quite extensively for food, are rarely far from escape routes to trees. Their groups thus differ in size from those of the true savannah-ranging species: they are small enough to require relatively small home ranges, and one may suppose, in the absence of any other evidence, that the food density factor is a major one in determining group sizes. Probably the proportions of adult males to adult females have little to do with predator defence but only with the mating pattern and the system of social organization in which this plays a part.

While there is some evidence that arboreal species such as the Colobus (Booth 1957; Ullrich 1961; Hall, personal observation) are to be found in very small groups of about ten with small home-ranges, so little is yet known about their social organization, and intergroup relations, that no correlations can be suggested, nor indeed is it reliably known what the range of variation is in any arboreal species. Thus, this numerical trend as between arboreal and terrestrial species (to which, anyway, the patas is a conspicuous exception) is far from significant because of the unevenness of the sampling. No analyses of group compositions for arboreal species are available.

Probably the most important point for final emphasis in this section is the rather obvious one that the species which, in terms of habitat utilization, are most adaptable and therefore to be found most widely distributed will show a very extended range of numerical size, and even, it seems, some quite significant regional variations in group composition. Linked with this is a complexly determined kind of social organization which is sufficiently flexible to allow of relatively stable relationships in very large groups. The converse of this proposition, that the very locally distributed species have a numerically smaller range and an inflexible kind of social organization has still to be verified or refuted. The advantage of making such analyses and comparisons for the most-studied, mainly terrestrial, species, is that these suggest a great variety of problems for further field and experimental study. These could not be recognized as definable problems until the present accumulation of data on a few species became available.

Intragroup Behaviour

We have discussed social organization in our reference species as it is reflected in numerical sizes and group compositions, and as it holds together in some species for large parts of the year independently of primary sexual motivation amongst the adult males and females. In no species, except the chimpanzee, is there any positive evidence of significant changes of membership between group and group, such changes as do occur being of rare occurrence. Further, there is very little evidence indeed, at present, as to the splitting of groups in the wild, though the Japanese workers have carefully followed the course of such splits in a few of their groups, and have carried out an important study of the process of group formation and of the effect of releasing a group in a new area (Sugiyama 1960; Furuya 1960; Kawai 1960). The latter kind of experiment is of the greatest value in determining how the social structure of a group is worked out until a stable order is achieved, and should be carried out, with experimental variations, in semi-natural or natural conditions with other species.

Starting again from Zuckerman's (1932:233–234) first attempt at a systematic account of the factors determining social organization in the non-human primates, we find his view stated as follows: "Every ape or monkey enjoys a position within a social group that is determined by the inter-relation of its own dominant characteristics and those of its fellows. The degree of its dominance determines how far its bodily appetites will be satisfied. Dominance determines the number of females that a male may possess, and except on occasions when there is a superfluity of food, it also determines the amount a monkey eats." This view of dominance was derived mainly from data on baboons, notably the *hamadryas* groups studied at the London Zoo, so that its validity must be examined both by reference to the more elaborate and varied environmental settings provided by natural conditions and by comparison with other species.

As a general statement, it can hardly be doubted that, in monkey and ape groups, as in the societies of other vertebrate animals, individual status in the group varies significantly with age, sex, oestrous condition, physical health or weakness, and so on. However, the dominance concept we know to be highly complex in the varied forms of its expression, even within the baboon genus (Hall 1962c; Hall and DeVore 1965; Kummer and Kurt 1963). If relative dominance of an adult male is rated on the basis of criteria analogous to the peck order in domestic fowls, we can assign a rank to the animal in terms of two kinds of competitive situation: (1) priority of access to special foods; and (2) priority of access to an optimally receptive female. These are the situations in which Zuckerman observed dominance to be expressed in zoo groups. However, it is clear from field observation that the real social function of such a dominant animal is far more important to the group than its expression in these situations can indicate. Thus, we can distinguish several other situations, with responses varying notably between species, where the dominant animal is conspicuous: (3) preventing serious fights within the group; (4) protecting mothers with infants from interference by other group members; (5) coming to the fore when the group is threatened by a predator or by some other source of danger, and prominent alertness in watching for such danger; (6) threatening or chasing an "alien" of the same species or of a conspecific group; and (7) taking the initiative in "leading" a group. Aside from these situations in which dominance is expressed by particular, easily recognizable behaviour patterns, the more subtle forms of the relationship between individuals is expressed in the communication repertoire of the species, as by the act of mounting, being presented to or cringed to, being groomed, and so on. For several species, for example mountain gorillas, macaques and baboons, the dominance of the adult males over all other classes of animal in the group is fairly clearcut, although the rankings amongst these males are often not linear but complicated by "alliances" between two or more males and by differing orders in dominance according to the type of situation (Hall and DeVore 1965). Further, the relationships amongst the adult females, in which some kind of at least temporary hierarchy is often apparent, are complicated by their relationship with the adult males and by their sexual or maternal situation. Nor is it by any means always possible to assign the major dominance functions within a group to the males alone, because there is at least one instance (in the Minoo β group of Japanese macaques) where an adult female was the α animal, and it is highly likely, in the one-male patas group, that the adult females play an important part in maintaining order within the group, the male's watchfulness being primarily directed toward disturbances and dangers from *outside* the group.

While the integrating functions of adult males are prominently expressed in rhesus and baboon groups, they are far from prominent in other species. Jay (in press) noted, in one group of common langurs, only five dominance interactions amongst the adult males in one week, as compared with a *daily* rate of eight in a nearby rhesus group. She considers that dominance relations are much less rigid in langurs than in baboons and rhesus. The dominant (silverbacked) male gorillas of Schaller's (1963) study usually asserted themselves only by attenuated gestures, rarely by more forceful aggressive action, and adult females were sometimes dominant over the younger (blackbacked) males. Gartlan (personal communication) is doubtful whether anything directly comparable to the dominance pattern of rhesus and baboon is to be found amongst the adult males of the Lolui Island vervet population. Goodall (1965) noted the rarity of aggressive and submissive interactions amongst her chimpanzee population, only seventy-two instances being observed in the twenty-eight months of her study to that date. Chimpanzee males normally show a great deal of tolerance in their behaviour towards each other, this characteristic being especially remarkable during mating—as, for example, on the occasion when seven males (one an adolescent) copulated in succession with one female, no signs of aggression being observed amongst them.

The more tolerant, and perhaps as a consequence more flexible, type of relationship amongst the adult males is usually considered to be reflected, as in the bonnet macaques (Simonds 1965) and perhaps the vervets, by a nearly equal ratio of adult males to adult females within the group structure. However, there may turn out to be important qualifications to this, perhaps linked with significant differences in the tensions within groups of the same species, as might turn out to be the case with the Murchison baboon groups where the ratio is nearly one to one. Further, it is far from clear, at present, whether the single large patas male is aggressive to individuals in his group. In fact, not a single instance of baboon-like aggressiveness within the group was observed in over 600 hours of observation. It will be realized, however, that a group that is stable in its environment is one in which, for a time, such aggression may simply not be manifested. One would suppose that, in the patas, the aggression is shown only very rarely and then in extreme form by driving out maturing males. Even in baboon groups in the wild, many hours may pass without any signs of aggression, but its readiness to occur is clearly to be seen when there is competition for an oestrous female, or when tension is experimentally created in a group by presenting it with a disturbing or frustrating situation to which a male may react by redirecting his aggression onto subordinate animals. What is abundantly clear from all the studies is that actual fighting is extremely rare in nature, for the reason that stability in the group is normally maintained by threat or "inhibited" biting only. Even a change in dominance, as several studies have shown (notably some on the Japanese macaque) can be achieved by repeated threat, and removal of an α animal is usually followed by the number two male taking over his position without dispute.

The adaptiveness of these variants in the dominance pattern, as shown in the different species, can only be assessed in relation to the totality of factors operating upon the species in its natural setting. We have already referred to one such factor, namely the aggressive-defensive potential of baboon males in relation to ground predators and the selective value of an especial wariness or watchfulness in those species that rely on escape or concealment. In the latter case, with the probable exception of the patas, such wariness is not necessarily pre-eminently the function of adult males, but may be observed in any members of the group who happen first to detect the disturbance. The alarm is then shared by vocalization or by movements to which all individuals are immediately alerted. In species with such a survival pattern of communication behaviour, the advantage of pronounced sexual dimorphism and fighting ability in the males is obviously negligible.

We can only conclude, at this stage, that the social adaptations shown in the varying patterns of dominance, from the conspicuous adult male hierarchies of baboons and rhesus to the lack of any such demonstrable relationships in other species, can readily be understood only within the ecological framework with all its complexity of food-getting, sheltering and resting, avoidance of predators, and the changing seasonal internal pattern of births and mating. Zuckerman's (1932) original formulation requires modification to fit the variations we can now discuss, and even more significant modifications may come in future as studies of arboreal species are completed.

Intergroup Behaviour

Bourlière (1955:235) has pointed out that it is necessary to analyse in detail the relationship between the kind of social hierarchy characteristic of groups within a species and its territorial behaviour, ". . . for there seem to be many links between these two manifestations of aggressiveness within the species." Tolerance in its most prominent form seems to be shown in the loose, temporary groupings of chimpanzees. Gorillas also are distinctly tolerant of exchanges of individuals from group to group, and so, it seems, are the Lolui Island vervets. The adult male *hamadryas* is, perhaps, at the other extreme in showing an unceasing watchfulness over females straying away from his group, punishing such a stray very severely by biting and beating (Kummer and Kurt 1963). Adult male *P. cynocephalus* and patas react vigorously to the presence of an "alien" adult male, but a juvenile male baboon was accepted into a strange group after only one brief threat charge by the α male (Hall 1962c).

Proceeding, then, from dominance as expressed within the group to behaviour toward alien individuals and finally to behaviour towards another group, we have to consider various grades of intraspecific social relationship culminating in those conventionally designated as "territoriality" (Carpenter 1958b:228, 242) or territorial behaviour. Carpenter views ". . . territoriality primarily as a behavioural system which is expressed in a spatial-temporal frame of reference." Such a definition is probably too general, just as the dominance concept has to be stretched far beyond its original reference if it is to fit the variety of social interactions within our sample of monkey and ape groupings. Only in this general form is his conclusion justifiable that ". . . on the basis of available data territoriality is as characteristic of primates' behaviour as it is of the other vertebrates." As DeVore (1963a) points out, Carpenter's definition includes both the concept of territory and that of home range which are usually to be clearly distinguished in mammalian group studies. Bourlière (1955:100) defines the home range as ". . . the area over which the individual or the family group normally travels in search of food. A fundamental negative characteristic differentiating it from the territory is that the home range is not the exclusive "property" of the individual that frequents it. Thus, it is not defended by its occupant against other members of the same species, and several home ranges may overlap without giving rise to conflict." In this sense, as DeVore (1963a) says, a monkey group can have an all-year-round home

TABLE 1–5   RELATIONSHIPS OF INTRAGROUP SOCIAL ORDER AND
BETWEEN-GROUP BEHAVIOUR IN SOME SPECIES OF
OLD-WORLD MONKEY AND APE

Species	Intragroup	Between-Group
Pan troglodytes	Loose, temporary groupings, relationships between individuals being largely tolerant and unaggressive.	No between-group hostility; vocal demonstrations; "home-range" applicable only to population, not to groupings.
Gorilla gorilla	Relative dominance of silver backed males, asserted with minimum threat; occasional fighting between individuals, but with no resultant injury.	No between-group hostility; no vocal demonstrations; but highly variable behaviour—sometimes mingling of individuals, sometimes ignoring, occasional aggressive bluff-charges and weak aggressiveness; "home-range" applicable only to population, not to groups.
Papio cynocephalus	Complex dominance relations amongst adult males, both in terms of aggressiveness and other social characteristics; sub-adult males are peripheral.	Highly variable; sometimes extensive overlap of home ranges; occasional aggressive chase; vocal demonstrations in woodland habitat; mutual tolerance, or mutual avoidance, depending upon ecological conditions.
Papio hamadryas	Exclusive adult male dominance within one-male unit.	Tolerance of many one-male units on same sleeping cliffs.
Macaca mulatta	Very similar to *P. cynocephalus.*	Highly variable; actual fighting between groups observed when very close contact occurred in Temple areas, sometimes considerable home-range overlap (up to 80 percent); similar to *P. cynocephalus;* no vocal demonstrations.
Macaca radiata	Similar to *mulatta*, but, in the small sample observed, a probably less aggressive manifestation of dominance amongst adult males; sub-adults remain within group.	On five occasions of contact between groups, visual alertness and watching by males, then withdrawal of one group; no aggression; no vocal demonstration; overlap of home ranges.
Macaca fuscata	Similar to *mulatta* and *P. cynocephalus;* sub-adult males peripheral.	Home-range overlap; vocal demonstrations on group contact; no actual aggression other than threat; intergroup relations said to be determined by relative dominance.

TABLE 1–5—*continued*

Species	Intragroup	Between-Group
Erythrocebus patas	Exclusive one-male dominance only rarely aggressively expressed within group, though sub-adult males must be driven out of the group; probably complex relationship to adult female hierarchy.	In limited sample, only slight home range overlap; long-range alertness for presence of another group, and immediate chasing by dominant group, immediate withdrawal by other group; no close range contact ever seen; barking by adult male only *after* contacting extragroup male or another group.
Presbytis entellus	Dominance relations amongst adult males much less clearcut than in baboons and macaques, and very rarely demonstrable in aggressive interactions.	"Whoop" vocalizations by adult males; peaceful intergroup meetings; home range overlap varying in degree from "extensive" to "slight."
Cercopithecus aethiops	Uncertain complexity of dominance amongst adult males, but not marked by frequent aggressiveness.	Peaceful interactions; sometimes at close range.

range which extensively overlaps with that of a neighbouring group, but included in this home range may be "core areas" which are behaviourally of quite a different significance to the group and into which another group would rarely, if ever, penetrate. Nevertheless, the operational definition of "territory" is an area which is "defended" from encroachment, and it is only occasionally possible to discern any such behaviour between groups even of species, such as rhesus and baboons, whose social organization, within the group, is characterized by a dominance hierarchy not uncommonly reinforced by overt aggression. The danger of using a concept so extensibly is that it will lead to an oversimplification of observations and of analysis and interpretation of them. It is thus necessary to proceed with caution in considering our comparative evidence summarized for characteristic within- and between-group behaviour for a selection of species (Table 1–5).

In species where the adult male dominance is most noticeable within the group, behaviour of group to group varies considerably from occasion to occasion, region to region. DeVore and Hall (1965) have observed entirely tolerant encounters and even, temporarily, mingling of some members of baboon groups at watering places. In areas where the maintenance needs of groups do not necessitate contact, as in the Cape Peninsula habitat and elsewhere, contacts seem simply to be avoided. Where one large group, at

Murchison, had been foraging almost to the middle of the known home range of the usual occupant group that was much smaller in size, it withdrew rapidly on sighting the latter, some of the males of the latter advancing towards it with frequent barking. Thus, the relationships between groups are, in normal ecological conditions, regularized without intergroup aggressiveness, and such frequent meetings as regionally occur may be assumed to lead to a more or less complete habituation of extra-group aggression in the males.

Regulation of behaviour between rhesus groups takes place in the same way, the smaller group, for example, on Cayo Santiago usually giving way to the larger at food hoppers. The only instances of severe intergroup fighting are those recorded by Southwick *et al.* (1965) in the Temple area habitat where overlap of ranging between two groups was of the order of eighty per cent, and close contact between them sometimes accidentally occurred, although it was usually avoided.

In the few instances when one patas group sighted another, the larger group instantly followed the big male in chasing the smaller away, the male himself thereafter positioned himself high in a tree and uttered repeatedly a dog-like bark heard on no other occasion. One might thus suppose that the exclusively one-male system of these groups is correlated with an unusual degree of spacing between groups; possibly this really represents, in another form, the pronounced antagonism of one adult male to another, whether in his group or in another group, whereas the *cynocephalus* baboon and the rhesus have a several-male group system based on only occasionally manifested threat or aggression. As an experimental demonstration which may have some social significance, it has been observed (Hall 1962*a*) that the adult male of a captive patas group habituates, on any single occasion, to his mirror image, but later observations (Hall, personal observation) have shown that he never fully habituates to the reflections of himself on metal doors or glass, even after several weeks of living with them.

While "territorial behaviour," in the usual definition, may turn out to be characteristic of patas groups, it is only rarely manifested by baboon groups, presumably because alternative methods of maintaining distance or group coherence are just as effective. Baboon males in the Urungwe region of riverside woodland in Southern Rhodesia often bark repeatedly in the early morning, while still at or near their sleeping trees. Group location vocalizations, if that is what these turn out to be, are given by common langur males (Jay 1965) and by colobus. These do not seem to occur in vervets, even where several groups are located in clumps of trees within an area of a few hundred yards. While this vocal spacing effect reduces the likelihood of group contact, it would only be advantageous in wooded habitats, and it is not yet known how general this is amongst arboreal species.

The study of the interrelations of social organization in groups, and behaviour between groups, is a fascinating problem, the intricacies of which are only just becoming apparent. There is a very strong case for researches on group and intergroup dynamics in selected natural habitat areas. The excellent beginnings of the Japanese studies should be greatly extended. Social experiments, few of which have been attempted in the field, are known to be feasible, and must be used in trying to discern, objectively, what it is that underlies the normally observed stability in the wild populations.

DISCUSSION

The main impression from a comparative treatment of these four related aspects of social organization is of the complexity of the factors that determine both the typical pattern of different species, and the variability of pattern seen within the widely distributed species. This can only be described as an "impression" because sampling of evidence is inadequate for every single species. The basis for more precise comparison, using quantitative data that has come from really long-term studies and data from several species within the same genus, is still not available. Yet certain broad outlines for tentative comparison are discernible.

In the baboon genus, *Papio cynocephalus* is remarkable because it has spread, without speciation, over a very wide range of habitat. While a great deal of further research on populations of the species in different regions, including forest habitat, the semi-desert bordering the Southern Sahara, and the "pocket" regions within the Sahara itself at Tibesti and Ennedi (Monod 1963), needs to be carried out, it is already evident that here is a highly "successful" form of social organization which can be fitted into a variable ecological framework, allowing of coherence of group structure over a numerical range far greater than that known for any other species under fully natural conditions. It follows also, from its very wide distribution, that the social organization can maintain its basic form in areas where mating and births occur all the year round and in regions where seasonal availability of food, and possibly other factors, make it more advantageous for the populations to show a distinct birth peak, if not a discrete breeding season. What is equally impressive with these overall adjustments is the evidence of intergroup adjustments, almost always peaceable, which, on a group scale, probably reflect the same important learning processes, of social habituation and social conditioning, which are so much in evidence in the behavioural interactions within the group itself.

While it is, perhaps, inevitable that the baboon and macaque genera feature most prominently in the present comparison, the very striking and varied social adaptations of other genera, such as the chimpanzees and gorillas, the patas, the vervets, and the langurs, draw attention most forcibly to the need, both for more field work and for more precise experimental studies of their social behaviour. Although three separate field studies of the chimpanzee have very recently been carried out, it will not be possible to piece together all the evidence on the wild and the captive behaviour of these animals until Goodall has published the full account of her findings. While it is already evident, from her preliminary publications, that they show in higher degree than any other non-human primate certain "intellectual" skills, such as use of, and even modification of, tools for food-getting, their informal social organization, combined with their physical adaptations, has been far less "successful," in the distribution sense, than that of the non-tool-using baboons, macaques, and vervets.

Our view of the mountain gorilla, likewise, is one of an animal which, in terms of the laboratory definition of intelligence, impressed Yerkes and others very strongly, and which, in the wild, lives a life that is easy-going and offers little challenge to its supposed intellectual powers. Perhaps one of the notable characteristics of *Papio cynocephalus*, of some macaque species, and of the vervets, is their readiness to adapt, if allowed, to man-created changes in their environment, whereas, so far, this seems much less in evidence in the "superior" anthropoid apes. Possibly, a most important clue to the relative success of all these animals will come from the study of the fundamental characteristics of the natural social environment, making the group, or variable grouping, the unit of study, instead of concentrating experimental attention upon individual performances. The success of baboons, relative to chimpanzees, is a consequence, not of individual prowess, but of the fitness of the social organization.

In species such as the langurs and patas, we see again important variations in terms of group and intergroup behaviour, these being reflections of their adaptations to predator situations, food needs, and so on. But the range of comparisons is still so slight that there is little more to do in concluding comment than to re-emphasize the need for sustained investigations of more species, and of the same species, with the aid of experimental and observational programmes of group behaviour in captivity, closely linked with long-term field projects. When these have been carried out, it is not improbable that the perspective may revolutionize some of the conventional concepts of this branch of comparative study, while, in the process, demonstrating beyond doubt the unreality of making any social behaviour comparisons of these animals without a detailed knowledge of the ecological circumstances of their natural life.

A final comment concerns the value of drawing upon comparisons both with nonprimate animals and with man. Probably by far the most fruitful, at this early stage, will be the task of discerning the similarity of the principles underlying the social adaptations of other non-human group-living vertebrates, for, once the similarities are thus in focus, the most significant differences may become apparent. The task of comparison with human groups takes various forms, and may include the reconstruction of primitive, pre-hominid, pre-tool-making society, or the selection of very free, uncritical analogies as between present-day human groups and those of contemporary apes and monkeys. Both forms, and others, will derive their validity directly in proportion to the progress of critical analysis and original experimental and observational study of the social organization of the more adaptable species. The clues for reconstruction and for analogy may be pieced together by selection of the relevant interrelationships in several differently adapted species, and clearly not from the anthropoid apes alone.

2

BEHAVIOUR AND ECOLOGY

OF THE WILD PATAS MONKEY,

ERYTHROCEBUS PATAS, IN UGANDA*

K. R. L. Hall

Prior to the present study, no systematic field data were available on the behaviour and ecology of *Erythrocebus patas*. This monkey, widely distributed over the grass and woodland savannah regions of West and East Africa, appears to be unique in some of its physical and social adaptations to a terrestrial mode of life. In three main study periods, 640 hours of observation were carried out on groups in the Murchison Falls National Park. Small samples of data on baboon and vervet groups in the same area were obtained. Numerical sizes of patas groups ranged from 9 to 31, mean 15. In no group was there more than one full-grown male. Groups were followed for many successive day-ranges, distances travelled varying from group to group, season to season, with a maximum of about 12,000 m and a minimum of 500 m. Home range size of one group was 5200 hectares. Groups tended to use a different area of the home range each night, and individuals dispersed far apart in taking up night resting positions in trees. The day activity pattern comprised two main feeding periods, with a rest period of one to three hours in the hottest time. Drinking at water holes or other sources was infrequent.

Infants less than three months old occurred only up to June, and were commonly seen in March and April. Infants aged 3 to 12 months, and juveniles, engage frequently in long, active bouts of play-chasing, wrestling, and bush-bouncing—almost all play is on the ground. Grooming amongst them is common, its social pattern being similar to baboons. Submissive gestures are very rarely seen, baboon-like presenting and being mounted not

*Reprinted with permission from *The Journal of Zoology*, 1965, 148:15–87.

occurring. Threat-attack is mainly by adult females, very rarely by the adult male. Vocalizations audible at about 100 m occur very infrequently (about two to four a day, compared with 25 to 50 for baboon groups).

The adult male patas plays the part, for the group, of watchdog. Whenever the group is disturbed, or approaches new areas, he may reconnoitre from a high point several hundred metres away from the group. When disturbed by the observer, he has a noisy, bouncing display on bushes and trees, and probably a form of diversionary display by running away from his group and from the observer. In the group, he is spatially peripheral, except when day resting, mating and grooming, and the adult females habitually initiate directions and times of group movement. Their function is essentially that of looking after themselves, their infants, and the juveniles, while that of the adult male is very strikingly that of watching for predators or other patas groups of baboons, etc. Isolated adult males and one all-male party of four have been observed. Spacing between groups is such that inter-group encounters are exceedingly rare (two occurrences only). Reaction consisted of chasing by the larger group, rapid avoidance by the smaller. A contralto bark is uttered repeatedly, in short series, by the adult male of a group only, it seems, on encounters with extra-group patas.

The patas' adaptations of swift locomotion, silence, concealment, and dispersal, contrast very clearly with those of the much noisier, larger, more aggressive baboons in whose groups there are usually several adult males.

Further research on the species is required from West Africa, and captivity studies must be used to determine the precise nature of the social organization amongst the adults and the processes of socialization.

INTRODUCTION

The comparative study of the old-world monkey species which have a mainly terrestrial way of life may be of particular evolutionary interest in showing the variety of physical and social adaptations that have developed to fit the different ecological niches. Of the terrestrial species of Africa so far studied in the wild, the greatest concentration of data has been upon the baboons, which are very successful ground-living primates, in terms of adaptability to a wide range of habitat, and their way of life is considered to give some insight into the problems which confronted early man (DeVore and Washburn 1963). The Desert baboon, *Papio hamadryas,* studied in Ethiopia by Kummer and Kurt (1963), shows very interesting contrasts in behaviour and social organization with the baboons of Kenya and Southern Africa, which may be correlated with its different ecology. Nevertheless, there is a fundamental similarity in the social, as in the physical, adaptations of all the *Papio* species that have been studied.

No studies are yet available of the other large terrestrial monkeys, namely the mountain-dwelling gelada, *Theropithecus gelada,* and the Central West African forest species, *Mandrillus sphinx* and *leucophaeus.* From their physical characteristics, one might expect to find again some fundamental similarities of social behaviour in the baboon pattern, but with special adaptations appropriate to their way of life.

Apart from these large monkeys, there are only two African species (aside from *Macaca sylvana* of North Africa) that are classed as mainly terrestrial. One of these, the very widely distributed *Cercopithecus aethiops,* the Vervet or Grivet, is, in many areas, based on thickets or forest edges from which it makes forays into the savannah. The other, *Erythrocebus patas,* sometimes called the Red, Red Hussar or Military monkey, is, from the accounts of its habits and distribution, at least as terrestrial in its way of life as the baboons. Though about twice the size of the vervet, it is just about half the size of the baboon. Its particular interest for field study, therefore, has been to compare its ecology and behaviour with, on the one hand, that of the baboon, on the other, that of the vervet.

No systematic field study of the patas in any part of its distribution had previously been carried out. The animals have been described as very shy, extremely difficult to hunt (Tappen 1960), but evidently not difficult to trap, because they are nowadays used extensively for commercial medical purposes. Since April 1962, a group of eight patas has been set up in the Bristol Psychology Department for social behaviour and social learning studies. This seems to be the first time the species has been used for behaviour study in captivity, and there has been great value in the possibility of checking captivity observations with field data, and *vice versa.*

DISTRIBUTION

A review of the available literature on the distribution of patas (Tappen 1960) indicates that the species occurs, more or less continuously, over the savannah country north of the equator. It is found from Senegal in the west to the Sudan in the east, then south in Uganda and W. Kenya to the northern-most part of Tanganyika. The southern limit to its range over the middle of Africa is the forest belt of South and West Cameroon and Congo, and likewise its distribution towards the coast of West Africa seems to follow the High Forest limit of Keay's (1959) vegetation maps, according to Booth's (1956) data. The northern limits of the patas along the edge of the Sahara have only been vaguely determined (Monod 1963), but the scanty evidence indicates that, in certain regions, they occur to the north of the limits of *Papio* and certainly of *C. aethiops,* and that in general, they range in the savannah only to the edge of the forested country into which these other species penetrate.

It is necessary to consider in more detail the distribution evidence for particular regions, so that some estimates of the variations in habitat can be made, especially for comparison with baboons and vervets. The northern limits are of some interest in the Sahara region because it seems that a few isolated populations have survived in what are now probably marginal habitat areas. Dekeyser (1950) reports their occurrence in Air, within the Sahara, and considers that here the patas' food supply differs markedly in quantity and quality from that of unisolated populations. As these patas live in a very limited area, he thinks they must be in serious competition with the baboons whom they always seem to avoid. Here also, the patas frequent rocky country unlike their normal habitat. There is, however, no definite evidence of patas still surviving in Tibesti in the Sahara, where baboons are still to be found (Huard 1962).

Further east, and into the Sudan, they are reported at the southern edge of Ennedi, with baboons occupying the more central regions of Ennedi itself. Still further east, patas, baboon, and vervet are reported from Gebel Marra, an area isolated in arid country and said to be similar in habitat to Southern Sudan. There are no published data on the northern limits in the Nile regions of the Sudan, but Huard cites Cloudsley-Thompson for a limit of 11°N in the vicinity of the Blue Nile, but no occurrence from Ethiopia.

From the Sudan south, the eastern limit is uncertain. It seems doubtful if, in Kenya, it now occurs east of about 36°E. Percival (1928) observed it near Makindu, 37°E but even at that date, he described the species as "extremely rare" in Kenya. The southern limits, on the eastern side, reported from northern Tanganyika at about 2°S 35°E are doubted by Tappen (1960) who points out that the record from this area is from 1905, and that no more recent information is available. In Uganda, its limit south is the right bank of the Victoria Nile complex of lakes and rivers, but it occurs both to the west and east of the Albert Nile, and presumably in savannah and woodland savannah in a north westerly curve around the Congo forest limits, but no reports are available from this area.

Tappen (1960) considers that the abrupt termination of the species range to the south in Uganda is difficult to correlate with environmental differences between that region and the southern half of the continent where the other two savannah monkey species, the baboon and vervet, are found in abundance. Indeed the habitat of the Murchison Falls National Park where patas occur only north of the Victoria Nile is essentially the same as the southern part where they are not found. Whether or not patas will cross rivers or streams is not known, but it is known, from the present study, that patas never venture into the riverine vegetation belt on which baboons and vervets are based. In Uganda, the species occurs in the districts of Acholi, Teso, West Nile, Lango, Madi, and Karamoja.

Detailed local information is also available for Ghana and the Cameroon. In the former, Booth (1956) records their occurrence as far south as the juncture of the Guinea savannah zone with the high forest, which brings them to about 100 miles from the coast, at about 6°N. In the latter, Jeannin (1936) describes the species as common in the northern savannah, and the

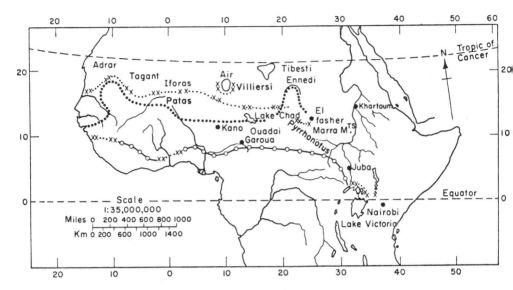

Fig. 2–1. Distribution limits of *Erythrocebus patas;* the northern limit into the Sahara is from Monod (1963); southern limits are estimated from Forest limits (Keay 1959), except where the surveys cited in the text have given locations.

·····, Probable northern limit of papio; ××····××, approximate patas distribution as far as is known from surveys and field study; O———O, approximate southern limits of patas as judged from vegetation zones.

1962 brochure on the Game Reserves of the North Cameroon reports them as common in five of the northern reserves. Tappen (1964) reports its occurrence in Sierra Leone, presumably toward the north-east.

While it looks as though the species may be continuously distributed from Senegal right across Africa to the Sudan, then south to the Victoria Nile, there are still huge areas in the supposed range from which no data are available (Fig. 2–1). Because, as we have found in the present study, patas can utilize savannah areas where baboons rarely, if ever, penetrate, because they seem to be far less dependent on water sources than baboons, and because they require only a few widely scattered trees of quite small size for their night-resting, it seems likely that the species may be continuously distributed much further into the arid zones to the north than the baboons, although baboons survive in a few isolated regions of rock habitat in the Sahara itself.

From the present information, therefore, we can conclude that patas are to be found almost exclusively within the following vegetation areas of savannah and steppe of the northern equatorial and tropical zones, as described by Keay (1959):

Type 25: Wooded steppe with abundant *Acacia* and *Commiphora;*

"Vegetation classified under this heading covers large tracts between the desert and subdesert types on the one side and moister woodland types on the other."

Type 20: Undifferentiated: relatively dry types: climatically, most of them come between Type 25 and the moister types of woodlands, as for example, Types 16 and 17 below; although acacias are often frequent, there are many broad-leaved trees, such as species of *Combretum* and *Terminalia.*

Type 17: Woodlands of *Isoberlinia doka* and *I. dalzielii,* with tall grass savannah, sometimes with *Borassus* palms, in wide valleys and strips of evergreen forest fringing the streams.

Type 16: Woodlands of relatively moist type, with a dense growth of tall grass.

Broadly, these areas comprise climatic zones where rainfall is moderate, with severe dry seasons. The extent of the species' penetration beyond Type 25 into the subdesert steppe (Type 31) is, as Monod (1963) has said, not yet known. All these main areas are covered with grasses ranging in height from about 80 cm to 3 to 4 m which, in most places, are seasonally burnt.

TAXONOMY AND PHYSICAL CHARACTERISTICS

Most taxonomists have assigned the monkeys designated Red, Patas, Hussar, Military, or Nisnas, to a separate genus, *Erythrocebus,* with one species, *patas,* and three or more subspecies. Osman Hill (personal communication) proposes in his classification to recognize a single species, *E. patas,* with the following subspecies: *patas; villiersi; pyrrhonotus; baumstarcki.* Pocock (1907) considered the patas had many basic physical similarities to the genus *Cercopithecus* in which he then included it as one species. The same writer later (1925) assigned the patas once more to a separate genus, apparently on the basis of comparing limb, hand and foot characters with those of the *Cercopithecus* genus.

The most recent revision is that of Verheyen (1962) who retains the patas in the *Cercopithecus* genus, on the basis of cranial characters. The gist of his evidence is that, although there are certain differences in cranial characters as between patas and *Cercopithecus* spp., these are of absolute magnitude, not of relative proportion, and therefore provide no ground for patas being excluded from the genus. If this is indeed the argument, it seems insufficient to outweigh the contrasts in other anatomical features. Buettner-Janusch (1963:34), however, supports this classification: "The unique features of *C. patas* are probably best explained as modifications in a basically arboreal *Cercopithecus* monkey for a largely terrestrial way of life. To some extent *C. patas* resembles the highly terrestrial baboon in its locomotor behaviour and mode of existence. Field studies of this interesting monkey . . . should go far toward elucidating this (taxonomic) problem." Washburn and Hamburg (1965:17), while maintaining patas as a separate genus, emphasizes its close relationship with *Cercopithecus,* the species having ". . . adapted to ground life by high-speed locomotion, a most interesting adaptation that is unique to the patas monkey."

The extent to which ecological and behavioural data on the wild patas can be used to support such taxonomic arguments depends upon the availability of similar evidence on *Cercopithecus* species. The species of this genus which most nearly resembles the patas in its way of life is *aethiops,* the vervet, on which field studies have only just been completed. No other *Cercopithecus* species have yet been studied (systematically) in the wild.

Physically, the patas are of long-limbed, slender build, contrasting with the much heavier, stockier physique of baboons, and the smaller, more thick-set vervet. Pocock (1925:679) notes particularly the length of the patas forelegs as compared with other *Cercopithecus* species: "A comparison between them forcibly suggests the differences in aspect between a Cheetah and the larger species of *Felis* of about the same size, such as a Puma or a Leopard." These physical proportions of the patas are shown by Dekeyser's (1950) measurements of an adult male specimen from Air, the fore and hind limbs being, respectively, 580 and 550 mm, head and body length 620 mm, and length of tail vertebrae 670 mm. Jeannin's (1936) measurements of an adult male taken in the Cameroon (750 and 700 mm for head and body, and tail vertebrae, respectively) support Dekeyser's view that the Air specimen was smaller than average.

Body weights of the Bristol laboratory animals (Table 2–1) show that that of the adult male is rather more than twice that of any of the adult females, and that this sex differentiation is early apparent in that a male at age 18 months is already nearly as large as a female aged about 42 months, and a male of about 42 months is already two-thirds as large again as the female of the same age. One adult male weight (10 kg) from West Africa is given by Bigourdan and Prunier (1937). The baboon sample, from Northern Rhodesia, shows that the adult sex weight proportion for the two terrestrial species is very similar, while there is much less discrepancy between the sexes in the arboreal *Cercopithecus ascanius.*

Fur colouration varies considerably between individuals, and between age-sex classes. Crown of head, nape, back and sides varies from a bright brick-red to brown or light brown, this being mixed with grey in older adults. The underside fur, inside fur of the limbs, around the rump and the rear of the hindlegs, is much lighter in colour, being conspicuously pure white in the adult male, and light brown or fawn in females and young males. The rear view of the adult male in the wild, when he is standing or moving, contrasts very strikingly with that of the other much smaller animals of the group, for the white expanse shows up very vividly against the grass and bare ground. No white is visible in the other animals as they move across country. The adult is also easily distinguishable from the others by a mantle of long fur

TABLE 2–1   BODY WEIGHTS FOR A LABORATORY GROUP OF PATAS MONKEYS, BY AGE AND SEX, WITH COMPARATIVE FIGURES FOR ADULT BABOONS* AND ADULT REDTAIL MONKEYS**

Sex	Estimated or Known Age (years)	Weight (kg)	Sex	Estimated or Known Age (years)	Weight (kg)
		Patas			
Male	Adult	12.6	Female	Adult	7.1
	3.5	7.85		Adult	6.5
	1.5	4.68		Adult	5.35
	0.8	2.0		3.5	4.85
		Baboon			
Male	Adult	34 (mean, $N = 4$)	Female	Adult	15 (mean, $N = 5$)
		Redtail			
Male	Adult	4.2 (mean, $N = 38$)	Female	Adult	2.9 (mean, $N = 36$)

*DeVore and Washburn, 1963
**Haddow, 1952

around his shoulders and neck, and his overall fur colour tends to be a darker reddish-brown. The canine teeth of the adult male are well developed (31 mm for the upper canines, Dekeyser 1950). The scrotum, clearly visible from the rear when he is standing, is bright blue, as it is in *C. aethiops*.

Facial colouration and the fur surrounding it also varies considerably. In the Uganda animals of the field study, faces were black or dark grey, with a white patch on the top of the nose. The laboratory animals, all from West Africa, have light to dark grey face colour, with no white nose patch. The eyebrow ridge fur is black, contrasting with the light or white skin of the upper and lower eye-lids in the "threat-face" expression characteristic of these and other monkeys. On the upper lip, the white moustache, which presumably gave rise to the popular name of Military monkey, is a conspicuous feature in the adult male, but is also to be seen in the adult females.

In the field, sex differentiation, except between adult males and adult females, is much less easy than in baboons. The callosities of the male patas, as of *Cercopithecus* species, are separated by a comparatively wide area of soft integument (Pocock 1925), and therefore are indistinguishable, in the field, from those of females. In the laboratory, the scrotum and penis of the young male when aged 3·7 years were still only visible when he sat facing the observer with his legs apart. Similarly, in the wild, juvenile or young adult males could only be reliably identified from a similar viewpoint when they were sitting on tree branches at fairly close range.

There are no overt signs of the approximately 30-day female cycle except menstruation (Zuckerman 1932)—no sexual swellings as in baboons and mangabeys, and no colour changes in the sexual skin. Gestation period is stated by Jeannin (1936) to be seven months, but he does not give the number of cases from which the figure is derived. This seems to be long, if reckoned at 210 days, because Chacma baboon gestation averaged 187 days (Gilbert and Gillman 1951) and Zuckerman (1932) reviews evidence for Rhesus macaque (164 days), and Hamadryas baboons (171 days), with even the upper range figures not exceeding 193 in the Chacma. In the case of one infant born to the female of the laboratory group who conceived it in the group, gestation was estimated to be 170 days (Goswell and Gartlan 1965). This seems to accord with the expected figure.

The fur colour of the two infants born to the laboratory animals, and of those in the wild groups in March, April, and May, is dark brown, the colour changing gradually to a light grey-brown up to about three months of age. In classifying infants in the field, an infant one is the designation of any infant still with distinct traces of the dark phase, that is, up to about three months as judged from the laboratory animals. An infant two is the second phase when the lighter colour is achieved, and this phase is arbitrarily taken to continue to the end of the first year of life. Animals in their second year of life are classed as juveniles. Judging from the growth rate of the laboratory animals, it seems that the female reaches full size at about three and a half years, the male not until about five years. Whether the female can be classed as sexually mature at that age or earlier is not yet known. The adult male of the laboratory group tried to mate with the young female when she was about two and a half years, and thereafter, but no pregnancy has yet resulted. It seems that sexual maturity in the young male may be reached by about four years. Nothing is known of the longevity of the species in captivity.

The hands and feet of the patas are adapted to the terrestrial way of life. Pocock (1925) emphasizes these adaptations as shown in the length of the palm and sole (Dekeyser's 1950 specimen had hand and foot lengths of 100 and 160 mm, respectively), in the shortness of the terminal digits, the reduction of the hallux and pollex and the development of the plantar pads. Functionally, it has been suggested (Napier 1960) that terrestrial life may have increased the fine control of the hand in many primates, including man. Bishop (1962), using captive patas to test this hypothesis, found a high degree of success on precision grip tests. Hall and Mayer (1966) extended these tests on the laboratory patas. The shortened thumb is used very efficiently against the side of digit 2 in picking up small objects or threads.

No experimental evidence is available as to the patas' sensory capacities, and there is no detailed account of the structure of the brain which could be used for comparison with those available for baboons and Rhesus.

UGANDA HABITAT

Data on vegetation types and on climate, are taken from the excellent Atlas of Uganda (1962). Description of the Murchison Falls National Park habitat is based on the Uganda National Parks Handbook (1962) and on personal observation. Details of vegetation will be given only for the main field study areas of the Murchison Falls National Park (Acholi District). From information on the general Uganda distribution of the patas, the species is to be found in country where the vegetation types range from steppe to woodland, with intermediate types of thicket, grass savannah, and wooded savannah.

Steppe, the "driest" vegetation in Uganda, is characteristic of the more arid stony parts of Karamoja which is largely a flat plain, altitude 1000 to 1200 m, with some isolated peaks up to 2500 to 2700 m. The vegetation is mainly *Acacia-Lannea* tree and shrub steppe, dry *Acacia* savannah associated with *Hyparrhenia* spp. and with *Themeda,* and *Chrysopogon* grass steppe. The climate is characterized by an intense dry, hot season from November to March when streams dry up; the rainy season is April to August, with an average rainfall of between 50 and 100 cm.

In the districts in which the field study was carried out, Acholi and Teso, two types of wooded savannah predominate, the *Combretum* and *Butyrospemum* savannah, associated with *Hyparrhenia* spp. Here, there are scattered shrubs 2 to 5 m high in grassland, scattered trees 5 to 12 m high, or an open canopy of trees 5 to 12 m high overlain by grass. Included in the Acholi distribution, however, is an area of Woodland where the trees are relatively dense, with canopy height varying from 9 to 15 m and with a grass layer that is, in places, only just continuous. The country is mainly flat, altitude 1 to 1200 m, with few hills. Rainfall averages about 125 cm p.a., falling on 140 to 170 days in the year. The rainy season is April to October, with peaks in April–May and August. Rainfall is, in the main, convectional and an afternoon and evening occurrence.

There is thus, in the Uganda habitat, a variety of countryside and climate from the arid regions of low rainfall and intense dry season where thornscrub predominates to the Woodland and Woodland savannah where trees are plentiful and rain occurs in every month of the year.

In the Murchison Park itself, the study areas lay to the north of the Victoria Nile from Paraa, the Park H.Q., in the west to Karuma Falls in the east. The habitat comprised: (i) woodland; in the Pamdero area is found *Terminalia glaucescens* woodland which has a tall and annually burnt undergrowth of *Hyparrhenia* grass; this merges into (ii) mixed tree and shrub savannah, as in the rest of the Pamdero area and between Chobi and Karuma; the trees here are mainly of *Terminalia, Prosopis* and *Combretum* spp., while the commonest shrubs are *Lonchocarpus laxiflorus* and *Combretum binderanum;* grasses are mainly *Hyparrhenia* spp. (iii) *Hyparrhenia* grass savannah, which now forms the bulk of the Murchison Park, and which merges with (i) in the home ranges of patas groups in the Paraa area.

Likewise, within the ranges of the patas near Paraa, deciduous thicket occurs on exposed sites along heavily eroded areas. It consists mainly of thorny *Harrisonia* and *Acacia* bushes, with the *Combretum aculeatum* shrub which has small winged fruit; in the gullies, evergreen shrubs predominate. The commonest trees are *Tamarindus indica* and *Acacia sieberiana,* with an occasional *Euphorbia candelabrum.* Running down from, and through, the savannah to the Victoria Nile and to its tributaries, the Namsika and Emi Rivers, there are extensive areas of erosion of both the sheet and gully type. The sheet areas formed grassless sides or slabs, with cliffs and gullies where the savannah started above them, with *Tamarindus* trees predominating and broad expanses of grass towards the middle of the valleys along which, in many places, were water holes and wallows.

During most of the study period at Murchison (June to September 1963), the savannah grass was fairly long, 2 to 3 m at Pamdero, about 1 m elsewhere; in the long grass areas, observations were made from the top of the frequently occurring termite mounds, these being 2 m or more in height. However, at this time, the groups in the Paraa region were spending much of the day feeding on and around the erosion areas and valleys, hence observation was often very good, and contact with the groups could be fairly easily maintained.

Over great areas of the Murchison woodland savannah habitat, most of the trees are dead or dying. The primary causes are said to be an excessive elephant population and fire. The *Terminalia* trees, which seem to suffer most heavily, have thick bark which is normally able to withstand the annual fires that burn the grass around them and which is normally not palatable to elephants. However, the elephants have here started to rip the bark off the trunks, and the effect of this, followed by fires which scorch the exposed cambium, has been to kill the trees over large areas.

Climatically, Murchison, north of the Victoria Nile, is very similar to the rest of Acholi. Rainfall (Pakwach station, at NW corner of the Park; all available data to 1961, Uganda Atlas) averaged annually about 100 cm with January and February less than 2 cm, December and March about 5 cm with peaks of 14 cm for May and 11 cm for August. The rain occurred mainly in late afternoon and evening, leaving a fairly heavy precipitation on the grass the following morning. Water-holes or wallows, used regularly by the large mammals, were never completely dried up at any time of the study, and these were to be found along the middle of most of the erosion valleys. Much of the main course, and almost all the side courses, of the Emi and Nansika rivers were completely dry, except after heavy rain when they became briefly impassable and torrential.

Temperature shows little seasonal variation, the highest monthly maximum being 32 °C in January and lowest maximum 27 °C in July. The highest minimum is about 15 °C in March and lowest minimum 11 °C in August. In the field, shade temperatures were recorded during the day up to 36°C near Paraa, but on many days there were intermittent light breezes which cooled the air over the savannah, though not in the erosion valleys. The Chobi-Karuma area is about 1000 feet in altitude more than Paraa, and temperatures by day and night were notably cooler.

The fauna of the Murchison habitat include very large numbers of elephants, and large herds of buffalo. Oribi are very common, and other antelope regularly seen within the patas home ranges are Jackson's Hartebeeste, Uganda kob, Waterbuck, Bushbuck, Redbuck and Bush duiker. One or more Black rhinoceros were seen most days, being commonest at Chobi-Karuma where giraffe also occur. Warthog were very common.

Lion and leopard were seen only occasionally. Hunting dogs occurred on only two occasions in patas areas—there being only two animals. Cheetah do not occur.

Hippopotamus in huge concentrations are to be found in the Victoria Nile, and single animals were sometimes encountered during the day several kilometres inland.

Of the other species of monkey in the Park, baboons and vervets were mainly based on the riverine trees and shrubs of the Victoria Nile, but foraged well into the savannah.

Of the many species of bird, several ground-nesting species, such as plovers, bustards, quail, and night-jars, might have eggs and young preyed on by the monkeys, as likewise might tree-nesting species, but we have little information on this. Birds of prey commonly occurring included the large Martial eagle, but the Crowned eagle, *Stephanoetus coronatus,* known to prey heavily on *Cercopithecus* spp. and Colobus in woods and forests (Haddow 1952), was not observed.

Snakes were seen only twice in the savannah, but Monitor lizards and other small species were common.

Only brief mention of the Teso district habitat is necessary. It is a fairly densely populated agricultural area in which crops such as maize, millet, cassava and cotton, are grown, and there are many banana plantations. All these are reputedly fed upon by patas groups which escape, when chased, into Forest Reserves and thickets where vervets also occur. Baboons are no longer found except in isolated pockets where there is dense cover and some rocky outcrops. According to Mr. A. Stephens, who worked at the Serere Agricultural Research Station for over 30 years, baboons were previously common, and gradually decreased in numbers with the spread of agriculture. The patas population appeared to him to have notably increased in Teso. It is therefore probable that the patas, because of their smaller size and elusive habits, have been able to spread as the baboons have been eliminated.

FIELD WORK

On present-day standards, the work reported in this paper should be classed as a preliminary field investigation. Being concerned with a species not previously studied, choice of study location was a critical preliminary step. The general area of Uganda was selected, because Uganda has seemed to be the best area in which to organize a programme of comparative study of the patas and of some of the *Cercopithecus* spp., namely *aethiops* and *mitis*. The present sample of data is limited to one small area of the species, and to a relatively short span of time, with no data for the months of October through to February, inclusive.

Prior information had indicated that, patas being reputedly common in the Teso District, a start should be made in working that area, based on the Agricultural Research Station, Serere. A comprehensive survey of the area showed that patas were relatively common, but two factors made field work in the area very difficult: (1) population density of Africans working small holdings and shambas: the patas, frequently raiding crops, were periodically harried and hunted by the human inhabitants, and were therefore extremely wary in most areas; (2) the close vegetation cover of trees and thickets in most areas, which made it impossible to maintain contact with a patas group for the succession of day-ranges necessary to give worthwhile ecological and behavioural information.

At the time of first visiting the Murchison Falls National Park (1 June 1963), the grass was already long but, as described later, it turned out to be perfectly possible to locate groups and, in some areas, to follow them without losing contact throughout the day. The Park had obvious advantages over any other likely study area in East Africa—patas only occurring in one other Park, that of Kidepo in North Karamoja—namely that there would be no interference from human inhabitants, that the patas were to be seen in an environment which included a great variety of other animals, including possible predators, and that the Park staff were able to offer excellent working facilities. In view of the major objective of the study, which was to obtain as much detailed observation of patas social behaviour and ecology as possible

TABLE 2-2   STUDY PERIODS, LOCATIONS, AND OBSERVATION HOURS FOR PATAS, BABOONS, AND VERVETS

Stage	Location	Period	Field Days	Observation Hours			Main Objective
				patas	baboons	vervets	
		1963					
Preliminary	Teso district	March–April	17	17	—	3	Survey
I	Murchison (Paraa)	June–July	35	211	50	2	Search for groups; concentration on one population area
II	Murchison (Chobi)	July–August	17	55	12	33	Search for new groups; data on baboons and vervets
	Murchison (Paraa)	August–September	30	248	—	—	Intensive study of one group
		1964					
III	Murchison (Paraa)	March–April	19	107	3	2	Follow-up study; search for new groups.
		Total	121	638	65	40	

within a limited period, all field work was thereafter concentrated upon the Murchison population.

Study Period

Field work fell into four main stages, and the objectives of each stage varied as to the need for, and the possibilities of obtaining, particular types of information became apparent (Table 2–2). The number of hours of observation made while in contact with the groups varied considerably according to the objective. Many days of searching for new patas groups yielded little or no observation. Successive days of following a group on its day range from dawn to dusk provided up to 12 hours more or less continuous observation which varied in its yield of information according to the situation of the group. Data were obtained on baboon and vervet groups, which were very much easier to locate than patas, so that a local sample could be used for comparison with the patas.

The longest run of successive days' observation was 28 on Group IV in Stage II, providing about 250 hours of contact. Group II was observed for 109 hours in Stage I, and 103 hours in Stage III. Groups in the woodland savannah of Pamdero and Chobi were specially difficult to follow, because the grass was very long and there were few areas where the animals came for long periods into the open. In Stage III, the grass was short, after being burned in December 1963, and observation conditions were excellent. In Stages I and II, though the savannah grass was fairly long, Groups II, III and IV were found to spend quite long periods most days in foraging around and over large erosion areas where the animals could be clearly seen.

Field Methods

While there are general working rules relating to the field study of any monkey or ape species, the particular methods applicable to a species not previously studied have to be learned in the course of study and adapted to the habits of the species as these become apparent. The patas, being exceedingly shy and silent, offered a different problem from baboons. Baboons, in any area where they are not shot at or otherwise molested by humans, tend to habituate very readily to the observer. They are likewise easy to locate because of a much greater regularity of habit, and because they bark loudly on being disturbed. The only possible way to study the patas was, once having located a group, to follow it on foot for as long as contact could be maintained or until a sufficient sample of observations had been achieved. As the group usually spent each night in a different part of the home range, it was most economical of working time to follow it until it had stopped its ranging in the late afternoon so that it could be relocated in the same area the next morning. The routine of the field work was thus to leave camp in the Land Rover in the early morning, park it at the track side point nearest to the group's night resting area, then spend the day following the group on foot. The terrain of the Park was such that groups could not have been followed in the Land Rover. When searches were made for new groups, these were systematically carried out in the form of long circuits on foot from and back to the Land Rover. Most sightings of new groups were made by long-distance spottings of one or more patas in trees or walking over erosion sheets. As home ranges turned out to be very large and day ranges sometimes covered several miles, it was possible to walk all day searching without making any contacts.

Tolerance distance of patas groups varied according to the terrain and to degree of habituation. In Stage III over short grass country offering very little cover, Group II was difficult to approach nearer than 200 m. In woodland savannah, individual animals could be observed at 100 m, even shortly after first contact. In the Teso district, even closer approach was sometimes possible, presumably because the animals were used to the presence of human beings. Habituation after many successive days of observation of Group IV led to a reduction of observation distance from *c*. 400 to *c*. 100 m on average, with occasional periods of shorter range observation when the group was resting. Whether it would be possible to reduce distance to much less than 100 m is very doubtful because of the shyness of the animals. Use of hides is out of the question, because of their ranging habits, and likewise the Japanese method of provisioning would scarcely be practicable, even if desirable.

On every occasion, except for a few short reconnaissances, the observer, at Murchison, was accompanied by an African ranger who carried a rifle. This was a precaution required by the Park Warden against the possibility of attacks by buffalo or rhino in the long grass. The ranger employed on about 90 percent of all the field work, an Acholi of long experience, turned out to be a very great asset because of his very thorough knowledge of the topography and of the habits of the large mammals of the Park, elephant, buffalo, rhino, and so forth, which were encountered daily, and were duly circumvented without ever losing contact with the patas group.

In recording field notes in journal form, it became useful, as knowledge of the patas habits increased, to attempt simple quantification, on prepared score sheets, of the day's activities, and of social behaviour events such as grooming, play, and aggression. Distances travelled and the directions taken on the day range were charted as described in the relevant sections.

Conditions for photography were difficult because of the height of the grass and the shyness of the animals. Still photographs were taken with a Leica M.3 and associated lenses, and with a Russian Zenit 35 mm camera body with the MT01 500 mm lens. This lens proved excellent, because no tripod was necessary in using it. No cinefilming was attempted, as this would in itself have been a major undertaking for which valuable observation time could not be spared. No tape recordings were made because patas vocalizations audible at the usual observation distance were so infrequent. A 9 × 50 pair of Ross binoculars was used for all observations.

NUMERICAL DATA

Sizes of Groups

No reliable information, based on actual counts, has been available on the numerical sizes of patas groups, but several estimates have appeared, examples of which are: (i) small bands of 8 to 15; Uganda, Game and Fisheries Department Report for 1954–55; (ii) companies of 10 or 12; Uganda, Bere (1962); (iii) small parties of five or six individuals, seldom more; Kenya, Percival (1928); (iv) bands of 10 to 20 individuals, rarely more; West Africa, Bigourdan and Prunier (1937); (v) bands of 20 or so; Cameroon, Jeannin (1936); (vi) "Bands . . . at times gather into aggregations of more than 100"; apparently for West Africa, Tappen (1960:102), but the source of this statement is not clear from the text, (vii) "Large troops of these monkeys roam about the grassfields in northern Assumbo"; West Africa, Sanderson (1940). Sanderson (personnel communication, 28 May 1962) also says: "In Nigeria, these monkeys . . . live in huge bands—I would say up to 200 on occasions."

The differences between the estimates listed in (v) to (v) and (vi) to (vii) is very striking. In the first group, 20 is the maximum and five the minimum figure reported both for East and West Africa. No large aggregation of the order of (vi) and (vii) have ever been reported from East Africa and their absence is confirmed by the present study. However, regional differences of the order of magnitude suggested by these statements are definitely known to occur in baboon populations (Hall 1963b; DeVore and Washburn 1963), but large groups of baboons may temporarily subdivide, or temporary, purely local aggregations of several groups may occur at water-holes or pools in regions where water is seasonally very restricted. This suggests the possibility that, in patas likewise, seasonal aggregations of several distinct groups might be seen around water, each group, as in the case of baboons, moving off into its own home range after drinking.

The task involved in counting the individuals of a patas group varies greatly, as stated in the *Field work section,* with the terrain over which the group is moving. Repeated counts were made of groups on which long periods of observation were concentrated. The problem of obtaining an adequate sample, in terms of number of groups, is illustrated by the fact that it was possible to get reasonable counts of more baboon and vervet groups than patas in the Murchison study periods, simply because vervets are far more common and of predictable occurrence in particular areas, and baboons far more conspicuous and also more common. The 5200 hectare home range size estimated for patas Group II, when numbering 31 animals, compares with not more than about 3900 hectares in open savannah country for a large baboon group (perhaps numbering 60 to 80), and very much less for smaller baboon groups (DeVore and Washburn 1963). Where patas habitat overlaps extensively with that of baboons and vervets, as in the woodland savannah of the Chobi-Karuma area, the relative difference is very clear. In 17 days' field work there, only one patas group was located, after prolonged search over all likely areas to north and south of a 15 km stretch of track, as well as 8 km to W. of where the track ended. Baboon and vervet groups were sighted every day, and usually on several different occasions. Patas, in certain areas and times of year, may give the illusion of commonness, because a particular group may be seen several times, at different places, crossing a track or sitting near it.

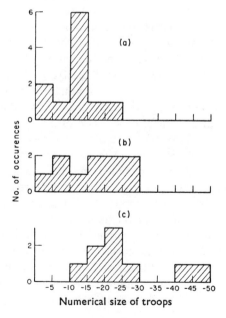

Fig. 2–2. Frequency data on group sizes for patas, vervets, and baboons at Murchison. (a) Vervets ($N = 1$); (b) patas ($N = 10$); (c) baboons ($N = 9$).

Reliable counts of eight different groups, excluding the all-male party (see below), were obtained at Murchison, and Group II was recounted in Stage III, March/April 1964, after an interval of nine months. In Teso, one small party, apparently consisting only of females and juveniles, was counted and two groups were separately counted, but, as the groups were counted at locations on separate days only about 2 km apart, it is evidently possible that these were one and the same group counted and recounted with an observational error of two such as was very likely to occur in woodland savannah. A summary of the numerical data (Fig. 2–2) includes the baboon and vervet samples obtained at Murchison. Data provided by Mr. J. M. Savidge from his survey of the fauna of the Kidepo National Park, Northern Karamoja, fall within the same range, the largest group being 28+. Mean and range of variation of vervet and patas groups counted in Stages I and II are closely alike, while the baboon sample gives a mean of about twice the size and a corresponding range of variation the upper limit of which is far higher and the lower limit is at about the mean size for the other two species.

While the means for patas and vervets show little difference, the statistical pattern of group sizes varies considerably between the species (Fig. 2–2, which also includes the baboon sample). It is quite clear that the samples of patas groups, both in terms of numbers of groups counted and in terms of recounting groups of the same population at different seasons and after long intervals of time, fall far short of what is necessary for even an elementary understanding of the population dynamics. In the Stage III period, in which the maximum time available was just over three weeks, only one group was recounted from Stages I and II, though prolonged searches were made for the other groups, one of which was briefly sighted, the remaining field time being spent on getting comparative data on ranging by Group II and on trying to locate new groups. Hence, the data of Fig. 2–2 must be treated as merely suggestive as to possible critical points of numerical size and social organization in terms of which the species may be found to differ. It is, for example, possible that a point of subdivision of a patas group occurs when it reaches 25 to 30. Two parties, quite separate from groups, numbering five and seven animals, were found in the course of the study, one in Teso, one in Murchison. Neither included an adult male. To what extent this splitting was temporary, and even accidental (through losing contact with the main body), cannot be known. The next two groups, in order of numerical size, consisted of 9 and 11 animals, and each included one adult male. Not a single group occurs between 11 and 20, in contrast to the vervet sample in which six out of the 11 groups fall within this range. One of the most important matters for further study of a patas population will be to determine the consistency and variability of groups in terms of size and composition over a long period of repeated censuses.

Constitution of Groups

Accurate analysis of age and sex classes in the patas groups is fundamental to understanding their social organization. Because there appears to be a birth peak, or even a discrete birth season, in the Murchison population, there has been no difficulty in counting the numbers in the age classes of infant one, infant two, and juvenile. Difficulty does arise after about age three years, because of the differential growth rate mentioned earlier, and because identification of sex at this stage could not always be reliably made in the field. Bearing this in mind, it has nonetheless been possible, by drawing upon all our presently available sources of information from the field and from the laboratory group, to make certain inferences about the patas group constitution and the changes that may take place in it as the young males reach maturity.

(1) ADULT MALES. The bare information from the field data is that, in every patas group, from Group VIII numbering nine animals to Group II numbering 31 in Stage III, there has been only one adult male. These males are, as the description earlier has stated, very conspicuous animals rather more than twice the size of the adult females.

In each group, however, there have been at least one, sometimes two, animals which, from study of the physical characteristics and appearance of our laboratory young male, were almost certainly of this category. In each of the two small parties of five and seven animals, there was also what appeared to be one young adult male, but the rest were adult females, juveniles or infants.

In addition to these young and full-grown adult males that belong to the bisexual groups or parties, isolated single adult males were occasionally encountered within the patas group home ranges but far from where the group was then ranging. One such male was observed at Chobi on two occasions, and was followed for one hour and for 35 minutes to ensure that he did not belong to a group somewhere in the vicinity. The group whose home range included this area was located 2–5 hours later, about 2–5 km from the isolate. There were three other records of isolate adult males in the home ranges during the study period; in two of these, the group was far away from the area; in the third, the isolate was discovered in the long grass by the adult male of Group III and raced away.

An important finding in Stage III, in the Pamdero woodland savannah, was of an all-male party of four animals; these were seen in the course of a search for Group I, sitting in the lower branches of the trees, or on termite mounds or fallen branches; on our slowly approaching them, they did not move away, and we were able to approach to 100 to 150 m; J. S. Gartlan, who was with the writer, independently checked the sex of all four animals, and we were able to establish that the party consisted of one full-grown adult male, two near-adult males whose fur colouration was similar, but their size was somewhat smaller, and one young adult male. The genitals of the three larger animals were clearly visible; those of the young animal were clearly visible when he sat on a branch facing the observer and opened his

TABLE 2–3 ANALYSIS OF PATAS GROUPS BY AGE AND SEX CLASS

Group Identification	Home Range Location	Date of Analysis	Adult Male	Young Adult Male	Adult Female	Juvenile	Infant 1	Infant 2	Total in Group
I	Pamdero	1.6.63	1	1	8	6	1	3	20
II	Paraa	12.6.63	1	2	12	5	0	2	22
III	Te Okot	12.4.64	1	1(+?1)	12	6	5	5	31
		6.7.63	1	2?	4	4	0	0	11
IV	Nansika	16.8.63	1	2?	5	3	0	0	11
		27.8.63	1	2	7	4	0	6	20
V	Chobi	5.9.63	1	2	7	6	0	5	21
		Aug. 1963	1	1	6	3	0	3	22
				(+8 juveniles, young adults and adult females)					
VI	Emi		0	1	2	1		1	5
VII	Air strip	2.4.64	1	(no adequate analysis made)			7		30
VIII	Tangi	11.4.64	1	(uncertain)	2	(uncertain)	2		9
B	Atira	4.4.63	1	1	8	13	1		26
				(+2 adults s.i.)					

Number of Animals in Each Age/Sex Class

legs to scratch inside the thigh. We kept this party under observation for two hours. We then walked on long circuits all over the Pamdero woodland area, and did not find any patas group. It is therefore certain that this all-male party was quite separate from any others.

There is no means of estimating accurately the number of surplus, isolate males, or of all-male parties, in a large population area. It is inevitable that sightings of such animals will be rare, because they must be most likely to occur well away from the vicinity of any of the groups.

In Murchison, isolate adult baboon males were also occasionally seen, but, so far as is known, all-male parties have never been observed in baboon populations anywhere.

The pattern of social organization that goes with the apparent exclusion of adult males from patas groups will be discussed later.

(2) AGE/SEX ANALYSIS OF GROUPS. In most cases, many successive days of observation were necessary before an adequate age/sex analysis of a group could be achieved. In the Chobi-Karuma woodland savannah, Group V was observed for over 50 hours without such an analysis being possible, because they were feeding mostly in grass of 1–5 m high and more. In such circumstances, it is necessary to wait till the group passes over bare ground or a short grass area, when it is usually possible to obtain the total count and the rough analysis in terms of adult males, adult females with infants, and so on.

In the Paraa areas of open grassland and erosion valleys, opportunities for such analysis were much better. When, as sometimes occurred, the whole of a group went into one big tamarind for the day resting period, it was possible to take up a position 75 to 150 m from them, and to classify each animal as it descended from the tree—usually, the descent of a group was spread over at least 30 minutes, sometimes up to an hour or more. It was largely on the basis of repeated observations of this sort that it became possible to recognize all the adults and young adults of Group IV as individuals.

All available data are summarized in Table 2–3. The age classes are those designated earlier (*Taxonomy and physical characteristics*). Only occasionally was it possible to determine sex in juveniles and infant two's, and then only to know that one of these was probably a male, so that no sex division is valid in these categories. There is never any problem in distinguishing the adult male from the other animals of the group, for the reasons already given. The young adult males were, in general, fairly easily distinguishable from the adult females by their larger size, including longer limb. Only very occasionally, however, was it possible to observe the genitals of these young adults—when sitting on branches—whereas those of the adult male were easily visible from the rear whenever he was standing or moving. By exclusion, that is, by counting of the adult females with whom infant one's and two's were closely associated and whose teats were elongated, there still remained one or two adults or young adults in almost every group whose sex was indeterminate (s.i.), and who could have been either females of about three to three and a half years or males two and a half to three years. In the table, date of analysis refers usually to one day on which most of the animals of a group were reliably classified, but often supplementary observation on many later occasions led to some revision.

A summary of the main points from the data of Table 2–3 is as follows:

(1) The patas adult sex ratio, when excluding the young adult males, ranges from 1:4 to 1:12 in the five groups for which accurate figures were obtained. Comparison in this respect with the four baboon groups of Murchison for which adequate data were obtained shows a highly significant species difference, there being 28 adult males to 39 adult females in the groups, that is, an overall ratio of 1:1–4, with a variation from 1:1–0 to 1:1–6. A sample of four baboon groups from Southern Africa (Hall 1963b) shows a greater disparity, the total of adult males being 26 against 72 adult females, giving a ratio of 1:2–8, and variation from 1:2–2 to 1:5–5 (overall ratio 1:2–8, variation from 1:2–2 to 1:5–5 for four groups) but no baboons (except *hamadryas,* Kummer and Kurt 1963, in a different form of social organization) have the one-male group social system.

(2) The age structure of the patas groups in terms of the numbers of infants classifiable as one or two differs significantly as between the group counts and analyses made at Murchison in April 1964 and those made at any other time of year. Thus, in Stage III, there were 14 infant ones in four groups totalling 70 animals. In Stages I and II, there was only one infant one in six groups totalling 100 animals. This infant one was observed at the beginning of the Stage I study period, and no further records of infant one's occurred between then and the end of the Stage II period.

This observation suggests that there is a birth peak or even a discrete birth season in the patas population of Murchison, The Warden of the Park reported that very small infants began to appear in Group II about January and February 1964.

HOME RANGES AND DAY-RANGING

Patas have been described as semi-nomadic in their use of habitat. This idea was presumably derived from the fact that patas groups, unlike baboons, were never found to be in the same area for long periods. The term implies that a group does not have a definable home range, but, as no field work has been done on the species, it was premature to apply it or any other term. From the Murchison area, we now have sufficient data to indicate that patas groups, within the limits of the study period, range in a basically similar fashion to baboons, but with some highly significant differences that may be correlated with other different adaptations as between the genera.

Day-Ranges

Day-ranges were recorded by the observer in following a group from the time it left its night-resting area in the morning to the time it settled in another, or occasionally the same, night-resting area in the late afternoon or evening. Compass-bearings were taken at successive points throughout the day-range, and distances between points were either visually estimated or sometimes paced. The chart of the day-range was plotted in the evening, and the whole series of ranges was checked with the main features of the terrain and the distances between them on the Murchison Falls National Park map, Sheet 30/1, Uganda 1:50,000. Air photographs of the areas were also used for identifying details of the terrain, such as the erosion gullies and sheets, and the extent of particular vegetation zones. Accurate distance estimation was found to be difficult in the open savannah country. A pedometer would not have helped materially, because of the need to make detours. Periodic checks of visual estimates by camera range-finder and pacing were useful, but the main check came in comparing the chart of bearings and distances with the map.

The sample of 58 day-ranges charted for eight hours or more during the three stages of the study period shows that there is a considerable variation between groups, and also a very notable variation within a group (Group II) at different times of year (Fig. 2–3). While the modal tendency for the whole sample is 2000 to 2500 m, the home range utilization pattern

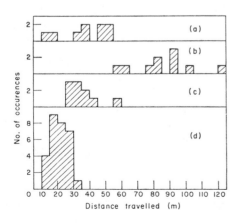

Fig. 2–3. Distances travelled by patas groups, Murchison, in 58 day-ranges observed for 8 hours or more. (a) Other groups: 8 day-ranges in Stages I and II; (b) Group II, 10 day-ranges between 26.4.64 and 5.4.64; (c) Group II, 10 day-ranges between 11.6.63 and 21.6.63; (d) Group IV, 29 day-ranges between 8.7.63 and 14.9.63.

evidently varies so much from season to season, area to area, that the complete range of variation in the sample is from 700 m (Group IV, 24–8–63) to 11,800 m (Group II, 31–3–64). Patas, like baboons, may spend several hours feeding in a particular area of trees and shrubs when fruits, berries, etc., are abundant. But, when foraging across the open grassland, as in the case of Group II in Stage III when the grass was short, they may move steadily throughout the day, starting off early in the morning and ending late in the afternoon, with the exception of the usual resting period in the hottest hours of the day.

The short day-ranges of less than 2000 m of which there were 21 out of the 29 recorded for Group IV, were spent in foraging amongst the long grass and *Combretum* shrubs above the valleys or in or around the edges of erosion valleys where the beans of *Tamarindus indica* were a major item of diet. Likewise in the Pamdero woodland savannah, the group there ranged only short distances because there was abundant fruit on trees of the *Ficus* and other species, whereas the Chobi group, in similar habitat, two months later travelled between 4 and 5000 m per day and obtained no food from the trees, other than ants on scored areas of bark.

The sample of five day-ranges for the Murchison baboons varied from about 2500 m to 5500 m. The two vervet day-ranges observed at Chobi were less than 2500 m. Baboons in South Africa may range up to about 11 km, when moving from one main feeding area to another, but the average is about 5 km (Hall 1963). It is not known that baboons will, for several successive days, travel the kinds of distance over which the patas Group II went in March and April 1964.

Home Range

Within the limits of this study, it is possible only to assert that the patas group on which the most field data were obtained each ranged by day and rested at night in a large area of country which, at the time, it alone utilized and occupied. Thus, each group may be supposed to remain, at least for long periods, within its own area, and other groups are to be found in adjacent areas. The evidence as to the range occupied by Group II Paraa during Stage I and then again by what may be assumed to be the same group augmented by the season's crop of births during Stage III supports the view that patas here, like baboons here and elsewhere, occupy a home range. The size of the range, and the pattern of its use, may vary from season to season. Its central areas are highly unlikely to be penetrated by any other group. The groups of adjacent areas have been observed in circumstances in which there has been no possibility of mistaken identity—as when Group VII, numbering 30, was first contacted, followed, and counted, on the morning of 2.4.64, after being sighted late the previous evening by the

Warden. On the same morning, the observer first located Group II, numbering 31, at its sleeping area, then went by Land Rover to the point where Group VII had been and walked until Group VII was found and subsequently counted. He then returned by Land Rover to the area where Group II had been two hours previously, and relocated it about 600 m away. It seemed just possible that Groups II and IV were the same group consistently using, over quite long periods of time, different parts of one very large home range. No sighting of the two groups separately on the same day was obtained. But there are three pieces of evidence which make this extremely unlikely:

(i) The fact that there is very little overlap between the home ranges as plotted from 20 day-ranges (Group II) and 28 successive day-ranges (Group IV).

(ii) While a visiting colleague, Mr. T. Wilson, followed Group IV on its day range, the observer searched the Group II home range and found fresh patas spoor and evidence of recent feeding.

(iii) Though difference in the total numbers in the two groups (22 in Group II, 20 in Group IV) could have been due to loss or to observational error, the quite considerable difference in the group composition (Table 2–8) was not thus accountable.

When the day-range sample has been large enough, as with Groups II and IV, a pattern emerges which indicates that, although over a succession of days a group may wander over a large area and never end up twice in the same night-resting area, there may sometimes be "preferred areas," though of quite a wide extent as fits their night dispersal habits, to which they are found to return on many occasions. Figure 2–4 shows how, for a ten-day sample of Group II day-ranges and night-resting areas in Stage III, and a sample of 13 successive days for Group IV in Stage II, there is some clustering of night-resting locations. This follows from a home range utilization pattern in which, sometimes, the group goes over and around a given feeding area for several days in succession, then moves on to another area and repeats the process. Group IV, for example, had, during the 28-day observation period of Stage II, three extensive areas of valley with shrubs, thickets, and trees, around which it did most of its day-ranging, spending a few days in or near one, then moving across the savannah to the next valley, and so on. But, in spite of this relative concentration upon one area for a few days in succession, it was still quite exceptional for the group to return to precisely the same place for two successive nights. For one night, they might be located to north of the valley around which they were temporarily based, for the next far to south of it out in the savannah, and so on. Apart from the dispersal of the animals at the night-resting area, and the great number of these areas, the utilization in feeding has some general resem-

Fig. 2–4. Samples of day-ranges and night-resting locations for Groups II and IV.
■– – –■, Night-resting locations and day-ranges, Group II, Stage III;
●———●, same for Group IV, Stage II; —|—|—|—|—, motor road.

blance to the pattern shown by the C group baboons in South Africa (Hall 1963*b*).

The notion of "core areas" within the home ranges of baboon groups (DeVore and Hall 1965) carries with it a kind of differential behavioural topography of the home range. A "core area" may be a place of special security and weather shelter for the group, to which it may return day after day at the end of the day-range. In the mountainous habitat of the Cape, the area is based upon a steep cliff, or a rocky escarpment or kopie. According to the nature of the terrain, there may be one or several such areas in the home range. Such areas have been thought to be only rarely penetrated by a neighboring baboon group, but we have found that a particular sleeping cliff may be used by two different groups on different occasions when one of the group has been at another part of its home range.

Even allowing for a considerable regional variation in the structure and utilization pattern of baboon home ranges, it seems that there is nothing comparable to the patas habits at Murchison, where almost any part of the home range away from the middle of the valleys may be used for the night-time dispersal of group members. The difference in the home range pattern as between baboons, vervets, and patas was made specially clear from see-

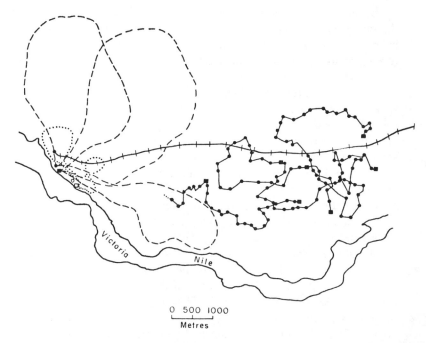

Fig. 2–5. A comparison of the day-ranging pattern for baboon, vervet, and patas groups at Chobi, Murchison. ●— — — —■, Baboon day-ranges; ●·····■, vervet day-ranges; ●———·———·———■, patas day-ranges. —|—|—|—, motor road.

ing groups of the three species in the Chobi-Karuma area (Fig. 2–5). The baboon and the vervet group returned regularly to the same clusters of trees along the Nile bank every night on which observations were made—and were still doing so when Gartlan (personal communication) spent three weeks in the area in July 1964, a year later. The patas group passed each night in a different area of the woodland savannah, and never went nearer to the bank than about 400 m in the course of its day-ranges. No patas group has so far been encountered in Murchison near the riverine vegetation or in the heavily wooded parts of some of the valleys. The baboon groups near Paraa likewise regularly returned either to tree clusters along the Nile or, in one case, to a tree cluster by the Emi river. Baboon groups range far into the savannah from these home bases, but there are many areas of savannah and erosion valley ranged by the patas where baboons were never seen. Thus, in the 28 consecutive days of observation of Group IV, not a single baboon group was sighted, only one isolate adult male baboon being seen twice in the home range. Patas Group II, on the other hand, met baboon groups several times in the southern third of its home range, but never in the northern two-thirds which was further away from the Nile.

Vervets were often seen in the Chobi woodland savannah, but the pattern the one group showed was similar, on a much smaller scale, to that of the baboons, namely ranging out during the day into the savannah, then returning to the river bank. This particular group never went far from trees, and rushed back to trees whenever it was frightened. It tended to feed and rest during the latter part of the day along the Nile bank. Small parties of vervets were sometimes found far into the grass savannah away from the river, but they were always near small gullies with a few trees. Thus, although baboons and vervets overlap with the patas home ranges, and eat some of the same foods such as berries and fruits, there are large areas of *Combretum* bush grass savannah and erosion valley where only patas have been seen. The vervet still remains a tree or thicket-based monkey, in spite of its sometimes quite long grassland excursions. The patas, one may say, is essentially, by contrast, a ground-based monkey who sometimes uses trees or thickets for food and shade. The escape behaviour of the two species usually shows this clearly—patas running down trees and away across the ground, even in woodland, vervets running up into trees.

The full extent of the home ranges of the patas groups is not yet known for any except possibly Group II. The area ranged over by Group IV in Stage II is certainly only a part of its home range, a thorough search of the area in Stage III failing to locate it. Likewise, Group III had moved elsewhere by Stage III, during which only a brief sighting, interrupted by a heavy storm during which we lost the animals completely from view, was all we obtained of it or Group IV. The Group II home range covers about 5200 hectares—considerably larger than most baboon home ranges. Group III, in Stage II, was in a kind of "buffer" position between the Group II and IV areas, the extent of overlap being as shown. If the Group II home range is typical in size, as seems likely from the very small patas population of the whole area, the density is not more than 30 patas to 5200 hectares. The whole patas population of the Paraa—Te Okot—Buligi—Tangi area may be little more than the five groups shown, that is 110 patas in 311,200 hectares.

DAY ROUTINE

The daily pattern of activities of the patas groups differs in some important respects from that of baboons, and differs also in some ways from what we at present know about the vervets.

So far as possible, the events of the patas day-ranges were recorded so that they might be used for some quantitative representation of the hour-by-hour pattern, as in the baboon study (Hall, 1962*b*,*c*), the preliminary study of vervets (Hall and Gartlan 1965), and in a field study of the Howler monkeys of Barro Colorado (Bernstein 1964). The data thus obtained are expressed in proportion to the total number of observation hours spent during each day-hour in the Murchison Stages I, II and III. At this latitude, $2°\ 17'$ N, sunrise and sunset time variation is negligible, and the day can be divided into 12 day-hours. Between 55 and 68 observation hours were spent at each day-hour from 0801 to 0900 to 1601 to 1700, with 20 observation hours before 0800 and 40 after 1700.

Activity Pattern

In the patas groups, there were four types of activity which could be usefully quantified per day-hour throughout the day-range: (1) distance travelled by the group (in metres); (2) prevalence of feeding by members of the group, estimated in terms of all or most of group, several (about half), and few (less than half); on the prepared score sheet, prevalence was noted for each ten-minute period, the results converted to weighted scores of three, two, and one for all, several, or few, respectively, and totalled for the day-hour; whether the feeding was in a tree or bush into which the animals had climbed, or on the ground, was also noted; (3) prevalence of social grooming and (4) of social play was likewise estimated at each ten-minute period, in terms of the number of grooming pairs and grooming clusters, and the number of play episodes weighted by the number of participants (thus, in a ten-minute period, there might be only one play episode, but, if it involved six animals, it would be scored as three, as would three more or less independent play episodes each only involving two animals).

In Stage III, with the grass very short, and conditions for observing the activities of all or most of Group II optimal, the task of quantifying was relatively easier and particular attention was paid to this. The pattern that emerges for the four types of activity (Fig. 2–6*a*) scores for which are expressed per observation hour at each day-hour, has several points requiring comment:

(i) The day-resting period usually occurred from about 1300 hours, and lasted about two hours, sometimes longer; feeding was considerably reduced over this period, being observed in a few animals when, as was usual, the shade trees for resting were Tamarinds.

(ii) Feeding activity went on fairly consistently up to the rest period, going up to a second peak in the later afternoon—a pattern that fits closely to the one described by Haddow (1952) for *Cercopithecus* species in Uganda. The small sample of data on *Cercopithecus aethiops* at Chobi showed the same trend.

(iii) Just less than 25 percent of all feeding took place in trees or in shrubs into which the animals climbed.

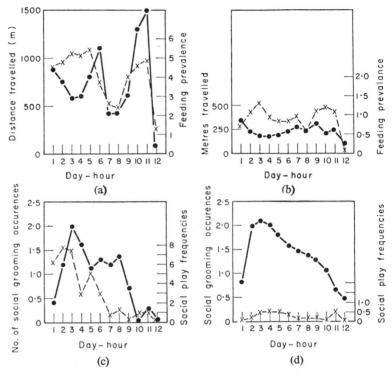

Fig. 2–6.   Graphic representation of activity pattern for day-hours 1 to 12 in terms of metres travelled; feeding prevalence; social grooming and social play frequencies.
(a) Patas Group II; (b) all other patas data.
(a), (b): ———, feeding prevalence; −×−−−×−, metres travelled
(c), (d): ———, social play frequencies; −×−−−×−, social grooming occurrences.

(iv) Social play, mainly amongst juveniles and infants two's, was very prevalent during the first three hours, that is up to 1000 hours, then decreased markedly as the day-range continued; play was not common in or under the day-resting shade trees.

(v) Social grooming likewise showed a peak in the first three hours of the day-range, but remained fairly steady in frequency of occurrence through the day-resting period, then dropped sharply to near zero in the last three hours.

(vi) The very great reduction of social play affects, as stated, mainly juveniles and infant two's, the reduction of grooming affects mainly the adults; both reductions go with a notable concentration upon feeding at that time of day; though the feeding peak is not as high then as in the first part of the day-range, for some reason this group moved much greater distances during the 10th and 11th hours than at any other time of day.

In Stages I and II, with the grass of the savannah long, conditions for obtaining a quantitative picture of the day activities in terms of (ii), (iii) and (iv), were, for some periods and some parts of the home-ranges, less satisfactory (Fig. 2–6*b*). The feeding prevalence pattern bears a general similarity to that of Group II in Stage III, with two main peaks, and a period from the fourth to the eighth hours where feeding was less prevalent because, as the record of particular day-ranges shows, a rest period usually occurred at some time between 1000 and 1500 hours, and sometimes there were two shorter rests in one day. The grooming pattern, however, correlates closely for the Stage III sample and the total of data on the four main groups observed in Stages I and II, even in terms of absolute frequency, the reason being that social grooming occurred mainly on tree branches and the top of termite mounds. This contrasts very sharply with the order of data on social play. As this play is almost entirely of chasing over the ground, play-wrestling on the ground, and so forth, and was therefore easy to observe in Stage III, it either actually did not occur nearly so frequently in Stages I and II, or it could not be nearly so frequently observed because it occurred mainly in grass long enough to obscure much of the activities of the young animals. It is certainly possible that play is reduced in frequency and prevalence in the long grass country simply because a play episode, as we know from our laboratory group and from Stage III field observations, is set off by a visual "invitation" to play consisting of a series of "bouncing" movements on the ground. Restriction of visual social stimulus would therefore reduce the likelihood of play being started and would prevent its spreading throughout the age-groups most likely to be involved. Whatever the explanation may be, it is certainly a curious fact that in, for example, the 28 successive day-ranges on Group IV in Stage II, there were no long series of play interactions at any time on any day such as characterized almost every day in Stage III.

Spacing between Individuals

The "spread" of a group on the ground or in trees varies very markedly at different times in the day-range, during different kinds of feeding, in short grassland or woodland, in day-resting and night-resting. In Stage III, when moving over the short grass areas, Group II, with 31 animals in it (five of them, the infant ones, being always very close to the mother or clinging ventrally to her), was usually very widely dispersed. Estimates, in terms of the directional axis of group movement and the lateral spread of individuals about this axis, were often of the order of 500 × 300 m. However, as will be discussed later (under *social organization*), one part of the group might forage at about 800 m distance from the remainder. As the total distances covered in the day-ranges at this time of year show, the foraging pattern was mostly a steady movement over the ground, individuals keeping within visual distance. In Stages I and II, the spread was usually much less than this, even in "open" country such as the erosion valleys, and was judged rarely to exceed 200 × 200 m in woodland savanna or *Combretum* bush country where grass was long. Such judgments in the more "closed" country must evidently be of uncertain reliability, but they are based on the appearances of animals, at quite frequent intervals, up from the grass and onto trees, bushes, or termite mounds.

Day-Resting

The time during the day-range at which a group would rest probably depended upon factors such as proximity of suitable shade trees and amount of food obtained by the group in the first feeding period. Though the patas were not averse to sitting in full sun on termite mounds or on the branches of dead trees when grooming around noon or later, there was usually some period of actual resting in a shade tree during the hottest hours from about 1300 hours. Often all the animals of the group would climb up into the canopy of one large shade tree, usually a Tamarind, so that dispersal was minimal during the day-resting period. Sometimes two or three such trees in a cluster served the group. During this period, some grooming might occur, and infants would be nursing from their mothers, but most of the animals could be seen resting in a variety of sitting and reclining postures amongst the branches. The duration of such resting was usually between one and two hours, but sometimes about three hours—on 23.8.63, Group IV spent from 1240 to 1556 hours in one shade tree; on 7.9.63, Group IV made no move between 0915 and 1240 hours, after feeding for 90 minutes previously. Rest periods were shorter in the long day-ranges of Stage III, but there were sometimes two such periods in the day. Juveniles or infants may begin to move down and up the trunk of the tree occasionally as the rest proceeds, and eventually adults may start to descend. Descent, and resumption of the day-range, was usually a gradual process that might take 30 minutes or more, though occasionally the move away was fairly abrupt and rapid, with consequent difficulty for the observer in making contact.

Night-Resting

Early in this field study, it began to appear that the night-resting habits of the patas differed most interestingly from those of baboons and vervets. The point has already been emphasized that a patas group rarely occupies the same areas on successive nights. The day-resting pattern suggested that the group might all go up into one or a cluster of trees such as Tamarinds which are mainly to be found along the sides and towards the middle of erosion valleys. The night-resting pattern turned out to be completely different. Groups were never seen to go at evening into the denser areas of tree and shrub occasionally found in the home ranges, and usually avoided even the more scattered trees along the erosion valleys, moving up towards evening onto the savannah, and dispersing into several different trees. The dispersal area occupied by a group during night-resting, as judged from observations up to dusk and from daybreak, appeared to be at least as large as the area of their spread over the group when feeding during the day. The pattern was thus precisely the opposite of what occurred in day-resting.

Before this dispersal habit was known, there was sometimes difficulty, in the mornings, in relocating a group which had been observed till late the previous day. We learnt that the best method was simply to go to the area and wait there, if none of the patas was in sight, and they would gradually come into view as they moved out of the trees onto the ground. If we searched by walking around and beyond the area, we were likely to frighten some of them, and all would go out of sight in the grass.

Time of dispersal of a group at the end of the day-range was much later in the long day-range series of Stage III than in the shorter series of Stages I and II. In Stages I and II, a group often reached the general area in which it was to pass the night by about 1700 hours. Feeding did not cease then, but continued in a kind of radiating pattern within the area, individuals being widely dispersed, and moving about the area, but the group as a whole not moving. In Stage III, the group as a whole moved, feeding, until about 1800 to 1830 hours, sometimes even later. In the morning, Group II in Stage III began its day-range about 0715 to 0730 hours, and the groups in Stages I and II began between 0730 and 0800 hours.

The conclusion of feeding and the dispersal into sleeping trees was a gradual process that might go on for more than an hour. By the very fact of the wide dispersal between members of the group at this time, it was never possible to locate every individual of one of the larger groups before sunset at about 1900 hours or between sunrise at about 0700 hours and the time they began to move onto the ground. Nevertheless, the general pattern is clear, though some details of it are lacking—for instance, the position of the adult male in relation to the location of others of the group. Dispersal distances between individuals in the trees varied with the spacing of the trees. From the locations of individuals in Group IV, Stage II, and Group II, Stage III, the size of the dispersal area was sometimes at least 250,000 m^2, that is, a night resting density for the group of about one monkey in 10,000 m^2. We have no evidence that the spacing varied during the night. No group was known to shift its area as between the evening and the following morning.

On most occasions where the majority of a group was in view towards evening, it was the adult females with infant one's or two's who were among the first to climb up into the trees in the sleeping area. Here, they groomed the infants and allowed them to suckle. Thus, on 5.9.63, Group IV, a mother with an infant two climbed into the upper branches of a dead tree on the savannah above the erosion valley where some of the group were still feeding at 1755 hours; at intervals from then until 1825 hours, three other adult females, each with an infant two, each climbed up into a separate tree. On 13.9.63, individuals of Group IV began to take up positions in trees in the middle of a large stretch of savannah from 1715 hours in the following order: adult female with infant two; adult female; two adult females; young adult male; adult female with infant two. Each pair or individual was in a separate tree.

The dispositions were such that one adult or juvenile or one adult female with an infant was to be found in one tree. Two adult females, each with an infant, were once observed, at 1900 hours, on one tree, and the two adult females of the 13.9.63 dispersal remained in the one tree till observation ended that evening at 1910 hours. On 18.6.63 there were parties of four, four, and two patas of Group II in three trees of a cluster, but most others appeared individually and in mother-infant pairs from trees further away. Occasionally, there would be some movement of individuals after climbing into the trees, but, in general, they remained high up in the trees they had selected at least until observations ceased at dusk.

During the day-resting period, the adult male, as we have seen, is usually in the same shade tree as all the other animals of the group. In the evening and the early morning, he was never seen to be associated with the adult females and their infants, and never appeared in or out of a tree in their vicinity. When describing in detail the role of the adult male patas in the groups (see *Social organization* section), his watchfulness is the most prominent feature of his behaviour. Towards evening, as a group approached the area in which they were to pass the night, this male was sometimes conspicuously thorough in the way he surveyed the whole area. He has been observed, on several occasions, to run 400 to 600 m down a valley away from the rest of the group, who remained where they were. He took up a position high in a tree from which he scanned over the area, sometimes for about 30 minutes. He then either came back to nearer the group, or remained where he was as the others dispersed into trees. It seems reasonable to suppose that this behaviour is with reference to possible predators, such as leopard, although it might also be in relation to the possibility of other patas being in the vicinity. As no group ever contacted another group near sleeping areas, and as no leopard was known to have been sighted by patas, it is impossible to particularize about the objectives of this behaviour.

A very notable general feature of patas behaviour is the almost complete lack of any vocalizations audible to the observer. On no occasion was any vocalization heard morning or evening. The general adaptive significance of this silence can be considered in relation to the adaptiveness of the dispersal behaviour of the patas at night. Dispersal away from the middle of valleys and into many separate trees may be considered to be an anti-predator adaptation which would ensure that, if a leopard were to catch one animal in a tree, it would be very unlikely to catch any others in the other trees, whereas, if a leopard were to come upon the whole or most of a group in one tree, it might kill several. Tinbergen (1956) pointed out that procryptic animals of many species tend to scatter, and since this is done by a variety of means, the effect of scattering seems to have survival value. This certainly seems to be the case with the patas.

Leopard spoor was quite commonly found in the patas home-ranges, and leopards were three times seen during the day resting in trees in these areas. The fact that the groups rarely spent two successive nights in the same area would also reduce the likelihood of a leopard locating a group. No data on predation by leopards on patas are available. One patas skeleton was found in an area where a leopard had recently been seen. Other factors than predator-avoidance which might account for an adaptation that seems to go so strongly against the cohesive forces that bind the individuals in the group are difficult to envisage. However, it is possible that the frequent passage of elephants during the night might have also disposed the groups to avoid congregating in one or two trees.

Comparison with Baboons

The main differences in the day-routine adaptive patterns as between the Murchison patas groups and the baboons of Murchison and of the Cape, South Africa (Hall 1962*b*), are sufficiently distinct to indicate that they are much greater than the intraspecies differences likely to be found regionally. On the baboon day-ranges at Murchison, it was found that the groups fed fairly steadily throughout the day, as in the Cape, though there might be several individuals sitting and not feeding when the group was spread over a feeding area in which it remained for an hour or so. Certainly there was no evidence here of a regular day-resting period, and the far greater amount of food required by a baboon group would be one factor accounting for this difference.

The clearest difference concerns the night-resting habits. The Murchison baboons congregated in a few large trees, quite close together, on the banks of the Nile, towards evening, and the groups that were followed near Paraa and at Chobi mostly returned to the same trees night after night.

The morning and evening grooming peak noted in the Cape and the Kenya baboons (Hall and DeVore 1965) goes with the tendency to congregate at these times near the sleeping place, and therefore would not be expected in the patas who, conversely, are dispersed toward evening and even in the morning when about to start on the day-range do not cluster together.

INTERACTIONS WITH OTHER ANIMALS

The Murchison Falls National Park habitat, as described earlier, abounds with large mammals and encounters between patas groups and some of these animals were a daily occurrence. Examples of patas behaviour in relation to these animals will be given, and in relation to birds, and to baboons and vervets. No reactions to snakes or Monitor lizards were observed.

Potential mammalian predators that occurred in the Park were leopard and Hunting dogs. As the latter were so scarce, they could hardly constitute any danger to the patas. Nothing is, in fact, known about predation on patas other than by man. No predator-prey interactions were recorded in the present study. It is usually assumed that leopard prey on patas, but the only first-hand observation of an encounter (Percival 1928) strongly suggests that the leopard was far from intent on hunting them. Percival and his brother watched, from a station-house in Kenya, a leopard being followed by a party of patas who were "scolding" it. Apparently describing the same episode (Percival 1924), he says the patas were following the leopard through the open thorn bush, where trees were too far apart for them to stay aloft in their pursuit, so they ran from one tree to the next after it.

All the observations of the present study indicate that individual patas and groups of patas vary in their responses to the non-predatory animals according to the particular circumstances of the encounters. Such encounters must evidently form a part of the local tradition of the groups, by whom the appropriate behaviour is readily acquired from day-to-day experience. In general, patas, like other animals, are guided in their behaviour towards the other mammals by the direction of movement, or lack of movement, of these in relation to themselves, as well as by other such obvious cues as distance, sudden appearance, and so on.

Interactions with Nonprimate Mammals

Encounters can be classed, with reference to the result observed in the behaviour of the patas, as: conditioned alertness; usually neutral; and variable, but tending to avoidance. Others were so infrequent as to give no indication of the range of behaviour variations, as, for example, when two mongoose appeared foraging close to an adult female patas with an infant two near her; she grabbed the infant up to her belly, and ran away as did another adult who also saw them; later, the same two mongoose approached another infant two that was separated from its mother by a chasm one metre wide across which she had already jumped; neither the mother nor the infant reacted towards or away from the mongoose.

Conditioned Alertness

Washburn and DeVore (1961*b*) have reported that the frequent close association between baboons and Impala in Kenya provides natural protection against predators in open country, while, in forest areas, Bushbuck may play the same role. Baboons are always ready to given warning barks which alert not only the baboon group but the ungulates that may be near it. Patas, however, have never been known to bark or to give any other "warning" calls that would be audible beyond about 100 m (that is, the "chirrup" call which elicits immediately alert and watchful behaviour in the laboratory patas).

In the short grass season of Stage III, patas Group II was near to, or in easy viewing or auditory range of, Oribi every day. It was repeatedly noted that the Oribi's alarm-whistle, usually uttered with reference to the observer, immediately alerted many of the patas who looked in the direction the Oribi was looking, usually standing on hindlegs or climbing to vantage points on termite mounds or trees. If the Oribi ran away, however, the patas, after identifying the cause of the alarm call, at once resumed whatever activity they were doing. This behaviour of the patas is based presumably on a simple conditioned response, but there is no evidence that the association of patas and Oribi was anything other than due to the circumstance of sharing a common feeding area. It was never clear, however, that the patas responded in similar manner to the alarm calls of any other antelope.

Neutral, but Wary

A neutral relationship characterized most of the encounters with the large mammals such as elephant, buffalo, and rhino. None of these animals ever appeared to react directly towards the patas, except on a single occasion (buffalo, see below). In this, the behaviour of patas on the ground is similar to that of baboons (Washburn and DeVore 1961*b* and personal observation at Murchison), but baboons are more "casual" than patas, sometimes just stepping out of the way of feeding elephants when the latter are only a few metres from them.

Patas Group IV, during the 28-day series of observations in Stage II, encountered elephant herds or individual elephants every day at varying degrees of proximity. The patas' reactions varied from indifference to watchfulness to avoidance, as in the following instances:

(i) A young bull elephant, in a party consisting of a cow, calf and another young elephant, winded a buffalo in bush nearby, and charged the buffalo, trumpeting and ear-flapping, making it move far away. The charge took the young bull through the area where the patas were feeding. Several climbed onto bushes and tree stumps, and stood on hindlegs watching, but the group did not move away from the area, nor did individuals run away.

(ii) The patas group, during the day-range, climbed into a large fruit-bearing tree in which they started to feed very actively. One adult female was at the top of the canopy, watching a herd of elephant who were feeding 200 to 300 m from the tree. After 23 minutes of fruit-eating, the patas began to descend rapidly and ran away through the grass. A few of the elephants approached right under the tree, and ate the fallen fruits. The adult male patas was the last of the group to leap down from the tree as the first of the elephants came beneath it. The patas sat on stumps and bushes in the vicinity of the tree, and, as the elephants moved away, the adult male patas remained sitting on the branches of a dead tree about 3–5 m above the head of one of the herd that passed directly below him. After watching the movement of the elephants away from the tree, the whole patas group returned up into the canopy and resumed feeding there.

(iii) The patas group spent two to three hours feeding in *Combretum* bush savannah in an area of a few scattered trees, while elephants were standing under the shade of these trees or were browsing from the bushes. Two patas already resting in a tree climbed higher into the canopy as an elephant came directly below them. A mother with an infant two at her belly was distinctly nervous on this occasion, running up into one of the large trees whenever elephants came near her.

Although elephants were never observed to react towards the patas, on one occasion a crashing noise of branches being shaken violently was heard from a large tree in which some patas were resting and under which a full-grown elephant had come to stand. A peculiar "choking" vocalization was heard from the patas.

Reactions to rhino were similarly variable. A juvenile patas was once seen sitting on a termite mound 10 m from a feeding rhino. On another occasion, most of Group IV, wandering along close to a wallow area, raced back, some of them as far as a cluster of Tamarinds 100 m away, when a bull rhino walked slowly to the wallow. But an adult female with an infant two remained on top of a two metre thornbush only 15 m from the rhino, and others stayed on the ground at about 50 m where they stood on their hindlegs watching the rhino. When the rhino settled into the wallow, some of the patas passed close by him, though most accelerated their pace to a gallop when directly in front of him. It was noticeable that the juveniles and infant two's quickly lost their nervousness, approaching to the edge of the wallow to eat the red mud. When, shortly after, a cow rhino with her calf approached the wallow, some of the patas were again nervous, one adult female racing away, leaving an infant two who tried to cling on to her belly to follow her as fast as it could. On other occasions, rhinos were watched, if approaching, otherwise ignored.

When patas encountered the large buffalo herds grazing or resting along the valleys, the adult male patas were often very watchful, particularly when there was any movement of the herd, and other patas, when a group was feeding in the grass, would frequently look out from fallen tree branches or mounds, and never approached closer than about 100 m from the buffalo. Although evidently cautious of a herd's movements, in areas where trees were few, a patas group has, on several occasions, passed right through the middle of a large herd, going very fast and keeping close together through a "gap" between parts of the herd. Only once was a buffalo, a solitary bull, seen to react to patas, by jerking his head upwards towards those sitting in a tree above him.

Single hippopotamus only were encountered during the day by patas, because of the patas habit of avoiding the riverine vegetation, and the patas just kept out of the way when one of these animals was on the move.

With all such encounters, the patas' behaviour is, with individual exceptions, no more than a keeping of adequate distance to avoid being trampled or, presumably, the possibility of being dislodged from a tree by a feeding elephant. No threat movements by these large mammals were seen to be directed toward patas, and, with the one exception of interrupted feeding at a fruit tree, the day routine was not apparently altered in any respect by their presence.

Avoidance

The only direct movements toward patas, in the form of chases or perhaps mock attacks, came from encounters with various species of antelope. Hartebeeste frequently chased individual patas for short distances, making them climb onto bushes. Bushbuck were particularly prone to do this with patas, and also with baboons, sometimes chivvying different individuals of a patas group repeatedly and for quite long periods. One episode lasted 83 minutes, but the patas group did not leave the area, individuals simply scampering away as the bushbuck charged in their direction. Even Duiker and Oribi have sometimes chased patas, but Redbuck and Waterbuck have not been seen to do so. On one occasion, the adult male patas of Group II chased an

Oribi that was coming toward him as he was feeding on the grass. This Oribi had several times previously chased adult females and infants in the area. When Warthog have approached, patas have usually moved out of the way, and only once was a brief chase seen when a young Warthog ran after a juvenile patas.

Interactions with Birds

There is no evidence that any species of eagle preys on patas. The large Martial eagle, *Polemaëtus bellicosus,* was seen occasionally flying over or perched in trees near where a patas group was feeding. No change in behaviour was observed in the patas, and certainly no avoidance or special alertness, except when one of these birds flew over with a Banded mongoose in its talons. Then, several patas, including the adult male, stood on hindlegs watching. When a Wattled plover, *Afribyx senegallus,* was repeatedly diving, uttering its loud alarm call, low over the head of a Martial eagle perched on a tree top, making the eagle bow its head to avoid being struck, patas on the ground nearby paid no attention. Mackworth–Praed and Grant (1957) include in this eagle's diet small antelope and jackals, so that it would not have been surprising if the patas had been more wary of its presence.

Most interactions with birds involved air-harrying of patas, notably by the Drongo, *Dicrurus adsimilis,* the Grey kestrel, *Falco ardosiaceus,* and the Grey hornbill, *Tockus nasutus.* Patas usually ignored these common but harmless threats, but young patas have occasionally struck out fiercely with their hands at the birds, and sometimes have chased after these birds or plovers when they were settled on the ground. Two factors may perhaps give rise to this kind of interaction: one, that patas are reported to eat eggs and young birds (Percival 1928), and were once observed in the present study eating eggs from a nest in a tree; two, that some of the species, for example the Grey hornbill and Bruce's Green pigeon, *Treron waalia,* are frequently associated with patas in feeding off fruits of trees such as *Ficus,* and the Grey kestrel and the hornbill have both been observed feeding on insects in short grass, where patas also feed on grasshoppers, and so forth.

Interactions with Baboons and Vervets

On the rare occasions when a baboon group approached directly an area where patas were feeding, the latter withdrew rapidly. Patas Group II in Stage III was foraging over short grass along a valley. A group of 34 baboons came into view about 500 m from them. At first, the patas continued foraging on the ground, then climbed into a cluster of Tamarinds. When the baboons continued steadily in their direction, apparently heading for some fruit trees, the patas rapidly descended, with the baboons still 300 m from them, and galloped out of sight. We followed the patas, and located them 20 minutes later about 1000 m further on. A similar rapid withdrawal took place when a baboon group approached a fruit tree in which the patas were already feeding. The patas disappeared into a gully, along which they must have run, reappearing on the far side 500 m away. The baboons did not threaten or bark at the patas—evidently no such display was necessary. In the light of this behaviour by the patas, the statement in the 1954–1955 report of the Uganda Game and Fisheries Department that even baboons have a healthy respect for the patas can scarcely be supported. This statement is based on one instance in which a baboon group is described as moving away from a pool when a large male patas came to drink there. Lack of sufficient detail of this encounter makes this interpretation of cause and effect uncertain. It is clearly possible that the baboons had finished drinking when the patas arrived.

The other interactions observed, of which there were only two, making a total of four in the whole study period, were much less definite, probably because in them the baboons were not moving directly towards the patas, but parallel to them. The longer of the two episodes lasted nearly two hours. Patas Group II were feeding along the side of a valley. A group of 46 baboons came down the middle of the valley, stopped, fed on Tamarind beans, rested there, and squabbled noisily. They seemed to ignore the patas completely. Some juveniles of the patas group came within about 100 m of the nearest baboons. The adult male patas was watchful, but the group did not withdraw on this occasion, and eventually moved away to continue its day-range. On the fourth occasion, the patas, while continuing to feed, watched a baboon group going along past them at about 300 m. No threat behaviour or vocalizations have occurred with reference to the other, either on the side of the patas or of the baboons on these occasions. No doubt the patas know the probable behaviour of the baboons encountered in their home range with some accuracy, so that they do not unnecessarily take evasive action.

The only definite encounters with vervet groups occurred in the Woodland savannah at Chobi and Pamdero. There is no evidence that vervets withdrew from patas, or *vice versa*. In Stage I, patas Group I and a vervet group were between 80 and 150 m from each other for nearly an hour. During this period, patas and vervet watched each other, but there were no vocalizations and no alarm or threat behaviour. The vervets began to feed on the figs in one of the trees, these being one of the main food items at this time of the patas group. In the more open grassland habitat, where vervets were rarely seen, no encounters with patas were observed. On two occasions, volleys of calls that were probably from vervet groups were heard, apparently when the patas group that we were following had come into contact with them. On both occasions, the adult male patas barked repeatedly—a rare occurrence that otherwise was recorded only when a patas group encountered other patas. As the behaviour of the vervets was not observed, the data are inconclusive, and there remains from the present study insufficient evidence as the usual relationship between the two species.

Because of their way of life which, at Murchison and in West Africa (Booth 1956), brings them only to the edges of forest, and of riverine thicket and tree clumps, patas are very unlikely to encounter monkey species other than baboons and vervets.

FEEDING AND DRINKING

The schedule of diet obtained for the patas at Murchison is very far from complete, because it has been made up from direct observation only, then collections of a specimen whenever possible for later identification. No stomach content samples were obtained, because it was not feasible to try to shoot any of the animals during the field study. Direct observation has obvious limitations when the animals are feeding in long grass. From the foraging habits of the groups, it is clear that, within the seasonal limits of the study period, grasses, berries, fruits, beans and seeds formed the bulk of the diet, this being supplemented by occasional finds of mushrooms, by licking up ants, catching grasshoppers, rarely catching small lizards, once only eating the eggs of a tree-nesting bird, and occasionally eating chunks of red mud. Table 2–4 gives the main dietary items recorded, and indicates those items known also to be part of the diet of the Murchison baboons. Easily the commonest food other than grasses is the pods and fruit pulp of the Tamarind. It was rarely possible to obtain specimens of the small plant or grasses eaten. Although there are several items which patas and baboons were eating during the study period, the difference in the ranging habits of the two species probably prevents much dietary overlap on a quantitative basis. While both species eat the beans of *Tamarindus indica,* the patas get them mainly from trees which baboons have not been seen to visit, and patas eat grasses in areas where it is doubtful if baboons ever penetrate. There are, no doubt, many foods which baboons obtain from the riverine vegetation where patas do not go at all. In the savannah, baboons often gnawed and ate the very tough sausage-shaped fruit of *Kigelia aethiopica* and occasionally ate the small fruits of *Balanites aegyptica,* neither of which patas have eaten. The former is probably much too tough for the patas jaws. A detailed ecological study of two species in the Murchison area would be of great interest.

As the seasonal and group differences in day-ranging distances indicate, the feeding pattern varies considerably. Much of the feeding time of Group II in Stage III was spent over short grassland. Though most of the food was taken from the grass itself or from small plants growing amongst it, it was impossible to be sure which items they were selecting. That there was usually

TABLE 2–4   SOME FOOD ITEMS OF PATAS GROUPS, MURCHISON
(B INDICATES THOSE ALSO EATEN BY BABOONS)

Plant Species	Parts Eaten	
Tamarindus indica	Pods, fruit pulp	B
Crataeva adansonii	Fruit	B
Ficus natalensis	Berries	
Ficus glumosa	Fruit	B
Teclea nobilis	Berries	
Syzygium owariense	Fruit	B
Harrisonia abyssinica	Berries	B
Combretum aculeatum	Seeds	
Acacia sieberiana	Seeds	
Cassia mimosoides	Pods	
Acacia senegal	Leaves	
Celtis integrifolia	Berries	
Hyparrhenia filipendula	Grass seeds	

Note: parts of several other grasses were eaten, but specimens were not obtained

Other items

Mushrooms:
Lepiota species indeterminate	Large size, diameter *c.* 150 mm
Cantharellus species indeterminate	Small size

Insects:
"Grasshoppers"
Ants	Licked from scored areas of tree trunk

Lizards:
Agama agama	and possibly other species

a selection of particular plants was evident from the fact that, when walking over such an area, the patas would pick off blades or stems only at about 10 m intervals. Sometimes, the action of the animal showed that it was looking for and occasionally finding some insects. In the woodland savannah of Pamdero in Stage I, Group I did much of their feeding from the fruits and berries of trees. In the Chobi-Karuma area in Stage II, the patas only fed once from fruits or seeds in a tree.

Feeding Behaviour

Patas, like baboons, obtain almost all their food by hand, and rarely by applying the mouth directly to it. Many of the plant items, such as seeds found on the bare ground of erosion areas or on tall grasses or in low bushes, are small and require an effective coordination of the shortened thumb in relation to the fingers in the act of picking up or plucking. When foraging over short grass or erosion areas, they usually feed at a steady walk, visually searching the area just ahead of them and plucking the food objects with one hand. Like baboons, they often stand on hindlegs, when feeding on the ground, so as to reach up with the hands to pull down seeds from tall grasses or from small bushes. Like baboons also, though the action differs in detail, food objects that are gritty or dusty are rubbed between the hands before being placed in the mouth. Sometimes a tall stem of grass or long twig of a tree branch is pulled down towards the feeding animal by one hand and held while the other hand is used to take off the food item. There is little in all these feeding movements to distinguish patas from baboons, though baboons, with their greater strength, pull, tug and dig roots and grasses from the ground and from banks in a way that patas have not attempted.

When a cluster of large mushrooms, evidently a much-prized food, was found by a patas group, several interesting social and manipulatory aspects of their feeding were shown. First, relative status was to be seen in that an adult female who had not yet obtained a large mushroom might chase another adult female or a young adult male with the effect, occasionally, of making the holder drop all or part of it. With the large mushrooms, such chases several times resulted in the pursued animal running away on its hindlegs holding the mushroom in both hands. It was, in fact, very rare for any animal other than the adult male or the probably "senior" adult females (those with infants) to obtain possession of a big mushroom. Second, the time taken in eating these mushrooms was as long as 20 minutes on occasion, the feeding animals eating every part including the stem. In spite of the "competitiveness" occasionally seen, no fight occurred. The adult male was once sitting 2 m from an adult female who was busily eating a large mushroom, and he made no attempt to get it from her or to chase her away. Infants sometimes sat below the adult females that were eating them, and picked up small pieces that were dropped. Infants sometimes tried to grab larger pieces, but were never permitted to get them. Third, these were the only occasions on which any of the patas were seen to carry food or any other object in the mouth while walking or running. Baboons at Murchison carry objects in this dog-like manner sometimes—usually the large *Kigelia* fruits.

The cat-like quickness and agility of patas was seen most clearly in their occasional chasing and pouncing on small lizards found under the bark of dead or dying trees, usually *Prosopis* species. It was also noted in their pouncing on grasshoppers, or swiping with one hand, often from a bipedal stance, at flying insects. Sometimes a patas has leapt high into the air trying to catch such an insect.

When eating the red mud found on some banks or at the edges of wallows, the patas usually put their mouths directly to it and chewed it or licked it. The action is the same as in drinking or in licking the salt crystals from the edge of pools.

The spacing between individuals when feeding varies enormously in patas groups according to the terrain. In the short grass season of Stage III, Group II was estimated as being spread out over 100,000 m² at times (see below). When feeding on mushrooms, as described above, or in fruit-bearing trees, inter-individual distances were greatly reduced so that relative rank might become temporarily apparent. Thus, the adult male and a few of the adult females would usually be the first to go up into a fruit tree. As stated above, and also in the *Aggression section,* the organization within the group is such that, even in restricted feeding areas, the spacing is so well-ordered that threat is rarely ever seen. The feeding activities of a group are co-ordinated by such social processes as facilitation, secondary conditioning and observational learning.

The role of the adult male is again conspicuously demonstrated in the course of day-ranges when the group is approaching a new feeding area, such as an erosion valley, across the savannah. He would take up position high in a tree, sometimes 400 m or more away from the group, from which he surveys the whole area for as much as 15 minutes. In such a position, he is clearly visible to the group. When he descends, he comes back towards the group, and they all move into the valley.

Drinking

The patas has been supposed to be much less dependent on water availability than baboons. Bigourdan and Prunier (1937) report the occurrence of patas during the dry season in areas of West Africa completely devoid of water, whereas the baboons at that season remain fairly close to water because they are said to need drink every day.

At Murchison, apart from observations of a special type of drinking seen in Group I in Pamdero (see below), during the whole of the Stages I and II study period a group, or individuals from a group, was seen to go to water holes, wallows, pools or puddles to drink on only four occasions:

Group III	12.7.63 at 1335 hours	
Group IV	22.8.63 at 1322 hours	
Group IV	4.9.63 at 1152 hours	
Group IV	9.9.63 at 1430 hours	

Thus, Group II, in 109 observation hours, never visited water, Group IV, in 282 observation hours, visited water three times. As already stated, no patas group ever went near the Nile or near the Nansika river where there were always plenty of shallow drinking places. On two occasions when Group II went alongside the Emi river bed, none of the animals went to drink at the pools. Group IV, on many hot, dry days, ranged close to pools or wallows in the middle of valleys without going to drink. When they did go to drink, the adult male approached the water alone, the group remaining about 200 m away. He looked over the area for several minutes from a vantage point in a tree. When eventually he descended and went to the pool to drink, the rest of the group ran down to the water and also began to drink. The briefness of the usual drinking is also very striking, individuals being timed to remain at the water from 10 to 30 seconds only. This seemed a remarkable example of the role of the adult male in surveying an area presumably of potential danger to the group and of the group's apparent recognition of this role—the behaviour of the adult male and of the group is very similar to what has sometimes been observed at night-resting places (see previous section).

Probably the water-content of their food, and the dew or evening precipitation of rain that remains on the vegetation in the morning, must provide sufficient water at this time of year when, also, the groups were ranging relatively short distances during the day. Captive patas, however, drink regularly, and the wild-born captive juvenile, when taken out to follow Group IV on a day-range, became very distressed and had to be given drinks from our water-bottles on several occasions. Probably the wild groups are habituated to a low level of water intake.

In Stage III, when there was no rain and the day-ranges were much longer, Group II drank at pools on two occasions (1130, and between 1120 and 1220 hours), and probably drank (disappeared out of sight in a gully at a point where there was a pool) on three other occasions (0900, 1135 and 1630 hours). On two days, most individuals both drank from salty puddles and licked salt crystals around the edge.

An interesting variation in drinking was seen in Group I in the Pamdero woodland savannah, June 1963. Individuals, on three different days, obtained water by dipping one hand repeatedly into holes in the trunks of trees where water had collected. The action differed between individuals. Some, on withdrawing the hand, licked off the moisture from the fur of hand and forearm. Others used the hand as a kind of scoop by curling the fingers inward toward the wrist. A similar use of the hand as a means of obtaining water from a tank was observed by the writer in Rhesus monkeys on Cayo Santiago, but it seems unusual in wild monkeys and was not seen in other patas groups.

The fact that these patas groups went so rarely to the water sources in the valleys, even when they were ranging close to them, suggests that there may be some special hazard for them associated with such places. This is also indicated by the watchfulness of the adult male, and by the briefness of the drinking. Baboons showed no such caution at Murchison, some of them being seen to drink from pools or wallows on all the full day-ranges in the Paraa area.

LOCOMOTION AND POSTURES

Being adapted to life on the ground, and to escape by running or by concealment rather than by collective defence or threat by adult males, as in baboon groups, the primary form of locomotion is quadrupedal walking, cantering or galloping. Their speed of galloping over the savannah grass is very impressive, and there is little doubt that they must be the fastest of all primates when running away from danger, or when chasing after another group of their own species. Tappen (1964) reports driving his vehicle alongside a patas with the speedometer registering a steady 55 km/h. A fast pace across country can be sustained for long distances, even by the adult females with their infant two's carried ventrally, as when moving away from a baboon group. The long limb structure in proportion to the body makes them appear greyhound-like in their stride when "hurdling" over the grass. When startled and running away, some of the group will usually rise briefly onto their hindlegs to look back over their shoulders at the source of disturbance, while continuing their rapid progression forward. This "stutter" in the fleeing locomotion is really a quick leap with the body raising up briefly to the bipedal position, enabling the animal to see over the top of the grass.

In the normal locomotion on the ground, the tail is held in a downward curve below the horizontal. Infants, when running about, often have their tails waving about above the horizontal.

The alert posture, when standing on the ground, consists of rising onto the hindlegs, with body fully upright, a position giving maximum height for viewing, and one which they can easily maintain for up to 30 seconds. Bipedal stance is common when feeding, and they can run bipedally, when chased by another patas, holding a large object such as a mushroom between their hands.

Except in grooming parties, which often occur on termite mounds, resting and reclining postures are mainly seen in the trees.

Patas climb readily into trees, for feeding, or resting, or looking around. As most trees in their habitat are spaced at 50 m or considerably more apart, it is usually impossible for them to go direct from one tree to another along the branches.

Occasionally, however, patas will jump across gaps of 6 m or so between the upper branches of two trees, and they are adept at walking along thin branches. Their method of ascending or descending tree trunks is adapted to the tilt of the trunk and its girth. They climb thick perpendicular trunks with a wide, frog-like spread of arms and legs inching up it slowly, and likewise descending slowly in the same manner, head uppermost, until a few feet from the ground when they leap down, landing on the hindlegs first with the body at about 45° from the horizontal and arms held out in front to take the second impact. Only rarely do they jump to a four-point landing, this usually occurring in young animals. If the trunk is sloping, they will usually run up it, or run down it head first. The tail is often used as a slight brake for such descents, being wound around branches, or, in walking or running along a narrow horizontal branch, the tail may move upwards to about 45° or higher, presumably as an aid to balance. Their movements in trees appear to be those of a ground adapted animal. Only very young animals have been seen to swing on branches briefly by the arms alone. Young animals may descend from small bushes by a kind of somersault in which they kick off from the bush and land on all fours on the ground.

As we have noted in the laboratory group, patas are able to leap with great agility to cling onto the side walls at about 3–5 m above ground, while even the infant two's have several times leapt to the floor over distances which measure about 5 m in the arc of the legs. Only one accidental fall was observed in the wild. The adult male of Group IV, when agitated by the presence of a tame juvenile male patas with the observer, fell about 9 m onto hard ground when the dead branch of a *Prosopis* tree broke under his weight. The fall had no apparent effect on him.

Resting postures in trees or bushes accommodate in great variety the long limbs of the patas. In the fork of a tree, the legs may be stretched up one branch so that the feet are at about the same height as the head, with the body bowed forward and the hands resting near the feet. The animals may sit on a horizontal branch in at least four ways: (1) lying flat along it, dog-like; (2) sitting bolt upright, with legs dangling below the branch (like a bather on the edge of a swimming pool; (3) sitting astride the branch; (4) sitting with knees up under the chin. As with baboons, relaxed sitting is with the back bowed, alert or tense sitting with the back straight and head raised.

Sleeping positions during the day-resting period, or as seen at dusk, may be in any of these postures, and are usually taken up in the fork of trees or at branch intersections.

In the following sections dealing with various aspects of the social behaviour of wild patas, occasional reference will be made to the detailed account of the behaviour repertoire of a captive patas group (Hall, Boelkins, and Goswell 1965). The field data provide the broader social context for the captivity observations, and add much that could not be known from captivity study alone.

SEXUAL BEHAVIOUR

The evidence, from field studies, on the nature of the annual reproductive cycle of monkeys and apes (Lancaster and Lee 1965), is, as the authors point out, inadequate except in the case of the long-term studies of free-ranging Rhesus monkeys on Cayo Santiago (Koford 1963*a*) and of the Japanese monkey populations (data are contained in the Lancaster and Lee review not previously available in English translation). The two macaque studies show that there is a discrete birth season of a few months each year, and no births at all outside of this period. Sade (1964) has also established that there is a seasonal cycle in testes size in the Cayo Santiago Rhesus colony, and that the cycle of large testes and small testes corresponds to the cycle of true copulations and births. The samples of data available from wild baboon populations (Zuckerman 1932; Hall 1962*c;* DeVore 1962) indicate only that there does not appear to be a discrete birth period in the areas studied, that births may occur in any month of the year, but that birth frequencies may vary significantly from one period to another (DeVore; for Kenya (1962) Wingfield (1963) for Southern Rhodesia). No adequate data on copulation frequencies or testes sizes at different seasons are available.

In the present field study, it was impracticable to collect samples of adult female patas for analysis of state of pregnancy. The only data bearing upon birth seasonality are the numbers of infant ones at different stages of the study (Table 2–3). In Stage III, these represent 20 percent of the total of all animals in the groups, as against less than 2 percent in Stages I and II. Births to patas females after capture in West Africa most frequently occur in January and February, according to the records of the Wellcome Research Laboratories, Beckenham. The three births to females in the Bristol group have all been in January, one of them being conceived in captivity. Though both field and captivity data are inadequate they point to the likelihood of a birth peak in the dry months of December, January, February at Murchison, and they do not rule out the possibility of a discrete birth season. If, as in the macaque studies, true copulation frequencies should correspond to the birth frequencies, the incidence of the former should be much greater in a period around June, July and August. Likewise, it might be expected that "soliciting" of the adult male by receptive females would be more frequent at this season. In the wild, mounting and thrusting by the adult male and "soliciting" by the adult females were infrequently observed in any part of the study. However, such data as were obtained (Table 2–5) show that these behavioural indications of mating were seen to occur only in July, August and September, and not at all in June or in March and April. Also, mounting with pelvic thrusts was only observed between 8 July and 19 August. This slight amount of positive evidence, taken with the negative evidence and with the highly significant proportion of infant ones seen in the groups in Stage III, does at least suggest that the annual reproductive cycle of the species at Murchison may be similar in form to that of the macaques.

Of the seven occasions of mounting, and mounting with pelvic thrusts, two took place on the branches of trees, five on the ground, three took place between 1100 and 1300 hours, and the other four after 1500 hours. The

TABLE 2–5   OCCURRENCES OF SEXUAL BEHAVIOUR BETWEEN THE ADULT MALE AND ADULT FEMALES OF PATAS GROUPS, MURCHISON

Dates of Occurrence	Groups Observed	Soliciting (S) by Adult Female	Mounting (M) and Pelvic Thrusts (T) by Adult Male		No. of Episodes	No. of Observer Hours	No. of Occasions Adult Male is Active Groomer of Adult Female
1963							
1 June–5 July	I, II	—	—		0	240	1
5 July–13 July	III, IV	—	M	T	3	80	2
		—	M	T			
		—	M				
15 August–31 August	IV	S	M	T	7	160	14
		S	—	T			
		S	M	T			
		—	M	T			
	Female evades male		M				
		S	—				
		S	—				
1 September–14 September	IV	(1) S	—		3	140	19
		(2) S	—				
		(3) S	—				
1964							
24 March–12 April	II	—	—		0	100	7

Note: Stage IIA, Chobi, is not included in the data. No sexual behaviour was observed, but the conditions for observing were far too difficult for negative information to be of any value.

chances of the observer seeing this behaviour would be greater when the group is resting or gathered around trees feeding.

Mounting only, and mounting with thrusting, was observed by young adult males on adult females on three occasions (one at Serere, April, the others in early July). A juvenile male mounted with thrusting on an adult female once, and there was one instance of mounting with no thrusting (both April). Infant two's were occasionally seen to mount each other or to mount juvenile or adult females.

Grooming in which the adult male is involved with adult females as the groomer is known from observation of the laboratory group to occur infrequently except in relation to sexual behaviour. Hence, frequencies of such grooming interactions (Table 2–5) in the wild groups might provide a further indication of the presence of sexually receptive females in whom the adult male is actively interested. However, inspection of the table does not support a close relationship between the two sets of frequency data. The highest incidence of adult male grooming adult females is toward the end of Stage II when no sexual behaviour by the male, was seen though "soliciting" by a female was observed three times. Also, in Stage III when no sexual behaviour was recorded, the adult male was actively grooming an adult female on seven occasions. Possibly the adult male may be involved in such non-sexual grooming much more frequently in a wild group, for instance with females with their infant ones, than in the restricted social circumstances of the laboratory animals.

From field observation, there is little to add to the detailed account of the female's behaviour when "soliciting" mating by the adult male and of the postures and actions of the adult male in copulation (Hall et al. 1965). The female's cringing half-run, with short quick steps, towards the adult male was usually seen in the wild as she approached him along a tree branch during the day resting period. On nearing him, she would sit with her back to him, and arched forward, her cheek pouches out, and the jaw thrust forward, as she turned her head to look at him. This puffing-out of the cheeks is accompanied, in the captive females, by a wheezing, chortling sound going with the expiration of breath—a sound never heard in the wild because inaudible at about 6 m.

In the wild groups, a female has repeated the soliciting behaviour several times to the adult male without him necessarily responding. It has never been seen to occur except to the one adult male of the group.

There are many detailed differences in the components of mating behaviour described for Chacma baboons (Hall 1962c) and for patas. Amongst the most noticeable are the fact that the patas female does not run away from the male as he dismounts, her position of readiness for mounting is a forward crouch, and her tail always remains down and between the male's legs when he is mounted. He does not raise himself off the ground when mounted, as does the male baboon who grips the thighs of the female with his feet. The patas female's soliciting behaviour has no closely corresponding sequence in the behaviour of the female baboon or vervet.

In the field, it was never possible to be certain precisely as to the whole sequence of events in the patas mating. For example, it could not be determined whether there were occasional single copulations by the adult male with a receptive female, or whether there were series of mountings with intromission and pelvic thrusts, the end of each series occurring when ejaculation took place, as in the Chacma baboon and the Rhesus macaque. Our laboratory observations made it quite clear that the characteristic pattern in the captive group was a copulation series in which mounting with pelvic thrusts would occur about once every two minutes until ejaculation took place. Statistical data show that the frequency per day of such copulations increases to a peak in the two or three days after mating with the particular female had begun, then rapidly wanes to zero. Although this pattern seems basically similar to that of the Chacma baboon, there is the very significant social difference that, in the patas group, there do not seem to be any sexually mature but younger males who will mate with the females prior to their reaching maximum receptivity. While we cannot be entirely certain about this, because of the difficulty of getting a sufficient sample of data, we can be certain that there never was more than the one adult male in any of the groups and that soliciting by adult females was never seen except towards the adult male. Aside from the ideal situation arising in the field in which a wild group could be observed at so close a range that even its activities in shade trees or long grass could be seen, it seems that only data from a captive group in which young, but sexually mature, males were present as well as the full-grown adult male can provide the answer.

In the laboratory group, it has been regularly observed that when the adult male begins to be sexually interested in an adult female he is far readier to threaten facially or make lunging threat-gestures toward any other animal of the group that comes near him. Even infants are threatened in this way, though very rarely at other times. In the wild, some of the infrequent threat-behaviour episodes in which the adult male was involved have occurred in the same kind of situation, but on three occasions the adult male of Group IV, when attempting to mount and mate with one of the adult females, was charged at and threatened by several other adult females and, once, by some juveniles. Because such interactions could have an important bearing on the social organization of a patas group, one example will be given in detail: 7.8.63, 1700 hours; adult female approached the adult male several times with soliciting behaviour sequence; he mounted her, and was at once threatened by two other adult females and by some juveniles; he dismounted, and made a threat-charge at one female who ran away; he then leapt against a small bush, in the side-bouncing display to be described below, and rebounded from it; he then went up to another adult female and put his nose up to her ano-genital area; two other adult females in turn did the soliciting sequence to him. On another occasion, the female he had mounted herself turned on him and was joined in threatening him by two other females.

Nothing comparable to this has been seen in baboons. The only "harassing" of an adult male baboon who is in consort with an oestrous female seems to come from other adult males, though the female herself may be threatened by other adult females. It is possible that the female hierarchy in some patas groups, in some seasons, leads to sexual competitiveness amongst the females themselves and the aggression thus aroused in them is redirected against the male. Redirection of aggression is very common amongst socially ranked members of groups of baboons and is frequently seen in the laboratory patas group. An intensification of the aggression amongst the adult females would seem specially likely to occur if there were a limited mating season during which several females might become sexually receptive within a fairly short period. This intensification of aggression amongst the females might also account for the readiness of the adult male to threaten any animal coming near to him while he is mating. There is no evidence from the field study that extragroup males have ever approached a group, either at the times when mating has been in evidence or at any other time.

The genitals of the adult male of the laboratory group often attract very close attention from the young adult male, the juvenile male and the infant male. When he is not sexually interested in a female this close visual attention and sometimes touching with the hand, does not result in threat by the adult male. This interest seems to be exclusively shown by the young males, though the soliciting female will groom the adult male's genital area very thoroughly.

FRIENDLY BEHAVIOUR

This behaviour is characterized in all monkey species systematically studied by approach of one individual to another, without threat intention and with gestures or expressions that anticipate physical contact such as sitting together or grooming. Although lack of tension is evident in many such interactions, particularly between habitual friendly associates, hesitancy and nervousness may sometimes be seen in the approach of a subordinate to a more dominant animal, and ambivalent behaviour indicative of fear or even hostility as well as of a wish for friendly contact may sometimes occur.

Grooming is easily the most frequent behaviour of this category in wild patas. As we have seen, the grooming frequency in the patas group tends to decrease gradually in the course of the day-range. In the Murchison

TABLE 2-6   GROOMING FREQUENCIES FOR BABOONS AND PATAS COMPARED, WITH INTRA-SPECIES VARIATIONS WHICH, IN PATAS, ARE ASSOCIATED WITH DAY-RANGE DISTANCES

Species	Location	Group(s)	Date	Observer Hours	No. of Grooming Events	Numerical Size of Group	Grooming Events per Observer Hour	Mean Day-Range Distance (×100 m)
Baboons	Cape	S	1960	197	294	26	1-5	43.5
Baboons	Murchison	Three	1963	57	43	19, 24, 42	0-8	43.3 (but modal is 45-50)
Patas	Murchison	II	St. I	110	88	22	0-8	30.5
		II	St. III	100	48	31	0-5	82.1
		IV	St. II	240	585	20	2-0	15.5

baboon groups, the day pattern is similar to that of the South African baboons, with a greater concentration of grooming in the first few hours of the day, then another concentration towards evening. Inter-species quantitative comparisons of totals or means of grooming interactions are difficult to evaluate because of seasonal changes, numerical size differences, and so on, which make the variance within the species quite considerable. Data samples are summarized (Table 2–6) to show the differences between species and within species. Patas Group IV, in Stage II, averaged four times as many grooming interactions per observation hour as Group II in Stage III. The larger the day-ranging, the fewer the grooming events.

Within the patas groups, analysis of the age and sex class of the grooming participants, when these were clearly discernible, shows the adult females were very frequently involved in these interactions, both as groomers and as recipients of grooming (Table 2–7). The social pattern appears similar to that analysed for the baboons of S group, Cape, 1960, (Hall 1962*c*) although there were no infants in that group at the time, and sexual behaviour was much more frequent with concomitant grooming between sex partners. From the patas data, it was not clear whether young adult males

TABLE 2–7   ANALYSIS OF GROOMING PARTICIPANTS IN TERMS OF FREQUENCY OF DIFFERENT AGE AND SEX CLASS ACTING AS GROOMER AND AS RECIPIENT FOR PATAS, MURCHISON, AND FOR BABOON GROUPS

			Recipient				
Groomer	Adult Female	Infant	Young Adult or Juvenile	Adult Male			Total
Patas groups, 1963/64							
Adult female	174	156	85	51			466
Young adult, juvenile, infant	30		9				39
Adult male	19						19
	223	156	85	51			524
			(+9)				
Baboons, S group, Cape, (*N* = 26)				(α)	Young adult male		
Adult female	62		27	23	17		129
Juvenile	3		2				5
Adult male (α)	24						24
Young adult male	5						5
	94		29	23	17		163

were involved in grooming. In the laboratory group, the young male has, occasionally, groomed the adult male very thoroughly, and has sometimes participated in grooming with adult females. Patas grooming has mainly been on trees or termite mounds, and grooming clusters of several adult females with their infants are of common occurrence. The adult male has not been seen in such clusters, but he may occasionally be groomed by two females simultaneously. In the laboratory group, the senior of two females may chase another away from the vicinity of the adult male when both females wish to groom him.

As in the Chacma baboon, the amount of time which the adult male patas spends grooming an adult female is far less than the reverse relationship. Out of 57 timed observations on the Murchison patas groups, in 31 occasions the adult female averaged 4.3 minutes in grooming the adult male, and in 26 occasions the adult male averaged 0.8 minutes in grooming the adult female. The corresponding modal figures for S group, Cape, baboons, were of very much the same order (Hall 1962c:304, Fig. 4).

The postures and actions involved in patas grooming behaviour (Hall *et al.* 1965) appear to differ from those of Chacma baboons as follows (the differences being described for the patas):

(i) Lipsmacking is usually inconspicuous, slow and soundless (laboratory group).

(ii) "Inviting" grooming, for example adult male approaching an adult female, consists of standing in front of, or sitting with back to, her; the adult male's tail may be raised vertically when she begins to groom his ano-genital area as he stands (laboratory group and wild).

"Inviting" by one adult female to another can consist of the above or of approaching and sitting very close to the other (laboratory group).

(iii) The arms of the recipient are sometimes, from the seated position, held straight above the head so that surfaces under the arms can be groomed (wild).

(iv) When a patas wants to groom another whom it has approached, it may begin by taking firm hold with one hand of the top-knot of fur on the crown of the head and pulling the head down so that the nape of the neck can be groomed with the other hand (laboratory group and wild).

Any area of the body may be groomed, the recipient adjusting its position appropriately by standing, lying on the side, etc. The receptive female may pay more attention to the genital region of the adult male. Recipients are, as in other species, very relaxed when being groomed, but nervousness by a would-be groomer approaching a "senior" is shown by frequent head-movements of glancing towards and glancing away from the senior.

Other friendly behaviour seen in the wild and in captivity is the approach of one animal to the other, and stretching of the head forward so that its mouth touches that of the other. This gesture has no direct relation to food, except sometimes when it is done by an infant to its mother when she is feeding. It occurs specially between adult females, and, in the laboratory group, it does not seem to be initiated more frequently by a subordinate than by a senior in a pair who are habitually on friendly terms. In the wild, this gesture has been seen often, but it has rarely been possible to identify reliably the participants. Occasionally females have done it to the adult male. As between adult females, the approacher may actually push her body so close to that of the recipient as to force the latter into a lying position. The gesture sometimes, not always, precedes grooming.

The number of grooming interactions and the duration of grooming events as between particular partners are, amongst adults, usually regarded as significant behavioural indicators of social relationships within a group. These relationships, which may be of particular interest amongst the adult females of wild patas groups, have not yet been possible to determine except in the laboratory.

SOCIAL PLAY

In making behaviour comparisons between different types of animals, play is sometimes said to be one of the characteristics supposedly indicating relative evolutionary progress. Thus, Thorpe (1962:50–51) says: ". . . it is not too much to say that the prevalence of play in a species of animal is itself a very good indication of the degree of its mental evolution" because play is a major example of ". . . the process of freeing appetitive behaviour from rigid subservience to the primary needs." Play, however, is a very broad term which includes almost any activity which, to the observer, seems to have no immediate objective. It therefore includes the manipulation of non-food objects, and the whole variety of sensorimotor performances that are "exploratory." It also includes the complex social interactions that take place amongst young animals and sometimes between young animals and adults, these being thought to be highly important in the process of socialization of the young and possibly in establishing relative ranks amongst the young which might carry over into the adult hierarchy.

In wild patas groups, there has been very little opportunity to see any examples of manipulation or exploration of objects or features of the environment that were not more or less directly associated with primary needs, and the same is also true of wild baboon groups. Much of the day, as we have seen, is spent in moving about the home range in search of food, or in resting. The surplus energy of the young patas is almost entirely spent in social play interactions which involve a most vigorous exercising or practising of speed and agility of ground locomotion which can be readily seen as an adaptation for survival from day-hunting predators such as cheetah or hunting dogs. The "arena" for this quite spectacular play of the young patas has almost always been a large open stretch of grassland with a few bushes or an erosion sheet or erosion gullies. Young baboons in the Cape play mainly on or near their sleeping cliffs in the morning or evening, though they may also play-chase and somersault over sand-dunes or cliffs in the course of the day-range.

The fact that the alertness of the patas, and the particular local conditions at Murchison, would make it highly improbable that predators have much success in killing them, may not invalidate the argument that social play of this kind is adaptive. Washburn and Hamburg (1965) have suggested that such "excess" energies and skills are required to be at their peak for just that rare emergency when it does occur. But, while much of patas play may be a preparation for escape from predators, it also involves a great deal of play-biting and wrestling which may be preparatory for attaining social rank within the group, and, in the case of the male, may contribute towards the decision whether he stays in the group at all or is temporarily eliminated from it.

No clear answer to such questions of function can be given from field study, but field study provides the necessary ecological and group context so that social experimental situations can be devised to test these several hypotheses in captivity. We can here simply describe the kinds of social play in wild patas, and indicate how, in its general or its detailed aspects, it differs from that of baboons.

The components and sequences of play in the patas groups were:

(i) *"Inviting"* play—usually by bouncing, on the same spot, quickly from hands to feet to hands, and so on, with the limbs held straight, and glancing towards the other animal; the inviter, often the older of the two animals, then leaps away and races over the grass with the other chasing after it.

(ii) *The play-chase*—the usual sequel to (i), and carried out at full speed over the ground.

(iii) *Play-wrestling*—typically with each player on hindlegs, facing each other, a grappling with hands around shoulders and arms, then sometimes one, sometimes both, rolling over on the ground; two juveniles wrestled thus for two minutes, trying to "throw" each other; the play face almost always accompanies these wrestling bouts, the mouth being open, but with no threat of face or limb, and mock-biting often occurring.

(iv) *Play-sparring*—actual slapping movements with the hands may accompany or precede mock-biting and wrestling.

(iii) and (iv) are vigorous, but entirely non-threat replicas of actual fighting that has occurred betwen adults of the laboratory group.

(v) *The play bounce* is a very high-speed version of the on-the-spot "invitation" bounce—the animal, at full gallop, hurls itself sideways against a

sapling or small bush so that the hands contact the bush first, being immediately followed by the feet, the effect being that the animal catapults itself
sideways before continuing to gallop away. In the laboratory, exactly the
same action is done against the walls of the room or the sides of cages,
but, in the wild, the springy bushes were evidently preferred, because no
side-bouncing was seen from tree trunks or cliff sides. The effect of this
very fast movement is to bring about a very swift change of direction, but
one which, in play-chase, is usually exactly followed by the chasing animal.
Occasionally, the bounce is done from the top of a bush onto which the
animal has leapt. What seems to be exactly this kind of action is carried
out by the adult male patas in the totally different situation of diversionary
or possibly threat display with reference to the observer (see later section).
In the laboratory group, it has been repeatedly and very noisily performed
by a young adult female against the sides and top of a cage in which another adult female was confined. The young adult female had been continuously, and effectively, provocative and aggressive towards the older
female when the two of them were free in the room.

The speed and grace of these play sequences in a wild group, often continuing amongst six or more of the young animals for periods of up to 30
minutes without respite, is such as to have no parallel in any other terrestrial
monkey. Players may run at full gallop for 200 m or more away from the
others before circling back to the grass and *Combretum* bush arena around
which the play is centred. Play groups of Group II in Stage III have often
gone on with their activities about 400 m from the adults while the latter
are feeding. As we have seen from the day-activity data, play is most prevalent when the group is already well on its day-range, between 0900 and
1100 hours, diminishing to almost zero in the afternoon. Though minor play
interactions may occur mostly amongst infants around or in the day-resting
trees, all major play sequences are on the ground. The tempo of play builds
up very clearly as more and more of the young animals become involved.
   In the wild, no vocalization audible to the observer ever accompanies
these play sequences. In captivity, it is just possible to hear a "nickering"
noise, audible at about 3 m, when the young animals are play-wrestling.
   Neither the bouncing "invitation" to play, nor the running side-bounce,
have any known equivalent in baboons or vervets. Indeed, much of the character and tempo of the whole play sequence seems to be peculiar to the patas,
though play-wrestling, biting and chasing occur in many monkey species.
The so-called patas "dance", referred to in non-systematic descriptions of
captive individuals, is presumably the stereotyped pivotting back and forward
on straight limbs that occurs in some caged animals. In the laboratory group,
the juvenile male and the young adult male both do this movement over and
over when removed from the group room and confined separately in a cage

for test purposes. It appears then to be a frustration response in a very active animal.

The frequency with which the different age classes of patas groups were involved in play interactions shows the juveniles to be far the most active participants, then the infant two's, then young adults (Table 2–8). However, adult females occasionally engaged in play with younger animals, though never with each other, and mothers sometimes briefly tussled with their infant ones. For example, in Group II, 5.4.64, an adult female "invited" play by looking back at juveniles who were already playing, and she raced away with the juveniles chasing after her. The play of an infant one as it gets near to the stage of joining in play with other infants is often quite rough as it pulls her head or bites her arms or jumps on her. She will sometimes

TABLE 2–8   SOCIAL PLAY INTERACTION FREQUENCIES BY AGE CLASSES IN PATAS GROUPS, ALL STAGES, MURCHISON STUDY

	Juvenile	Infant Two	Young Adult	Adult
Juvenile	99	57	11	6
Infant Two	57	8	3	6
Young adult	11	3	6	1
Adult	6	6	1	3
Total	173	74	21	16

retaliate by mildly biting it, or she may give little play bounces inviting the infant to play with her. Play interactions have almost never been seen to involve the adult male. Only once, in Group IV, when play by young animals was very active and vigorous all around him, the male gave a play-bounce and cantered away with some of the young ones briefly following him. In the laboratory group, it has been noted that even the adult female of highest rank may initiate play during the two or three days prior to her becoming sexually receptive and soliciting the attention of the adult male.

As such play as has been observed in the wild patas groups seems to fit closely into the adaptive pattern of the species as inferred from all the field data, just as the play of baboons is adapted to their particular way of life, there seems no valid reason for considering the play behaviour patterns of these animals or the frequency of their occurrence as having any evolutionary significance apart from the way of life. They may have as much or as little bearing upon the problem of origins of "intellectual" play of the human kind as similar behaviour in the nonprimate mammals.

AGGRESSION

It is now becoming clear from the accumulations of field data on several different species of monkey that the manifestations of aggression within groups vary enormously from species to species, and within a species according to the environmental conditions (Hall 1965*a*). The patas is no exception. Conditions have been set up in the laboratory, by altering the composition of the group, removing one animal, introducing another, and so on, as a result of which great tension is temporarily created with aggressive episodes occurring repeatedly and actual fights taking place between adult females. Conversely, it has proved possible to establish in the laboratory a "stable" group of six animals, modelled on a small wild group, consisting of an adult male, three adult females, a young adult male and a juvenile male. In this group, relative ranks are so clearly organized that even threat is rare, and fighting never occurs. In the wild, the situation is intermediate between these two experimental extremes, in that the groups are larger and the day to day pattern of events is much less regular than for the stable laboratory group.

As in the other sections of this paper, data from the laboratory group study will be used only where they seem to clarify or amplify particular points in the field study, the main concern of the present section being to characterize the role of aggression in the wild patas groups, to compare this role on the basis of quantitative data and qualitative description with that seen in baboon groups, and thus to prepare the way for the account of patas social organization.

Threat-Attack Repertoire

The detailed account of facial expression, gestures, intention movements, vocalizations, and actual fighting of captive patas (Hall *et al.* 1965) illustrates the range of behaviour indicative of aggression, from very low to high intensity, in the species. Some of the behaviour patterns have not been seen in the wild. Actual fighting was never observed. Vocalizations uttered in high intensity threat-attack episodes in the laboratory by the aggressors have not, except for occasional brief snarling, been heard in the wild, partly no doubt because such episodes were very rare, partly because the vocalizations, including even the rapidly repeated huh-huh-huh of the adult male, might not be audible at more than about 100 m, and partly because even fighting between adult females in the laboratory has often not been accompanied by any vocalization whatever. All this is in very marked contrast to the tremendous hubbub of barking and squealing in a baboon group when threat-attacks occur, and even when no fighting takes place.

A point that must be added to the laboratory account, being derived from a later stage of laboratory observation, concerns the differentiation between the behaviour shown when *one* animal is directly attacking another, and when one animal is trying to "enlist" others of the group to join in attacking the other. The former behaviour appears to be entirely non-vocal, consisting of steady approach with threat-face, etc. In the latter case, when the would-be aggressor is turning its head to look towards others who may support her, the huh-huh calls are almost invariably uttered.

In the wild groups, as in the laboratory, aggressive intent by a "superior" animal is manifested simply by walking towards the subordinate, this being sufficient to make the latter move rapidly away. A quick cat-like striking with the hands is also a common aggressive gesture, one of the participants in such an encounter usually withdrawing without actual physical engagement. Occasionally in the wild there is a "surprise" attack by one female who pounces onto the back of another that is feeding or otherwise off its guard and gives it a quick nip which again is sufficient to send the victim away so that no fighting ensues. Most of the behaviour episodes in which, in the wild groups, such threat-attack gestures occurred were clearly brief, and evidently adequate, reinforcements of relative social rank. There has been repeated verification of this from laboratory observation of social interactions.

One of the major differences in the threat-attack interactions of patas and baboon may be related to the fact that patas seem to have no appeasement or submissive gestures whereby they can signal to a superior animal their intention to be submissive. Presenting does not occur, the fear-grin may occur only when actual threat has occurred, and mounting by an adult male, other than in the sexual context, does not occur. The young adult male patas of the captive group may cringe and squeal when looking at and going toward the adult male, but this seems to be the only behaviour in the whole repertoire which may be classed as an intermediate gesture of the kind that is so prominent a feature of baboon social behaviour. It is likely that this difference is significantly related to the different social organization of the two species.

Frequency of Aggression

The frequency data from the field study will be based on all instances in which, other than in play interactions, any degree of threat-attack behaviour has been observed, including walking towards, chasing, slapping at, or lunging at, the intended victim.

A total of only 49 episodes, usually of very brief duration, was recorded in the whole period of 627 observation hours of Stages I, II and III at Murchison. Table 2–9 analyses these episodes as far as possible in terms of aggressor and object of aggression and the type of behaviour manifested by each.

TABLE 2–9   ANALYSIS OF ALL AGGRESSIVE EPISODES OBSERVED IN PATAS GROUPS
IN STAGES I, II AND III

Aggressor's Behaviour

Aggressor	Victim	No. of Occasions	Standing/Sitting Threat Gestures	Walking/Chasing Approach	Total No. Contact	Slapping/Grappling	Biting	Total Contact
Adult female	Adult male	11	1	10	11	0	0	0
Adult male	Adult female	7	4	3	7	0	0	0
Adult female	Adult female	13	1	8	9	4	0	4
Adult female	Young adult/juvenile	6	0	4	4	1	1	2
Young adult/juvenile	Young adult/juvenile	5	0	2	2	2	1	3
Adult sex indeterminate	Adult sex indeterminate	7	2	4	6	1	0	1
Total		49	8	31	39	8	2	10

Victim's Behaviour

Aggressor	Victim	Runs Away	Runs Away, Then Counter-threat or Side-bounce	Counter-threat	No Reaction (stays, ignores)	Total
Adult female	Adult male	4	5	1	1	11
Adult male	Adult female	5	2	0	0	7
Adult female	Adult female	9	2	1	1	13
Adult female	Young adult/juvenile	3	0	0	3	6
Young adult/juvenile male	Young adult/juvenile	3	0	0	2	5
Adult sex indeterminate	Adult sex indeterminate		Not recorded			—
Total		24	9	2	7	42

Several interesting features stand out in this analysis:

(i) only ten out of 49 threat-attacks resulted in actual contact with the victim, and, of these, two only led to brief biting with no visible damage inflicted, the other eight being hand-slaps and attempts at grappling;

(ii) victim's behaviour was, in 24 out of 42 occasions, simply to run away;

(iii) there were 11 instances of brief counter-threats, six being by the adult male in response to chasing by adult females, and two of these six included a side-bounce by the adult male off a bush as he ran away;

(iv) on not a single occasion did the adult male contact adult females, or *vice versa,* in the total of 18 aggressive interactions amongst them;

(v) adult females were involved as aggressors in 30 of the 49 episodes (probably more, as the sexually indeterminate adults were almost certainly female in several of the seven cases), and the high proportion of these directed at the adult male (11 out of 30) is a very significant quantitative indicator of the role these females may play in the organization of the group;

(vi) on only seven occasions was the adult male aggressive toward adult females, and never toward any other class of animal in the groups.

Causes and Nature of Episodes

Precisely what sets off a particular aggressive episode has usually been difficult to determine in the field. Three types of situation only have clearly led to such interactions:

(i) Threat-attack by a mother toward a juvenile or young adult engaged in rough play with her infant two.

(ii) In special food areas that are spatially confined, as where a cluster of mushrooms has been found, adult females or the adult male may threaten sufficiently to keep others away from the spot (five occasions, four of them with adult males as aggressor).

(iii) When the adult male is sexually interested in a female, he may threaten any other animals that come near, and, as previously described, adult females and sometimes young adults may "harass" the adult male when he has attempted to mate. What it is in the social system that produces this kind of interaction is by no means clear. It is possible, as already suggested, that these "attacks" are a result of the tension created amongst the females when several are simultaneously receptive. However, there is strong evidence from studying the laboratory group that "alliances" amongst the females can be firmly established so that an aggressive lead by one of them is likely at once to produce aggression by the others against the victim.

Other instances seem simply to arise out of the ranking amongst the adult females, so that, for example, a superior female that wants to join a grooming cluster may cause a female subordinate to her to move quickly out of the way.

The general nature of the episodes is partly evident from the frequency data, and partly from the fact that these episodes are almost always of very short duration. Chases rarely persist more than about 50 m, and usually are much shorter. Slapping usually involves one or two quick movements, and the only two instances of biting each involved one brief nip. These are thus the sufficient expressions of status that maintain the required social distance amongst the individuals of the group. Counter-threats by the adult male, when he has been chivvied by some of the females, are particularly interesting because they have never involved more than turning to stand at bay, this being sufficient to halt the females without contact being made on any occasion. Precisely the same counter-behaviour has been observed in the laboratory male when closely threatened by two adult females. He has turned at bay after leaping away from them, showing in full face towards them the threat-expression of staring, displaying the white eyelids, and gape-yawning at them with head lowering. He has slapped at them with his hands to keep them away, but has never grappled with or bitten them. Even one of these adult females, half his weight, has produced this reaction in him by a snarling threat-attack.

The side-bounce of bushes, seen twice in the adult male when running from females, and several times when in close proximity to the observer who has disturbed him and the group by coming too near, is difficult to interpret. While it may certainly serve as a part of threat-display, its "origin" may lie in its being one of several kinds of response to frustration or conflict.

Interactions with Extra-group Patas

The size of the home ranges of the groups at Murchison made the likelihood of encounter between two groups very slight indeed. Only two such encounters were observed in the whole period, both concerning Group IV ($N = 22$) and Group III ($N = 11$). On the first occasion, Group IV was foraging over short grass hillocks at the head of a long valley, spread out by *c.* 150 × 100 m. Suddenly, the adult male galloped to the top of a hillock ahead of the group, and stood, in alert posture, muzzle raised, looking intently down the valley for *c.* 30 seconds. The rest of the group waited near him. After gape-yawning once, he galloped very fast indeed straight down the valley over the short grass with the others following like a pack of hounds. No vocalizations were heard. We followed the group as fast as possible and sighted in the distance what turned out to be Group III moving very fast away from the area. Group III continued to move fast, without feeding, for about a mile, when they reached the area where they passed the night.

On the second occasion, we were with Group III who were in or near to day-resting trees on one side of a valley. Suddenly the adult male became very alert, and the others descended from the trees and ran away to the west, followed, last, by the adult male. On searching through binoculars the far side of the valley at which they had been looking, we located Group IV.

It is obviously impossible to know whether such hasty avoidance and such determined chasing as was seen on these two occasions is typical of patas group interactions. But because there is so little chance of such encounters taking place, there is no opportunity for habituation to occur such as is evident in the interactions of baboon groups around water pools in Southern Rhodesia (Hall 1963b).

On one occasion only was an isolate adult male seen in contact with a group, this probably being an accidental encounter when Group III began to come up the side of a valley and the adult male of the group, standing high up in a tree, caught sight of the isolate who raced away quite close by the observer. The group male showed considerable agitation in his behaviour during the next hour, being very watchful from high up in trees, gape-yawning repeatedly and bouncing noisily down from the branches. It was particularly noticeable that the other members of the group scampered out of his way whenever he came near them—quite in contrast to the normal, tolerant relationship. Later, the group male, continuing his agitated, very watchful behaviour, climbed into a Tamarind 200 m from the group, who were feeding, and uttered a muffled, high-pitched bark, at about one every two seconds for series of up to ten. He kept this up for 35 minutes. It can scarcely be doubted that this was an aggressive vocal display directed at the extra-group male.

Comparison with Baboons

Apart from certain very clearly-defined differences in the threat-attack behaviour repertoire of baboons and patas (Hall et al. 1965) and the already noted difference in the vocal accompaniment of such episodes, there are some major differences of frequency, intensity, and form of the interactions, which must reflect most importantly on the different social adaptations of the two genera.

The baboon group most nearly comparable in numerical size and age-sex class constitution to the patas groups of the recent study is S group, Cape (Hall 1962c), which numbered 26 in 1960, 35 in 1961. There was, in that group at those times, only one full-grown adult male, with a few younger adult males, and several adult females, and the usual proportion of young animals. The adult male was clearly "dominant" over all other animals of the group in terms of the various behavioural criteria used. The group could be defined as stable in its social relationships with respect to baboon standards of stability. In this group, 167 aggressive episodes were recorded in 190 observation hours, that is, about one episode per hour. In the patas groups, there were 49 episodes only in over 600 hours, that is, rather less than one episode per day-range of ten hours. In the Murchison baboon groups, where conditions of observing were very similar to those for the patas, there were 24 aggressive episodes in less than 60 hours, that is, about one episode every 2–5 hours. Even allowing for the fact that, at certain periods, aggressive interactions amongst patas could not have been clearly seen because of long grass, there were many successive days of more or less uninterrupted observation of most of the adults in the groups during which the very low total frequency of aggressive interactions was amply confirmed.

Comparing the age-sex class frequencies of aggressive interaction (Table 2–10), the most significant difference between the species seems to lie in the interactions between the adult male and adult females. The victim of threat-attack by adult females in the patas group was the adult male on 11 out of the 31 occasions on which they were the aggressor (35 percent), whereas on only two occasions out of 110 was the baboon male harried by adult females, both being the direct result of attacks by him on one of their number. Also, the baboon male attacked adult females far more frequently in proportion than did the patas male, and the statistical comparison of these frequencies for the adult male: adult female interactions is highly significant (chi^2 = 49–5, $P < 0$–001). In other words, the balance of aggressiveness is very strongly weighted to the baboon male against the females as victims, whereas the weighting is the other way round in the patas interactions.

TABLE 2–10   FREQUENCIES OF DIFFERENT AGE-SEX CLASS AGGRESSIVE INTERACTIONS IN PATAS, AND BABOONS, S. GROUP, CAPE, 1960

Aggressor	Victim	Patas	Baboon
Adult male	Adult female	7	37
	Others	0	15
Adult female	Adult male	11	2
	Adult female	13	104
	Young	6	4
Others	Others	12	24
	Total	49	186

Not only does the Cape baboon sample of data indicate that, in actual frequency, aggression is far more common than in patas, but that aggressive behaviour was very much more severe, particularly when the adult male went into action. As analysis of the episodes showed (Hall 1962*b*, Table 16,

p. 318), the adult male baboon grappled with his hands and beat his adult female victims on 11 occasions, and actually bit the female on six other occasions. These episodes were usually very noisy and very rough, yet did not result in any observable physical injury. Contact aggressive reactions were relatively few in the interactions of the female baboons (22 out of 104 episodes). No attacks of this severity were seen in the wild patas.

Comparing the interactions between groups is difficult because of lack of data on the patas. As is now well known, baboon groups vary in their behaviour to each other very greatly with circumstances, interactions in some areas showing a high degree of tolerance. But the fact that the patas male will not tolerate other adult males in or near his group, combined with the two observed interactions between groups, suggests that these animals are, at least locally, strongly territorial in their behaviour.

ANXIOUS AND WATCHFUL BEHAVIOUR

Behaviour which is intermediate between threat and escape is often difficult to classify. In wild monkeys, this is usually recorded when an observer approaches slightly within the tolerance-distance of a group, so that some members of the group become particularly alert and watchful, and, in some species, a few individuals may make threat-intention movements or ambivalent gestures indicating an alternation of threat—and escape—intention. Possibly also curiosity may sometimes be involved in the sense at least that the animals try to keep the source of disturbance in sight. In such situations, young baboons or vervets, usually males, may vocalize loudly and repeatedly, and may show some threat display. The adult males rarely do so unless the intensity of the disturbance to the group is increased. In effect, the disturbance is usually shown first in the behaviour of the animals peripheral to the group, and these may also show "nervous" behaviour, such as quick glances back toward others in the group, rapid scratching of the body or tail, and so on.

In very clear contrast to baboons, it is the adult male patas of the group who is alerted and shows watchful and "nervous" behaviour in such circumstances. Others of the group very rarely do so, because their normal reaction in this kind of situation is to move away or conceal themselves. There has been no single instance where patas have shown threat intention movements towards the observer, except in so far as the displays of the adult male to be described below can be thus interpreted.

The watchful behaviour of the adult male patas in relation to possible predators or, presumably, to the possible presence of baboons or of extragroup patas has been described in the context of night-resting, drinking at an open water source, and approaching a new feeding area. When the group has been disturbed by the too-close approach of the observer, only the adult male has shown the following two main types of behaviour, the second of which probably only occurs at a rather high level of arousal.

Looking Round, "Yawning"

Typically, the alerted male climbs into the upper branches of a tree from which he can survey or "scan" the whole area. When searching a new area prior to the group going to it, his position is likely to be far away from the observer, who remains near the group. When doing this with reference to the observer himself, he may take up position in a tree quite close to the observer, and from this he may look all over the area and only occasionally towards the observer. This behaviour, described as "scanning" (Hall 1960) in male baboons, was so called because the animal's gaze seems to wander, as its head turns laterally, over a very wide arc. It appears, in baboon and patas, to indicate a general arousal or orienting response. In patas it is completely silent behaviour, in baboons barking is likely to occur.

In such a situation, the patas male gape-yawns over and over again. This behaviour, fully described in captivity (Hall *et al.* 1965), may occur in some form or other in any of the laboratory group animals, when they are tense, or slightly disturbed, and it can be clearly distinguished from the threat-gape which is one component of the facial expression, including staring and displaying the white eyelids, and which is directed straight at the other animal or person. In the wild, it is only the adult male who can be seen doing this from his vantage-point, and the circumstances of its occurrence in the wild and in captivity strongly indicate that it is an "anxiety" or tension indicator. Percival (1928) noted the high frequency of "yawning" in captive patas as compared with other monkeys and ascribed it to the "boredom of captivity." "Anxious" yawning does occur in other monkeys, such as baboons (Bolwig 1959; Hall 1962c) but far less frequently and conspicuously, and it must also be distinguished from the gaping, with the wide open jaws and canine teeth exposure, which is sometimes a part of male baboon threat display (DeVore 1962).

In the wild male patas, the frequency of the gape-yawn in the watching situation is remarkable, as three examples will indicate: (i) Adult male sitting in the tree *c.* 50 m from observer, with group further ahead; he gape-yawned 26 times in 17 minutes, the frequency reducing from 15 in the first five minute period. (ii) Adult male standing on the top branches of a 15 m tree at *c.* 75 m from observer; he gape-yawned 32 times in 12 minutes, and continued to do so less frequently during the next 18 minutes, after which he descended and went after the group. (iii) In the early morning as we approached the group, the adult male, already 100 m from the group, ran further away, and climbed to the top of a Tamarind from which he looked over the whole area; he gape-yawned at intervals timed between 17 and 25 seconds during the first three minutes, and only occasionally glanced towards us; he then shifted his position in the tree and sat with his back to us, stood, looked around and away from us, and gape-yawned 21 times at intervals between 10 and 55 seconds.

These were typical examples of the adult male's behaviour in the early stages of following a group, before it became to some extent habituated to the observer's continued presence. The points to emphasize are that the gape-yawn is not *directed* towards the observer, it is not accompanied by threat-gestures or expressions, it is often accompanied by other behavioural signs of nervousness, such as body-scratching, tension of posture, etc., and it is never, in these circumstances, accompanied by barking or any other vocalization. Whereas, in baboons, loud and repeated barking by many different animals, including watchful males, is the almost invariable response to this kind of situation, the silent gape-yawn of the patas male seems to be the adaptive alternative of a species that relies mainly on concealment and alertness and escape to avoid human predators.

Display and Diversion

Just as, in the gape-yawn and watchful behaviour, the patas seems to differ very clearly from the baboons both in the form and frequency of response, so in the occasional sequel to this, the patas male has shown a conspicuous kind of display which, from its reference to the observer, bears a general resemblance to the distraction behaviour of some species of birds, and which seems to have no precise equivalent in other monkey species.

When the patas male, in his tree or bush quite close to the observer, starts to descend, he may bounce conspicuously and noisily on the branches, making them shake vigorously. On reaching the ground, he has occasionally galloped very close by the observer, sometimes doing a full-speed side-bounce off a bush (as described in the play sequences of the young animals), then has continued to run far away from the observer and the group so that, sometimes, the observer has been between the group and the adult male. Possibly the noisy bush or tree-bouncing may be the patas equivalent of similar demonstrations by male baboons, vervets, and Rhesus macaques, and usually considered to be displays of threat. The unusually close approach to the observer might also be interpreted as threat, although no *direct* threat behaviour at the observer has been seen. The running far away from the observer and the group, however, may perhaps be explained as, in effect if not in intent, a distraction or a diversion which, because the male is such a conspicuous animal, might draw off the attention of day-hunting predators sufficiently to allow the group itself to escape.

Because this behaviour may be an adaptation peculiar to the patas, details from field notes are given:

(i) Patas group, Atira (Teso district) 3.4.63. When this group was first contacted in the evening, the adult male watched the observer intently from a tree, looked round, gape-yawned repeatedly, descended to the ground, and ran into a thicket ahead of the observer (*c.* 25 m away). He again descended to the ground, noisily crashing the branches in doing so, galloped away, and side-bounced off a sapling. The observer walked slowly after the male. When *c.* 10 m from another thicket, there was a crashing sound of branches being violently shaken, and the adult male leapt to the ground and galloped very close indeed, at *c.* 3 m, past the observer and in the opposite direction to the route which the group was taking. There was no vocalization.

The next morning, the observer recontacted this group, and started to follow it on its day-range, keeping at 100 to 150 m. A young adult male suddenly bounced noisily down from a tree at 40 m, galloped away, climbed another tree where it stood looking round, gape-yawning repeatedly, then sat looking towards the observer. The penis of this animal was erect—a not unusual occurrence in this kind of situation. This is the only occasion on which any animal of a group other than the adult male has taken part in this kind of display. The adult male himself now appeared, crashing noisily to the ground from a tree at *c.* 60 m. He uttered a bull-like whoo-wherr roar or growl, and ran a short distance ahead of the observer who continued slowly following the group. Then the adult male galloped noisily through the grass from behind the observer, shaking the bushes by side-bouncing off them, and climbed into another tree where he bounced noisily on the branches. Later in the day, it was evident the adult male was still sometimes watchful, because he came through the grass once towards the observer. The observer stopped, and the adult male stopped at 12 m, stared, looked round, and galloped away.

These sequences, in an agricultural area, where the patas probably saw Africans almost every day, strongly indicate threat-display rather than distraction. Sequences at Murchison, on the other hand, where patas groups had little or no human contact until the field observations began, never showed these very close approaches by the adult male, but were of the diversionary or distraction kind.

(ii) Group IV. On the few occasions of the 28-day series in which, inadvertently, the observer came too close to the group in long grass, or got between two parties of the group, the adult male sometimes did the noisy bouncing in a tree, once with the effect of breaking off dead branches against which he had been pushing vigorously so that they fell to the ground, but nowhere near the observer, and sometimes the ground version of this in side-bouncing off bushes. In most cases, however, these displays occurred just before the animal jumped to the ground and galloped sometimes far

away across the savannah, with the rest of the group remaining where it was. This appears to be a special case of the watchfulness that the adult male shows in other circumstances, such as approaching water or in a new food area, but its coming rather regularly after the noisy bouncing display suggests at least the possibility that it may have a survival value as predator diversion.

(iii) One further special instance illustrates an extreme of agitation by the adult male of Group IV when we took a captive juvenile male patas with us attached to a long lead in following the group on its day-range. The purpose of this was to try to induce some of the group to come very close to the juvenile, and possibly, later, to accept it into the group. Though some of the adult females came to about 30 m at the beginning, the general effect of this was to increase the agitation of the adult male, so that he repeatedly bounced on and shook branches of the trees on which he perched, and once, as a consequence, broke off a large dead branch with the vigour of his arm movements, and fell with it to the ground 15 m below. He also uttered the muffled whoo-wherr call, and, for one period of three minutes, gave the dog-like bark at very high frequency—a vocalization only otherwise heard when the adult male has seen other patas.

MOTHER-INFANT BEHAVIOUR

The fundamental processes of socialization of the patas infant, through the stages of increasing independence of the mother after the infant two stage and the very active engagement in social play then and in the juvenile stage, can only be sketched in broadest outline from the present field study, supplemented by some observations on two laboratory-born infants. The differing patterns of socialization described by Jay (1963a) for the Common Indian langur, *Presbytis entellus,* and for the Kenya baboon, *Papio anubis,* by DeVore (1963b), indicate how important is a knowledge of these developmental interaction processes in the wild groups for an understanding of the factors determining the social organization of the groups. The Japanese workers, in their analyses of social interactions in *Macaca fuscata* groups, have emphasized two very important processes of social learning in the early phases of mother-infant relationships. One is the acquisition of food habits both by the infant observing the mother and by the mother observing the infant. Infant baboons follow the mother closely during the second stage of their lives, feeding where she feeds, and using the same actions as she uses (Hall 1962c). The other is the acquisition of social rank which, according to Imanishi (1960) and others, is largely determined by the rank of the mother, because the mother's attitudes and behaviour in relation to the other adult females and the adult males will directly affect those of her infant.

The thorough analysis that is required of the processes of socialization in the patas infant can probably only be achieved by observation and experiment in the captive group such as is now a major part of the Bristol programme. The present field study provides the background of the social adaptations and ecological conditions in which the wild-born infant grows up.

In the Murchison groups, infant ones were always to be seen clinging to the belly of the mother, head towards the front, tail between her legs or curled around her thigh. At about three months' age, the infant begins to spend much of the day closely following the mother as she searches for food, and, at this stage, it begins to take solid foods as well as continuing to suckle from her periodically—mainly during the day-resting period, during short halts when grooming clusters are formed, and in the evening when she and the infant ascend into the sleeping tree. When the mother is frightened, as in the case of the sudden appearance of some other mammal (such as the mongoose episode previously described, or of a rhino), or when the group is crossing a road, she is likely to grab the infant up to her belly and carry it thus, even at the second stage, for quite long distances. The occasions when infant twos have been observed to be carried by their mothers for the longest distance have been when a group has run away from baboons or has run after another patas group. Occasionally a mother with an infant two has been separated temporarily from the group. This occurred in Stage I with Group II.

The group waited for more than an hour, the adult male sitting in a Tamarind looking back in the direction from which she eventually appeared. When she did reappear, she uttered the "moo" call, which seems, from laboratory observation, to be a social contact or contact-need call. The group then moved on its day-range. Baboon adult males are known occasionally to carry infants on their backs. No instance of patas infants clinging to any but an adult female has been seen. When the mother with a young infant climbs into a tree to rest or feed, the infant still clings to her ventral side, and there has been not a single instance, even of the briefest duration in this study, in which the infant, either in the first or the second stage of its life, has ridden on the back of the mother. As is well known, baboon infants tend to ride mostly on the mother's back from about the fourth month. Sanderson (personal communication) says that in West Africa, patas females, like baboons, have their infants riding on or clinging to their backs. If this is a regional difference for the species in the West and East African parts of its distribution, it is an important and unexpected one.

The beginnings of play in the patas are to be seen in relation to the mother (see previous section). During the second stage, the mother will sometimes nip the nape of the neck of her infant, or slap it with her hands, either when it persists in trying to suckle, or when it plays roughly with her. The infant is sometimes checked by her by being held by the tail or limb. Play interactions are seen amongst the infant twos, and between them and the young of the previous year, now juveniles, and the mother will occasionally threaten a juvenile or another infant two if play is rough and her infant squeals. The squeal of the infant usually acts immediately in arousing threat-attack behaviour by the mother. In the laboratory group, this alertness of the mother has been much in evidence, but declines in frequency of manifestation as the infant gets more and more independent of her.

No "protective" behaviour by the adult male patas of wild groups towards mothers with young infants has been observed. In baboon groups, mothers with infant ones tend to keep close to adult males. The adult male is ready to attack, beat, and bite, an adult female who may threaten or attack one of the mothers near him. In Stage III of the patas study when Group II included several infant one's, no instances of this kind of behaviour were observed. It was, in fact, rare for the mothers with young infants to be close to the adult male at any time, though they tended to keep much closer to each other during the day-range than they did to others of the group, such as the juveniles. This apparent lack of protective association between the adult male patas and mothers and infants fits the rest of the field data regarding the role of the adult male in the group.

Quite in contrast to the langurs described by Jay (1963a), patas mothers do not allow their infant ones to be picked up and carried about by other females. She reports that passing round of infants occurs very soon after birth. In Chacma baboon groups, Hall (1963b) has described the "greetings" approaches made mainly by other adult females to infant ones and their mothers. The "greeters" were permitted to pick up the infant, usually by the hindlegs, and touch its rump with their mouths, "embrace" it, and so forth. On one occasion only, in patas group II, 29.3.64, an adult female approached an infant one near its mother, held it briefly with both hands while standing on hindlegs and glancing twice at the mother—glances such as these are usually seen in subordinate animals anticipating possible threat or attack. Nothing comparable to the baboon interactions has been observed.

If, as our data have suggested, there is in patas a limited season of perhaps two or three months in which most of the infants are born each year, it is possible, as DeVore (1963b) has indicated for baboons in Kenya, that most of the social interactions of the infant as it becomes independent of the mother will be with age peers rather than with siblings. This likelihood would be increased if patas females, like baboons and vervets (Gartlan personal communication), usually only give birth to an infant every two years. As we have seen, however, from analysing the play interactions of patas, infant twos freely engage in all forms of play with juveniles and, less often, with young adults.

The study of the socialization process is nowadays recognized as bearing very significantly indeed upon the role and status of the individual monkey when it comes to maturity in the group. Imanishi (1957) has suggested that, in Japanese monkey groups, a young male, in order to enter into the central part of a group, must be accepted by the dominant females. If he is the off-spring of a very high-ranking female, acceptance by the other females who are lower in rank is likely to be greatly facilitated. In our laboratory patas group, adult female ranks are very clearly defined, but the effects of the mother's rank on the ultimate status of the infant is not yet known. A long-term study of the socialization process in the captive group is required before we shall be in a position to identify clearly which of several factors are of critical importance to the achievement of "dominance." That the adult fe-males could have crucial selective influence as to which male remains in the group as the sire of their offspring is suggested below, but it is impossible without several years of further field and captivity observation to determine how such selection occurs. Jay (1963a) has suggested that the lack of pos-sessiveness of langur mothers towards their infants may be a very significant determinant of the tolerant form of the langur social organization. Thus, it is emphasized that infant socialization can only be an integral part of the social adaptation complex of the species. Hence, it may well be significant that the wild-born patas mothers in captivity are extremely possessive towards their infants, and this might strongly suggest that the highest ranking female, so long as she retained this rank, would influence very positively the social position of her male infant. But the time factor here might be critical. A male reaches sexual maturity at about four years of age. If his mother was of high rank at his birth, but was superseded by a younger female before he reached maturity, it is possible that the early social conditioning would not be effective in keeping him within the group. This possibility is suggested to illustrate how complex the factors may be which determine whether or not a male, on reaching maturity, remains in or is ousted from the group.

VOCALIZATIONS

Communication of intentions and of status within a patas group is mainly carried out by means of visually perceived gestures or movements. The patas social adaptations have favoured a vocalization repertoire most of the dis-tinctive calls of which are audible to the human observer at very short dis-tances (Hall *et al.* 1965). These calls are such as would, with difficulty, be heard, or located, by a ground predator, but are such as can communicate certain general needs within the group. Play, including play-fighting, is, as we have seen, completely silent. Threat or attack episodes in the wild are completely silent. The approach of humans is never reacted to vocally in such manner as to give away the presence of the group. We can describe their general vocal pattern as one of adaptive silence in which muted calls have occasional function. This fits clearly into the other adaptations of dispersal and high speed locomotion. Patas may hide silently in long grass when disturbed, and young animals have twice been found by the Warden of the Murchison Park crouched motionless on the ground, only their tails giving away their position. On each occasion, he was able to pick up the animal by the scruff of the neck.

As we know from the laboratory group, the patas repertoire of calls is about the same in number as that of baboons and Rhesus macaques. But, even in the laboratory, they are rarely uttered. The only "vocal" animal in the group is a juvenile male who was hand reared, in isolation from his mother and the other patas, for three months while still at the infant one stage. This suggests the possibility that, in the wild state, a strict economy of vocal habit may be acquired very early through the interaction with the mother. The inhibition of vocalization is likewise suggested by the special provocation necessary to elicit the far-carrying bark of the adult male, as described below.

The field study data on vocalizations are as follows:

(i) Day-to-day frequencies of audible vocalization. Frequencies were noted of all types of vocalization occurring in full day-ranges of patas and baboon groups at Murchison, observation distances being more or less the same for the two species. As already indicated in previous sections, the patas, at distances of 100 to 200 m from the observer, appear for many hours on end almost completely unvocal. Aggressive episodes, which are anyway infrequent, are often carried out without vocalization—this being confirmed from laboratory data, whereas baboon aggression elicits almost always loud vocalization both from aggressor and victim. Not only are audible vocalizations in patas groups therefore very rare, but are usually extremely brief, for example, a single squeal from an infant, instead of the crescendoes of squeals quite often heard in baboons. As examples of comparative frequencies, there were 25 and 50 distinct vocal episodes in two of the baboon day ranges. Of these, six and five were direct reactions to the observer, 19 and 45 to interactions within the groups or towards other animals (for example, the group once went shrieking and barking after a solitary buffalo which they appeared to have driven out of the undergrowth). On eight successive days with a patas group, there were no vocalizations audible on five, and only a total of five for the other three days. None of these was with reference to the observer, and there never was a vocal reaction to the observer by the Murchison groups even on encountering a group for the first time. In fact, the only vocalization that was presumably "caused" by the observer's presence was the whoo-wherr growl of the adult male of the Teso group. Most patas vocalizations were "want" calls from infants or brief squeals from infants or juveniles, usually in response to nipping by adult females from whom they have tried to suckle.

(ii) Calls heard in the wild only. These, elicited by situations which do not arise in captivity, were observed when or after a patas group encountered

another group or individual male patas. The barking of the adult male of the patas group, higher pitched than that of the male baboon, may occur repeatedly, at about 1/sec for "volleys" of about 20, then decreasing rapidly. The male has, when thus barking, always been stationed high up in a tree where he is very conspicuous, and it has never been heard from the ground. On another occasion, the successive volleys consisted of 35, 20 and 16 barks, then in shorter series for a total of 17 minutes.

On the occasions when the cause of the barking was certainly identified, it was the sighting of another small patas group or party in the distance (once) of a single adult male patas who fled from the area (two occasions), and of the captive juvenile male patas out with the observer on Group IV's day-range.

A more muffled and only a few times repeated vocalization by the adult male (that described as whoo-wherr, because of its distinct two-phase characteristic rather more drawn-out than the double-bark of the baboon) may perhaps be a less intense form of the bark. Judging from the movement of the barker's jaws, the "whoo" is a loud phase made on expiration of air, the "echo," as it were, occurring as the jaws close. This we have seen occurred when the observer was close to the adult male of the Atira group, and once when Group II in Stage III had retreated from an oncoming baboon group.

On two other occasions when the adult male of a group was barking repeatedly, others of the group were uttering a kind of higher-pitched chittering or scolding vocalization that has not been heard at any other time. On neither occasion, however, was it possible to see what had caused this highly unusual vocal behaviour. It could well have been due to a sudden encounter with some animal, such as vervets, a solitary baboon, or even, presumably, a predator.

SOCIAL ORGANIZATION

The final product of the adaptations of the patas recorded in the Murchison habitat is the patterning of the social relationships within the group and between the groups and isolates forming the local population. This centres around the role of the adult male and the adult females, and the relations between them. So far as can be seen, this results in a form of social organization which, in some respects, is unique amongst present day primates that have been studied in the wild. These unique features are to be expected from the fact that they differ considerably in their adaptations to ground living from other terrestrial or partly terrestrial species, such as baboons, vervets, and macaques. They are primates who have evolved survival patterns similar to those of some other terrestrial and herbivorous mammals of the savannahs, such as antelope or hares, while retaining some of the basic primate characteristics such as manipulatory skills, ability to climb trees, and the sexual reproductive cycle with long infant dependence. The significance of their social play on the ground is particularly impressive, and points perhaps more clearly than any other factor to their being adapted more thoroughly even than baboons to living in open savannah country.

The One-male Unit

A unit consisting of one adult male and several adult females and their young is described by Kummer and Kurt (1963) as the basis of the social organization of the hamadryas baboons. The points of difference between the species will be discussed later. The patas breeding unit consists of one adult male and up to twelve adult females. The extra males live either as isolates or in small bachelor parties, and no "peripheral" or "complemental" males that keep contact with the group, such as are found in baboon and rhesus groups, have been observed. This suggests that the patas social system is, as a breeding unit, the most exclusive of any so far recorded in monkeys or apes. It is also presumably the most economical in that a male weighing about twice as much as an adult female is likely to require twice as much food. From the size of the home ranges utilized by patas groups at Murchison, one might see the patas one-male unit as the basic social adaptation that ensures the survival of the population economically, including in relation to predators. The presence of more than one adult male in a group would not be economical in terms of food resources or, in a species adapted to swift locomotion, silence and concealment, in terms of predator protection. The obvious difference to the rut mammal harem system is that, in the patas so far as we know, the adult male stays with the group throughout the year, whether or not there are sexually receptive females in that group.

Several important questions remain to be answered in the patas system. If, as the field data suggest, there is a birth season and possibly a mating season, even though they are not discrete as in the Rhesus and Japanese macaque, a quite considerable change might take place in the social organization of a group in and out of the seasons, at least with respect to the adult male's relationships with the rest of the group. Certainly we find the adult male of Group II in Stage III, March and April, keeping very much further away from the others during the day-range than he, or other in-group adult males, did at other times of the year. But it seems probable that the reason for this is the long-distance view available to the animals in the short grass country, allowing of far greater spacing out in search of food. And, further, the distance of the male away from the group is perfectly compatible with his defensive function as a watcher and diverter rather than as an aggressive protector.

At present, we can only guess as to the process whereby a male becomes the one accepted in the group as the breeder and watcher. Possible factors in relation to status of the mother have been mentioned. Extra males can be presumed to be driven out by the in-group male and to be kept away by him from the vicinity of the group, until such time as he loses his sexual potency or otherwise fails to maintain his position *vis-à-vis* the extra males. A male that has been driven out is presumed to have a reduced chance of survival against predators, but there is absolutely no evidence on this point, and it is reasonable to suppose that a strong extra male would, at least when there are sexually receptive females in the groups, be continually on the look out for a chance to attract such females to him.

Apart from the possibility of an extra male competing directly with an in-group male, there are two other likely ways in which a continuing process of selection amongst the males may take place. One is by remaining in the group, under the protection of the adult females, and, on reaching sexual maturity, driving out, with their aid, the older animal. The other, and more likely, is that, when a group has become so large that it contains several more adult females than the in-group can cope with, these females may drift away from the group and be joined by one of the isolate males. Possibly the temporary "splitting" of Group II on several occasions was an indication of such a tendency.

The normal lack of aggressiveness of the adult male within the group is clearly comprehensible in that he has, at the time, no rivals with whom to compete. The spacing between the groups is so great that there is extremely little chance of females straying from his group to another group, whereas, in the hamadryas population, the one-male units are sometimes in very close proximity, and the male may severely chastise any of his females who strays. It seems, therefore, that the aggressiveness of the patas male is very closely linked with, or is an integral part of, his sexual behaviour. As we have noted, the threshold of aggression of the laboratory male is greatly lowered in the period when he is mating with a receptive female. It follows that the "territorial" behaviour of the patas is probably, in fact, that of the adult male who is reacting towards a rival, though in-group, male. The exclusive one-male mating system here is linked with a very strong dispersal tendency as between groups, this being itself determined by the totality of the ecological factors. The large size, conspicuous appearance, and large canine teeth of the male patas, would seem to have been selected for in evolution primarily as sexual characteristics, not for aggressive defence against predators. Secondarily, however, the large size and conspicuous appearance are advantageous as a focus of attention for the rest of the group and as an effective part of diversionary display.

The Adult Females

In the patas one-male unit, the ranks of the various adult females are, from laboratory observation, clearly defined at least over relatively short periods

(Hall 1965c). In view of the special watchful-defensive functions of the adult male, and his frequent remoteness from the group, the adult females may be expected to have the essential function of maintaining the coherence of the group, the male being, from the point of population survival, relatively expendable. In this context, then, the adaptiveness of a strongly organized ranking system amongst the females is evident, whereas, in a baboon group with several adult males who form the inner structure of the group, with the females and their infants staying close to them, there would seem to be no advantage in so clear-cut a hierarchy. Nevertheless, it is an oversimplification of the social organization to say that the patas packs are ". . . bossed by old females" (Sanderson 1957:118). As we have seen, the adult male is pre-eminent in any situation where another group or another male are concerned, or where the group is perceived by him to be threatened by a predator. In short, apart from mating, his role is with any threat from outside the group, whether from congeners or other, and hardly at all with what goes on in the group itself. Unlike baboon males, he has not been seen to interfere in squabbles amongst females or to protect a mother with infant from threat-attacks by another female.

Sanderson (personal communication) has enlarged on his statement by saying that an adult female almost always seemed to "lead" the groups he saw in West Africa. There is ample confirmation of this in the present study. On many occasions when a group had halted, as in a day-resting tree, it was one or more of the adult females who were the first to descend and move off across the savannah. In such instances, the adult male might follow after most, or all, the rest of the group had gone after the leading females. The distances that separated the leading females from the adult male were sometimes considerable. Thus, in Group II, two adult females moved away from the day-resting trees at 1420 hours. By 1520, these females had gone 500 m away from the tree in which the adult male still remained. Only at 1540, that is, 80 minutes after the females had led off, did he descend and move after the others. Occasionally, however, it appeared that the group would not move away if the adult male remained in the tree. So, the adult females of Group II moved about 400 m on the day-range, but then waited until the male followed them. This does not invalidate the notion that the females "lead," but it points to the probability that they would not normally go beyond visual contact with the adult male. Occasionally also, Group II split up temporarily. The most notable occurrence was when a part of the group with adult females leading ranged in a westerly direction over the grassland, while a few others went with the adult male on a northerly bearing. Eventually, the first party, with which the observer remained, was completely out of sight of the male's party. But, instead of altering direction north, they continued slowly west, the male and his party changing their direction to rejoin them.

This kind of "leading" of the day routine fits clearly into the total social pattern as we have described it. The possessiveness of the adult females towards their infants, and the clearly structured status relations between the females, though complicated by "alliances," seems to ensure the compactness of the group as relatively independent of the close presence of the adult male, leaving him free to roam sometimes far away from them.

The general pattern as between the adult male and the adult females thus seems clearly defined. But it is complicated by the already noted fact that the females may sometimes threaten or chase the adult male, usually when he has been trying to mate with one of them. A notable feature of the patas organization in the laboratory group is a generalization or redirection of aggression by, for example, the no. 2 female against the no. 3 as a direct consequence of no. 1 having attacked no. 2. This is a well-known feature of other monkey groups, there sometimes being a kind of chain reaction along the hierarchy when the equilibrium of the group is disturbed. It is possible that the "ganging" of females against the male is, in fact, at first directed at the female with whom he has been mating, and is then switched to him. As already reported, in the wild groups, such threat sequences against the male never resulted in his counter-attacking them, although he might turn and check them.

On present evidence, the preliminary conclusion is that we have, in the patas groups, a distinctive form of social organization, as between the adult male and the adult females, which may well be the extreme of a type of social adaptation to ground living. The resemblances to some forms of ungulate social organization are evident, but the differences lie particularly in the characteristic behaviour of the adult male. Where survival depends upon the economy of the one-male unit, it is perhaps to be expected that there should be what seems a remarkable degree of discipline in the social organization, as shown in the night dispersal system and in the way in which the group awaits the adult male's "lead" when approaching water or a new feeding area.

COMPARISON WITH BABOONS

At several points in the foregoing sections, direct comparisons have been made with the Chacma baboon (*Papio ursinus*) and the baboons of Kenya and Uganda (*P. anubis* and *cynocephalus*). Such comparisons are easiest to draw, and perhaps most reliable, when they are made by the same observer from data obtained on the different species, and probably most vividly made when, as in Murchison, it was possible to obtain data on the baboons and patas as they utilized areas of the same habitat. A close familiarity with the work of DeVore on the Kenya baboons, which has been synthesized in joint publications by DeVore and Hall, Hall and DeVore (1965), dealing with both the Kenya and Southern Africa data, has made it possible to at-

TABLE 2–11   A SUMMARY OF THE MAJOR ADAPTATIONS OF PATAS AND THE BABOONS OF SOUTHERN AND EAST AFRICA

Adaptation	Patas	Baboons
Physical	Slim build; high-speed ground locomotion; sexual dimorphism: male 13 kg, female 6.5 kg	Sturdy build; large size; very skilful rock climber; sexual dimorphism: male 33 kg, female 16.5 kg
Reproductive cycle and sexual characters	Female cycle about 30 days; no sexual swelling; pronounced local birth season, and possibly mating season; gestation 160 days	Female cycle about 30 days; pronounced sexual swelling; possibility of local birth season, but regionally variable; gestation 180 days
Distribution	Northern equatorial Africa, south of Sahara	Whole of Africa, south of Sahara
Habitat	Steppe and savannah from arid to woodland; only on fringes of thicket and forest; probably avoids rivers	Veld, mountain, savannah, woodland, and sometimes forest-based; not in equatorial rain forests (Congo, and so forth)
Home range	Up to 52 km² for group of 30; no "core areas"; some overlap between groups	Average of 8.40 km², but no data for arid regions; "core areas" of security and feeding
Day-ranging	Varies from 500–12,000 m	Approximately same range of variation
Day activity	Two main feeding periods; day-resting period of 2–3 h	Most of day spent in feeding, with no long or regular resting periods
Night resting	Dispersal at dusk over savannah; sleeping place changed on successive nights; no assembling in morning	Congregation at dusk on rock faces or tall trees; in some areas, same sleeping place used on many successive nights; congregation in the morning
Numerical data	Mean group size 15, range 6–31; one adult male, several adult females, several immatures	Very large group may occur (up to 200); mean 25–30; several adult males and several females and immatures; Young males may be peripheral to group, but belong to it
Extra-group animals	Isolated adult males; all-male party	Isolated adult males; no all-male parties recorded
Feeding	Mainly vegetarian; insects, lizards	Mainly vegetarian, but also small mammal prey; diet probably more varied than patas
Drinking	Very rarely to standing water, never to rivers	Regularly to standing water and sometimes to rivers

TABLE 2–11—*continued*

Adaptation	Patas	Baboons
Interactions with other animals	Nothing known of predation; leopard probable; in some area, cheetah and Hunting dogs; they give way to baboons	Occasional individual loss to leopard, Black eagle, crocodile, or python recorded
Sexual behaviour	Mating rarely seen; soliciting by adult female; "harem" system of one male, several females	Mating frequently seen; some variation in mating partnerships, and not an exclusive harem system
Friendly behaviour	Grooming is frequent, but spread over day; chiefly a female activity; indicative of relative status	Similar; in addition, "greetings" behaviour sequences
Play	Reaches a peak 1100–1200 h; very vigorous, high-speed, almost entirely on ground	Peaks early and late, that is near sleeping place, and usually on cliffs or trees
Aggression	Rare occurrence, then usually only slight contact, and no fighting; episodes silent, brief; no attacks by adult male	Frequent, noisy, rough, often by adult males
Mother-infant behaviour	Infant always on ventral side of mother; possessiveness of mother; no "sharing" with other females; no protection, by adult male	Infant early on ventral, later on dorsal side of mother; mother and infant protected in centre of group; attractive to other females
Vocalizations	Adaptive silence; two calls heard per day; repertoire of muted calls; barking by adult male only at other patas	Up to 50 loud vocalizations per day; strong vocal display at human beings
Social organization	One-male breeding unit; male as watcher and diverter; females "lead" day ranges; male often remote from group	Several-male breeding unit; males as aggressive defenders of group; females and infants in centre of group with some adult males, with other males more peripheral

tempt a general summary of the adaptations of patas and baboons (Table 2–11) which may serve as a guide to further field and captivity studies. Inevitably, such a summary has many defects. Regional sampling of the adaptations of baboons is still inadequate, with no field data at all for the whole of West Africa, while the patas sampling is from one preliminary study confined to one small region of the East African distribution. No data for *P. hamadryas* are included in the table, because, at the time of writing, only the one short account of the year's field work by Kummer and Kurt (1963) is available. There are no systematic data whatever available on the two *Mandrillus* spp.

While comparison with the terrestrially-adapted baboons or baboon-like monkeys may be a useful first stage, a very important second stage will come when the field studies of Gartlan in Uganda and Struhsaker in Kenya of *Cercopithecus aethiops* become available. At present, the most prominent difference in social organization of patas and vervets is based on different group constitution. A vervet group of 20 to 25 animals would have several adult males in it, and even the modal group of about 12 animals would have three or four such males. There are also many important differences in the behaviour repertoires, but, as stated earlier in this paper, it is impossible to use such differences for taxonomic argument as to whether patas is a Cercopitheque species or a separate genus until adequate data samples on other *Cercopithecus* species such as *mitis*, are available. Our present evidence certainly strongly suggests very clear and important differences in the ecology and behaviour of patas and vervet, as well as in that of patas and baboon.

We have said that the patas has evolved to extreme form amongst monkeys a particular complex of adaptations to ground living. This complex contrasts in many important features from that which makes up the kind of ground plan of baboons and macaques. The major contrast seems to lie in the physical adaptation for high speed ground locomotion, and the associated adaptations of evasion by concealment, by dispersion, and by silence. Correlated with these is the uniquely interesting watchful and perhaps diversionary behaviour of the adult male, and the probably closely-organized social system of the adult females who, with the young animals of the group, never take part in such behaviour but remain quite separate from the adult male during these activities. The very small amount of aggression, and, when it does occur, its usually non-contact variety, compares very markedly with the baboon group the adult males of which can be exceedingly rough in "disciplining" the group and exceedingly effective in combined defence-attack against predators (see Washburn & DeVore 1960, film entitled *Baboon Behaviour*). Further, the spatial arrangement of a several male baboon group is for females with infants, juveniles, and highest ranking males to form the centre of the group, while younger or lower ranking males tend to be in the van, in the rear, or at the sides when the group is on the move: "Thus, without any fixed or formal order, the arrangement of the troop is such that the females and young are protected at the centre. No matter from what direction a predator approaches the troop, it must first encounter the adult males" (Washburn and DeVore 1961*b*:64). A similar type of spatial organization is described for the Japanese macaques. In patas groups, we have seen that extra males were never in contact with groups, indeed were encountered very far away from them.

Relations between groups likewise contrast very clearly. Baboon groups frequently tolerate the presence of other groups, or at least rarely act hostilely towards them unless "trespass" within the home range has been considerable. The fact that several adult males learn to tolerate each other within a group is probably another aspect of the same basic adaptation. An adult male patas can be assumed to be exceedingly intolerant of other adult males, just as he, and the group with him, is very agitated and aggressive towards other groups when they encounter them.

Amongst baboon populations in very harsh habitat, such as Southwest Africa, group sizes are small (average about 23), and such groups have only one full-grown male. This, however, is only a regional variation, and the social organization still fits the general plan. The only species so far known to be consistently organized on the one-male-unit system appears to be *P. hamadryas* (Kummer and Kurt 1963). But the organization of these units within the population is entirely different from that of the patas population in that the units are frequently associated loosely with one another, at sleeping places and one day-ranges. It is true that juvenile and subadult males and some adult males without females live outside such units, but would be classed as on the periphery and not as completely isolated as in the case of the patas all-male-party and the single adult males.

The importance of the contrast between the patas and baboons is in emphasizing the quite different survival pattern of the two genera. Baboons, being based on rocky escarpments or cliffs or on large tree clumps, use the savannah or woodland from these bases, and rely for daytime security on the defensive power of adult males and on the alertness of peripheral males. Patas are truly creatures of the savannah itself, and there are no areas within the home ranges which are specially favoured because of the security they offer.

FURTHER RESEARCH

The research tasks envisaged, and the methods required in undertaking them, have a bearing upon the general course of nonhuman primate ecology and behaviour studies. The present study is classed as preliminary, but has been assisted by observations of the laboratory group, while the behaviour of this group in a very restricted environment has attained significance through the possibility of comparing results with the field data.

First, specific problems for further field study are:

(i) Extensive sampling of areas of probable distribution of the species, particularly along the southern edge of the Sahara. The species is now much in demand for medical researches and tests. Although its range is geographically large, the numerical density may, regionally, be very small. If areas are found where the population density is much greater than in Uganda, there may turn out to be very significant population differences in ecology and social organization for different regions.

(ii) Intensive study, preferably by more than one observer, is required on one population area, so that group structure can be precisely determined by observing identifiable individuals over a long period. Similarly, changes in the composition of groups, particularly in terms of the in-group male and the extra males, can only be ascertained by the simultaneous observations of two or more field workers. If there is a mating season, it is to be expected that there may be, in some groups, changes in the social pattern. Possibly the extra males move closer to the groups, and possibly, at this time, new groups are formed.

Second, specific problems that can probably only be answered by long term study of a captive group include:

(i) Detailed analysis of the processes of socialization and social learning in general, including the relation of mother's to offspring's status.
(ii) Analysis of causes and circumstances of status changes within the group.

Third, it is clear that certain general problems, such as the use of ecological and behaviour data in taxonomic discussion, and the whole task of comparison between the species that are primarily terrestrial in their adaptations, require a far more thorough species sampling than is at present available. But not only is an increased *range* of data required. The data of field studies need to be much more clearly formulated on a quantitative basis which takes account of intra-specific variations before more appropriate generalizations than those that have been in existence for many years can be attempted.

Since Zuckerman's (1932) account, there has been no systematic evaluation of the nonhuman primate data in relation to the data available on non-primate mammals and other vertebrates. As stated earlier, the patas adaptations to ground living bear some obvious resemblances to those of herbivorous mammals, and the "distraction display" of the male, if that is what it is, to similar displays in ground-nesting birds. Ethological analysis may also show that there are patterns of social stimuli, for example, eliciting aggression in the adult male or mating behaviour, or protective behaviour by the mother, which have a clear but limited adaptive function in the group. No doubt some of the vocalizations would fall into this category. To suggest such possibilities is in no way to reduce the significance of learning as an adaptive process in the behaviour of the wild group. On the contrary, it merely serves to emphasize what, in other comparative animal behaviour studies, is nowadays obvious, namely that the processes of learning, particularly social learning, are geared to the ecological conditions within which the species can survive. They are simply the neurophysiological extensions of the primary adaptations. In the form in which they are seen in the wild, they are assuredly the product of the group experience of many generations. How does the adult male patas "know" the behaviour appropriate to him in the group? Probably as a result of complex, long-term observational learning. There are many such important problems which can scarcely be answered except by experimental study. At least the problems that are important, and that are susceptible to experimental treatment, can be seen from even preliminary field study of the species.

The field study was supported by a grant from the Wenner-Gren Foundation for Anthropological Research, New York. Research on the laboratory group of patas, unpublished data from which are cited in the text, has been supported by the Medical Research Council, and the help of Mrs. M. J. Goswell in analysing the field data has been made possible by the same source.

Field work in the Murchison Falls National Park, comprising almost all the data in the present paper, was kindly authorized and facilitated by Colonel C. D. Trimmer, D.S.O., Director of the Uganda National Parks. Mr. Roger Wheater, Warden of the Park, was unfailingly helpful in providing facilities for the work, including accommodation at the Park H.Q. and at Chobi camp, and the services of the Park rangers. Mr. John Savidge, Scientific Officer of the Parks, provided information as to possible locations of patas groups. A special acknowledgement is due to Joseph, the Acholi ranger, who accompanied the writer throughout most of the fieldwork at Murchison, and whose knowledge of the Park was of great value.

At Makerere University College, I thank Professor L. C. Beadle, and Dr. and Mrs. Rowell, for their help and hospitality, and Dr. W. C. Osmaston and Miss Ann Tallantire for identifying botanical specimens.

At the Agricultural Research Station, Serere, I am grateful to its Director, Mr. Arthur Stephens, for his help, and to Mrs. Stephens for her kind hospitality.

3

EXPERIMENT AND QUANTIFICATION

IN THE STUDY OF BABOON BEHAVIOR

IN ITS NATURAL HABITAT*

K. R. L. Hall

The baboon, *Papio cynocephalus,* being probably the most widely distributed of any species of nonhuman primate in Africa, is adaptable to a very considerable range of habitats. So far, these habitats have been adequately sampled from only Kenya and Southern Africa (DeVore and Hall 1965) no systematic data on ecology and behavior of the species being available from any area of its extensive distribution south of the Sahara in West Africa. In the Cameroun, Spanish Guinea, and Gabon, the mandrill and drill take the place of *P. cynocephalus,* the habitat here being rain forest. The species is, however, reported to occur in forested areas of the Congo, and is known to adapt readily when introduced to coniferous forest—as it has done in the Cedarberg Mountains and on Table Mountain in Cape Province, South Africa, where it feeds quite extensively upon the seeds removed from the pine cones. Other areas of its distribution from which no adequate data are available include Northern Rhodesia, Nyasaland, Tanganyika, Southern Sudan, Angola, Mozambique, and Ethiopia. Only a small sample of data is available for Uganda (Hall 1965c), where groups base their home ranges on mountains or rocky hills, as in the province of Karamoja, or on forest patches or riverine forest, as in the Murchison Falls and Queen Elizabeth National Parks. Some completely isolated small popu-

*Reprinted with permission from *The Baboon in Medical Research,* H. Vagtborg, ed. Austin: University of Texas Press, pp. 29–42.

lations or even single groups are to be found in the agricultural provinces, for instance in Teso district, and interesting survival populations are reported within and on the edge of the Sahara on the rocky massifs of South West Tibesti, on Ennedi, and on Aïr (Monod 1963).

The purpose of the present article is to take as a lead this evidence of the adaptability of *P. cynocephalus*, to consider its implications with special reference to the ecological conditions pertaining in my own areas of study in Uganda and Southern Africa, and to discuss the uses and limitations of experiment and quantification as a means of obtaining objective data on the species which can be used for comparison within the species and with other terrestrial species such as mandrill, drill, gelada, and hamadryas.

Even within the Southern African distribution, habitat differences are very marked (Hall 1963a). In Southwest Africa baboons are found ranging over the arid thornveld, where edible vegetation is seasonally extremely limited and where some groups use cattle-drinking troughs as their main water supply. Temperature variations in winter are from about 80°F during the day to below freezing at night—a drop of about 50°F. In the temperate areas of the Cape, where animals occur right down to the coast of the Cape Peninsula and intermittently along the coast eastwards to Natal, the diet of the species differs very considerably from that of populations in other parts of Africa. In Southern Rhodesia, there are considerable differences in habitat between baboon populations along the Zambezi river banks—where groups use trees as night resting places, and often feed along the river banks and sometimes in shallow water of pools—and populations living in the woodland savannah farther to the south.

In the Murchison Falls Park of Uganda (Hall 1965c), baboon groups, based mainly on tree clusters along the banks of the Victoria Nile and its tributaries, range far into the savannah grasslands and woodlands for food.

Some notable dietary differences are to be found for each region, and home-range utilization varies considerably from area to area according to the nature of the terrain. And, as is now well known (DeVore and Hall 1965), baboon groups show, in certain areas, a remarkable adaptability to human habitation, crops, and motor vehicles; their positive responses are very easily maintained, allowing very close range observations, when occasionally reinforced by food.

It is in this context, then, that we shall now consider our objective of obtaining precise information about the behavior of the species. The behavior we observe in the natural population is a product of modifications and refinements of a basic repertoire brought about by the continuing interactions of individuals in their group life, of the group with other groups with which it has contact, and of the group with other species of animal—significant as potential predators, as food objects, as providing warning signals, and so on. The repertoire is also basic to the group learning processes concerned with the "map" of the home range, and with the location of food, water, and sheltering places. As a result of the accumulation of data now available on this species, we are in a position to work out problems for intensive investigation which bear particularly upon the learning processes of the group and upon the ways in which the group provides the essential setting for each and every act of learning by the individual that belongs to it. This is, and needs to be, a radical change of emphasis from the usual laboratory procedure of starting to study the learning process of the individual monkey or ape when group influences are eliminated from the experimental situation. It is tantamount to saying that we are interested primarily in the individual differences in behavior that are determined by the social situation.

The proposition therefore is that the group is the basic unit for the study of learning processes, species characteristics behavior patterns having operationally defined capacities for variation in terms of different contexts. However, it follows from this approach that quantification of the basic ecological and behavior data must be attempted in the stable natural group, before experimental variations can be systematically used to bring about special or unusual social situations.

FIELD OBSERVATION AND QUANTIFICATION

The relationship of field and experimental observation has been classed as a continuum from noninterference to maximum interference with the natural life of the animal (Schneirla 1950). The general problems of representative sampling of monkey and ape behavior for purposes of comparison have been reviewed at length elsewhere (Hall 1963b). The ordering and classification of data, with some statistical evaluations of an elementary kind, is possible in the noninterference stages of field work, and some examples of how this has been attempted and how it might be done more effectively and extensively will be given in reference to our species. Let us start by pointing out that our objective, for *P. cynocephalus,* is to obtain truly representative samples of the species which will accurately reflect the degree of variation in different areas and under different conditions. Although verbal, rather than numerical, statements—as, for example, that baboons are less tolerant of observers in one area than another—can give an impression of difference, these are quite inadequate scientifically. It is, perhaps, important, first and foremost, that field observers should be trained to think quantitatively, for this will affect their whole approach to the task and need in no way vitiate accuracy of their qualitative descriptions. For this reason one of the most important stages in prefield training should be an exercise in quantifying observations on a group in captivity. The skill of the field worker then comes in his ability to adapt his methods from the "ideal" situation in which he has learned them to the vicissitudes of the natural group study situation.

Selected examples of field quantification are now treated with comments as to their further application and improvement:

(1) Numerical Data

The species shows a remarkable degree of variation in group sizes from area to area (DeVore 1965; Hall 1963d; Hall 1965c). The observational problems in arriving at accurate counts of groups in the field are well known. The major problems remaining here are the obtaining of large sample counts from other areas of the distribution, and the long-term census of populations in the same area over successive years. So far as is known, such a census is, at present, only being carried out by DeVore and his associates (DeVore 1965) on the Nairobi Park population. This kind of time-sampling is particularly important in areas such as Southwest Africa, where ecological conditions can alter drastically from year to year. The dynamic relationships of groups within a population area should be studied by following up relative group sizes when one group has been experimentally eliminated or reduced in size. This should be done, for example, in the Cape Nature Reserve of South Africa, where individuals of the southernmost group are periodically shot or trapped as a means of reducing damage to visitors' cars.

Accurate analysis of group constitution in terms of age and sex classes is obviously essential for the reconstruction of the social pattern in the groups, and for the determination of whether there are seasonal trends in births indicative of regional differences. Although, for example, such analyses strongly indicate birth peaks in the Kenya, Uganda, and Southern Rhodesia populations, we have too little data at present on which to base any conclusion as to seasonality, or otherwise, in the Cape populations of South Africa. The fact that births are known to occur in all months of the year in this region is quantitatively insufficient to indicate whether there are statistically significant differences in this respect from one season to another. Adequate samples require month-by-month counts for several years in order to get data comparable to that on births and mortality in the Cayo Santiago rhesus population (Koford 1965).

(2) Home-Range Charting

DeVore and Hall (1965) have recorded day-range distances and night-resting places for their groups in Kenya and South Africa, which indicate the kinds of utilization of the home ranges, the sizes of the home ranges, and the distances traveled by groups. The patterns given by the charts show considerable differences from group to group and within the same group from season to season. It should be possible to refine this kind of quantification, as suggested by Calhoun (personal communication), by working out the charts of group movement on an hour-by-hour basis from dawn to dusk. Such a time-movement chart would show the rate of movement for any hour of the day, and would be interpreted in terms of the kinds and frequencies of activity going on throughout the day. This would graphically indicate time spent in travel, resting, and so on; it could be used for seasonal comparisons of the same group, for comparisons between large and small groups, and for comparisons between groups in different habitat areas. It is important that the field worker should be prepared to record his data in this way, distance judgments being recorded at the time of observation and checked against a large scale map of the area. Distance judgment is difficult in the field because of terrain differences, and range-finding equipment, other than that on standard cameras, is probably not sufficiently portable. Pedometers are impractical because of the diversions that the observer usually has to make in walking across country after a group. Only on especially favorable terrain, as in the Nairobi Park, is it possible to follow a group throughout its day range in a motor vehicle. Nevertheless, reasonable estimates can be obtained, as was found by the writer in following baboons, vervets, and patas monkeys on foot in Uganda.

(3) Time-Sampling of Group Activity

As stated with reference to home-range charting, the picture of the "typical" routine of a baboon group can be given objectively in terms of movement-rate over the ground and in terms of prevalent activity of the group at different times of day. As examples of activity quantification in the field, it was found (Hall 1962b) that grooming is far more persistent during the first two or three hours of the day, while the group is at or near its sleeping cliffs, than at any other period. A secondary grooming peak occurs when the group gets near to its sleeping place at the end of the day. In the intervening period grooming occurs sporadically, as when a group rests for a short while. About 80 percent of day time is spent by most adult individuals in a group looking for and eating food. Young baboons tend to spend relatively less time in feeding, and more time in playing with each other. Aggressive episodes are likewise more frequent, as also is copulation, early in the day. By such approximations of quantification, based on counting, it should be possible to construct a statistical profile of group activity—proportional, obviously, to the number of observation hours in the study period at each hour of daylight. What is typical in the routine of a group of baboons in one region may well be shown to differ quite markedly from groups in other habitat areas. For example, much less time is spent around the sleeping cliffs in the early morning by baboon groups in the winter in South-west Africa, with temperatures at near freezing, and less social activity was observed at this time of day. In tropical regions of high midday tempera-tures there may be indications of regular day resting, this not being a feature of the South African groups.

Overall frequency data on behavior such as copulations, aggressive epi-sodes, and so on, are important for regional comparisons, and for within-group comparisons over a long period. It has, for example, been noted (Hall and DeVore 1965) that adult male baboons in the Cape engage in a series of copulations with estrous females, with intervals of a few minutes be-tween each copulation of a series. Thus the mating pattern seems, in this race, to be directly comparable to that recorded for the rhesus on Cayo Santiago (Carpenter 1942*b*), whereas, in Kenya, copulations were far less frequent and apparently did not occur in series.

Aggressive episodes require quantification so that it is possible to desig-nate comparative frequencies both between groups and within groups, when there are changes in the group situation. Hall (1962*c*) pointed out how ag-gressive episodes among the females in a group increased more or less di-rectly in proportion to the number of copulations by the male with the one female who was then in estrus. Also, when an alien baboon was near the group the male's aggressiveness to other baboons in his group occurred about thirteen times more frequently than in the 190 observation hours prior to this occasion.

It is evident that careful definition of the events to be quantified is of great importance. Provided that this is done, however, it will be realized that these simple methods of frequency recording can have considerable use for comparative purposes from one field study to another. They also make the data obtained in the field more readily comparable with what can be easily obtained from captivity group studies. Refinements can be introduced with such procedures by the timing of individual episodes, by the breaking down of the episodes into components of behavior, and by intensity ratings. For example, the time spent in actively grooming is shown to be far greater for adult females than for adult males (Hall 1962*c*), and it tends to be much more superficial when the male is doing it.

(4) Analysis of Behavior Repertoire

A particularly useful kind of preliminary quantification can be carried out within the group in the process of describing and analyzing the com-munication behavior patterns and sequences, the social stimuli which elicit them, and the responses which follow them. As Altmann (1962*a*) has em-phasized, for example, with reference to tactile signals in rhesus monkeys, and as Marler has clearly described as a general point of method in the analysis of nonhuman primate communication (Marler 1965), careful statistical data on sequence patterning of the behavior that precedes and follows these tactile signals (very prominent in baboons and macaques) is required in order to discover what information these signals communicate. While there is nothing new about such quantification as applied to ethological studies of lower vertebrates and invertebrates, the amount and kind of data is only just becoming sufficient to make it feasible for application to the baboon in its natural environment.

In considering the friendly behavior of baboons, as shown by grooming and greetings—both of which primarily involve tactile signals, with visually perceived signals preceding approach and contact—we find (Hall 1962c) that it is possible to elicit, in a natural group, no less than twelve different components of behavior between individuals, nine of which involve actual contact (that is, tactile signals), as shown by embracing and the nuzzling of the genital-stomach area. It is also necessary to determine between which individuals or classes of individual such sequences occur as well as in what social situations they occur. Again, frequency counting can help in comparing situations within the group, this kind of behavior being observed only rarely where stable social relations appear to exist, but occurring at a high incidence when infant ones are present.

A similar kind of quantitative treatment is necessary in delineating the behavior patterns that appear in situations of conflict or frustration. It is well attested for several species of monkey that certain kinds of behavior, such as scratching, yawning, and fumbling of food objects, recur in situations where analysis indicates that other kinds of motivation, such as tendencies to escape or attack, may be primarily aroused. It is necessary, however, to distinguish the normal occurrences from those that appear in the conflict type of situation, and this can be done only by careful attention both to frequency and intensity differences. Thus, scratching of the back or tail may be more rapid and far more frequent per time unit when the baboon is manifestly ill at ease than when it is engaged in its routine activities of food-seeking or resting. Such quantitative comparisons are easy to work out in captivity situations, but there is nothing to prevent the field worker from obtaining similar data either in the course of observing social interactions in the wild group or in the instigation of conflict or frustration by experimental interference with the group.

It is reasonable to conclude that there are no data at present on *P. cynocephalus,* in the wild or in captivity, which is comparable in exactness of description and in quantitative finesse to that which has been produced for the rhesus macaque in seminatural conditions (Altmann 1962a; Hinde and Rowell 1962; Rowell and Hinde 1962). Until such data are available from wild baboon groups it will be impossible to accurately compare the social behavior of groups of different races or different habitats, or to assess with any precision the effects of field experiments on social behavior. As a further example, the analysis and quantitative treatment of the vocalizations of our species in the wild have proceeded little further than the preliminary descriptive stage, and it must be remembered that quantitative differences are likely to be particularly significant in our appraisal of regional differences in communication behavior.

FIELD OBSERVATION AND EXPERIMENT

We have already touched upon minor experimental interferences with the natural behavior of baboon groups, as in considering the effects of the presence of an alien baboon or of the elimination of individuals within a group in order to determine the effects upon the population structure. Field experimental variations may, however, be far more comprehensive than this. They may take the form either of the observer taking advantage of an indirect change in the group's environment—that is, one brought about by such natural causes as habitat destruction or by such incidental man-made causes as the flooding of habitat at Kariba (Hall 1963*d*)—or of the observer deliberately creating a situation intended to modify the group's behavior.

The first type of situation illustrates particularly well Schneirla's point about the interrelationship of field and experimental observation. Unfortunately, however, in baboons little advantage has been taken of studying groups under such conditions. The Kariba flooding produced some data on the disintegration of group life, but observation could not be made, in the field study time available, of the course of change in group behavior as food availability decreased and home range sizes were drastically reduced. Similarly, no data are available as to the consequences of home range devastation by fire or by prolonged drought. There is little doubt that major experimental changes of the home range environment could lead to important information as to the troop's adaptability—the time it takes for group behavior changes in ranging, diet, and other activities to take place—and the effect on the social organization, particularly as represented by the behaviour of the dominant males. However, there is no a priori reason to suppose that changes would be initiated by the older males; it is more likely, as judged from the exploratory zeal of younger males of Cape groups, that these younger males might furnish the lead for group adaptation under unfamiliar conditions.

The second type of situation already has many examples from studies of Japanese macaques which could well be applied to baboons. Testing for relative dominance of pairs of adult males by giving a special food incentive is a common example, and one used by DeVore in Kenya and by Wingfield

(Wingfield 1963) on groups in the Cape and in Southern Rhodesia. Experimental interference of this, and the other sorts to be described, may be required either to obtain information directly and with some measure of observer control, which can be obtained only very rarely or inadequately by the usual field methods, or to elicit unusual responses, which may indicate the underlying structure of the group relationships not apparent under normal stable conditions.

The writer has already reported on a few minor experimental tests on wild baboons (Hall 1962*b;* Hall 1962*c;* Hall 1963*d).* Though preliminary and unsystematic, the results were promising because they indicated quite clearly how a planned series of field experiments could be carried out with a group so well-habituated to the observer as to allow him to sit in their midst, while ignoring him completely. It is certainly necessary to follow up such interesting response differences to live snakes and scorpions as are shown by the Cape baboons, on the one hand, who avoid these creatures, and the Southwest Africa baboons, who eat scorpions and legless lizards and are reliably reported to eat back-fanged sand snakes. These cultural differences are of great interest, but field observation alone can merely broadly indicate what they are in different areas, whereas experiment is necessary to determine under precisely what conditions particular aversions or preferences develop, and, especially, how the learning processes involved are affected by the group situation (that is, the role of social facilitation and inhibition).

It is, further, of great importance to assess accurately the learning capacities of baboons in the natural environment. Their adaptability is quite unrealistically tested in the usual laboratory tests of conditioning, discrimination, and so on. Quite informally, the writer has tested the delayed reactions of young baboons by luring them away from the rest of the group with a high-incentive food, such as a banana. It is simple then to conceal pieces of banana by covering them with soil, while the baboons watch carefully, then drive the baboons away from the place and keep them away for several minutes. When the baboons venture to the place their speed and accuracy in locating the food can be readily assessed. In more controlled experiments, which would follow from these simple observations, it would be necessary to vary the conditions systematically, for example, to eliminate olfactory cues, to study the effect of increasing the delay and the number of food objects concealed, the spacing between them, and so on. Operant conditioning or tool-using experiments can also very easily be carried out on an habituated wild group, and techniques of avoidance conditioning might be developed in the field as a useful aid in keeping baboons away from crops.

It is now very well attested that baboons occasionally kill and eat small mammals and fledgling birds. It is also highly probable, from the accounts of eyewitnesses in South and Southwest Africa, that lambs are killed quite regularly by baboons. While much more field evidence is required of the circumstances and frequencies of occurrence of this carnivorous tendency, it would also be invaluable to study the stages of the acquisition of such a habit in groups not known from field observation to show the tendency. As in the Japanese studies of the propagation of a new food habit in their macaque groups, the spreading process of the habit is itself of great interest and can readily be studied experimentally.

The dynamics of the social organization of baboon groups offer a particularly important area for experimental study in the field. Introduction of alien baboons or even of a new group can provide fascinating insights into the social organization. A group should also be transported to a new habitat area and released so that the observer could follow up its adjustments to the unfamiliar conditions. Many such experiments could best be done as part of a long-term program based on a research station in the natural habitat. A considerable amount of information which is already available from the Cayo Santiago and Japanese Monkey Center studies, can be usefully applied in setting up comparable programs of research in Africa. The baboon is likely to be, in many ways, the most interesting of all the monkeys as a subject for field experiment.

CONCEPTUAL FRAMEWORK

Important quantitative and experimental studies of rhesus macaque groups in seminatural and captivity environments have demonstrated many possibilities for extending such techniques to the study of baboon groups in the wild. Our knowledge of baboons in their natural habitats is such as to indicate a multitude of behavior problems which can best be solved by the quantifying of observations and by experimental manipulations. There is little doubt that important advances will be achieved by a flexible and imaginative adaptation of such techniques to the field situation; but, in order that the researches of both laboratory and field investigators can be integrated, it is necessary to examine the behavior concepts in terms of which the results can be analyzed and hypotheses framed. Most of the aspects of adjustability that have been examined in this paper appear to involve rather simple processes of learning, such as habituation, and classical and instrumental conditioning. But they are occurring in the group environment, and thus, whatever the goal-object may be, it is basically social learning that is involved.

Social learning is, at present, too general and imprecise a conception to be more than broadly descriptive of a whole range of behavior modifications that go on in the baboon from birth to maturity to death. In its most elementary form it seems to involve the facilitation or inhibition of an existing behavior pattern, so that a measurable increase or decrease of occurrence or of amplitude of the behavior can be observed in different social situations. In its more complex form it probably involves refined discriminations of cues in the behavior of one animal, for example a dominant male, which have to be acted on by subordinate animals in avoiding punishment. Although quantification of definable social events in a group is an important way of striving for some precision in observation technique, this is only the prelude to the more profound experimental analysis of how the social relationships in a group arise and are altered through individual experience.

Much is written in the experimental work on animal learning about the nature of reinforcement. A realistic view of reinforcement of learning in a natural group of baboons makes it abundantly clear that there are likely to be as many types of reinforcement as there are situations in which learning can be demonstrated to take place. Grooming or being groomed is reinforcing; chasing or being chased is reinforcing; playing with another baboon or with a physical object, such as a stick, is reinforcing. The natural progress of learning in the group probably bears little relationship to what has so far been demonstrated in the laboratory. The methodological, technical, and conceptual aids of the laboratory investigation may perhaps be put to the service of the field investigation with important results for our knowledge of baboon behavior.

4

TOOL-USING PERFORMANCES

AS INDICATORS

OF BEHAVIORAL ADAPTABILITY*1

K. R. L. Hall

INTRODUCTION

The use by an animal of an object or of another living organism as a means of achieving an advantage has been commonly regarded by comparative psychologists as an indication of intelligent adaptability. The mediating object is required by definition to be something extraneous to the bodily equipment of the animal, and its use allows the animal to extend the range of its movements or to increase their efficiency. Phrases like "functional extension" have been applied to such performances, whose crucial characteristic is manipulation of something in the environment, in appetitive or aversive behavior or, much more rarely, as part of an instinctive display or nesting operation.

Many problems arise as to the origin, in ontogeny and phylogeny, of such

*K. R. L. Hall (1963), "Tool-using Performances as Indicators of Behavioral Adaptability," *Current Anthropology* Vol. 4, No. 5, pp. 479–494.

¹This paper was prepared while the author was a Fellow at the Center for Advanced Study in the Behavioral Sciences, Stanford, California, in 1962–63, and was supported by a PHS research grant (M-5502, Evaluation of Literature on Primate Behavior, National Institutes of Health, U.S. Public Health Service). The author acknowledges particularly the help of his colleague at the Center, Dr. George Schaller, in calling attention to several references and in commenting upon certain points in the manuscript, and he thanks Mr. Robert H. Krear, Department of Biology, University of Colorado, for allowing him to quote from his unpublished observations on tool-using in the sea otter.

performances. It is rarely clear whether a performance is characteristic of a species, or whether individual variations due to local ecological conditions modify it. Nor is it clear whether a performance, once it has occurred in an individual given or in a group of animals, can be transmitted to form a "tradition," in the sense of a habit learned and retained, or whether the more likely evolutionary process is selection, on the basis of the advantage of the performance; in the latter case, the learning is a matter of trial-and-error application of the tendency, comparable to the way in which any number of inherited tendencies may be ecologically employed. Thorpe (1951, 1956) has examined much of the evidence along these lines, with particular reference to birds. In the present paper it is intended to carry the analysis into the realm of nonhuman primate behavior; some of the well-authenticated studies of other animals will be cited to give the necessary comparative perspective.

On evaluating performances as falling inside or outside the category of tool-using, it will be evident that they vary greatly in their flexibility and apparent behavioral complexity. All performances are conventionally excluded if they involve simply applying a "primary" object, for example, food, to a "secondary" object, such as a rock. Thus, the snail-breaking by thrushes or the dropping of shells by gulls or crows onto a hard surface can be excluded. Included can be performances as manifestly unlike as the carrying of actinians in the claws of crabs and the enlisting of aid among chimpanzees in the cooperative solving of problems beyond the ability of a single chimpanzee, or the inducement of one chimpanzee by another, through food-begging or threat, to bring it food.

TOOL-USING OTHER THAN FOR DEFENSE
OR FOOD-SEEKING

The classic example of tool-using in insects, that of the solitary wasp, *Ammophila urnaria,* was reported by Peckham and Peckham (1898); to be sure, Williston (1892) had already made similar observations on another species. In each instance, the act consisted of holding a small pebble in the mandibles and using it as a hammer to pound dirt into the nest burrow. The Peckhams commented (1898:223): "We are claiming a great deal for *Ammophila* when we say that she improvised a tool and made intelligent use of it, for such actions are rare even among higher mammals. . . ." Whether this is to be counted as an "individual" achievement rather than characteristic of a species is not certain, and the problem is not, at this level, of importance except in the way it parallels the situation in "higher" animals. So unexpected and interesting were these observations to the early comparative psychologists that they tended to jump to the conclusion that "intelligent purpose" and "perception of the relation of means to an end" (Morgan 1900) were involved, while McDougall (1923:91) was somewhat more lyrical, saying:

> Are we then to regard each of these two wasps as a lively *bahnbrechende* genius, leading their species onward to the use of tools; individual sports comparable to the man, or ape, who first took a stone in his hand to crack a nut and so foreshadowed the genius of Nasmyth? I see no other plausible interpretation of the facts.

The best known and most reliably reported instance of tool-using among birds occurs in the Satin bower-bird, *Ptilonorhynchus violaceus*. This species was said by Chisholm (1954:381) to use a "tool," such as small wads of bark, to aid in the painting of the inside walls of its bower. He commented:

> . . . it had been supposed that these served the office of a brush, but it is now thought more probable that each one acts as a cork, or stopper, to prevent the paint oozing from the tip of the mandibles while the bird is plastering the walls of the bower with the sides of the bill.

Marshall's study (1960:207) provides the behavioral context of these performances in the Satin bower-bird species, as well as a very full description of them:

> . . . many, but not all, adult males begin to plaster their bower with a thick, black, tacky material made from a mixture of charcoal compounded with saliva. With a bark wad held between the tips of the beak, the plaster is forced between the mandibles and so transferred to the inside sticks of the bower.

A similar kind of behavior is reported of some male members of the genus *Chlamydera:* painting their bowers with dry grass mixed with saliva. These performances occur during displays which serve partly to attract females to the display grounds, partly to repel other males, so that pair-formation can occur: "Remarkable as they are, the bowers and display paraphernalia of bower-birds are no more than an extension of the territorial and display impulses to be found in other birds" (1960:208), and the whole performance of bower-construction and painting is interpreted by him as the outcome of a "displaced nesting-drive," the male taking no part in nest-building or incubation. Marshall commented that bower-birds are no more intelligent than other highly developed passerine species, and there is, indeed, no valid reason for supposing they might be simply on the grounds that an elementary act, definable as tool-use, is incorporated into the display. The *rarity* of any such performance among birds or other animals in such a context suggests that it is a special case of behavioral adaptation which has no particular significance in the evolution of "intelligent" tool-using.

Seemingly the only instance in this miscellaneous category known in mammals is that of the Burmese elephant, which, according to Williams (1950), picks up a long stick with its trunk to scratch its body. Although in captivity monkeys and apes are known to cover themselves with sacking or other materials, apparently as protection from cold or wet, no such instances are known from field studies.

TOOL-USING AS A PART

OF AGONISTIC BEHAVIOR

Not a single authenticated instance of tool-using as an element in agonistic behavior is known in animals other than that of the monkeys and apes which use a tool in repelling predators or intruders. According to Duerden (1905), the carrying of actinians by the crab *Melia tessellata* may have protective function. The crab travels with the actinians expanded and directed forward, sometimes waving them from side to side; when irritated, it moves its chelipeds toward the source of irritation, thereby placing the actinians in what may be considered the most favorable aggressive or defensive attitudes. It is possible, however, that this function is secondary and incidental, for the crab reacts in the same way whether it is carrying the actinians (as food-getting "instruments") or not.

In considering such evidence as there is of the "agonistic" use of objects by monkeys and apes, trying to analyze the observations in terms of function and context of the act, we should first examine reports on wild animals, in which no training by or imitation of human beings is presumably involved. Some of the sources of information (Table 4–1) are personal observations of trained field-workers, others, those of naturalists and hunters (Wallace; Merfield and Miller; Hingston), and the rest, of unknown source. The two major field studies of baboons (DeVore 1962; Hall 1962*b*, 1962*c*) include no observations of agonistic object-use. In both of these studies, the investigator's objective was to study the baboons without disturbing them by his presence, and hence, the very situations most likely to elicit agonistic behavior in a group usually were lacking. The unexpected presence of parties of travelers or soldiers in baboon country may produce great agitation in the animals, eliciting a more intensive reaction.

In analyzing the function and context of these "primitive instrumental acts" (Carpenter 1934), we shall need to refer chiefly to the few studies in which sufficient detail of observation is available. In general, it is implicit in most early reports that the animals roll stones or drop or throw branches and other objects *with intent* to hit or drive away intruders. Aim or purpose in the act is assumed, and hence the whole act is usually thought of as intelligent or learned rather than instinctive or emotional. Lacking detailed and careful observation, one alternative was that these happenings are the "accidental" result of some agonistic behavior pattern characteristic of the species. Thus, excited macaques may dislodge stones in scrambling up a slope away from an intruder, or members of an arboreal species may chance to break off branches while making threatening gestures. Zuckerman (1932) inclined to the view that the many instances of this sort of behavior could be explained as the more or less accidental outcome of emotional displays, and thus did not need to assume the animal's perception of a relationship between such acts and the possible consequence of driving away an intruder.

This explanation seems correctly to emphasize the emotional origin of such acts but probably incorrectly assumes that animals noted for their learning ability would not readily carry out the emotional gesture with a very elementary directedness rather than in a supposedly random fashion.

Analysis of two sets of observations may help to clear the way for a critical evaluation of the status of the behavior involved. Carpenter (1935) describes the reactions to man of red spider monkeys in Panama as including the following: (1) barking; (2) frequently, approach; (3) in trees within 40 to 50 feet of the observer, shaking of the branches associated, almost invariably, vigorous scratching; and (4) "breaking off and dropping of branches . . . close . . . to the observer." "This behavior cannot be described as throwing, although the animal may cause the object to fall away from the perpendicular by a sharp twist of its body or a swinging circular movement of its powerful tail." Sometimes the dropping is delayed for a few seconds, as an observer approaches; feces and urine are also dropped. All are "instrumental acts" carried out with reference to objectives.

This account indicates that: (1) the approach of the monkeys is an aggressive action; (2) the vigorous scratching represents a displacement activity, which is known experimentally to occur in agitated monkeys that, because of caging, are unable to act out their escape or aggressive tendencies more directly (Hall 1962a), (3) shaking of the branches probably represents a redirection of the aggressive tendency; (4) breaking off and dropping the branches would seem to be a natural carryover of the aggressive movements, no new type of movement being involved; (5) the delay in dropping and the imparting of direction to the branches is "purposive" or "instrumental" in the elementary sense that the consequence of this variation is anticipated as being more rewarding than the consequence of no aiming; in other words, a simple process of operant conditioning is at work, whereby the "aimed" variation is reinforced over the "unaimed."

The objections to such a formulation stem mainly from the lack of information as to the frequency and variability of "directed" performances in these animals. Nevertheless, the learning postulated is of so elementary a kind that all it requires is a very slight modification in the agonistic behavior repertoire apparently characteristic of the species in such circumstances. It is not easy to imagine simpler learning performances, given the usual threat-gesture system of monkeys, for no new act is involved.

TABLE 4–1   SOME SOURCES OF EVIDENCE ON THE AGONISTIC USE
OF OBJECTS BY MONKEYS AND APES IN THE WILD

Species/genus	Author	Behavior and Situation Recorded
Gorilla	Merfield and Miller (1956)	When hunted, tearing off branches and flinging in direction of hunters below, "after peering about to locate them accurately"
	Schaller (1963)	Various forms of throwing of branches in agonistic display; not reported to be directed at source of disturbance
Orang-utan	Wallace (1902)	Throwing down of branches and heavy fruits in direction of intruder
	Schaller (1961)	Breaking off and hurling branches in direction of the observer
Gibbon	Carpenter (1940)	Breaking off and dropping dead branches in direction of observer
Howler	Carpenter (1934)	Breaking off and dropping dead limbs toward observer, also defecation and urination from directly above observer
Red Spider	Carpenter (1935)	Breaking off and dropping branches close to observer
Cebus	Kaufmann (1962)	Dropping nuts and debris onto coatis
Baboons	Brehm (1916), Hornaday (1922), and other sources of unknown reliability	Geladas meeting Hamadryas and rolling stones down upon them; rolling of rocks toward human intruders
Macaques	Kinnaman (1902), quoting another source Hingston (1920) Joléaud (1933) and other sources of unknown reliability	Deliberate tilting-up and rolling of stones down slope; throwing down of pine cones by Japanese monkeys at passers-by
Patas	Boulenger (1937)	Directing "fusillade" of sticks, stones and so forth on river travellers in W. Africa

For all other species of new and old world monkeys, only a single, very brief statement about the behavior of a *Cebus capucinus* group on Barro Cororado Island has added to our knowledge. During his two-year study of coatis, Kaufmann (1962) on one occasion saw the monkeys chase some coatis from a tree, then go on to drop nuts and debris from a *Scheelea* palm onto them. The coatis ignored the shower except to pounce on and eat the ripe nuts that were included. This observation is of particular interest in view of the reputation of *Cebus* in laboratory experiments and because it is the first by a naturalist of behavior of this type involving nonhuman intruders.

Among the apes, Wallace's observations (1902) on the orang-utan and Schaller's confirmation and elaboration of them (1961:82) suggest a similar pattern. One of Schaller's observations was as follows:

> A female with a large infant spent 15 minutes throwing a total of about 30 branches varying in size from twigs to limbs 10 feet long and 3 inches in diameter. Considerable effort was expended at times in tearing off the larger branches. Limbs were thrown in three ways: (a) she merely held the branch at her side and dropped it limply; (b) she looked down at me and swung the branch like a large pendulum, and at the peak of the arc closest to me she released it; (c) she lifted branches either as high as her chest or above her head with one hand and hurled them down forcefully. Whatever interpretation is given this behavior, there is no doubt that it induced me to jump nimbly at times and that it kept me effectively away from beneath the tree.

Wallace's account concerned the throwing down of branches and of the fruits of the Durian tree by an adult female with young ones near her; and he supposed that the ape's parental instinct may have been specially aroused. However, the essential features of the situations in which this and the resulting behavior occur are similar to those in the Red spider monkey account, namely disturbance by a human intruder eliciting agitation and redirection of aggression onto the most readily available objects, and an effective directing of the objects toward the observer.

The explanation already proposed seems to need no revision to include the orang-utan data or any other data of similar performances in free-ranging monkeys or apes. This does not imply that such displays always or even usually have a "direction." Schaller's (1963) full account of the mountain gorillas' repertoire of gestures in such circumstances does not suggest that branches or leaves are, in the physical sense, aimed at the observer. The amount and kind of learning involved in "aiming" are such that many other mammals below the primates might achieve this behavior very readily *if* they had happened to evolve the sort of manipulatory and agonistic repertoire which seems to be a general simian characteristic. To underline this point, we may briefly consider the agonistic and the feeding repertoire of baboons in the wild (Hall 1962b, 1962c). First, baboons frequently turn over stones when searching for food. Second, they may pull violently back and forward on tree branches or rocks while staring at and otherwise threatening an observer. Third, they may hit away, with a swift underarm movement, a noxious or unfamiliar small object or living organism as a sequel to, or component of, a startle behavior sequence. These three aspects of their behavior readily dispose thse animals to the simple instrumental act involved in tipping a rock toward an intruder. There would be no mystery if it were shown that baboons or chimpanzees, for example, throw sand, stones or sticks, toward a predator on the same horizontal plane. All that is necessary is that the hitting-away movement be combined with the most elementary of feeding acts, that of grasping some object in the hand and "aiming" it in the same way that a threat-gesture or movement is usually directed *toward* an adversary. Because the use of objects as missiles has tended to be confused with the use, and even fashioning, of objects as offensive weapons, the complexity of the behavior involved seems to have been greatly exaggerated.

Linking behavior of this kind with that observed to occur spontaneously in captivity adds very little to the over all picture. Many reports are available of agonistic scooping/throwing in captivity (Kortlandt and Kooij 1963), but all that need be added as commentary is that horizontal aiming is an extension of the threat-display, involving nothing more than the coordination of two acts basic to the repertoire. Brandishing of a stick and using it to beat another animal, as described by Cooper and Harlow (1961) in an individual *Cebus fatuellus* and in several chimpanzees, is an interesting elaboration of threat-display against other animals, but the significance of such performances must again be regarded first in their functional context, and only later against the supposed evolutionary background. The kind of brandishing action reported is very similar to that which baboons (Hall 1962b) and other monkeys and apes may engage in throwing a sack or a stick over a food-object.

We are not primarily concerned here with sifting through the varied kinds of evidence and deciding as to their reliability and accuracy. It is not yet possible to make valid comparisons of the various species or for example, of terrestrial monkeys and anthropoid apes, of old world or of new world types, and the like, with respect to their "ability" to engage in this kind of instrumental behavior. Chimpanzee, capuchin, and baboon may turn out to demonstrate this propensity more readily and more flexibly than other nonhuman primates, but it is all too easy to fit the inadequate observational evidence into whatever evolutionary model one chooses—as Kortlandt and Kooij (in years) have done. It is simply the interaction of the processes of learning with the components and sequences of the naturally practiced behavior repertoire that requires a clear and straightforward analysis. The key to the instrumental learning successes of many types shown in the wild and in captivity by these animals is the exploratory-manipulatory tendency, of a quite general kind, which makes it easy for transfer or generalization to take place from one kind of situation to another, and over a wide range of objects or stimuli. Although we can thus simplify the behavioral analysis in such a way as to show that performances of the kind reported are readily to be expected in these animals, it still remains necessary to consider very carefully the kinds of environmental conditions which elicit or inhibit or just fail to elicit these performances.

TOOL-USING IN EXTENSION

OF THE FEEDING REPERTOIRE

The use of an object as a means of obtaining food which the animal cannot reach or which if within its reach, the animal cannot obtain directly is, contrary to the preceding class of performance, reported in birds in several instances, occasionally and rather uncertainly in marine invertebrates, and once only, with two other insufficiently substantiated instances, in subprimate mammals. For monkeys and apes, there is an extensive experimental literature, many observations on animals in captivity, and extremely few field data that provide evidence for analysis. The data will merely be sampled, as in the previous section, to illustrate points that seem significant for the whole comparative picture. Inevitably, this means paying most attention to the areas where most reliable knowledge is available.

The case of the crab, *Melia tessellata,* and actinian "commensalism," described by Duerden and others, is a curious example of the use of a living organism as a tool to aid the feeding of another. Although Duerden says the crabs do not restrict themselves to one species of anemone and may also, as already noted, hold them forward as a kind of defensive aid, the performance need not be classed as more "intelligent" than other sorts of behavioral adaptation to ecological need in which no tool or accessory is involved.

In birds, there are two sorts of performance which have been much discussed, namely, the string-pulling achievements of *Parus* and other passerines, and the use of a cactus-spine or twig as an extention of the bill to probe out insects or larvae in the so-called Galapagos woodpecker-finch, *Cactospiza pallida.* The former type of behavior clearly has some parallel in the probable factors involved here and in similar performances of primates. There may be an "inherited tendency" to pull upon and manipulate with beak and foot grasses, hair, bents, and other long flexible materials, in the course of nestbuilding or perhaps in obtaining certain sorts of food. This factor and practice can be supposed to account for the ease with which some of these birds seem immediately to tackle the task of pulling in a string on the end of which a bait is attached. We may note that the direct pulling-in of a string or stick to the end of which the food-object is attached seems to be a task requiring very little modification of existing repertoire other than trial-and-error application.

The tool-using performances of the woodpecker-finch are usually considered a remarkable example of behavioral adaptation to fit it into the special ecological circumstances of the Galapagos Islands bird population. According to Lack (1947, 1953), this primarily insectivorous finch resembles a woodpecker in that it climbs up and down vertical trunks and branches in search of its food. But whereas the woodpecker, having excavated in a branch with its beak, inserts its long tongue into the crack to get the insect out, the finch has evolved the alternative method of picking up a cactus spine or twig, holding it lengthwise in its beak and poking it up the crack, dropping the twig to seize the insect in its beak as it emerges. It has been seen to reject a twig if it proved too short or too pliable, and sometimes the bird carries a spine or twig about with it, poking it into cracks or crannies as it searches one tree after another. Bowman (1961:33) added further observations on this behavior. He saw it most frequently in the dry season in the arid zone, where almost every bird of the species was seen carrying a cactus spine in its bill. He also reported two cases of what appeared to be attempts of the bird to adjust the size and shape of its probe to fit the cranny or crack in which it was searching: (1)

> One such bird was holding a spine about six inches long. Only about two inches of the spine protruded from the tip of the bill, the remainder passed along one side of the face and neck. Apparently the bird realized that the stick was excessively long, for it made an unsuccessful attempt to twist off approximately three inches of the spine by holding it with the feet.

(2) He quotes an observation made by Mr. Kastdalen (1956:33):

> I was looking at a finch the other day, and he convinced me that the stick habit is intelligent and not instinctive. One of them was working in a hole . . . which seemed to be full of bugs, so he had to drop its stick several times to catch the bugs. Each time it went for a new stick, but after a few times it came with a forked stick, and tried to get it into the hole a couple of times, but in vain. Then he saw what was wrong and turned the stick around and broke it off at the fork, and started working.

Ignoring the terminological points about the bird's "realizing" what it was doing and the distinction between "intelligent" and "instinctive," it is evident that something definable as "tool-making," that is, an attempting to work upon the tool-object, is here involved. However, it is likely that nothing more worthy of note is involved in such an attempt than what is routine in of nest-constructing activities.

While it is indeed remarkable that this finch should have evolved a behavioral adaptation supposedly more appropriate at the primate level of evolution, the chief significance of such a performance, in the comparative behavior framework, is perhaps to emphasize the fact that *tool-using as such,* and even tool-making, taken outside of the total behavioral context in which it occurs, is not a criterion of adaptability that should be assigned any special weight. If in rare cases a species of crab or bird evolves a behavioral, rather than a physical, adaptation to deal with some ecological condition, this may be interesting evidence of the versatility of evolutionary processes but involves no more complex type of *learning* than, one may suppose, the sort of trial-and-error adjustments which these "remarkable" species have in common with other crabs and other birds.

Among subprimate mammals, we have already cited Williams' (1950:78) report of elephants using sticks to scratch their bodies, and he also describes how "Many young elephants develop the naughty habit of plugging up the wooden bell they wear hung around their necks with good stodgy mud or clay so that the clappers cannot ring, in order to steal silently into a grove of cultivated bananas at night." While the performances of elephants in captivity indicate that their potential in tool-using is probably greater than that of any other nonprimate animal, there is no sysematic evidence of the variety of their performances in the wild. It can merely be noted in passing, however, that the way in which they pull down or push over trees to get at foliage otherwise beyond their reach is an "instrumental act" at least on a par for behavioral complexity with patterned string or string-pulling performances. It is also, for the elephant, a much more economical way of feeding than would be, say, its attempt to knock off fruit or leaves by brandishing a stick in its trunk.

Apart from elephants, another class of mammal that may be found to use tools as a feeding aid in the wild are bears. The readiness with which they stand on hindlegs and use their paws in manipulations would predispose them to develop such skills where need arises, and Harington (1962) interestingly reviews the evidence that polar bears dislodge or pick up and cast down blocks of ice onto the heads of sleeping walruses. The only subprimate mammal for which there are reliable reports is the sea otter, *Enhydra lutris*. Studies made of its feeding habits show that in the Aleutians as well as in California, mollusks form a substantial part of the diet. In California, abalones are also commonly brought up and eaten, but it is not known whether rocks are used to aid in the process of removing these large shellfish from their sites. Fisher (1939:28) was the first to give a detailed account of this animal's use of a stone as a tool:

> It is a not uncommon thing to hear a sharp clicking sound and then to locate its point of origin . . . This sound is always made by an otter that is trying to crack open something with a very hard stonelike shell. The object that the otter has in its paws is too small to see—possibly it is some mollusk. The object is held with both paws and with full arm action from well over the head it is brought down hard on a piece of rock that rests on the otter's chest. These pieces of stone are brought to the surface at the same time as the food. It may take several severe blows before the object is cracked enough for the otter to get the food out. These rocks are not small but appear to be almost as large as the large abalones. When the otters roll over they hold both the rock and the food on their chests. This clicking sound is so distinct that it can be heard for some distance above the noise of the waters.

Murie (1940) confirmed this observation on the California animals, and Hall and Schaller (1964) have obtained quantitative data on this performance; they reported that it is usually mussels that are banged against the rock anvil, although occasionally other animals, such as spiny lobsters, may be pounded in this way. Krear (personal communication), who spent from late July until mid-December 1957 on Amchitka in the western Aleutians, watching sea otters most of the time, observed only one young animal traveling with its mother that used a rock as a tool: "The immature was observed on three occasions to bring rocks to the surface, and on these he would pound and crack his food items, most of which were little blue mussels." It is probable that the mussels in the Aleutians did not require tool-use of the sort so frequently seen off the California coast, but that the propensity for such performances is readily available, as is strongly indicated by Kenyon's account (1959) of how an adult otter, captured in the Aleutians, used rocks as anvils on which to pound clams.

The sea otter data suggest very little at present as to the origin, variability, and other characteristics of this behavior. So far as is known, no developmental observations are available, other than the one instance quoted. It is also likely that the pup acquires the habit by observing the behavior of its mother, for it swims for many weeks very close to her, takes food from her chest, and is occasionally offered food by her (Hall and Schaller 1964). It is thus highly probable that the pup must learn its discriminations of food objects and of behavior appropriate to deal with them by observing the corresponding behavior in the mother. The fundamental dependency relationship is such that "following," both perceptually and in the locomotor and manipulatory senses, is necessary for the pup's survival. This is generally true of mammals and is mentioned here only because it may help to explain the origin of the habit.

Considering now the nonhuman primates, detailed evidence from field studies indicates that only one, the chimpanzee, uses tools; this it does in reference to a probably minor feeding behavior, probing termites out of holes with twigs. Beatty (1951) reported that chimpanzees in Liberia break open palm nuts by hammering them with rocks, and Merfield and Miller (1956) described how chimpanzees poke long twigs into the entrance holes of the ground nests of bees and withdraw the twigs coated with honey. The distance at which this observation was made was 50 yards, using binoculars. Pitman (1931) mentioned seeing a free-living gorilla using a stick to obtain fruit otherwise out of its reach, but Schaller (1963) had no record of such behavior in 12 months of field study.

This lack of evidence of tool-using comes as a surprise to the many investigators familiar with the ease with which other species of great ape and several species of monkey learn spontaneously in captivity, as well as with progressive training procedures, to use sticks, sacks, boxes, or even live rats (Klüver 1937) to haul in food objects otherwise out of reach. *Cebus capucinus* and perhaps other *Cebus* species appear to be particularly adept in this respect (Klüver 1933; Bierens de Haan 1931), while individuals of the *Papio ursinus* species (Bolwig 1961; Hall 1962*b*) show a similar kind of aptitude. The surprise of the laboratory investigators is due to the apparent discrepancy between the *potential* that these animals have for such performances when given situations designed to elicit them in captivity and their failure to make use of the potential as an aid in increasing their dietary repertoire in the wild. Two of the main factors accounting for this discrepancy are: (1) Systematic field evidence is still far too scanty for us to know how great the discrepancy is; for example, very little is known of the details of the feeding habits of free-ranging *Cebus*. (2) The discrepancy is not a behaviorally significant one but is rather due to a misconception as to the degree of transfer or generalization involved when the wild-born animal is given the usual run of instrumentation tasks in captivity. This point requires a brief elaboration.

If we take as an example the natural feeding behavior of the baboon and the more or less continuous processes of exploration and manipulation of objects that go with it, some of which have already been mentioned, we find that the animal is practicing, either in play or in actual feeding, a variety of skills which are readily generalized in the experimental situation. The young ones carry sticks or branches in their mouths or in one hand and do not use them in feeding. All of them at some time or other break dead branches from bushes in searching for food, as when, for example, they are searching for larvae or ants' nests (Hall 1962*b*). They push over slabs of rock, and they tend to investigate almost any strange manipulable object that lies in their path. They pull upon telegraph wires, open the doors and windows of unoccupied huts and cars, and so on. In short, they show a generalized tendency to fiddle with and try out objects that may or may not be instrumental in obtaining food. These animals appear to have a surplus of exploratory-manipulatory energy for which there may seem to be no immediate ecological need. However, it is perfectly feasible to suppose that it is just this kind of generalized activity which has enabled baboons to be sufficiently adaptable to survive over large areas of Africa in a very wide variety of habitats, for example, allowing them to be omnivorous in some regions (although they are classed as predominantly vegetarian in all areas where the diet has been adequately scheduled, according to Washburn and DeVore [1961*a*] and Hall [1962*b*]). Thus, given the behavior reportoire the baboon is known to possess, the learning involved in obtaining food that is out of reach would appear to be of a rudimentary kind.

Similar evidence as to the maturation of the necessary manipulatory coordinations (Schiller 1957) and as to the effective role of natural and instrumental practice (Nissen 1931; Birch 1945) has been put forward for the chimpanzee, and there is no need to review it. One comment of Schiller's (1957:275) is particularly appropriate, however, because it indicates how, in chimpanzees and other species, the "emotional" repertoire of gesture may be readily utilized in differing contexts:

> That a chimpanzee breaks off a branch if excited has nothing to do with his desire to get the food [in an experimental situation]. Once he has the stick in his hand, he will use it sooner or later. Such a sequence can easily be reinforced in a couple of trials, then it appears to be a coherent, continuous pattern.

GENERAL EVALUATION

Tool-using performances have tended to be treated as though they represented some kind of behavioral homology at the different levels of organism in which they have been recorded. This view seems to be incorrect, however, because it seems evident that the application of a common term to so varied an assortment of performances has led to the glossing over of fundamental differences in adaptive significance. While the criterion of tool-using is no longer used by anthropologists to signalize a supposedly critical stage in the transition of ape to human, it is still not unreasonably inferred that tool-using was an important behavioral adaptation somewhere in primate evolution, and that the *making* of tools derived from a prevalence in tool-using far in excess of that now discernible in any living nonhuman primate (Washburn 1950). For anthropologists, behavioral evidence of living nonhuman primates in the wild is thus of interest to the extent that it indicates "transitional" ingredients of essentially hominid characteristics such as the carnivorous tendency and tool-using (Oakley 1951).

In the general framework of animal evolution, we have seen that instances definable as tool-using occur in highly specialized ecological settings, as in the woodpecker-finch, crab-actinian commensalism, and probably the *Ammophila*. These are basically behavioral adaptations that are probably produced by trial-and-error learning, like that commonly found in almost all living organisms. These adaptations do not appear to give their possessors any selective advantage over other species which have evolved alternative forms of adaptation. Rather, they simply enable their possessors to survive at a certain population level in their ecological niches. In other words, such performances are only worthy of special note because of their entirely superficial, indeed one might almost say fortuitous, resemblance to human tool-using. The case of the string-pulling performances of some passerines is of the same order. While one allows that birds of the *Parus* genus, as an example, show a certain aptitude in this kind of problem, as in others, such as pecking open milk bottle tops, no one, but for the human analogy, would probably be disposed on this ground to give this species a specially high rating for adaptability. As others have clearly indicated (Thorpe 1956; Tinbergen 1960), birds may evolve certain rather restricted propensities enabling them to learn through what one might call a special aptitude. The natural practice of food-seeking and nest-construction may fit into the scheme. A performance classifiable as tool-using may in fact be less significant as an adaptability indicator than one which cannot strictly be so considered, such as the performances of thrushes, gulls, or crows in breaking open hard food-objects.

The observations of the sea otter were reviewed at length to refute the view that its performance indicated that a new process had appeared at the *Mammalian* level of evolution. The apparent uniqueness of this performance and its occurrence in the context of a particular marine ecological situation for which the animal shows other peculiar behavioral and physical adaptations, such as lying on the back when feeding, indicate that there is no reason to judge this animal's performances as of any greater evolutionary significance than those for which other marine mammals, such as seals and dolphins, are noted.

In the evaluation of what is known about the nonhuman primates' performances and potentialities, we have to consider two main types of tool-using: that in the service of agonistic behavior and that in obtaining food. It is in the former category that by far the most evidence is available, suggesting that "instrumental acts" with some degree of direction or purpose are quite a widespread and general characteristic in monkeys and apes, as a straightforward function of fear-threat motivation and manipulatory endowment. And indeed it seems, as the quotation from Schiller indicated, that we have here a behavioral adaptation of a fairly general and simple kind which evolved primarily in the context of agonistic tendencies toward opponents that inhibit direct attack. Associating this with the fact that no such instances have been reliably reported in any other class of animal, one can infer that this is the fundamental behavioral situation from which all other instances of primate tool-using have been derived. There is, in most monkeys at any rate, an arousal of fairly strong agonistic tendencies in any food-to-be-gained situation in which they are frustrated. They tend easily, in such circumstances, to show displacement activities or redirections of aggression (Masserman and Pechtel 1953), and their tool-using attempts often consist of throwing actions which are hardly distinguishable from threat-gestures. It will be only through systematic developmental studies of young primates that we shall be able to trace the course of these performances and to study the relationship between frustration responses and the emergence of tool-use in general.

SUMMARY

Tool-using performances in animals have often been considered important indicators of relative intelligence, but no comparative analysis of their probable origin and place within the total ecological and behavioral setting has been available. The usual definition has tended to emphasize features that performances at different phyletic levels have in common, while glossing over the underlying and even overt differences.

The many examples in the literature are sampled with reference to the use of tools: (1) in agonistic behavior; (2) in extending the feeding habits of a species; and (3) in courtship display (Satin bower-birds), nest-hole construction (*Ammophila* spp.), and, possibly, body care (elephants).

Examples of the second category include what appear to be special behavioral adaptations that are functionally equivalent to physical extensions or modifications, as in the case of the crab-actinian relationship in *Melia tessellata,* the Galapagos woodpecker-finch, *Cactospiza pallida,* and possibly also in the sea otter, *Enhydra lutris.* To varying degrees, the tool-using adaptation has importance in the life of the species. In the crab and the finch, it seems to involve a basic feeding adjustment, while in the sea otter it is reportedly used only with respect to one major item of food, mollusks, and it may be much more prevalent in the southern limits of distribution than in the north. Among nonhuman primates in the wild, tool-using of this sort is rare, not being known in baboons and macaques, and only reliably reported, among the anthropoid apes, in the chimpanzee which appears to use a food-getting tool to obtain a supplementary rather than a staple item of diet.

Examples of the first category occur only in nonhuman primates. In systematic field studies in the wild, "primitive instrumental acts" of breaking off and casting down branches, twigs, or leaves in the direction of the observer have been reported of howlers and red spider monkeys, gibbons, and orang-utans. Gorillas include throwing gestures in their complex and apparently stereotyped displays when disturbed, but no "directing" toward the source of disturbance has been noted. Terrestrial monkeys of the *Macaca* and *Papio* genera have been reported to push or roll stones towards intruders. There are, however, no detailed field observations of this behavior, and, if it occurs, it is probably elicited in groups of monkeys that are highly disturbed and unused to human intrusion and would not be seen under the noninterference conditions in which the field observer usually tries to work.

Controversy over the reliability of the evidence on tool-using, particularly in nonhuman primates, and over the explanation of such instances as are irrefutable, seems to stem from the following: (1) a tendency to overestimate the significance of such performances as indicators of behavioral adaptability, largely because of the urge to discover equivalences to stages in human evolution; (2) a failure to analyze in detail the context and function of such performances. It is suggested that the "primitive instrumental acts" involve only an elementary form of operant conditioning imposed upon the agonistic repertoire of the species, and that "direction" of aim with objects is no more surprising than the fact that threat gestures without objects are normally aimed at an intruder.

The discrepancy, commented upon by laboratory investigators, between the apparent ease with which many monkeys and apes use tools to gain food in captivity situations and their apparent failure to use this propensity to advantage in the wild, has no real significance. Possibly the "primitive instrumental acts" provide the primary emotional bases from which any kind of tool-using arises, the transfer to other situations, such as food-getting, being conditioned by the way in which the animals manipulate objects not directly related to food.

The present evaluation of the comparative data has, as its purpose, the clarification of the confusion caused by inadequacy of behavioral evidence and by the biasing of such evidence to fit some evolutionary scheme. The hypothesis that the "emotional" use of tool objects by monkeys and apes may provide the lead to an understanding of the origins, in phylogeny and ontogeny, of such performances in human beings is suggested by the fact that no comparable agonistic performances are known in any other class of animal. On the other hand, tool-using as a feeding adaptation occurs in several different types of animal but has so far proved very rare in monkeys and apes.

ABSTRACT

Use of an object by animals as a functional extension of their limbs in order to obtain food or to facilitate some other goal seeking activity has quite commonly been reported as an especially significant indicator of intelligence or complex learning ability.

The present review has selected well authenticated examples of tool-using behavior from different types of animal, such as wasps, crabs, birds, subprimate mammals, and nonhuman primates, and examined the context of their occurrence and the apparent complexity of performance involved. These performances have been concerned with: a) attainment of food; b) offensive or defensive use against predators or intruders; c) miscellaneous functions such as self-grooming, courtship, nest-building. Categories (a) and (b) contain by far the most instances, and (c) has very few indeed.

The problem, in attempting a comparative analysis of such instances, is to evaluate the performance within the whole context of the animal's capacities and the way these are expressed in various ecological settings. The evidence cited is primarily from naturalistic studies, that from restrictive settings, such as Zoo or laboratory, being adduced only in emphasizing discrepancies. As an example, baboons have, so far, not been seen to demonstrate tool-using in the wild in their food-seeking behavior, but they do so readily when given the opportunity in captivity. They thus have a potential which their natural surroundings perhaps only rarely bring into action, whereas chimpanzees demonstrate their capacity for this kind of performance in diverse ways both in the wild and in captivity.

Certain performances by nonprimate animals, such as the Galapagos woodpecker-finch or the California sea otter, indicate that tool-using of a very effective, though presumably restricted, kind can evolve in animals having a narrow habitat range, and in whom, therefore, other significant aspects of adaptability may be missing. Further, from assessing the many instances of category (b) and the very few instances of category (a) in wild monkeys and apes, it was tentatively suggested that the emotional offensive-defensive type of tool-using might have had primacy in evolution over that of food-getting and the other miscellaneous instances. A review of this sort, with a suggestion of this kind, is put forward anyway chiefly as an attempt at clarification which may lead to much further detailed studies, experimental and naturalistic, of the animals in question.

As always in describing complex behavior and in deriving models or inferences from the description, the profusion and confusion of terminology are difficult to sort out neatly or clearly. But the objective of this review will have been achieved if, in deliberately avoiding the use of controversial terms, it has been possible to show the need for a fresh research approach to the comparative study of behavioral adaptability in animals with a view to working out much more satisfactorily than at present the bearing that such evidence may have upon fundamental questions of human evolution.

5

AGGRESSION IN MONKEY

AND APE SOCIETIES*

K. R. L. Hall

INTRODUCTION

The term "aggression" in its precise sense refers to fighting and means the act of initiating an attack (Scott 1958). However, as is clear from other contributions to this Symposium, the kinds of behaviour shown by different species of animal in trying to gain ascendancy over conspecifics often fall far short of actual fighting, at least in the natural environment, being expressed in ritualized displays and threat intention movements which are seemingly effective in furthering the survival of the species. In other words, aggressive behavior is usually, under the ecological conditions of natural feeding, breeding, and defence, adaptive.

In considering the evidence on aggression in the nonhuman primates, no discussion on the Prosimiae will be included, and examples will be taken from those species of monkey and ape on which most systematic field data are now available. Even for these species, however, much remains to be learned about the factors which determine the forms and frequencies of aggression in the natural living groups or populations, the behavioural data being almost entirely at the essentially descriptive stage, with very few studies being taken further, by experiment or controlled observation, to the analysis of causes.

*Reprinted with permission from *The Natural History of Aggression,* J. D. Carthy, Ed. Published for the Institute of Biology by Academic Press, London and New York, 1964.

Monkeys and apes, in common with other animals including man, demonstrate aggressiveness by a variety of actions and expressions involving face, limbs, and the whole body. Threat, as the prelude to attack, is expressed in species-characteristic behaviour patterns, including vocalizations, the repertoire of these now being fairly well known for the rhesus macaque (Hinde and Rowell 1962; Rowell and Hinde 1962) in a captive group situation, for baboons (Hall 1962; Hall and DeVore 1965; DeVore 1962; Kummer 1957; Kummer and Kurt 1963), for patas monkeys (Hall, Boelkins, and Goswell, 1965), for gorillas (Schaller 1963), and for chimpanzees (Goodall 1965). Other species that are or have been thoroughly studied in the wild, such as the common langurs, and the vervets, at present lack a detailed inventory of their attack-threat behaviour, and only very recently has an account appeared in English of the communication behaviour of the Japanese macaque (Miyadi 1963). In terms of thorough ethological description and analysis, all these studies are in some degree deficient, but, for the present purpose of attempting to work out the role of aggression in the natural populations, there is sufficient information for a broad assessment, though not for a detailed quantitative comparison.

Again as in other animals, we find that aggression is expressed not only in direct and seemingly unequivocal forms but in indirect ways where, as is very commonly the case, other motives than to attack are also aroused in the situation, or where direct attack is frustrated. Thus we see from field studies many instances in which a redirection of aggression occurs away from the primary objective or cause of aggressive arousal. For hamadryas baboons, this has been well described by Kummer (1957), and for other baboons by Hall and DeVore (1965). It probably occurs in all species, but the clearest examples, as in the baboon studies, are manifested when a dominant animal is inhibited from attacking another animal of its group of more or less equal status, and diverts its attack onto subordinates. Where, from the context of the behaviour, the motives of attack and escape are simultaneously aroused, both may receive expression in alternating behaviour patterns, or neither may receive expression, only signs of nervousness, such as increased scratching, food-fumbling, and possibly yawning (Hall 1962a), being in evidence.

Elementary derivatives of threat-intention, or nervousness, or both, have been recorded for several species, as, for example, when branches, twigs, leaves, pebbles, or faeces, are dropped apparently with reference to the position of the human observer (Hall 1963b). Throwing, or even stick-brandishing, is not uncommon in captive monkeys and apes. Most of these acts seem to have the purpose, where purpose rather than the accidental outcome of agitation can be established, of getting rid of a disturbing stimulus, and not of attacking it. In trying to characterize the nature of aggression in these species, the behavioural "status" of such acts as these is not at issue, although it may later require brief discussion in considering certain implications for human evolution.

No discussion in detail will be included on one limited aspect of aggression, namely the killing of other animals for food. This propensity has been fully authenticated for baboons (Washburn and DeVore 1961*a;* Dart 1963), and for chimpanzees (Goodall 1965), the victims being buck of various species, sheep, and, on two occasions, other nonhuman primates (baboon eating a vervet monkey; chimpanzees eating a red colobus). The reasons for omitting further discussion of this interesting habit are, firstly, that far more evidence is required, and could fairly easily be gained, for regional variations in baboons in this respect; secondly that it is not clear at what level of prey we need to look for some evolutionary significance—for example, patas monkeys hunt and eat lizards, vervets eat eggs and fledgeling birds, and so on; thirdly, it is not clear that this propensity has any bearing upon the major aspects of aggression with which we are concerned, namely aggression within and between groups of the same species.

It is similarly very difficult to know how any of these monkeys and apes deal with predators. Goodall (1965) has no evidence that chimpanzees are attacked by leopards. Schaller (1963), though recording that mountain gorillas are occasionally killed by leopards, has no data as to how a gorilla group reacts on detecting their presence. Baboons have been described by Bolwig (1959) as teasing lions. Washburn and DeVore (1962) have a film record of encounters between baboons and lions and cheetahs. Stevenson-Hamilton (1947) observed a large cheetah being chased away by a large male baboon after the former had tried to cut out some juveniles from the group. Loveridge (1923:728) describes the "mobbing" of a leopard by E. African baboons, "the four old baboons surrounding a leopard and striking at it with their hands." It is also widely known that baboons will turn on dogs that threaten their group. Except for baboons, however, there is so little evidence of defensive aggression in monkeys and apes that we cannot attempt any comparison on this basis as between species. The other large terrestrial monkeys, such as mandrills, drills, and the gelada, have not yet been studied in the wild, and the data on this aspect of aggression in the hamadryas is not yet available from the Kummer and Kurt study. All the evidence suggests that the terrestrial patas monkeys must rely on dispersal and concealment to avoid leopards or hyenas or hunting dogs (Hall 1965*b*, 1965*c*), and it is difficult to imagine that this species would do otherwise if encountering cheetahs. Nothing seems to be known about the behaviour of macaque species towards predators.

It is usually supposed that the pronounced sexual dimorphism apparent in baboons (the adult male with well developed canines, being about twice as large and heavy as the adult female) is the consequence of selection pressures derived from their savannah-ranging habits and the need for defence against the large carnivores (DeVore 1963*a*). Correlated with this is a highly-developed aggressive potential. Equally, if not more, important, however, from the point of view of group survival, would seem to be the very strong social facilitative effect amongst the males consequent upon aggressive arousal by one of their number against a predator-stimulus. All the males are likely to join in the attack if the intensity of arousal is high, but it seems that only the younger, peripheral males may initiate and maintain alarm and defensive behaviour on other occasions, the dominant males remaining in the background. A similar facilitative build-up of attack is reported for chimpanzees in captivity (Yerkes 1943), and is no doubt well documented for other species.

In patas, likewise, the sexual dimorphism of the adults is very pronounced, with comparable differences in the canine teeth development, but it seems probable that this functions very differently in the context of group survival. In each of the groups so far studied, there has been only a single full-grown male whose conspicuous size and colouration seemed, from his behaviour, to function in diverting attention from the group and in enabling the group itself to maintain contact in the long savannah grass by marking on him as he sat or stood high up in some tree. It is difficult to imagine, from the slender physique and the elusive habits of the patas, that this male alone or the group with him would resort to attacking any of the large carnivores as a means of defending themselves.

REVIEW OF FIELD DATA

The field study evidence will be discussed primarily in terms of the role of aggression within the group and between groups of the same species. On the whole, relationships between groups of different species of monkey or ape are characterized by tolerance or just ignoring each other. Multi-species aggregations are not uncommon in certain forested habitats (Haddow 1952; Reynolds 1963), and Hall (1965*c*) saw no instances of aggression as between groups of baboons, patas, and vervet monkeys when these encountered each other in the woodland savannah. It is, of course, likely that groups which encounter other species groups regularly in their habitat know very well the tolerance limits to be observed on such occasions. Between-species chases, or withdrawals by one species group from the vicinity of another, do occur, but inter-species group fights have only, it seems, been reported for geladas against hamadryas baboons in Ethiopia (quoted by Zuckerman, 1932:195), but such accounts need verification. It is difficult, likewise, to know how much truth there is in the many stories from different parts of Africa in which baboons are reported to have attacked and even killed human beings. Male baboons, in particular, may become quite fearless if conditioned to expect food from human beings, and may attack a person in trying to get food (as has occurred at the Cape, South Africa). No field observer has, however, reported being attacked by uncontaminated wild groups. On the contrary, these groups tend, initially, to be very shy, and only gradually, with habituation, allow of close approach.

(1) Baboons and Macaques

In dealing with all examples from the field literature, aggression within species groups and between species groups will be treated as two distinct but closely related aspects of the same social process. It has generally been considered that the baboon and macaque genera contain species which are more overtly aggressive in both within-group and between-group interactions than any other monkey or ape species. As has been already stated the ground-ranging habits, taking groups away from refuges of trees or cliffs, are suggested to have set a premium on the collective aggression of adult males. So far as the genera are concerned, however, it is to be noted that the species of macaques show, from the sampling of rhesus, Japanese, and bonnet, very considerable variations in the extent to which aggression seems to be expressed in the wild groups. Further, from captivity reports, both the stump-tailed macaque, *M. speciosa* (Kling and Orbach 1963) and the pig-tailed, *M. nemestrina,* are docile and easy to manage in captivity in comparison with *M. mulatta.*

In the baboon genus, systematic field studies are at present available on *hamadryas* in Ethiopia, on *cynocephalus* in Kenya, and on *ursinus* in Southern Africa. Other large terrestrial species sometimes included in *Papio,* but more usually given separate generic status, are the mandrill, drill, and gelada, on which no field data are available. In reviewing the evidence that is available, one cannot fail to be impressed by the apparent regional variability in aggressiveness shown by *Papio* groups, and it is necessary to be very careful in evaluating these differences in the light of ecological variants that may determine them.

The description concept that most nearly represents aggression in its various forms in these animals is that of dominance. The ordering of relationships within baboon groups of *ursinus* and *cynocephalus,* as outlined by Hall and DeVore (1965), indicates that the large adult males do, on occasions, behave aggressively to other members of their group in a variety of different situations, as where priority of access to a special food incentive or a fully-oestrous female is at issue, or where a female with a young infant has been molested by another female, or where there is a quarrel amongst subordinate members of the group. However, it is obvious from many days of observation of these groups that the routine behaviour of their members is controlled as much by a conditioned expectation of reprisal for what we may call a non-conformist action than by overt threat or attack. When dominance relationships amongst the adult males are clearly established, threat episodes amongst them will be rare, the subordinate simply keeping away from the superior, as in the food-test situation shown in the Washburn and DeVore film. Dominance is manifested aggressively as between the males when tension is aroused by the presence over a period of days of only one female in oestrus, "harassing" threat sequences occurring, as reported by DeVore (Hall and DeVore 1965). Relative rank amongst the males is also complicated by temporary alliances between, for example, two males who act together in threatening another male who, individually, is described as superior to either of the other two. Fighting amongst the adult males is extremely rare, the demonstrations between them consisting mainly of, to the onlooker, impressive, noisy chases without physical contact being made. These "threat displays" are probably less stereotyped than those described for other nonprimate mammals, but are likely to have the same social significance. Discipline within the group is usually very adequately maintained by threat, or by beating and biting of the subordinate on the nape of the neck which very rarely result in any visible injury to the victim.

The overall picture of group organization in these animals is of a sensitive balancing of forces, the balance being achieved by the social learning of individuals in the group from time of birth to adulthood, so that infringements of the group norm are rare. When they occur, they may be severely punished *if* the victim is caught. Even changes in dominance rank amongst the males are reported to occur as a consequence of persistent harrying rather than by fighting. In other words, physical prowess may not be actually tested, the confident usurping animal achieving his end simply by some of the forms of threat display and moving towards the other animal. What exactly is the social context from which such a usurpment takes place is not yet known. From the Japanese macaque studies, it is likely that the confident attitude of the to-be-dominant male is engendered by his being the offspring of a female who is high in the female hierarchy and hence is closely associated with the already dominant males.

As no full account of the *hamadryas* study is yet available, it is possible only to point out that dominance relations amongst males are quite differently organized in this species. Because the social unit is the one-male party, the male having with him a few adult females and their offspring, dominance is manifested aggressively mainly in the adult male herding his females and preventing any from straying to other units. This exclusiveness is an alternative method of avoiding tension leading to fighting between the males.

Relationships between baboon groups are characterized by mutual tolerance or mutual avoidance according to the nature of the habitat. Where water needs have to be satisfied at a common source, as happens in Southwest Africa, Southern Rhodesia, and Kenya, groups may even intermingle temporarily, then divide up and go their separate ways into their home ranges. Where, as in the Cape of South Africa, or in Murchison Falls Park, Uganda, the need for congregating does not normally arise, groups very rarely meet. Although they overlap into each other's home ranges, and even use the same sleeping cliffs on different nights, they keep apart from one another. No aggressive interactions between groups have ever been recorded by Hall and DeVore (1965) in over 2000 hours of observation.

What has been said is not intended to imply that baboons are not potentially aggressive to one another. It is all too well known that, in the unnatural restriction of physical and social space of the usual captivity conditions, lethal aggressiveness may occur. As a recent example of this, fighting broke out in a group of 17 baboons at the Bloemfontein Zoo when an "alien" adult male and adult female were introduced into their midst, as a result of which most of the animals were killed or died of their injuries (van Eel, personal communication). The point, of course, is that the natural regulation of numbers within a baboon population, and within the groups that it comprises, is usually achieved entirely by means short of actual fighting. Animals so socially conditionable as baboons have a highly articulated system of appropriate behaviour patterns towards each other, within groups and between groups, so that this tremendous aggressive potential is rarely manifested toward species members.

The social system of the rhesus macaques and the Japanese macaques appears to be similarly constituted. According to Southwick *et al.* (1965), the peculiar habitat of the Temple rhesus groups that they studied led to as much as an 80 or 90 percent overlap of the home ranges of adjacent groups but these usually avoided contact with each other, as Altmann (1962*a*) observed to be the case with the Cayo Santiago colony, and the "subordinate" group tended to move away as soon as it saw the approach of the more dominant group. Occasionally, however, fairly close contact was not quickly enough avoided, and severe fighting between the two groups would occur. In 85 days of observation, there were 24 severe fights between two of the groups and numerous minor scraps. Normally, the adult males began the fight, but females and juveniles would become involved. Severe wounds often resulted, and most adult males bore wound scars around the face, shoulders or rump. Wounded individuals were fewer amongst rhesus groups in rural habitats and forest areas, where spacing and protective covering greatly reduced the likelihood of intergroup contacts. Baboons have not been studied in a comparable natural situation, but it is reasonable to suppose, by interpolating from captivity situations to the natural ones, that similar manifestations of intergroup aggression would occur.

We have already noted how important a part social facilitation seems to play in the cumulative effect of aggressive encounters. Southwick *et al.* noted that most of the inter-group fights were initiated by young adult (subordinate) males who would normally be the first to contact each other, because of their peripheral position *vis-à-vis* their own group. The sounds of fighting, particularly the vocalizations, would bring more and more animals on to the scene.

From the many years of study of the Japanese macaque groups, group interactions, characterized by tolerance or avoidance, appear to be very similar to those of baboons and of rhesus in habitat areas other than the urban and Temple. Changes in relative dominance as between adult males of a group usually proceed without fighting, and removal of an α male is likely to be followed by a take-over of status by the No. 2 male of the group. The idea that these males, or those in baboon and rhesus groups, achieve their dominance by fighting for it seems mainly to have arisen from inaccurate observations. Threat displays amongst baboon males, for example, may be exceedingly noisy and vigorous, and give the casual observer the impression that a kind of dog fight is going on.

For the only other macaque species studied (*M. radiata,* studied by Simonds, 1965), aggression within and between groups appears to be of much lower intensity and frequency than in rhesus. Males approach each other for grooming and play, and young adult males are not forced out to the periphery of the group, as in *fuscata, mulatta,* and baboon groups. The only threat behaviour recorded between these groups occurred when a young male dropped out of a tree into the wrong group, and was chased away. Contacts between groups were observed on five occasions. When they met, the young males and the adult males would move towards the other group, and then sit and look at each other, with distances sometimes of only about 20 feet separating them. Then the males of one group would begin to drift back in the opposite direction, and the groups would separate. No inter-group fighting was observed. Home range overlaps between groups was of the order of 20 percent only, compared with the 80–90 percent of the Temple rhesus. Probably this spacing difference is a critical factor. A baboon group in the Murchison Falls Park was observed to chase another, much larger, group when the latter had encroached almost to the middle of the former's home range. This is the only occasion on which a short chase by a baboon group has been observed. Other contacts between these two groups, near the respective home range limits, were of the sort already described as typical of the baboons.

While allowing for the probability that the aggressive potential may differ in degree from species to species within the macaque genus, and perhaps also regionally in the baboon genus, such differences cannot be comparatively assessed without a thorough knowledge of the ecological circumstances of the group that are being studied and compared. Under the most widely prevailing natural conditions, none of these species show aggressive interactions between groups. Where sampling has not yet been very extensive as in the bonnet macaque study, it remains possible that other environmental variants may be found to produce a more aggressively characterized social organisation. In all studies so far available, however, the effectiveness of the natural controlling mechanisms are in evidence, so that reduction of numbers through actual fighting is rarely seen, and the necessary degree of group cohesion can usually be maintained by occasional threat or by chastisement short of physical injury. While it seems highly likely that there are genetic differences in aggressive potential as between monkey species, the pattern of conformity achieved by members of a group that live together all their lives is such as normally to ensure that fighting is extremely rare.

(2) Other Monkeys

Perhaps the most striking comparison with baboons and rhesus at present available comes from study of the terrestrial patas monkey, *Erythrocebus patas* (Hall 1965*b*). Overlapping extensively with baboons and vervets in the Murchison Falls Park woodland-savannah habitat, the species may be expected to have to deal with the same kind of survival problems. Physically, the full-grown patas male is less than half the weight of the full-grown baboon male, but stands almost as high off the ground, and has well-developed canine teeth. These animals are probably the fastest of all primates in running along the ground, being built on the greyhound pattern, rather than for fighting. The adult females are only half the size of the adult males. In each group so far observed, there has been only one large male with several adult females and young animals. Numerical sizes only went up to 23 animals, with an average size for 7 groups of 15 animals. Baboon groups in the same area had a far greater proportion of adult males. In a baboon group totalling 24 animals, there were six large males and nine adult females.

These considerations make it clear that the patas group could not survive predation by leopards or hyenas except by the habits observed in the field, namely dispersion, silence, watchfulness and concealment. Whereas a baboon group tended to cluster together high up in trees by the Nile bank at night, the patas remained out in the savannah, an individual going up into a tree as much as 400 yards distance from the next individual of the group. The group would reassemble about one hour after sunrise, and set off after the adult male on the day range through the long grass and into the erosion valleys. Isolated adult males are occasionally seen near a group or far away from any group.

Within the groups not a single threat-attack by an adult male was observed in over 500 hours of observation. In contrast to the noisy barking and squealing baboons, the patas group is, to the human observer at about 100 yards distance, almost completely silent throughout the day range. As we know from study of a laboratory group of the species (Hall, Boelkins, and Goswell 1965), the patas have several distinctive vocalizations in their repertoire, but these are audible only at very short ranges. On not a single occasion, again in striking contrast to baboons, has there been an audible vocalization from the large male or any other animal in the group when the observer has first encountered them or walked too close to them. No animal within these groups had any visible scar or injury. Again in marked contrast to baboons, females or young animals do not show any submissive postures or expressions if the large male passes near to them, nor do they tend to move out of his way. Our laboratory data suggest that adult females may play an important part in regulating the social relationships within the group, and the field data suggest that this large male's main function is watchfulness for predators rather than exerting any aggressive dominance within the group.

On the other hand, the large male patas was immediately aggressive and uttered a higher-pitched baboon-like bark when viewing an isolated male patas or another patas group. No fights were ever seen, nor would ever be likely to occur in such terrain, the isolate or the other group retreating very fast indeed. The patas groups range over a large area of savannah up to about 12 square miles in extent, and, the country being so open, close-range contact between groups is extremely unlikely, especially as the large male tended regularly to go high up into any tree that was available, from which he watched the surrounding countryside.

It would be premature to suggest that this is the "typical" pattern in patas groups, because sampling of other areas, particularly in West Africa, is necessary. Nevertheless, the physical and behavioural adaptations of the patas are clearly understandable in the kind of environment in which they have been observed. In such country, spacing between groups is easily maintained by long-range watchfulness, and there is little or no opportunity for between-group tolerance to be achieved, as in baboons, by a process of habituation. The social order is such as fits the particular environmental needs, and does not require overt aggression to maintain it. Evidently at some stage maturing males must be eliminated from the group, either through aggressive action by the large male, or, conceivably, by concerted action by the adult females. Probably the answer to this important problem can only be provided in the captive group setting.

In keeping with the general picture so far outlined, other monkey species, such as the common langur of India whose physical characteristics and routine behaviour would likewise dispose it to escape or avoid predators, also show far less overt aggression within groups than do baboons and rhesus. "Social relations in a North Indian langur group are not oriented primarily to protection of the individual by group action. Unlike macaques or baboons, a langur protects himself as an individual most effectively by dashing up the nearest tree, instead of depending for protection on large adult males with well-developed fighting powers. Relations among adult male langurs are relaxed. Dominance is relatively unimportant in langur daily life and most of the activities which occupy an individual's time are unrelated to dominance status. Aggressive threats and fights are exceedingly uncommon" (Jay

1965:53). Jay was able to compare langur group behaviour directly with that of rhesus groups in the same area, noting that in the latter aggressive reactions in the group were frequent, and fighting was often severe. In this area, the langurs might spend as much as 80 percent of the day on the ground, but, as noted, and in contrast to baboons and patas, tended to remain close to trees into which they could easily find refuge. Tolerance between langur groups was likewise the prevailing behaviour.

It will be realized that, so far, only species which spend much of their day time on the ground have been considered, but these samples are sufficient to indicate that it is not terrestrial habit as such which links with aggressive potential but the complex array of physical and behavioural adaptations.

Of the primarily arboreal species, only the South American howlers have been sufficiently studied to afford direct comparison with these Old World species. From Carpenter's (1934) study, it is apparent that dominance relations amongst adult male howlers are far less clearly defined than they are in baboons and rhesus, actual fighting or any form of overt aggression being very rare indeed. Spacing between groups seems to be maintained chiefly by the vocal demonstrations of howler males, and this fits in with the forest habitat which does not allow of visually-derived spacing to be effective. It is an interesting fact that adult male baboons in groups studied in the fairly close woodland areas bordering the Zambesi River (Hall, 1963*b*) likewise tended to bark persistently in the early morning, these vocalizations being taken up by males of other groups in the vicinity which were completely out of sight of each other. Such vocal demonstrations very rarely occurred in the open terrain of other parts of Southern Africa.

(3) Anthropoid Apes

The study by Schaller (1963) of gorilla groups in a mountain habitat and by Goodall (1965) of a chimpanzee population in a savannah habitat provide important information as to the role of aggression in these primates.

From Goodall's data, it seems that the chimpanzees, in contrast to all the monkey species we have discussed, are loosely organized in temporary parties. Aggressive and submissive interactions between individuals were infrequent, and the concept of a dominance hierarchy amongst the males cannot be substantiated even within the temporary groupings. In the whole of the very long study period, only 72 clear-cut dominance interactions were observed in which one male gave way before another with respect to food or to place. Threat gestures, including vocalizations, were occasionally recorded. Nothing comparable to the between-group tensions sometimes observed in monkeys was recorded, adult males going peacefully from one grouping to another. Even during mating, tolerance between males was in evidence, as when several of them copulated in turn with the same oestrous female. As described by Hall and DeVore (1965), such a situation amongst baboons would almost certainly lead to great tension amongst the males, and, in most groups, the dominant male would have a temporary but exclusive consort relationship with an oestrous female, tending to keep away from the rest of the group, and thus avoiding interference.

The social organization in gorilla groups is similar to that of the monkeys, groups tending to retain their entity. However, although a dominance order is in evidence as between the silver-backed males and younger black-backed males, it is rarely exerted aggressively and interactions between groups were usually entirely peaceable, and sometimes occurred at very close range. The ranging habits of these gorilla groups differed markedly from those of the monkeys, because a group might in successive days, wander over a wide area, its course taking it criss-crossing amongst the paths taken by other groups. Thus, gorilla group home ranges not merely overlap with each other, but seem to be communally shared amongst the gorilla population. No monkey species so far studied has shown a comparable home range pattern, each monkey group, though overlapping with its neighbours, tending to remain most of the time in an area exclusive to its own use.

CONCLUSION

Although the sample of data we still have available from which to draw comparisons is very limited, and includes only one arboreal species, it is probably sufficient for certain general points to be raised. In common with the comparative treatment of social organization as a whole, it is now obvious that the characteristic expressions and frequencies of aggression within and between groups cannot be meaningfully considered without detailed reference to their ecological context. The large size, the food needs, and the ranging habits of baboons require them frequently to go far away from shelter areas of trees or rocks. Controlled aggressiveness in this context is a valuable survival characteristic in that it ensures protection of the group and group cohesion. Indeed, in a situation where threat to the group arises, the adult males are immediately prominent and the remainder tend to cluster close together. The slim build and speed of the patas who range about as far in a day as a baboon group is correlated with quite a different set of behavioural adaptations, and the physique and habits of langurs and howler likewise are adapted to a relatively unaggressive way of life which is reflected in their social organization. In all the species, however, inter-group spacing is achieved, with the peculiar exception of the Temple rhesus, without fighting, and dominance, in some cases, as between groups ensures the withdrawal of one, just as it ensures the withdrawal of the subordinate individual.

The apes are difficult to place in comparison with the monkeys. Their physical adaptations of great size and strength are far superior to any monkey's, but they are in many respects perhaps less adaptable to survival in the contemporary environment. The relative placidity of the gorilla, coupled with great bulk, slow movement, and apparently restricted diet, put it at considerable disadvantage with the baboons or indeed with the rhesus, patas, or langur. The chimpanzee, with its high rating on the human comparative scale of intelligence, is apparently able to use tools for food-getting and even for defence, and yet lacks other characteristics of social organization and adaptability which must rate it as less successful than the baboons.

The question, of course, arises as to what our knowledge of the different forms that aggression takes in these wild primates has to tell us about the evolutionary role of aggression in the prehominids or early hominids. The closest parallel seems to be discernible in the baboons whose social organization is such as to allow of large groups (up to 200) maintaining their coherence without the aggressiveness of the adult males being in any way dangerous to the survival of the group. The same is true of the relationships between baboon groups, and it is, indeed, a remarkable fact that aggressive interactions between them are so rare, even when ecological needs require frequent and close contact. Probably the most important point to emphasize is that the inhibitory control system of baboon social organization is so effective that their lethal fighting potential is rarely released. One of the most significant tasks for future research will be to work out, under experimental conditions in captive groups, exactly what are the factors of spacing and social learning which determine the natural equilibrium. This equilibrium can, as is already known, be very easily disturbed, and it is necessary that group experiments be conducted to elucidate the tolerance limits in these animals and in other species. If the accounts cited by Dart (1936) and Oakley (1951) for the predatory behaviour of baboons in South Africa can be systematically reinforced in long-term field studies, we have one more line of evidence to support the view, long ago put forward by Carveth Read (1917), that the prehominids may have had many of the characteristics of a wolf-like primate, the nearest contemporary parallel to which is the baboon. The chimpanzee, whom one might assess as academically superior to the baboon, seems to lack other adaptations of a physical and social kind which have resulted in its being biologically less successful.

BIBLIOGRAPHY FOR CHAPTERS 1–5

Altmann, S. A., 1959, "Field Observations on a Howling Monkey Society," *J. Mammal.*, **40**:317–330.

————, 1962*a*, "A Field Study of the Sociobiology of Rhesus Monkeys, *Macaca mulatta*," *Ann. N. Y. Acad. Sci.*, **102**:338–435.

————, 1962*b*, "The Social Behavior of Anthropoid Primates: An Analysis of Some Recent Concepts," *The Roots of Behavior*, E. L. Bliss, ed. New York: Harper and Row, pp. 277–285.

Andrew, R. J., 1962*a*, "Evolution of Intelligence and Vocal Mimicking," *Science*, **137**:585–589.

————, 1962*b*, "The Situations that Evoke Vocalization in Primates," *Ann. N. Y. Acad. Sci.*, **102**:296–315.

————, 1964, "The Displays of Primates," *Evolutionary and Genetic Biology of the Primates*, Vol. II, J. Buettner-Janusch, ed. New York: Academic Press, pp. 227–309.

Atlas of Uganda, 1962, Government of Uganda.

Beatty, H., 1951, "A Note on the Behavior of the Chimpanzee," *J. Mammal.*, **32**:118.

Bere, R. M., 1962, *The Wild Mammals of Uganda*. London: Longmans.

Berlyne, D. E., 1960, *Conflict, Arousal and Curiosity*. New York: McGraw-Hill.

Bernstein, I. S., 1964, "A Field Study of the Activities of Howling Monkeys," *Animal Behaviour*, **12**:92–97.

————, and W. A. Mason, 1963, "Activity Patterns of Rhesus Monkeys in a Social Group," Animal Behaviour, **11**:455–460.

Bierens de Haan, J. A., 1931, "Werkzeuggebrauch und Werkzeugherstellung bei einem nierderen Affen *(Cebus Hypoleucus Humb.)*, *Zeits. für vergleichende Physiologie*, **13**:639–695.

Bigourdan, J., and P. Prunier, 1937, *Les Mammifères Sauvages de l'Ouest Africain et leur Milieu*. Paris: Paul Lechevalier.

Bingham, H. C., 1932, "Gorillas in a Native Habitat," *Publ. Carnegie· Inst. Washington*, **426**:1–66.

Birch, H. G., 1945, "The Relation of Previous Experience to Insightful Problem-solving," *J. Comp. Psychol.*, **38**:367–383.

Bishop, A., 1962, "Control of the Hand in Lower Primates," *Ann. N. Y. Acad. Sci.*, **102**:316–337.

Bolwig, N., 1959, "A Study of the Behaviour of the Chacma Baboon, *Papio ursinus*," *Behaviour*, **14**:136–163.

————, 1961, "An Intelligent Tool-using Baboon," *South African J. of Science*, **57**:147–152.

————, 1963, "Bringing up a Young Monkey *(Erythrocebus patas)*," *Behaviour*, **21**:300–330.

Booth, A. H., 1956, "The Distribution of Primates in the Gold Coast," *J. West African Sci. Assoc.*, **2**:122–133.

————, 1957, "Observation on the Natural History of the Olive Colobus Monkey, *Procolobus verus* (van Beneden)," *Proc. Zool. Soc. London*, **129**:421–430.

Boulenger, E. G., 1937, *Apes and Monkeys*. New York: McBride.

Bourlière, F., 1955, *The Natural History of Mammals*. London: Harrap.

————, 1961, "Patterns of Social Grouping Among Wild Primates," *Social Life of Early Man*, S. L. Washburn, ed. New York: *Viking Fund Pub. in Anthropology, No. 31*, pp. 1–10.

————, 1962, "The Need for a New Conservation Policy for Wild Primates," *Ann. N. Y. Acad. Sci.*, **102**:185–189.

Bowman, R. I., 1961, "Morphological Differentiation and Adaptation in the Galapagos Finches," *Univ. Calif. Publ. Zool.*, **58**:1–326.

Brehm, A. E., 1916, *Tierleben, Band 4: Saugetiere*. Leipzig und Wien: Bibliographisches Institut.

Buettner-Janusch, J., 1963, *Evolutionary and Genetic Biology of Primates*, Vol. I. New York: Academic Press.

Carpenter, C. R., 1934, "A Field Study of the Behavior and Social Relations of Howling Monkeys *(Aloutta palliata)*," *Comp. Psychol. Monogr.*, **10**(2):1–168.

————, 1935, "Behavior of the Red Spider Monkey *(Ateles geoffroyi)* in Panama," J. Mammal., **16**:171–180.

————, 1937, "An Observational Study of Two Captive Mountain Gorillas," *Human Biology*, **9**:175–196.

————, 1940, "A Field Study in Siam of the Behavior and Social Relations of the Gibbon *(Hylobates lar)*," *Comp. Psychol. Monogr.*, **16**(5):1–212.

————, 1942a, "Characteristics of Social Behavior in Nonhuman Primates," *Trans. N. Y. Acad. Sci.*, **4**:248–258.

————, 1942b, "Sexual Behavior of Free-Ranging Rhesus Monkeys, *Macaca mulatta*," *J. Comp. Psychol.*, **33**:113–142.

————, 1942c, "Societies of Monkeys and Apes," *Biol. Symp.*, **8**:177–204.

————, 1945, "Concepts and Problems of Primate Sociometry," *Sociometry*, **8**:56–61.

————, 1952, "Social Behavior of Nonhuman Primates," *Colloq. Inter. Centre Nat. Rech. Sci. Paris*, **34**:227–246.

————, 1953, "Grouping Behavior of Howling Monkeys," *Extrait des Archives Neerlandaises de Zoologie*, **10**:45–50.

————, 1954, "Tentative Generalizations on the Grouping Behavior of Nonhuman Primates," *Human Biology*, **26**:269–276.

————, 1958a, "Soziologie und Verhalten freilebender nichtmenschlicher Primaten," *Handb. der Zool. Berlin*, Band 8, Tiel. **10**(11):1–32.

————, 1958*b*, "Territoriality: A Review of Concepts and Problems," *Behavior and Evolution*, A. Roe and G. G. Simpson, eds. New Haven: Yale University Press, pp. 224–250.

————, 1962, "Field Studies of Primate Populations," *The Roots of Behavior*, E. L. Bliss, ed. New York: Harper and Row, pp. 287–294.

Chance, M. R. A., 1960, "Köhler's Chimpanzees—How Did They Perform?" *Man*, **60**:130–135.

Chisholm, A. H., 1954, "The Use by Birds of 'Tools' or 'Instruments'," *Ibis*, **96**:380–383.

Čihák, R., 1963, "Development of the Dorsal Interossei in the Human Hand," *Československá Morfologie*, **11**:199–208.

Collias, N. E., and C. H. Southwick, 1952, "A Field Study of Population Density and Social Organization in Howling Monkeys," *Proc. Amer. Phil. Soc.*, **96**:143–156.

Cooper, L. R., and H. F. Harlow, 1961, "Note on a Cebus Monkey's Use of a Stick as a Weapon," *Psychiat. Rep.*, **8**:418.

Dart, R. A., 1960, "The Bone Tool-Manufacturing Ability of Australopithecus Prometheus," *Amer. Anthrop.*, **62**:134–143.

————, 1963, "The Carnivorous Propensity of Baboons," *Symp. Zool. Soc. London*, **10**:49–56.

Dekeyser, P. L., 1950, "Contribution à l'étude de l'Aïr," *Mém. Inst. Africa Noire*, **10**:388–426.

DeVore, I., 1962, "The Social Behavior and Organization of Baboon Troops," unpublished Ph.D. thesis, University of Chicago.

————, 1963*a*, "Comparative Ecology and Behavior of Monkeys and Apes," *Classification and Human Evolution*, S. L. Washburn, ed. New York: Viking Fund Pub. in Anthro. No. 37, pp. 301–319.

————, 1963*b*, "Mother-Infant Relations in Free-ranging Baboons," *Maternal Behavior in Mammals*, H. L. Rheingold, ed. New York: Wiley, pp. 305–335.

————, 1965, "Changes in the Population Structure of Nairobi Park Baboons," *The Baboon in Medical Research*, H. Vagtborg, ed. Austin: University of Texas Press, pp. 17–28.

————, and K. R. L. Hall, 1965, "Baboon Ecology," *Primate Behavior: Field Studies of Monkeys and Apes*, I. DeVore, ed. New York: Holt, Rinehart and Winston, Inc., pp. 20–52.

————, and R. B. Lee, 1963, "Recent and Current Field Studies of Primates," *Folia Primat.*, **1**:66–72.

————, and S. L. Washburn, 1963, "Baboon Ecology and Human Evolution," *African Ecology and Human Evolution*, F. C. Howell and F. Bourlière, eds. New York: Viking Fund Pub. in Anthro. No. 36, pp. 335–367.

Duerden, J. E., 1905, "On the Habits and Reactions of Crabs Bearing Actinians in Their Claws," *Proc. Zool. Soc. London*, **2**:494–511.

Etkin, W., 1964, "Theories of Socialization and Communication," *Social Behavior, and Organization Among Vertebrates*, W. Etkin, ed. Chicago: University of Chicago Press, pp. 167–205.

Fisher, E. M., 1939, "Habits of the Southern Sea Otter," *J. Mammal.*, **20**:21–36.

Forster, A., 1916, "Die Mm. Contrahentes und interossei Manus in der Säugetierreihe und beim Menschen," *Archiv für Anatomie und Entwickelungsgeschichte*, 101–378.

Frisch, J. E., 1959, "Research on Primate Behavior in Japan," *Amer. Anthrop.,* **61:**584–596.

Furuya, Y., 1960, "An Example of Fission of a Natural Troop of Japanese Monkeys at Gagyusan," *Primates,* **2**(2):149–180.

Game Reserves in N. Cameroon, 1962, brochure.

Gilbert, C., and J. Gillman, 1951, "Pregnancy in the Baboon *(Papio ursinus),*" *S. African J. Med. Sci.,* **16:**115–124.

Goodall, J. M., 1962, "Nest Building Behavior in the Free-Ranging Chimpanzee," *Ann. N. Y. Acad. Sci.,* **102:**455–467.

————, 1963, "Feeding Behaviour of Wild Chimpanzees. A Preliminary Report," *Symp. Zool. Soc. London,* **10:**39–47.

————, 1965, "Chimpanzees of the Gombe Stream Reserve," *Primate Behavior: Field Studies of Monkeys and Apes,* I. DeVore, ed. New York: Holt, Rinehart and Winston, Inc., pp. 425–473.

Goswell, M. J., and J. S. Gartlan, 1965, "Pregnancy, Birth, and Early Infant Behaviour in the Captive Patas Monkey, *Erythrocebus patas,*" *Folia Primat.,* **3:**189–200.

Haddow, A. J., 1952, "Field and Laboratory Studies on an African Monkey, *Cercopithecus ascanius schmidti* Matschie," *Proc. Zool. Soc. London,* **122:**297–394.

Hall, K. R. L., 1960, "Social Vigilance Behaviour in the Chacma Baboon, *Papio ursinus,*" *Behaviour,* **16:**261–294.

————, 1962*a,* "Behaviour of Monkeys Towards Mirror-Images," *Nature,* **196:**1258–1261.

————, 1962*b,* "Numerical Data, Maintenance Activities, and Locomotion of the Wild Chacma Baboon, *Papio ursinus,*" *Proc. Zool. Soc. London,* **139:**181–220.

————, 1962*c,* "The Sexual, Agonistic, and Derived Social Behaviour Patterns of the Wild Chacma Baboon, *Papio ursinus,*" *Proc. Zool. Soc. London,* **139:**283–327.

————, 1963*a,* "Observational Learning in Monkeys and Apes," *Brit. J. Psychol.,* **54:**201–226.

————, 1963*b,* "Some Problems in the Analysis and Comparison of Monkey and Ape Behavior," *Classification and Human Evolution,* S. L. Washburn, ed. New York: Viking Fund Pub. in Anthro. No. 37, pp. 273–300.

————, 1963*c,* "Tool-Using Performances as Indicators of Behavioral Adaptability," *Curr. Anthro.,* **4:**479–494.

————, 1963*d,* "Variations in the Ecology of the Chacma Baboon, *Papio ursinus,*" *Symp. Zool. Soc. London,* **10:**1–28.

————, 1965*a,* "Aggression in Monkey and Ape Societies," *Natural History of Aggression,* J. D. Carthy and J. F. Ebling, eds. London: Academic Press, pp. 51–64.

————, 1965*b,* "Behaviour and Ecology of the Wild Patas Monkey, *Erythrocebus patas,* in Uganda," *J. Zool. London,* **148:**15–87.

————, 1965*c,* "Ecology and Behavior of Baboons, Patas, and Vervet Monkeys in Uganda," *The Baboon in Medical Research,* H. Vagtborg, ed. Austin: University of Texas Press, pp. 43–61.

————, R. C. Boelkins, and M. J. Goswell, 1965, "Behaviour of Patas Monkeys, *Erythrocebus patas,* in Captivity, with Notes on the Natural Habitat," *Folia Primat.,* **3:**22–49.

————, and I. DeVore, 1965, "Baboon Social Behavior," *Primate Behavior: Field Studies of Monkeys and Apes,* I. DeVore, ed. New York: Holt, Rinehart and Winston, Inc., pp. 53–110.

————, and J. S. Gartlan, 1965, "Ecology and Behaviour of the Vervet Monkey, *Cercopithecus aethiops,* Lolui Island, Lake Victoria," *Proc. Zool. Soc. London,* **145:**37–56.

————, and M. J. Goswell, 1964, "Aspects of Social Learning in Captive Patas Monkeys," *Primates,* **5**(3–4):59–70.

————, and B. Mayer, 1966, "Hand Preferences and Dexterities of Captive Patas Monkeys," *Folia Primat.,* **4**(3):169–185.

————, and ————, 1967, "Social Interactions in a Group of Captive Patas Monkeys *(Erythrocebus patas),*" *Folia Primat.* **5:**213–236.

————, and G. B. Schaller, 1964, "Tool-Using Behavior of the California Sea-Otter," *J. Mammal.,* **45:**287–298.

Hansen, E. W., and W. A. Mason, 1962, "Socially Mediated Changes in Lever-Responding of Rhesus Monkeys," *Psychol. Rep.,* **11:**647–654.

Harington, C. R., 1962, "A Bear Fable," *The Beaver,* 4(Winter):4–7.

Harlow, H. F., 1959, "Basic Social Capacity of Primates," *The Evolution of Man's Capacity for Culture,* J. N. Spuhler, ed. Detroit: Wayne State University Press, pp. 40–52.

————, 1960, "Primary Affectional Patterns in Primates," *Amer. J. Orthopsychiatry,* **30:**676–684.

Harrisson, B., 1960, "A Study of Orang-utan Behaviour in Semi-wild State, 1956–1960," *Sarawak Mus. J.,* **9:**422–447.

————, 1962, *Orang-utan.* London: Collins.

————, 1963, "Education to Wild Living of Young Orangutans at Bako National Park, Sarawak," *Sarawak Mus. J.,* **11:**220–258.

Hewes, G. W., 1961, "Food Transport and the Origin of Hominid Bipedalism," *Amer. Anthrop.,* **63:**687–710.

Hill. W. C. O., 1960, *Primates, Vol. 4. Cebidae, Part A.* Edinburgh: University Press.

Hinde, R. A., and T. E. Rowell, 1962, "Communication by Postures and Facial Expressions in the Rhesus Monkey *(Macaca mulatta),*" *Proc. Zool. Soc. London,* **138:**1–21.

————, and N. Tinbergen, 1958, "The Comparative Study of Species-Specific Behavior," *Behavior and Evolution,* A. Roe and G. G. Simpson, eds. New Haven: Yale Univ. Press, pp. 251–268.

Hingston, R. W. G., 1920, *A Naturalist in Himalaya.* Boston: Small.

Hornaday, W. T., 1922, *The Minds and Manners of Wild Animals.* New York: Scribner.

Huard, P., 1962, "Árcheologie et Zoologie: Contribution á l'étude des singes au Sahara Oriental et Central," *Bull. Inst. Africa Noire,* **24**(B)(1–2):86–104.

Imanishi, K., 1957, "Social Behavior of Japanese Monkeys, *Macaca fuscata,*" *Psychologia,* **1:**47–54.

————, 1960, "Social Organization of Subhuman Primates in Their Natural Habitat," *Current Anthrop.,* **1:**383–407.

Jay, P., 1963a, "Mother–Infant Relations in Langurs," *Maternal Behavior in Mammals,* H. Rheingold, ed. New York: Wiley, pp. 282–304.

————, 1963*b*, "The Indian Langur Monkey, (Presbytis entellus)," *Primate Social Behavior,* C. H. Southwick, ed. Princeton, N.J.: Van Nostrand, pp. 114–123.

————, 1965, "The Common Langur of North India," *Primate Behavior Field Studies of Monkeys and Apes,* I. DeVore, ed. New York: Holt, Rinehart and Winston, Inc., pp. 197–249.

Jeannin, A., 1936, *Les Mammifères Sauvages du Cameroons.* Paris: Lechevalier.

Joléaud, L., 1933, "Etudes de Géographie Zoologique sur la Berbérie. Les Primates: Le Magot," *Congrés Internatl. de Geographie, Paris* 1931. Comptes. rendus, Vol. II, Part 2:851–663.

Kaufmann, J. H., 1962, "Ecology and Social Behavior of the Coati, *Nasua narica,* on Barro Colorado Island, Panama," *Univ. Calif. Publ. Zool.,* **60**:95–222.

Kawai, M., 1958, "On the Rank System in a Natural Group of Japanese Monkeys, (I) The Basic Rank and Dependent, (II) In What Pattern Does the Ranking Order Appear On and Near the Test Box," *Primates,* **1**(2):111–148.

————, 1960, "A Field Experiment on the Process of Group Formation in the Japanese Monkey *(Macaca fuscata)* and the Releasing of the Group at Ohirayama," *Primates,* **2**(2):181–253.

Kawamura, S., 1959, "The Process of Subculture Propagation among Japanese Macaques," *Primates,* **2**(1):43–60.

Keay, R. W. J., 1959, *Vegetation Map of Africa.* London: Oxford University Press.

Kenyon, K. W., 1959, "The Sea Otter," *Ann. Rep. Smithsonian Inst., 1958,* pp. 399–407.

Kinnaman, A. J., 1902, "Mental Life of Two *Macacus rhesus* Monkeys in Captivity," *Amer. J. Psychol.,* **13**:173–218.

Kling, A., and J. Orbach, 1963, "The Stump-tailed Macaque: A Promising Laboratory Primate," *Science,* **139**:45–46.

Kluver, H., 1933, *Behavior Mechanisms in Monkeys.* Chicago: University of Chicago Press.

————, 1937, "Re-examination of Implement-Using Behaviour in a Cebus Monkey After an Interval of Three Years," *Acta Psychologica,* **2**:347–397.

Koford, C. B., 1963*a*, "Group Relations in an Island Colony of Rhesus Monkeys," *Primate Social Behavior,* C. H. Southwick, ed. Princeton, N. J.: Van Nostrand, pp. 136–152.

————, 1963*b*, "Rank of Mothers and Sons in Bands of Rhesus Monkeys," *Science,* **141**:356–357.

————, 1965, "Population Dynamics of Rhesus Monkeys," *Primate Behavior: Field Studies of Monkeys and Apes,* I. DeVore, ed. New York: Holt, Rinehart and Winston, Inc., pp. 160–174.

Köhler, W., 1925, *The Mentality of Apes.* London: Kegan Paul.

Kortlandt, A., 1962, "Observing Chimpanzees in the Wild," *Sci. Amer.,* **206**(5):128–138.

————, and M. Kooij, 1963, "Protohominid Behaviour in Primates," *Symp. Zool. Soc. London,* **10**:61–88.

Kummer, H., 1956, "Rang-Kriterien bei Mantelpavianen," *Rev. Suisse Zool.,* **63**:288–297.

————, 1957, "Soziales Verhalten einer Mantelpavian-Gruppe," *Schweiz-Zeits. Psychol.,* No. 33:91.

————, and F. Kurt, 1963, "Social Units of a Free-living Population of Hamadryas Baboons," *Folia Primat.*, **1:**4–19.

Lack, D., 1947, *Darwin's Finches.* Cambridge: Cambridge University Press.

————, 1953, "Darwin's Finches," *Sci. Amer.*, **188:**66–72.

Lancaster, J. B., and R. B. Lee, 1965, "The Annual Reproductive Cycle in Monkeys and Apes," *Primate Behavior: Field Studies of Monkeys and Apes,* I. DeVore, ed. New York: Holt, Rinehart and Winston, Inc., pp. 486–413.

Loveridge, A., 1923, "Notes on East African Mammals, Collected 1920–1923," *Proc. Zool. Soc. London,* 1923:685–739.

Mackworth-Praed, C. W., and C. H. B. Grant, 1957, *Birds of Eastern and North Eastern Africa.* London: Longmans.

Marler, P., 1965, "Communication in Monkeys and Apes," *Primate Behavior: Field Studies of Monkeys and Apes,* I. DeVore, ed. New York: Holt, Rinehart and Winston, Inc., pp. 544–584.

Marshall, A. J., 1960, "Bower-birds," *Endeavor,* **19:**202–208.

Mason, W. A., 1960, "The Effects of Social Restriction on the Behavior of Rhesus Monkeys. I. Free Social Behavior," *J. Comp. Phys. Psychol.,* **53:**582–589.

Masserman, J. H., and C. Pechtel, 1953, "Neuroses in Monkeys," *Proc. N. Y. Acad. Sci.,* **56:**253–265.

McDougall, W., 1923, *Outline of Psychology.* New York: Scribner.

Merfield, F. G., and H. Miller, 1956, *Gorilla Hunter.* London: E. Arnold.

Miyadi, D., 1959, "On Some New Habits and Their Propagation in Japanese Monkey Groups," *Proc. 15th int. Congr. Zool. (Lond.),* pp. 857–860.

————, 1963, "Studies on the Social Life of Japanese Monkeys," *Proc. Amer. Assoc. Adv. Sci.,* Dec. 27.

Monod, T., 1963, "The Late Tertiary and Pleistocene in the Sahara and Adjacent Southerly Regions, with Implications for Primate and Human Distributions," *African Ecology and Human Evolution,* F. C. Howell and F. Bourlière, eds. New York: Viking Fund Pub. in Anthro., No. 36, pp. 117–229.

Morgan, C. L., 1900, *Animal Behavior.* London: E. Arnold.

Morris, D., 1962, *The Biology of Art.* New York: Alfred A. Knopf.

Mowrer, O. H., 1960, *Learning Theory and the Symbolic Process.* New York: Wiley.

Murie, O. J., 1940, "Notes on the Sea Otter," *J. Mammal.,* **21:**119–131.

Napier, J., 1960, "Studies of the Hands of Living Primates," *Proc. Zool. Soc. London,* **134:**647–657.

————, 1962, "The Evolution of the Hand," *Sci. Amer.,* **207:**56–62.

————, 1963, "Early Man and His Environment," *Discovery,* **24**(3):12–18.

Newsweek, 1963, "Tooling up," May 27, p. 98.

Nissen, H. W., 1931, "A Field Study of the Chimpanzee," *Comp. Psychol. Monogr.,* **8**(1):122 pp.

Oakley, K. P., 1951, "A Definition of Man," *Science News,* **20:**69–81.

————, 1961, *Man the Tool-Maker.* London: British Museum (Natural History).

Peckham, G. W., and E. G. Peckham, 1898, "On the Instincts and Habits of Solitary Wasps," *Wisc. Geol. and Nat. Hist., Survey II.*

Percival, A. B., 1924, *A Game Ranger's Notebook.* London: Nisbet.

————, 1928, *A Game Ranger on Safari.* London: Nisbet.

Petter, J. J., 1962*a*, "Ecological and Behavioral Studies of Madagascar Lemurs in the Field," *Ann. N. Y. Acad. Sci.,* **102**:267–281.

————, 1962*b*, "Recherches sur l'Écologie et l'Éthologie des Lemuriens Malgaches," *Mem. Mus. Hist. Nat. Paris,* Series A, **27**(1):1–146.

Pitman, C. R., 1931, *A Game Warden Among His Charges.* London: Nisbet.

Pocock, R. I., 1907, "A Monographic Revision of the Monkeys of the Genus *Cercopithecus*," *Proc. Zool. Soc. London,* **1907**:677–746.

————, 1925, "The External Characters of the Catarrhine Monkeys and Apes," *Proc. Zool. Soc. London,* **1925**:1479–1579.

Read, C., 1917, "On the Differentiation of the Human from the Anthropoid Mind," *Brit. J. Psychol.,* **8**:395–422.

Reynolds, V., 1963, "An Outline of the Behaviour and Social Organization of Forest-Living Chimpanzees," *Folia Primat.,* **1**:95–102.

————, and F. Reynolds, 1965, "Chimpanzees in the Budongo Forest," *Primate Behavior: Field Studies of Monkeys and Apes,* I. DeVore, ed. New York: Holt, Rinehart and Winston, Inc., pp. 368–424.

Romanes, G. J., 1882, *Animal Intelligence.* London: Kegan Paul.

Rowell, T. E., and R. A. Hinde, 1962, "Vocal Communication by the Rhesus Monkey *(Macaca mulatta),*" *Proc. Zool. Soc. London,* **138**:279–294.

Sade, D. S., 1964, "Seasonal Cycles in Size of Testes of Free-Ranging *Macaca mulatta*," *Folia Primat.,* **2**:171–180.

Sanderson, I. T., 1940, "The Mammals of the North Cameroons Forest Area," *Trans. Zool. Soc. London,* **24**:623–725.

————, 1957, *The Monkey Kingdom.* London: Hamish Hamilton.

Schaller, G. B., 1961, "The Orangutan in Sarawak," *Zoologica,* **46**:73–82.

————, 1963, *The Mountain Gorilla.* Chicago: University of Chicago Press.

————, 1965, "The Behavior of the Mountain Gorilla," *Primate Behavior: Field Studies of Monkeys and Apes,* I. DeVore, ed. New York: Holt, Rinehart and Winston, Inc., pp. 324–367.

Schiller, P. H., 1957, "Innate Motor Action as a Basis of Learning," *Instinctive Behavior,* P. H. Schiller, ed. New York: International Universities, pp. 264–287.

Schneirla, T. C., 1946, "Problems in the Biopsychology of Social Organization," *J. Abn. Soc. Psychol.,* **41**:385–402.

————, 1950, "The Relationship Between Observation and Experimentation in the Field Study of Behavior," *Ann. N. Y. Acad. Sci.,* **51**(6):1022–1044.

Scott, J. P., 1958, *Aggression.* Chicago: University of Chicago Press.

Simonds, P. E., 1962, "The Japan Monkey Centre," *Current Anthrop.,* **3**(3):303–305.

————, 1965, "The Bonnet Macaque in South India," *Primate Behavior: Field Studies of Monkeys and Apes,* I. DeVore, ed. New York: Holt, Rinehart and Winston, Inc., pp. 175–196.

Southwick, C. H., 1962, "Patterns of Intergroup Social Behavior in Primates, with Special Reference to Rhesus and Howling Monkeys," *Ann. N. Y. Acad. Sci.,* **102**:436–454.

————, M. A. Beg, and M. R. Sidiqi, 1961, "A Population Survey of Rhesus Monkeys in Villages, Towns and Temples of Northern India. A Population Survey of Rhesus Monkeys in Northern India II. Transportation Routes and Forest Areas," *Ecology,* **42**:538–547, 698–710.

————, M. A. Beg, and M. R. Sidiqi, 1965, "Rhesus Monkeys in North India," *Primate Behavior: Field Studies of Monkeys and Apes*, I. DeVore, ed. New York: Holt, Rinehart and Winston, Inc., pp. 111–159.

Stevenson-Hamilton, J., 1947, *Wild Life in South Africa*. London: Cassell.

Sugiyama, Y., 1960, "On the Division of a Natural Troop of Japanese Monkeys at Takasakiyama," *Primates* **2**(1):109–148.

Tappen, N. C., 1960, "Problems of Distribution and Adaptation of the African Monkeys," *Current Anthrop.*, **1**:91–120.

————, 1964, "Comment on Hall (1964)."

Thorndike, E. L., 1898, "Animal Intelligence: An Experimental Study of the Association Processes in Animals," *Psych., Rev. Monogr. Suppl.*, **2**(4).

Thorpe, W. H., 1951, "The Learning Abilities of Birds," *Ibis*, **93**:1–52, 252–296.

————, 1956, *Learning and Instinct in Animals*. London: Methuen.

————, 1962, *Biology and the Nature of Man*. London: Oxford University Press.

Tinbergen, N., 1956, "On the Functions of Territory in Gulls," *Ibis*, **98**:401–411.

————, 1960, "Behavior, Systematics, and Natural Selection," *Evolution after Darwin*, Sol Tax, ed. Chicago: University of Chicago Press, pp. 595–613.

Uganda: Annual Report of the Game and Fisheries Department 1954–1955, Entebbe.

Uganda National Parks Handbook, 1962, 3d Ed.

Ullrich, W., 1961, "Tur Biologie und Soziologie der Colobusaffen *(Cologus guereza caudatus* Thomas 1885)," *Der Zool. Gart. Leipzig*, **25**(6):305–368.

van Hooff, J. A. R. A. M., 1962, "Facial Expressions in Higher Primates," *Symp. Zool. Soc. London*, **8**:97–125.

Verheyen, W. N., 1962, "Contribution à la Craniologie Comparee Primates," *Anal. Mus. Afr. Cent., Ser.* (8)**105**:1–255.

Vevers, G. M., and J. S. Weiner, 1963, "Use of a Tool by a Captive Capuchin Monkey (Cebus appella)," *Symp. Zool. Soc., London*, **10**:115–117.

Wallace, A. R., 1902, *The Malay Archipelago*. New York: Macmillan.

Washburn, S. L., 1950, "The Analysis of Primate Evolution with Particular Reference to the Origin of Man," *Cold Spring Harbor Symposium on Quantitative Biology*, **15**:67–78.

————, and I. DeVore, 1961*a*, "Social Behavior of Baboons and Early Man," *Social Life of Early Man*, S. L. Washburn, ed. New York Viking Fund Pub. in Anthropology, No. 31, pp. 91–105.

————, and ————, 1961*b*, "The Social Life of Baboons," *Sci. Amer.*, **204**(6)62–71.

————, and ————, 1962, *Baboon Behavior*, Film, Berkeley: University of California.

————, and D. Hamburg, 1965*a*, "The Implications of Primate Research," *Primate Behavior: Field Studies of Monkeys and Apes*, I. DeVore, ed. New York: Holt, Rinehart and Winston, Inc., pp. 607–622.

————, and ————, 1965*b*, "The Study of Primate Behavior," *Primate Behavior: Field Studies of Monkeys and Apes*, I. Devore, ed. New York: Holt, Rinehart and Winston, Inc., pp. 1–13.

Williams, J. H., 1950, *Elephant Bill*. New York: Doubleday.

Williston, S. W., 1892, "Notes on the Habits of Ammophilia," *Entomological News*, **3**:85–86.

Wingfield, R., 1963, "Social Behaviour of Some Catarrhine Monkeys, with Particular Reference to *Macaca* and *Papio*," unpublished Ph.D. thesis, University of Bristol, England.

————, 1943, *Chimpanzees: A Laboratory Colony*. New Haven: Yale University Press.

Yerkes, R. M., and A. W. Yerkes, 1929, *The Great Apes: A Study of Anthropoid Life*. New Haven: Yale University Press.

Zuckerman, S., 1932, *The Social Life of Monkeys and Apes*. London: Kegan Paul.

————, 1933, *Functional Affinities of Man, Monkeys and Apes*. London: Kegan Paul.

PART TWO

STUDIES
OF VARIABILITY
IN SPECIES BEHAVIOR
Comments

Phyllis Jay

One of the relics of the theory that most primate behavior is instinctive was the notion that the behavior of a whole species might be meaningfully described on the basis of a small sample from a single location, and even that the behavior of a genus might be inferred from the behavior of such a sample of the behavior of a species. Today it is clear that learning is important in social behavior and ecological adaptation, and that the behavior of even a species can not be described on the basis of limited samples. Hall's papers represent this newer point of view. In retrospect, it is remarkable how well some of Carpenter's generalizations have stood up in spite of the short length of his studies.

The major concern of *Primate Behavior: Field Studies of Monkeys and Apes,* edited by Irven DeVore in 1963 was to describe norms of behavior among a variety of species of free-ranging nonhuman primates. The present volume, written only three years later, adds field observations of seven species that had not been studied at the time the earlier book was written. In 1963, moreover, there was very little information on the extent to which the behavior of a species varied from one location to another. In ten years we shall probably be able to discuss the cause and extent of variation in behavior patterns and adaptations that now seem to be unitary and unvarying.

Our notions of what constitutes an adequate study have been elaborated in the last ten years as a result of the diversity of projects from which information is available. Some types of study are obviously more likely to provide the answer to one question than to another. Essentially different kinds, as well as quantities, of information are yielded by long- and short-term efforts, and the differences are further compounded by whether the investigator attempts to manipulate variables experimentally in the field or restricts his efforts to naturalistic observations. A study lasting years spans individual variations in behavior that in an overview can be melded together to reveal broad patterns and generalizations that could not possibly be gleaned from a few months in the field. For example, as a result of such long-term studies general statements could be made about patterns of social behavior associated with genealogical relationships. Three types of studies —the very short problem-oriented study, the year-long one in which an annual cycle is observed and during which some changes may occur, and the still longer one during which young mature and adult status and activities change—are needed for the special problems they pose and the information they yield.

It is becoming possible to relate field and laboratory research to questions on the adaptive significance of variations in behavior—how variations arise, what advantages they have so they become established in group behavior, and how they are perpetuated from one generation to the next. The long list of field projects being pursued and those being planned include studies specially designed to investigate dimensions of variability in several populations of the same species. In still other studies the observer, who does not have years to wait for special events to occur, deliberately induces change (see Chapter 11). It is also time that we began to give attention to changes occurring within populations of animals living in changing habitats. Some of these situations pose problems in short-term adjustment, but other circumstances may present a threat to the survival of species living in the area. Animals can be observed where, for example, forests are being chopped down, poisoned, or drastically changed by man, or where other animals are dramatically changing the habitat, as elephants do by removing trees and turning woods into grasslands. Such observations should be made in addition to those of the relatively static adjustments of groups living in essentially untouched areas of forest and savanna.

In the past, to arrive at norms of behavior, emphasis almost had to be on locating study areas where animals occupied an environment as similar as possible to the one in which they lived before man altered much of the land's surface. Certainly those choices of study areas included locations where man had effected change, but an attempt was made to work where this interference was minimal. Studies in relatively stable and untouched areas were, and are, essential if we are to understand a species' behavior, but we must also study changing behavior, an aspect of investigation that was perhaps a luxury in the early days of primate studies.

The amount of variability in living nonhuman primate behavior may seem to pose additional problems to the anthropologist interested primarily in the evolution of human behavior. It might be assumed that reconstruction would be far easier if all monkeys and apes acted in the same ways. In fact, however, a realization of the diversity of behavior and our attempts to understand causes of variability become aids in the study of evolution. Interspecific variation in behavior assists in reconstructing the most probable early patterns of behavior, while intraspecific variations help in determining relevant and significant selection pressures on behavior.

Hall (1963c) was concerned with the reasons for difference in group size in the chacma baboon living in different locations in South Africa. He documented variations in ecology and social behavior, and was concerned with the learning mechanisms underlying the maintenance of social traditions as the latter pass from generation to generation. He asked a series of questions: Which of the apparent factors of variability might reflect observer bias? Which ones were related to ecological conditions unique to each location? What aspects of variability were due to actual genetic diversity among groups or populations?

Even assuming genetic variability in a total population, the consequent social behavior of individual groups (that is, the expression of this genetic and behavioral complex), depends upon local conditions. A comparison of primarily tree-living monkeys with mainly ground-living forms shows that the latter generally exhibit greater variations in behavior and a wider range of adaptation to local conditions. To take predominantly ground- or tree-living characteristics as diagnostic of greater or lesser ability to live successfully in a large number of habitats is a rough generalization that, it is hoped, will soon be replaced by more specific knowledge of what factors are involved in the ability of a species to maintain itself in these habitats. It may be assumed, however, that if this ability characterizes ground-living baboons and macaques, it must have been even more characteristic of populations of tool-using early men such as *Australopithecus*. An understanding of variability gives clues of this kind for reconstructing transitional forms that no longer exist and whose behavior cannot be understood by direct study. (Reconstruction of the evolution of some aspects of behavior is discussed in Chapters 16, 17, and 19.)

In the present papers the study of two species, *Cercopithecus aethiops* and *C. mitis,* offers a particularly good illustration of how comparisons of local variation and adaptation enrich the understanding of behavior. If comparisons had been limited to a single locality, the ability of *C. aethiops* to vary and adapt would not have been apparent. Nor would such comparisons have shown the apparent repeated inability of certain varieties of *C. mitis* to adapt to drier conditions. But field data alone were not sufficient for the analysis; it also required the study of captive animals.

The comparative study of primate behavior has witnessed its share of irksome problems in communication among scientists, but none of these problems are unique or insurmountable. Rather, they are part of the growing pains besetting any rapidly developing new science. Some semantic difficulties are becoming apparent as an increasing number of studies are undertaken and the results published. The reader will notice differences in the way individual authors use certain terms. The genesis of some of these discrepancies is apparent, since the ranks of observers are drawn from many countries with different languages, and from diverse traditions and disciplines. Differences in terminology are due both to diversity of behavior of the animals and to differences in observer interest and emphasis. In gathering examples from field and laboratory studies to make comparisons among species (or even among groups in one species), one finds that terms used to describe components of, for example, threat, are often not comparable. Sometimes different terms are used to describe the same gesture, or various gestures are lumped under one term, particularly when the descriptions are for a species observed by different people in several locations. This is not a criticism of individual observers, but it does indicate a need for more detailed and reproducible analyses to determine whether the behavior patterns under consideration are comparable. We must see whether play, aggression, or appeasement (to name a few) really mean the same things to all observers. It is possible, although unlikely, that these terms may turn out to be subjective labels which we as humans have selected for categories of activities that we assume to be valid on the basis of our conceptions of human behavior.

Consider an example of proliferation of terms. Persistent local social groups of nonhuman primates have been referred to as groups, troops, hordes, families, harems, and by other terms as well. In some cases, social groups of identical composition have been described by several of these terms. There are special instances when it is not always clear just what term is most accurate, and these uncertainties may reflect a lack of understanding of the behavior. In the case of the chimpanzee in the Gombe Stream Reserve it is difficult to describe the local population as a troop, a term commonly used for baboons and other monkeys (Goodall 1965; Hall and DeVore 1965). The local population in Van Lawick-Goodall's study area is divided into small groups of shifting composition, most of which are not stable for long. This may be typical for the chimpanzee since comparable social groups in the Budongo Forest were observed by Reynolds (1965). On the other hand, Hamadryas baboons (Chapter 11), gelada baboons, and patas (Chapter 2) live in small, relatively stable groups that include only one adult male, several immature males, and several mature and immature females. One-male groups are characteristic of at least segments of other species such as some south Indian langurs (Chapter 8) and some *C. aethiops* (Chapter 10). Hamadryas, however, come together into very large aggregations in the evening when they move back to sleeping cliffs. Within this largest grouping there are divisions larger than one-male units; these intermediate-sized units may correspond in some respects to the social groups among other baboons described as troops by DeVore (1962) and as groups by Hall and DeVore (1965). Given the many terms referring to social groups it is essential, whatever term is used, that an author describe the composition of the group and the conditions under which the group lives.

Another problem involving labels needs mention, and this one centers on the concept of "territory." The relationship of primates, or for that matter mammals in general, to the land or space they occupy is complex. It is futile to argue over definitions of home range, territory, or core area—or any other term used in reference to the use of space—without considering the biological basis of the behaviors. The relation of primates to land is not adequately described by the rigid types of space use defined for some birds. Very important differences in the use of diverse habitats occupied by one species may be obscured if only descriptive accounts of group movements are available. It is equally as important to know why and for how long an animal goes somewhere as it is to know where the animal goes.

As a term that focuses attention on certain types of behavior in primates, "territory" is perhaps most useful as a label indicating only the general problem to be investigated, the relation of animals to land or space. Because observers have meant many different things by this term, problems have arisen in attempts to compare accounts of behaviors with this label from one species or genus to others. Instead of using this word alone, since it has such distinct attributes from its use in bird studies, it might be useful for us to be more specific and to add a modifier to designate precisely what we are describing. For example, "habitual territory" could refer to the area usually used by the social group or by the solitary primate. "Core territory" would apply to the part of land most used, either in terms of frequency of visits or amount of time spent there; this would include locations of essential elements for survival such as food, water, sleeping places, refuge, or locations for other important activities. "Defended territory" would then refer only to the part of the territory that is defended, if any is. "Shared territory" would apply to the area utilized by several social groups at the same or different times. Traditionally, a species has been described as "territorial" if it defends always or during certain seasons of the year; whether or not most monkeys defend aggressively, however, depends on the particular circumstances. Clearly it is not always accurate to classify a species simply as territorial or nonterritorial.

It is possible to denote both individual territory and group territory in the ways suggested. The use of a modifier will keep the meaning clear, and this may well be worth an extra word. New conditions can be met by a new modifying word rather than by debate as to whether or not the phenomenon is "territorial."

The following chapters deal with aspects of variability at several different levels in primate social behavior. Ellefson and Mason (Chapters 6 and 7, respectively) report on the social behavior of the gibbon and of a South American monkey, *Callicebus.* The gibbon is remarkable in the lack of variation in composition of each social group and in its extreme defense of territory. There are many axes of variability among primates, and the gibbon and *Callicebus,* unlike most monkey and ape genera, both engage frequently in loud—and the gibbon in prolonged—vocal displays between members of adjacent groups at the edge of their territory. The small American monkey offers remarkable parallels to the gibbon in this behavior, raising the question of whether there are basic primate patterns that repeatedly have been modified in the course of evolution.

Yoshiba (Chapter 8) presents new information on the striking differences in behavior between the closely related north and south Indian langurs. The south Indian langurs he studied represent an extreme in the relationship of a normal social group to extra-group males, and it is not clear at present whether this is a common langur pattern or a local situation, perhaps caused by great overcrowding. Frisch (Chapter 9) gives an overview of behavior patterns specific to certain groups of Japanese macaques, and he stresses the importance of individual and group variability. Data from Japan provide our best information on the importance of learning in the observed variability in patterns of behavior. Many of these patterns have been learned in the context of acquiring new feeding habits and new foods, and their spread throughout the group has been recorded. As mentioned earlier, Gartlan and Brain (Chapter 10) are concerned with the social behavior of two *Cercopithecus* species (*aethiops* and a variety of *mitis*) that provide a fine comparison of one very adaptable species with one more fixed in its environmental requirements. Kummer (Chapter 11) describes differences between the hamadryas and *cynocephalus* baboon; the former shows extremes of ecological adaptation in the form of one-male groups and huge sleeping aggregations. Van Lawick-Goodall (Chapter 12) outlines major features of chimpanzee gestural communication, its richness and the great apparent variation in the use of complex and often very subtle gestures in the characteristic repertoire. This chapter on chimpanzee communication is presented in Part Two because of the striking individual variations Van Lawick-Goodall has observed.

Our investigations should eventually allow us to understand the origins of variation—not only those that are genetic and the result of selection in the course of the evolution of the species, but also those that are wrought by environmental factors operating in the life span of the individual. It is difficult to assess which behavior modifications are due to environmental factors in the face of great variation characterizing many aspects of behavior. The scope of our task in seeking to understand variability in species behavior should be apparent from the following chapters. The behavior of most species is rich and potentially variable, and to this must be added a substantial amount of individual variation. Our emphasis on the high degree of variability in the behavior of nonhuman primate species may help us appreciate variations in behavior natural to the species *sapiens*.

Although the emphasis in the papers of this section is on variability and modification of behavior, it is important to keep in mind that morphology and physiology underlie behavior, and that a substantial proportion of this (especially the sensory and perceptual apparatus) is common to most primates. For most genera, life consists of familiar patterns of behavior within an intimate organized social group in a well-known location; it follows the same daily routine month after month.

6

TERRITORIAL BEHAVIOR

IN THE COMMON

WHITE-HANDED GIBBON,

HYLOBATES LAR LINN[1]

John O. Ellefson

INTRODUCTION

Gibbons occupy a unique position among nonhuman primates. They are the smallest, by a factor of ten, of the anthropoid apes; they are probably the most primitive and yet by far the most successful of the apes in number and distribution. Gibbons are arboreal (with insignificant exceptions); this is reflected in many unique anatomical and behavioral specializations. Until offspring are born, the gibbon primary social group and the species basic

[1]The fieldwork on the ecology and social behavior of gibbons was supported by a United States Public Health Service research grant, MH 08507–01, and a National Institute of Mental Health, U.S.P.H.S., Predoctoral Fellowship, MPM 17,336. The study was undertaken in Malaysia, primarily in the state of Johore. Over 2000 hours of direct observations were logged.

I would like to acknowledge the work of my predecessor, Dr. C. Ray Carpenter, who studied *Hylobates lar* in Thailand in 1937 (Carpenter 1940). Although the duration of his study was relatively brief (six months), he observed and recorded most of the important behavioral adaptations in this species. I was able to corroborate Carpenter's findings and to substantiate some of his hypotheses. As further work on a subject often does, my fieldwork revises and expands some of the earlier work. However, as far as I can now discern, Carpenter's fundamental findings on group size and territoriality, in the strict sense, remain unassailable.

reproductive unit are the same—mated adult pairs. In human terms, gibbons practice monogamy. This is unique among Pongidae and Cercopithecidae.

This paper deals with territoriality, the most important aspect of gibbon social behavior which, in its pervasiveness and intensity, is unique in gibbons among the Cercopithecoidea.

Territorial behavior must have been a central issue in gibbon phylogeny; it continues to be a focal point in the ongoing daily social behavior of this genus.[2] Unless the behavior that comprises territoriality is recognized, analyzed, and understood, little can be grasped concerning the evolutionary event that is *Hylobates*.

GROUP DEFINITION

A gibbon population is a mosaic of interacting small groups. Social behavior and social communication in a gibbon species can be defined only if at least two (preferably, more) groups living adjacent to one another are under observation. The importance of intergroup social relations in gibbon life cannot be overstated.

Most social behavior occurs within the gibbons group which, as Carpenter (1940) has stated, is composed of an adult male, an adult female, and offspring (numbering from one to four). The behavior that is of central concern here occurs between two or more of these primary social groups, and thus does not conform to Altmann's (1962a) definition of social communication. Nevertheless, I do not hesitate to call it social behavior. This behavior consists of patterns of communication that are readily discernible and are acted upon by nongroup members. Individuals of all adjacent groups as well as members of the animal's own primary group are recognized and responded to as individuals.

Some nonspecific communicatory acts, especially those involved in activities such as grooming and copulation, are exchanged only between primary group members; others, such as the "conflict-hoos" (vocalizations) of adult males, occur only between adult males of different primary groups. Still others, such as the "great-call" (vocalization) of the adult female, may serve simultaneously as social communication in both intragroup and intergroup activity.

The problem that emerges is not that a social group cannot be defined, but rather that a social group (a communicating society) varies in composition depending on the pattern of communication in question; that is, the "frontiers of communication," in Altmann's (1962a) sense, that serve to

---

[2]Genus is appropriate here since Carpenter's and my brief observations on other species of gibbons lead me to hypothesize that all species of *Hylobates*, including siamang, manifest territorial defense behavior.

delineate a society vary in *H. lar* according to the behavior under consideration. Paradoxically, even though in most aspects of social behavior *H. lar*
is a species composed of well-defined, closed social groups, it also displays
extremely important social adaptations that have derived phylogenetically
from intergroup social interactions. Moreover, the ontogeny of parts of these
intergroup social behavior patterns continues to depend on intergroup social
contact.

TERRITORIALITY

Students of animal behavior use the term "territoriality" differently; I use
it to mean the *defended* tract of land habitually used by a primary group.
Territory is distinguished from "home range" (Burt 1940)[3]—that is, the
area utilized by a social group—by the fact that a territory is defended by
behaviors collectively termed territoriality.[4] *Behavior* is crucial to any
concept of territoriality. Territorial behavior is concerned with the establishment, maintenance, and defense of territory boundaries. Central to gibbon
territoriality are the behaviors that occur in intergroup conflicts.

Many of the behaviors that comprise a typical gibbon *inter*group
encounter are restrained and subtle. Because the behaviors displayed in
conflicts are rather stereotyped (probably even ritualized in some aspects)[5]
an observer might be led, as I was at first, to conclude that the animals are
engaged in some sort of relaxed *intra*group social exchange. It was not until I
had observed several such exchanges that I discovered that *two* primary
groups were interacting. Even then the antagonism, which is now so apparent
to me, was not patent. After seeing several more encounters I began to realize
that these adult males were confronting one another, that the behavior being
displayed was intense, and that some sort of contest was being waged. I then
witnessed an adult male catching, shaking, and biting another adult male; it
became apparent, since fighting was a possibility, that these meetings be-

[3]"The home range of an animal . . . is that area about its established home which is
traversed by the animal in its normal activities, for food gathering, mating and caring
for the young." (Burt 1940)

[4]"Territoriality can exist only when there is a defense of all or part of the home
range of an animal. This defense is directed primarily against members of the same
species." (Burt 1940) "An animal has territoriality if it demonstrates advertisement,
isolation, intolerance, and fixation." (Nice 1933:89) "Territoriality is based on both a
positive reaction to a given space and, within that, often, on a negative reaction to in-
vaders of the same species, except for mate or mates. Varied types of territorial defense
are known among birds when 'any defended area' is regarded as being a 'territory.' "
(Allee *et al.* 1949:412)

[5]This ritualization and stereotypy serve to order conflict proceedings so that they
rarely break down into contact aggression.

tween adult males were pervaded by aggression. On several occasions subsequent to this intergroup expression of extreme overt aggression, I heard shrieks and squeals of fear emitted by a male being chased, as the male chasing him closed in on him; these vocalizations were given even though contact was not made. Although fighting occurred in somewhat less than one percent of all intergroup conflicts and fear squeals by adult males in only an additional 8 percent, overt aggression occurs often enough to function as the ultimate sanction.

The characteristic great-call of gibbon females (the loud, shrill, wailing crescendo that fills the forest each morning) serves several functions, the most important being that of location. It is simultaneously a proclamation ("here we are") by the callers, and a signal ("there they are") for the hearers.

Southwick (1962) has emphasized the intergroup *avoidance* function of howler (*Alouatta palliata*) calls. For gibbon calls the function is often the opposite. A group, the adult male taking the lead, sometimes moves a hundred yards or more to make contact with another group that is giving morning calls, including the female's great-call, if that other group is on or near a territory boundary. The move is rapid and nonstop. Because territories do overlap (about 14 percent or slightly more than the 10 percent reported for howlers by Collias and Southwick 1952 and Altmann 1959), a foreign group may be inside an overlap area, or no man's land. Often two groups that have begun their morning calls close to one another move toward each other as the bout of calling proceeds. Groups change the direction of their foraging pattern in order to make contact with another group that has been detected through aural or visual cues. Adult males sometimes move several hundred yards away from their groups to watch or to participate in an intergroup conflict occurring between two other groups. Such events indicate that gibbon vocalizations, especially the great-call, serve a fundamentally different function from those proposed for howler vocalizations. These events are indications that gibbon social behavior contains elements of territorial defense.

Typically, a gibbon group engages in one major feeding bout before morning calls are given. This feeding bout ends at approximately 7 A.M. The group then either moves from the food source and begins to forage away from the past night's sleeping area, or it begins a grooming session. Because groups tend to sleep centrally in their territories, movement away from sleeping locations is likely to bring a group toward one of its territory boundaries. The starting times of intergroup conflicts indicate that arrival at a border usually occurs before midmorning. It is a rare day in which a group does not spend some time on one of its territory boundaries.

After grooming or foraging has been under way for awhile, morning calls begin. Morning calls, including the females' great-call, are given on 85 percent of all days; they last for an average of about 15 minutes. If the adults have been lower than the upper canopy prior to morning calls, they move up as calls progress. The calls are broadcast. Other groups are likely to be doing the same since gibbon calls stimulate other gibbons to call, both within the group and with outside groups.

The average size of the *H. lar* territories in the Malay Peninsula is approximately 250 acres. In Carpenter's (1940) main study area in Northern Thailand, the average size of a territory was 110 acres. In all Malayan study areas territory size ranges from 40 to 300 acres. Because of this relatively restricted territory size, a gibbon group is rarely more than a mile from another group. Great-calls can be heard for at least a mile on most mornings, so intergroup auditory contact is always imminent.

Approximately 85 percent of all intergroup conflicts begin before 10:30 A.M.; about 92 percent of the first great-calls of the day also occur before this time. The correlation is not fortuitous. Morning calls precede 36 percent of intergroup conflicts by less than one hour, and an additional 6 percent by less than two hours. Of the remaining 58 percent intergroup conflicts beginning before morning calls were given, 36 percent occurred as groups met while foraging along a common territory boundary; 17 percent began when one group came upon another group eating in a disputed food source in a boundary no man's land; and 5 percent started when a group's attention was drawn to an intergroup conflict already under way between two other groups at a point where three territories met.

In summary, calls, foraging patterns, sleeping arrangements, and territory size serve to bring gibbon groups together into situations that elicit territorial behavior.

On the average, the adult male of one group encounters and enters into conflict with the adult male of another group on every other day. The actual pattern is often a clustering; on several consecutive days intergroup conflicts occur, and then for several days there are no intergroup conflicts. On the days that conflicts occur there is usually one intergroup conflict per day, regardless of subsequent great-call bouts. One reason for this is that at the end of an intergroup conflict the two groups usually move back into the central part of their territories where they rest and forage peacefully.

Intergroup conflicts always occur near a territory boundary in a no man's land. The no man's land, or territory overlap, varies in width from 25 to 75 yards depending on the placement of food sources and topographical features. Intergroup conflicts never extend deep into a group's territory. In fact, I have never seen one group deep within the territory of another group for any reason. Although chases among battling adult males may carry as far as 100 yards into the territory of one or the other, they never go farther; and the dominant, chasing male always hastily returns to the no man's land or to his own territory. He returns whether or not a counterchase has been initiated by the subordinate male. Most of the time spent in intergroup conflicts is spent near a boundary in a no man's land.

INTERGROUP CONFLICT EXAMPLES

Suppose, then, that adjacent groups have finished their first major feeding bout of the day, completed their first morning-call bout, and begun to forage toward a territory boundary. The whereabouts of another group is detected, or has previously been detected, through audio-visual cues,[6] and the conflict proper begins. The following examples are taken from field notes.

The times given are all A.M. The noted times are not equal intervals, and are not meant to be time samples. All animals involved in the conflict are under observation throughout the entire encounter, and all behaviors pertinent to the conflict are noted. When there is an apparent lack of notations, a seeming gap in the description, it can be assumed that the two combatant adult males are sitting or hanging and quietly looking around emitting low-intensity vocalizations.

December 8, 1964

7:35   Group IV[7] is foraging in the west-central part of its territory. (See Fig. 6–1 for the locations of territories, boundaries, and intergroup conflict areas.) Group I[8] is giving morning calls 80 yards west of this area. The Group IV male and female are grooming. The Group IV male looks toward Group I.

7:50   The Group IV female emits a few hoo's as a prelude to her great-call.[9] She calls, and at the end of the call she swings around a little. The Group IV male follows her call with two soft hoots.[10] The Group IV male defecates, urinates, and moves down the slope, northwest toward Group I. Conflict-hoos[11] begin by the Group IV male and the Group I male. The

[6]Unlike the rhesus groups studied by Southwick (1962), a gibbon group is rarely surprised by another conspecific group. Groups become aware of one another while they are still at least 50 yards apart. Calls and good visibility from the upper canopy allow groups to become aware of each other.

[7]Group IV is composed of a black adult male, a buff adult female, a buff subadult male, and a black juvenile male.

[8]Group I is composed of a black adult male and a black adult female.

[9]To list and fully describe all gibbon vocalizations is beyond the aims of this paper. I shall, instead, describe briefly in footnotes the vocalizations occurring in the intergroup conflicts as they first appear. A "hoo" is a medium-to-loud vocalization emitted in several contexts by all ages and both sexes. When given by a female as a prelude to her rising, wailing crescendo, or "great-call," it seems to function as a kind of warming-up exercise.

[10]An adult male usually follows his mate's great-call with a series of loud, long "hoots." During an intergroup conflict, his follow-up is often attenuated and sometimes absent. He seems preoccupied with other behaviors.

[11]A "conflict-hoo" is usually emitted in rapid series of gradually increasing volume, at a rate of about two per three seconds. It is the most characteristic adult male vocalization during conflict proceedings. When not otherwise engaged in conflict, adult males emit this sound almost unceasingly.

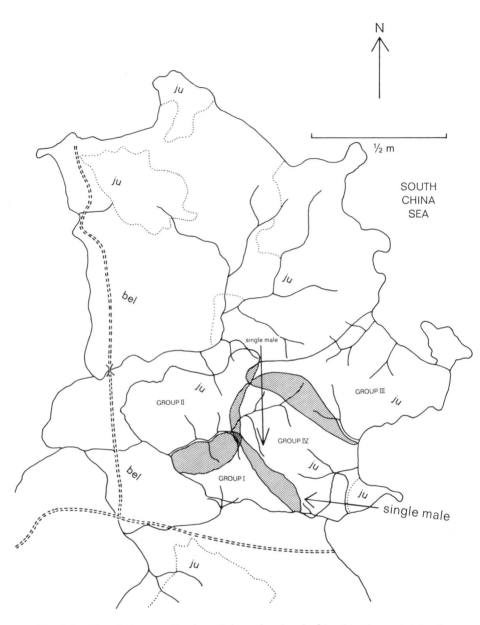

Fig. 6–1. The study area, Tanjong Triang, is a head of land jutting out into the South China Sea on the east coast of the Malay Peninsula. The promontory is comprised of approximately 1000 acres; about 700 of these acres are rain forest. The gibbons utilize only about two-thirds of the forest. Territories are demarcated by heavy lines. Territory overlap is indicated by hatching; this area is coterminous with "intergroup conflict area" and "no man's land." (Roman numerals refer to primary groups.) There are 15 gibbons in the area: one group containing two adults; two groups containing two adults and one young; and one group containing two adults and three young (the third young was not born at the time of the conflict example); and two adult males, each living a solitary existence.

Group IV male moves 50 yards northwest into the territory overlap area or no man's land. Both males continue conflict-hooing.

7:58   The Group IV female gives a great-call. The Group IV male moves slowly east a few yards.

8:00   The Group IV female, subadult, and juvenile are 40 yards southeast of the conflict. The Group I female has not appeared. (She was not seen during the entire encounter.) The males continue conflict-hooing and swing to and fro, each dangling by one arm. They look around in all directions, appearing calm and relaxed.

8:07   The Group IV female gives a great-call and swings around a little. The Group IV male hoots softly once. He returns to the rest of Group IV. The Group IV juvenile grooms the Group IV male's neck. The Group I male sits in an adjacent tree and looks toward Group IV. The males are about 15 yards apart. The Group IV male conflict-hoos and moves a few feet closer to the Group I male.

8:12   The Group IV female gives a great-call; the Group IV male hoots softly four times. The Group I male moves a few yards west, back into his own territory. The Group IV male moves to his female and solicits for grooming; she grooms him. The Group I male hangs 20 yards away and swings around with abandon on one arm; he twists his body around as much as 360 degrees in either direction while maintaining the same hand grip. The Group IV male lies on his back and is groomed by his female; he watches the Group I male from this upside-down position. The Group I male moves to the branch tip in his tree that is closest to the Group IV adults, swings to and fro, and conflict-hoos. (See Figs. 6–2 and 6–3.)

8:18   The Group IV juvenile grooms the Group IV subadult. The Group I male moves away from Group IV a few yards, and defecates and urinates. The Group IV female grooms the Group IV subadult. The Group IV male rejoins the fray, and both males swing around vigorously, 10 yards apart, conflict-hooing.

8:26   The Group IV female gives a great-call and swings around; the Group IV male hangs and gives conflict-hoos. The Group IV female swings down closer to the conflict scene, and then moves back again. The Group IV juvenile moves to the Group IV male and squeals softly.[12] He sits beside the male and looks toward the Group I male. The Group IV male places his right arm around the juvenile. The Group I male makes a short rush toward the Group IV male and the juvenile but stops several yards short of them. The Group IV male and juvenile retreat a few yards. The Group IV juvenile then moves away from the conflict area into his father's territory.

8:30   Light sprinkle. The Group IV male chases the Group I male briefly. A large branch breaks under the Group IV male as he pursues the

---

[12]This soft "squeal" is usually emitted by a subordinate animal as it approaches a dominant animal if the subordinate animal intends to come within touching distance of the dominant animal. It is used intragroup only.

Fig. 6–2. An adult male hanging and emitting conflict-hoos. (*Photograph by John O. Ellefson*)

Group I male. The Group IV male catches onto another branch and continues the chase with no break in his forward motion. Then there is another chase; it is difficult to tell who chases whom; the males pop in and out of the same tree rapidly. The Group I male moves into the Group IV male's tree; the Group IV male chases him out. The Group I male chases the Group IV male back again (see Fig. 6–4). The Group IV female has been nearer the Group I male than the Group IV male during this chase exchange. The conflict moves 30 yards away from her.

8:51   Both adult males swing around and conflict-hoo 10 yards apart. The Group I male moves southeast a few yards, and then circles around back to the same spot. The conflict shifts from northwest to southeast 100 yards, paralleling a territory boundary. The Group IV male makes a short rush toward the Group I male, stopping several yards short. He then moves back to his prerush position. The Group I male gives way slightly.

8:56   The Group IV male moves east; the Group I male follows, but does not chase.

Fig. 6–3. An adult male swinging around and emitting conflict-hoos. (*Photograph by John O. Ellefson*)

Fig. 6–4. An adult male starting a chase. (*Photography by John O. Ellefson*)

9:05   The males continue to conflict-hoo, sit, hang, swing around, and look at each other. It rains hard, halting activity for ten minutes.

9:15   The conflict begins anew. The Group I male is doing most of the conflict-hooing and moving around. The Group IV male sits around, then moves 5 yards toward the Group I male and hoos.

9:17   The Group IV male chases the Group I male 30 yards northwest. The Group IV male returns southeast and joins the rest of Group IV who have been eating and foraging slowly east for the past 20 minutes. The Group IV juvenile is sitting in a tall tree from which he has been watching the conflict proceedings.

9:30   Group IV forages east along the territory boundary shared with Group I. The Group I male is tagging along 30 yards behind.

9:37   The Group I male moves noisily along behind. The Group IV male turns around and heads back toward the Group I male.

9:40   Conflict-hoos begin again.

9:42   The Group IV female gives a great-call and swings around; the Group IV male also swings around at the end of his female's call and follows that with soft hoots. The Group IV male moves east again; the Group I male does not follow, and the conflict ends.

January 27, 1965

The members of Group I have slept in the northwest corner of their territory, 50 yards from a large fruiting tree that had been the focal point of conflicts between Group I and Group II[13] for several consecutive days.

6:59   The members of Group I move north from their sleeping place toward yesterday's disputed tree. The Group I male moves into the tree and begins to eat. The Group I female remains sitting 30 yards south of the disputed tree. Group II is arriving from the north.

7:15   The Group II female, 50 yards north of the disputed tree, gives a great-call; the Group II male follows with several hoots. Group II moves closer to the disputed tree.

7:16   The Group I male moves out of the disputed tree toward the south as Group II moves into the disputed tree.

7:17   The Group II female gives a great-call; her male follows with several hoots. The Group II female eats in the disputed tree. The Group II female is calling a lot this morning. Group I is not calling.

7:21   The Group II female gives a great-call; her male follows with several hoots. The Group II male moves south through the disputed tree toward the Group I male. The Group I male is sitting 30 yards south of the disputed tree.

7:24   The Group II female gives a great-call; the Group II male follows with several hoots. The Group I male swings around and conflict-hoos softly now and then.

7:26   The Group II female gives a great-call; her male follows with several hoots. The Group I male defecates. Group II eats and calls.

7:29   The Group II female gives a great-call; the Group II male follows with several hoots and swings around.

7:37   The males conflict-hoo, sit, hang, and swing. Each is in his own tree.

7.45   The Group I male defecates and moves around to the northwest.

7:53   The Group I male moves a few yards closer toward the disputed tree. The Group II male, who has moved back into the disputed tree to eat,

---

[13]Group II is composed of a black adult male, a buff adult female, and a buff infant.

moves out of the disputed tree, and heads south toward the Group I male. The Group I male retreats south 20 yards rapidly. The Group II male does not pursue.

7:59   The Group I male defecates and urinates. One minute later he does so again.

8:11   The Group II female gives a great-call. The Group II male and female swing around; they have been eating in the disputed tree. The Group II male moves out of the tree and chases the Group I male to the south.

8:17   The Group II male, after moving north a few yards, moves south toward the Group I male again.

8:25   The Group II female gives a great-call; her male follows with several hoots. Both males swing around, 10 yards apart. No chase occurs. The Group II female moves north out of the disputed tree back into her territory. The Group II male chases the Group I male south, then circles north and joins his female. Group II breaks into loud morning calls.

8:28   The Group II female gives a great-call; the Group II male emits five hoots. The Group I male moves north, urinates, and enters the disputed tree. The Group II male rushes south and chases the Group I male south and out of the disputed tree.

8:29   The Group II male moves north and rejoins his female. Again Group II calls loudly.

8:30   The Group II female gives a great-call; the Group II male follows with six hoots. The Group I male moves back into the disputed tree. Once again, the Group II male rushes south and chases the Group I male south from the disputed tree. The Group II male had moved 50 yards north of the disputed tree prior to this chase. The chase extends 40 yards south of the disputed tree. The Group II male moves north and rejoins his female. Group II calls loudly once more.

8:33   The Group II female gives a great-call; the Group II male follows with seven hoots. The Group I male moves north into the disputed tree again.

8:34   Group II moves 100 yards north of the disputed tree; the Group II male does not return south again.

8:35   The Group II female gives a great-call; the Group II male follows with seven hoots. The Group I female, who has sat 50 or more yards south of the conflict scene during the entire conflict, moves into the disputed tree with the Group I male; both eat steadily for about an hour.

9:40   Group II comes rushing up the slope from the north, driving Group I from the disputed tree and toward the south. (No contact had occurred between the groups since 8:37. Each group had gone about its own activities prior to the chase.) The members of Group I move about 100 yards southeast into their own territory, and call a little. Group II stays in the disputed tree and calls loudly. The conflict ends.

DISCUSSION OF INTERGROUP CONFLICTS

In 15 percent of the 126 intergroup conflicts, three groups were involved simultaneously. In these conflicts the dominant group's adult male drove off one or both of the other adult males. Sometimes, after the subordinate groups dispersed, they came back together and continued the conflict between themselves. The dominant group went on its own way foraging.

Prolonged conflict-hooing by the adult males (33 minutes on the average) precedes the first chase of an encounter. This prechase period is foreshortened when groups meet in a situation directly involving a food source; it is protracted when a food source is not involved. These factors suggest that an excitation threshold must be reached before a chase, or other clearly overt forms of aggression, can occur. Sometimes it appears that, rather than building tension, the opposite function is being served by the conflict-hooing; the males appear to be dissipating tension as they swing around in seeming casual abandon, hooing softly. On a few occasions males have continued this activity for an extended period, with the conflict ending at the prechase stage. The males appear to become bored with conflict behavior, and gradually drift off to eat or groom with the rest of their group, who have tired of the conflict proceedings and have moved away. Usually conflicts contain some definitive and more aggressive moves by the adult males; for example, in 63 percent of the intergroup conflicts there is at least one chase among the adult males. Most often one male makes a short rush toward the other male, then swings back; the other male reciprocates, and gradually tension is built up and a chase ensues. Rarely, in less than one percent of the 126 conflicts, contact and actual fighting occur.

During the initial conflict-hooing session, the males put on an acrobatic display that includes twisting and dangling around on one arm and swinging rapidly around a particular arboreal pathway (usually a circular or oval route of from 10 to 20 yards). It appears to be a ceremonial display or a ritualized set of behaviors designed to make the males highly conspicuous. Only during a chase is a male's speed and agility more evident than it is during these displays.

In 14 percent of the intergroup conflicts large dead branches are broken off by the adult males during their displays and subsequent chases. The branches crash to the forest floor. I have never seen a male falter or lose his balance after one of these branches breaks under him, which leads me to surmise that this behavior is also part of the display. It can be considered an intention movement, since one fighting tactic (seen most often and most clearly in the play-fighting of the young) is to force one's opponent down by pushing, kicking, or dropping. Moreover, during normal, nonconflict locomotion it is extremely rare that an adult gibbon mistakes a dead branch for one that will support it.

There is some tactical maneuvering by the males as they display-swing and hoo. It is, for example, advantageous to be higher than one's opponent at the beginning of a chase because some of the height can be converted into acceleration by dropping down as the chase begins. Chases are usually from the upper canopy downward.

In the conflict examples described, there were no prolonged chases; some chases occurring in other conflicts extend 200 or more yards around a large oval route paralleling a territory boundary. In these longer chases the combatants often end up in precisely the same prechase positions.

Some of the grooming that takes place between the adult pair of a group during an intergroup conflict appears to be as relaxed as that in a nonconflict situation, that is, the normal grooming pattern. At other times conflict grooming takes on the appearance of a displacement activity. The adult male moves to his female and presents tensely for grooming; the female grooms him briefly, and the male goes quickly back to the fray. Although in these latter groomings the male has apparently not relaxed, he may have received moral support or reassurance. It may be significant that the least dominant male in the study area, the Group I male, receives no support of any kind from his mate. She neither vocalizes during conflicts nor grooms him; she always stays well clear of the intergroup conflict area.

In the second intergroup conflict example given, note that the Group II female called frequently, and that at the peak of one of her great-calls her male chased the Group I male. The great-call, regardless of the time of day or the context, nearly always precipitates vigorous swinging around, primarily by the adults of the group calling. In an intergroup conflict this call is likely to set off a chase. Usually the male of the calling female chases the opposing male. Both grooming and calling, as well as mere presence on the scene, by the adult female seems to lend support to her mate during intergroup conflicts. Occasionally a female closely accompanies her mate as he chases another group or male. Nevertheless, these intergroup conflicts are predominantly the domain of the adult males. It is a clear-cut case of behavioral sexual dimorphism.

The second intergroup conflict example is unusual in the obvious dominance of one group adult male over another, as exemplified by the chases. It is slightly unusual also in that the single fruiting tree was so obviously the conflict incentive. Also uncommon was the repeated return of the Group II male to the disputed tree in order to chase the Group I male from it. In part these returns may have been made because the Group II male had not been able to eat his fill from the tree during the encounter, owning to constant harassment by the Group I male, and therefore he wanted to stay and feed. The Group II female had eaten her fill and had moved away, and the Group II male was undecided whether to continue the conflict over the tree or to move on with her. An hour later Group II did return to the disputed tree, lending credence to this interpretation because a group rarely returns to a food tree after so short a time interval.

SELECTION AND SURVIVAL MECHANISMS

A few figures should serve to establish the importance of the various behaviors involved in gibbon intergroup conflicts, that is, gibbon territorial behavior.[14]

Gibbon intergroup conflicts, as the primary manifestation of gibbon territoriality, occupy a substantial amount of a male gibbon's active hours. Once an adult male gibbon is mated, he spends 6 percent of his waking hours directly engaged in intergroup conflicts. I stress the time spent by the adult males because it is they who carry the burden of the conflicts. Intergroup conflicts occur at the average rate of every other day; they last an average of one hour and ten minutes.

The average amount of time spent per day in an intergroup conflict does not adequately reveal the strain on a male during certain fruiting seasons when foraging patterns bring groups together daily for many days at a time. It is significant that at a day's end the adult males often forage and eat from a half-hour to an hour longer than the rest of their group. In addition to this testimony to the greater energy expenditure on the part of adult males, there is more dramatic evidence of the physical toll taken in intergroup conflicts. Half the adult males in the study area have one or more wide scars in their lips just over the canine teeth. The females have none. Carpenter (1940) emphasized the predominance of torn ears among adult males over adult females in his study area. Frisch (1963b) points out the predominance of broken and damaged canine teeth among adult males compared with adult females.

One function of the prolonged intergroup conflicts between the adult males of opposing groups is to allow the female and young of the dominant male's group to feed in a disputed food source. Presumably, the group that has first access to a food tree on any given day obtains the best fruit, the ripest fruit, and sometimes all the edible fruit. The gains are not completely one way, however; the dominant male has usually been kept out of the food source by the harassment of the subordinate male, and has not been able to eat. (See the second intergroup conflict example.) This takes a physical toll from him and leaves his portion of fruit in the tree. The subordinate male has limited the amount of food the dominant group has been able to take; he has

---

[14]These figures, which will be averages for the most part, do not indicate individual and group variation that is evidenced in all gibbon behavior. It should be borne in mind that variation does exist, sometimes in broad latitudes.

hindered, however slightly, territorial encroachment. The members of the invading group have been kept uneasy; they have not been able to make themselves at home.

The seeming abundance of plant food in a tropical rain forest is partly illusory. Although gibbons eat parts of more than 150 plant species, as well as many insect species, the absolute number of individuals of each species within one-third to one-half square mile is small. Given somewhat over 4000 species of trees alone in the Malayan forest (Richards 1952), it is not difficult to see why the number of individuals of each species is low. Individuals of a species are often scattered or appear in scattered clumps. This necessitates trekking (moving over relatively long distances at a single stretch) by a gibbon group, from one individual or clump to the next during a day's foraging. Moreover, all individuals of a plant species are not in the same reproductive state, which further reduces the number available at any one time.

Gibbons concentrate their feeding on three or four species at a time; the fruiting seasons of different species range in duration from a few days to several months. The great bulk of the 150 food species plays only a minor part in the over-all diet; these minor sources are selected when the animals are foraging from one primary source to another, or when they are satiated with staple foods.

Within each territory, there are very few of the major plant food species; and so far as I could tell, the gibbons[15] eat most, if not all, of the ripe fruit in these trees each day. Not much of the ripe fruit falls to the ground. When preferred food sources are on a territory boundary they are constantly the focus of intergroup disputes. It is significant that although a gibbon group and leaf-monkeys (langurs) or macaques can often eat near one another in the same food source with little antagonism, gibbons from two different groups can never eat simultaneously in the same tree. When two gibbon groups meet at the same food source aggression is always the rule. This fact illustrates the conspecific nature of territorial behavior so often stressed in definitions of territoriality. The limits of gibbon territory size are effectively set and maintained by this intolerance toward adult nonmate conspecifics.

Regardless of the absolute amount of food involved in any single conflict, food is one major conflict incentive. The primary aim of the dominant group in an intergroup conflict is to gain food; the primary task for the subordinate group is to inhibit that act. That many intergroup conflicts occur without direct reference to a food source demonstrates that food is not always the proximal incentive. Since there were no appreciable territory shifts in the fifteen months the animals were under observation, territory expansion per se

[15]Gibbons compete for their food with several species of squirrels, leaf-monkeys, *Presbytis obscurus,* and long-tailed, crab-eating macaques, *Macaca irus.* According to J. L. Harrison (1955) and Lord Medway (personal communication), vertebrate zoologists in Malaysia, the last-named should be called, *M. fascicularis.*

was not an effective proximal incentive. Territorial expansion-contraction, when it does occur, probably comes about gradually and almost inadvertently as a result of the constant vying over food sources near common borders.

One reason that there were no territory boundary shifts is that even though some males were unquestionably dominant over others, subordinate males never failed to respond to the challenge of conflict presented by the appearance of another group. Regardless of the odds, gibbon males engage in territorial behavior because they are male gibbons, and territorial encroachment is thus slowed.

Group dominance depends almost wholly on the individual prowess of the adult male, although his dominance may be partly affected by the united front his group presents. A male's dominance also fluctuates depending on the depth to which a conflict (most often in the form of a chase) has penetrated his territory; this factor is analogous to the behavior found in many territorial birds.

The territory of Group IV (which was comprised of four individuals) is twice as large as that of Group I (comprised of a pair), suggesting that sometimes as group size increases, more territory may be needed to maintain the group. (Territory enlargement may also be necessary under some unusual fluctuation in the food supply.) This again emphasizes that there are definite limits to the abundance of the rain forest, and that the abundance of food is balanced by the abundance of animal life partaking of it. Territory expansion would require a dominant male. The Group IV male fills this requirement.

Any increase in territory size leads to further behavioral burdens on the adult male. As territory size increases, the length of the boundary increases, and the task of policing the boundaries becomes more difficult. This job falls to the adult male. There is an absolute limit to the amount of space a male can effectively guard; for gibbons, this space limit seems to be about 300 acres.

Given the limits of territory size imposed by an intolerance of adult nonmate conspecifics and by the border-policing abilities of the adult male, group size must be curbed at some upper limit. In *H. lar* the limit is six.

A clear indication of the primary curbing mechanism is provided by Group IV. In this group the subadult male is most harshly treated by the adults with regard to feeding. The subadult is forceably kept out of fruiting trees until the other male, female, juvenile male, and infant are through eating. As time passes, the subadult spends more and more time foraging on the periphery of the group. He is sometimes 300 yards or more away from the others for prolonged periods of the day. As time progresses this tendency increases. He becomes peripheralized. By the time a young adult has become fully peripheralized, that is, when he has been moved out of his natal territory, the primary group in its territory can accommodate a newborn. Two adult males live singly on the peripheries of the study area, an indication of what happens to the peripheralized individuals from the final point of peripheralization until they are mated (see study area map). In this way the behavioral mechanisms involved in territoriality are utilized in curbing increase in group size.

The large group, Group IV, moves from half again to twice as far as the smaller groups during a day's foraging. This added burden falls on all group members, with the exception of clinging infants, and can be thought of in terms of food-getting efficiency.

To summarize, the proximal influences maintaining or changing territory size are an intolerance of adult nonmate conspecifics, the dominance of the adult male, and the fluctuating abundance of food as it affects the group's food-getting efficiency. Group size is maintained below an upper limit (six) by some of the same mechanisms—mainly, through antagonism toward adult nonmates that is extended to the maturing young, especially in feeding situations.[16]

PHYLOGENETIC CONSIDERATIONS

It seems reasonable to assume that an equitable food-getting arrangement is one of the major survival factors underlying gibbon territoriality. One primary function of this territorial behavioral complex is to maintain and to insure a ready food source for each primary group.[17] If this is so, food-getting behavior, with special emphasis on territoriality and the unique gibbon mode of locomotion, was a primary selective factor in *Hylobates* phylogeny.

Although adequate documentation is lacking, the fossil evidence indicates that the progenitors of today's gibbons had differentiated from a more generalized form by the Miocene (Simons 1964).[18] As shown by the Miocene form *Pliopithecus,* these early possible representatives of gibbons were small and agile, as small or smaller than extant forms. They were arboreal forest dwellers.

A corollary line of evidence bearing on the antiquity of the gibbon lineage is the stereotype of behavior in intergroup encounters and territorial conflicts. Not only is it obvious that individual adult males have developed stable dominance patterns vis à vis one another during their ontogenies, but it is also

[16]An amplified discussion of gibbon group size is in preparation by the author.

[17]Another major survival function served by the gibbons' territorial behavior is to insure a tight-knit population structure for breeding purposes; groups are attracted to, as well as repelled by, other groups, thus providing neighbors whose offspring are available to form new mateships at sexual maturity (Wynne-Edwards 1962).

[18]Some recently discovered fossils and a re-examination of the old suggests that gibbon phylogeny may be traced back into the Oligocene (Simons 1965). However, these suggestions are based almost wholly on teeth, jaws and cranial fragments; postcranial fragments are needed to demonstrate gibbon ancestry conclusively at this time depth.

evident that the over-all form of intergroup conflicts is quite rigidly determined, that it is in fact deeply rooted in the phylogeny of the genus. If the intergroup encounters among rhesus monkeys studied by Southwick (1962) are compared with those of *H. lar* it is obvious that the rhesus monkeys are not programmed phylogenetically for efficient territoriality; conversely, gibbons have evolved an elaborate behavioral complex for dealing with frequent intergroup encounters. There are built-in mechanisms that allow gibbon groups to live close to one another, to come into frequent contact with one another, to go through protracted territorial ceremonies, and yet to do all this with a negligible amount of contact aggression. It has taken evolutionary time for this well-ordered system to come into existence.

Extant gibbons are superbly adapted for terminal branch feeding. The critical adaptations in this regard are those that allow extreme freedom of movement in the joints of the upper extremity, especially the shoulder. Presumably this terminal-branch niche was available because it was not exploited or was not exploited efficiently. This opening provided the selection pressures that led to the emergence of the complex series of anatomical adaptations seen in gibbons today. The anatomy of a brachiator has often been viewed as primarily a locomotor adaptation. It is more than this; in gibbons it is primarily a feeding adaptation, and as such is central to their way of life (Washburn 1963).

Like most adaptations, the anatomical brachiation complex is a compromise that resulted from the molding by many, and sometimes conflicting, selection pressures. What gibbons gained in the ability to fully exploit a food niche through their feeding-locomoter adaptations, they lost in the ability to move long distances efficiently; that is, they lost the ability to trek efficiently. All species of Anthropoidea in the study area *H. lar, Presbytis obscurus,* and *Macaca irus* (see footnote 15) have a thorough knowledge of arboreal pathways. When required to move rapidly all species are fast. Gibbons are faster than the macaques in the upper canopy and on terminal branches; but the macaques are equally fast or faster in the middle reaches of the forest, and are much faster on the ground. (Gibbons never use the ground to move from place to place.) The leaf monkeys are faster than the gibbons in moving from tree to tree at all forest levels. It is my contention that brachiation is not as efficient as quadrupedalism when animals are moving long distances through the forest.

Siamang may represent the maximum extreme in body size that can operate efficiently in a brachiating mode of rain-forest living.[19] Gorillas in their evolu-

---

[19]The orangutan, *Pongo pygmaeus,* is a special case of a large, almost wholly arboreal anthropoid. So little is known of its forest behavior that it would be meaningless to attempt to fit it into this theoretical framework. I think no one would dispute the fact that orangs have not achieved, or at any rate not maintained, anything approaching the biological success of gibbons. The orangutan is reportedly in danger of extinction, whereas gibbons thrive in hundreds of thousands in Southeast Asia.

tionary course have come to the ground (Schaller 1963). Chimpanzees, however, eat in the trees and spend as much as 75 percent of each day there, but when they trek they usually come to the ground (Goodall 1965; Reynolds and Reynolds 1965). Chimpanzees and gorillas use both arms and legs in a quadrupedal sequence when moving on the ground. This mode of locomotion is more suitable and more efficient for them than brachiation because of their large body size.

It is impossible to know whether territoriality was present in the ancestors of modern gibbons prior to the series of anatomical changes that led to their present-day specializations. However, it seems reasonable to assume that as trekking became more and more difficult because of these anatomical changes, the establishment and maintenance of a territory gained in adaptive value. Territoriality is as old in the gibbon lineage as the feeding-locomotor specializations that allow them to exploit a terminal branch-feeding niche efficiently. Given these features (anatomical specializations and territoriality), small group size is a necessity. The lack of variation in gibbon group size indicates that there continue to be severe selection pressures acting to maintain this state. The present-day success of gibbons in numbers and distribution suggests that this constellation of traits evolved and was highly successful in the distant past.

SUMMARY

Gibbons of the species *Hylobates lar* manifest territorial defense behavior. Examples of intergroup conflict are provided as background for discussions of adaptive mechanisms (both proximal and ultimate) involved in gibbon territoriality. Comments are made on some aspects of a possible phylogeny of the gibbon behavorial-anatomical complex related to territoriality. Fossil, anatomical, and behavioral considerations suggest that this complex of traits is well established, and hence comparatively old.

7

USE OF SPACE

BY CALLICEBUS GROUPS[1]

William A. Mason

INTRODUCTION

All behavior must necessarily occur in space, although species differ markedly in the kinds of environments they select and the way they use the space within it. Some animals make more elaborate and subtle uses of space than do others. For the primates, strongly social creatures and much dependent on vision, spatial adjustments enter into almost every detail of everyday life. Spatial factors are intimately involved in feeding, resting, and sleeping; they play an important part in behavior toward predators, and are prominent features of social relations, both within and between groups.

Here, we are principally concerned with the social aspect of the use of space. In nonhuman primates, free-living social groups are defined in part by spatial criteria, but the arrangement of individuals within these groups—the degree of dispersion, the presence of clusters, and their composition—varies with the particular species. Similar variation can be seen in the use of space by the group as a whole. Interspecies contrasts have been shown in the size of the group range, in the manner in which the range is utilized, and in the relation between the ranges of neighboring groups.

Spatial relations within a group are technically more difficult to study quantitatively than is the spatial behavior of entire groups, and it is probably

[1]The research reported here was supported by National Institutes of Health Grants FR00164, GM11328, and TW00143.

for this reason that most attention has been given to the group phenomena of range and territoriality. It is only here, in fact, that a reasonable overview of interspecies trends and variations is possible.

Before considering the findings on the use of space by primate groups it will be helpful to review briefly some of the basic concepts that have been used in studying spatial phenomena in the field. Range is defined as the area traversed by a group in the course of normal feeding and maintenance activities (Burt 1943). According to current usage we can distinguish *daily range* (the *distance* covered in a single day's travel) from *home range* (a composite measure usually expressed as the *area* encompassed by multiple daily ranges) (DeVore and Hall 1965). Within the home-range concept some authors recognize *core areas* (regions used frequently, perhaps exclusively, by one group) as distinguished from other parts of the home range that are used less intensively and that often overlap considerably with the ranges of adjacent groups. Within the core area it is often possible to identify certain "fixed points" such as water holes, sleeping trees, or food sources that play a special part in group activities. Inasmuch as range concepts refer to the frequency and distribution of locations or activities in geographic space, they offer no special problems of definition, although, as would be expected, each can be measured in several ways (Odum and Kuenzler 1955).

Territory, in contrast to range concepts, admits no straightforward definition. Most field primatologists accept the recommendations of Noble (1939), Nice (1941), and Burt (1943), that territory be defined as any area defended against encroachment by conspecifics. This definition seems clear enough at first glance, but when looked at more critically it will be seen that both key terms are imprecise. "Defense" is usually taken to mean any form of fighting, threat, or agonistic display elicited by and directed toward extragroup conspecifics. "Area" can be equated with "boundary," "home range," or "core area" or presumably can refer to any specific locus within a group's habitual range. Thus loosely defined, territorial defense may be difficult to distinguish in practice from other instances of intergroup antagonism that occur whenever two groups meet, regardless of where they happen to be.

The data now available on spatial phenomena in primate groups suggest the following conclusions: (1) *Home range:* Few, if any primates are nomadic. A group habitually confines its activities to a circumscribed, definable area. The size and stability of the home range varies widely with species, and is undoubtedly influenced by local factors such as food supply, topography, population density, and presence of predators, as well as by the size of the group. The home ranges of adjacent groups characteristically overlap. (2) *Core areas:* Within the home range of many species (for example, langurs, baboons, and macaques) one area or more can be found that is used intensively by one group and is rarely, if ever, penetrated by adjacent groups. The tendency to form core areas may be more widespread in monkeys and apes than current information suggests, since the concept has only recently come into general use in primate field research (Kaufmann 1962). (3) *Territoriality:* Because of the ambiguities already noted in the concept of territorial defense, there is considerable room for differences of opinion with respect to primate territoriality. Even so, it is clear that earlier views of territorial defense as a widespread phenomenon among primates must be sharply qualified. The regular conjunction of intergroup aggression (or aggressive displays) and specific spatial loci, which is the essential criterion of territorial defense, has been claimed for only a handful of primate species, and has been demonstrated in even fewer. The gibbon is the best-known example of a territorial primate, and probably the least controversial.

The remainder of this chapter will consider recent findings on a South American monkey that like the gibbon appears to be territorial in the strict sense. Such species are of interest in their own right, but in addition they offer a special opportunity to investigate the interrelations between social behavior, ecology, and the use of space. Territory as an ecological phenomenon cannot be sharply distinguished from the core area, which, as we have seen, is present in many primate species. The significance of a territory, as compared with a core area, lies in the means through which the area is created and maintained. Unless we are willing to make the doubtful assumption of a unitary "territorial instinct" operating independent of other facets of behavior, we would expect the territorial primate to show a variety of distinctive behavioral attributes acting in concert to create or support its territorial inclinations. Presumably, these behaviors are reflected in many basic adjustments—ecological, social, and spatial. When a greater number of territorial species are known, it may be possible to view primate territoriality (again in the strict sense) as one element in a more general pattern of adaptation. Our objective here, however, is the more limited one of describing the major features of the use of space by a single territorial species.

GEOGRAPHIC DISTRIBUTION, STUDY SITE, AND SUBJECTS

The genus *Callicebus* may have originated in southeastern Brazil; from there it spread north (Hershkovitz 1963). Today, these small monkeys —known popularly in English as Titis—are found over a large section of the South American continent. From their southern limit in the upper Rio Paraguay basin in Mato Grosso, Brazil, and in Paraguay, they extend north into Colombia, Venezuela, and extreme northwestern Brazil; from their western limit near Rio Tocantins in the state of Pará, Brazil, they extend east into parts of Bolivia, Peru, Ecuador, and to the base of the Andes in Colombia (Hershkovitz 1963). They show considerable regional variation in coat color and markings, but the most recent taxonomic statement made concerning these animals definitely recognizes only two species inhabiting the Orinoco and Amazon forests (*C. moloch* and *C. torquatus*), and the possibility of a third species (*C. personatus*) in eastern Brazil (Hershkovitz 1963).

Naturally, not all of the huge area within the *Callicebus* range can be expected to provide suitable habitat, but information on these animals is so meager that little can be said about the nature of their ecological preferences and needs. The abundance of *Callicebus* in the region where the present study was conducted suggests that ecological conditions were adequate for these monkeys, perhaps even favorable, although this is not the impression that one receives on first acquaintance.

The study site was in the great plains area or llanos of Colombia, a few miles east of the town of San Martin. The major commercial activities in the region are the production of cotton, rice, and cattle. The study site was within a cattle ranch, Hacienda Barbascal. Barbascal, in addition to thousands of acres of cleared and natural grassland, contains many forested areas in the form of isolated groves surrounded by savanna, and narrow galleries along the rivers and streams. An aerial view of the region is presented in Fig. 7–1.

Monkeys found in the forests at Barbascal include *Alouatta, Aotus, Cebus,* and *Saimiri,* as well as *Callicebus. Ateles* and *Lagothrix* were said to be in the area, although I never saw them at Barbascal. I found both species, however, about 100 km northeast, near the town of Puerto Lopez.

My attention was first drawn to *Callicebus* during a visit to Barbascal. They are diurnal, and the species at Barbascal (*C. moloch ornatus*) were marked so distinctively that it would have been hard to overlook them (Fig. 7–2). I became interested in them as possible subjects for scientific study for several reasons. First, they were highly vocal. One morning, for example, I counted 45 separate calls between 05:17 and 06:45, coming from three forests around our camp. The 15 calls in this series that were timed had a mean duration of 59.1 seconds. Secondly, whether we encountered the monkeys in small forests or in large ones, they were always in small parties, most often of three or four animals. Size differences usually suggested that only two of the animals were fully mature. Finally, there was a strong suggestion from the consistent location of calls on different days and from successive contacts with groups in the same specific areas of the forests, that *Callicebus* ranges were small and stable. In short, the species seemed to combine three unusual traits: the family-unit pattern of social organization, extensive vocal activity, and localization of groups within a small area. To secure further information on these characters, three small forests were selected for investigation. The largest of these, Socay Forest, covered approximately 17 acres, and it was studied most intensively.

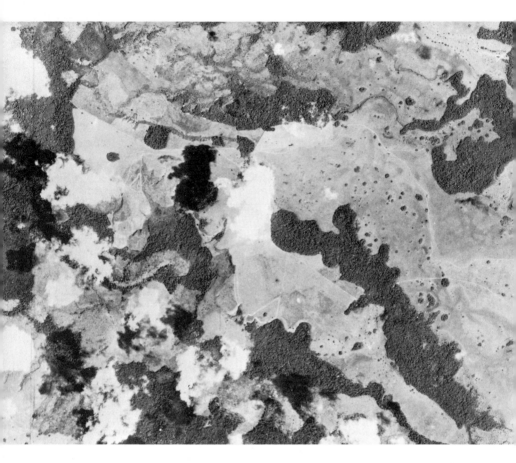

Fig. 7–1. Aerial view of study site. (*Photograph by William A. Mason*)

POPULATION OF SOCAY FOREST AND
DISTRIBUTION OF GROUPS

Among the first objectives of the work in Socay Forest were the determination of population size, and the number, location, and composition of groups. The procedure followed was to spend several days with a group, thus obtaining repeated counts of group size, as well as some indication of location and movements. Early in the study the practice of marking trees was adopted, especially food and lodge trees, which were then located on a map of the forest. Using these trees as reference points, and aided by a field compass it was possible to obtain fairly accurate records of animal location and to describe the direction and extent of gross travel movements.

Fig. 7–2 (a and *b).   Callicebus moloch ornatus. (Photographs by William A. Mason)*

The first adequate group count was made in May 1964, and the census was completed on August 2, 1964. The results established that there were 28 callicebus monkeys in the forest, arranged in nine spatially distinct groups of from two to four animals each.[2] The approximate location of groups within the forest and their composition at the time the census was completed is shown in Fig. 7–3. Group location did not change during the study period,

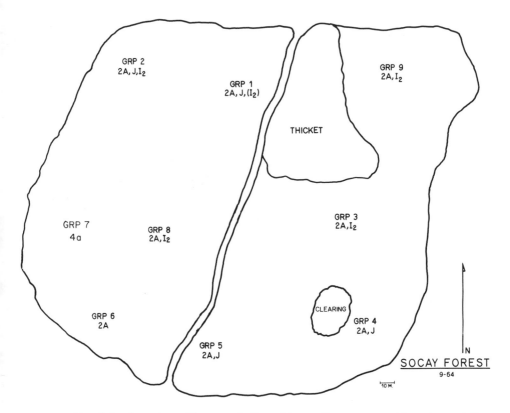

Fig. 7–3. Location of 9 groups in Socay Forest. Group composition at completion of census. A = adult, J = juvenile or subadult, I_2 = late infant, no longer carried. Age class of animals in group 7 was uncertain.

and counts made at intervals throughout the study period indicated that group composition was also quite stable: One infant died, another was presumed dead, and two subadult or young adult animals disappeared. The only additions to groups were the result of births (Mason 1966).

[2] So far as I could determine, no other primate species were permanent residents. Although on several occasions I saw one or two *Cebus apella,* they never remained in the forest for more than a few days.

USE OF SPACE: OVERVIEW

The nine groups of *Callicebus* in Socay Forest should be viewed as a community in which each group occupied and made intensive and virtually exclusive use of a limited portion of the total available space. The space occupied by individual groups was, in turn, differentiated by well-defined patterns of use. Groups could be found before dawn in a limited number of lodge trees in which they habitually spent the night. Following the vocalizations with which the day typically began, groups moved along customary pathways and into familiar food trees. During the morning, feeding was often interrupted by meetings between neighboring groups, and these too occurred with predictable regularity in certain locations.

Toward midday, feeding declined and groups entered certain trees (not necessarily those used as night-time lodge trees) where they rested (often sitting quietly with their tails twined), slept, or groomed. Later, they returned to the food trees and resumed feeding, which continued intermittently until dusk when the animals entered a lodge tree, twined tails, and settled for the night.

USE OF SPACE: SELECTED GROUPS

To provide a more objective and detailed illustration of the use of space in *Callicebus,* I propose in this section to examine the behavior of Groups VI, VII, and VIII, all found in the southwest sector of Socay Forest (see Fig. 7–3). The primary data are derived from a total of 139 observation hours or four all-day sessions with each group, distributed between July and December of 1964. Although this data sample is too small to justify great confidence in the specific quantitative values reported, the magnitude is representative of the more extensive data from the study as a whole.

Social Distance within Groups

Callicebus is an extreme example of what Hediger (1964) calls a contact animal. There is no clear evidence of dominance within the group; members show a high degree of social tolerance for each other; and they seem to act most of the time so as to maintain social proximity. Animals follow each other closely while traveling. They feed together in the same trees, and during rest periods they are often in contact or only a few meters apart. Even on those comparatively rare occasions when an adult increased the distance between itself and a near-adult by chasing or biting, the result was usually transient, the younger animal returning within a few minutes to groom or twine tails with the adult that had previously chased it. At night, group members slept side by side on the same branch with their tails twined.

It is desirable to support the impression of strong social cohesiveness with some sort of quantitative evidence, if only to provide a basis for comparison with other species. To this end, I tried to make regular notations in the field of interindividual distance, but the effort was not entirely successful. In the mornings, when the animals were traveling rapidly or interacting with neighboring groups, I seldom had time to make careful estimates of social distance. At midday, when the tempo of activity was more relaxed, a different problem arose; at that time groups often selected rest trees that were heavily overgrown with vines so that they could easily disappear into these for an hour or more. When this occurred it was probably correct to assume that at least some of the group members were no more than a few meters apart, but unless this could be established with some confidence in the particular case, no judgment was made.

To provide a measure of social distance for the twelve days considered here, the smallest distance recorded between two or more group members during each 15-minute period throughout the day was determined. Of the total of 570 such intervals potentially available, social distance could be estimated in 289 intervals. In 256 of these intervals, or 90 percent, social distance was 3 m or less. Inasmuch as the chances of obtaining a definite estimate of social distance are better when animals are together, this value may be too high. On the other hand, the value of 45 percent, obtained when all 570 intervals are considered, is almost certainly too low. Probably a reasonable estimate is that group members are within from 1 to 5 m of each other 60 to 80 percent of the time during the day, and are within 1 m or less during the nocturnal sleeping period, extending roughly from 18:00 to 05:30.

Travel Patterns

To determine travel patterns the successive points at which the animals were found throughout the day were plotted, and these points were connected with straight lines. In these plots, position changes of less than 5 m were disregarded, and the animal leading the travel was used as a reference point. Travel estimates by this method are conservative inasmuch as they do not reflect departures from the most direct route, which occurred frequently.

To appreciate travel patterns in *Callicebus* it will be necessary to make a distinction between *path length* (total travel, regardless of direction) and *travel distance,* defined as the straight-line distance between the two most remote points in a day's travel. In most primate field studies both measures are subsumed under the concept of daily range.

Path length is shown in Table 7–1. The lowest daily value, 315 m, was obtained by Group VI, and the highest, 870 m, by Group VII. The average for 12 days is approximately 570 m, which is substantially higher than the mean daily travel distance of 100–200 m reported for howler monkeys, but well below the 3 miles reported for baboons (Altmann 1959; Bernstein 1964a; Carpenter 1934; DeVore and Hall 1965).

TABLE 7–1 PATH LENGTH AND TRAVEL DISTANCE

		Path Length (m)		Travel Distance (m)
Group VI				
7/31		315.0		90.0
8/7		395.0		85.0
8/22		520.0		90.0
9/23		470.0		65.0
	Mean	425.0	Mean	82.5
Group VII				
8/3		390.0		100.0
8/4		870.0		100.0
8/24		805.0		110.0
9/29		485.0		80.0
	Mean	637.5	Mean	97.5
Group VIII				
8/25		360.0		65.0
8/27		690.0		80.0
8/28		830.0		85.0
12/10		680.0		85.0
	Mean	640.0	Mean	78.7
Mean		567.5		86.2

Of greater interest than path length, however, is the relation between path length and travel distance. Figure 7–4 shows the pathways of each group during the four-day sample. It is obvious that travel takes place within a small, clearly circumscribed area. For animals traveling a direct route throughout the day, path length and travel distance would be equal. In the

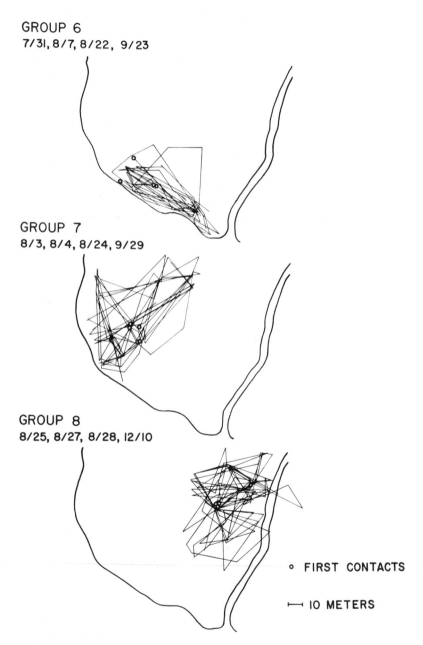

GROUP 6
7/31, 8/7, 8/22, 9/23

GROUP 7
8/3, 8/4, 8/24, 9/29

GROUP 8
8/25, 8/27, 8/28, 12/10

○ FIRST CONTACTS

⊢—⊣ 10 METERS

Fig. 7-4. Pathways on the days indicated for groups 6, 7, and 8. Open circles mark the location of the first contact at the beginning of each day.

present data, daily path length was never less than 3.5 times larger than travel distance, and on the average it was nearly 7 times larger. Although each group traveled daily at least the equivalent of the distance between either the north-south or east-west limits of the forest, on no day did the travel distance exceed 110 m (see Table 7–1).

Home Range

The area enclosed by a line connecting the peripheral points and pathways of a group's four daily ranges defines its home range. Home ranges were about one acre for each group: they were 3201, 5093, and 4762 square m for Groups VI through VIII, respectively. Even allowing for the possibility that home ranges would have been somewhat larger had a larger sample been used, these data show that *Callicebus* ranges are quite small—a mere fraction of the gibbon's home range of 40 acres or more. (The gibbon's range is among the smallest reported for primates.)

In spite of the small area of its home range, *Callicebus* does not use all parts of it with equal frequency. There is some suggestion of differential use in Fig. 7–4, but the pattern becomes clearer if the time factor is taken into account. To do this a grid representing 10-m squares was imposed on a map of the forest, and group locations were plotted on this grid; the first location noted in each 15-minute interval throughout the day was used as the basic datum. Of the total of 570 such intervals potentially available, 486 (85 percent) provided information on group location. According to these data, groups were found in only 62.8 percent of the total area of their home ranges. But the amount of total home range that was used frequently is even less than this value suggests, as can be seen in Fig. 7–5. The shaded squares of this figure (selected in order of decreasing frequency of use) account for 75 percent of each group's locations, yet these squares cover less than 26 percent of the total range of any group.

The finding that *Callicebus* spend a disproportionate amount of time in certain areas is in accord with the subjective impression that the home range is a complex and highly differentiated structure for its occupants. Its elements are used selectively, and some of them play a special part in the daily routine. Some of the shaded areas in Fig. 7–5, for example, contained favorite rest trees used regularly throughout the study period. Such trees were usually overgrown with vines, but there were similar trees within the range that were not used intensively, suggesting that preference was as much a matter of custom, as a response to the specific characteristics of the trees. Other shaded areas shown in Fig. 7–5 represent the location of clusters of food trees that were visited for brief periods nearly every day, and often several times in a day. Again, these were not the only food trees available, and their selection seemed to be based on established patterns of use as much as on the availability of food.

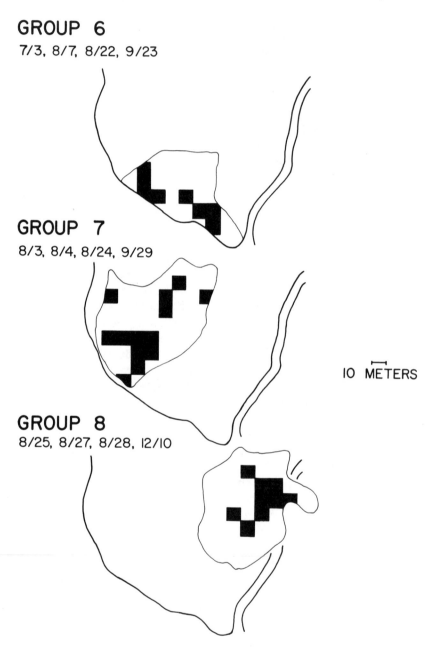

GROUP 6
7/3, 8/7, 8/22, 9/23

GROUP 7
8/3, 8/4, 8/24, 9/29

GROUP 8
8/25, 8/27, 8/28, 12/10

⊢⊣
10 METERS

Fig. 7–5. Shaded areas accounting for 75 percent of group locations.

Intergroup Relations

In *Callicebus* the amount of overlap in the ranges of adjacent groups is small, both absolutely and in relation to total area of the home range. The largest overlap in the present data, 222 square m, occurred between Groups VI and VII. This is only 7 percent of the home range of Group VI, and less than 5 percent of the total range of Group VII. Because of the limited sample from which these data are taken, the estimate of overlap is probably low; but in any case it is reasonable to assume that adjacent ranges seldom overlap by more than 20 percent, a value that is well below the 60–80 percent reported for many Old World primates, or for the howler, the only New World monkey for which comparable data are available (Carpenter 1934, 1965; Hall 1965c).

The crucial evidence for the territorial tendencies of *Callicebus* is closely tied to these small overlapping areas at the boundaries of the home ranges. Here groups met frequently and engaged in an elaborate and extended display in which calling, rushing, and chasing were prominent elements. Such intergroup confrontations characteristically began with two of the groups rapidly converging toward each other, then stopping a few meters apart. As the groups approached each other the animals of one group would draw together, and then sit with their sides touching, facing the opposing group. Calling was probably most often initiated by the male, but his mate certainly participated, and both animals showed signs of extreme agitation. Vocalizations were loud and sustained. Piloerection, arching of the back, stiffening or bowing of the arms, and tail-lashing frequently accompanied the calling, and the rushes, counter-rushes, and chases that normally occurred during the confrontation were carried out with great vigor. In spite of the apparent intensity of these activities, fighting was infrequent and never severe. During a chase, the pursued was seldom caught, and even when it was, the contact was brief (1–2 seconds), and no serious injuries resulted. Wounds, torn ears, and the other residuals of aggression that are so common in many terrestrial species were never seen in the monkeys of Socay Forest.

During the twelve days considered here, a total of 20 confrontations were observed among the three groups. Their locations are shown in Fig. 7–6. Eleven confrontations occurred between Groups VI and VII, six between Groups VII and VIII, and three between Groups VI and VIII. It will be noted that all the confrontations between the last two groups fall outside the area of overlap between their ranges. The explanation for this is that only the pathways of the subject group were used to determine ranges. Thus on 23 September when I was following Group VI a confrontation occurred with Group VIII in the southeastern third of the range of Group VI. Conversely, when I was following Group VIII, two confrontations with Group VI took place just outside the indicated area of overlap between their ranges.

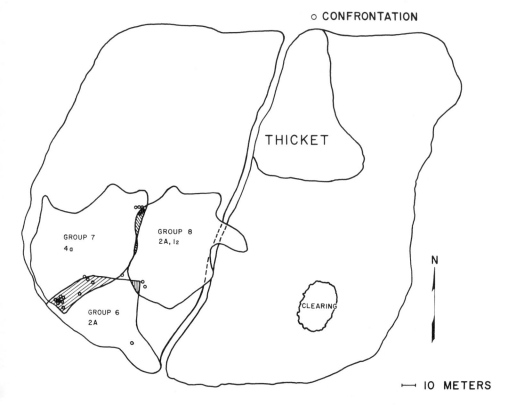

Fig. 7–6. Overlap of group ranges. Circles indicate the sites of confrontations between the three groups.

In Fig. 7–6 are shown only those confrontations in which the three groups were involved with each other, although during the same period they also met with other groups: Group VI met with Group V, Group VIII met with Groups I, II, and V, and Group VII met with Group II. In three of the confrontations between Groups VII and VIII, Group II also participated, joining with them in the area shown in Fig. 7–6.

SOURCES OF TERRITORIALITY

Territoriality, as Carpenter (1958) remarked, is a higher order system dependent upon many specific behavioral determinants. In *Callicebus* these determinants are only partially understood, but enough is known to suggest that they are numerous, and that they are present at the community, group, and individual levels of organization.

As would be expected, the clearest view of territorial elements can be had at the community level, and the most obvious of these elements is the confrontation. The confrontation—an agonistic display elicited by and directed toward neighboring groups, and occurring with predictable regularity at the boundaries between ranges—fully qualifies, according to current usage, as a form of territorial defense. Strictly speaking, however, there is little evidence that defense plays an important part in the motivation or causation of the confrontation; the motivation seems to be intrinsic. Apparently all that is required to produce a confrontation is two groups in proximity and in the proper "mood" (the mood is most often right in the mornings). When these conditions are met the groups converge, chase, and call, and then withdraw into their areas to resume the daily routine. There is seldom any suggestion of an invasion, nor does the confrontation end with a victor and a vanquished. Whatever its causes, however, there is little question that one of the functions of the confrontation is to help maintain the home range as a stable and exclusive preserve of the resident group.

Other factors presumably operate at the community level, and contribute to the same end: The "dawn calls" and the vocal "chain reactions" (Mason 1966) may serve as forms of territorial marking. At least they provide the observer with reliable information on group location, and there is no reason to suppose that they do not do so for the monkeys. Scent marking is also a possibility, although here the evidence is less secure. Callicebus monkeys seem to have the structural equipment for scent marking (a sternal patch of glandular tissue), and they rub this area against branches by pushing or dragging the body forward. Apparently some substance is deposited, for the animal performing the response often pauses after a stroke to sniff or mouth the place it has rubbed. Furthermore, one receives the compelling impression that the performer is transported during the act, much as a cat seems to be when it encounters catnip. The fact that chest-rubbing most frequently occurs after an encounter between groups is suggestive of a marking function, but unfortunately for this hypothesis the response is not always performed at boundary areas, nor has any animal been observed reacting to a spot rubbed by another. Nevertheless, it is hard to believe that such a pattern plays no part in territorial behavior. Perhaps chest-rubbing imparts to the home range an odor that is recognized by the occupants, or, possibly, by providing the performer with an especially intense experience closely linked with a physical object in its home range, it serves to enhance the individual attachment to place.

Even though community relations supply the most dramatic evidence of *Callicebus* territoriality, they are only one aspect. Territoriality for *Callicebus* is a way of life, and it must draw upon many factors outside the arena of community relations. Chest-rubbing might be one of these. In general, we might speculate that at the group and individual levels the most important factors in the territorial pattern are those that result in a strong and specific attachment of the individual to its mate and to the place where it lives.

Of the two forms of attachment, that for the mate is revealed most clearly under field conditions. The behaviors that characterize the relationship between a mated pair are remarkable for their subtlety and variety. There is the close coordination of behavior during feeding, progressions, and confrontations with other groups; there is tail-twining and frequent and prolonged bouts of social grooming; there is nuzzling, hand-holding, foot-grasping, and lip-smacking; there is the obvious evidence of distress when a monkey is separated from its mate; and there is the unequal division of parental labor in which the male carries the infant at most times (the exceptions being when it is being suckled or groomed).

The ties to place are less obvious, but I am sure they too are strong. On one occasion, for example, we captured the male in a two-animal group. The female remained within the customary group range for several days, until she too was captured only a few meters from the tree where we had taken her mate.

Naturally, the normative data alone do not permit a careful assessment of the factors that contribute to the territorial mode in *Callicebus*. However, comparison with another territorial primate, the gibbon, lends confidence that many of the traits seen in *Callicebus* are related parts of a single pattern of adaptation (Carpenter 1940; Ellefson Chap. 6 this vol.). Gibbon groups are organized around an adult male and female who differ little in physical appearance and dominance status. Groups are apparently stable, and they occupy a relatively small home range that overlaps only slightly the ranges of adjacent groups. Like *Callicebus,* the gibbon has a rich vocal repertoire that plays an extensive part in relations between neighboring groups.

In view of the large phyletic gap between gibbons and *Callicebus*, the resemblances between them can only be regarded as convergent evolutionary reactions to similar selective pressures or environmental opportunities. It remains to be seen whether other territorial primates will display a comparable configuration of traits.

8

LOCAL AND INTERTROOP

VARIABILITY IN ECOLOGY

AND SOCIAL BEHAVIOR

OF COMMON INDIAN LANGURS[1]

Kenji Yoshiba

INTRODUCTION

The common Indian langur or Hanuman langur, *Presbytis entellus,* belongs to the subfamily Colobinae, together with langurs and leaf monkeys of Asia, and colobus monkeys of Africa. So far it is the best studied species of the subfamily.

Although the boundaries of geographical distribution of the species are not clearly defined, it is known that they are distributed over most of north India and throughout peninsular India as far south as Cape Comorin. They can also be found in Ceylon, if we consider the southeastern form, or *priamus,* as one variation on a subspecific or racial level.

Langurs are extremely adaptable and live in vegetation zones ranging from dry scrub with only occasional low trees, to thick wet forests. They are seen as high as 11,000 feet above sea level in the foothills of the Himalayas and in fields of snow (Jay 1965*b;* Hingston 1920). As a result, considerable variability in their ecology and social behavior can be expected.

[1]The fieldwork for this study was financed by Rockefeller Foundation grant RF60229.

Jay studied the langurs in north India for 18 months from October 1958 through April 1960. From November 1958 to November 1959 she observed three groups in the forest near Orcha village, Bastar District, Madhya Pradesh. From December 1, 1959 to March 30, 1960, she undertook intensive observations on one group near Kaukori village, 14 miles from Lucknow in Uttar Pradesh. During her study period Jay also made brief observations of langurs in Nagpur, Kondagaon, and Narayanpur in central India, and checked these areas periodically for 16 months.

The langurs living in the forest near Dharwar, Mysore State, were observed by us (D. Miyadi, M. D. Parthasarathy, S. Kawamura, Y. Sugiyama, and me) from June 1961 to March 1963. We made a brief survey at Sagar and Yellapur, Mysore State, in a part of the evergreen forests to the southwest of Dharwar, and we made occasional checks along the Poona-Bangalore road. Ceylon gray langurs were studied by S. Ripley in 1962 and 1963.

Jay recorded additional data on langur behavior at Dharwar in February 1963. A visit to Kaukori was made by me in January 1960 and by Sugiyama in October 1962. We undertook a brief group count around Raipur (in central India), and a few days' survey at Orcha in November 1962.

The langurs in Jay's study area belong to the northern form; those in our study area belong to the southern form. They differ markedly from each other in the way the tail is carried, as Jay (1965*b*) describes; the tail of the Dharwar langur is carried up with the end pointing down and behind the monkey, whereas that of the northern langurs is carried over the back toward the head in a large single loop. The head of the Dharwar langur does not have the cone-like peak of fur, and is usually round like that of the northern forms, which seem to have longer hairs around the face and head. In this respect they differ from the southeastern form, which has a prominent peak of head fur, and was once classified as a separate species, *P. priamus*. The boundary between the northern and southern forms is considered to be the Tapti and Godavari rivers.

Extensive data on langur population structure and other aspects were collected from many troops in which the members were not individually identified. At Dharwar, data were mainly collected at roadsides.

Detailed observation of many aspects of social behavior was difficult and often impossible in the Orcha Forest owing to restricted visibility, but conditions at Kaukori were excellent for that purpose (Jay 1965*b*). Conditions at Dharwar Forest were generally good and sometimes excellent for detailed observations of social behavior.

Observation methods used in the two field studies were essentially the same. Data on social interactions were collected by Jay and by us from troops in which the members were individually identified. At both study areas, habituation of the monkeys to the observers was made mainly by the repeated and gradual approach of the observer to the monkeys. In Jay's area

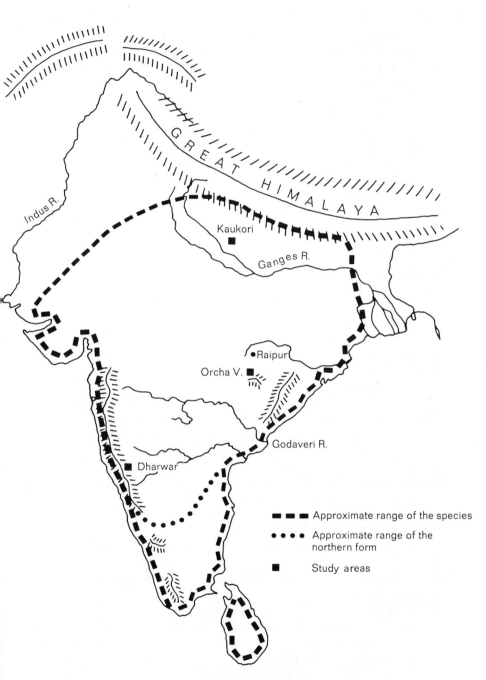

Fig. 8–1.   The study areas of the common Indian langur.

no attempt was made at feeding langurs with the exception of the last few weeks at Kaukori. At Dharwar two troops (Troops XL and XLI) were given peanuts daily for the last few months. Attempts were also made to feed other Dharwar troops, but were not successful. These troops accepted only wild bamboo shoots found within their home range in small quantities. Bamboo shoots were given several times to troop number 1, and twice to Troop V. During the last dry season water was given daily to Troops XL and XLI, and occasionally to Troop I, but not to the others.

The observations of behavior included in this chapter were obtained mainly from Troops II, V, and XXX, which were not fed or supplied with water. Observations of Troop XL and XLI are included in the section on dominance where artificial feeding is mentioned. Data obtained from Troop I are also referred to, but only where the results are found to be the same as those obtained from the troops that were not fed.

ECOLOGY

Climate and Vegetation

Orcha is situated in the Abjhmar Hills at an altitude of 2500 feet. Kaukori is in the Gangetic Plain at 400 feet above sea level. Dharwar is in the western part of the Deccan Plateau, on the east-side slope of the Western Ghats at an altitude of about 200 feet. All three localities have a tropical monsoon climate, but there are some differences in the local climates.

Annual rainfall at Orcha is about 80 inches. It is from 30 to 50 inches at Kaukori, and about the same or a little more at Dharwar Forest. At Orcha, about 75 percent of the annual rainfall is recorded during the rainy monsoon season. Monsoon rainfall accounts for from 70 to 80 percent of the annual rainfall at Kaukori, and for 90 percent at Dharwar. There are from 1 to 4 inches of winter showers at Orcha, less than that at Kaukori, and almost none at Dharwar.

Maximum temperature in summer ranges from 90° to 100°F at Orcha, from 100° to 118°F at Lucknow, and from 100° to 105°F at Dharwar. The summer climate at Orcha is comparatively moderate with some shade and humidity, whereas it is rather severe at Kaukori and Dharwar, with dust storms and strong winds. Conditions are especially severe at Dharwar Forest, where almost all the trees shed their leaves and where there is little rainfall in summer. In winter it is colder at Kaukori, with lower temperatures and more wind, than at Orcha and Dharwar.

The natural forest at Orcha is moist deciduous forest, and that at Dharwar is dry deciduous forest. The natural vegetation at Kaukori, though little of it is left, is classified as dry scrub forest (Puri 1960).

Fig. 8-2. The forest at Dharwar in the dry season. (*Photograph by Y. Sugiyama*)

Human Influence and Interspecific Relations

Orcha is a tribal area with a very low human population density. Only 3 percent of the land is under cultivation. It includes large reserved forests where hunting is not permitted, and it is very rich in wild life, including such animals as the tiger, leopard, wild dog, and hyena. In contrast, the Kaukori area has a high human population density, and 98 percent of the land is under cultivation, leaving almost no natural vegetation. It is in part open fields with little brush or scrub, but in some places there are large mango orchards with scrub undergrowth. As a result, there are few wild animals left. At Dharwar Forest, human population density is comparatively low. The forest forms an eastern tip of a large mass of west Deccan forests. To the east of the forest there are open areas with cultivated fields and scrub forests (see Fig. 8–2). About 10 per cent of Dharwar Forest is under cultivation, and about 20 percent consists of teak plantations, some of which have recently been cleared. There are some wild animals such as tigers and jackals, although these are not as abundant as they are at Orcha.

At all three localities langurs are not hunted by man, although they are chased when they enter cultivated fields or men's houses. The langurs at Orcha have little contact with man, and their reaction to an observer's

Fig. 8-3. The langur at Kaukori (adult female). (*Photograph by Y. Sugiyama*)

Fig. 8-4. A Dharwar langur (juvenile female). (*Photograph by Y. Sugiyama*)

approach is flight or concealment in treetops. At Kaukori, the langurs are accustomed to man, although they do not tolerate people coming too close to them unless food is thrown or the people are not paying attention to them. At Dharwar, the reaction of the langurs to a human observer differs from place to place. Where there are frequent contacts between monkeys and man (as at the forest fringe or near villages), the langurs do not run if an observer does not come too close to them, and will come to tolerate his presence after a certain period of repeated contact. Where the langurs have had less contact with man they will run away or hide as soon as an observer approaches.

As for possible predators, there are tigers, panthers, and wild dogs at Orcha, and tigers at Dharwar. According to George Schaller (personal communication), of the 335 tiger feces collected in Central Kanha Park, India, 21, or 6.2 percent, contained langur hair; and of 22 leopard feces collected in the same area, 6, or 27 percent, contained langur hair.

The rhesus macaque lives in the same area as the langur at Orcha and Kaukori, and in the same areas as the bonnet macaque at Dharwar. The ranges of groups of the two species, the langur and the macaque, overlap somewhat at Orcha and Kaukori, and almost completely at Dharwar. At all three localities, the relations between the langurs and the macaques are peaceful, and groups of the two species can mix freely without threat or aggressive behavior, although their requirements (such as food or sleeping trees) sometimes partly overlap.

Usually langurs and macaques do not pay much attention to each other, even when feeding on the same trees, although two rhesus macaques were observed living in the langur troop at Kaukori, and at Dharwar langur juveniles were seen playing with juveniles of the bonnet macaque.

Population Density

At Orcha the average population density of langurs may be calculated from average troop and range sizes to more than 16 per square mile. Kaukori apparently has the lowest population density of all three localities, as the Kaukori troop of 54 langurs was the only langur troop in that area, and was recorded with an area of approximately 8 square miles. Including 3 nontroop males, the population density of the langurs around Kaukori is calculated as about 7 langurs per square mile. The average population density in Jay's study areas (665 langurs in 29 groups), is given as at least 12 individuals per square mile (DeVore 1963a).

At Dharwar, however, the langur population density, calculated from repeated counts of the troops observed at roadsides on the same section of a road, is about 43 individuals per square mile in the open area and about 220 individuals per square mile in the forest (Sugiyama 1964). The part of the forest in which we made intensive and continuous observations had a population density of 349 langurs per square mile, with 111 langurs (7 troops and one male group) living in about 0.3 square mile. Some of the forest is not used by langurs because it has recently been disturbed by humans, so the real density of the area may be between 220 and 349 langurs per square mile. It is at least 13 times as high as that at Orcha, and much higher than that at Kaukori (Sugiyama *et al.* 1965).

Group Structure

At all three localities langurs were observed living in both bisexual and unisexual troops. The size of a bisexual troop varies from 5 to 50 in the forest area of Orcha and the surrounding hills in Bastar District, with the average being from 18 to 25. At Kaukori the troop size is 54, and in the dry central regions it is from 13 to 120, with the average from 25 to 30. Troop size at Dharwar ranges from 6 to 32, with the average being about 15 or 16.

In Jay's study area more than 1000 langurs were counted in 39 troops; at Dharwar about the same number were counted in 63 troops. Troop size at Dharwar tends to be smaller in the forest than in the open areas (Sugiyama 1964).

A total of 53 adult males were observed living outside the troop in Jay's study area. They were observed either living alone or in male groups of from 2 to 10, with the average size from 4 to 5 (Jay 1965*b*). At Dharwar about 120 adult, subadult, and juvenile males were observed living outside the troop. They were observed in male groups of from 2 to 59 langurs, with the average from 11 to 18. Many groups, including the largest, contained juvenile males as young as one year. Size and membership of male groups often changed; a large group tends to split into two or more smaller groups of various sizes and age combinations.

At Orcha and in the surrounding hills, troops with more than 2 full-adult males seem to be more frequent than troops with only 1 adult male. A troop larger than 20 usually has more than 2 adult males (Jay, personal communication). The Kaukori troop has 6 adult males, and in a dry central region a troop with more than 2 adult males appears in higher frequency than at Dharwar, where the predominant pattern of troop structure is the one-male troop. Of 63 troops counted, 46 (73 percent) had only 1 adult male. In those troops with more than 1 adult male, the number of adult males varied from 2 to 7; it is suspected, however, that some of these troops were in the process of social change when observed, and that the presence of more than 2 males in the troop was only temporary. Not all these multi-male troops were observed later (at the time of rechecking); instead, one-male troops were seen in the same troop ranges. However, in 2 troops that were studied intensively the subadult males that had been immature when the study started became fully adult toward the end of the observation period; thus each of these troops came to have two adult males.

Compositions of the Kaukori troop (three Orcha troops, and six Dharwar troops) are shown in Table 8–1. Females over four years of age and males over six are counted as adult. It was chiefly with these troops that intensive observations on social behavior were made. On an average, there were between 1.5 and 2 adult females for each adult male in the bisexual troop in Jay's study area, and from 4 to 5 adult females for each adult male in the troop at Dharwar. At Dharwar the ratio of adult females to adult males, including nontroop males, is about 3 to 1.

TABLE 8–1   COMPOSITIONS OF THE TROOPS MOST INTENSIVELY
STUDIED AT EACH LOCALITY

Troop Name	Adult		Subadult		Juvenile		Infant	Total
	Male	Female	Male	Female	Male	Female		
Kaukori	6	19	2	3	5	5	14	54
West Orcha	3	5	—	1	2	2	6	18
North Orcha	6	9	1	2	—	5	5	28
East Orcha	2	4	—	1	—	—	3	10
Dharwar No. 1	1	7	2	8	2	3	4	27
Dharwar No. 2	1	7	—	4	—	5	6	23
Dharwar No. 3	1	6	—	1	3	3	—	15
Dharwar No. 4	1	8	—	1	—	—	6	16
Dharwar No. 5	1	8	2	2	5	5	—	23
Dharwar No. 30	1	9	1	—	6	3	5	25

Food and Water

In its food habits the common Indian langur is highly adaptive and shows marked differences from place to place.

At Dharwar, there is a tendency to utilize as stable food sources the common or dominant plant species of the dry deciduous forest, such as *Zizyphus rugosa, Zizyphus xylopyra, Phyllanthus emblica, Cassia auriculata,* and the like. If the common plant species of the area are well utilized at each locality, there can be a variation in langur food habits corresponding to the wide range of vegetation of the langur's habitat areas.

For Orcha troops the forest supplies 99 percent of the food. Crops constitute 90 percent of the Kaukori troop's food source, whereas at Dharwar Forest they comprise 0 to 20 percent of the langurs' food.

Fig. 8–5. The forest at Orcha. (*Photograph by Y. Sugiyama*)

Fig. 8–6. The open land near Raipur, Central India. (*Photograph by Y. Sugiyama*)

Leaves are the main diet of the langurs in all localities, but when leaves are not sufficient, langurs also eat flowers, buds, bark, and fruit. At Dharwar, in the dry season when few leaves are left, they can live on fruit, buds, and bark.

At Orcha there is a water supply throughout the year. At Kaukori the langurs take advantage of artificial water sources that remain in the dry season. At Dharwar Forest all water sources dry up in summer, and the langurs live without drinking water for four or five months.

At Orcha and Kaukori no animal food was recorded. At Dharwar Forest the langurs were once observed eating small black caterpillars on teak trees, and at other times they were seen eating gall leaves of *Terminalia tomentosa* with insects in them. However, these occasions were rare.

Daily Activities and Troop Range

There seems to be no basic difference in daily activities among the three study areas. Langurs tend to be more active in the morning and toward the evening, and less so in midday.

At Kaukori and Orcha a troop usually moves from one to two miles a day (Jay 1965*b*), whereas at Dharwar a troop usually moves about half that far, or even less.

There is a great difference in troop range between Jay's study area and ours. In Jay's area the home range of a troop varies in size from approximately 0.5 to 2.5 square miles in the forest area, to as large as 5 square miles in the open area, with average sizes of from 1 to 3 square miles. Home range is plotted from continuous tracings of the daily travel of each troop—for example, for 80 consecutive days at Kaukori, and for more than a year at Orcha (Jay 1963*b*, 1965*b*). Size of the home range per troop member averages from 0.033 to 0.176 mile.

To get data on the home ranges of 6 troops at Dharwar, we followed each troop continuously for 43 consecutive days. Later, over a period of 18 months, we checked each troop for several days at intervals of from 2 to 3 months, a total of 73 days for each troop. Other data on home range were collected from another troop by more or less continuous observations for more than a year; the results were similar. At Dharwar the home range of each troop varies from 0.04 to 0.126 square mile in size, with an average of 0.072 square mile. Size of the home range per troop member varies from 0.002 to 0.006, with an average of 0.004 square mile. The home ranges of troops in Jay's study area are from 14 to 41 times as large as those in Dharwar Forest. Average size of the home range for each troop member is from 8 to 41 times as large. The smallest home range of a troop in north India is still 4 times as large as the largest one at Dharwar.

At all three localities there are core areas (Jay 1965*b*) within the home range of each troop that are frequently used, and other parts of the home range that are seldom used. The home ranges of adjoining troops may overlap extensively, but core areas do not.

At Orcha (Jay 1965*b*) there is a definite seasonal use of different parts of the range, and a change of core areas from dry seasons to monsoon seasons. At Dharwar Forest, however, the same parts of the range are equally used, and core areas do not change throughout the year if the troop itself does not change (Sugiyama *et al.* 1965).

At Dharwar each troop defended its core area against neighboring troops, whereas at the other localities they did not.

The male groups at Dharwar seem to have no fixed range, but move over much wider areas than do bisexual troops. At Dharwar the range of a male group usually included the home ranges of several bisexual troops.

At Orcha the langurs may spend approximately 30 to 50 percent of the day on the ground, and at Kaukori as much as 70 to 80 percent, whereas at Dharwar they spend only 20 percent to 40 percent of the day there. At Dharwar they move approximately 10 times faster and more than three times as much on the ground as in the trees.

Birth Season

In central India births are concentrated in April and May, but troops in Bastar district contained newborn infants in most of the months of the year (Jay 1965*b*). At Dharwar we also observed newborn infants in most months, but with higher frequencies between December and April. Births are concentrated in from two to six months in each troop, but the season varies from troop to troop and from year to year, even with the same troop (Sugiyama *et al.* 1965).

After social change occurred at Dharwar sudden and marked increase of sexual activity was always observed. This shows that the sexual behavior of langurs is influenced not only by seasonal factors, but also by social factors.

SOCIAL BEHAVIOR

Maternal Behavior and Infant Development

There seems to be no fundamental difference between Jay's data on maternal behavior and ours. In every troop at Orcha, Kaukori, and Dharwar the passing of black infants between the mothers and other females of the troop was observed. At Dharwar an infant is sometimes kidnapped by a female from another troop.

At Orcha and Kaukori the infant is weaned from the eleventh to the fifteenth month. All social ties are completely severed between the mother and her infant when the infant is about two years old, and its mother gives birth to another infant (Jay 1962 and 1965*b*).

At Dharwar weaning is not yet completed as late as the twentieth month (Sugiyama, in press), and on two occasions two-year-old juveniles were observed suckling side by side with a newborn infant. According to Sugiyama (Sugiyama, in press) the tie remaining between the female juvenile and her mother is still strong when she is two years old, but is severed before the juvenile is three.

At Orcha and Kaukori the differences in behavior between male and female can be observed as early as the third to the fourth month (Jay 1962), but at Dharwar it is only after the sixth month that any sexual difference in behavior can be observed (Sugiyama 1965).

Relations between the Young Male and the Adult Male

At Orcha and Kaukori no behavior was observed to suggest that the social unit for the care of the newborn included the adult male. Adult males are indifferent to a newborn, and are seldom seen near one (Jay 1962, 1965*b*).

At Dharwar it was observed that when a newborn infant was taken by a female from a neighboring troop, it was usually difficult for the mother to get her infant back. When she approached the female holding her infant, she was chased by the leader male and by the females of the troop. In such a case, the leader male of the mother's troop always followed her and threatened or attacked the kidnaper's troop.

When an observer picked up a newborn infant that had fallen from a tree the leader male of the troop, together with the infant's mother, attacked the observer while other troop members paid little attention to it. Also, it was always the leader male that came forward to attack an observer when he showed the troop a black infant from another troop (Sugiyama 1965; Yoshiba, in press). However, this behavior of the leader male might be defense of the members of the troop against external threat, and might have occurred in Jay's study area also under the same conditions (Jay, personal communication). A north Indian langur adult male will defend any individual in the group when that individual is threatened with danger from outside the group. Adult males of the Dharwar troop also seem to be indifferent to a newborn of the troop but they are more often seen close to the young monkeys.

Jay also reports that the male infant has no contact with the adult males until he is approximately ten months old. After that time the infant displays a characteristic approach to adult males of the troop. The infant male runs up to a standing or walking adult male, mounts the adult, and then, as the infant dismounts, the male sits and the infant runs around to face the adult, and the two embrace. At first approaching, touching, mounting, and embracing occur one by one in the infant's developmental stage, and once all of them have been displayed they occur thereafter either as a series or as separate events. One adult male may be mounted and embraced by as many as four infants and juveniles in rapid succession. This approach is displayed by the young male until he is approximately four years old (Jay 1963*b*, 1965*b*).

At Dharwar it was observed that the infant is quite free to approach the adult male of the troop who tolerates and sometimes even plays with him. The infant older than four months follows the leader male when he is making a display jump, or squeals constantly and tries to approach him when he is whooping (Sugiyama 1965; Yoshiba, in press). At Dharwar no juvenile or infant male was observed mounting an adult male in the troop. The squealing approach of the infant and the juvenile male to the adult male was observed only when the adult was display-jumping or whooping. Touching or embracing was also sometimes seen on such occasions. It seems that the relations between the young male and the adult male of the troop at Dharwar are more relaxed and intimate than those of the Orcha and Kaukori troops.

In a male group at Dharwar, however, a characteristic approach was observed on a few occasions between the juvenile males and the adult male. The juvenile approached a moving adult male, mounted its hindquarters, and then embraced him. Embracing alone between the juveniles and the adults in the male group was observed more often.

Harassment of Sexual Behavior

In Jay's study area the consort pair may be harassed by less dominant males who run about the pair and bark, threaten, and slap at the consort male. The aggressive behavior of a harassing male is directed almost exclusively at the consort male, and not at the estrous female. This behavior is displayed by both the adults and subadults of the troop.

At Dharwar, the consort male is not harassed by subadults or by the juvenile males in the ordinary bisexual troop. However, in a new troop formed by three adult males from a male group and adult females from more than two bisexual troops, the copulation between the predominant male and a female was harassed by less dominant males which ran about the pair making loud cries. When the male group temporarily mixes with a bisexual troop, copulation between the troop females and the nontroop males is harassed by males of the all-male group. As many as six adult, subadult, and juvenile nontroop males surround the copulating pair and grunt, squeal, bark, embrace, push, and pull down the mounting male; he then dismounts, threatens, and sometimes chases them away, but as soon as he mounts again they come running back.

However, at Dharwar the adult and subadult females in an ordinary bisexual troop often harass the consort male. They gather round the pair and try to embrace, push, and pull at the hair in the head, chin, or other parts of the body of either the male or female. Consequently, the male is often pulled down from the female or the female pulled away from him, and the copulation is interrupted. Sometimes estrous females harass the consorting pair; nonestrous adults and subadults do also. The same behavior can be observed in a newly formed troop or in a troop that is in the process of social change.

Dominance

Jay (1965*b*) reports that the dominance hierarchy is relatively well defined among adult males in the troop. In the Kaukori troop the status of each of six adult and two subadult males is well defined and constant for long periods of time. The high-status male is able to take positions, food, and estrous females from other males. When he is tense and irritated he is surrounded by a wide area of potential threat or personal space into which another monkey cannot enter without danger of being threatened by him.

According to Jay (1965*b*), the male dominance hierarchy may be determined accurately by observing aggressive and submissive behavior. Subtle gestures indicating dominance include grimacing, staring, biting the air, slapping the ground, bobbing the head, lunging in place, chasing, slapping, biting, wrestling, making a dominance pause, and putting a hand on another monkey, all with or without vocalizations. Gestures displayed by subordinate males are grimacing, avoiding visual contact, turning the head or looking away, turning the back, moving the tongue in and out of the mouth, embracing, walking away, presenting, and running away; these are done either in silence or with grunting or belching.

Jay (1965*b*) also states that adult male dominance is established and maintained with a minimum of aggressive behavior. Subtle pauses and hesitations are predominant in dominance interactions. When a male is relaxed he does not maintain an area of personal space. The number of completed copulations does not always correspond to the dominance rank of the adult male.

Only one major shift in dominance hierarchy was observed in 16 months of observation of the Kaukori troop; the most dominant male changed status with the next dominant (Jay 1965*b*).

At Dharwar we did not observe dominance between adult males in the troop because all the troops on which we made intensive observations were one-male troops. The only dominance interactions we observed were between the subadult males and the adult male of the troop. However, this dominance relation can be observed only when the troop is fighting with another troop, facing a dog, or in a similar state of tension. On such occasions the subadult male may come to the front with the leader of the troop in order to face the enemy. Sometimes antagonistic interactions between the leader and the subadult males can be observed, but more often the subadults and the leader sit close together. The subadults may cooperate with the leader in intertroop fighting; the subadult males may also make display jumpings or whoops with the leader male. Usually, no personal space around the adult male can be observed, and the subadult can often be seen near the adult male. Grooming behavior associated with dominance interactions was not observed, but sometimes subadult males were seen to groom the leader male in more relaxed contexts (Kawamura, personal communication; Yoshiba, in press).

At Dharwar, dominance hierarchy among adult males was observed in the all-male groups. Membership in the male group is not always constant, but relations between the adult males (or between the adult and the subadult males) are peaceful and relaxed, with few antagonistic interactions. Some males have close relationships with other males, whereas others are indifferent to each other. Usually subtle dominance interactions can be observed between them; for example, the dominant male can take favored positions from the others. Threat and other aggressive behavior is rare; mounting, embracing, presenting, or moving away are more common. At Dharwar, animals were never observed moving their tongues in and out of their mouths.

When they mix with females of the bisexual troop, relations among the nontroop males become more antagonistic. The adult males threaten each other by grinding their teeth or bobbing their heads; the juvenile males squeal. Often the males fight each other, and the dominance interactions are more aggressive and unstable. The dominant male can copulate with the female in estrus, displacing the others; but his dominance is not firmly established, and he has to fight repeatedly with the others. As a result of fighting, some of the males leave the area and avoid further interaction.

Jay (1965*b*) states that it is not possible to assign a female to a position in the female dominance hierarchy except within a general level of dominance that includes females of approximate rank. An individual female occupies a rank within a general level; she is dominant over these females in a lower level, and submissive in most situations to the females in the next higher level. Relationships among females within one level are often poorly defined and may vary slightly in short periods of time. The hierarchy of small troops usually presents a cross section of age grades, and tends to be linear with most or all females of unequal status.

The very dominant female is able to take food whenever she wants, and when she is irritated or tense she is often avoided by less dominant females. Nevertheless, the female dominance hierarchy is relatively unstable and poorly defined. Dominance is often a matter of degree, and an adult female that is dominant in one situation may not be in another. Temporary alliances of two or more adult females were observed in dominance interactions (Jay 1965*b*).

Dominance hierarchy among the females seems to be even less clear at Dharwar than in Jay's study area. Levels of dominance were not observed, nor were any dominant females that had precedence over the others in taking food or position. On the contrary, when they fed on wild bamboo shoots all the females and juveniles would gather around the monkey holding a shoot and would reach out and try to tear a piece off; even the one-year-old juvenile was able to pull off a piece from a shoot held by the fully adult female. Another antagonistic interaction was observed around favored spots on a tree; usually neither threat nor aggressive gesture was observed, but one animal merely pushed the other's body aside. In such interactions no particular female seemed to establish dominance over others. When we fed peanuts to two langur troops, the troop members fought and struggled with each other repeatedly. Even the male was often pushed and slapped by adult and subadult females. No precedence of a certain individual over the others in taking the food was observed. Here the relation between age grade and dominance is not clear.

At Dharwar, in ordinary and stable bisexual troops, no alliances of more than two females in dominance or aggressive interaction were observed. However, such alliances were often observed in a new troop formation in which females from different troops gathered to form a new troop with a nontroop male. Usually in this situation the females from the same troop tended to join in alliance against the females from other troops.

Spatial Distribution

At Orcha and Kaukori the troop members sometimes disperse over a wide area, and it takes some time before an observer is sure that the monkeys observed belong to the same troop or that all the members of the troop are observed (Jay, personal communication).

At Dharwar a close distance is maintained between troop members, and the range of the troop's dispersion seldom exceeds 150 feet in diameter.

Jay (1965*b*) also reports that the subadult male, although he has free access to any part of the troop, spends most of the day on the edge of the troop, and is near the adults only when they are resting quietly.

At Dharwar the subadult males are often seen at the center of the troop and near the leader male. There seems to be no spatial differentiation of the position each troop member occupies, with the exception that the leader male is usually observed near the center when the troop is relaxed, and at the edge of the troop when it confronts another troop, a male group, or a possible predator. The position the subadult male occupies in the troop seems to be near that of the adult leader male.

Intergroup Relations

In north and central India langur troops are separated very effectively by their daily routes and patterns of range use. Thus they seldom come together in the forest or in the open fields. At Orcha an effective spacing mechanism that allows troops to determine each other's position is a deep, resonant "whoop" vocalization produced by adult males when a troop is about to move suddenly or for a long distance. When two troops are in the same area they do not threaten each other although the larger troop usually takes precedence, and the smaller troop remains at a distance until the larger one moves away. Members of two troops may eat together in the same trees or drink from the river with no display of aggression. On three occasions two troops were observed to meet and mix together without any aggressive behavior other than the adult males grinding their canines. When several troops use the same areas around water reservoirs their interactions are peaceful (Jay 1963*b*, 1965*b*).

In contrast to this, at Dharwar intertroop encounters are daily affairs. More than once a day (on the average) a troop meets another troop at the overlapping area of the ranges of the two troops. "Whoop" vocalization is used as a display against other troops or against male groups at a distance, and it is also elicited when a troop is suddenly disturbed (as by a passing automobile). Usually display jumps accompany or follow the vocalization. Vocalization is also used as a threat in intertroop encounters at short distances. It does not necessarily function as an intertroop spacing mechanism.

When two troops meet, the leader male of each troop threatens the other troop by grinding his teeth, grimacing, and biting the air. As tension increases, one of the leader males will suddenly rush into the other troop and make a display jump, often chasing a member of the other troop. The leader of the invaded troop will then chase the intruder, which soon returns to his troop. Then the two troops part after exchanging a few more threats. Usually no troop members (with the exception of the leader male) are involved in the intertroop aggression, but sometimes adult and subadult females will fight the leader male or the females of the other troop. The subadult male sometimes cooperates with the leader. When the leader males start to threaten each other, male and female juveniles often run forward squealing, and embrace the juveniles of the other troop.

Usually there is a dominance hierarchy between adjoining troops. The submissive troop tends to avoid meeting the dominant one, or easily retreats from it at the overlapping area of the ranges. However, the submissive troop will defend its core area when the dominant troop approaches it.

Intertroop aggressive encounters seldom develop into severe fights between members of the two troops, but sometimes the leader and the females of one troop will slap and bite those of the other troop, although no animal is usually hurt in such encounters. The most severe intertroop fight ever observed at Dharwar was one between a newly formed troop and Troop V, from which some of the females had shifted to the new troop; these females fought fiercely against the leader and the females of Troop V.

Contacts between three nontroop males and the Kaukori troop were observed. One of the nontroop males attempted to follow the troop on two occasions, each time being repelled by the adult males and one old female of the troop. The fighting that occurred during these contacts was the most severe Jay ever observed among langurs (Jay 1965*b*).

Also at Dharwar, the relation between the bisexual troop and the all-male group is more aggressive than that between bisexual troops. The troop leader gets nervous when he sees an approaching male group; usually he immediately runs to the male group, leaving the other members of the troop behind, although the subadult male of the troop sometimes follows him. The troop leader stops at some distance from the nontroop males and threatens them by grinding his teeth, biting the air, and display jumping accompanied by whoops and belching. After that he rushes to them and chases one of them. Very often the male group runs away when the troop leader approaches, but sometimes they counterattack when the leader runs into the group. The troop leader can be attacked by some of the nontroop males from behind when he turns his back to some while chasing others. A severe biting fight may follow, which often results in serious injury to one side or the other. As a result, many of the nontroop males have scars on their bodies or faces, torn or cut ear lobes, severed upper lips, broken canines, or ripped tails. When defeated, the leader male turns and runs back to his troop, followed by the male group. Nontroop males then enter the troop, and the leader runs farther away, all males of the troop (including one-year-old juveniles) following him. While the leader threatens them from a distance, the nontroop males mix freely with the adult and subadult or juvenile females of the troop. They chase the females, the juveniles squealing all the time. There can be a slapping and biting fight between the nontroop males and the females, but grooming and copulation are also observed between them. The troop leader repeatedly threatens the invading males, and rushes to fight them. Usually the male group will retreat after two to five hours of contact with the troop; the troop leader will then return. Sometimes when the leader is severely wounded he is chased away altogether, and the male group stays with the troop for some time. On several occasions such encounters resulted in permanent social change.

Social Change

In Jay's study area, langur troops were stable and constant throughout the observation period of 18 months. No major change in troop structure was observed (Jay 1965*b*).

At Dharwar, however, during a field study of two years, more than ten major social changes were noted, six of which were directly confirmed by observation. In many other instances we suppose from indirect data that social changes had most likely taken place.

Social changes in Dharwar langur troops were always caused by contact between male groups and bisexual troops. There were changes of troop leaders; three troop leaders were chased out permanently by a group of nontroop males which then fought each other until all but one of them left the troop. There were divisions of troops or new troop formations in which a nontroop male became a leader of a new bisexual troop made up of some of the females of the troop he had attacked; the attacked troop leader remained the leader of the balance of the troop. On one occasion, adult and subadult females from other troops joined the new troop. Sudden and marked increase in sexual activity always followed these changes.

On three occasions of such social change, the new leader of the troop seriously injured all the infants and some of the one-year-old juvenile females. They were attacked and caught from behind while clinging to their mothers' bellies. The mothers escaped without getting hurt and deserted their injured infants, which were not seen the next day (Sugiyama 1965). When the leader male of Troop II was experimentally eliminated, the leader male of an adjoining troop became the new leader, and killed all the infants. This indicates that killing the infant is not necessarily behavior characteristic only of the nontroop male. Infant killing by the new leader was not confirmed in all cases of social change. On one occasion, infants born before the social change were not attacked for as long as the observation continued. On another occasion, in a male group of seven nontroop males, an adult male was seen holding a newborn infant while its mother sat by his side. The infants born *after* the change of the leader male were never attacked by the new leader, although it was certain that they had no genetic relation to him (Sugiyama, in preparation; Yoshiba, in press; Kawamura, unpublished). The motivation of the new leader to attack the infants is not clear; it was observed, however, that a mother that had lost an infant was soon in estrus and copulated with the new leader, whereas a lactating female seldom was sexually active (Sugiyama, in preparation).

We estimate that at Dharwar Forest such social change may occur in a troop with a frequency of once every three to five years. Troops may have only one adult male with females and with neither subadult nor juvenile males, or they may lack a certain age class of both males and females. We presume that such troop composition may be the result of social change, including the killing of the infants by the new leader.

When the male leader of a troop is expelled by nontroop males, all the males of the troop, including one-year-old juveniles, leave the troop. If the bisexual troop divides into two, the young males always go with the leader. On one occasion, without any aggression the leader male and all the other males of a troop were observed to be with the male group that had expelled them from their own troop. It was likely that they joined this male group. At Dharwar, social change may be the most important factor in a troop male's decision to leave the troop, and to become a nontroop male.

Social Organization

As already stated, the one-male troop is a predominant pattern in troop structure at Dharwar, whereas at Kaukori and Orcha each troop has two or more adult males. Fewer adult males are integrated within troops, and more males live outside troops at Dharwar than at Orcha and Kaukori.

We also made brief counts of langur groups in the vicinity of Raipur, central India, where some of Jay's counts were made, and found that nine out of sixteen troops (56 percent) were one-male troops (Sugiyama 1964). If we base our guess only on these figures, they suggest that the one-male troop is rather common in central India. However, these data were collected over 360 miles of roads in three days, and if the Raipur-Bislapur Road (48 miles in length) is considered alone, only three out of nine troops were one-male troops. Therefore, it is possible that differences between the results of Jay's troop counts and ours may be partly due to differences in methods, including the sampling process. However, there is another possibility. If a particular area of limited size is considered, there could be a significant difference in the ratio of the one-male troops to the multi-male troops. Further studies are to be made to clarify these points, but at present it is safe to say that one-male troops are seen far more frequently at Dharwar than at Orcha or Kaukori.

The adult males in the troops at Orcha and Kaukori are taken to have been born into the troop and to have remained continuously in the same troop, rather than to be former nontroop males that have succeeded in entering the troop. This assumption is based on the fact that it is impossible, or at least very difficult, for a nontroop male to enter into the troop. He can do so only by causing a social change, which would most probably result in a one-male troop.

At Dharwar it is more difficult for the males to remain in the same troop because social changes are more frequent. If a troop is stable, and its male infants remain in the troop until they become fully adult, that troop may become a multi-male troop. However, this happens far less frequently at Dharwar than at Orcha or Kaukori.

The stability of a troop may be closely related to the number of nontroop males in an area, and vice versa. The success of the nontroop males in entering a troop depends on their number in relation to the number of adult males already in the troop. The number of nontroop males depends in turn on the frequency of social change that expels the males of the troop causing them to become nontroop males. Males seem to leave the troop more frequently because a social change has occurred, and less frequently out of preference or antagonism between the troop males.

When nontroop males enter the troop after having expelled its leader (either temporarily or permanently) sooner or later all—or all except one—will leave the troop. Often they are chased out, but they also leave the troop even though there is not much aggressive behavior.

In Jay's study area adult and subadult males separate from females during a dominance fight; at this time interaction between the two sexes stops. As soon as fighting ends, normal social interactions are resumed (Jay 1965b). It is significant that the males do not leave the troop, but stay on after a dominance fight; it seems that there are stronger social bonds among the males of the troop than among the nontroop males. The social bond between the troop males and the rest of the troop members is far stronger than between nontroop males and the troop females that temporarily come together.

Dominance hierarchy may function as a social bond in langur groups. At Orcha and Kaukori dominance hierarchy can be seen among the adult males and between the adult and subadult males of the troop, although it is subtle and seldom expressed. Female dominance hierarchy can also be observed, although it is less obvious than that of the males. At Dharwar, dominance hierarchy is clearly seen only among the nontroop males of the male group. Dominance interactions between the adult and the subadult males of the troop are obscured, and the females of the troop seem to have no dominance hierarchy whatsoever.

When the nontroop males mix with the females, antagonism among the males is much stronger than when they are by themselves; and their dominance hierarchy does not seem to regulate such strong antagonism sufficiently to keep them from fighting each other. Among the bisexual troop members, dominance is expressed sometimes by physical attack, and is not always effective enough to prevent actual fighting.

At all localities the adult and the subadult females engage in relaxed mutual grooming. They seem to spend much more time in this way in Jay's study field than in ours. The relations among the females at Dharwar are quite relaxed. Juveniles, infants, and adult and subadult males in the troop are also involved in relaxed grooming.

The troop males have less contact with the infant-ones and seem to pay less attention to them at Orcha or Kaukori than at Dharwar. The relation between the infant-twos or juvenile males and the adult male of the troop is more tense at Orcha and Kaukori, and more relaxed and intimate at

Dharwar. The subadult male has a tenser relation with the adult male and occupies a more marginal position in troop life at Orcha and Kaukori than at Dharwar. At Dharwar the relation between the subadult and the adult male of the troop is more relaxed and more intimate, based on dependency and tolerance carried over from their juvenile stage. At Dharwar it is less likely that the subadult male will leave the troop as a result of antagonism for the adult male, or of his own accord, than it is at other localities. However, it is possible that if a subadult male in the troop at Dharwar remains in the troop until he becomes fully adult, the relation between him and the leader male of the troop will be more tense and antagonistic, and the dominance relation between them will be more clearly defined.

Social learning must also be important as a factor in troop cohesion (Hall, this vol.; Washburn and Hamburg 1965*a*). Differences in troop traditions, processes of socialization, the temperaments and personalities of the mothers or of the adult males in the troops may be reflected through social learning in differences among langur troops in social behavior and social structure. It can be understood that the difference in the socialization process between the adult male brought up in the more stable multi-male troop at Kaukori and the adult male brought up in the one-male troop at Dharwar (or in the all-male group from the early juvenile stage) may be reflected by the difference in their social behavior.

In the Kaukori troop the adult females sometimes break up the play group of infants and juveniles. Such adult interference in play is more frequent in small langur troops with few young members where play groups must include infants and juveniles of unequal size and strength (Jay 1965*b*). As this example shows, patterns of social interactions among the troop members may be directly influenced by the troop size or troop structure, and they may be indirectly influenced by them through social learning.

The relation between the social organization of a local langur population and the need for defense against possible predators is not yet clear. There is a possibility, however, that the higher proportion of one-male troops to multi-male troops and the larger number of nontroop males at Dharwar compared with Orcha may be related to decreased importance of protection from predators as a function of the troop. It is also possible that the higher tension between the young males and the adult males in the Kaukori troop may be related to the greater amount of time they spend on the open ground, as compared with troops at Dharwar.

Comparison and Conclusions

Table 8–2 shows the main differences between Orcha and Kaukori and Dharwar. These three localities differ significantly in natural vegetation, human influence, langur population density, troop size, troop structure,

size of troop range, time spent on the ground, relations between the young
male and the adult male, intertroop relations, stability of the troop, and so
forth.

TABLE 8–2 COMPARISONS OF THREE STUDY AREAS

Characteristics	Orcha	Kaukori	Dharwar
Summer conditions	Moderate	Severe	Severe
Winter conditions	Moderate	Severe	Moderate
Annual rainfall	80 in.; 75% in monsoon	30–50 in.; 70–80% in monsoon	30–50 in.; 90% in monsoon
Natural vegetation	Moist deciduous forest	Dry scrub forest	Dry deciduous forest
Human influence	Very weak	Very strong	Rather strong
Other wild animals	Tiger, leopard, and so forth, abundant	Almost none left	Tiger and so forth, survive in decreased number
Langur population density	7–16 per sq mi	7 per sq mi	220–349 per sq mi
Troop size	22 (average)	54	16 (average)
One-male troop	Less common	—	Common
Nontroop male	Very few	A few	Many
Sex ratio of adult troop members	6 females to a male	3 females to a male	6 females to a male
Home range of a troop	1.5 sq mi Seasonal change of core areas	3 sq mi	0.072 sq mi No seasonal change of core areas
Percent of time on ground per day (approx.)	30–50%	70–80%	20–40%
Weaning age	11–15 months		20 months
Infant male/adult male relations	More tense with less contact and characteristic approach		More relaxed
Juvenile male/adult male relations	More tense with characteristic approach		More relaxed
Subadult male's position in troop social life	Extremely marginal with less contact with the adult male		Near that of the adult male with more contact

TABLE 8–2—*continued*

Characteristics	Orcha Kaukori	Dharwar
Harassment of sexual behavior	By adult and subadult males of the troop	By females of the troop or nontroop males
Male dominance hierarchy	Clearly defined and constant among the adults and subadults of the troop	Not clear between the adult and the subadult of the troop; defined but unstable among nontroop adults
Female dominance hierarchy	Observed but poorly defined	Seldom observed
Intertroop relations	Peaceful and tolerant with less frequent encounters	More aggressive with frequent encounters
Relation between the troop and nontroop males	Very aggressive; nontroop males more easily expelled	Very aggressive, with occasional success of nontroop males in entering the troop
Frequency of major social changes	Low	Very high

However, this does not mean that there are basic differences in the langur's ecology or social behavior pattern in these localities. On the contrary, the differences can be more easily understood as the result of different degrees of emphasis on patterns common to all the localities, as suggested by Jay (1965*b*). Differences in degree of emphasis on certain tendencies or patterns of langur behavior can be caused by differences in natural and social environments, and may alter, in turn, the degree of emphasis on other patterns. Thus, the difference in one aspect of the langurs' ecology and social behavior may be closely related to that in others.

The much higher population density of langurs at Dharwar Forest may be related not only to natural conditions, but also to the effects of human influence, either through the decrease of predators or through the recent destruction of parts of the forest, which has forced some of the langurs to concentrate in a small area of adjoining undisturbed forest. The higher population density may be closely related to the smaller size of home ranges of the troops. The size of the home range is determined partly by the requirements of the troop—by the amount of available food, water sources, desired length of travel, sleeping trees, and so on—and partly by the relation with adjoining troops. At Dharwar the latter factor functions more strongly in limiting the size of troop range. The higher population density is also closely related to the social organization of the local langur population at

Dharwar forest, with a higher proportion of one-male troops and more nontroop males. Such a social organization pattern is related in turn to a higher frequency of major social change and of the particular behavior pattern that ensues.

Infant killing by the new troop leader in the process of a social change is difficult to understand, but it may be related to a stronger emphasis on some of the behavioral tendencies common to all male langurs. The fact that the leader male of a troop came to attack the observer when he showed him a newborn infant from another troop suggests that the adult male or the leader male of a troop can be more aggressive to an infant of another troop than to an infant of his own troop. Therefore, it is possible that the new leader of the troop can be more aggressive to those infants born before he has become the leader than to those born after, recognizing the former as different from the latter. Moreover, the new leader's attack on infants may be connected with his high sexual activity (Washburn and Hamburg, this vol.). The infant is attacked while clinging to its mother's belly. In some troops of Japanese macaques, such as the Takasakiyama or the Koshima troop, the adult male is commonly observed to attack the estrous female in order to establish consort relations with her. Although such behavior is not seen in ordinary langur troops, it is likely that similar behavior may occur in particular situations, such as in social change. The langur male seems to be more aggressive when he is sexually excited. As has been mentioned, stronger antagonism develops among the nontroop males when they are together with females than when they are alone by themselves.

However, at present the correlation between a certain pattern emphasized at one place or in one situation, and other patterns is only guessed at and not clearly defined. The adaptive value of a particular behavior in a certain environment, such as the killing of infants by the new troop leader, is not yet clear.

The differences in the ecology and behavior of the langurs of Jay's study area and of ours are stressed, but there are also variables in behavior between different troops within the same locality. Presently available data are not sufficient to warrant detailed intertroop comparisons of langur social behavior, such as the ones made on Japanese macaques (Frisch, this vol.). It is not clear to what extent the intertroop variabilities of langur behavior are based on the traditions of each troop or on the personality of the important troop members (such as the leader).

To clarify these points, further studies are to be made. Laboratory studies on social learning or on the relations between aggressive behavior and sexual activity may be of great help for this purpose.

9

INDIVIDUAL BEHAVIOR

AND INTERTROOP VARIABILITY

IN JAPANESE MACAQUES

John E. Frisch, S.J.

The aim of this chapter is to examine recent studies on Japanese macaques for information on the nature and potential evolutionary significance of behavioral variability as found between troops of the same primate species. Particular attention will be paid to the role played by individual animals in determining these troop-characteristic items of behavior.

The intensive and prolonged study of the behavior of more than 30 troops of Japanese macaques makes this species of primates one of those whose behavioral variability is presently best known. Variability has been reported in many sectors of behavior: feeding patterns, degree and expression of dominance, social organization, ease with which new food habits are acquired, child care, and so forth. (For a brief review of these intertroop differences, see Frisch 1959, 1963a, and also Kawai 1964.)

The size of wild troops of Japanese monkeys oscillates from 13 to 700 members. Although the social structure of these troops is uniform (regardless of size) Kawai (1964) recognizes three different types of social organization: troops in which the distinction between the central and the peripheral part is very rigid, troops that show no clear separation between these two parts and where class distinctions are correspondingly more blurred, and troops that are intermediate between the two previously mentioned types.

This variability in social organization manifests itself in a number of behavioral items: whether or not the nonleaders among the males are allowed in the central part of the troop, together with the leaders and females, what is the minimum distance between the members of the troop, the frequency of mounting between males, and so forth.

It is apparent that part of the behavior typical of a group can be traced to genetic factors. This is particularly clear for some behavioral items. For instance, during the first three weeks of life the same vocalizations and the same reactions to stimuli were found to occur in two new-born Japanese macaques, one brought up in isolation by a human worker, and the other by its mother. In later development also, the time when each pattern of vocalization appears seems to be identical and therefore presumably genetically determined. Some differences in the timing are seen, however: baby animals raised by their mother emit a characteristic mother-calling sound only several months after birth (when they learn to play by themselves away from the mother or when they stray from her or the troop); man-raised animals, on the other hand, emit this sound from the first day after birth when they are separated from their natural mother, and later when they miss the human foster-mother. Again, the mother-raised monkey emits long and loud sounds of merry excitement at feeding time, while the man-raised monkey emits, at most, a few low grunts (Takeda, personal communication). Moreover, the animal raised apart from its mother may lack a certain group of vocal patterns possessed by the animal raised by its mother (Takeda 1961).

The various expressions of dominance likewise seem to be innate. Asami (1964) observed the development of two infant females raised together, but apart from their group of origin. The rank between the two infants was found to vary during development according to changes in physical strength, corresponding in this case closely to the changes in body weight. The various behavioral items characteristic of dominance in Japanese macaques appeared first in the one, and then in the other individual, as their ranks changed. The same experiment (with the same results) was repeated on two infant males. Incidentally, it may be worthwhile to report that Asami (personal communication) noticed that male infants begin to show more aggressiveness than female infants the sixth month after birth.

Observations on Japanese macaques show also that one must proceed very carefully before deciding that a given item of behavior is innate. Activities as basic as the selection of foods, the use of the cheek pouches, and the feeding by the female of its newborn baby must apparently be learned. Kawai (1960) reports that it took some time for a group transferred from Yakushima Island to Inuyama (Aichiken) to identify with ease the edible plants and fruits of the new environment. The newborn infants showed none of the hesitation and bewilderment of their elders. Kawamura (1965) reports the case of an infant raised together with its mother (apart from other animals) that never made use of its cheek pouches. Later, when it was placed in a cage with another monkey it found hardly anything to eat at first, since the other animal quickly stuffed its cheek pouches with most of the distributed food. It was not long, we are told, until the sight of the other animal's eating behavior taught the infant the use of its own cheeks.

The examples given above illustrate the difficulties that may attend the clarification of the nature of a given behavioral difference. Yet, this clarification is of paramount importance. Natural selection will act quite differently upon a stereotyped innate behavioral pattern and upon a behavioral item that expresses a flexible response susceptible of adjustments to environmental conditions, either physical or social. This will be especially true if environmental changes are relatively rapid.

In this connection, however, it must be pointed out that although the possibility of explaining intertroop differences as adaptations to the respective local environments should not be lightly discarded, no precise correlation has so far been detected between the troop-typical behavioral items and given ecological conditions.

Kawamura (1965) suggests tentatively the possibility of a correlation between the low social tension found in Shodoshima-K troop and its habit of sleeping in a cave. On the other hand, the increase in size of the Takasakiyama troop from 220 to 700 members during the twelve-year period of observation did not affect the basic structure of the troop.

While environmental influences appear to exert at best a very limited influence on the peculiar behavioral pattern of a troop, adoption of a new type of behavior by an individual has often resulted in a durable modification in the pattern of behavior characteristic of the entire group. To this interesting phenomenon, related to the subject of social learning discussed by Hall (this vol.), we shall now pay special attention, for it is thought to be rich in implications for our understanding of hominid origins.

INTRODUCTION OF NEW FOOD HABITS
BY SOME INDIVIDUALS

Itani (1958) has studied and reported in detail how a new feeding habit—in this case, candy-eating—came to be acquired by the wild troop of monkeys in Takasakiyama. From the very beginning of the experiment, more than 50 percent of the one- to three-year-old infants took the offered candies, as against only one female (out of 66) and three males (out of 37). One year later, 92 percent of the infants were eating candies (100 percent of those born that year), as against 50 percent of the females and 32 percent of the males. When this male group is broken down in social classes, the importance of individual contacts for the acquisition of new food habits is clearly shown:

among the young males, for instance, those in closer contact with the juveniles and infants show the highest rate of acquisition (50 percent), whereas those farthest removed from the center of the group, and therefore having fewest contacts with infants and juveniles, show the lowest rate of acquisition (20 percent).

Both the influence of an individual animal in introducing a new food habit in a troop and the importance of individual contacts in the transmission of this food habit are made clear in the case of "wheat-eating acculturation" reported by Yamada (1957). In contrast with the slow spread of the candy-eating habit reported for the Takasakiyama group, wheat-eating spread to an entire group of Minoo Valley (near Osaka) within four hours. This difference in rate of acquisition can reasonably be attributed to the fact that here the habit was introduced by the leader of the troop. Transmission from dominant to subordinate animal occurs more readily than in the opposite direction. Here too, as in Takasakiyama, the greater frequency of individual contacts with the animal introducing the new habit determined the speed of acquisition of this habit: dominant adult females (closer to the leader) acquired the habit first; infants (moving freely through the group) acquired it from their mothers or their playmates; subordinate females (farther removed from the leader) picked up the habit eventually from their infants.

The influence of a particular individual may of course inhibit as well as facilitate the adoption of a new food habit. Kawamura (1965), comparing the slow acquisition of a new food habit in Takagoyama (Chiba-ken) to its quick acceptance in Group A of Minoo Valley, remarks that also in Takagoyama some juveniles and infants, and some peripheral males rapidly started eating the new food. On that occasion, however, they were violently attacked by the leader. This attack probably accounts for the fact that although much of the distributed food (persimmons) was eaten at the beginning of the experiment, *all* individuals suddenly ceased to accept them. It is also noteworthy that monkeys ate the persimmons from trees in farm gardens, but refused to take any fruit offered by man.

INFLUENCE OF AN ANIMAL'S "PERSONALITY"
ON THE BEHAVIOR OF THE TROOP

The last quoted example leads to the consideration of cases in which the behavior of the entire group has been found to be modified by the peculiar attitude of one or some of its members.

The relative frequency of atypical behavior in Japanese macaques has led Japanese workers to talk of the "personality" (Itani 1959) of each individual monkey or of "personal differences" (Miyadi 1964). The apparent existence of such individual patterns of behavior raises a number of questions: to what extent is a given item of behavior unique? What is the importance of this type of behavior in the over-all behavior of an individual? How does it influence the behavior of the group? Is it transmitted to other animals, or to those of the next generation? Inversely, how much free margin does the structure and behavior of the group leave for the development of individually characteristic behavior? Does it allow or even encourage "innovations" by individual animals?

That individually characteristic behavior, especially when it is that of the top-ranking leader, may have an important influence on the behavior of the entire troop has been established by the detailed observations on the changes that occurred in the Takasakiyama troop upon the death of the old leader (Itani *et al.* 1963) The pattern of nomadism was substantially altered, as can be seen from Fig. 9–1. The way in which the troop used the customary feeding ground, which had remained relatively constant during the last four years of the life of the former leader (Jupiter), suddenly changed after his death and the accession to power of Titan, the new leader. Other changes not shown in Fig. 9–1 also occurred, such as lesser aggressiveness of males towards females (Itani *et al.* 1963). It should be remarked, however, that factors other than the "personality" of the new leader may also have been involved: for example, the ever-increasing population and the old age of the new leader.

Although the causal link between the turnover in leadership and these changes in troop behavior is not yet well understood, there is little doubt that the new leadership is to some extent responsible, and that the so-called "personality" of the new leader is also involved.

INFLUENCE ON THE TROOP'S BEHAVIOR
OF INDIVIDUALS OUTSIDE OF THE TROOP

So far, we have considered cases in which some individuals within a troop determined new patterns of behavior in the society of which they were members. There are also instances in which individuals exterior to the troop seriously influenced the behavior of this troop.

A case in point is the second fission that occurred in Troop A in Takasakiyama in 1962. From the summer of 1962 a solitary male began to approach the troop and in Itani's (1963) words, "started recruiting females and young males from the periphery." Little by little, a new troop was formed whose movements became slowly distinct from those of the troop of origin. An autonomous ranking order between the young males was established from the beginning.

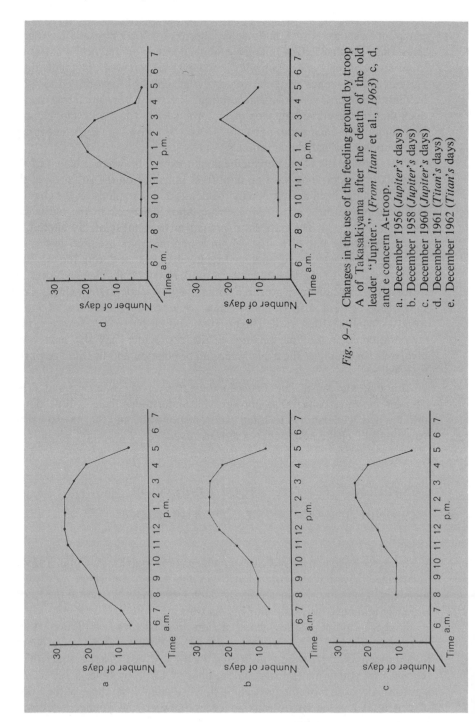

Fig. 9-1. Changes in the use of the feeding ground by troop A of Takasakiyama after the death of the old leader "Jupiter." (*From Itani et al., 1963*) c, d, and e concern A-troop.

a. December 1956 (*Jupiter's days*)
b. December 1958 (*Jupiter's days*)
c. December 1960 (*Jupiter's days*)
d. December 1961 (*Titan's days*)
e. December 1962 (*Titan's days*)

INVENTIVE BEHAVIOR

Particular mention should finally be made of a type of behavior that has so far been observed carefully in only one locality and that illustrates most aptly the role of some individuals in modifying the behavioral pattern of a group.

The monkey colony on Kôshima Island, off the south-eastern coast of Kyûshû, is today perhaps the group that has had the least contact with human beings among those "provisioned." The island is uninhabited, with the exception of a family of fishermen. A feeding station was established near the seashore eleven years ago, but, fortunately, the colony has so far been spared the curiosity of tourists. Until four years ago, the monkeys of Kôshima only rarely entered the sea. Then one day some of them tried swimming, probably in search of sweet potatoes that had been thrown into the sea. Two years later there were only 13 members of the group of 50 (all of them adult) that did not enter the sea; all the others had acquired the habit by imitating the animals that had first started to swim.

About one year after the establishment of the feeding station on the beach, a sixteen-month-old female began to wash the sand from the sweet potatoes by plunging them into a small brook that was running through the beach toward the ocean. This "washing behavior" spread gradually through the group beginning with the younger animals, and replaced the mere rubbing of the potatoes with the hands, which had been customary in this group, as it is in others. After four years, the new habit had spread to one-half the animals, and after nine years to 71 percent. More significantly, the habit is now shared by 80 to 90 percent of all animals born since it was first observed.

A further modification in the process of cleaning the sweet potatoes occurred when some monkeys began washing them in the sea water (Figs. 9–2 and 9–3). Some seemed to perfer this new method to the former one, perhaps, as has been suggested, because of the salty taste of sea water. Even when the food lay scattered on the sand near the brook, some animals took the potatoes all the way to the sea. In so doing, they occasionally walked on their hind legs, as most monkeys do at times, carrying the food in their hands. Later, as the monkeys began to enter the sea more frequently, the posture of walking erect in the water and holding the potatoes in the hands became more and more common. Subsequently, erect bipedal walking became more frequent on land also, and the most agile individuals are reported to walk distances of up to fifty meters.

Perhaps the most striking invention by the troop on Kôshima has to do with the eating of wheat. Picking up the wheat scattered on the beach proved to be rather tiresome work, the more so since sand almost inevitably got mixed with the food. A solution to this problem has been found: the monkeys

Fig. 9–2. Potato-washing behavior on the shore of Koshima Island. (*Photograph by M. Sato*)

Fig. 9–3. Potato washing behavior in a puddle of water in a hole on a rock. (*Photograph by M. Sato*)

carry the wheat to the sea and plunge it into the water; the sand falls to the bottom of the water thus separating from the wheat, making it easy to eat the remaining and purified wheat. The workers of the Japan Monkey Center insist that this method of sifting the sand from the wheat has never been taught or shown to the monkeys. If this is true, we certainly witness here a sort of behavior that it is difficult to call by any other name than "invention."

We want to call direct attention to the way in which a pattern of behavior initiated by an individual animal may spread within a relatively short time to the major part of a group. The examples cited above also allow us to identify the conditions under which these changes in behavioral patterns occurred.

First, the adoption of new habits, as well as the occurrence of inventive behavior, has always followed upon some alteration in the environment and living conditions of the group, resulting here from the provision of food. The new items of behavior can therefore be interpreted as adaptive responses of the group designed to take full advantage of the new ecological conditions.

Second, new items of behavior are seen to have developed from previously present behavioral patterns. Walking bipedally and also swimming are sometimes observed in macaques, although only for short distances. These habits, present occasionally, have been intensified in Kôshima to the point of becoming "habitual." Similarly, cleaning away the dirt from edible objects appears to be a common habit in macaques. It is only a short step from mere rubbing in the hands to rubbing in water (that is, washing). Again, wheat-sifting can be regarded as an extension of the process of "potato-washing" in sea water.

A third characteristic in the inception of new behavior is that the behavior usually appears first in a child or young individual from which it spreads among other young animals, then to their mothers, and finally to the other adult animals. The "plasticity" of behavior found in children, and well illustrated by their play activities seems, therefore, to have an important role in the acquisition by a group of new items of behavior and their adoption by the majority of its members.

The particular case of the Kôshima troop helps us to see that the new items of behavior acquired by a group that make it different from the other troops must be attributed to the combined action of a number of factors: environmental (the change in environment brought about by artificial feeding), historical (what the past behavioral patterns were like), and ontogenetic (the role of the immature individuals in introducing new habits). A factor that has often escaped the attention of the student of behavior in the wild, however, is the different capabilities of given individual animals. Preliminary surveys appear to indicate that there is a broad correlation between inventive behavior and aptitude to solve laboratory-type psychological problems. It is not clear to what extent these individual capabilities have a genetic basis.

CONCLUSION

These observations on the role of individual behavior in modifying the behavioral patterns of a troop should prove of great significance for an understanding of the origins of hominid behavior.

Obviously, the influence of individuals in controlling or modifying the behavioral patterns of their group will play a major role when environmental changes require a rapid adaptation of the group's behavior to new requirements. It would seem that such adaptive modification of the group's behavior is best effected when the influence of some individuals is potentially great, and when these individuals are left enough freedom for departing from traditional patterns of behavior.

Japanese macaques apparently show more such individual and social flexibility than do the langurs (Yoshiba, this vol.). Recent observations by Jane Goodall show such flexibility to be even more characteristic of chimpanzees.

It would seem that, as we reach higher levels of primate evolution, we discern the emergence of the type of capabilities that may have helped the early hominids to meet the challenges offered by the new ecological conditions that attended upon their emergence from nonhominid ancestors.

The ecological shift from forest to savanna, or at least the successful exploitation of the latter environment, is now commonly regarded as one of the main factors in the hominization process. It is important to visualize the behavioral background that would enocurage the type of behavior required by this new ecological adaptation. The latter would seem to call for more than ordinary exploratory tendencies and curiosity, an inclination to experiment with unknown objects and situations—qualities that would enable the dwellers in savannah country to invent appropriate responses to the new challenges offered by the savannah environment. Flexibility in behavior (individual and social) may be essential for allowing these qualities to develop, hence the importance of studying the nature and extent of behavioral variability in both the close and more remote relatives of the first hominids.

10

ECOLOGY AND SOCIAL

VARIABILITY IN *CERCOPITHECUS*

AETHIOPS AND *C. MITIS*[1]

J. S. Gartlan and C. K. Brain

INTRODUCTION

It is only comparatively recently, with the completion of adequate field studies of different primate genera, that the considerable variation in social organization and behavior within the order has become fully apparent. Perhaps the most important single result of this has been the necessity to discard simple, unitary explanations of primate social cohesion and the consequent attempt to fit the observed variability into an evolutionary framework.

This change in emphasis has meant that attention has been directed first to studying a given species in different habitat areas within its geographical range, and second to examining ecological and behavioral differences between closely related species. Definitive answers to these problems can result only from intensive study programs of a topical nature (Washburn and

[1]The fieldwork reported from East Africa was carried out by J. S. Gartlan, and that from Southern Rhodesia and South Africa by C. K. Brain. The small colony of *C. aethiops* was established and observed by Brain. The large colony in the Johannesburg Zoo was observed by M. Lyall-Watson, who contributed a report, acknowledged with thanks, part of which is incorporated into this chapter. G. Jackson's valuable aid in describing the ecology of Chobi and Lolui is also gratefully acknowledged.

Hamburg 1965); the studies reported here are very incomplete, and to that extent must be regarded only as indicators of tendencies rather than as established facts.

TAXONOMY, DISTRIBUTION, AND HABITAT

Cercopithecus monkeys (Guenons) are restricted to Africa and along with about fifteen other species constitute the continent's largest primate genus. Typically, they are monkeys of high rainfall forest, occurring well within the tropics and with only two species showing any marked northward or southward extension of this geographic range. These species are *C. aethiops* and *C. mitis,* both of which extend as far south as Cape Province and north into Ethiopia. All other species are found to the north of the Zambesi and Cunene rivers, and do not penetrate farther south than about 15°S.

The species group *Cercopithecus aethiops* in recent taxonomy contains five subspecies: *C.a. aethiops* L., *C.a. tantalus* Ogilby, *C.a. sabaeus* Scopoli, *C.a. pygerythrus* Cuvier, and *C.a. cynosurus* Scopoli. These common gray or green monkeys of Africa have characteristically black faces and white side whiskers, the color of the fur varying between gray and tawny to greenish gray. The adult males of the last two subspecies also have a patch of reddish brown under the base of the tail, in addition to the normal bright blue of the scrotum. The classification followed here is largely that of Dandelot (1959), with minor modifications. The use of the concept "subspecies" (Tappen 1960) is justified here merely for practical purposes—to impose what must be regarded as essentially an arbitrary boundary on what is in effect a cline.

C. mitis is more restricted, and the geographical range is more fragmented; thus it is easier to justify the use of the subspecies concept on the ground that local differentiation has occurred. In Kenya, for example, *C.m. kolbi* is separated from *C.m. neumanni* by the Rift Valley, and it seems likely that differentiation has occurred since the separation. Most taxonomists now recognize about twenty subspecies of this monkey. *C. mitis* are generally darker in color than *C. aethiops,* with an extensive range of high-pitched twittering vocalizations, long tails, and the long silky fur that is often a characteristic of animals living in rain forests (Fig. 10–1).

The geographic range of *C. aethiops* extends from the highlands of Ethiopia and the semiarid regions of the Sudan to southern South Africa, and from Senegal to Somalia (Fig. 10–2). Starck and Frick (1958) record *C. aethiops* as the most widespread primate of Ethiopia; they observed the species up to a height of 9000 feet, and as far north as 15°N. Monod (1963) records them "north of Khartoum." As it is unlikely that they reach 20°N, the most reasonable estimate in the absence of direct evidence would

Fig. 10–1. A subadult samango carefully examines a seedling plant it has plucked from the ground.

seem to be that the northern limit of distribution is about 17°N. The species is not found in the lowland rain forests of the Congo basin or in those of the west coast, except along water courses.

C. *aethiops* has a much wider environmental tolerance than C. *mitis,* and occurs in a variety of different habitats, but is characteristically an animal of riverine vegetation (Lundholm 1950; Meester *et al.* 1964). The biotic types inhabited include tropical rain forest, lowland evergreen forest, montane evergreen forest, savanna woodland, temperate grassland, thorn forest and scrub, and Mediterranean evergreen vegetation in parts of South Africa having winter rain. Forests are not inhabited homogeneously by C. *aethiops,* the tendency being for them to utilize the fringes, especially where these adjoin grassland. Riverine gallery forest is a highly characteristic habitat, the adaptive significance of which is demonstrated along the Orange River.

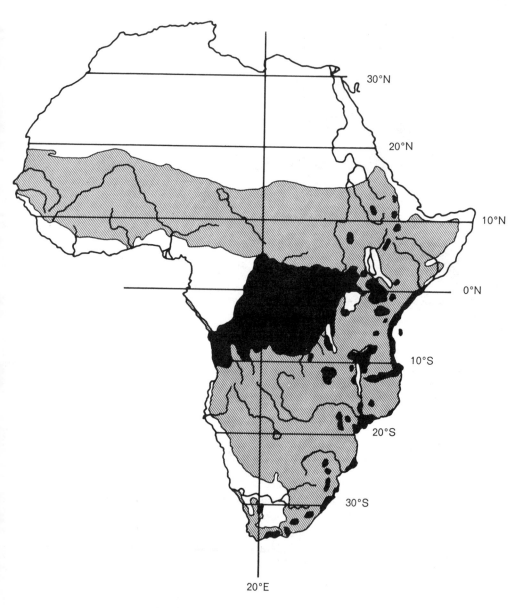

Fig. 10–2.   Distribution of *C. aethiops* (crosshatched) and *C. mitis* (solid blocked). Partly from distribution data and partly estimated from ecological data.

The lower 200 miles of this river flows through country of great aridity and desolation; here the countryside is so impoverished that no monkey could exist, yet by remaining in the narrow strip of riverine vegetation *C. aethiops* extend to the sea.

Habitat variability and atypical or impoverished environments are probably one of the main sources of social variability. Pitman (1954), for example, records *C. aethiops* from papyrus swamp; T. S. Jones (personal communication) has observed them living in mangrove swamps in West Africa. It is clear that such conditions demand the acquisition of particular skills in any population living there, and will alter normal patterns of feeding and movement; they will also almost inevitably affect the social characteristics of the population. However, in order to determine the precise causal factors affecting the social structure, the relationship of the animals to the environment must be carefully worked out, and few studies of primate social organization have established adequate criteria to do this. It may be noted here that because of the more stringent environmental requirements of *C. mitis,* if environmental factors are accepted as causal in social variability, one is less likely to find variable social systems within this species.

The distribution of *C. mitis* is generally discontinuous and coincides with areas of evergreen forest. Relatively few are recorded north of 10°N, and those are in isolated areas of Ethiopia (Starck and Frick 1958). Except for the population in the rain forests of Central West Africa, the species is generally confined to the eastern part of the continent. As Tappen (1960) has remarked, a discontinuous distribution of this kind (Fig. 10–2) implies that the various segments were continuous at a time when climatic conditions were different. Separation of the population has clearly been in effect for some time and subspecies are now described from many of the isolated populations. In East Africa, subspecies have also been described in altitudinal bands on the various mountain ranges, Haddow (1952, 1956).

The typical habitat of *C. mitis* is evergreen forest, but they also inhabit montane and bamboo forests (for example, the Ruwenzori Mountains of Uganda). Although populations may inhabit lowland forest or savanna woodland, it would seem that when this species comes into contact with *C. aethiops* it is generally the latter that succeeds in occupying the habitat.

ADAPTATIONS AND HABITAT VARIABILITY

The *Cercopithecus* monkeys as a genus are mainly arboreal, moving through the forest canopy with ease and seldom descending to the ground. This is largely true of *C. mitis,* although in discontinuous patches of forest they are often seen running rapidly across open ground. *C. aethiops,* however, spend a great deal of time on the ground and moving about between trees—hence one of their popular names, "savanna monkey." Jolly (1964) emphasizes this further when he gives them an "arboreality rating" similar to that of the macaques, indicating the extent of their anatomical specialization for variable habitat conditions. In degree of terrestrial adaptation, they are intermediate between the more arboreal species of the genus (such as *C. mitis)*, and the closely related patas monkey *(Erythrocebus patas)* of the dry savanna country.

Jolly (1964) gives anatomical evidence for this in his comparison of various measures of the three species types, with the following results. The length of the upper and lower arm was found to increase with increasing terrestriality, although the former measure failed to distinguish between *C. aethiops* and *E. patas.* The difference in this respect between *C. aethiops* and the more arboreal species of the genus was demonstrable only at the 5 percent level. In the latter measure, however, *C. aethiops* was not different from the arboreal species, although they differed markedly in this from *E. patas.*

When the length of the foot was compared with the length of the lower leg it was found that the arboreal guenons had significantly higher values for this measure than did *E. patas.* The difference between *C. aethiops* and the arboreal guenons, however, were not significant. Relative total leg length illustrated very clearly the intermediate position of *C. aethiops,* which could not be shown to be significantly different in this respect from either the arboreal guenons or *E. patas;* however, leg length in *E. patas* was significantly greater than that in the arboreal *Cercopithecus* species.

The ratio of lower to upper leg length in *C. aethiops* was found to be significantly smaller than in either *E. patas* or the arboreal guenons; this would tend to suggest that the species is not representative of the primitive stock from which the more arboreal and terrestrial forms have diverged, but rather that this intermediacy reflects a specialization for a habitat that has a degree of variability in the vertical axis. The last measure presumably represents an efficient adaptation for this type of environment.

Therefore, even at this level we have two very different types of specialization, the latter of which seems important in that it appears to represent anatomical generality as an efficient adaptation to a nonuniform habitat. The more common case is to find (as in *C. mitis)* anatomical specialization for a uniform habitat. Much of the remainder of this chapter will be devoted to examining the social results of this particular adaptation and to contrasting it with the direction taken by *C. mitis.*

As has already been pointed out, the genus *Cercopithecus* is in general a forest and arboreal one, and there can be no reasonable doubt that at one time the ancestors of *C. mitis* also lived in forests. Although there is a wealth of fossil cercopithecoid material from the Transvaal Caves, forms likely to be ancestral to *C. aethiops* are strangely lacking (Freedman 1957). This makes it difficult to judge when the transition from forest to savanna life first occurred.

We know now that marked changes in climate characterized the early part of the Pleistocene in Africa. To primates capable of fairly rapid adaptation the situation presented many possibilities, but to those already highly morphologically adapted to one particular ecological niche, the disappearance of that niche, or its further restriction, would almost certainly result in additional fragmentation of the population at best, and extinction at worst. It is evident that anatomical generality of the type evolved by *C. aethiops* would be one of the most advantageous conditions with which to meet the rapidly proliferating savanna.

It should be borne in mind, however, that the environments a savanna-dwelling species might encounter would vary from forestlike conditions to grassland areas in which there would be seasonal aridity and consequent food shortages. Other primates (*Theropithecus gelada, Papio hamadryas,* and *Erythrocebus patas,* for example) do exist in such arid areas. These species have all dealt with the problems in broadly similar fashion (Crook in press; Kummer and Kurt 1963; Hall 1965*a*). They have all developed the one-male group system, this being more economical than a six ratio of 1:1, where there is extreme pressure on food resources; one male can fertilize many females, and this economy is further increased if the male is larger in size and thus useful in group defense (J. H. Crook and J. S. Gartlan, in preparation). Increased sexual dimorphism, however, results in a social system that may be more or less restricted by the anatomical and morphological characteristics of the male. There must also be mechanisms for the exclusion of adult males from groups—mechanisms that are not necessary in more productive habitat areas. In much the same way, a high degree of specialization for an arboreal habitat will also restrict the social variability of the species and will ensure social organization of a particular type (a fairly loose and fluid group with a sex ratio that approximates to unity).

As a species *C. aethiops* has to deal with environments of all types between the extremes of forest and grassland. It lacks the anatomical specializations that to some extent specify the type of social organization of which a species is capable. This anatomical generality and relative lack of sexual dimorphism is a physical adaptation for a wide and variable environment; the major and most important adaptation, however, is the correlated flexible social structure.

C. aethiops and *C. mitis* are a pair of species that would presumably respond differently to adverse climatic change. Present evidence indicates that *C. aethiops* would be able to tolerate a fair amount of climatic dessication—perhaps responding by increased sexual selection with more pronounced male dimorphism and a correlated gradual rigidification of the social system. The geographical range of *C. mitis,* however, would shrink with the shrinkage of the forests to which they are adapted. It seems possible that if one were able to make an exhaustive behavioral and ecological comparison of the species in areas where they occur together it would be possible to elucidate more exactly the basis of *C. aethiops'* adaptability. Some forest and savanna areas provide almost laboratory conditions for a study of this sort.

PARTICULAR STUDIES

Studies of both wild and captive populations of *C. aethiops* were undertaken by the joint authors in East Africa and in Rhodesia (Fig. 10–3), and a small captive group was also studied by the first author at Bristol University. One of the most important findings of these studies was the difference in social behavior between populations of ecologically rich and poor areas, and, perhaps more important, that the behavior of the species under captive conditions seemed to approximate that which would be

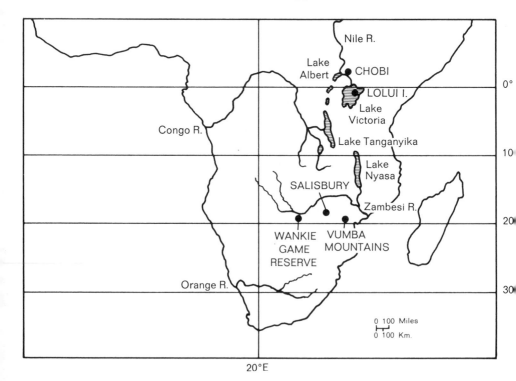

Fig. 10–3. Map of study locations.

expected under extreme ecological impoverishment. An attempt is made here to correlate the behavioral differences with attempts at adaptation to the various ecological circumstances.

These findings raise the important question of the validity of generalizing from cage studies to the species in general without examining the ecological conditions of cage life and comparing this with the complex and delicately balanced situation in the wild. It is not unreasonable to suggest that the transition from wild to cage life involves more adjustment than would a simple transfer of a wild animal between the extremes of ecological conditions to be found within the geographical range of the species concerned. Several generalizations based on evidence from captive studies are examined in the light of evidence from field studies, and frequently accepted assumptions such as the male's being the "nucleus" of wild primate groups are seen to need further field evidence.

Finally, the mechanisms of group integration and the relationship of sexual selection to sexual dimorphism and group dynamics are examined in the light of the evidence from the field studies reported here.

Lolui Island: An Ecologically Rich Area

One study of the ecology and behavior of *C. aethiops* in the wild was carried out on Lolui Island, Lake Victoria (Hall & Gartlan 1965). This is the southernmost island of the Butembe–Bunya group in Busoga County, Uganda. Lolui has an area of about 11 square miles (Fig. 10–4), and was evacuated by the human population in 1908 because of the presence of *Glossina fuscipes* and associated trypanosomiasis epidemics. It has not been permanently resettled to the present day, and is therefore an ideal situation for the study of the indigenous *C. aethiops* population and its relationship to the ecology of the island.

Lolui is a granitic feature, the highest point of which reaches 3950 feet. The present formation of the lake dates from middle-late Pleistocene times when the plateau was partially submerged as a result of the back-tilting of its drainage due to warping (Bishop and Posnansky 1960). The lake level was then reduced to about the present level with the development of the Nile outlet at the new lowest point of the watershed. Archeological evidence (Posnansky, personal communication) suggests a land bridge during the Middle Stone Age (40–10,000 B.C.), as stone tools of nonindigenous materials such as phonolitic lavas and banded shales (probably originating on the Kenya mainland) are found on Lolui. These tools are characteristic of preboatbuilding man, and one must therefore assume land connections at that time. However, as Lake Victoria is one of the shallowest of the East African lakes, fluctuations in level with consequent temporary land bridges always remain a possibility.

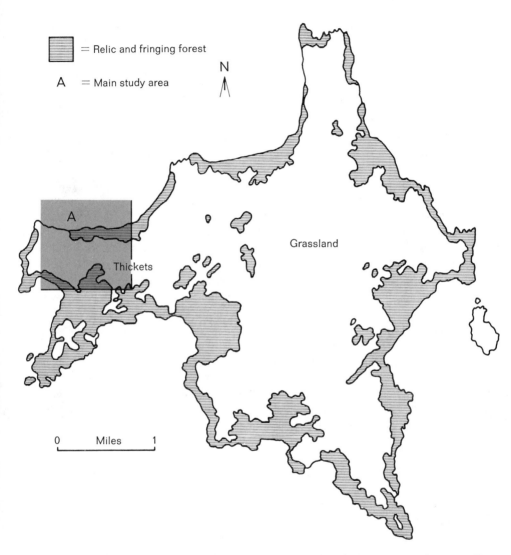

Fig. 10–4. The principal vegetational areas of Lolui Island showing the distribution of forest, thicket, and grassland.

The *C. aethiops* population could therefore have been introduced by man, or on floating logs or papyrus mats, or, conceivably, by swimming if the island remained isolated after the formation of the lake. Haddow (personal communication) records a group of *C. aethiops* swimming in the Kavirondo Gulf area of Lake Victoria; Hall (personal communication) records their diving and swimming in Lake Kariba; and van Lawick (personal communication) has observed them bathing on Lolui Island.

It would appear that the island was fairly isolated culturally until the second half of the second milennium A.D., which would suggest a certain amount of indigenous cultivation, and this is borne out by the archeological evidence. Boundary stones, numerous grinding holes, earth terraces, and the like, all suggest a period of fairly intense agrarian habitation. This resulted in the deforestation of the island except in rocky areas and areas along the coast unsuitable for cultivation to which, presumably, the monkey population was restricted. This state of affairs apparently lasted until the time of evacuation. The coastal margins of the island are still forested (Fig. 10–4), as are the rocky areas; but there has been an encroachment of thicket vegetation from these areas into the grassland. This is ideal *C. aethiops* country (Fig. 10–5).

The relic forest has strong affinities with the moist semideciduous forests of the Mengo mainland on the west shore of the lake; it is characterized by tall forest trees, climbers, and specialized flora of the forest floor. There are numerous climbers in the forest including *Saba florida* and *Uvaria virens* and a well-developed forest-floor flora with several grasses and legumes *(Sansevieria* sp. and *Haemanthus multiflorus)*. Linking the patches of relic forest along much of the shoreline is fringing forest dominated for the most part by *Alchornea cordifolia,* and often including taller trees such as *Antiaris toxicaria, Maesopsis eminii, Canarium schweinfurthii,* and *Anthocleista schweinfurthii.* The vegetation of the thickets and fringing forest is almost all animal dispersed (Jackson & Gartlan 1965).

There are four main grassland types, each characterized by a particular grass that is more or less dominant. These grasses are *Loudetia kagerensis, Andropogon dummeri, Hyparrhenia dissoluta,* and *Eragrostis blepharoglumis. E. blepharoglumis* is a grass of damper, better drained areas, and on Lolui is restricted to the areas surrounding drainage lines. It also occurs at the base of termitaria and around thickets in all parts of the island, suggesting a different microclimate in these restricted areas.

The thickets on Lolui are associated with animal dispersion of fruits and seeds. Careful examination of thicket species has revealed only one species not dispersed in this manner, and that only in thickets close to relic forest areas. The monkeys, being mainly frugivorous on Lolui, are the chief dispersal agents; their feeding habits and preferences are thus responsible for thicket initiation and composition, as will be described later.

Most of the behavioral study on Lolui was carried out on the northwest peninsula of the island (Fig. 10–4). A total of 32 *C. aethiops* groups lived in this area. An analysis of the type and proportion of the vegetation cover in this part of the island made it possible to estimate the probable total of groups supported by the island. Analyses of the sizes of the groups in the peninsula and of a series of 46 groups counted in all parts of the island during the first month were used to estimate the total group population. This estimate was 212, the sizes varying from a minimum of 6 to a maximum of 21 (Fig. 10–6). Assuming this distribution to be valid for the entire

Fig. 10–5. *a*. Part of *C* Group's home range on Lolui Island. Note the thicket growth over the rocks and termitaria.

b. Thicket and grassland contact area. The thicket is composed exclusively of monkey food species.

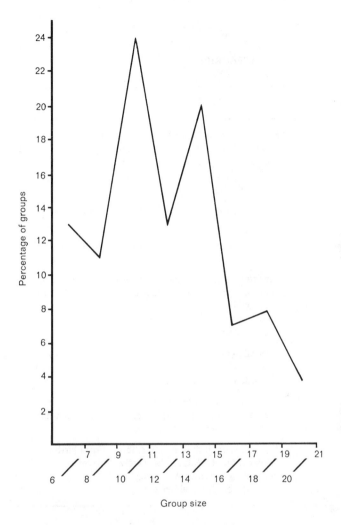

Fig. 10–6. Percentage of groups of given sizes on Lolui Island.

population, the estimate so obtained of the total population size is of 2514 individuals, or about 230 per square mile.

It was possible to count completely 18 of the 46 groups initially surveyed. An analysis of these 18 by age and sex classes showed that the over-all sex ratio of adults and juveniles was nearly 1:1, there being some discrepancy in favor of females in the adult ratios (1:1.4). Immature animals (Table 10–1) account for about 45 percent of the total composition of these groups. The proportion in the remaining 28 groups that it was not possible to count completely was of the same order, giving an

TABLE 10–1 TABLE OF PHYSICAL CHARACTERISTICS: CRITERIA
USED TO DIVIDE THE POPULATION INTO AGE–SEX
CATEGORIES

Category	Definition	Age
Adult male (A♂)	Physically mature and fully grown. Canines fully developed. Scrotum completely descended and bright blue. Adult coloration of perineal region. Voice deep.	Fifth year +
Adult female (A♀)	Physically mature and fully grown. Nipples elongated.	Fourth year +
Subadult female (S♀)	Physically mature and fully grown. Nipples not elongated.	Third year
Juvenile male (J♂)	Physically not fully grown. Scrotum small and purple rather than blue. Voice rather high pitched. Alarm barks given readily and persisting after adult males have ceased calling.	From eighteen months through fourth year
Juvenile female (J♀)	Physically not fully grown. Alarm barks given readily and persisting after adult males have ceased.	From eighteen months through second year
Infant two (I2)	Physically immature. Peer orientated. Found in play groups. Returns rarely to mother. Weaned.	From four or five months to eighteen months
Infant one (I1)	Physically small; dark in color; face and ears pink. Leaves mother rarely. Not weaned fully. A source of interest to adult females.	From birth to four or five months

over-all percentage of 44.3 immature animals. These figures suggest that the maximum group size suitable for the conditions of Lolui is about 21 individuals. Groups that become larger than this, either through births or through animals' joining the group, probably split. It is of interest to note that the modal group size (ten to eleven individuals) is about half the size of the largest groups, which might suggest that after reaching this figure the groups tend to split into two halves. The difference in ratios between adult males and females is not a result of differential predation, as there are no monkey predators on Lolui. It reflects the fact that males are less closely attached to groups and move between them, becoming temporary solitaries.

A typical group of *C. aethiops* on Lolui might consist of eleven individuals;

two adult males, four adult females, and five juveniles and infants. This group will inhabit a vegetation clump or an area in the relic or fringe forest, but will spend a large proportion of time foraging in the grassland. The day range is confined to a territory that is fairly small, but clearly defined and strongly defended.[2]

Chobi: An Ecologically Poor Area

Another but shorter[3] study of a *C. aethiops* population was carried out at Chobi, which is located on the north bank of the Nile 32° 10′ E in an area of savanna woodland characterized by a high density of *Terminalia glaucescens*. The actual banks of the Nile, however, carry a vegetation that is dependent on the presence of the river and that has affinities with the climatically wetter areas of Uganda.

Terminalia glaucescens savanna woodland is the highest vegetation community and is found at varying distances from the Nile, from a few hundred yards to three miles away depending on the degree of damage done by elephant. *T. glaucescens* is very susceptible to elephant damage, and when barked or pushed over does not appear to regenerate to any extent from coppice.

The grass cover is tall and tufted, and the species are those associated with overgrazing. The height of the grass is important in the daily life of the *C. aethiops* population. Nearer the Nile there are considerable stands of tall *Acacia sieberiana* with the same grass cover as the *Terminalia* woodland. On the much broken and eroded banks of the Nile is a relic community that represents a thinned-out riverine vegetation including many of the food species of the monkey and baboon population. It is here that the monkeys generally spend the night, and also some part of the day foraging, usually moving out through the grassland to the *Acacia* and *Terminalia* woodland at some time during the day.

In this relic forest area the trees are often badly damaged and there is colonization by *Securinega virosa* and *Hoslundia opposita* with the spiny climber *Capparis lilacina* and *Ipomoea cairica*. There are some grasses that are closely grazed (such as *Cynodon dactylon* and *Brachiaria decumbens*), and in the less accessible erosion gullies there are dense stands of the reedy *Panicum deustum*.

The variations in the vegetation seen at Chobi are brought about by the grazing pressures of the numerous game animals (Fig. 10–7). The principal diet component of elephants is grass and herbs, but they cause considerable damage to tree species. *Terminalia glaucescens,* a main diet component of

---

[2]More than 1300 hours of direct observation were completed on Lolui.
[3]This study comprised 120 observation hours.

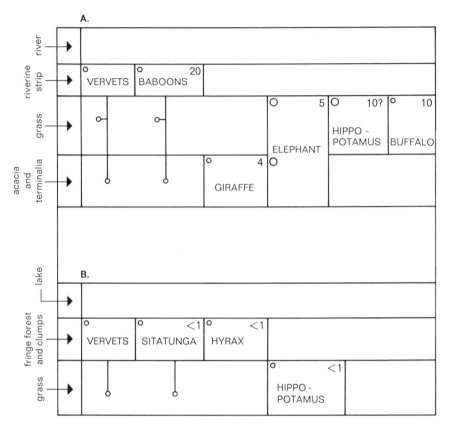

Fig. 10–7.   Ecological relationships in two habitat areas of *C. aethiops:* A. Chobi
and B. Lolui. Horizontal strips represent ecological zones and the
animals that exploit those zones. The circle in the top left of each
rectangle represents the level of exploitation by that particular species
(o = an adequate level of exploitation, O = overexploitation). The
number in the right hand corner of each rectangle represents the
number of individual animals of that particular species that can be
expected to be found feeding within a given *C. aethiops* troop's home
range during seven days.

the monkeys, is very susceptible to elephant damage, and dies when barked;
it is also easily uprooted. Large areas of the Murchison Falls National Park
that were once dominated by this tree are now, to all intents and purposes,
treeless *Hyparrhenia* grassland.

   Combretum guienzii and *C. binderanum* are broken down by the
elephants, and give rise to a regrowth form that can be described as elephant
coppice, which is fairly leafy and survives if not overgrazed.

Several animals other than elephants and including giraffes feed on the coppice regrowth vegetation; with increased feeding pressure the coppice growth is suppressed. This leads to the apparent elimination of tree species in the grassland, but in fact careful transecting in grassland reveals the presence of numerous very suppressed shoots of all major tree species found in *Acacia* and *Terminalia* savanna woodlands.

Hippopotamus (of which there are very many at Chobi) are grazing animals exerting a great pressure on the grasslands near the river and up to a distance of from four to five miles away. The extent and pressure of grazing is largely responsible for the grass communities found at Chobi. Nearest the river there is complete annihilation of grass cover with subsequent sheet erosion. Where any grasses survive it is usually *Cynodon dactylon,* especially near the termitaria. Inland of the eroded areas, grazing pressure has converted the grassland to a tufted low ground cover dominated by *Sporobolus pyramidalis,* which at Chobi extends as far inland as the *Terminalia* savanna woodlands with a gradual merging into grass covers normally associated with this woodland.

The monkeys and baboons feed from several tree and shrub species, as well as on grass. On the Nile banks the relic forest provides several fruiting species, and some of the climbers also provide a source of food. In the savanna woodland *Acacia sieberiana, Gymnosporia senegalensis, Bridelia sclevoneura, Piliostigma thonningi, Annona senegalensis, Securinege virosa, Phyllanthus discoideus,* and *Vitex fischeri* are all potential sources of food. Many of this group are now at a considerable distance from the river across the *Sporobolus pyramidalis* grassland, or they exist as geophytic survivors without fruits. *Acacia sieberiana,* however, still exists close to the river, and the leaves and fruits are a main diet component of both baboons and monkeys.

ECOLOGICAL FACTORS AND THE POPULATION

Lolui and Chobi are two environmental areas supporting populations of *C. aethiops* in very different conditions. Chobi is an impoverished and deteriorating habitat, whereas Lolui is rich and regenerating. The primary result of conditions at Chobi, specifically the removal of trees and the thinning out of grass, is that each monkey group needs much more space for survival than it does on Lolui (Figs. 10–8 and 10–9).

Foods eaten at Chobi that are probably of little nutritive value are papyrus root, acacia gum, and bark. The principal diet components are grass and *Terminalia* and *Acacia* leaves, and there is direct competition with baboons for these, as there is also for the small supply of fruit. The

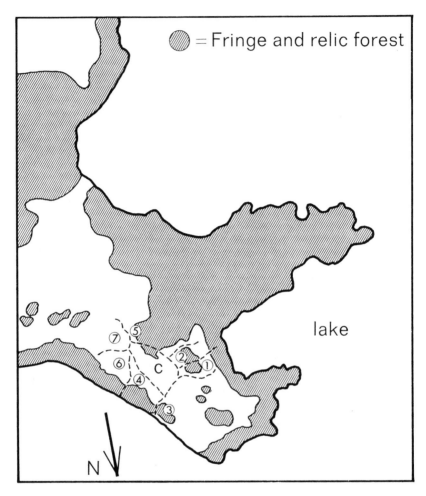

Fig. 10–8.   Northwest corner of Lolui Island showing territory size of eight groups of *C. aethiops*. Compare amount of tree cover with Fig. 10–9.

C. aethiops population of Chobi is noticeably unhealthy when compared with that of Lolui, and the animals seem out of condition; there is also a high frequency of growths and tumors among the population.

At Chobi, groups are very often dispersed in their home ranges, which are much larger than the territories on Lolui. Distances of 500 meters were once observed between members of Group I, and distances of from 200 to 300 meters were common. It is clear that such conditions affect the social cohesion of a group, and in an area such as this where predators are not rare it is most necessary that group unity be maintained. One result of this situation was the development of a signal system; adult animals starting to

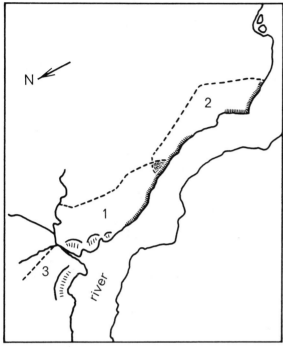

Fig. 10–9. Chobi area showing home range sizes of three *C. aethiops* groups (on same scale as Fig. 10–8). Note lack of tree cover.

$\widehat{\text{\tiny{IIII}}}$ = Erosion areas

$\text{\tiny{IIII}}$ = Riverine strip vegetation

⊛ = Areas of home range overlap

walk through the grass often moved the first few yards with their tails held vertically, an efficient means of locating their position for other members of the group. (In other areas this signal was only observed in agonistic situations, where it nevertheless also acted as a focal point for the group.) Also, the mother-infant bond seemed to be more intense at Chobi, which is perhaps necessary where the group is habitually more dispersed. The "jealous reaction" of infants was more commonly seen there. When the infant saw the mother either begin to groom or to be groomed by another animal, it would stop whatever it was engaged in, run up to the grooming couple, and attempt to suckle the mother. If it was allowed to do so, this usually brought the grooming session to a natural conclusion. Copulation was also once interrupted in this manner by an infant's jumping at a mounted and thrusting male, who then dismounted and moved off without any signs of aggression toward the infant. The long-term results of strong interanimal bonds in an environment such as this (where the group is often physically dispersed) are probably of great adaptive significance.

0   3m.

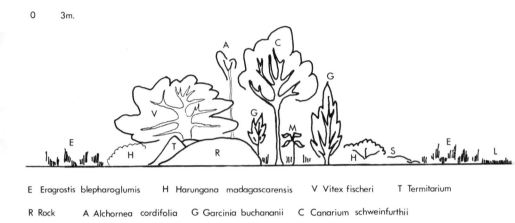

E   Eragrostis blepharoglumis   H Harungana madagascarensis   V Vitex fischeri   T Termitarium

R Rock   A Alchornea cordifolia   G Garcinia buchananii   C Canarium schweinfurthii

S Saba florida   L Loudetia kagarensis   M Maesopsis eminii

Fig. 10–10.   Typical thicket in grassland on Lolui Island showing typical profile of thicket.

The far-reaching results of the interaction between a population and the environment are not unilateral, as is shown by an examination of the relationship of the Lolui population to the ecology of the island. Here the monkey population is expanding its food resources as a result of the reforestation, which is the consequence of its feeding habits. Thickets are often established with rocks and termitaria as foci (Fig. 10–10); these areas provide a more advantageous habitat for the young seedlings than does open grassland with respect to protection from fire, improved drainage, and soil that is brought to the surface through the layer of quartzite sand and gravel covering it. The typical thicket complex is one in which a few tall *Canarium* trees dominate a dense understory of *Garcinia, Vitex,* and *Pachystela brevipes,* with *Harungana madagascariensis* at the margins and *Saba florida* and *Uvaria virens* climbers within.

The monkeys, in their forays into the grassland, use the termitaria and rocks as resting places where they do much grooming, and as lookout spots over the tall grass; much urination and defecation occur here, and the high seed content of the feces (Table 10–2; Fig. 10–10) is left in an environment in which it is most likely to succeed when it germinates. Established thickets are usually joined together by the climber *Saba florida,* which sends out pseudostolons into the grassland.

The island is thus being reforested from the fringing and relic forest toward the center by the action of the monkeys. This process has almost certainly been continuing since the removal of the human population in

TABLE 10–2   ANALYSIS OF MONKEY FAECES FOR MAY 1963
AND APRIL 1964, LOLUI ISLAND.

	May 1963		April 1964	
Seeds	Number	Dry wt (g)	Number	Dry wt (g)
Saba florida	37	49.1	48	58.20
Harungana madagascariensis	63	1.2	18	0.40
Vitex fischeri	30	20.5	3	1.70
Popowia buchananii	20	4.0	—	—
Uvaria virens	8	1.6	1	0.15
Wrinkled pea type	22	1.4	—	—
Chipped seeds	12	0.2	—	—
Residue				
Fibrous matter, plant remains, insect remains,* sand		37.3	—	19.56
Total		115.3		80.01
Ratio (seeds: residue)	1:0.48		1:0.32	

SOURCE: From G. Jackson and J. S. Gartlan (1965).
*Insect remains absent from the 1964 sample.

1908. The expansion of the monkey population has been accompanied therefore by a corresponding increase in food resources that are particularly concentrated. This, taken in conjunction with the rapid increase in the monkey population, has resulted in a highly characteristic organization of the population. The groups have territories that are extremely small when compared with those of mainland groups, and are well defined and strongly defended.

CAPTIVE CONDITIONS AND ENVIRONMENTAL RESTRICTION

The mechanisms of social interaction and the more extreme results of environmental restriction can best be studied under captive conditions. Two studies of captive populations of *C. aethiops* will be considered here; they will subsequently be referred to as the "small" and the "large" groups.

The Small Group

The small group was set up and studied by the second author in Salisbury, Rhodesia (Fig. 10–3). An attempt was made to select individuals of different ages and both sexes in such a way that the final group would be similar to a small natural one. All the monkeys had been born wild and reared in human company from a very early age. Vervet monkeys (a local name for *C. a. pygerythrus*) are shot in large numbers on Rhodesian farms. Thus the infants were obtained when their mothers, to which they were clinging, were killed.

Wild groups usually include some old monkeys of both sexes. Initially, several attempts were made to incorporate fully adult or aged individuals into the small group. These attempts proved unsuccessful, and resulted in very severe fighting. Finally it was accepted that the only way to produce a stable and integrated artificial group was to start with one adult male (Robert) and one adult female (Belinda) who appeared compatible, and then to add a group of juveniles and infants of both sexes. Several years would have to elapse before the age structure of the group would become normal, but at least the final group would be integrated, and thus of value for the behavioral study.

With the exception of Capunk, who came from the Lusaka area of Zambia, all seven monkeys of the small group (Table 10–3) originated in

TABLE 10–3   MEMBERS OF SMALL CAPTIVE GROUP LISTED IN
CURRENT ORDER OF DOMINANCE

Name	Sex	Position in Social Order	Date of Birth
Capunk	M	1	December 1960
Belinda	F	2	November 1958
Chi Chi	F	3	December 1960
Johnny	F	4	Late 1959
Herbert	F	5	Late 1960
Robert	M	6	Late 1958
Mathew	M	unplaced	December 1961

Rhodesia. During the last few years the social order of this group has remained remarkably stable, with only two clearly defined changes occurring. One of these changes involved a group attack on Robert (the oldest and largest male in the group), which was precipitated when he persistently followed Belinda, a behavior that began when she first came into estrus. Similar attacks were also observed in Uganda with the attackers concentrating their bites on the knees and elbows of the victims. Although the wounds sustained were generally of a minor nature and often failed to break the skin, the victim would be cold to the touch and in a state of extreme shock; at this point it would be impossible to revive the animal, and it would die. That this did not occur with Robert is probably a result of the relatively larger cage area in which this group was kept. It is likely that this behavior is pathological, and the result of extreme overcrowding under cage conditions; it is unlikely to occur in nature.

One of the most important observations of primates to have been made in recent years concerns the process of subcultural propagation (Kawamura 1959). This behavior is significant in that it represents a learned adjustment to environmental circumstances, and underlines the extreme importance of the mother-infant relationship in the spreading of adaptive habits. This is especially important in species with a flexible social system that is capable of accommodation to changes in ecological conditions by changes in such aspects of the social system as the sex ratio, the amount of aggression, and the type and frequency of interactions. A secondary consideration concerns the environmental conditions that make such behavior necessary; it may be, for example, that tool-using in a primate population is more an indicator of environmental deficiency than of the "mental capabilities" of the population concerned. Kawamura reported food-washing as one instance of a subculture among the Japanese macaques; it was interesting to note that one monkey of the small group of *C. aethiops,* Chi Chi, also started to wash her food.

The floor of the cage was covered with a thin layer of white sand, and the food that fell from the feeding platform usually became encrusted with it. Most of the monkeys would try to remove the excess sand, particularly from beetroot, by rubbing it with their hands or against the inside of the forearm. Chi Chi, however, was seen to pick up the pieces of beetroot, carry them to the water trough, and then rub them under water. Over a period of three months this became a well-established pattern (Fig. 10–11). She has since then been dipping most of her food into the water before eating it. So far the procedure has not spread to other members of the group, although there have been opportunities for it to do so. Capunk has been observed going up to Chi Chi while she was busy washing food, taking it out of the water, and eating it himself. So far Chi Chi has not bred; when she does, it is possible that the washing behavior will be passed on to her offspring, as it was with the Japanese monkeys.

The Large Group

In 1964 the Transvaal Provincial Administration introduced legislation that made it illegal for private persons to own or keep a primate in captivity. As a result of this legislation the Johannesburg Zoo was inundated with

Fig. 10–11.   Female vervet ("Chi-Chi") washing a piece of beetroot in the water trough to remove sand from its surface.

Papio ursinus and *C. aethiops.* More than 70 *C. aethiops* were accepted, and a large circular aviary was emptied to provide space for them. The cage contained an artificial hollow rock pile 20 feet high that was covered with clusters of branches reaching from the ground to the highest point in the cage. Wooden shelves were placed at strategic points inside and outside the rock cavern. Fifty-seven healthy individuals were simultaneously released into the cage in November 1964 to form a group; they will subsequently be referred to as the "large group."

As the expansion of a population brings about qualitative differences in the organization, so the expansion in size of area occupied by a population can also affect social structure. On the one hand, all attempts to introduce unfamiliar adults into the small group failed, partly owing to the cohesion within the group, and partly owing to the lack of space in which the introductions took place. On the other hand, several adults (males and females) were introduced into the cage occupied by the large group when it had already become established and, in spite of initial aggression, these introductions succeeded. This was mainly because there was sufficient room for the animals to avoid immediate close contact with aggressive residents. They were also protected in some measure by the population cushion of the large group, and were thus able to "lose themselves in the crowd."

Because of the peculiar origin of the 57 *C. aethiops* thrown together to form the large group, there was an abnormal sex ratio. There were only 11 fully adult females and 30 adult males. It was expected that this preponderance of adult males would give rise to much aggression, but there was considerably less fighting than had been expected. This may be attributed in part to the large size of the colony cage, and in part to the fact that all the monkeys were introduced to a strange area at the same time, and none had the opportunity to establish territorial claims prior to the arrival of the others.

TERRITORIAL BEHAVIOR

With the establishment of the large group, scent-marking of the new cage area was observed, confirming the observations made on Lolui. In the caged group several of the adults, both males and females, moved slowly about the unfamiliar area subjecting it to close visual and olfactory scrutiny. These monkeys were seen to rub their cheeks and the angle of the lower jaw against the rocks, branches, and wire in the cage. It is well known that many ungulates possess a preorbital gland whose secretion has a territorial demarcation function, and a scent-marking of territory has been described in Prosimii, but not in any higher primates. Although no gland is visible in *C. aethiops,* it seems likely that the area of skin at the angle of the jaw is glandular in nature. Histological investigations of this possibility are now in progress.

The small, rigidly defined and defended territories of *C. aethiops* on Lolui have previously been described (Jackson & Gartlan 1965) (Fig. 10–8). The scent-marking described for the large group in the Johannesburg Zoo was also observed there, but this seemed to be a lower intensity version of full intensity territory marking, which was done with the chest in a very characteristic posture. This behavior was only observed in places that had previously been determined as the group's territorial boundary on other behavioral grounds. A branch was generally the object marked, although on one occasion a rock was used. The position of the animal doing the marking would be modified according to the type and position of the object. In the rock-marking incident, which was performed by an adult male, the animal stood bipedally with arms spread wide and horizontal to the ground and with the chest close to a rock, which he sniffed very slowly and carefully; his hindquarters were then moved away from the rock by his bending forward and bringing his chest into contact with the rock. The animal then straightened up slowly, rubbing his chest against the rock as he did so. Each rub was followed by a sniff, which was in turn followed by a rub. When branches were marked (and this was observed in both male and female adults) the animal held itself very close to the branch with its arms round it, and alternately sniffed and rubbed. The whole behavior had the appearance of being peculiarly intense, little notice being taken of other animals or noises while it was in progress. Marking sometimes continued for two or three minutes in an unbroken sequence.

Another territorial display observed on Lolui was called "jumping around," and perhaps corresponds to branch-shaking in the Rhesus macaque. It generally occurred in the context of territorial disputes and was always performed by an adult male, although less complete versions were occasionally performed by females. The usual site for this was the crown of the highest tree in the neighborhood of the dispute and within the demonstrator's own territory. The adult male would climb swiftly and noisily to the top of the tree and would then jump around the perimeter of the crown, sometimes making two or three complete circuits; leaves and branches would often be knocked off. The display was often terminated by a spectacular leap from the high canopy to the understory, sometimes a drop of twenty or thirty feet. Occasionally the male, while engaged in this display, would jump on or otherwise disturb an animal of his own group and would then often be chased by the animal concerned (most frequently an adult female).

It is likely that these territorial displays occur only under conditions of a certain amount of ecological stress. In the captive group, probably the newness of the environment and its relatively small size were the functional causes of marking, and on Lolui the exceptionally small size of the territories was probably causal; neither marking nor jumping around was observed as a complete performance at Chobi.

SCENT AND OLFACTION

Scent and olfaction, in addition to their role in territorial display, seem to play a relatively large part in the day-to-day behavior of a *C. aethiops* group. Sniffing of strange objects is often observed, and adult females seem to sniff their infants when they have been away from them, probably as a means of identifying them. The most frequently observed behavior pattern incorporating olfaction, however, is the very common mouth-to-mouth sniffing. The two individuals approach each other cautiously and extend their heads, lips pursed but faces otherwise relaxed, to touch each other on or around the mouth. This is generally a greeting response and is sometimes accompanied by lipsmacking, but on Lolui it has been used to find out what food an animal is eating; on one occasion after sniffing the mouth of an animal eating the flowers of *Saba florida,* a fairly uncommon food, the other individual went straight to a *Saba* plant, picked some flowers, and started to eat. The equivalent gesture in *Papio ursinus* has become incorporated in an elaborate greeting display (Hall 1962*b*).

SOCIAL ORGANIZATION
AND INTRAGROUP RELATIONS

Within any group of *C. aethiops* the social organization will have certain fundamental integrative mechanisms, and will depend also on ecological conditions. Under conditions of extreme crowding, for example, there is an increase in aggression, which results in the group's being less cohesive in some respects, although aggressive acts unite the aggressors in a very striking way. As a result of this increased aggression, some males will probably be driven out or become more or less peripheral. Because there is comparatively little restriction on the direction of aggression in *C. aethiops* and apparently little ritualization of aggression, some system of early warning is needed so that the threatened animal may be aware of impending aggression in order either to defend itself or to flee. This need may account for the development of the white patch of skin around the eyes of *C. aethiops* that makes both the intensity and the direction of the threat very clear; this feature is especially noticeable when the threat face of *C. aethiops* is compared with that of *C. mitis* (Fig. 10–12).

Variations in the strength of threats are associated with variations in the levels of conflicting emotional components. The most aggressive threat is the attack face (Van Hooff 1962) in which the mouth is tightly closed, the eyes wide open, and the eyebrows drawn together in a frown. This often precedes actual physical combat. Animals in which the attack and flee components are more or less evenly balanced show some combination of the "attack face" and the "scared threat face," as described by Van Hooff. When the tendency to flee is predominant and actual flight is prevented (as often happens under captive conditions), the animal concerned may crouch close to the ground with lips retracted into the "grin face" and eyes almost closed. In exceptional circumstances the animal assumes the "fetal position" of complete submission with eyes tightly closed.

Fig. 10–12. *a.* Threat expression of an adult samango (*C. mitis*). There is no differential skin pigmentation to accentuate the eyes.

b. Threat expression of an adult vervet. (*C. aethiops*). Raising of the eyebrows displays areas of white skin around the eyes, in startling contrast to the general blackness of the face.

COMMUNICATION

In a monkey group there is a constant interchange of signals that indicates the emotional state of individual members of the group, their intentions to other members, and their relationship with the environment.

It seems likely that with increasing terrestriality and tightening of group structure there may be an increased reliance on facial rather than on vocal communication. Reliance on facial communication, which would be adaptive in avoiding the attention of potential predators, both necessitates and tends to maintain certain aspects of the social system—primarily its integrity as a unit and its physical closeness, since facial expressions are efficient signals only over short distances. Such reliance also requires the development of "visual aids" such as the white eyepatches and the red-brown bar under the tail, and behavioral signals such as walking with the tail erected. These factors ensure that the social organization of savanna animals will be both qualitatively and quantitatively different from that of arboreal animals. This difference is illustrated by *C. mitis,* which has a varied repertoire of high-pitched vocal signals and relatively immobile facial musculature. *C. aethiops,* as would be expected from its wide environmental tolerance and flexible social structure, seems to be highly variable. Struhsaker (personal communication) records 36 distinct vocal signals from the species at Amboseli, for example, certainly more than occur at Lolui or Chobi, even allowing for individual differences in classification. Completely terrestrial species often have few vocal signals, and what there are seem to be long-range predator warnings, as in *E. patas. T. gelada* is apparently an exception to this (Crook personal communication), although perhaps secondarily so.

There is abundant evidence that primate ancestors were exclusively arboreal, and as the problems of forest life are much the same irrespective of geological time, it seems reasonable to assume that adaptations that are widespread in many different present-day primate groups may also have been characteristic of primate ancestors. One of the basic problems of forest life is that of efficient communication under conditions of low visibility. The solution to this problem, a solution that has been evolved by many present-day primates, has been the development of fairly elaborate high-pitched calls. It seems reasonable to assume that this sort of solution was at some time characteristic of the forest-dwelling ancestors of the *Cercopithecus* genus, and that the partial change to visual communication in *C. aethiops* followed the change of habitat from forest to savanna. It is likely that the emancipation of the vocal signaling system associated with the transfer to communication by visual expression and the correlated group closeness was one of the germinal influences on the formation of protohominid hunting groups where the importance of silent, directional communication that could be used selectively would be of great adaptive significance. In other words, this development makes possible elaborate dyadic communication, as distinct from mass response to emotional calls. The vocal system would be freed from purely "emotional" communication, although still retaining that function; this would open the way to the development of nonemotional language (Lancaster, this vol.).

Social behavior can be seen to be a function of the interaction of the population with the environment. To the extent that both environmental requirements and the patterns comprising the normal behavior repertoire are the results of evolutionary selection, it is clear that changes in one aspect would almost inevitably involve changes in another. For example, aggression that results from crowding at concentrated food sources may be alleviated by long-term changes in the social repertoire, as well as by changes in the environmental requirements of the species, perhaps involving morphological evolution.

The total social pattern of a wild monkey group is a balance of the needs of the individuals and the needs of the group. It is necessary to spend a certain number of hours per day feeding, to make movements of the entire group to a waterhole to drink, and to mobilize certain individuals for the defense of the group. The group is a unit made up of individuals familiar with each other, many of which are born, live, and die within the same social group.

To be removed from such a unit and caged in a very small area with unknown animals, to have restricted and short feeding times, to have no space in which to escape from aggression, and to have no need to explore these limitations must cause extreme social stress. The introduction of another animal into a group kept under such conditions generally results in severe fighting and, not infrequently, in death either from "stress diseases" or from the exacerbation of infections and conditions that in the wild would not be lethal. An indicator of the extreme physiological involvement is the normally bright-blue scrotum of the adult male which may, under captive conditions, turn to a pale putty-white color, a process that can occur in about seven to fourteen days in captive animals.

HYPOTHESES FROM CAPTIVE STUDIES
AND EVIDENCE FROM THE FIELD

Theories of primate social integration frequently have been based on observations made under captive or cage conditions (Gartlan 1964). The conclusions thus reached have generally been that the male is the nucleus of the group, that he is "dominant" and punitive, and that he maintains his females as a unit by means of aggressive acts. These views stem largely from

Zuckerman's (1932) work on *Papio hamadryas,* which has in many details been confirmed by Kummer's recent findings (Kummer and Kurt 1963). However, the social organization of *P. hamadryas* seems to be an adaptation to life in the ecologically rather barren areas of Ethiopia. In other words, the habitat of *P. hamadryas* in the wild comes near to conditions of captivity in its environmental impoverishment. The danger then is in failing to recognize that these patterns express different levels of adaptation to the same type of circumstance, in considering them as normal instead of extreme patterns, and in generalizing to the entire order.

In impoverished areas it is likely that the patterns of social organization of *C. aethiops* would approximate that of *P. hamadryas,* as the peripheral males gradually expanded their feeding ranges leaving a nucleus of adult females, infants, and juveniles with one or two adult males. It is likely that this is also what would happen in captivity if the conditions of captivity permitted males to move away. Since they cannot, they are subjected to aggression with the results often seen under captive conditions—severe wounding or death.

There is some evidence from the field to support hypotheses about the nucleus of social groups and about the age-sex structure under relatively impoverished conditions. The evidence from Lolui points clearly to the fact that there the nucleus of a social group is the infants and juveniles with the adult females; the adult males come and go. In one of the chief groups studied, only one adult male remained with the group throughout the study period, and a total of five adult males was associated with it during that time. It also appeared that most copulations were by males who joined the group. The figures are as follows: A ♂ 1 was with the group throughout the entire study period (April 1963 to May 1964) and was observed to copulate only once, in spite of his being fully adult and apparently in the prime of life. The other two adult males with the group at the beginning of the study were A ♂ 2 and A ♂ 3; A ♂ 2 left in November 1963 to join neighboring Group VII, and was not observed to copulate; nor was A ♂ 3 who left in February 1964. In August 1963 A ♂ 4 joined the group, and copulated eleven times; A ♂ 5 joined in November of the same year, and was observed copulating four times. Such intergroup changes are only likely to be observed when intensive studies of individual groups in which each group member is known are undertaken. This phenomenon has also been recorded by Rowell (personal communication) in baboons, by Schaller (1963) in gorillas, and by Hazama (1964), who records the disappearance of more than 20 leading males from Arashiyama during 1954 to 1956. It is significant that this behavior occurs on Lolui where territorial behavior is so strong, because if there were any limiting factor on interchange of adult males between groups, territorial behavior might be expected to provide it. It took about four months for A ♂ 4 to become fully integrated into the group; before this he would move with the group, but would have very little social interaction with it. Neither he nor A ♂ 5 was subjected to aggression severe enough to cause wounds.

There is also evidence that group size within *C. aethiops* is correlated with ecological conditions, although precise evidence is not yet available. It is significant, however, that north of the equator groups reaching a size of more than 50 animals are rare, whereas south of the equator sizes of up to 100 are not uncommon. R. C. Wingfield (personal communication) gives a range of from 7 to 51 for the Lake Kariba and Victoria Falls area (N = 9), whereas on Lolui (N = 46) the range was from 6 to 21 with a mean of 11. Hall (personal communication) gives a mean of 11, with a range of from 4 to 23 for the Murchison Falls National Park (N = 10). A count of three groups at Chobi by the first author gave the figures 13, 16, and 25.

It seems that large groups (over 50) are restricted to the subspecies *C.a.pygerythrus* and *C.a.cynosurus,* and as these two subspecies are the ones in which there is most dimorphism in male color (no evidence is yet available on differences in size) it is tempting to seek some correlation between the two observations. If this does in fact represent an equilibration towards the one-male group system in extratropical and climatically more variable areas, then one would expect a corresponding difference in sex ratios of these larger groups. There is, however, little information about sex ratios in these more dimorphic subspecies. Wingfield (personal communication) gives the A ♂ to A ♀ ratio of three of his groups, the only ones that he was able to count completely. The figures are 1:7[1], 1:7, and 1:2. On Lolui the ratio approximates unity, and the figures for the three groups counted at Chobi are 1:2, 1:1.5, and 1:1.7. In other words, in this admittedly unsatisfactory sample only one of the Central African groups had a sex ratio as high as 1:2, whereas only one of approximately 50 East African groups had a ratio as low as this. This is consistent with the hypothesis of increased peripheralization of males under conditions of stress.

GROUP INTEGRATIVE MECHANISMS

In spite of the emphasis that has been placed on variability and the mechanisms of dispersal, there are mechanisms that are more or less invariant and that promote group unity. The unity of a group when attacking a common enemy has already been mentioned, and it is under these conditions that group unity is most necessary. Another important integrative mechanism is the comparatively late development of the infant in primates, which tends to make the infant-mother bond strong and enduring. The presence of an infant in a group also has a very strong cohesive influence on adult and juvenile females. They will remain constantly close to it, waiting for their turn to pick it up and handle it, and at the first sign of danger they are

[1]Mean of two counts taken at an interval of 12 months.

fearless in coming to the infant's assistance. All females are attracted by young infants and attempt to get close to them, usually by approaching and grooming the mother, thus gradually working closer to the ventrally clinging infant. The females that are most interested in infants and are most persistent in their attempts to take them from their mothers are adults that have not had infants of their own. These females are frequently clumsy in their handling of the infant, holding it upside down in the ventral position with the head toward their groin, or failing to put it high enough on their chest when carrying it ventrally, and thus having to support it with one arm while walking. Most mothers are unwilling to part with their infants until about the fourth week after birth, but there are large individual differences in this, and some old and experienced mothers allow two- or three-day-old infants to be held by other females. There was no passing of the infant between other females. No interest in infants was ever exhibited by adult or subadult males. On one occasion, however, an adult male allowed three infant-twos to play on him as he lay on his back on a rock. This continued for several minutes but the male did not participate, and eventually moved off. Adult females are not only interested in infants, they are also very protective towards them. On one occasion, for example, the second author was trying to catch an infant in its cage for a routine weight check when for some reason the young monkey became alarmed and let out its distress squeal; this precipitated a simultaneous and fearless attack by all the females in the group. On another occasion an infant suffered an epileptic fit and finally collapsed on the ground; the females grouped around it and prevented anyone from entering the cage until it had recovered. There will usually be some infants in a wild vervet group to exert a constant cohesive effect on the group's females.

Another integrative factor is that of sleeping associations. When the weather is cool, vervets habitually sleep in small clusters with their arms around each other for warmth. In the small caged group the high-ranking monkeys formed one cluster and the subordinates another. Cool or cold nights, which are often encountered in the extremes of *C. aethiops'* geographical range, will consequently serve to accentuate group cohesion.

Another factor that is traditionally supposed to act as a group integrative mechanism is sexual behavior, a hypothesis that stems from Zuckerman (1932). In *C. aethiops,* copulation is not as common as it is in the baboons. There are not the same external signs of estrus in adult females as in *Papio,* and consequently the elaborate social behavior associated with these signs is missing. Presenting, in the sense that it occurs in the baboons, does not occur in *C. aethiops,* although a cryptic form is sometimes observed. There is no evidence of the "consort pair" type of relationship commonly observed in baboons, and there is no succession of males copulating with a single female.

Copulation in *C. aethiops* is rather difficult to observe; the animals are relatively shy and are easily disturbed by external circumstances (for example, alarm barks generally result in copulation attempts being discontinued). It was possible, therefore, to get information of any degree of reliability only from groups that were so well acquainted with the observer that copulation was uninhibited. One such group was one on the north-west peninsula of Lolui. Only 11 complete copulations were observed in this group through the entire study period. There was a distinct birth season on the island, with births occurring between May and November (almost 80 percent of adult females were carrying infant-ones in August). The adaptive significance of this seasonality is not clear, as the onset of the birth season does not appear to coincide with a period of particularly abundant food. Lolui is also just south of the equator, with very little variation in day length throughout the year to act as a synchronizer. If sexual behavior does act as an integrative mechanism, it is certainly a much less potent integrative force than it is with the baboons; it occurs much less frequently and is probably seasonal. Females also do not pass from male to male during estrus.

COMPARISON OF PROBLEMS OF EXISTENCE
IN FOREST AND IN SAVANNA

There is no question that life on the savanna is more hazardous than that in the evergreen forests. Arboreal monkeys that spend their time high up in the forest canopy and do not descend to the ground even to drink, lead very sheltered lives with very little danger from predators. As Haddow (1956) pointed out: "It is remarkable how few predators are known to attack African monkeys in nature, with the exception of ground-haunting species such as the baboons, the great apes, the Grey Monkey, and l'Hoest's Monkey." Haddow was here commenting on the situation in the forests of equatorial Africa, but this statement seems to apply farther south where *C. mitis* also occurs. Here, as farther north, the greatest danger to the arboreal monkey is the Crowned Eagle, *Stephanoetus coronatus*. It may be seen in most forests, flying silently among the tree tops and demonstrating remarkable maneuverability for a bird of its size. Human hunters aside, no predator seems to constitute a serious threat to *C. mitis* in the forest canopy.

The same cannot be said of *C. aethiops* in the woodland savanna where they normally live. Here they fall prey to a great variety of predators. In place of the Crowned Eagle is the Martial, adapted to the relatively open spaces of the savanna. In addition, there are numerous other birds of prey, together with all the normal predators—terrestrial and arboreal, diurnal and noc-turnal. The life of the vervet in the savanna is hazardous, thus necessitating particular survival qualities both in the individual and in the group.

Apart from the question of predation, problems of regular food and water supply are present, especially in the extremes of the geographical range. It is doubtful whether *C. mitis* ever needs to drink at all except in the dryest weather; it obtains moisture instead from the forest food, as well as from the mists and rainstorms that characterize the habitat. Vervets, however, in most parts of their extra tropical range can be seen to drink almost daily to counteract the dryness of their food and atmosphere.

The staple diet of *C. mitis* seems to include a greater proportion of leaves than does that of *C. aethiops*. In Rhodesia, October is the most difficult month for monkeys, being at the end of the dry season and before the rains begin. Even at this time the lot of *C. mitis* is far easier than that of *C. aethiops*. During October in the evergreen forests of Rhodesia's eastern sector, *C. mitis* were seen to feed very largely on the leaves of the large forest tree, *Albizia gummifera*, of which there was an inexhaustible supply. They would strip off handfuls of the small leaflets as they went along. At the same time, in the dry woodlands of Rhodesia's western sector, vervets were eking out a precarious existence on dry Mopane seeds and fruit of the baobab trees (Fig. 10–13). In doing so, a group was seen to travel a distance of 11 miles in one day (Brain, in press). Such circumstances are certainly an incentive to a carnivorous way of life, and vervets eat a greater variety of insects and small mammals than do *C. mitis*. Yet they do not show the same degree of predation that DeVore and Washburn have described in East African baboons (1963).

SOCIAL RESULTS OF SAVANNA LIFE

The most important group adaptation to the problem of savanna life seems to be a general tightening of group organization associated with a change from vocal to visual communication except for alarm purposes. Troop membership clearly protects an individual both through the efficient location of predators and in defense against them. A single monkey is much more likely to be taken unawares by a predator than is a member of a group, hence the adaptive significance of peripheralization; solitary males are more vulnerable to predation, thus easing pressure on food resources. As discussed elsewhere (Brain, in press), either of the two typical alarm calls of the vervet is of very great group significance. The low-intensity version, given at the sight of a distant predator or an unusual object, is a quiet, whispered call made with the lips drawn back. Its effect in alerting other monkeys is enormous, while its quietness is clearly important because it does not readily draw the attention of the predator to the position of the monkeys.

It has not been found possible so far to study the group organization of *C. mitis* in the wild state, although such a study by P. Aldrich-Blake is now in progress in East Africa. Two main difficulties have been encountered: First,

Fig. 10–13.   *a.* Vervet monkey habitat in the western sector of Rhodesia: dry Acacia and Mopane woodland.

b. This photograph, taken on the Vumba Mountains in the eastern districts of Rhodesia, shows a characteristic, discontinuous patch of evergreen forest inhabited by *C. mitis.*

the problem of keeping the group under prolonged observation while it passes along about 50 feet above the ground. Second, the problem of distinguishing males from females; in adult vervets this is not difficult, but with *C. mitis* it is almost impossible.

One of the more interesting objectives for future research would be an elucidation of the type of interactions that occur between *C. aethiops* and *C. mitis* groups. Normally, in large areas of evergreen forest, contact between the two species will be infrequent, but in areas like the eastern districts of Rhodesia forest patches are small and discontinuous (Fig. 10–13) with the result that the ranges of vervets and *C. mitis* frequently overlap. In some of the Rhodesian Vumba forests (Fig. 10–3) exotic grenadilla vines have multiplied and spread into the primary forest; when these are in fruit, vervets move up into the forests to feed. Interactions between troops can be observed at times like this, and preliminary study suggests that when vervets appear the *C. mitis* groups either move away or move upward, feeding perhaps 60 feet from the ground, while the vervets forage lower down. In the same area, wattle plantations frequently adjoin patches of forest and both vervets and *C. mitis* visit them to feed on flowers and perhaps on young leaves. Such areas should prove extremely fruitful for studies on group contact. Normally, however, interspecific contact can be avoided in the forest since there is, in effect, a double-story habitat. *C. mitis* can feed in the canopy while the vervets use the lower levels. Such an arrangement cannot exist in the woodland since the upper canopy is lacking and the two species would be in direct ecological competition. Riparian forests along many of the larger southern African rivers seem to provide the sort of habitat in which *C. mitis* could exist, but it is here that the vervets are particularly well established. Along some of the very largest rivers, however, the forest may be so well developed that both species can occur, and in fact both have been observed in forest on the banks of the Zambesi near the Luangwa confluence (R. W. Rankine, personal communication). Such contact would be exceptional, however, on the larger rivers to the south.

CONCLUSIONS

In southern Africa tolerance to a varied environment was a distinguishing characteristic of primitive man and of some early hominids. It seems possible that the *C. mitis–C. aethiops* comparison may provide an analogy for the two fossil australopithecines, *Australopithecus* and *Paranthropus,* which seem to have occupied respectively very similar ecological niches to the present-day species *C. aethiops* and *C. mitis.* Further research on the two present-day monkey species may therefore provide further hypotheses about the probable course of human evolution.

More directly, however, the main contribution of research of this nature lies in elucidating the relationship between ecological conditions and correlated social structures. Social behavior is deeply rooted in the evolutionary history of the species; it does not exist in a vacuum, but is the means by which species are adapted to the efficient exploitation of particular niches in just the same way as the evolution of physical structures permits this. But in *C. aethiops* we have a species that, in common with several other present-day primates, has evolved a physical structure that enables it to deal efficiently with a variable environment. The evidence is that the anatomical generality that permits this is matched in this species by a flexible social system, the origin of which is presumed to have been the need for efficient exploitation of the proliferating savannas during the Pleistocene. The problems of savanna life are complex, but those species that have met them successfully have become geographically widespread with a relatively high level of social development.

SUMMARY

The field studies of primates, which have increased greatly in number during the last decade or so, have concentrated on many different species rather than on confirming findings of work already completed in the field. As a result of this, very few systematic studies comparing the ecology and social organization of populations of single species in different habitat areas have been attempted. However, in recent years there has been an increasing tendency for different workers to study similar species in different habitat areas, although this has often been the result of chance rather than design. Such studies have revealed an amount of social variability that was perhaps unexpected, since it was assumed that the uniformity observed in captive and caged groups would also hold true for wild groups. These replicated studies have generally been carried out on fairly widespread terrestrial species rather than on arboreal animals; in India this has meant that the macaques and langurs have been studied in different areas, and in Africa the baboons and vervet monkeys. Differences in social organization and behavior among different populations of the same species have been described, and have been found to be greater than differences between species. Perhaps the best example of this type of variability is Jay's description of the common Indian langur as compared with the findings of Sugiyama (1964).

The widespread distribution of *C. aethiops* ensures that it comes into contact with environments and habitats of all types between the extremes of arid grassland and forest conditions. To determine the degree of social flexibility exhibited by the species, it is necessary to study populations in these different areas, and to analyze the relationship of the populations with the environment and the place of the population in the ecosystem.

The discovery of social variability in primarily terrestrial species (such as vervets and macaques) is leading currently to attempts to explain this in evolutionary terms. It must first be remembered, however, that the variability of these terrestrial species may to some extent be an artifact reflecting the lack of knowledge of the social organization of arboreal species. But this lack is not complete, and what evidence there is suggests that the typical structure in forest is a loose and rather small group. For the social structure of primates living in the arid areas around the perimeter of the Sahara, especially Ethiopia and the Sudan, the evidence is clear. Three species are commonly found there: *Papio hamadryas, Theropithecus gelada,* and *Erythrocebus patas.* These species are anatomically specialized, and also have evolved a highly characteristic one-male-group system. Single males are economical in areas where food supplies are seasonally in short supply, they can fertilize several females, and the economy is further increased if the males are dimorphic and useful in group defense.

Anatomical evidence is presented to show that *C. aethiops* is intermediate between the more arboreal species of the *Cercopithecus* genus (such as *C. mitis),* and the closely related patas monkey *(Erythrocebus patas).* This does not indicate a primitively generalized nature from which both the more terrestrial and more arboreal species might have diverged, but is an efficient specialization for life in a variable habitat.

Information from studies of two populations of *C. aethiops* in different habitat areas is presented to show the difference in social structure between the two populations. These differences are then correlated with the different ecological conditions, Chobi being an impoverished and deteriorating habitat and Lolui a rich and regenerating one. It is pointed out that the interaction between a species and the environment is not unilateral; the effects of the bilateral interaction are described for Lolui island, where this interaction is resulting in the progressive reforestation of the island.

Studies of captive groups are then reported, and it is hypothesized that many of the most common and severe behavior patterns exhibited under cage conditions represent attempts by the population to adjust socially to conditions that approximate severe environmental restriction in the wild. It is hypothesized that the fighting commonly observed in *C. aethiops* represents equilibration to the one-male-group system that is appropriate under conditions of environmental impoverishment. The a priori assumptions of primate social uniformity can be seen to have their origins in this equilibration process. Many captive and laboratory primates are the widespread and presumably socially labile species that would be expected to equilibrate under cage conditions.

Behavior patterns (such as scent-marking of cages) are described for captive groups, and tend to confirm the hypothesis that captive conditions approximate severe ecological stress. Information about the sex ratios of groups living under different environmental conditions is clearly important if the hypothesis of equilibration under environmental impoverishment is to be upheld. Although only scanty evidence is available on this matter, there is a suggestion that in East Africa the ratio usually approximates unity, whereas farther south in Rhodesia and South Africa where dry seasons are relatively severe the sex ratio may be as high as seven or eight females to a single male. The subspecies in these areas are also more dimorphic than they are farther north. The mechanism by which this equilibration is achieved is considered to be the relatively loose attachment of adult males to the social group, the nucleus of which is considered to be adult females, their infants, and juveniles. Evidence of the interchange of adult males between groups is increasing, and it is possible that it is a fairly widespread and general phenomenon. Even on Lolui, where territorial behavior was very strong, changes of adult males among groups was not an uncommon occurrence. It is assumed that the males that become solitaries through peripheralization by extending their feeding ranges during the severe dry seasons or by being driven out by other members of the group are more subject to predation than are animals living in social groups. This will contribute toward easing the pressure on scarce food resources.

It is considered that the evolution of these particular social and physical characters began during the Pleistocene and was a response to the particular ecological conditions of that time, permitting the efficient exploitation of the rapidly proliferating savannas. The social results of savanna life are thought to have been fundamental and to have been evolved (as the most efficient means of exploiting this wide and variable habitat) as a parallel solution by many of the savanna species. These social results are thought to have been important in the evolution of prehominid hunting groups and in the development of human language. Some of these social mechanisms are exhibited by present-day savanna species such as *C. aethiops,* and the study of such species may well throw light on the social evolution of early man.

11

TWO VARIATIONS IN

THE SOCIAL ORGANIZATION

OF BABOONS[1]

Hans Kummer

On the basis of morphological characters, Jolly (1963) divides the genus *Papio* into two species groups: the *hamadryas* group, including only one species, and the *cynocephalus* group, which includes all the other forms. The social organizations of both groups have recently been studied in the field. That of the cynocephalus has been studied by Hall (1962a, 1962b, 1963c) in South Africa, and by DeVore (1962) and Altmann (unpublished manuscript) in Kenya. The social organizations of the hamadryas have been studied by Kummer and Kurt (1963) in Ethiopia. From the available descriptions (Hall and DeVore 1965; Kummer, in press) it appears that the two species groups arrive at two essentially different types of social organization by a differential use of a very similar set of social behavior patterns. This chapter attempts a first grasp of this difference as a program for future research, rather than as a presentation of conclusive statements.

The cynocephalus baboons studied so far live in highly stable groups averaging from 40 to 80 individuals. Groups keep apart from each other on their daily ranges, and only rarely does an individual leave his group and enter another. Within the groups, the individual relations of the adults are centered around the dominance order of the adult males who consort with the

[1]The field of study on hamadryas was supported by a grant of the Swiss National Science Foundation, and by contributions of the G. and A. Claraz-Foundation and the Schweizerische Naturforschende Gesellshaft. I wish to thank Dr. Stuart Altmann and Dr. Irven DeVore for their specifications on the behavior of cynocephalus baboons.

females for a few hours or days during their estrus. Each male's success in establishing such temporary consort pairs with fully adult females during their periods of maximum turgescence is determined by his fighting ability and, in some groups, by his capacity to enlist the support of other males. These abilities—to fight and to gain support—together determine the male's actual place in the dominance order, and thus his success in breeding.

The hamadryas organization as observed in the western quarter of the species area differs markedly from this pattern. Stable, detached groups of 40 to 80 individuals are not obvious in these hamadryas populations. Instead, one finds inconstant troops of approximately 130 individuals that sleep together on the same sleeping cliff. During the day, any number of a troop's members may leave the main body and spend the following night with another troop on a neighboring cliff. The second obvious difference is the fragmentation of each troop into small "one-male units," each of which consists of an adult male, several females, and their young offspring. These family-like units (which are even formed in zoo colonies) are highly stable for months, their members remaining together at all times, even within the troop. Apart from these two main differences in organization there are morphological differences between cynocephalus and hamadryas. In particular, sexual dimorphism is more pronounced in hamadryas. It includes not only body size and dentition, as in the cynocephalus baboons, but also a large mane of conspicuously lighter color in the male (Figs. 11–1 and 11–2).

The wide distribution of the cynocephalus type of organization in the genera related to *Papio,* as well as among the New World monkeys, suggests that this type of organization is the older pattern from which the hamadryas type branched off as a specialization to the dryest part of the area inhabited by baboons (Figs. 11–3 and 11–4). According to their characteristic habitats, the cynocephalus and hamadryas are also referred to as savanna baboons and desert baboons, respectively.

THE FRAGMENTATION OF THE HAMADRYAS

TROOP INTO ONE-MALE UNITS

In the one-male unit, the adult male leads his one to four females in and with the troop. Only rarely does the unit move away from all the other troop members. Alone and within the troop, the male herds the females together by frequently looking or staring at them. The females usually follow him closely, but once every few days a female may lag behind or move away 20 or more feet. The male then reinforces her following response by attacking her with a bite in the nape of her neck (Kummer and Kurt 1963, Fig. 11–5). This

Fig. 11–1. An adult Kenyan male grooms an estrous female during their temporary consort relation. (*Photograph by Irven DeVore*)

neck bite is occasionally observed in cynocephalus baboon, but here it is only one of several kinds of bites; it is not correlated with the female's straying away from the male, and the female does not respond to the bite by following the aggressor. Cynocephalus males do not herd the females in their group.

Although two or even many more one-male units of the hamadryas may rest and walk close to each other day and night, the degree of their behavioral isolation from each other is striking. Even two units that separate from the troop together and walk side by side for days avoid mixing. The average frequency of social contacts across units is less than 10 percent of the contact frequency within each unit. No fully adult hamadryas baboon was ever seen to groom or copulate with an adult of another unit. Communications between the units are exchanged mainly by their adult male leaders.

Whereas the females within the cynocephalus group communicate with each other and show some evidence of a dominance order, the contacts of a hamadryas female are virtually restricted to the other members of her unit. Only occasionally does she inspect a young infant in a neighboring unit,

Fig. 11–2. Hamadryas male herds his unit. (*Photograph by Hans Kummer*)

threaten a juvenile when passing by, or groom a female juvenile of another unit for a few seconds. In one day, a female has an average of seven such contacts with baboons outside her unit, most of them very short and of low intensity. Fights among females of different units do not occur, and the few female fights within the unit are fought by enlisting the support of the male. This statement applies to cynocephalus females as well, if "unit" is replaced by "group." Thus, the adult hamadryas female is actually not a member of her troop, but only of her unit, which she follows regardless of the troop (Figs. 11–1 and 11–5).

The fragmentation of the troop into one-male units is fully realized only among the adult hamadryas baboons. Infants, juveniles, and subadult males are not herded by the adult males and may make contacts throughout the troop. Their grouping patterns show some characteristics of the cynocephalus organization. Like young savanna baboons, they assemble in play groups where infants and juveniles of different one-male units meet. Additional cynocephalus characteristics appear in the sexual relations among the juveniles, relations that resemble the "consort pairs" formed by adult cynocephalus baboons. The adult hamadryas male—like the cynoce-

Fig. 11–3. Kenyan baboons foraging among ungulates near a grove of large sleeping-trees. (*Photograph by Irven DeVore*)

phalus male—shows little interest in juvenile females even of his own unit if it includes adult females. Thus, the juvenile hamadryas female is allowed to leave her leader and to consort with a juvenile male whom she seeks out for copulations, but she remains only for a few minutes at a time and rejoins her unit between copulations (Fig. 11–6). As subadults, the hamadryas baboons no longer engage in temporary consort relations. By this time the female is no longer allowed to leave her male. The male subadult loosely follows a certain one-male unit, and he is sometimes groomed by a female member; but he rarely has a chance to copulate because of the group leader's intolerance.

An immediate consequence of the vertical fragmentation of the hamadryas troop is the restrictions it imposes on some lateral grouping tendencies of the adults in the troop. The restrictions on cross-unit consorting and female fighting have already been mentioned. Another limitation is that placed on grooming between adults. Whereas adult cynocephalus males very rarely groom one another (Altmann, personal communication), adult hamadryas males before and past the age of leading a unit tend to pair up and to pass most of their social time in grooming each other. This habit still survives into the "initial," immature stage of the one-male unit, but it is completely abandoned once the male is a leader of adult females (Fig. 11–7). The

Fig. 11–4. A sleeping-cliff of hamadryas baboons surrounded by a thin acacia brush. (*Photograph by Hans Kummer*)

most frequent subgroupings found in cynocephalus baboons are grooming clusters of females (Fig. 11–8), mothers with young infants often being the centers of attraction. In the hamadryas organization this tendency, although apparent, is thwarted by the intolerance of males to the spatial mixing of their units (Fig. 11–2). Only when a hamadryas female finds herself close to a mother in a neighboring unit does she repeatedly leave her male for a few seconds to inspect the infant; grooming between adult females of different units was never seen. Only the juvenile females, who may temporarily leave their leaders, will visit and groom adult females of other units.

DIFFERENCES IN THE SOCIALIZATION OF FEMALES

The troop members most affected by the hamadryas organization are all females past the juvenile age. The earliest observed difference between the social surroundings of cynocephalus and hamadryas females is in the degree of the juvenile's participation in play groups. The hamadryas play group is made up mainly of males; for instance, a count of nine such groups with

Fig. 11–5. After having entered his sleeping place, an adult hamadryas male stares at a lagging female of his unit while the other female hurries to groom him. The cynocephalus female will soon be free to leave and to contact other members, while the hamadryas female is permanently fenced in by the herding activity of her male. (*Photograph by Hans Kummer*)

infants and juveniles up to the age of three years resulted in a total of 49 males versus 6 females. Without more data on the composition of play groups in cynocephalus, only one difference is certain: Whereas cynocephalus females engage in group play up to the age of three, hamadryas females older than one year rarely appear in the play groups (that is, they appear only if such groups are formed around a subadult or single adult male). It would be premature to state that there is a causal relationship between the hamadryas females' limited social experience in play groups and their failure to develop into independent and freely moving troop members, but the possible concurrence of the two differences should be noted.

About two-thirds of all hamadryas females from one to three years of age are already consorts of an adult male in a one-male unit. Even by one year of age, many a hamadryas female has become the first consort of a young but fully grown adult male who forces her into consortship by attacking her persistently until she commences to follow. The one-year-old female is not yet sexually mature, and no copulations occur in these "initial" units at first. The duration of the nonsexual phase, however, is brief because in many hamadryas females the first sexual swelling is shown already at the age of two years, which is about one and one-half years earlier than in cynocephalus

Fig. 11–6. A one-year-old hamadryas male grooms an estrous
three-year-old female between
copulations in a temporary consort relation. This grouping tendency is common to both species,
but troop fragmentation in hamadryas suppresses it among the
adults. (*Photograph by Hans
Kummer*)

Fig. 11–7. Two young hamadryas adults, both leaders of initial units, groom each other while
their juvenile females play a few
yards away. Both types of cross-
unit contacts survive only into
the first months of the units' existence. (*Photograph by Hans
Kummer*)

Fig. 11–8. In Kenya three adult females come together in a temporary grooming cluster. (*Photograph by Irven DeVore*)

females. Whether there is a causal connection between this apparently premature consort role and the early appearance of the sexual swelling could easily be tested in the laboratory. By the age of two years, the juvenile females in the initial unit copulate with their males, but none of the females was ever observed with an infant. Although the swelling of these half-grown females is of normal appearance, they are still not capable of bearing young, whatever the physiological reason.

Typical of the hamadryas organization is the high frequency of child care behavior by subadult and young adult males. In the initial unit, the one-year-old female flees into her male's arms when another baboon threatens her, and rides on his back across passages in the sleeping cliff, which she cannot negotiate because of her small size (Figs. 11–9 and 11–10). Such "maternal" tendencies are already prominent in the young subadult hamadryas males. They sometimes pick up a black infant, and hug and carry it at a safe distance from the mother and her leader. The same tendency is later shown by young adult males before they have any females of their own. Five young juveniles of both sexes that we trapped at one cliff and released near another were all caught and mothered in the described way, each by another young adult male. Thus, the "maternal" behavior of the male toward his first consort is a continuation of similar behavior at an earlier age. "Child care" motivations in the male are one important root for the formation of the one-male units in hamadryas (Kummer 1966). In the cynocephalus baboons studied by Hall and DeVore (1965:86) child care behavior in males is rare; Altmann (personal communication) saw it more often in Amboseli, but even there it has no part in the establishment of a female-male relation.

Figs. 11–9 and *11–10.* Initial unit. The young adult male gives his one-year-old female a gestural invitation to climb on his back; he then carries her across a difficult passage in the sleeping-cliff. (*Photograph by Hans Kummer*)

If the cynocephalus pattern is taken as a baseline, the social position of the hamadryas female can be summarized as follows: She participates in "play" groups more rarely and leaves them about one year earlier than the cynocephalus female. Her first sexual swellings also appear at least one year earlier. Hamadryas females are secluded, protected, and herded within a small segment of the troop from the early or late juvenile stage, and remain so throughout their lives. In the initial phase of their lives in a one-male unit, their relation with the leader often simulates behavior typical of an infant and her mother. Female dominance relations only appear within each unit.

This difference in social status of adult cynocephalus and hamadryas females is nicely illustrated by a preliminary series of cross-troop transplantations. When DeVore (personal communication) released four strange cynocephalus females in front of a cynocephalus group, one of the group's dominant males chased them away. This is also the first response met by strange cynocephalus males trying to enter a group (DeVore 1962; Altmann, personal communication). In contrast, four strange hamadryas females released individually in front of a hamadryas troop were caught, and then permanently herded by individual males. This is not the response met by a strange hamadryas male (who is not accepted either), but the reception found by a strange infant or juvenile.

THE RELATIONS BETWEEN
THE ADULT MALES

Whereas each cynocephalus male may function for and as a member of the entire group, each hamadryas male, in some respects, serves only his own one-male unit. The questions are: (1) Which functions shared by all males in the cynocephalus group are taken over in the hamadryas by the individual unit leader? and (2) In which other functions do the hamadryas males still cooperate on the troop level?

Male reproductive functions clearly belong to the first category. In cynocephalus males, most successful copulations with most fully adult females are made by the most dominant males of the group. In the hamadryas, the mating frequency is not related to a dominance order. Of the adult males 80 percent are unit leaders and the exclusive adult mates of their females. In contrast with the savanna baboons, free-ranging adult hamadryas males have never been observed to threaten or fight each other over a female in estrus, or to attempt copulation with another male's female.

Protective functions are less clearly decentralized. Since, by our presence, we involuntarily protected the hamadryas against predators, the comparison is limited to observations on protective behavior against conspecifics. In cynocephalus groups, strange baboons were chased away by the dominant males. In contacts with predators the dominant males were also the first to step forward, and were then joined by the other males of the group. This concentration of protective functions was reflected in the behavior of the cynocephalus females: Mothers with small infants were most often found near the dominant males in the center of the group. In conflicts between hamadryas troops, each unit leader at first herded his own females and fought only opponents that approached them. In the later stages of large-scale fights, however, the one-male units joined each other to form several bands that fought each other in simple arrays (Fig. 11–11). The hamadryas females, within the limits set by the herding behavior of their leaders, also exhibit the centripetal tendency of the cynocephalus females: When the troop is moving, the females of peripheral units tend to stay between their leader male and the center of the troop.

A third major function of the adult male baboon, the coordination of the troop's or group's movements, by its nature cannot be delegated to the individual unit leader. Despite their fragmentation in other contexts, large parties of hamadryas travel in a coordinated fashion; in fact, the travel formation of hamadryas troops is at times more compact than any marching order observed in cynocephalus groups (Figs. 11–12 and 11–13). The manner of coordination is essentially the same in both species, the more dominant males walking in the center or—in the hamadryas—in the rear of the column. The less dominant and younger males walk ahead of the party, steering with reference to the dominant males behind them. For the hamadryas, the mechanisms of troop movement are known in some detail. The coordination among the unit leaders is probably more elaborate, but not essentially different from the cynocephalus system.

The partial shift of male functions to the unit leaders obviously has its impact on their relations. Whereas cynocephalus males function within a complex but obvious dominance system, the hamadryas troops surprised us by revealing no clear, pervading order of male dominance. An order of function on the troop level could be based on only one criterion—the prevailing influence of the older adult males on the time and direction of the troop's movement. Young males are active in initiating troop movements, but the troop only moves when the older males follow them from the center. After what has been said in this section, this is less surprising than it seemed at first. An order of roles is obvious in the one function where the males cooperate on the troop level, but it is not found in the context of the reproductive function, which is entirely delegated to the one-male unit. The correlation between reproductive activity of hamadryas males and their dominance in directing the troop's travels is actually negative. The young males, although having little influence on the troop's movements and being very attentive to the behavior of the older males, lead more females and, therefore, probably produce more offspring. With increasing age, the hamadryas male herds his unit less intensively, and the number of his females decreases, while his influence on troop movements is increasing. Two of the females we released were taken over by the same young leader of low status, but no other male fought him, neither when he caught the females nor in the following weeks.

The major question is: Why is it that the unit leaders and the single males in hamadryas do not compete for estrous females, a kind of competition that is one of the most prominent issues in the relations of cynocephalus males? In other words, what inhibitions permit the close coexistence of stable one-male units? To this there is as yet no answer. A hint may be found in the fact that when an entire one-male unit was transplanted into a strange troop, its leader was fought by the resident males until they had taken his females.

DIFFERENCES IN THE SOCIALIZATION
OF MALES

Against the background of the cynocephalus organization the most prominent characteristic of the hamadryas male's life cycle is the tendency of two males of different age to associate with each other.

At the early subadult state (about the fourth year of life), the cynocephalus male changes from the rough play activity in the peer group to a behaviorally peripheral and pugnacious life. This change is also observed in the hamadryas males of the same age, but with a marked lack of aggressive behavior in both situations. From the age of four onward, most hamadryas males attach themselves to a certain one-male unit, becoming what we call a "follower." The followers of several neighboring one-male units frequently meet each other for grooming and a form of male-to-male presenting that, in the adult males, communicates the imminent departure of the presenting male. Aggression among the followers is rare.

In *his* one-male unit, the subadult follower concentrates on the females. He approaches them for grooming, and, if not observed by the unit leader, for copulation. As the follower reaches early adulthood his contacts with the females become less frequent and finally disappear. Instead, he enters into contact with the leader of the unit when the troop is moving. His place in the walking unit is now more constant since the females tend to line up between him and the leader.

The tendency to form such "two-male teams" persists throughout the life cycle of the adult hamadryas male. There are teams in which the younger male leads one juvenile female (initial unit) while his partner is a male in his prime, and has three or four adult females. In others, a male in early prime is accompanied by a full set of females and an old male with one or no females.

Fig. 11–11. In a large-scale fight provoked by artificial feeding, a hamadryas group of 750 splits up into fighting bands. The band on the right is pursuing the band on the left. (*Photograph by Hans Kummer*)

Fig. 11–12. A foraging cynocephalus group is evenly dispersed on a plain in Nairobi Park. The group is still coherent. No subgroups are apparent. (*Photograph by Irven DeVore*)

Fig. 11–13. A hamadryas troop leaves its sleeping cliff in a densely packed column. (*Photograph by Hans Kummer*)

Fig. 11–14. One-male unit of the same troop during the day. The troop has split up beyond the limits of coherence. (*Photograph by Hans Kummer*)

Eight such two-male troops were followed long enough to observe that the older male invariably had more influence on the direction of the march, regardless of the relative number of females that accompanied the two of them.

Up to and including the stage in which the younger male has a juvenile female, he does not participate in directing the party's travel, but just tags along at the end of the column. In such a team, the older male again and again walks back to the younger one, presents to him, and thus causes him to move on or to follow in a new direction. Only at a later stage does the younger leader take the front position, initiate movements, and indicate directions. One is tempted to speculate that the two-male team serves as the framework in which the younger male learns the social techniques of the unit leader, and later those of the male troop member. Social units with only two males of different age obviously are the smallest units in which adult male traditions can be passed on. The trend toward the smallest functioning unit is apparent here, as it is in the fragmentation of the troop into the units with only one protector. A complete dispersion into these minimum units was never realized in the lusher western part of the species area where we observed the hamadryas, but the population appears organizationally prepared to realize it under more severe conditions.

Two-male teams have not been found in savanna baboons. The "central hierarchies" described by DeVore include more than two males, and their most obvious function is the mutual support among a dominant set of males in aggressive encounters.

Summarizing the relations among the males in both species we find that the decentralization of male functions in hamadryas is complete as to reproduction, and at least partial as to the protection of females and young. Accordingly, these functions are no longer performed according to an order of dominance. The only obvious criterion that establishes such an order among the unit leaders in the hamadryas troop is the degree of influence on the time and direction of the troop's movements, and this influence is related more to age than to aggressiveness.

ECOLOGICAL AND EVOLUTIONARY CONSIDERATIONS

One would like to understand the pathway of evolution that led to the differences outlined above. The following hypotheses are centered on two questions: (1) Which are the specific ecological potentials of the hamadryas organization? and (2) Assuming that the hamadryas evolved from ancestors organized along the present cynocephalus pattern, do we still find in modern hamadryas a possible homologue of the closed, stable group?

Even in the relatively favorable western part of its habitat where we made our studies the hamadryas (without being hunted) has a lower population density and undertakes longer daily travels than the savanna baboons in Kenya and South Africa (Table 11–1). One may tentatively conclude that

TABLE 11–1   NUMERICAL DATA RELATED TO THE ECOLOGY OF CYNOCEPHALUS BABOONS IN KENYA AND SOUTH AFRICA, AND OF HAMADRYAS BABOONS IN ETHIOPIA. THE FIRST FIGURE GIVES THE CENTRAL TENDENCY OR THE AVERAGE, AND THE FIGURES IN PARENTHESES INDICATE THE OBSERVED MINIMA AND MAXIMA. THE SECOND LINES GIVE THE NUMBER OF GROUPS OR TROOPS ON WHICH THE OBSERVATIONS WERE MADE.

	Kenya (after DeVore)		South Africa (after Hall)	Ethiopia (after Kummer and Kurt)
	Nairobi	*Amboseli*		
1. Population density (per sq mi)*	10	25	7(?)	4.7
	9 groups	13 groups	S-group	6 troops
2. Number of available sleeping locations per unit number of individuals	2–12 per group, continuous along rivers		6 per 26 individual	6 per 450 individual
			S-group	6 troops
3. Length of daily range in miles	3		3.0–3.9	8.3
Min and max	(1–9)		(1.5–7.2)	(6.2–12.2)
No. of ranges	75		30	8
No. of units (g) or (t)	4 (groups)		2 (groups)	2 (troops)
4. Sex ratio of adults (M:F)	1:2.5		1:4	1:1.4
Min and Max			(1:2.2–10)	
No. of units (g) or (t)	5 (groups)		5 (groups)	6 (troops)
5. Group response troop size	40–80		33.5	136
Min and Max	(9–185)		(15–80)	(12–750)
No. of units (g) or (t)	26 (groups)		15 (groups)	19 (troops)

*In region without agriculture.

these differences reflect scarcity of food. Another difference is found in the density of available sleeping lairs (Table 11–1). Suitable cliffs and trees are relatively abundant in Kenya and South Africa. As a rule, hamadryas country offers no high and strong trees. All observed troops slept in cliffs, even where the local habitat offered apparently suitable trees. Where cliffs are abundant we found the hamadryas troops to be small (less than 80). In regions where cliffs are scarce, hamadryas baboons are able to congregate on one cliff in numbers from 400 to 750, which by far exceeds the largest cynocephalus groups observed so far.

Arid and flat country thus presents a difficult ecological problem. Although scarcity of food favors a population that scatters during the day, the scarcity of sleeping lairs requires that at night it concentrate in large troops consisting eventually of several groups. The hamadryas seems to solve the problem by a multilevel organization that permits the population to split and to reassemble at any time into units of any size (between ten and many hundreds) (Figs. 11–13 and 11–14). For example, two associated one-male units were first seen in a troop of 90 baboons; they then passed three days in isolation as a two-male troop of 12, and finally merged into a troop of about 80 on another cliff.

In the cynocephalus populations of Nairobi and the Cape there are no sub- or super-units below or above the group level. In a few arid areas in Amboseli, however, where groves of sleeping trees are more scarce, half a dozen or more cynocephalus groups may converge on one grove at dusk and disperse again the next morning (Altmann, personal communication). By joining each other at night, these groups realize one aspect of the hamadryas' flexibility, seemingly for the same ecological reasons. But they still differ from the hamadryas in lacking the ability to split and fuse below the group level. An analogy of the two extreme organizations is found in the structural difference between the more monolithic armies of the past and the multileveled, reversibly dispersable structure of modern infantry. The following details in the hamadryas organization suggest that units corresponding to the cynocephalus group are still present in hamadryas between the levels of the one-male unit and the troop:

1. In large-scale fights, the troops invariably were seen to split up into bands numbering from 20 to 90 animals (Fig. 11–11). These bands, and not the troops, fought each other.

2. Large troops of 300 and more baboons split into three or more sharply separated columns soon after the departure from the cliff.

3. "Subtroops" of constant size were repeatedly encountered on the daily range. For instance, a subtroop of 42 baboons, which was part of a relatively stable troop of more than 100, was followed on three occasions. It always included the same old male who was the principal director of the subtroop's movements.

4. The procedure that decides the direction of the troop's departure

never involved all the males of a large troop. Contacts were exchanged only within sets including approximately ten neighboring males. As soon as one of these sets had "reached a decision" and departed, the rest of the troop would get up and follow the departing set.

It is possible that these fighting and traveling bands are the homologues of the original groups of the cynocephalus type. They correspond to the cynocephalus group in size, and the contexts in which they appear suggest that they are socially more significant than the troops. In the course of evolution they would have broken up into one-male units, on one hand, and, on the other hand, they would have developed a mutual tolerance that permitted groups to use the same sleeping lairs (as do the Amboseli baboons). Our observations have shown that this tolerance is generally limited to a set of neighboring sleeping rocks. Some neighboring troops freely exchanged parties; two others once occupied the same cliff, but then got into a large-scale fight and separated during the night. Another troop withdrew when it found a cliff occupied and walked seven miles to its usual rock, arriving at nightfall. It is obvious that not all bands or troops are ready to share the same cliff. Close contact between strange troops may result in fights over the females (Kummer, in press) and thus threaten the most stable element of the organization, that is, the one-male units. If in hamadryas there are remainders of an older organization of the cynocephalus type, they will very likely be found in the bands described here.

The hamadryas *troop* does not correspond to the cynocephalus group. It is mainly an ecologically determined association of more constant units, having itself no stable membership. Its size depends on the number of sleeping cliffs in the area and often reaches numbers where thorough interindividual acquaintance and contacts are unlikely. No organized behavior of entire large troops has been observed, with the exception of the common departure in the morning. In troops of more than 300 even the departure is not integrated, and parties leave at different times and in different directions.

By what changes of individual behavior the transition to the hamadryas system was effected is not yet clear, although we can assume that the ritualization of the neck-bite and the increased "maternal" tendency of the adolescent male play important roles in establishing the system of one-male units.

SUMMARY

This chapter compares the social organizations of the desert baboon *Papio hamadryas,* and the savanna baboons of the species group *cynocephalus,* as they are known from preliminary field studies.

The social unit of the savanna baboon is the stable group that rarely splits or fuses with another group. Two differences characterize the probably more recent hamadryas specialization—the fragmentation of each hamadryas "band" into one-male units, and an increased tolerance between neighboring bands, which permits them to assemble in large troops on a few sleeping cliffs.

Several effects of the fragmentation are evident. Contacts that are common among adult cynocephalus baboons of the same group are strongly inhibited or suppressed among hamadryas adults of different one-male units, even within the band. Functions concentrated in the dominant males of a cynocephalus group are delegated to individual unit-leaders in hamadryas. Adult hamadryas females are herded and controlled by their unit-leaders and thus excluded from active membership in the band.

Two hypotheses are given: (1) The hamadryas band, which appears in critical situations as an intermediate level between the one-male unit and the troop, may be the homologue to the original cynocephalus group; and (2) the hamadryas organization permits a routine change between the extreme dispersion into small foraging parties (one-male units) and the extreme concentration in large sleeping parties (troops). This "fusion and fission" capacity may be especially adapted to a habitat where food is sparse and sleeping lairs are scarce.

12

A PRELIMINARY REPORT

ON EXPRESSIVE MOVEMENTS

AND COMMUNICATION IN

THE GOMBE STREAM CHIMPANZEES[1]

Jane Van Lawick-Goodall

INTRODUCTION

Primates have a wide range of expressive movements and calls, many of which have a communicative function; that is, they appear to have some effect on other individuals that see or hear them and thus they may help to maintain interindividual relationships within the social structure as a whole. Each of these movements and calls is likely to be affected, both in structure and in probable function as a signal, by a number of variables: the environ-

[1]The work was carried out in Tanzania, East Africa, and I am grateful to the Tanzania government officials in Kigoma and to the Tanzania Game Department for their cooperation. The research was financed initially by the Wilkie Foundation and subsequently by the National Geographic Society, and I express my gratitude to both organizations.

I should also like to thank Dr. L. S. B. Leakey, Honorary Director of the National Museum Center for Prehistory and Palaeontology, who initiated the expedition; Baron Hugo Van Lawick for his valuable photographic and film record and for his assistance in all aspects of the research; my assistants, Miss Edna Koning and Miss Ivey; and the African research. Finally, I am indebted to Professor R. A. Hinde, Sub-department of Animal Behaviour, Cambridge University, for his helpful criticisms during the early stages of this manuscript.

mental and behavioral situation at the time, and the motivational state and individuality of the sender and of other members of the group. Moreover, primate signals invariably occur in clusters:

> In most situations it is not a single signal that passes from one animal to another but a whole complex of them, visual, auditory, tactile, and sometimes olfactory. There can be little doubt that the structure of individual signals is very much affected by this incorporation in a whole matrix of other signals. (Marler 1965:583)

The data to be presented here were obtained during 45 months of observation (between 1960 and 1965) of free-ranging chimpanzees at the Gombe Stream Chimpanzee Reserve, Tanzania, East Africa. This reserve consists of about 30 square miles of rugged mountainous country, stretching along the eastern shores of Lake Tanganyika and supporting a small population (probably between 100 and 150) of *Pan troglodytes schweinfurthi,* the Eastern or long-haired chimpanzee.

The animals may be divided into the following main age classes on the basis of behavioral characteristics: infant, juvenile, adolescent, and adult.

The infant (0 to 3–3½ years) suckles, is transported by the mother (either continuously or occasionally), and sleeps in the same nest with the mother at night. During its first six months the infant is almost completely dependent on the mother for food, transport, and protection. At about six months it makes its first movements away from her, but remains extremely dependent for the following six months. Locomotor patterns develop rapidly, and the infant commences to eat some solid foods during the second half of its first year. Social interactions with other individuals are frequent; the infant may be patted or groomed by adults, and played with, groomed, and carried by older infants, juveniles, and adolescents. An infant frequently approaches individuals joining its group to "greet" them. The white tail tuft is fully developed and at maximum length by the end of the first year. In the second year the infant begins to walk beside the mother for short distances, and the proportion of solids eaten increases. Other individuals continue to show tolerance. During this year most if not all of the gestures used by adult chimpanzees during interindividual interactions appear. During its third year, the infant rides less and less frequently on the mother's back. By the end of the year, its diet differs little from that of the adult. Older individuals are still generally tolerant, but the infant receives a number of gentle rebuffs and behaves with increasing caution. It is still protected by the mother.

The juvenile (3–3½ to 6–7 years) is no longer dependent on the mother for food or transport and makes its own nest at night. The mother still protects her offspring on occasions, and the juvenile continues to move around with her for most of the time. Rebuffs from older individuals become increasingly severe. The white tail tuft gradually becomes less conspicuous.

The adolescent period is from 6–7 to 11–13 years. In the male chimpanzee the period of adolescence is fairly well defined and can be said to commence with puberty (about 7 years) and to continue until the individual is socially mature and becomes integrated into the adult male hierarchy. In the female adolescence is not easy to define, but probably commences between 6 and 7 years. During the first year or so of adolescence the female may show a very slight swelling of the anogenital region, but this in no way approximates a normal sexual swelling and does not arouse attention from the males. At a later period of adolescence the female shows the normal external features of the estrous cycle.

These chimpanzees are nomadic in that they normally sleep in a different place each night and, although for the most part they keep within the same general area, they follow no regular circuit in their daily search for food. The distance and direction of this daily wandering varies with the availability of food; thus when a tasty fruit is ripe in one part of the reserve only, some chimpanzees may move far beyond their normal home range in order to feed there (see also Goodall 1962, 1963, 1965).

The entire chimpanzee population of the reserve can best be described as one loosely organized group or community within which all or most individuals are familiar with each other and may from time to time move about together. With the exception of infants and young juveniles, which normally move around with their mothers, each individual within this community is an independent unit since it may move about on its own from time to time. In fact, mature and adolescent males are frequently encountered alone, and mature and adolescent females are also, but less frequently. Individual chimpanzees often join to form temporary associations that may remain stable for a few hours or a few days. These may consist of any combination of age-sex classes and may number from 2 to more than 30 (the average being 6). Membership within such temporary associations is continually changing as individuals or numbers of individuals move off, either to travel about on their own or to join with other chimpanzees.

There are certain individuals that may associate with each other on many occasions (thus an adolescent moves around more often with its mother than with any other single individual), but the only association that is stable over a number of years is that of a mother and her younger offspring (van Lawick-Goodall, in press).

The temporary nature of chimpanzee associations results in an *apparently* loose social structure (Goodall 1965; Reynolds and Reynolds 1965). However, when regular observations became possible on the interactions between the various individuals it gradually became evident that the social status of each chimpanzee was fairly well defined in relation to each other individual. In other words, it was often possible to predict, when for example two chimpanzees met on a narrow branch, which animal would gain right of way; that animal could then be described as the dominant one of the two.

At the beginning of the study it was decided that for close-range observation it would be necessary to habituate the chimpanzees to the

TABLE 12–1   INDIVIDUALS OBSERVED VISITING THE FEEDING AREA, APRIL 1964—MARCH 1965

Adults	No. of Observations	Adolescent	No. of Observations	Juveniles	No. of Observations	Infants 0–1	No. of Observations	Infants 1–3	No. of Observations
				Males					
David Graybeard	383	Faben	641	Fifi	673	Flint	666	Merlin	272
Mr. McGregor	377	Figan	631	Miff	283	Goblin	201	Sniff	20
Mr. Worzle	365	Evered	431						
Mike	323	Pepe	340						
J. B.	292	McD	221						
Leakey	287	Charlie	206						
Humphrey	283								
Hugo	277								
Goliath	244								
Huxley	205								
Hugh	121								
Totals (11)	3157	(6)	2470	(2)	956	(2)	867	(2)	292
				Females					
Flo	666	Pooch	319			Cindy	49	Gilka	309
Melissa	390	Gigi	91			Jane	37	Little Bee	20
Olly	309	Sally	21						
Marina	272								
Mandy	218								
Circe	123								
Madam Bee	20								
Sophie	20								
Totals (8)	2018	(3)	431	(2)		(2)	86	(2)	329

presence of an observer. This was a lengthy process (Goodall 1965), but finally most of the apes continued their normal activities even when the observer was within 30 to 40 feet of them.

In 1962 a mature male, David Greybeard (all chimpanzees known individually were named) visited my camp to feed on the fruit of a palm tree; he returned each day until the fruit was exhausted. During one such visit he took some bananas from my tent, and after this my African staff left these out for him. When fruit on another palm in camp ripened he returned, again took bananas, and subsequently visited camp from time to time for the bananas alone; on such occasions he was sometimes accompanied by other chimpanzees. Gradually, more and more individuals followed him to camp, and in 1963 I decided to set up an artificial feeding area on a permanent basis.[2] It then became possible to make fairly regular observations on the different chimpanzees, since every time they were in the area they detoured to have a meal of bananas.

The number of chimpanzees visiting the feeding area gradually increased. Table 12–1 lists the 38 individuals that came most frequently between April 1964 and March 1965, together with the number of "observation periods" when it was possible to observe each one for longer than 10 minutes at a time.[3] Although the total number of these observation periods for each individual is not an exact measure of the amount of time the animal was observed, the totals for various age-sex classes provide an approximate index to the relative amounts of time during one year that I was able to observe males as compared with females, and so forth. These measures were used as a means of determining the relative frequency in each age-sex class of some of the gestures and postures that form part of the communicatory system of chimpanzees.

CALLS, FACIAL EXPRESSIONS,
AND AUTONOMIC BEHAVIOR

Here I shall briefly discuss three aspects of behavior that will be referred to throughout the chapter. I have not yet commenced a detailed analysis of calls and facial expressions, but the more obvious of these are listed in Table 12–2, together with the behavioral contexts in which they were most

[2]After a good deal of experimenting, the feeding area now comprises some 30 cement boxes half sunk into the ground, each containing from 10 to 15 bananas; these boxes can be opened by handles situated not less than 10 yards away. Thus when a large number of chimpanzees arrive at the same time each one can have a box opened for him. The boxes are widely spread out, and the area has been designed to stimulate as little abnormal aggressive behavior as possible.

[3]Individuals sometimes remained at or near the feeding area for several hours; the average mean length for observation periods during one year was calculated for three females and was between 45 and 55 minutes for each.

TABLE 12–2   SOME COMMON CALLS AND FACIAL EXPRESSIONS

Call or Sound	Expression of Face
A. Between relaxed individuals.	
1. *Soft grunt.*	Typical relaxed or alert face.
2. Very *soft groan*, "hm-hmmm."	Typical relaxed or alert face.
B. In connection with feeding.	
1. Loud barking sounds, with a wide range of variation in tone and pitch.	Mouth slightly opened at each sound; lips may be slightly retracted to show teeth.
2. Short, high-pitched, single-syllable *shrieks.*	Mouth wide open; lips retracted from teeth; corners of the mouth drawn back.
3. Soft or loud *grunts.*	Various jaw and lip positions during eating.
C. During nonaggressive physical contact with other individuals.	
1. "*Panting*," soft.	Lips may be very slightly parted.
2. "*Copulatory pants*," louder and hoarser than C.1.	Lips may be very slightly parted.
3. "*Laughing*," soft panting sounds which may become jerky panting grunts.	"*Play face*." At a low intensity the lower lip is retracted to show the lower teeth; at higher intensities the mouth is opened and lip retraction increases until all forward teeth may be exposed. Laughing does not always accompany "play face."
D. During various types of social activity (not obviously aggressive).	
1. Quiet "huu."	Lips pushed slightly forward.
2. Series of "*panting hoots and calls*." There are many variations; the calls may rise or fall in pitch, and are sometimes long and drawn out toward the end.	"*Hoot face*." Lips pushed forward into trumpet, but corners of mouth may be retracted during inhalation. At end of series mouth may open wider, lips covering teeth.
3. "*Panting hoots* with *shrieks or roars*." Same as above, but always rise in pitch and volume.	Same as above, but during shrieks and roars mouth is wide open and, in some individuals, teeth showing.
E. During aggressive behavior.	
1. (*No sound.*)	"*Glare*." Lips compressed, animal stares fixedly at another individual.
2. "*Soft bark*," single syllable breathy exhalation, like a cough.	Mouth half open; lips pushed slightly forward but covering teeth.
3. "*Waa bark*," loud single syllable bark.	Similar to E.2 but mouth wider open.

Situation in Which Normally Elicited	Observed Response of Other Individuals
1. Relaxed situation in group during resting, grooming, traveling, and so forth.	May repeat similar sound.
2. Same as above.	Same as above.
1. Eating or approaching desirable food.	May look toward or approach calling animal.
2. Arriving close to desirable food, when commencing to feed.	May look toward or approach calling animal.
3. Feeding.	May look toward or approach calling animal.
1. Social grooming. Also when approaching another animal prior to and during "kissing," "bowing," and so forth.	
2. Copulation.	
3. During charging display, drumming, and so forth; sometimes when males cross ridge between valleys.	When one individual approaches with a "play face" another may respond by playing.
1. As another approaches; response to group calling in the distance.	
2. As another approaches; response to distant calls; when arriving in group; during meat eating; when lying in nest at night.	Frequently may join in and also hoot. May reach out to touch calling individual.
3. During branch-waving and dragging displays, drumming, and so forth; sometimes when males cross ridge between valleys.	May join in; if subordinate to the calling animal, may climb a tree, or "hide."
1. Sometimes prior to chase or attack. Prior to copulation.	Approaches and presents for copulation in this context.
2. When threatening subordinate or other species of which it is not afraid.	Subordinate normally shows submissive behavior.
3. Similar to E.2. Also when threatening superior from a distance; when another chimpanzee is being attacked.	Looks in direction of disturbance; may make similar call.

TABLE 12-2—*continued*

Call or Sound	Expression of Face
4. "*Wraaah*" call, long and drawn out, clear "savage sounding" call.	Similar to E.3.
5. High pitched *scream calls;* may be short or long and drawn out, and may lead to glottal cramps.	Mouth half or wide open; lips retracted from teeth and gums; corners of mouth drawn back. May occur without sound.
F. During "anxiety" or "frustration" situations.	
1. "*Hoo call*," soft, low pitched single syllable sound; less breathy than D. 1.	Lips pushed quickly forward, animal stares at worrying stimulus.
2. "*Hoo whimper*," similar but lower pitched sound.	"*Pout face*," lips pursed and pushed right forward; eyes wide open and staring at mother or other individual.
3. "*Whimpering*," series of "hoo" sounds rather like whimpering of puppy at times.	Initially similar to above but then the corners of the lips are drawn back and lower lip retracted from teeth; "*whimper face*."
4. "*Crying*," loud hoarse yells and screams; may lead to glottal cramps.	Mouth wide open; teeth show.
G. During submissive behavior and when individual is frightened.	
1. "*Bobbing pants*," loud hoarse panting sounds.	Mouth half open or wide open; lips normally pulled tightly over teeth. Lips may be pushed forward slightly at end of call.
2. "*Panting shrieks*," loud screamlike sounds.	Mouth open; lips pushed slightly forward.
3. "*Squeak calls*," short high-pitched, squeaky screams.	"*Grinning*." Initially the lips are parted, the corners drawn back, and an oblong expanse of closed teeth shown. In more extreme form the mouth is opened and the lips retracted fully from teeth and gums.
4. (*No sound.*)	"*Silent grin*." Same as above without calling.
5. "*Screaming*," loud screaming with many variations; some screams have a rasping quality; some are long and drawn out. May lead to glottal cramps.	Mouth wide open; lips fully retracted from teeth and gums.
6. "*Infantile scream*."	Uncertain, but mouth open.

Situation in Which Normally Elicited	Observed Response of Other Individuals
4. When disturbed by presence of human; sometimes when two groups meet. Often followed by shaking branches.	May hurry towards the disturbance; may give same call or "waa bark."
5. When threatening superior or animal of another species of which chimpanzee is afraid; may look round to another chimpanzee for "support."	May hurry towards the calling individual and threaten or charge at the caller.
1. When chimpanzee suddenly hears or sees strange object or sound.	Looks in direction of the calling individual and may then peer around.
2. Infant searching for nipple, slipping, trying to reach mother, and so forth. Older ape when begging; when ignored after it has presented for grooming, and so forth.	Mother "cradles" or retrieves infant. Older chimpanzee may be given piece of food, or groomed.
3. When there is no response to the "hoo" whimper; when juveniles lose their mothers; after threat or attack.	May then respond to the begging behavior and so forth; or make reassurance gesture.
4. When juveniles are lost; during "temper tantrums" in juveniles; during "frustration" in older individuals.	Mother hurries towards sound; may reassure child in tantrum.
1. When a subordinate male "bobs" to a mature male.	
2. When chimpanzee approaches to show submissive behavior or to greet a superior.	
3. After threat or attack, while the subordinate is making submissive gestures. Female may make these sounds during copulation.	The dominant individual may touch or embrace the subordinate.
4. Similar to above.	Same as above.
5. When a chimpanzee is fleeing or being attacked; after the attack while making submissive gestures; in many types of aggressive interaction.	Same as above. The mother of a screaming individual, or a "friend" may approach to threaten or attack the aggressor.
6. When infant (during first few weeks of its life) gets a sudden fright, falls from the mother, and so forth.	Mother hastily cradles and embraces. May look down with "pout face" or "grin."

commonly recorded and the observed responses of other individuals. Each specific call or facial expression referred to in the text is described in this table.

Calls

The chimpanzee has a wide range of readily distinguishable calls. These express his "emotions" at the time, and although, as Andrew (1963*b*) says, they are not given "in order, for example, to warn fellows of impending danger, in a way a man might cry 'Look out'," nevertheless they often do communicate the mood of the individual to his fellows.

Rowell and Hinde (1962) stressed the fact that in the rhesus monkey there is the possibility of an almost infinite range of intermediates between the main sounds. Rowell (1962) showed that nine major calls given by the rhesus in agonistic situations actually constitute one system linked by a continuous series of intermediates. After analyzing some chimpanzee calls recorded by Reynolds in the field, Marler (1965) has suggested that in this species too there is a similar gradation of sound between some of the calls. I have not yet analyzed tape recordings of chimpanzee calls and therefore, as a temporary measure to clarify the present discussion, I have merely listed the more readily distinguishable sounds of the chimpanzee in Table 12–2.

It should be mentioned that not only is it possible to distinguish between males and females, and adults and youngsters on the basis of their "voices," but it is also possible to recognize each individual from a distance when he utters "panting hoots." Although there is undoubtedly some degree of individuality in most chimpanzee vocalizations, it may be significant that this is particularly obvious in calls that are mainly connected with long-range communication. Such individual differentiation may help in reuniting two animals after a separation.

It is relevant to this discussion that in one species of shrike (genus *Laniarius*), which inhabits thick forest, the two birds of a pair tend to develop a particular and individualistic repertoire of duet patterns, which may well aid their mutual recognition and help them to maintain contact in conditions where visual display is ineffective (Thorpe 1963).

Thus, although a certain amount of individuality is undoubtedly present in the calls and songs of most types of mammals and birds, it is possible that this characteristic may have particular adaptive significance for an animal that is not in constant, or nearly constant, visual contact with its partner or other members of the group.

Facial Expressions

The expression of a chimpanzee's face alters continually with relation to each new behavioral context, and, according to van Hooff (1962), is one of the most important parts of the body concerned with visual communication.

This is certainly true with regard to the subtler aspects; for instance, when a subordinate is begging from (or merely sitting beside) a superior, the subordinate is constantly watching the face of the other, presumably for slight changes of expression that may reveal a change in "mood."

The normal attentive facial expression of the wild chimpanzee is shown by the mother in Fig. 12–1. Other expressions range from a slight pouting of the lips (when, for instance, a young animal is denied food) to a wide open mouth with lips drawn back from teeth and gums (as when an individual screams at the top of its voice after an attack). Other expressions are listed in Table 12–2. There are, of course, expressions intermediate between all the main types. Often these intermediate forms can be observed in a complete sequence—when, for instance, a lost juvenile initially pouts its lips, then commences to whimper (Fig. 12–2), and finally "cries" loudly (Fig. 12–3).

Each chimpanzee can easily be recognized individually by its face structure. In addition, some animals showed expressions that were never seen in others. Thus one male frequently pressed his lips together, drew back the corners of his mouth, and "mock smiled." This was in no way related to the "play face," which has been referred to in the literature as "smiling" (Yerkes and Yerkes 1929), but occurred in a variety of contexts, none of which was associated with play or good temper. Some animals typically droop their lower lips when they are relaxed; others never do so. One mature male, when "determined" to get more bananas, progressively pushed out his lower lip farther and farther as he inspected box after box.

Autonomic Behavior

Chimpanzees show pronounced hair erection in a number of situations. These include arriving at a food source, meeting another group, suddenly noticing chimpanzees in the distance, hearing a strange sound, finding themselves in an unfamiliar situation, threatening or attacking an opponent, or during courtship prior to copulation. Sometimes only the hair of the back and arms may be raised; at other times every hair on the body stands on end.

In some of these situations (feeding, greeting, and courtship) male chimpanzees may show penile erections. Yerkes (1943) remarks that the external genitalia of the female may also become turgid during similar situations. In the field I once observed a slight swelling in the sex skin of an anoestrus female in response to prolonged inspection by a male (see p. 363).

Mature males, particularly during social excitement, sometimes emitted a strong smell, slightly similar to very pungent human sweat. Although I was often close to individuals when they were sweating in the sun, the odor was not detectable on such occasions. Schaller (1963) detected a similar smell, which he thought emanated from silver-Back males; he also concluded that normal sweating alone could not account for the odor.

Fig. 12–2. Juvenile with "whimper face" after losing her mother. (*Photograph by Baron Hugo Van Lawick;* © *National Geographic Society*)

Fig. 12–1. Three-month-old infant with "pout face." (*Photograph by Baron Hugo Van Lawick;* © *National Geographic Society*)

Fig. 12–3. The same juvenile shows a low intensity "cry face" as her distress increases. (*Photograph by Baron Hugo Van Lawick;* © *National Geographic Society*)

It should also be mentioned that when chimpanzees are frightened, as during a severe attack or prolonged chase, they may defecate repeatedly, and the excrement is usually diarrheic.

FLIGHT AND AVOIDANCE

When a chimpanzee is frightened, either by a superior or by some other animal or object in its environment, it shows a variety of flight or avoidance patterns in addition to the submissive behavior patterns. The form used depends on the situation and the individual or individuals concerned.

Flight

Flight is defined as a rapid progression away from an alarming stimulus. When the latter is another chimpanzee, flight is characteristically accompanied by loud screaming with the mouth open and the lips fully retracted from the teeth and gums. A chimpanzee fleeing a social superior may either rush along the ground and take refuge in a tree or, if the incident commenced in a tree, it may hurl itself through the branches and then to the ground. This is usually sufficient to shake off the pursuer, although sometimes the latter may persist.

When a chimpanzee flees from some new or alarming object in the environment he does not call out, although there may be some noise as he rushes through undergrowth or dead leaves. When the chimpanzees suddenly came across me (before they were habituated to my presence) they sometimes paused to stare before running off out of sight; at other times they rushed off for a few yards and then stopped to peer at me before vanishing silently into the forest. When I surprised them in a tree, they invariably climbed rapidly and silently to the ground and then ran off. Reynolds and Reynolds (1965) report "panic diarrhea" under such circumstances.

Startled Reaction

When a chimpanzee is alarmed by a sudden noise or movement nearby—from a low-flying bird, large insect, snake, or the like—the immediate response is to duck its head and fling one or both arms across its face or to throw both hands up in the air. A reaction similar to the first is observed in the gorilla (Schaller 1963) and in man, and one similar to the second is observed in the baboon (Hall 1962b). After a second the chimpanzee peers around, and if the stimulus is not dangerous he relaxes. Occasionally these reflex actions were followed up by a hitting-away movement with the back of the hand toward the object. This movement, probably defensive in origin, has been incorporated into the repertoire of threat gestures.

"Hiding"

Before the chimpanzees were completely tolerant of my presence they sometimes "hid" when I approached to observe them. Thus an individual who had been feeding in full view might either move behind a tree trunk (where he then continued to feed out of my sight, peering round at me every so often), or reach for a large branch, and pull it down between us. Both Christy and Schaller (Reynolds and Reynolds 1965) reported seeing chimpanzees climb into old nests when they saw humans; they then remained there, occasionally peering over the edge. Reynolds and Reynolds (1965) report that one female constructed a nest for hiding. The orangutan may also hide from humans in a nest (Harrisson 1962).

On some occasions I observed chimpanzees hiding in similar ways from individuals of their own species. One dominant male (Goliath), who had been sitting peering uneasily in all directions suddenly hurried silently away, hair erected, when two other mature males appeared. (These three males were well acquainted.) The two ran after him, and then moved about for a few minutes in the bushes where he had disappeared. After this they commenced to feed. Some minutes later I saw Goliath sitting behind a tree trunk a little way up the opposite slope. He remained there for ten minutes, occasionally peering around and looking at the others below. When one of them moved suddenly or looked up, he at once ducked behind his tree trunk.

On many occasions individuals were seen to move behind tree trunks or other large objects when violent social activities were taking place around them.

Creeping

Occasionally an individual that had been attacked or threatened tried to "creep" from the vicinity of its aggressor. One adolescent male tried to creep from a tree in this manner, proceeding with extreme caution and moving each limb slowly while peering in the direction of his aggressor. He kept his body close to the branch and "grinned" or whimpered every time the aggressor looked toward him. When the dominant male made a sudden movement (which was not made with reference to him) he stopped moving altogether. On another occasion a young female spent 15 minutes trying to creep away from the vicinity of an older female who had been presenting to her for grooming.

"FRUSTRATION" (OR BEHAVIOR
IN UNCERTAINTY)

Frustration is used here as a convenient heading under which to group behavior patterns that occur in conflict situations, when the animal is motivated by conflicting tendencies (Hinde and Tinbergen 1958): when fear of another individual prevents the chimpanzee from obtaining a desired objective; when the capabilities of the individual itself are insufficient to achieve a desired goal; or when another individual does not make the appropriate response to a communicatory signal.

An example of the first type of situation is when a dominant individual takes food in the possession of a subordinate—the latter may then be motivated by a strong aggressive tendency that is counteracted by its fear of the other. An example of the second type is when a chimpanzee is unable to get at bananas that it can see or smell inside a box. An example of the third type is when an infant, unable to make a large jump from one branch to another, looks toward its mother with a pout face and "hoo whimper" but is then ignored.

The various behavior patterns observed in the situations described consist in large part of actions that appear irrelevant to the situation and out of context (displacement activities), and actions that are directed away from the eliciting stimulus and that may involve redirection to other objects or individuals.

Scratching

The chimpanzee makes deliberate scratching movements, typically on the arm from elbow to wrist, from below the armpit to the elbow, or from thigh to belly over the groin. The more intense the anxiety or conflict situation, the more vigorous the scratching becomes. It typically occurred when the chimpanzees were worried or frightened by my presence or that of a high-ranking chimpanzee. Scratching, as the response to the presence of a human, has also been recorded in gorillas, baboons, and Patas monkeys (Schaller 1963; Hall and DeVore 1965; Hall and Gartlan 1965). It may be compared with head scratching in man under similar circumstances (Schaller 1963).

Yawning

The chimpanzee yawns repeatedly, looking either toward or away from the disturbance. This typically occurred as a result of my presence in individuals not fully habituated, and also in youngsters that were unable to take bananas in the presence of their superiors. Yawning in uneasy or aggressive animals occurs in gorillas, gibbons, baboons, rhesus monkeys, patas monkeys, and, rarely in vervet monkeys (Schaller 1963; Carpenter 1940; Hall 1962*b;* Hinde and Rowell 1962; Hall and Gartlan 1965). Yawning in man sometimes occurs in mild conflict situations (Schaller 1963).

Grooming

The chimpanzee makes rapid and normally ineffective grooming movements either on itself or on a companion. This behavior is often seen when a chimpanzee is waiting for a desirable food (such as meat or bananas). Similar behavior has been observed in chacma and olive baboons and in hamadryas baboons (Hall and DeVore 1965; Kummer, personal communication).

Masturbation

Males of all ages sometimes held and toyed with their erect penes in situations when they were apparently frustrated, and one female juvenile frequently made thrusting movements of the pelvis while rubbing her clitoris against a branch or the ground, usually when she was frustrated. A juvenile male occasionally made the same pelvic thrusting movements while standing quadrupedally and looking back between his arms and legs as his scrotum bounced against his penis; this always occurred when he was frustrated.

Rocking

The chimpanzee rocks very slightly, either from side to side or backward and forward (a matter of individual preference). At times the movements are barely perceptible and the individual may only move its head. The violence of rocking may continue to increase gradually, even though there is no corresponding change in the external stimulus eliciting the behavior. The most vigorous form of rocking occurs when the individual stands bipedally and sways from foot to foot, grasping a branch in one or both hands and waving this also from side to side. Rocking has been seen in a number of contexts, the most common being when indiviudals were frustrated in feeding situations or when they were uneasy in my presence. This rocking movement occurs commonly in captive chimpanzees, normally in situations when they are upset (Berkson, Mason, and Saxon 1963).

Shaking and Swaying of Branches

A branch may be swayed as a chimpanzee rocks its own body. Sometimes a whole sapling is swayed from side to side, with the chimpanzee either in the sapling or standing on the ground. At other times the branch-shaking is not accompanied by rocking, but the chimpanzee, while glaring at the eliciting stimulus, seizes hold of a nearby branch and shakes it violently. This behavior typically occurred as a reaction to my presence when the chimpanzees were uneasy. Shaking of branches has been observed in a number of other primates such as gorillas, red spider monkeys, baboon, and rhesus monkeys (Schaller 1963; Carpenter 1935; Hall 1962*b;* Hall and DeVore 1965; Hinde and Rowell 1962).

Charging, Slapping, Stamping, Dragging, Throwing, and Drumming

In frustration situations slapping, stamping, dragging, throwing, and drumming[4] may accompany the chimpanzee charge away from the eliciting stimulus. As he charges he may slap on the ground with his hands, stamp with his feet, seize and drag branches after him along the ground, and hurl rocks or branches. Finally, he may leap up at a tree and drum on the trunk or buttresses with his feet—usually the two feet pound down one after the other in quick succession making a double beat; there is then a slight pause before the next double beat. From one to three double beats are normal.[5] Two males, out of the eleven that visited the feeding area, beat their chests during such displays in a manner similar to that described for gorillas (Schaller 1963).

The context in which these actions were usually observed was when mature males were unable to open banana boxes or when adolescent males were unable to obtain food because mature males were close by. When one adolescent male was unable to get bananas he frequently whimpered, hurried some 100 yards away from the group, broke into a run, drummed on a tree, swayed branches, and stamped and slapped on the ground—meanwhile uttering "panting hoots" and screams; he then returned, apparently relaxed, to his group. An individual often seemed to be more relaxed after performing one or more of these display patterns.

Temper Tantrums

Temper tantrums are a characteristic performance of the infant and young juvenile chimpanzee. The animal, screaming loudly, either leaps into the air with its arms above its head or hurls itself to the ground, writhing about and

---

[4]Charging display which involved all or some of these patterns, occurred invariably when mature or adolescent males approached a desirable food source, when mature (and occasionally adolescent) males joined other chimpanzees, and at the onset of, or during, heavy rain.

[5]Frequently, when a number of chimpanzees traveling together come upon some favored "drumming tree" along the track (a tree with wide buttresses) each male in turn drums in this manner. This results in a whole series of one to three double beats with irregular intervals between each. Adult females have never been observed to take part in such drumming rituals, but an infant and a juvenile female were each seen to do so once.

often hitting itself against surrounding objects. The first temper tantrum observed in one infant occurred when he was eleven months old; he looked around and was unable to see his mother. With a loud scream he flung himself to the ground and beat at it with his hands. His mother at once rushed to gather him up. Mothers of older infants and juveniles, although they sometimes reached out to touch their offspring during a tantrum, frequently ignored the behavior. Yerkes (1943), when describing tantrums, comments that he often saw a youngster "in the midst of a tantrum glance furtively at its mother or the caretaker as if to discover whether its action was attracting attention." In captivity, individuals are less prone to indulge in temper tantrums as they grow older, and this was also true of wild chimpanzees. Adolescents on five occasions went into tantrums after being mildly attacked by mature individuals or after making submissive gestures and not at once being reassured. I saw only three mature animals display temper tantrums; these were subordinate males who had been attacked by superiors and who were obviously too afraid to retaliate. Temper tantrums in connection with weaning have been described for infant baboons and langurs (DeVore 1963; Jay 1963a).

Redirection of Aggression or Transferred Threat

A chimpanzee that has been attacked by a higher ranking individual or that has been unable to obtain food owing to the presence of a social superior may chase after, threaten, or actually attack an individual subordinate to itself. When mature males attacked infants or juveniles it was always in this context. This type of behavior occurs frequently in rhesus macaques and baboons (Altmann 1962a; Hall and DeVore 1965) and, less often, in other monkeys such as vervets or langurs (Hall and Gartlan 1965; Jay 1965b).

AGGRESSIVE BEHAVIOR

In a given group of animals aggressive behavior falls into three main categories: aggressive interactions with (1) animals of another species; (2) other groups within the species; and (3) individuals within the group itself.

The chimpanzees of the Gombe Stream Reserve normally ignore or avoid the larger mammals of the area (such as buffalo, adult bushbuck, and bushpig), and often ignore or tolerate the close proximity of the other primates. However, aggressive interactions between chimpanzees and baboons (*Papio anubis*) over food are fairly frequent. In addition, these chimpanzees are predators of some consequence in the area, and from time to time hunt and kill various types of monkey and the young of the bushbuck and bushpig.[6] The chimpanzees themselves, however, are not apparently preyed upon.

Since the chimpanzee population of the Gombe Stream Reserve comprises one loosely organized social group, I have no data on interactions between different groups of chimpanzees. When individuals or associations of individuals met, there was seldom any aggressive behavior; at such a time, if a member of one association did threaten or attack a member of the other, this could usually be traced to a previous aggressive incident between the two. Reynolds and Reynolds (1965) describe occasions in the Budongo Forest area when loud chimpanzee calling and drumming continued for many hours at a time. They suggest that this may have been associated with relatively unfamiliar groups gathering at a food source; however, they were unable to verify this or to determine whether aggressive behavior had occurred.

Frequency of aggressive interactions between the individuals of a primate group vary from species to species. However, in all for which data are available most squabbles are settled by threat gestures and submissive behavior, rather than by actual attack (Jay 1965a). At least in part, this is because individuals living in constant association know each other, and their relative social positions are determined by habit. In the chimpanzee, however, the picture is slightly complicated because the individuals comprising the community as a whole are constantly splitting up and reuniting in different associations. This means that all mature chimpanzees, whatever their status in relation to the group as a whole, may from time to time be the highest ranking individuals of a temporary association. A further complication of the pattern is that the social position of some chimpanzees depends, in part, on the presence or absence of certain other individuals. One mature male (J.B.) frequently associated with the top-ranking male (Mike). When the two were together J.B. normally dominated the other males with them, but when Mike was not with him, J.B. was often dominated by one of the other high-ranking males. There were other close associations of this type, in which the presence or absence of the higher ranking of the two influenced the status of the other. These fluctuations in status are presumably due to the higher ranking partner's willingness to go to the aid of the other on occasion.

Usually, however, even within this constantly changing pattern order is maintained by means of threatening gestures and displays rather than by physical conflict. It is in this context that the branch-waving display of the

---

[6]Red Colobus Monkey (*Colobus badius grauri*), nine times; young bushbuck (*Tragelaphus scriptus*), six times; young bushpig (*Potamochoerus koiropotamus* sp.), four times; female Redtail monkey (*Cercopithecus ascanius Schmidti*) with new-born or fetal infant, once; adolescent baboon, once. On other occasions it was not possible to identify the kill. During one year, the total number of known kills (not including birds) was 20; these were all made by one or another of the known individuals.

male chimpanzee as he joins other individuals may be adaptive, since it reasserts social status by bluff, rather than by actual fighting. The greeting behavior that occurs when individuals meet after a separation can also be considered within this framework.

Threat

In aggressive contexts, the chimpanzee has a repertoire of gestures, postures, and calls that appear to elicit submissive behavior in the individual they are directed toward. They are not normally followed by physical attack. Since behavior of this sort invariably involves a combination of such gestures, postures, and sounds, and since it was seldom possible to estimate the precise significance of each individual component in the complex, I have merely listed each one, together with the behavioral contexts in which it was most usually observed. Most of these gestures were also directed toward humans or baboons during aggressive interactions.

Glaring, which is described in Table 12–2, was frequently associated with other threat patterns; a fixed stare is a form of threat in other primate species and also in man (Andrew 1963*b*; Schaller 1963).

HEAD TIPPING is a slight upward and backward jerk (or dorsalward tipping) of the head, and is invariably accompanied by the "soft bark." It is a low-intensity threat that was never seen to result in attack, and was often made by a feeding individual when a subordinate approached too closely. Andrew (1963*a*) comments that a sudden noisy expiration of air (used as a threat) is common throughout the mammals, and he suggests that a tipping back of the head (as when a dog howls) may lower the epiglottis so that the main current of air can pass through the mouth. The gesture of head tipping in chimpanzees may have originated in this way.

ARM RAISING occurs when either the forearm or the entire arm is raised with a rapid movement; the palm of the hand is normally orientated toward the threatened individual, and the fingers are slightly flexed. The gesture is often accompanied by head tipping and the "soft bark" or the "waa bark." The context in which this occurs is similar to that described for head tipping.

HITTING AWAY is a hitting movement with the back of the hand directed toward the threatened animal, and is often accompanied by the "soft bark." It may occur when a subordinate approaches too closely to a male who is feeding, for example. The same movement may also be a defensive reaction when a chimpanzee is startled by a large insect, a snake, or the like.

FLAPPING is a downward slapping movement of the hand in the direction of the threatened individual. It can be accompanied by "grinning" and "squeak calls," screaming, or the "waa bark." This gesture frequently occurred during female squabbles, and often led to "slapping." It may also occur when a chimpanzee, after being attacked or threatened, has sought reassurance contact with a third individual more dominant than the aggressor; after such contact the attacked animal may "flap" in the direction of the attacker.

BRANCHING describes the chimpanzee's taking hold of a branch or twig and shaking it from side to side or backward and forward. It is normally directed toward animals of other species. However, Fig. 12–4 shows a juvenile "branching" an individual older than herself, but subordinate to her mother.

Fig. 12–4. Juvenile female "branching" adolescent female. The juvenile's adolescent male sibling is near her, and their mother is also close by. (*Photograph by Baron Hugo Van Lawick;* © *National Geographic Society*)

STAMPING AND SLAPPING have been described in the section on frustration. This sometimes occurred during an aggressive encounter, typically when a chimpanzee (particularly a female) chased a fleeing individual. The aggressor often gave panting hoots and calls, or screamed loudly.

THROWING of sticks, stones, or vegetation, apparently at random, frequently formed part of the frustration and charging displays of mature and adolescent males in the Gombe Stream area. In addition, I observed eight different individuals throwing articles toward an objective with what appeared to be definite aim, within a context indicating that the action was aggressive. An earlier paper on throwing (Goodall 1964) suggested that the chimpanzees threw anything that was at hand. This may be true, but subsequent data reveal that 51 percent of the objects I saw thrown by the chimpanzees during two years were large enough to intimidate baboons, and certainly humans! Nevertheless, the rarity of aimed throwing as compared with random throwing, together with the fact that I observed this behavior in only 8 out of 17 males and that only 5 out of 44 objects thrown with apparent aim hit their targets, suggests that this behavior is not highly developed. It can more appropriately be described as threat or intimidation, rather than actual attack.

BIPEDAL ARM WAVING AND RUNNING at another individual is a form of threat behavior. The chimpanzee may stand upright facing the threatened individual, and then raise one or both arms rapidly in the air while uttering the "waa bark" or screaming. At other times the chimpanzee runs bipedally toward the threatened animal, waving its arms in the air. This behavior was most usually directed against baboons, both at the feeding area and elsewhere, when they approached chimpanzees too closely.

THE BIPEDAL SWAGGER is typically a male posture, and occurs only rarely in females. The chimpanzee stands upright and sways rhythmically from foot to foot, his shoulders slightly hunched and his arms held out and away from the body, usually to the side. He may swagger in one spot or he may move forward in this manner. This posture occurs most commonly as a courtship display, but it also occurs when one male threatens another of similar social status. I observed the swagger 31 times in the latter context, and twice it was followed by actual attack. Twice during aggressive interactions between two females one swaggered at the other, and one female swaggered at a mature male.

THE SITTING HUNCH has been observed only in male chimpanzees. The displaying animal hunches his shoulders and raises his arms in front of him or to the side while he sits. This is the typical courtship display of the adolescent male. I observed only one male showing this posture as a threat in a nonsexual context, and that was during an aggressive interaction with a young female.

THE QUADRUPEDAL HUNCH is a stance in which the individual stands with back rounded and head bent and slightly pulled back between the shoulders.

The chimpanzee may then move forward slowly or in a rapid charge. This was usually a high-intensity threat to another individual of a similar social status, and was sometimes followed by attack.

Attack

During one year I recorded 284 instances of attack; the frequency of attack behavior in the different age and sex classes is shown in Table 12–3. Of these, 66 percent were almost certainly due to the abnormal situation at the artificial feeding area where high-ranking individuals did not always have access to a desirable food. Therefore, although these attacks throw an interesting light on the mechanics of behavior and the social status of various individuals, their frequency cannot be regarded as typical. Of the remaining 34 percent of attacks, 15 were redirected aggression, 5 occurred during branch-waving displays, and the others were observed in a variety of contexts; the cause of many attacks was not apparent to the human observer.

Table 12–3 and the accompanying histogram show the result of a preliminary analysis on some of the data on attack behavior. The analysis was carried out in the following manner:

1. The number of attacks made by each age-sex class on each age-sex class was tabulated. These results, together with the total number of attacks made by each class on each class are presented in a table.

2. In order to obtain a more accurate estimate of the relative frequency of attack by each age-sex class (that is, on all other classes) the following calculations were made.

a. The total number of attacks made by each individual was divided by the number of occasions on which that particular animal was seen (see Table 12–1).

b. The resultant figure was multiplied by 1000 (extrapolated) to give the number of attacks made by that individual per 1000 observations.

c. The range of the figures calculated in *b* for all individuals in each age-sex class is given.

d. The median for the figures calculated in *b* for all individuals in each age-sex class is given.

e. Procedures *a*, *b*, *c*, and *d* were then repeated in order to determine the relative frequency with which each age-sex class was attacked.

This method of analysis does not tell us whether the observed frequency of attacks initiated by a certain age-sex class and directed (by that class) toward another class is a consequence of the relative frequency with which each of the classes was observed; it does not, in fact, tell us whether the initiator of the behavior exercises selection.

Table 12–3 shows that mature males initiated attack about four and one-half times more frequently (per 1000 observations) than did adolescent

TABLE 12–3   DISTRIBUTION AND FREQUENCY OF ATTACK BE-
HAVIOR IN THE VARIOUS AGE–SEX CLASSES

One attacked	One Attacking						Total No.	Median (2)	Range (2)
	♂	Adol. ♂	♀	Adol. ♀	Juvenile	Infant			
Male	45	2	0	0	0	0	47	10.0	0–38
Adult male	52	11	9	0	0	0	72	31.0	8–95
Female	82	15	6	0	0	0	103	50.5	33–64
Adult female	6	2	3	0	5	0	16	17.5	31–66
Juvenile	14	15	3	2	5	0	39	3.5	39–46
Infant	4	0	1	0	7	0	12	5.5	15–26
Total attacks	203	45	22	2	17	0	289		
Median (1)	59	14.5	3	3	12.5	0			
Range (1)	16–120	0–34	0–30	0–6	0–25	0			

Median and Range (1).   Median number of attacks made by each age/sex class per 1000
observations, and the range for individuals of that class.
Median and Range (2).   Median number of attacks made on each age/sex class per 1000
observations, and the range for individuals of that class.

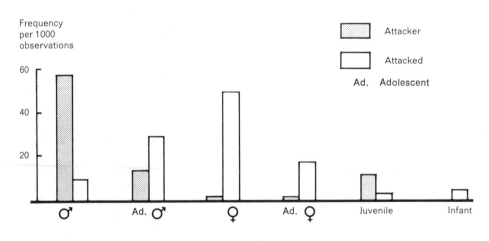

Histogram taken from Table 12–3 to show median frequency of attacking and being attacked in the different
age/sex classes.

males, and five times more frequently than mature females. It also shows that mature females were attacked more frequently (per 1000 observations) than was any other age-sex class, and that infants and juveniles were attacked significantly less often.

The range for the number of attacks (per 1000 observations) within each age-sex class indicates that some individuals are extremely aggressive as compared with some others. In particular, the old female (Flo) attacked approximately twice as frequently as all the other females combined. It may be significant that all the attacks recorded for juveniles were initiated by Flo's female offspring. The highest score for individual male attacks was that of the top-ranking male, Mike; the lowest was for David, a high-ranking but extremely nonaggressive individual. Other male scores all ranged between 41 and 87 attacks (per 1000 observations). Within the adolescent male class, the three individuals estimated as the eldest attacked far more frequently than the others.

The range given for the number of attacks on animals in the different age-sex classes suggests that some individuals were frequently involved as targets in aggressive incidents, whereas others normally avoided attack. Thus the nonaggressive male, David, was attacked less often than any other male except the dominant, Mike. The three youngest mature females (Mandy, Melissa, and Circe) each were attacked about twice as frequently as the three old mothers (Flo, Olly, and Marina).

Attacks were invariably of short duration, seldom lasting more than a few seconds; the longest attack lasted about one and one-half minutes. After a fight the aggressor often charged off, sometimes dragging branches behind him. The various methods of attack are listed below; most attacks comprise several of these components.

THE ATTACKING CHARGE. An attack is frequently preceded by a charge that is normally quadrupedal, silent, and fast. The hair of the attacking individual is usually fully erect at this stage, although on a few occasions it was sleek. In the five attacks by males during branch-dragging displays their charges were accompanied by hooting calls, and the victims (all females) were subjected to only a very mild form of attack (Figs. 12–5 and 12–6).

STAMPING ON THE BACK. The attacker seizes the victim by the hair and endeavors to leap onto its back. If this is achieved he then stamps on the victim with both feet. I have seen between one and three double foot-beats during such stamping, and the sound carries at least 50 yards. Occasionally, the male gives a final kick before moving off. Mature females were not seen to attack in this manner, but a juvenile female did so on several occasions.

LIFTING, SLAMMING, AND DRAGGING. When the victim is smaller than the aggressor it may be lifted bodily from the ground by its hair or limbs and

Figs. 12–5, 12–6 and 12–7. High-ranking mature male subjects an old female to low intensity attack on arriving at the feeding area. Her two-year-old infant is clinging on the ventral position. After briefly pounding on her back and then kicking her he immediately embraces her with one arm. (*Photograph by Baron Hugo Van Lawick;* © *National Geographic Society*)

slammed down again (Fig. 12–7). This may be repeated several times. The attacked individual may also be dragged along the ground by its hair or by one limb. Only mature males were seen to fight in this way.

BITING. During an attack the aggressor often puts his mouth to the body of his victim as though biting; normally, however, the only visible aftereffect is some saliva on the hair of the other. On only four occasions was serious biting observed: (1) once a male bit a female and left deep puncture marks in her arm; (2) another male bit an adolescent male in his foot, again leaving deep wounds; (3) an adolescent female bit the clitoris of a juvenile during a squabble; and (4) one mature male, during redirected aggression, dragged a juvenile female along with her foot in his mouth. On other occasions, however, chimpanzees were seen with puncture marks and gashes that might have been inflicted by biting. Yerkes (1943) frequently observed captive chimpanzees using their teeth during fighting, but records only one instance of a jaw-grip maintained.

HAIR-PULLING. The attacked animal may lose fairly large handfuls of hair during a fight. When females or youngsters squabble they sometimes grab at and pull on each other's hair (rather in the manner of human children), particularly hair on the head and shoulder region. In this context, also, handfuls of hair may be pulled out.

SLAPPING. One form of attack is a downward movement of the arm in which the palm of the hand slaps the body of the other animal. It occurs frequently when a female attacks another chimpanzee; both males and females may slap humans and baboons during aggressive interaction.

SCRATCHING. The chimpanzee may scratch by slightly flexing its fingers and drawing its nails rapidly across the skin of the victim. Only females were seen to scratch in this way. When the victim was human, such a scratch broke the skin; no visible marks were left on the skin of scratched chimpanzees.

Only 10 percent of the 284 attacks were classified as "violent," and even attacks that appeared punishing to me often resulted in no discernible injury apart from the occasional wrenching out of hair. Other attacks consisted merely of a brief pounding, hitting, or rolling (by hitting or kicking) of the individual, after which the aggressor often touched or embraced the other immediately (Fig. 12–8).

Most often the victims, screaming loudly, tried to escape from their aggressors. At other times they crouched during an attack, presenting their backs to the attacker and protecting their faces, limbs, and abdomens. This was particularly true of mothers with infants clinging ventrally (see Figs. 12–5, 12–6, and 12–8). In only 18 instances, when the fight was between two individuals of similar size and social status, did the attacked individual fight back fiercely.

SUBMISSIVE BEHAVIOR

This heading is used as a rather loose term to describe various nonaggressive postures and gestures that are directed toward a dominant chimpanzee in the following behavioral contexts: (1) When the subordinate has been threatened or attacked by the dominant individual (referred to as "appeasement" gestures); (2) when the subordinate approaches or is approached by, or passes or is passed by a high-ranking individual which has not, apparently, shown aggression toward the gesturing animal; and (3) when the subordinate, after being attacked or threatened, approaches a third individual of higher social status than the aggressor and makes gestures similar to appeasement gestures.

The various postures, gestures, and calls that are observed in submissive behavior of these types are described, together with the contexts in which they were normally seen.

PRESENTING. Presenting, in a non-sexual context, occurs when a subordinate individual turns its rump towards a higher-ranking one. It is a posture common to many primates, such as rhesus macaques, baboons, and langurs (Altmann 1962*a*; Hall 1962*b*;

Fig. 12–8. Mature male attacking adolescent female. Grasping her by hair and one leg he lifts her from the ground. The female is screaming loudly. (*Photograph by Baron Hugo Van Lawick;* © *National Geographic Society*).

Jay 1965*b*), in a variety of nonsexual situations. It was one of the most frequently observed elements in submissive behavior patterns among the Gombe Stream chimpanzees.

The posture of the presenting individual varies in relation to the situation. After a particularly severe attack the subordinate (screaming loudly with open mouth and lips retracted from teeth and gums) may back toward the aggressor from a distance of eight feet or more, looking over its shoulder. It then adopts the "extreme crouch," with all its limbs completely flexed and its head almost on the ground (Fig. 12–9). After a less severe attack, or when the dominance status of the two individuals involved in the attack is more nearly equal, the presenting posture is less extreme. The animal may stand with half-flexed limbs, looking back over its shoulder and "grinning" while screaming or giving "squeak calls," or showing the "silent grin," or whimpering.

After a low-intensity threat, the subordinate may flex its limbs only slightly while presenting; it may grin and give "squeak calls" or it may whimper. When a subordinate comes close to a higher ranking individual (usually a male) it may present with slightly flexed limbs (Fig. 12–10), or it may simply turn its rump toward the other with no obvious change in posture or facial expression (Fig. 12–12). A juvenile once turned her hind

Fig. 12–9. Adolescent male presents with the "extreme crouch" after being attacked by a dominant mature male. The latter reaches out to touch him with a reassurance gesture. (*Photograph by Baron Hugo Van Lawick;* © *National Geographic Society*).

quarters toward her adolescent sibling in this manner after he had mildly threatened her.

I have roughly analyzed 324 instances of presenting that occurred in the three types of behavioral contexts described earlier. Of this number, 32 percent occurred when the subordinate had been attacked or threatened (Category 1); 54 percent occurred when subordinates came into close proximity to high-ranking individuals (Category 2); and the remaining 14 percent occurred when subordinates, after being attacked, presented to a third individual (Category 3). Table 12–4 shows the percentage of the total number of presentings that fell into these three categories made by individuals of the various age-sex classes.

These data were further analyzed, and Table 12–5 shows the actual distribution of the presentings observed during one year. It will be noted that males seldom presented but were frequently presented to, and that females were seen to present more often than any other age-sex class (per 1000 observations). High-ranking males were presented to by individuals of all other age-sex classes (including lower-ranking mature males), but no male was seen to present to a female or adolescent. On two occasions a juvenile was presented to; on both occasions this occurred after the same juvenile female had threatened individuals older than herself, but subordinate to her

Fig. 12–10. Adolescent male reaches out to touch the genital area of a juvenile female who has paused to present to him as she passes by. Her limbs are half-flexed but her facial expression is relaxed as she looks back at him. (*Photograph by Baron Hugo Van Lawick;* © *National Geographic Society*)

TABLE 12–4 PERCENTAGE OF TOTAL NUMBER OF PRESENTINGS IN EACH AGE/SEX CLASS ELICITED BY THREE DIFFERENT BEHAVIORAL CONTEXTS

	Percentages of Presentings Category			Total Number
Age/Sex Class	1	2	3	of Presentings
Male	25	25	50	4
Adolescent male	68	22	10	48
Female	16	80	4	136
Adolescent female	56	43	1	40
Juvenile	55	43	2	35
Infant	10	90	0	61
Total				324

Categories (1) Subordinate had been attacked or threatened.
(2) Subordinate came into proximity to higher ranking individual.
(3) Subordinate, after attack, presented to individual of higher rank than its aggressor.

Fig. 12–11. Young mature female with start of ano-genital swelling presents, looking back over her shoulder, to an old mature male. (*Photograph by Baron Hugo Van Lawick;* © *National Geographic Society*)

mother who was close by. Table 12–5 also shows that there is a wide range for the individuals of the different age-sex classes, both in the frequency of presenting and in being presented to. Thus, one female (Melissa) presented twice as frequently as another young mature female, and all the young females presented more often than the older ones. The top-ranking male, Mike, was presented to most frequently. Among the adolescent males the range for the number of times presenting was directed toward them (per 1000 observations) varied from 44 to 50 times for the three oldest to 12 to 25 for the others.

BOWING, BOBBING, AND CROUCHING are shown by a subordinate when it is facing the dominant individual; these actions involve various degrees of limb flexion. On the few occasions when I saw an individual bob slowly, he stood briefly and bipedally, but with his body only slightly raised from the horizontal position. He dropped back onto four limbs, and as a continuation of the movement flexed his elbows until his chest was close to the ground. He then jerked himself back to the bipedal position prior to repeating the entire sequence several times; his knees were slightly flexed throughout. Usually these movements follow each other rapidly, and often the elbows are flexed and straightened while the hands remain on the ground. Any number (up to

Fig. 12–12. Adolescent female pauses to present as she passes a mature female; the latter peers at her genital area before briefly touching it. This is the most relaxed type of presenting. (*Photograph by Baran Hugo National Van Lawick;* © *National Geographic Society*).

ten) bobs is normal; the behavior is usually accompanied by "bobbing pants" or occasionally by "panting shrieks." This behavior is most commonly seen in adolescent males: occasionally low-ranking males bob, and I saw two females do so. It is a typical response of a subordinate animal when a high-ranking male moves into its vicinity (Fig. 12–13).

Bowing occurs when the subordinate goes up to a higher ranking individual and flexes its elbows to a much greater extent than it flexes its knees. It is usually associated with soft panting. It is seen frequently when a subordinate (particularly, a female) approaches a high-ranking male who has previously shown signs of aggressive behavior, or after he has performed a branch waving display.

Crouching is an extreme form of bowing: the subordinate flexes all limb joints so that its body is close to the ground. The animal normally pants, or it may "grin" and give squeak calls. Crouching appears in a context similar to bowing, but may also occur as appeasement behavior after an individual has been threatened or attacked.

A lowering of the body toward the ground in a submissive context occurs in other species of primate. Gorillas and baboons when frightened during aggressive interactions may crouch prone to the ground (Schaller 1963; Hall

TABLE 12–5   DISTRIBUTION AND FREQUENCY OF NONSEXUAL
PRESENTING IN THE DIFFERENT AGE/SEX CLASSES

One pre-sented to	One presenting						Total No.	Median (2)	Range (2)
	♂	Adol. ♂	♀	Adol. ♀	Juve-nile	Infant			
Male	4	44	90	20	24	40	222	71.0	16–170
Adolescent male	0	2	42	13	6	21	84	34.0	12–50
Female	0	2	3	6	4	0	15	3.5	0–15
Adolescent female	0	0	0	1	0	0	1	0.0	0–1
Juvenile	0	0	1	0	1	0	2	1.0	0–2
Infant	0	0	0	0	0	0	0	—	—
Total No.	4	48	136	40	35	61	324		
Median (1)	3	13	39	80	39	102			
Range (1)	0–4	9–38	10–220	98–132	37	55–150			

Median and Range (1).   Median number of presentings made by each age/sex class per 1000
observations, and the range for individuals of that class.

Median and Range (2).   Median number of presentings made to each age/sex class per 1000
observations, and the range for individuals of that class.

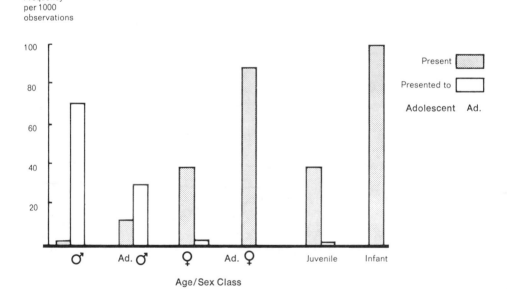

Histogram taken from Table 12–5 to show median frequency of presenting and being presented to in the different age/sex classes.

Fig. 12–13. Low-ranking mature male hurrying toward a high-ranking male (who shows hair erection) in order to "bob" as the latter passes him. (*Photograph by Baron Hugo Van Lawick;* © *National Geographic Society*)

Fig. 12–14. Mature female lays her hand on the back of a higher ranking female as the latter passes her. (*Photograph by Baron Hugo Van Lawick;* © *National Geographic Society*).

and DeVore 1965). In man, too, bowing has long been a submissive gesture, and until a few years ago even civilized peoples prostrated themselves when appealing for mercy.

SUBMISSIVE KISSING. Kissing, a pressing of the lips or teeth to the body of another individual, occurs in both submissive and dominant individuals. As a submissive gesture it frequently accompanies bowing or crouching, in which case the kiss is typically in the groin of the other individual. Sometimes when a chimpanzee moved close to a high-ranking individual (or vice versa), it touched the latter's face with its mouth. On rare occasions a female who had been threatened or startled by a sudden movement of a mature male kissed his hand when he reached out to touch her.

Behavior of this sort, described as "mouth to mouth touching," may occur in both dominant and submissive baboons (Hall and DeVore 1965; personal observation), and again until a few years ago man showed submissive kissing when he pressed his lips to the feet of his master or king.

HAND AND ARM MOVEMENTS. Various hand and arm movements are seen in a submissive context. The most frequently observed is when the subordinate reached out to touch a higher ranking chimpanzee; virtually any part of the body may be touched, but the head, back, or rump are the most usual. The subordinate usually pants as it touches the other, but may "grin" or make "squeak calls." This behavior is seen most commonly when a subordinate is passing or being passed by a high-ranking individual (Fig. 12–14). It occasionally occurred as an appeasement gesture when a chimpanzee had been threatened or mildly attacked.

Touching, in a similar behavioral context, was observed in the Gombe Stream baboons; during nonsexual mounting the mounted individual sometimes reached back and touched the other on the leg with one hand. In addition, when baboons presented in a nonsexual context, they frequently reached back one leg and touched the dominant animal on the thigh or even on the chest with one foot.

Another gesture observed in the chimpanzees is that of holding the hand toward a higher ranking individual without actually touching. The wrist and fingers are extended, and the hand may be held palm upward or, occasionally, downward. (The gesturing individual may also whimper, "grin," make "squeak calls," or scream.) This gesture, which was seen most often in females, occurred in a variety of contexts. When a mature male made a sudden movement a nearby female sometimes held her hand toward him. One female (Melissa) invariably held her hand out toward the highest ranking male in the group several times before moving off to get a hidden banana that she had noticed.[7] When a chimpanzee had been attacked or

[7]Sometimes we hid bananas in trees so that the young chimpanzees could find them while the others fed from the boxes.

threatened, it sometimes approached and held its hand toward an individual dominant to its aggressor.

Another gesture falling under this heading is "wrist bending": the wrist is flexed, and the back of the hand or wrist may then be held toward the lips of a dominant chimpanzee. In the typical submissive context this was seen only rarely, when females or juveniles approached mature males. However, a similar gesture was observed when juvenile, adolescent, or mature individuals reached toward infants (under one year of age), since they invariably did so with the backs of their hands, keeping the fingers bent away. In some instances this gesture seemed to be made with reference to the mother of the infant concerned, but further data are required before this can be substantiated.

Another movement in this series is "bending away." This occurs when the subordinate individual flexes its elbow and wrist, at the same time drawing its arm close to its body and leaning slightly away from the higher ranking animal (Fig. 12–15). This may be accompanied by soft panting, or, occasionally, by low-intensity grinning and squeak calls. Bending away was usually seen when mature males passed close to youngsters, particularly if the male showed, or had previously shown, some signs of aggression or frustration.

SUBMISSIVE MOUNTING. The subordinate holds the other chimpanzee around the waist, or lays its hands and lower arms along the back of the other from the rear. Normally it leans forward so that its chest is close to the other's back, and then gives thrusting movements of its pelvis. Both males and

Fig. 12–15. Adolescent male "bending away" as a mature male passes him. (*Photograph by Baron Hugo Van Lawick;* © *National Geographic Society*)

females have been seen to mount in a submissive context, usually after they had been charged or attacked. When the mounted animal was a male, the subordinate occasionally reached up with one foot to touch or grasp the other's scrotum.

REASSURANCE BEHAVIOR

In many circumstances one chimpanzee appears to be calmed or "reassured" as a result of touching or being touched by another.[8] The three main contexts in which such behavior is typically observed can be described under the following headings: (1) reassurance gestures made to a subordinate; (2) calming behavior directed toward a high-ranking chimpanzee; and (3) reassurance contact with individuals of any rank.

Reassurance Gestures Made to a Subordinate

A dominant individual may respond to submissive behavior directed toward it by a subordinate in any one of the following ways:

TOUCHING. The dominant animal reaches out to touch the subordinate with one hand or, on occasions, with one foot. The latter may be thus touched anywhere on its body, depending mainly on its position relative to the dominant individual at the time. Touching the genital area or rump is the typical response to submissive presenting; occasionally this involves an "inspection" of the vulva of the female. When the subordinate bows or crouches, it is normally touched on the head, shoulders, or back; when it holds out its hand, the hand is commonly touched or even held by the dominant animal (Figs. 12–16 and 12–17). Occasionally the higher rank-ing chimpanzee will touch the other with his toes; for example, when a female, in passing, presented to a reclining male he idly reached to touch her genital area in this manner.

PATTING. The dominant chimpanzee may reach out and make patting movements on the body, head, or face of the other with the palmar surface of its hand or fingers. These movements are slight and very rapid, and may be

---

[8]This may be related, sometimes, to the fact that the skin, at least in man, is a highly complex and versatile organ of communication. It has been suggested that the "sympa-thetic innervation, perhaps that of the sweat glands and capillaries, is also conductive to the viscera and to other organ systems" (Frank 1958). Certainly the rhythmic pat-ting and caressing of a human baby has a soothing effect (Frank 1958), and this may be compared with the calming effects of physical contact described in this section for chimpanzees.

Fig. 12–16. The female ("Melissa") holds her hand toward a high-ranking mature male as she approaches when her infant is two days old. (*Photograph by Baron Hugo Van Lawick;* © *National Geographic Society*)

Fig. 12–17. The mature male responds by reaching out to touch her hand. (*Photograph by Baron Hugo Van Lawick;* © *National Geographic Society*)

compared with those made by a human mother when patting her baby. Patting behavior typically occurred when the subordinate was extremely agitated (for example, when it had been attacked by the dominant chimpanzee and had then approached with a submissive gesture). Sometimes the subordinate was screaming loudly and on such occasions the dominant continued to pat for 30 seconds or more or until the screaming had died down. Figure 12–18 shows a nervous adolescent female being reassured in this way.

Mature and adolescent chimpanzees, particularly males, frequently responded to the approach of a small infant in this manner (Fig. 12–19).

EMBRACING. The higher ranking animal may embrace the subordinate with one or both arms from the front, the side, or the rear. This type of reassurance sometimes occurred after a mature male had attacked a female during an arrival branch-dragging display (Fig. 12–8). It was also the typical response shown by a mother when her infant was hurt or frightened.

REASSURANCE MOUNTING. The position is similar to that adopted during submissive mounting, but it is the subordinate animal that is mounted. This was the response to screaming and presenting on 21 occasions. Both mature and adolescent males sometimes placed their hands around infants and made thrusting movements over their backs when the infants screamed and crouched in submission.

REASSURANCE KISSING. In a reassurance context, kissing sometimes occurred during an embrace, and was occasionally seen as a response to a subordinate's reaching out its hand, at which time the dominant individual held and kissed the hand. Occasionally a mature male pressed his lips to the face of a female when she approached and slightly crouched in front of him, or after he himself had been kissed submissively. When the dominant individual responded to a submissive kiss with a similar gesture, this sometimes resulted in mouth-to-mouth kissing.

RUMP TURNING. The dominant animal turns its rump toward the subordinate, and may even back toward the latter. This was not a common response to submissive behavior, but it was seen sixteen times. On each occasion the behavior was apparently elicited by submissive postures or gestures on the part of the subordinate and sometimes resulted in submissive mounting. Seven times when rump turning was shown in response to presenting this led to the animals' pressing their bottoms together (Fig. 12–20); each of these incidents involved the same adolescent male. Three times this animal turned his rump when a mature female held out her hand toward him; she then touched his scrotum and he made thrusting movements on her hand.

Fig. 12–18. Adolescent female after being mildly threatened by top-ranking male ("Mike") turned away screaming and presented her rump. Mike reached out and touched her genital area; she turned back toward him, still uttering fear squeaks. As the final stage in this chain of events Mike is now touching her under the chin. After this the female was quiet. (*Photograph by Baron Hugo Van Lawick;* © *National Geographic Society*)

Fig. 12–19. Eleven-month-old infant approaches mature male who pats the infant under the chin. (*Photograph by Baron Hugo Van Lawick;* © *National Geographic Society*)

Fig. 12–20. Adolescent male turns his rump towards a female in response to her submissive presenting. (*Photograph by Baron Hugo Van Lawick;* © *Geographic Society*)

Submissive behavior did not always elicit reassurance gestures; sometimes the dominant individual ignored the subordinate altogether. On such occasions the latter either moved away or (particularly if it was a juvenile or young adolescent) maintained its submissive posture while continuing to scream or whimper until it was finally touched. Indeed, some chimpanzees went into temper tantrums if reassurance was withheld. This apparent "need" for reassurance contact sometimes resulted in an obvious conflict situation. Thus, after a particularly savage attack, an adolescent male often showed a tendency to approach the aggressor that was strongly counteracted by a tendency to flee; he therefore moved forward in a series of circles or zig-zags as he alternately approached and turned away from the dominant male concerned.

The underlying motivational state of the dominant individual that induces reassurance gestures of the type described here is unclear, but the effect on the subordinate is apparent in many instances. The two following examples will serve to illustrate this.

An adolescent male (Pepe) approached a mature male (Goliath) that was feeding on a huge pile of bananas. Pepe did not immediately take a fruit, but instead crouched, whimpering and screaming, while looking toward Goliath and occasionally reaching out one hand toward him. After a few moments Goliath reached out and began to pat the youngster on his face and head. After this, Pepe reached slowly toward a banana, but at the last moment jerked back and began to scream again. Goliath once more reached out and patted him for several seconds. Finally the adolescent stopped screaming,

Fig. 12-21. A high-ranking male who is trying to get at the bananas inside this box pauses and starts to utter "panting hoots." A subordinate joins in, at the same time reaching out to make a few grooming movements on the neck of the other. (*Photograph by Baron Hugo Van Lawick;* © *National Geographic Society*)

and, watching the big male carefully, gathered up a few fruits and moved away with them. Similar behavior was seen on many occasions.

The second example concerns the female Melissa. We have seen that she invariably held out her hand to a dominant male when she wanted to go and take a hidden banana; not until she had been touched or patted once or several times did she actually move away to take the food.

This type of behavior occurs in other primates. Dominant olive baboons sometimes reach out to touch a presenting subordinate (personal observation; DeVore, personal communication), and male hamadryas baboons may, perhaps, show a similar gesture (Kummer, personal communication). Langurs often reach out and place their hands on the body of a subordinate at the end of an aggressive interaction (Jay 1956*b;* Jay, personal communication). I observed a young red colobus approaching a large mature male that was feeding, and sit before him with slightly bowed head. The big male reached out and touched its head, after which the youngster moved past him and commenced to feed nearby. Lip-smacking in the rhesus monkey may have the effect of "reducing fear" in a subordinate, and a dominant monkey

Fig. 12–22. Adolescent male touches his own scrotum when he suddenly sees chimpanzees approaching in the distance. (*Photograph by Baron Hugo Van Lawick;* © *National Geographic Society*)

Fig. 12–23. Two males hooting in response to calls of chimpanzee. The mature male is reaching out to touch the higher ranking male. (*Photograph by Baron Hugo Van Lawick;* © *National Geographic Society*)

sometimes lip-smacks when a subordinate shows frightened grinning (Hinde and Rowell 1962). Man, too, may respond to an abject subordinate with a smile, a touch, a pat on the shoulder or, in some circumstances, an embrace.

CALMING BEHAVIOR. On several occasions a high-ranking male, after he had attacked some individual or performed violent charging displays was touched, patted, or groomed by other males. During such bouts of physical contact the male in question gradually "calmed down" (that is, he appeared to relax and slowly lost his hair and penile erections).

Reassurance Contact with Individuals of Any Rank

A chimpanzee may seek to initiate physical contact with another chimpanzee (often, but not necessarily, a higher ranking one) in a number of behavioral contexts when it is afraid, agitated, or intensely stimulated by social activity or the sight of food. The gestures most frequently involved in the behavior are touching, holding the hand toward another, embracing, mounting, and grooming movements. In addition, one adolescent male frequently touched or held his own scrotum or penis under such circumstances. This type of behavior is illustrated by the following examples.

When chimpanzees were suddenly startled (for example, by a strange noise or sudden movement) they frequently reached out to touch another individual. When some violent social activity broke out in a group (such as fighting or branch-dragging displays) individuals not participating often reached out to touch or make grooming movements on each other; sometimes one mounted or embraced a companion. The same patterns often occurred when chimpanzees heard or saw others in the distance (Fig. 12–23). When chimpanzees were confronted with an especially large pile of bananas or saw us opening a big box of the fruit, the individuals concerned not only touched, patted, kissed, or embraced each other, but invariably uttered loud food "barks" at the same time.

One mature male embraced a three-year-old infant three times—twice after the adult had been attacked by another male and once when he had a sudden fright from seeing his own reflection in some glass. Even contact with the infant had a marked effect in calming him.

When a chimpanzee hurried to touch a high-ranking individual after being attacked or threatened by a less dominant one, it often looked around after the contact and made threatening sounds or gestures in the direction of its aggressor. Similarly, when an infant was suddenly frightened it often ran to its mother and suckled her, briefly held her nipple in its mouth, or simply reached out to touch her; he then looked around at the alarming stimulus (van Lawick-Goodall, in press).

This type of contact-seeking behavior also occurs in other primates. On one occasion a gorilla was seen to reach its hand toward another when it suddenly saw a human observer; the second responded by taking the hand (Osborn 1963). An old baboon at the Gombe Stream Reserve was seen to reach out and touch another individual while threatening an observer (Miss Koning, personal communication). Hall (Hall and DeVore 1965) observed behavior in the chacma baboon that may be comparable; when a pair of animals was threatening another baboon, one sometimes briefly mounted the other, placing its hands lightly on its companion's back while standing slightly to the side and pointing its muzzle in the direction of the threatened individual. Man also shows a number of similar gestures in such situations. Frank (1958) notes that "a person who is strongly reacting emotionally, as in acute fear or pain, or grief, may be able to recover his physiological equilibrium through close tactile contacts with another sympathetic person." A small child may hold its mother's hand or skirt in the presence of strangers; similarly an adult may reach out and touch a companion or hold his hand when suddenly frightened or emotionally upset. In a different type of situation (probably comparable to a chimpanzee seeing a lot of food) two men may embrace or clap each other on the back when they suddenly hear good news.

EXPRESSIVE GESTURES OBSERVED
IN A SEXUAL CONTEXT

There are various gestures and postures that occur during sexual interactions between male and receptive female chimpanzees. (Many of these have already been described, as they occur also during frustration and aggressive behavior.) Of the 213 copulations or attempted copulations I observed in one year, males took the initiative 176 times, either by approaching the female with both hair and penis erect or by giving a "courtship display."[9]

Four courtship gestures have already been described: the bipedal swagger, the sitting hunch, branching, and glaring. Two other displays are (1) "tree leaping," when the male concerned (if he is in a tree) may execute a series of leaps and rhythmic swings through the branches, his body usually in an upright position while he faces in the general direction of the female; and (2) "beckoning," when the male, in a bipedal posture, raises one arm level with his head or higher and then makes a swift "sweeping toward himself" movement, his hand making an arc in the air.[10]

Females responded to 82 percent of the approaches or courtship displays of mature males, and to 77 percent of those of adolescent males by presenting for copulation (by remaining crouched where they were while the male approached or by running toward him and presenting). On eight occasions the males lightly touched females on their rumps before the latter presented. The percentage of success of the various types of displays of mature and adolescent males, that is, the percentage of those resulting in copulation, is shown in Table 12–6.

On 20 occasions, females ran away screaming when males approached to initiate copulation; on 10 of these occasions the males pursued until the females stopped and presented, on the other 10 occasions the males "gave up" and after shaking branches in the direction of the females moved away. On 12 occasions, females ignored courtship displays; the males concerned either persisted until the females presented, or they moved off.

On 37 occasions females solicited males. Typically, the female approached to within six feet, flattened herself in front of the male with her limbs flexed, and looked back at him over her shoulder. Five times the five soliciting females were ignored; four of them walked away, but the fifth persisted until the male mounted and copulated with her.

---

[9]This term is used simply as a means of describing postures and gestures commonly directed toward a receptive female prior to copulation; it is not intended to imply that these were observed only in a sexual context.

[10]This gesture is not unlike an exaggerated form of that made by females when they gather their infants into the ventral position.

TABLE 12–6   RELATIVE FREQUENCY OF VARIOUS COURTSHIP DISPLAYS AND OF SOLICITATION PRIOR TO COPULATION (OR ATTEMPTED COPULATION) BY MATURE AND ADOLESCENT MALES WITH RECEPTIVE FEMALES

Display	Percent of All Mature Male Displays	Percent of Success*	Percent of All Adolescent Male Displays	Percent of Success
Male approach	43	95	35	96
Bipedal swagger	20	78	6	100
"Branching"	8	94	24	61
Sitting hunch	1	100	15	73
Tree leaping	9	89	1	100
Beckoning	6	100	1	100
Glare	1	100	—	—
Initiated by female	12	83	19	100
Total Percentage	100		100	
Total Success		90		84

*Percent of success represents occasions when the male or female responded to the behavior.

The male copulatory position is not a stereotyped one; normally he mounts, places one hand on the female's back, and adopts a "squatting" position, his buttocks scarcely more than an inch from the ground and his body slightly inclined forward. At other times, however, males either placed both hands on the ground or both on the back of the female, or held on to a branch overhead with both hands. Occasionally copulation took place while the female stood quadrupedally with only very slightly flexed limbs; the male either stood behind her and leaned directly forward, his chest on her back and his arms encircling her body, or he stood bipedally behind her and copulated while holding onto an overhead branch.

During some copulations slow lip-smacking was observed in the male; three males invariably gave "copulatory pants" at the culmination of the sexual act (which was normally completed after 5 to 10 seconds). During intercourse, females sometimes looked ahead, sometimes looked around at the male, and often gave short high-pitched squeak calls with "grinning." After sexual contact females remained still, moved away calmly, or rushed off screaming. Copulation was sometimes followed by brief grooming by either partner.

One behavior pattern, "inspection" of the genital area, was frequently observed when a nonreceptive female presented to a male or stopped near him. Sometimes he merely put his nose near her vaginal opening and appeared to sniff; at other times he poked his finger into the opening carefully, and then sniffed the finger; occasionally he used both hands to part the lips of the vulva, and then poked, peered, and sniffed. Such behavior was often repeated two or three times; one male inspected 18 times in 10 minutes while the female reclined beside him.

Inspection seldom occurred when females had large sexual swellings. That the behavior is, in fact, related to the estrous cycle of the female is suggested by the marked increase in the number of inspections usually directed toward any one female at the first signs of sexual swelling. Inspection also occurred frequently in the period immediately following detumescence.

Mature, adolescent, and juvenile females sometimes inspected other females, particularly during greeting behavior; it was a common pattern on the part of infants of both sexes, especially when the female concerned had a sexual swelling.

Fig. 12–24.   Adolescent male "inspecting" the genital area of a female who has just arrived in his group. (*Photograph by Baron Hugo Van Lawick;* © *National Geographic Society*)

Fig. 12–25. Mature female grooming adolescent male in greeting. Her two-year-old infant has jumped onto the adolescent's "lap" and is closely embracing him. (*Photograph by Baron Hugo Van Lawick;* © *National Geographic Society*)

GREETING BEHAVIOR

Greeting behavior may be defined as the nonaggressive interactions (or, at least, with only a very slight element of aggression) that occur between individuals meeting after a separation. There are many postures and gestures in the repertoire of the behavior. They consist of bobbing, bowing, and crouching, touching, kissing, embracing, grooming, presenting, mounting, inspecting of the genital area, and, occasionally, hand-holding. In addition, males (rarely, females) may precede their greeting with some form of ritualized aggressive pattern, such as the bipedal swagger, the quadrupedal and sitting hunch, stamping, and so forth. Often, but not always, males show erection of the hair and penis prior to and during greeting. As two individuals approach each other they may utter soft or loud panting sounds, particularly the subordinate as it bows, crouches, or bobs. Sometimes both the dominant and the subordinate individuals may "grin"; the latter may also make "squeak-calls."

During a greeting, one or several of the postures and gestures listed may be displayed by both the individuals concerned; at other times the higher ranking individual may ignore the greeting behavior of the other. The 686 greetings that were observed during a seven-month period have been broken down into the 1065 actual gestures and postures of which they were comprised. Table 12–7 shows the observed frequency with which these

TABLE 12–7   DISTRIBUTION AND FREQUENCY OF GREETINGS GESTURES IN THE DIFFERENT AGE/SEX CLASSES

One to Which the Gesture is Made	One Making Greeting Gesture					Total No.
	♂	Adol. ♂	♀	Adol. ♀	Juvenile and Infant	
Male	139	50	176	16	32	413
Adolescent male	209	98	46	15	23	391
Female	12	11	81	22	16	142
Adolescent female	11	13	17	6	4	51
Juvenile and infant	27	13	8	14	12	74
Total No.	398	185	328	73	87	1071

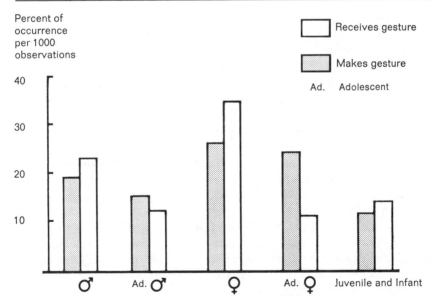

Histogram showing the relative frequency of making and receiving greeting gestures in the different age/sex classes. This is expressed as the mean percentage of occasions that each class made greeting gestures per 1000 observations.

gestures were directed toward each age-sex class by each class, and the frequency with which they were received by each of these classes. As the median frequency of greetings gestures in each of the classes has not yet been worked out, the histogram below the table shows only the mean percentage of occasions when each age-sex class initiated or was the recipient of greetings gestures (per 1000 observations). This does suggest that mature females show greeting gestures more often than do the other classes, and that greeting behavior is directed toward them more often than toward other classes. It also suggests that the two adolescent classes (particularly the females) are the most frequently ignored during greeting.

The particular gestures and postures displayed during a greeting depend partly on the age-sex class of the animals concerned, partly on their individuality, and partly on their mood at the time and the length of time for which they have been separated. Thus the more exaggerated gestures (such as embracing) are more likely to occur between individuals that are strongly attracted to each other (particularly if they have not seen each other for several days), than between two individuals that seldom interact socially in other ways. Swaggering and charging prior to greeting is seen more frequently when two associations of chimpanzees meet than when one animal quietly approaches a resting group.

Table 12-8 shows that although some of the gestures and postures (kissing, grooming, touching, and embracing) are displayed by all the age-sex classes, others are more or less limited to one or a few classes. Among adults and adolescents, presenting is almost entirely limited to females, whereas inspection is far more common in males. This suggests that there may be a sexual element in greeting behavior between males and females.

I have not yet analyzed the frequency with which each type of gesture was directed by individuals of each of the classes to each of the other classes, or vice versa, but Table 12–9 is an attempt to group greeting behavior into three main categories: (1) gestures made by subordinate chimpanzees to higher ranking ones; (2) those made by dominant individuals to their social inferiors; and (3) those seen when two individuals of similar social status greet each other.[11]

Table 12–9 shows that those gestures and postures that may appear in both submissive and reassurance contexts (such as kissing, touching, grooming, and embracing) were observed in all three types of greeting; those made only in submissive contexts were never directed by higher ranking individuals toward their subordinates, nor did they occur between animals of similar rank. This suggests that gestures and postures of submission and reassurance play a major role in greeting behavior, while the pregreeting displays, such as the bipedal swagger, add an aggressive element.

---

[11]Sometimes it was difficult to determine the social status of one individual in relation to the other at the time of greeting (for example, when an older chimpanzee greeted an infant the status of the latter was sometimes influenced by the proximity of its mother). Greetings involving two such individuals have been omitted from this table.

TABLE 12–8 FREQUENCY OF DIFFERENT GREETING GESTURES AND POSTURES IN THE AGE/SEX CLASSES, EXPRESSED AS A PERCENTAGE OF TOTAL NUMBER OF GESTURES RECORDED IN THE GREETING BEHAVIOR OF EACH CLASS

Gesture	Percentage of Occurrence				
	♂	Adol. ♂	♀	Adol. ♀	Juv. and Infant
Kiss	10.0	7	15	8	14
Groom	18.0	20	10	18	8
Touch	24.0	16	21	15	10
Embrace	12.0	9	8	9	8
Present	0.5	3	27	43	30
Inspect	19.0	19	2	1	21
Mount	5.0	8	—	6	1
Bob	0.5	14	—	—	—
Bow and crouch	1.0	4	7	—	—
Hold out hand	—	—	10	—	—
Hold hand	10.0	—	—	—	—
Total Percentage	100	100	100	100	100
Total No. Gestures	398	328	185	73	87

TABLE 12–9 TYPES OF GREETINGS GESTURES BETWEEN INDIVIDUALS OF SIMILAR SOCIAL STATUS, EXPRESSED AS PERCENTAGE OF TOTAL NUMBER OF OBSERVATIONS OF EACH TYPE OF GESTURE WHEN IT OCCURRED IN THE THREE DIFFERENT TYPES OF GREETING

Gesture	Subordinate Greets Dominant (%)	Dominant Greets Subordinate (%)	Similar Status (%)	Total No. Gestures
Bob	100	—	—	27
Crouch and bow	100	—	—	28
Present	100	—	—	87
Reach hand to	100	—	—	10
Hold hand	—	100	—	10
Mount	—	100	—	15
Kiss	60	30	10	82
Touch	41	51	8	189
Groom	30	60	10	120
Embrace	40	46	14	95

Greeting behavior may be considered adaptive in relation to the loose social structure of the chimpanzee community. When two individuals meet after a lapse of time that may have been anything from a few hours to a few weeks, some clear-cut gestures may be important or the re-establishment of a status recognition between them. When two humans greet, the basic principle involved is similar—the acknowledgment of a similar or different social standing of the person greeted. The deep bowing of the Japanese or the nodding of the head in Western civilization may have been derived from a submissive act (comparable to bowing or bobbing in the chimpanzee) that was originally intended to convey the meaning that no aggressiveness was intended (Schaller 1963). Similarly, reaching to shake an outstretched hand may have derived from some gesture of reassurance to an individual of lower rank (such as hand touching or holding in the chimpanzee). In fact, many of the greeting gestures described for chimpanzees have striking parallels in the greeting behavior of man.

SOME EXPRESSIVE MOVEMENTS THAT OCCUR IN OTHER CONTEXTS

There are gestures and postures that can be observed in behavioral contexts not mentioned in the previous pages. Some of these will be briefly outlined below.

In Social Grooming

The chimpanzee has a number of gestures and postures that apparently serve to elicit grooming behavior in another individual. In the most usual of these a chimpanzee approaches another and stands or sits, usually with head slightly bowed, so that some portion of its anatomy is placed in close proximity to the chosen partner. Most frequently presented in this manner are the head, back, and rump—those parts of the body that a chimpanzee cannot easily groom itself. Usually, such solicitation elicited a grooming response. Sometimes one animal simply approached and started to groom another chimpanzee; if the latter did not reciprocate after a few moments, the initiator frequently stopped grooming and adopted a soliciting attitude, or scratched some part of its body that was facing the partner. This often elicited grooming behavior and the two then groomed mutually.

There were many occasions on which an animal soliciting grooming was ignored; its reaction then varied, depending on its social status relative to that of the other chimpanzee and on its individuality. Thus when females were ignored by males they usually either moved away, started to groom the male, or groomed themselves. One female (Melissa), however, often rocked and whimpered if she was ignored, and sometimes reached out to poke the male concerned. This behavior invariably elicited a grooming response from the male. One male, on five occasions when his partner stopped grooming him, moved a few feet away and commenced to "branch" the other vigorously, at the same time showing full hair erection and glaring; each time, the partner got up immediately and began to groom again.

In Play Behavior

There are various gestures and postures associated with playful behavior.[12] These include the "play face," "laughing," and the "play walk." In play walking, the chimpanzee walks with a rounded back, head slightly bent down and pulled back between the shoulders, and takes small, rather "stilted" steps. Often there is a pronounced side-to-side movement as he moves forward, rather like the seaman's roll.

Play between youngsters was often initiated when one approached the other with the play walk or a gamboling-type run. When mature males initiated play with adolescents or juveniles they normally approached with the play walk and then reached out to prod or tickle the youngster. On the seven occasions on which mature individuals were seen to initiate play with other adults they always did so by "finger wrestling" (that is, they reached to the other's hand or foot and began to push, pull, and squeeze the fingers or toes).

In Food Sharing

Chimpanzees frequently show begging behavior when one individual (often, but not necessarily, a higher ranking one) is in possession of a food that is in short supply (such as meat or, at the feeding area, bananas). A begging individual may reach out to touch the food or the lips of the possessor of the food, or he may hold out his hand toward him (palm up), sometimes uttering small whimpers.

The response to such gestures varied according to the individuals involved and the amount of food. Often the possessor pulled the food away from the begging individual or threatened him. Sometimes, however, individuals detached pieces of their food and handed them to begging subordinates. Almost always when chimpanzees held their hands to the mouth of the possessor, the latter eventually responded by pushing out a half-chewed lump

---

[12]I have described as social play behavior that consists of nonaggressive interactions between two or more individuals, including one or a combination of the following: tickling, wrestling, mock-biting, sparring (hitting and pushing), and chasing.

Fig. 12–26. Juvenile puts her hands to the mouth of her adolescent male sibling, begging for the chewed food from his mouth. (*Photograph by Baron Hugo Van Lawick;* © *National Geographic Society*)

of food that was promptly chewed by the one that had begged. It was not uncommon to see a high-ranking chimpanzee reaching to the lips of a feeding subordinate.

The type of food-sharing described above, in which a dominant individual not only allows a subordinate to take a piece of food, but also may actually "give" a piece, is not reported for other nonhuman primates in the wild.

In Mother-Infant Communication

There are a number of movements, gestures, and sounds made by infants that appear to act as signals to their mothers, and others made by the mothers that serve as signals to the child. Some of these do not ordinarily occur during interactions between adults, and are discussed in detail elsewhere (van Lawick-Goodall, in press). Some of the more obvious of these communication patterns are the following: The mother may lightly touch her infant when she is ready to move off; the infant then normally responds by clinging to her. She may stand with bent knees, look back over her shoulder, and make a beckoning movement; such a signal is directed toward an older infant, which normally climbs onto her back as she moves off. She may, as she approaches thick undergrowth, touch the child when it is riding in the dorsal position; the youngster then slides round into the ventral position. When an infant first starts to make short exploratory trips away from the mother, either she or the child may seek to re-establish physical contact by reaching toward the other, usually showing a pout face and uttering a "hoo whimper" at the same time. When an infant being carried by its mother screams, the mother at once responds by embracing it tightly; if the infant is some distance away and screams, she rushes over to rescue it.

Gradually, during its second year the infant begins to show the expressive movements that are typical of interactions between the older chimpanzees of its community.

DISCUSSION

The preceding pages have done little more than provide an outline of the complex communicatory system of a free-ranging chimpanzee community; a great deal of analysis remains to be carried out on my existing data, and many more observations are needed from the field. However, even this incomplete picture suggests that tactile, gestural, and postural communication plays an important role in interindividual relationships. Thus it may be of value to discuss, tentatively, the origin and evolution of some of these communicatory patterns.

The importance of the role played by tactile experience in the development of the human infant, and subsequently in the development of human communications, has been discussed fully by Frank (1958). It is certain that tactile experience is of at least equal importance to the development of the nonhuman primate infant and of subsequent nohuman primate communication patterns. It has, in fact, been suggested that the infantile clinging response may be a major factor in the development of filial attachments in nonhuman primates. Thus it has been shown that in infant rhesus monkeys reared with an artificial cloth mother this response was one of the main determinants in the formation of filial attachment to the surrogate; it was further demonstrated that the opportunity to cling to the cloth mother, particularly when the subjects were frightened or upset, was an incentive for performing simple tests (Harlow 1960; Harlow and Zimmermann 1958). Certainly the clinging response, as well as a wide variety of tactile signals, plays an important role both in mother-infant co-ordination and in the formation of mother-infant social ties in the wild chimpanzee (van Lawick-Goodall, in press).

It has been suggested that some infantile responses, particularly clinging, may persist after the primate has become independent of its mother and may then be directed toward other individuals in the group. Thus they may form the basis for later aspects of sociability and social organization (Mason 1964). This theory is strengthened by the fact that, in stressful situations, chimpanzees reared with cloth mothers tended to cling to familiar inanimate objects, whereas under similar circumstances mother-reared chimpanzees ignored such objects, but clung to other chimpanzees or to humans. In its natural habitat the growing primate is "usually surrounded from infancy by individuals whose appearance and reactions to him are similar to those of the mother, thus providing seemingly optimal conditions for the generalization or extension of filial attachments" (Mason 1964).

Observations of chimpanzee behavior in the field led me to form the same hypothesis as that discussed above with regard to the derivation of some of the expressive movements described (particularly those pertaining to contact-seeking behavior). Thus a mature chimpanzee may embrace, reach out to touch, or mount another animal under similar circumstances and in more or less the same manner as a frightened or apprehensive infant runs to embrace and be embraced by its mother, reaches out to touch or grasp her hair, or stands upright behind her grasping her rump and standing ready to climb on if the situation warrants it. Figure 12–27 shows a juvenile laying one hand on her mother's back as she hears chimpanzees calling in the distance, and Fig. 12–28 shows a mature female laying her hand, in exactly the same manner, on the back of a young male in response to the same stimulus. It is possible also that some forms of "kissing" may have been derived from the infantile response of suckling, or holding the mother's nipple in its mouth when alarmed or hurt.

Many other expressive movements have not evolved from such primitive social responses. Let us consider, for example, presenting, bobbing, and bowing. It is suggested, tentatively, that these patterns may have been derived from conflict situations. Bowing and bobbing may represent a desire to approach a dominant individual counteracted by a desire to flee. The flexing of the elbows may be an intentional movement of flight and does, in fact, leave the individual in a good position to jerk away if necessary. (On many occasions when adolescent males hurried to bob to dominant males during greeting they did actually leap away when the male concerned started a charging display.)

Presenting, in a nonsexual context, may have evolved from a similar conflict situation, and here again, except in the "presenting crouch," the individual is in an excellent position for immediate flight. Zuckerman (1932) suggested that presenting in baboons (in nonsexual contexts) might represent an incipient flight movement in animals that were subordinate.

In this context it should perhaps be mentioned that a mature chimpanzee (particularly, a male) frequently tickles the skin at the base of the white tail

Fig. 12–27 (left). As another group of chimpanzees call in the distance, a juvenile places her hand on her mother. (*Photograph by Baron Hugo Van Lawick;* © *National Geographic Society*)

Fig. 12–28 (below). Mature female places one hand on back of adolescent male as another group of chimpanzees call in the distance. (*Photograph by Baron Hugo Van Lawick;* © *National Geographic Society*)

tuft of an infant when it approaches, and occasionally strokes its penis or clitoris. When the infant first shows presenting behavior (in the start of its second year) it may present several times in succession to the same adult, particularly if this results in "tuft tickling." This pleasant stimulus, which occurs as a result of presenting, may be related to the high incidence of infants' presenting to males (see Table 12–5). It is also interesting to note that the mature baboon frequently lifts up the hind legs of an infant in "greeting," and "kisses" its bottom (Hall and DeVore 1965). One might speculate, therefore, that this type of pleasant stimulation of the genital area of the infant may have played some part in the high frequency of rump presenting observed in frightened or upset adult chimpanzees and baboons.

Finally, there is one aspect of chimpanzee communicatory behavior that must not be overlooked—the similarity of many of these gestures and postures to some of those made by man. These similarities, which have been pointed out in the relevant sections in the text, do not lie solely in the structure of the movements themselves, but also, more important, in the frequently close correspondence of the behavioral situations in which they occur. It seems almost certain, therefore, that those gestures common to both man and chimpanzee formed part of the behavioral repertoire not only of early man, but also of an earlier primate type ancestral to both ape and man.

PART THREE

ANALYSIS OF BEHAVIOR
Remarks

Phyllis Jay

The results of years of observation and careful recording remain just a huge quantity of information until someone works through them, item by item, to draw from them generalizations about the regularities of behavior, and then discovers in them patterns of actions and activities. Without this, the original body of information—thousands of statements about what the observer saw—may be of very little value to the student of comparative behavior. Most fieldworkers are acutely familiar with a feeling of "where to begin?" after a year or more in the field and the accumulation of volumes of notes, photographs, and recordings. Obviously, different approaches to the study of behavior produce different quantities and kinds of data. A student who undertakes continuous observation of as much behavior as possible for a long time confronts a different situation from that of the student who goes to the field and asks a very precisely defined question. The latter may record only information he feels is pertinent to his question, either in check lists or some other brief shorthand manner. He finishes with a restricted amount of data, but all, hopefully, highly relevant to his question. There are as many approaches as there are investigators, and this section on behavior analysis represents only a few of the existing methods of analysis.

Hall was a pioneer in using laboratory experimentation in conjunction with field observation in analyzing behavior. His work shows the power, and also demonstrates the problems, of combining both methods. He sought to understand variation in terms of social learning and ecological modification of behavior. His field experience and experiments convinced him that any understanding of primate behavior must be based on observations of free-ranging animals, because this is the context in which normal learning occurs. This emphasis, so different from that of traditional experimental psychology, is discussed in detail by Mason. In spite of their differing emphases on larger issues of psychology, both men agreed that the field experiment may often be the crucial one, and Hall actually undertook to demonstrate this in his fieldwork.

Mason and Hall are very much concerned with differences between laboratory-oriented experimental psychology and naturalistic investigation, but actually this may be more of an issue to the experimental psychologist than to the anthropologist. To the social, cultural, or physical anthropologist and to the archeologist, field research is an integral part of training and of continuing research, and fieldwork is a normal part of investigation. It does not occur to most anthropologists *not* to have both experimentation and observation as complementary aspects of their work. The anthropologist is concerned with social systems, in contrast (as Mason reminds us) to the experimental psychologist who traditionally has been chiefly attentive to dyadic relationships. Vocabulary and conceptual techniques can be made to work to the advantage of both types of study, and the participants in this volume agree on the importance and necessity of both experimentation and observation in the study of behavior. All participants are concerned with the problem of determining which questions are best answered where and how cross-fertile and mutually intelligible techniques can be developed.

We are beginning to realize how necessary field experimentation is, even though this type of investigation has hardly begun. In monkeys most learning, but not all as Hall states, takes place in a social context. The kinds of learning are adaptive, and these adaptations can best be understood when they occur in their natural settings. This means that field studies are required, but, again, there has not been enough field experimentation. Although the rules of learning that interest the traditional psychologist cannot be ascertained in the field, knowledge of these principles helps the field investigator understand the development or ontogeny of the behavior modifications that he observes. Neither of these lines of investigation necessarily contradicts or excludes the other. An investigator who does not use all the available relevant information deprives himself of as complete an understanding of behavior as is possible.

Imaginatively planned fieldwork projects are needed because it is only in rare circumstances that observation coincides with natural crises. Man-made crises are far more frequent; Hall's study of the Kariba Dam's impact on local primate groups whose areas of occupation were flooded is a good example of an investigator's taking advantage of such a disaster. In our analysis of the integration of specific patterns of behavior into a general social system or habitat of a species, we do not have to rely upon the observation of usual everyday interactions or wait patiently for the rare event; nor do we necessarily have to go to a disaster area. Experiments can be designed to create precisely those situations needed to settle uncertainties as to which elements are important in an interaction or action; for example, we need to design experiments to find the factors that are key in influencing or triggering the changes of the reproductive cycle. Long before the development of modern primate studies the ethologist set a precedent for this with his detailed analysis of behavior through the use of experimentation in natural or near-natural conditions.

Primate studies stand to benefit enormously from the development of new methods and techniques of analysis developed in other fields of research. Some of these new techniques make it possible to investigate behaviors that previously had not been recordable and were not available as data to an observer. Field investigators have used some methods of recording, such as photography, for a long time, but not as fully as possible. Photography can be especially valuable as a means of detailed analysis of the components of interactions and in the comparative study of behavior. Film can be used with particularly good effect in a study, once the animals are well known and habituated to the observer and the observer is familiar with daily routines and with important behavior patterns of the species (in other words, when he knows what to film). Even then, nuances of actions or stance may easily escape the perception of the observer and become known only upon repeated viewing of film, especially in slow-motion projection. The Van Lawicks and DeVore have made excellent films suitable for use in teaching and research. Van Lawick's photographic record of chimpanzee behavior in the Gombe Stream Reserve is our most outstanding example of the value of having recorded behavior on film for further analysis and comparisons with other primates. These chimpanzee films make it possible to trace individual growth and development patterns over a period of four years. All the important aspects of chimpanzee behavior that have been observed have been filmed, and it is possible to edit footage on very specific topics.

Some difficulties in achieving comparable terms to describe behavior have already been mentioned. There is no substitute for direct observation of behavior, but since it is not possible to study many genera in one lifetime at first hand, the closest one can come to this is to see films on behavior. Each investigator could identify, as precisely as possible, exactly what he meant by a certain descriptive term, and he could illustrate it with a short film. Visually documented definitions could then be more nearly standard and could serve as a more useful set of tools in comparative studies.

As Washburn and Hamburg have suggested, human subjective categories of behavior are clear, useful, and least likely to be misleading when they are applied to behaviors of animals closely related to us. These behaviors are based on biological structures similar to our own, and even though learning during ontogeny trains the individual to respond more to stimuli that are important to its own species, our senses probably perceive most of the same cues. After training and experience every fieldworker becomes very sensitive to differences in sounds and gestures, and can interpret and predict many more social interactions than he could when first exposed to the behavior of an unfamiliar species. Modern cinematic and sound techniques of recording make it possible, in spite of discrepancies in perception, to analyze vocalizations and gestures minutely. Play is a universal activity, at least of young primates, and although it is one for which we have no adequate definition, most observers have little difficulty in deciding which actions should be included in this category. In fact, some play patterns of monkeys and apes are so similar to those of man that it is possible—and tempting—for a man and an animal such as a chimpanzee to enter into each others' games.

The advantage of having films that deal with special topics of behavior needs no elaboration. Teaching comparative primate behavior and training observers will be more stimulating and accurate when films are available. Any observer fortunate enough to have watched several different kinds of monkeys or apes realizes how much broader a perspective he brings to what he observes and to his analysis of information. Comparative films on play, aggression, mother-infant behavior, and a long list of other topics could be produced by the investigator who has actually done the research on the species and who is concerned with that particular behavior. Films also make our information available for comparative studies of man and other animals.

Now it is standard field procedure to tape-record primate sounds, making it unnecessary to describe general categories of vocalizations in words. Many subtleties and nuances of communicative calls are totally lost to our ears even after we are familiar with the animals. Baffling differences in reactions to what human ears hear as identical calls can be understood when recordings of these sounds are analyzed spectrographically, and the structure of each vocalization is then related to the social situation. The sound communication systems of primate species are highly adaptive and help enable each species to occupy its habitat, often permitting the sharing of areas with other primate species. Experimental use of recordings to elicit responses of groups or individuals can help us explore these relationships among and within species.

Telemetric devices for monitoring and measuring physiological changes in animals are being developed and perfected. These machines permit us to get an index of the responses of individuals, including those animals in a group that are not visibly reacting to what is happening. For the first time it will become possible to monitor and measure the involvement or physiological effect of an event on an apparently "nonparticipating" individual. The clues these measurements could give to social status and relationships are limitless.

They would aid us in answering questions such as: How much reaction has the infant of a subordinate (or dominant) female when the mother is attacked (or attacks)? Is a mother responsive to a threat directed toward an almost grown offspring? Are animals that appear to be eating quietly (ignoring a fight between two adult males) really unconcerned with what is happening? Several telemetric devices are being used in field conditions on pilot projects and are being refined for future use.

Drugs will undoubtedly also be of great value as a means of deliberately controlled alteration of behavior. When drug action is understood it should be possible to manipulate many if not most aspects of social and individual behavior by administering the appropriate drug in the correct dosage.

Kummer describes the selective trapping of animals and their subsequent release into new social groups. After animals have been trapped and transplanted it is possible to study both the behavior of the group that has lost members and the adjustment of the individual animals after they have entered a new social environment. There are countless possibilities of intentional alteration of group composition. It would be most interesting to remove adult males from groups that are used to defending their territories against other groups of the same species and to place them in groups whose traditional behavior does not include aggressive defense of territory. Many alterations in group composition and behavior are possible as means to discover the ways these patterns are developed and maintained. Lancaster (personal communication) plans to do this in her study of *C. aethiops* in Zambia.

Cross-species fostering, in which infants are raised by mothers of different species or subspecies, has been suggested by several workers (Jay 1965). Such experiments could give us better notions of the separate contributions of heredity and environment to the behavior of the species. These are just a few possibilities for field experimentation, but taken together they support the conviction that it *is* possible to investigate some aspects of internal states of the animals and their observed behaviors.

None of the following chapters deals mainly or even primarily with analysis of the behavior of captive animals. Emphasis here is on fieldwork, but the basic goal is understanding primates, and besides study in natural situations this requires judicial use of artificially established and maintained colonies of animals. Many questions can be investigated only under carefully controlled conditions, which are usually far removed from a natural habitat. Information from field research is essential for maintenance of animals in captivity. Adequate care for captive subjects involves far more than proper diet and keeping them alive. Subjects must be physically and socially healthy, and only from the field can we determine what constitutes healthy behavior, that is, what are normal types of behavior under different natural conditions.

By careful selection of the animals that are to constitute a social group in captivity, it is possible to omit or remove the hyper-aggressive animal in favor of more docile temperaments. There is a range of individual temperament in nature so a choice can be exerted in the selection of the nature of the captive group. It is possible to adjust for more or less aggressiveness and for qualities other than the extremes of behavior present under free-ranging conditions. It is essential to know the extent to which the captive group is similar or dissimilar to wild groups, and where the behavior of the colony falls within the range of behavioral characteristics of the species.

The laboratory or colony must be planned to allow adequate space and to meet the social requirements of the animals in terms of the particular experiment. Where it is important that breeding be maximally efficient and that socially as well as physically adequate adults be produced, special attention must be given to handling and maintenance. By the time free-ranging primates reach the laboratory they frequently are not physically healthy enough for experimental purposes and must undergo extensive and expensive processes of conditioning. At this time we do not have a precise understanding of the extent to which abnormal or faulty caging and mistaken animal handling and management, through trauma and insult to the animals, affects the physical and social well-being of the animal. In addition, we do not know how it affects the behavior of the captive subjects. We do know, however, that these effects can be so great as to reduce the animal to physical sickness and psychosis, if not to death. These matters are crucial; it is primarily from laboratory research that we gain our understanding of the internal workings, the psychological and physiological behavior of the individual. We carry this information to the field for a deeper look into the adaptive nature of these behaviors. Unless the laboratory information is based on healthy animals, it may be minimally relevant to the natural context.

The following chapters present many varied aspects of primate behavior, from detailed social interaction of a few members in a social group to complex patterns of behavior that allow communication among genera.

Hall is concerned with social learning as it occurs in the natural setting of a social group. Chapter 13 is the synthesis of much of his personal feeling on the appropriate process and setting for normal learning. Hall offers the caution to psychologists that they must guard against a science of learning that may only be valid in an artificial laboratory experimental situation. He states that "normal" primate learning takes place in a social group and not in an isolation cage, and this learning under normal conditions is essential to survival. Mason emphasizes the interrelationship of laboratory and field investigation and discusses in detail factors important to both kinds of analysis and some of the results that legitimately may be expected from each. Mason takes issue with Hall's contention that the laboratory study of learning behavior had not produced experiments that yielded information relative to social learning. Both men agree that historically, and at present, experimental and field approaches are in practice far apart and that this is unfortunate because both are indispensible in the study of social learning. As Mason points out, "there is no reason, in principle, why experiments cannot be performed in the field, nor does the laboratory environment preclude certain forms of naturalistic research." The traditional interest of psychologists has been with individuals rather than with groups, and in part this has been so because of a lack of awareness that the social group is the setting for most natural behavior, and, as such, is an appropriate locus for study. The prognosis for future coordination of field and laboratory study is good according to Mason, who outlines the basis for this prediction.

Marler is concerned with the adaptive value of communication and its roles in these relationships among and within species of monkeys and apes. He discusses patterns of spatial distribution as they relate to an understanding of the exploitation of an environment by populations of nonhuman primates living in an area. The importance of social communication, Marler points out, is related to the patterns of spatial distribution in that different types of signals transmit more or less efficiently over distances. Marler discusses signals that affect different types of spacing not only among groups but also within them.

Lancaster analyzes the structural basis for and evolutionary problems in the evolution of human language from a nonhuman base. The communication system of the nonhuman primates cannot be viewed as steps leading to human language, but instead has more in common with the communication systems of nonprimate mammals. After considering the nature of primate communication systems, Lancaster then discusses the nature of language and its anatomical basis. From this comparative discussion emerges an understanding that the most fundamental part of human language is not present in communication among the nonhuman primates or among any other nonhuman animal because the anatomical basis for the action of naming is lacking in other animals. The evolution of a system of names with most of the meaning carried in a single sensory modality has resulted in what we know as human language.

Washburn and Hamburg are concerned with the problem of aggression and with what can be learned from comparative studies of the nonhuman primates to help in the understanding of human behavior. They suggest that the study of aggression in nonhuman primates may be utilized as an effective instrument in gaining evolutionary perspective into the development of patterns of aggressive behavior. The role of aggression in determining relations among the members of a social group is discussed, as well as the role of aggression as a species-spacing mechanism.

Eibl-Eibesfeldt emphasizes the possible contribution of ethology to the study of primate, and especially of human, behavior; this is a tradition that has influenced many primate-behavior researchers. He suggests that exploring the behavior of the nonhuman primates by analyzing phylogenetic adaptations will offer research methods to apply to human behavior.

Hall has set the pace with his clear declaration of the adaptive nature of behavior, and of social learning in particular. Two other important behaviors, communication and aggression, can best be understood when viewed from an evolutionary perspective as adaptive; they are so viewed here. We are a long way from thoroughly understanding even some of the simplest aspects of behavior, but by the effective use of field observations and by experimentations both in natural conditions and in the more controllable confines of laboratory and colony, we will come closer to the understandings we seek.

13

SOCIAL LEARNING IN MONKEYS

K. R. L. Hall

If the psychologist is to make a general contribution to the study of primate social behavior distinguishable from that of zoologically or anthropologically trained investigators, it should be in a specialty of his field, namely, the study of learning.

The principles of learning, as we know them from the standard texts, still have a somewhat narrow species and situational reference; it is not very clear, therefore, how naturalistic social studies and experimental studies could be integrated. Many psychologists nowadays are sensitive to this problem, especially as it relates to human social behavior and the learning processes involved in that behavior. They now know that by aiming at experimental precision in the laboratory, before they have discerned some of the major problems that should be the objects of this precision, they are in danger of setting up a science of learning that is valid only in the experimental situation.

This awareness no doubt has been brought about by the influence of several trends in the other sciences concerned with behavior, as well as from within psychology itself. Psychologists studying the behavior of children, human social groups, and behavioral deviants, have not found the learning principles derived from the laboratory entirely adequate. Their problem is similar to that of the fieldworker on the nonhuman primates. Beset by the complexity of his data, he is conscious of the need to progress beyond the essential descriptive and classificatory phases by the systematic use of experiment and by integrating his findings with those of general behavior theory. The artificiality of laboratory learning situations has been frequently emphasized. Leuba (1955:28) for example, said: "Most human learning and development . . . does not occur when people are deprived of food or water for twelve or more hours, are given electric shocks, are under the influence of powerful neurotic drives, or are in any situations even remotely resembling these." A similar emphasis is given by Bandura and Walters (1963:109), from their studies of children's social learning: "generally speaking, it has been assumed, rather than demonstrated, that reinforcement principles apply within complex social settings and that they govern the social behavior of human beings in precisely the same manner as they regulate the responses of human and animal subjects in highly structured nonsocial laboratory experiments."

The influence of ethology in changing and expanding the view of learning has been, and continues to be, profound. It stems in part from a general biological orientation (the implications of which have not always been appreciated by psychologists) to the effect that learning is a product of evolution and is therefore an integral feature of a species' adaptations, and not something that can be studied independently of them. "This characteristic of animals, whereby their abilities for the learning of particular types of responses are related to their ecological requirements, is one of the fundamental points of emphasis of ethological studies" (Etkin 1964:186). As a principle of great importance, derived from comparative studies of bird behavior, Hinde and Tinbergen (1958:255) point out that ". . . many of the differences between species do not lie in the first instance in stereotyped behavior sequences but consist in the possession of a propensity to learn." Learning processes serve and are an extension of the processes of evolution. Comparative studies of primate learning only at their peril can ignore the biological frame of reference. Assessments of relative learning ability or "intelligence" in the nonhuman primates are usually irrelevant and inaccurate because they have ignored it, as well as for other reasons of method (Hall 1963*b*). For the lower vertebrates, as for the primates: "Evolution, through selection, has built the biological base so that many behaviors are easily, almost inevitably, learned" (Washburn and Hamburg 1965:613).

The group is the environment in which the young primate does his learning, and in which traditions of feeding, ranging, and the like are perpetuated; it is not unreasonable then to suppose that the starting point for learning studies on the primates—both observational and experimental, both in nature and in captivity—must be the social group rather than the isolation cage. The wild infant monkey or ape does not survive except in the group. Survival requires it to live socially and, preeminently, to learn socially and to do so not only in the long period of its dependence and growth, but also throughout its life. The emphasis here is not new, being a part of biological and anthropological thinking, but its implications have not been manifested in many primate behavior studies.

ADAPTABILITY OF WILD MONKEYS

If we are to increase the relevance of the experimental studies of primate learning we must consider first some of the major characteristics of the social life of wild primates to which learning is likely to have contributed most importantly. Interspecific differences are now known to be enormous, and it is as ridiculous to suppose that the talapoin goes through more or less the same processes of learning as the baboon as it would be to equate the ground-nesting plover and the great tit in this respect. However, there will be an obvious basic common factor in most primate species, namely the setting provided by a group around the mother-infant relationship, although in some species the social surroundings will be numerous and diversified (as presumably in a large baboon group), whereas it will be very limited in the family-party type of organization.

In field studies, as Washburn and Hamburg (1965) point out, the problem is that observations are primarily of the results of learning rather than of the process itself. Variations in the life of the group can be imposed by the investigator and the results observed, as in several of the Japan Monkey Centre studies. Unplanned variations, such as habitat destruction or drought, can significantly test the limits of adaptability of a population, but a sufficient experimental control is difficult to impose in natural conditions. We must therefore continue to rely mainly upon working out our ideas about the social learning processes by analysis of field data, with the intention of formulating these in such a way that they can be elaborated in the captivity situation. It is perhaps still necessary to point out that, when we try to analyze species-characteristic behavior and behavior of populations or groups of a species, it is always to be understood that genetic factors constitute a major source of variation, but that learning must operate in some manner and in some degree whatever the situation and however stereotyped a behavior may appear to be.

If we list some of the main features of the environment and the activities in terms of which we usually work our field data, it is fairly obvious that we are concerned with certain conformities or traditions. These are in part defined by the physical adaptations of the species, in part imposed by local conditions, and in part the product of intergenerational spread and continuation of habits that have proved serviceable in the local situation:

Feature (physical-social)	Conformities
Home range.	Routes of feeding areas, sleeping places, areas of contact with neighboring groups, day-ranging patterns, seasonal changes, danger areas.

Feature (physical-social)	Conformities
Food and water.	Discriminations of edible from inedible, ripe and unripe, manipulatory techniques, water locations.
Day-activity pattern.	Times of resting, times of activity, coordination of movement, rest, feeding, and so forth.
Other animals (different species).	Discriminations of predators or noxious creatures, tolerances of large mammals, warning cues from other animals.
Other, extragroup animals (same species).	Tolerance distances between groups, hibituation or avoidance or territorial display.
Size and composition of groups. Sexual reproductive characteristics. Individual social development. Group social interaction pattern, and social interaction code.	Processes of socialization continually involve familiarization with individuals in the group, appreciation of social distance, and social discriminations derived from conflicting impulses (*approach:* friendly, sexual; *avoidance:* fear, threat; and so forth).

What are the social learning processes chiefly involved in these conformities? These processes evidently differ between species; but they may, at this level of analysis, suggest a different way of looking at the problem. An accepted way of classifying learning processes is to break them down into forms that differ in kind and in complexity. Habituation, for example, is a very "primitive" means of adjustment, whereas insight or perceptual learning sometimes involves a restructuring of relationships (as in the chimpanzee instrumentation problem-solution) that appears to be of greater complexity and suggests an ability in the nervous system to mediate several alternative relationships between stimulus and response. Of these several processes each has its reference experiments, and they are experiments that usually have been derived from a particular type of situation of a nonsocial kind. When we are studying the complex interactional system of a monkey group, which comprises a kind of natural unity, we may suppose that any or all of the defined learning processes may be operating in the adjustments of individuals to their environment. However, we may also question whether we can obtain an entirely satisfactory account of conformities and adjustments in this social matrix by superimposing on it those learning categories. The doubt is precisely due to the nonsocial character of most of the experimental references. In Gestalt terms, for example, the social situation of a group of baboons cannot adequately be broken down into the sum of the performances of the individuals in it (conditioned response of A, plus conditioned response of B, and so on). It is clear that the social unity is the group, that the behavior of the individual is only comprehensible in terms of its membership in that group to which it has belonged since birth, and that changes in the composition of the group will in some degree affect all members of it. Where there is some kind of role differentiation and rank relationship in a group, as in baboons and patas monkeys, the Gestalt quality of the group is exceedingly clear. In a simple form, we have been able to demonstrate this repeatedly in our laboratory group of patas by observing the effects on the group of removing individuals, one at a time, and introducing or reintroducing individuals (Hall and Mayer 1967). The dynamic equilibrium of the whole pattern of relationships is temporarily disturbed and is then restored, but in a modified form. By withdrawing *A* from the group, you do not simply leave *B* plus *C,* and the rest in the same pattern of relationships, but in some degree you modify the whole relational system. In human group studies this dynamic view was most cogently expressed by Lewin (1935), but its implications for the study of social learning in the nonhuman primate group do not seem to have been properly formulated. Again and again, in observing a group of monkeys, whether in the field or in captivity, one is impressed by the more or less continual awareness of each member of the behavior, the distance, and the situation of the others. This is inevitable when the group is the natural and more or less constant unit.

If we extend the argument we may distinguish two main characteristics in the dynamic interaction processes, both of which contribute to the total pattern of group organization, the group organization itself being a dependent part in the greater organizational whole of the population. The coordination of the activities of the group and the general conformity of the habits of its members appear to be derived from very simple social learning processes. These we have described as following, social facilitation, and observational learning (Hall and Goswell 1964). The infant follows the actions of its mother, to some extent and for an early period "modeling" its actions and the directions they take or the objects to which they relate upon her behavior. Any animal's behavior in the group may be set going or facilitated by the perceived example of another member of the group. Any animal may observe the behavior of another, with or without awareness of its reference, and later may behave in the same manner in the same type of situation. These three processes, which intergrade one with another, constitute a more or less continuous interactional system through which survival habits of feeding, avoidance, dispersal, or aggregation are acquired. "New" habits are in this manner spread throughout the group. Although, in terms of the experimentalist's "trials," nothing could appear simpler than the learning processes here involved, in terms of the group the cumulative effect of repeated adjustments in this manner may be considerable. It is, as we know, easy to transform the meaning of some object from negative (avoided) or neutral (ignored) to strongly positive merely by the observing animal's seeing the positive behavior of another animal with whom it has a friendly relationship.

A second characteristic is that of the more active processes of adjustment going on within the social structure of the group. There are two examples we can use to illustrate it. Where rank relationships within the group can be clearly defined (as they can be in macaques) in terms of behavioral interactions, social distances, and so on, it has been suggested that the social behavior of the high-ranking mother favorably affects the chances that her offspring (or at least the males) will attain high rank in the group (Kawai 1958, as quoted by Imanishi 1960; Koford 1963*b*). Allowing for the likelihood that there are genetic predispositional factors involved, this means that the confidence or security, or simply the example of successful assertiveness afforded by the mother's behavior, serve to build up similar habits in the social behavior of the young. These habits then supposedly transfer to the interactions with agemates, and the "successful" young male remains in the group rather than going to the periphery or into isolation. The converse situation must also presumably produce the opposite effect.

Although there is no doubt that such cases do occur, and indeed would be expected from what we now know about social learning, it has to be appreciated once again that these social systems are anything but static and that the great advantage of observing these systems in action in the natural state is the complexity of the information they provide and the number of alternative hypotheses they may suggest. If we consider an extreme case, that of the one-adult male patas group, we do find in our laboratory group that the ranks of the adult females are over a period very clearly defined. The female is extremely possessive and protective toward her young. The behavior of the highest ranking female was such that when her son reached the age of about two years the pair of them were regularly in the ascendant over the adult male in feeding tests and positioning in the living room. The young male would even threaten the adult male without provoking retaliation. Immediately the mother was removed from the room or was confined in a small cage within the room; the social situation of her son changed radically, and the son accepted the change without its being necessary for others in the group to impose it forcibly upon him. He now takes his place in low rank. The son of the second ranking female in the group, although he is a year younger than the other, when his mother is present is in the ascendant over the first young male. At all times the one-year-old male, whether his mother has been in high rank or not, has been exceedingly bold, and the relationship between the two mothers (although entirely clear in terms of rank) is friendly and without tension, each having more or less equal access to the adult male.

If we now consider the much greater complexity of the wild patas group we have to suggest how it is that all males (with the exception of one) are eliminated from the group when they reach sexual maturity. There are several alternatives, any or all of which may operate according to the dynamic situation of the group and the population, which includes isolate adult males, and, once, a group of bachelors (Hall 1965*a*). Only four of the many possible combinations of events are shown below:

The following are some alternative interaction patterns whereby changes of ingroup adult males may occur in a wild patas monkey population:

$$
\begin{aligned}
\text{In-group adult } \male \quad &= A. \\
\text{Adult } \female\,\female \quad &= 1, 2, \text{ and } 3. \\
\text{Their sons} \quad &= B, C, \text{ and } D. \\
\text{Extragroup adult } \male\,\male \quad &= X \text{ and } Y.
\end{aligned}
$$

1. *A* attempts to drive out *B*.
    1, 2, and 3 combine in attacking *A*.
    > Then either
    B remains with the ♀ ♀ ; *A* leaves.
    > Or
    B leaves the group; *A* remains.
    > Or
    The group splits; some ♀ ♀ going with *A,* some with *B.*

2. Sons *B* and *C* reach sexual maturity at the same time.
    A attempts to drive out both.
    1, 2, and 3 combine in attacking *A.*
    > Then either
    B remains; *C* and *A* are left.
    > Or
    A remains; *B* and *C* leave.
    > Or
    The group splits.

3. ♀ 1 loses her ascendancy to ♀ 3 (younger).
    Her son, *B,* is still subadult.
    > Then
    Sons *B* and *D* reach sexual maturity.
    A attempts to drive out *B* and *D.*
    3 and other females attack *A.*
    > Then either
    B and *A* leave; *D* remains.
    > Or
    A remains; *B* and *D* leave.
    > Or
    The group splits.

4. *A* is killed by a predator.
    B, C, and *D* still subadult.
    > Then either
    X or *Y* join group.
    > Or
    Group splits, *X* joining one part, *Y* the other.

When these combinations of interactions are examined it is at once apparent that the ascendancy of a particular male depends upon a great many factors, and that the rank of the mother is likely to be only one of them. It must be pointed out that we know of the ranking behavior of the patas females only in the very restricted situation of the laboratory group. Where the spacing between individuals is as great as it is in the wild group, and where competition for food is very rare, it is possible that female ranks are ill-defined and that the high rank of females does not bestow any particular advantage on their young. The mother is scarcely in a position to further the social ascendancy of her son after he has grown beyond the juvenile stage, for he is rarely close to her. It is therefore possible that by their interactions among themselves the young males achieve social learning that is relevant to their social position on reaching sexual maturity. We can scarcely doubt, from what we have seen in the laboratory, that the reaching of sexual maturity is an exceedingly stressful situation both for the young male and for the whole group.

A further problem in social learning arises out of the special role that the adult male of the wild patas group has in watching for predators and for other patas. This male is usually very remote from the rest of the group, and behaves in a manner that is quite distinctive and unlike the other members of the group. This behavior must surely be learned, not simply by unguided trial-and-error, but from the young patas having observed the behavior of his predecessor in the group. If this is so, then the learning is acquired (without any obvious reinforcement at the time of its acquisition) when he is a juvenile or a subadult. The learning is latent because it does not come into effective performance until the young male becomes the successor to the adult male already in the group. The only clue we have to this process is from our observations of the behavior of the young male in our laboratory group. He is obviously attracted to the adult male, approaching close to him, but he is also obviously fearful and ready to flee at the first sign of antagonism from the adult. He is also, in a nervous way, ready to be aggressive. His behavior is thus clearly and repeatedly ambivalent, attraction, fear, and antagonism all expressing themselves in his gestures and movements. In human psychological terms we could suggest that there is a tendency for the young male to identify with the adult male. This would imply that the young one learns to match the behavior of the adult, the reinforcement for such learning arising from the arousal of quite intense conflicting motivation.

It has seemed useful to elaborate these examples as illustrations of the dynamic processes of learning and motivation that may have to be taken into account in the actual group situation. The major point requiring emphasis is that conflict of tendencies, sometimes in only mild degree, is not uncommon in the interactions of monkeys such as baboons, macaques, and patas, and that such conflicts may serve repeatedly to reinforce discriminatory social learning. The adaptability of a species, to use a term that comprehends all possible aspects of social learning, consists not only of the conformity patterns achieved in the routine activities of daily life, but also of the manner in which a stability in the social organization is acquired, maintained, and restored when social or ecological change occurs.

SOCIAL EXPERIMENT

If, in our field studies, we discern such social complexity and so many possible factors that interplay in social learning, we may wonder how far we can succeed in elucidating some of these problems by experimenting on captive animals. An alternative is, as has been mentioned, to try systematic experiments in the field. The difficulties of so doing are considerable, partly because wild groups are not available in many areas in such conditions that they can be observed for long periods at very close range, and partly because there is far too little control of the relevant factors. We wish to discover precisely how these animals learn with reference to one another, not merely how a group responds, for example, to an unusual situation induced by the investigator. The latter is an informal aid to the task of description, not a method of further analysis. So far no sustained experimental program has been undertaken with the primary objective of linking with the field data on a monkey species, with the exception of our own small beginnings on the patas monkey. There are, consequently, evident limitations in the experimental social learning studies that are available, both in terms of species (mainly rhesus macaques) and of situations used. We shall consider a few examples of such studies.

Observational Learning

The problems of method, the experimental limitations, and some of the difficulties involved in selecting relevant social factors for study have been reviewed elsewhere (Hall 1963a). As Harlow (1959:43) pointed out in discussing a discrimination problem-solving solution that was achieved as a consequence of the observer monkey (O) perceiving cues given by a model (M): "It is more than possible that the conditions existing in nature have been more favorable in terms of suitable social environment in this regard for producing imitative learning than have the conditions in the laboratory. Mother monkeys, for example, may have far more insight into the importance of these variables than do experimental psychologists."

One of the standard methods of experimenting is to use two cages or compartments. In one, M tackles the problem, achieving solution and obtaining food reward. At the same time, O observes M's behavior through a screen. After *M* has been removed or the screen has been obscured, *O* is given the opportunity to attempt the same problem. The correct performance by *O* may be significantly quicker or subject to less error consequent upon his having observed *M*. The location of the correct cue (that is, the cue in response to which *M* has been rewarded) has been indicated by *M*; without *M*'s example, *O* would have had to find it by trial and error. This type of result, on the one hand, appears to be a straight-forward confirmation of what we can see occurring daily in the interactions of young animals in our patas monkey group (Hall and Goswell 1964) or in wild groups of macaques or baboons. It appears to add nothing to our knowledge of social learning, except by isolating the animals from any other influences or distractions. On the other hand, a negative result (one in which *O* does not benefit from *M*'s performance) can usually be attributed to some factor such as *O*'s inattention, and cannot be explained as an inability to learn by observing.

It is possible to achieve results that are in one sense more meaningful by adopting a much less rigid experimental schedule. Negative or neutral response by *O* to an unfamiliar food object can be transformed into positive responses after *O* has watched *M*'s positive responses, even though *O*'s behavior continues to indicate some aversion (Hall and Goswell 1964).

In avoidance learning, Mirsky, Miller, and Murphy (1958) have demonstrated "communication of affect" from the startle and avoidance behavior of *M* to another monkey observing this behavior. *O* responds to the perceived "mood" of *M* after *O* has been conditioned to associate such a "mood" with unpleasant stimuli, such as shock. Our own results on the patas confirm this finding, and show that a previously positive response to a box by two young animals can change to a strong avoidance of that box after seeing their mothers reacting by startle to it. The startle was induced in the mothers by our having a live snake under a perspex cover that was visible to them when the lid of the box was lifted; it was not visible to the young patas, in a cage nearby. Similar results have been obtained when a positive response by *M* (such as opening the box lid) has resulted in shock, with *O* watching from an adjacent compartment. The point these results seem to make, although they are only preliminary, is that the young animal can learn to respond with avoidance to an object simply as a consequence of perceiving that avoidance in another monkey and without itself having experienced any unpleasant stimulation. This "vicarious reinforcement" seems indeed to be the probable process whereby the young in the wild group acquire their avoidance habits, and, to this extent, the findings substantiate what could only be set up as an hypothesis from field observation.

Expressions of mood or intention, positive or negative, may well serve as very important social indicators to the young monkey, and these expressions, rather than direct experience or primary reward or punishment (food or injury), may provide the reinforcement of discriminatory learning to approach or to avoid particular classes of objects. Whether such reinforcement can be classed as secondary (since the responses are derived originally from primary reinforcers of the usual kind) is still not clear.

Interanimal Conditioning

It is reasonable to suppose that the relative rank of two animals of a group, maintained assertively by one so that the other accepts a subordinate role, may be subject to change. Any experimental effect (for example, lobotomy, drugging, or induction of "neurosis") that substantially alters the behavior of the "dominant" animal may lead to such change. Murphy, Miller, and Mirsky (1955) have described the effect of punishment by shock of the dominant of a pair of rhesus monkeys associated with its seeing the subordinate at the far side of a glass screen. The shock could be terminated by the animal's pressing a lever, which results in the disappearance of the subordinate. Dominance was assessed before and after the experimental trials by the usual food tests. After the shock trials the subordinate in some pairings would take proportionately more food items than the dominant, reversing the pretest food relationship.

The question that at once arises from such findings is to what extent this change of rank, as thus determined, is specific only to the food-test situation or is generalized to other situations in which the two animals are placed. Smith and Hale (1959) found that there was no generalization from the same type of experiment on domestic fowls, and Hansen and Mason (1962) confirmed this on rhesus monkeys. We have also confirmed this lack of generalization with one pairing of adult female patas; although the postshock trials on the food test showed a marked change in favor of the subordinate female, as soon as the two animals were returned to the group in which they had been living before the experiment the ranks were immediately reasserted as before. Although it is perfectly possible that severe and prolonged shocking of the dominant animal in the visual presence of the subordinate would produce a change in rank that would carry over into the group situation, it is equally possible that the same amount of punishment would produce such a change without the view of the subordinate ever having been associated with the punishment. In other words, the shocked dominant would temporarily be reduced to a state of "neurotic" disturbance.

These experiments seem to suffer from two defects. First, they fail to consider in what ways rank relationships are really determined in the group, and the complexity and variability in such rankings. The food test is very far from being an adequate indicator of *social* rank. Second, they take no cognizance of the fact that the discriminatory learning processes that are likely to affect rank are not necessarily brought about by actual fighting or punishment, at any rate in wild groups, but through persistent interactions of a much subtler character. The data on the lack of generalization achieve at least the negative result of demonstrating that the other experiments were meaningless in reference to the group setting.

Studies of "experimental neurosis" per se have likewise failed to reveal much, if anything, that is relevant to the social environment of monkeys. The clash of competing or conflicting stimuli is usually brought about in the standard classical or operant conditioning situation. When the "normal" behavior of the monkey is thus disrupted it can usually be restored by a period away from the experimental situation, particularly if the monkey is returned to the group in which it has been living. Russian experimenters now appreciate the fact that the most lasting physiological disturbances in these animals can be produced where "natural" conditioned stimuli are involved, particularly those associated with the gregarious tendency of the animals (Miminoshvili, Magakian, and Kokaia 1960). If we are interested in using these animals to provide analogues of human neurosis, which is primarily a social condition, or to study the effects of sustained conflict or even mild conflict, it would indeed be appropriate to arrange for more relevant experimental variations.

INTEGRATION OF NATURALISTIC
AND EXPERIMENTAL SOCIAL LEARNING

With the exception of the series of studies from the Wisconsin laboratories, it would probably be true to say that experiments on monkeys relating to any aspect of social learning have contributed very little beyond the simplest confirmation or negation of hypotheses derived from field study. The experimental and the field situations are too far apart and bear too little relationship to one another. A more hopeful prospect lies in the opportunity to compare the social learning processes of groups of the same species kept in captivity under different environmental conditions. Meanwhile, we may at least attempt to see whether any integration is at present possible between the principles that seem to operate in the social organization of wild groups and the principles of learning derived from laboratory experiment.

Mowrer (1960) apears to have been the first experimental psychologist to attempt explicitly to apply his "theory" of learning to the task of explaining social behavior of primates. He examines in particular Carpenter's (1952) generalizations. The key statement from Carpenter concerns

> . . . the formulation of an important principle for understanding the dynamics of group integration: Namely, *that the drives, tensions or needs of one individual which are satisfied by activities of another individual or individuals of a grouping modify the previous adjustments between or*

among the individuals. This may be termed the principle of reciprocal interaction. (1952:243)

In any group the equilibrium in the relationships of the individuals composing it is a resultant of centripetal and centrifugal forces that, respectively, attract and repel. The former

> . . . attract the animals to each other, regulate their interactions and cause the society to persist as an identifiable group [whereas] . . . competition, conflicts, and various forms of aggression . . . operate . . . to differentiate the statuses of individuals, to create intra-group stresses and to cause some individuals to leave the society. (1952:244)

According to Mowrer this analysis

> . . . lends itself admirably to restatement in terms of revised two-factor learning theory. In fact, it is, in itself, almost such a statement. To begin with, there are the primary rewards and punishments which are mediated by group living. These are, on the one hand, food (especially for the young), shelter and mutual protection, and sexual gratification and, on the other hand, the aggressions which arise as a result of unregulated competition for the available rewards. To the extent that an individual experiences rewards in the group, various forms of stimulation associated with group life take on secondary reinforcement and tend to hold the individual in the group. To the extent that an individual experiences punishment in the group, the associated stimuli take on the capacity to arouse fear and tend to *repel,* or "expel," the individual. Hence the image of "centripetal" and "centrifugal" forces acting upon each individual in the group which thus determine, for the group as a whole, its stability or instability. (1960:384)

Mowrer goes on to point out that each individual in a group

> . . . learns to react selectively, discriminatingly toward other members of the group, while at the same time establishing attitudes of friendship or enmity on the part of others toward him. . . . Hence, in a stable, successful social group the total learning associated with life in the group is relatively great. (1960:385)

Much of what we have discussed earlier in this chapter, notably field studies data, seems, at least superficially, to fit Mowrer's formulation. "Secondary reinforcement" is so general a conception that it enables a learning theory to extend itself indefinitely so as to include learning that occurs in or results from situations in which no primary reward or punishment is evident. Thus the basic "trophallactic" situation (Schneirla 1946) of infant dependence on the mother, the "rewards" of which for the infant in security, comfort, food-getting, and the like are obvious, is considered extensible by some authors to account for the persistent social learning seen in the young as it grows older and loses close dependence on the mother. As drive-reduction and drive-induction are supposedly involved in reinforcement, the secondary reinforcers are derivatives of situations in which, for example, the young animal actually has been rewarded or punished.

Although Mowrer's is a useful attempt to cope with the complex social phenomena with which all field workers are concerned, it is doubtful if it is adequate to explain all that is probably to be included in the social learning of group-living primates. Further, the value of such a theory can be assessed mainly in terms of the hypotheses it suggests that ought to be testable in experiment, and so far, it does not appear to have led to anything new in this respect. This may be because the experimenters working along the Mowrer line have not been personally acquainted with the diversity of social behavior in a monkey group, and hence have been unable to formulate hypotheses from direct observation. Being essentially a drive-reduction (induction) theory, it focuses on problems of social learning in which the motivational factors causing approach or avoidance, hope or fear, are evident. It also probably suggests a framework in which the differential reinforcing effects of conflicting tendencies in social disciminatory learning can be set out for experimental testing.

Berlyne (1960:10) is likewise concerned with the role of conflict in learning, pointing out that conflict of several varieties, other than the more drastic forms described in the psychoanalytical literature, ". . . is an inescapable accompaniment of the existence of all higher animals, because of the endless diversity of the stimuli that act on them and of the responses that they have the ability to perform." In the monkey group there is a more or less continual interplay of friendly, sexual, aggressive, and fearful impulses, which require that they be balanced among the individuals. There is little doubt that these, rather than actual experiences of punishment and reward, serve to maintain the social framework, and, when the balance within the group is disturbed, permit relearning and modification by other means than fighting. Indeed, the significance of social conflict in social learning studies is something that might very well be investigated experimentally in ways more meaningful than those of the interanimal conditioning work so far attempted. The balancing of social inhibitions and excitations in a wild baboon group affords a remarkable illustration of effective social learning based on conflict.

Berlyne (1960) is also much concerned with the problem of exploratory behavior. Such behavior, in a wild monkey group, is scarcely ever carried out by an individual entirely without the awareness or the company of others; it is thus reasonable to suppose that this is simply an important propensity of the species which allows of some degree of flexibility, of opportunity to acquire new habits. It is serviceable to the group, and the learning is reinforced mainly by the friendly, attentive social context in which it occurs.

In summary, the fieldworker may begin with the assumption that all "normal" primate learning is, in essence, social. Where the individual primate is in temporary isolation learning a task without reference to any other member of its species, the learning is not normal. The primary reinforcement for all normal primate learning may come from its social context, the group in which the animal is born and nurtured. Even the sensorimotor activities of observing, manipulating, and exploring that are indicative of individual independence receive some facilitation, some inhibition, and some direction from the group setting. Conflict of tendencies (which varies with age and sex, with group situation, and with species' ecology and social organization) is likely to determine much of the discriminatory social learning with only occasional reference to such primary incentives as food or actual punishment. This paper presents some of the problems of integrating field and experimental studies, rather than attempting to answer them. Learning theory has been in one way too sophisticated, and in another way too limited to provide a useful basis from which to set up social learning experiments. Field studies may be analyzed with the purpose of providing experimentally testable hypotheses and may eventually contribute much to a more generally valid theory of social learning.

14

NATURALISTIC AND EXPERIMENTAL

INVESTIGATIONS OF THE SOCIAL

BEHAVIOR OF MONKEYS AND APES[1]

William A. Mason

INTRODUCTION

The study of primate social behavior is one of the most rapidly growing and exciting fields in the behavioral sciences today. Both the growth and the excitement owe much to the fact that the primates, because of their special status in relation to man, have attracted many different disciplines—anthropology, psychiatry, psychology, physiology, sociology, and zoology—that are contributing to and drawing upon research on monkeys and apes. Naturally, these groups vary in the extent and vigor of their involvement in the study of primate social behavior, but each has something to offer in the way of perspective, theory, content, or method. Thus far, no single discipline has dominated the field or has had an exclusive voice in determining the course of research; and this is as it should be, for we stand to gain much from the diversity of participating talent. There is even reason to hope that the primates will provide the focus for a new approach to the comparative study of animal behavior, cutting across traditional academic boundaries and accommodating many disciplines under the same roof.

If this is to be achieved, however, it is critical that a free and lively

[1]Preparation of this chapter was supported by funds received from the National Institutes of Health Grant FR00164.

exchange of ideas and information be maintained among the various participating disciplines. This will require special efforts, particularly because the field is growing quickly, and that growth is being carried forward by individuals representing contrasting viewpoints and different ways of approaching problems. Under such conditions there is always the risk that parochial interests may prevail, that communication may break down, and that legitimate and reasonable differences in attitude and aims may become confounded with judgments as to which approach is scientifically superior. Fortunately, this is not yet a serious problem in the study of primate social behavior, but the possibility that it may become one clearly exists.

One area that might become troublesome is the relation between field and laboratory approaches. It is an unfortunate peculiarity of primate research that these two approaches, which should supplement each other, have, in fact, developed independently. The problem is recognized, but recent treatments of it, notably by Hall (see especially Chap. 13), although provocative and praiseworthy in their aims, offer a critique that I believe is divisive and incomplete in spite of the cogency of some of the arguments. For example, Hall's statement that except for studies from the Wisconsin Laboratories ". . . experiments on monkeys relating to any aspect of social learning have contributed very little beyond the simplest confirmation or negation of hypotheses derived from field studies" is misleading. In the first place, even if experimental studies did nothing more than confirm or negate hypotheses derived from the field, they would be serving a most important function. Second, with a few minor exceptions, the social studies of the Wisconsin Laboratories have not been directly concerned with the learning process. And finally, many other laboratories have been responsible for experiments that are clearly pertinent to the question of social learning and go beyond anything yet described, demonstrated, or explicitly hypothesized on the basis of field data. To document the point, one need only mention Crawford's classic studies of cooperative problem solving in chimpanzees (1937); Delgado's demonstration that one monkey will learn to use intracranial stimulation of a cagemate to control the latter's aggression (1962); or the research by Azrin and his associates on the conditions eliciting social aggression and on the reinforcing effects of the aggressive act (Azrin, Hutchinson, and Hake 1963; Azrin, Hutchinson, and McLaughlin 1965). One problem in Hall's conclusion is that it dismisses the experimental literature too quickly, and by implication places it outside the realm of potentially useful information at the very time when we most need a careful and balanced appraisal of its significance for understanding the behavior of free-ranging individuals and natural groups. Similarly, Hall's ex cathedra pronouncements as to what constitutes "normal" learning (chapter 13), probably will not lead to any constructive change in the attitudes of learning specialists and could very well discourage nonspecialists from becoming more closely acquainted with a discipline that may have much to offer them.

RELATIONSHIP BETWEEN EXPERIMENTAL
AND FIELD RESEARCH: CURRENT STATUS

Hall is undoubtedly correct, however, when he points out that the experimental and field approaches are far apart. As yet, experimental research has not helped the fieldworker much in the conduct of his research or in the interpretation of his results, nor have the data collected in the field had an important influence on problems selected for experimental investigation in the laboratory.

It is easy to see why these two approaches have remained apart, but the separation is no less unfortunate for being understandable. A closer working relationship between them is not merely desirable, but is an essential requirement for continuing progress in the study of primate social behavior. Both approaches are indispensable; and neither can be complete without the contribution of the other.

We can find no evidence for a fundamental difference between experimental and field research. Whether the invesitgator works in the laboratory or in the field, his basic aim is to achieve a reliable, objective description of behavior. In either setting, observer bias and the effects of the observer's presence on the object of study must be evaluated. There is a common need for the replication of important findings, and for the use of situational variations as a means of checking, refining, or extending hypotheses; in either case, the accepted rules of evidence must be followed in the interpretation of results. Moreover, there is no reason, in principle, why experiments cannot be performed in the field; nor does the laboratory environment preclude certain forms of naturalistic research. The ethologists, in particular, have provided many illustrations of the feasibility of securing naturalistic data in the laboratory or performing experimental research in the field.

If the current separation between field studies and experimental research is not based on fundamental issues, why has it occurred? Historically, the two approaches have appealed to different workers and have been associated with different intellectual disciplines. Such a situation creates a favorable climate for the formation of in-groups and out-groups, and it is usual in these circumstances for the ins to develop strong views (usually expressed to other ins) on the competence of the outs, and on the value of their work. Insofar as the ins and the outs are aligned with "laboratory" and "field," this can only hinder the development of a more effective synthesis between these approaches. Among the factors that help create and preserve such alignments are personality characteristics, training, and professional identification.

CONTRASTS IN ORIENTATION: LABORATORY
AND FIELD

Personal Characteristics

The choice of a particular form of scientific activity is obviously conditioned by personal attributes and predilections. In respect to field and laboratory research, one can easily see how the scientist's personal characteristics might influence not only his preference for a particular approach, but also his judgment as to its scientific merit and utility.

The fieldworker must be able to accept solitude, physical discomfort, and frustration as normal parts of his daily routine. He is heavily dependent on his own resources in collecting and evaluating his findings and must be able to tolerate a high degree of complexity and ambiguity in his data, particularly in the early phases of research. The neat temporal separation between fact and interpretation, which is usually possible in the laboratory, is often unattainable in the field where the process of formulating, checking, and revising interpretations goes on continuously and is an inseparable and essential part of gathering information.

The whole trend of behavioral research in the laboratory is toward objectivity, and this has meant the formalizing and simplifying of the scientist's participation in the data-collecting process. Small wonder then that the experimentalist who has had no personal experience with free-ranging primates is inclined to doubt that the fieldworker, unaided by the instruments and controls of the laboratory, can really achieve an objective and reliable description of behavior. He may recognize the romantic appeal of the field, but views the research as excessively demanding, risky, and distressingly incomplete. Surely Carpenter must have had such persons in mind when he wrote: "The prevailing 'climates of opinion,' including scientific value systems and attitudes of the majority of our research colleagues, are of such a character as to impose an unusual burden of proof on us for the professional status of our achievements." (1950:1006)

The fieldworker might be expected to look upon experimental research as tame and pedestrian. What to the laboratory researcher is a necessary attempt to fill in details, he views as nit-picking, and he sees the experimental testing of hypotheses as a belabored attempt to prove the obvious. Finally, knowing something of the artificiality of the laboratory and the constraints it imposes on the animal, he is likely to question the value of experimental findings on the grounds that they lack ecological validity, and do not reflect normal and adaptive behavioral processes. In either case an objective basis for such attitudes can be found.

Training

Whatever the personal factors that enter into judgments about the scientific status of field and laboratory research, they are reinforced by the current arrangement for training graduate students. Each of the several academic disciplines that has an interest in primate behavior places its own peculiar stamp on the kinds of questions that are asked and the method of approach.

In general, fieldworkers are trained in departments of anthropology and zoology, both of which have strong traditional interests in field research. Both groups are concerned with the evolution of behavior, and are therefore sensitive to ecological variables and problems of adaptation. Most experimentalists come from comparative psychology—a discipline that has a deep commitment to quantitative laboratory analysis of individual behavior, and small enthusiasm for alternate approaches.

Selection of Problems

Nowhere is the influence of training more evident than in the selection and formulation of research problems. The major problems of contemporary psychology can be traced to the preoccupation of the classic philosophers. Many of the chapter headings in modern introductory textbooks bespeak this historical indebtedness. The senses, will, and intellect have been discarded as terms, but they have their modern equivalents in sensation and perception, motivation, and learning. The contrasts between contemporary scientific psychology and its historical antecedents are huge, and the differences, whether reckoned in number or significance, far outweigh the similarities. The important point in the present context, however, is that from its early prescientific beginnings down to the present, psychology's overriding interest has been the individual human being. Other animals have figured in psychological research chiefly as stand-ins for men: "The primary reason . . . for the use of subhuman animals in psychological experiments lies in the fact that more precise methods and more adequate controls can be exercised over animals other than man in the laboratory" (Harlow 1948:319). Such an attitude needs no defense. It has produced interesting and fruitful research in all branches of science and medicine and, without doubt, will continue to do so. Whatever knowledge we have of primate learning and sensory capabilities—and it is considerable—has been obtained within this framework. But, as has been pointed out by comparative psychologists such as Beach

(1960) and Schneirla (1952), the use of animals as substitutes for man inevitably leads the experimenter to select problems from human behavior and to formulate them in terms appropriate to man. In this sense, the traditional approach of psychological experiments with animals is deductive. Assumptions are made and criteria established that define the necessary and sufficient conditions for demonstrating a particular phenomenon (attachment, cooperation, communication, imitation, and the like), and with this accomplished the experimental methodology is, in principle, capable of providing an unequivocal measure of the phenomenon *as defined*.

With respect to its contribution to animal behavior, this formalistic approach has three obvious limitations: First, it fails to take into account the special propensities, abilities, and limitations of the subject species (or does so only incidentally, as in the design of the apparatus or the selection of incentive conditions). Second, it often fails to examine alternate methods for determining the range or generality of the effect. And third, it tends to overlook the context or situation as a source of behavioral determinants. Thus the traditional psychological approach to animal behavior can be characterized as nonevolutionary, nonecological, and narrowly anthropocentric. It is much less concerned with understanding the origin and nature of species-specific attributes involved in the adjustments of a given species to a complex, real-life situation than with describing and analyzing abstract traits or capacities of the isolated individual that have relevance to man.

That the fieldworker should find this approach alien to his own interests and activities is not surprising. In its essential features the field study follows the inductive method of classical biology, in which the selection of specific classes of information and the elaboration and testing of formal hypotheses is deferred until a comprehensive overview of the material is available. Field conditions are such that they tend to direct attention toward groups, rather than individual organisms. Although the fieldworker might agree that social phenomena are ultimately reducible to statements about individuals, he is far more impressed with the organismic quality or Gestalt of the group (Hall, Chap. 13), and with the overwhelming importance of the social and physical contexts as determinants of group behavior. The fieldworker aims at an account of group reactions. Animals are necessarily viewed within a social matrix, and individual behavior is of interest chiefly to the extent that it reflects or determines the activity of other members of the group.

If these characterizations of field and experimental research are correct, it is easy to see why the dialogue between the two approaches has not been more lively and fruitful. Although both are ostensibly concerned with social behavior, their immediate goals are not the same. The experimental approach has been directed chiefly toward a causal analysis of individual behavior, hence the extensive use of dyads, the arrangement of experimental situations into "demonstrators" and "observers," and the close connection between social experiments and the procedures and constructs used in investigations with single organisms. The naturalistic field study has dealt with groups, and it has been most successful in exploiting its unique opportunities to obtain information on predation, diet, role of seasonal factors in social behavior, group size and composition, range, territoriality, and the relations between groups—problems that are beyond the reach of most laboratory research.

It would be presumptuous to suggest that either group abandon its traditional interests. Both approaches are supplying needed information on important questions. At the same time, if we are to have a true interchange between laboratory experiment and field research, it is clear that new possibilities must be explored. As a first step we might begin with an examination of the language that is used to describe, classify, and measure primate social phenomena.

RESPONSE CLASSIFICATION AND DATA LANGUAGE

The Choice of Descriptive Units

Three primary dimensions have been used to describe primate social characteristics: (1) Enumeration or classification of individuals within definable social units leading to statements of group composition, central grouping tendencies, and sex ratios (Carpenter 1954); (2) arrangement of individuals in space, exemplified by the diagrams presented for Japanese monkeys (Imanishi 1960); and (3) specific responses or patterns of responses, elicited by, directed toward, or having some effect on other individuals. To deal with the dynamics of social behavior these dimensions can be considered in relation to each other and within a temporal framework.

Group composition and grouping tendencies are difficult to approach in the laboratory. They are significant problems in fieldwork, but they comprise only a small part of the total range of information with which most field studies are concerned. Measurement of spatial variables, although of great potential importance, has not been exploited systematically in the laboratory or in the field. The response dimension remains as the most versatile and widely used means for describing primate social phenomena, and the most promising avenue now available for discovering ways of bringing about a closer working relationship between field investigations and experimental laboratory research. It will be useful to begin by reviewing the general problem of response definition and measurement in behavioral research. More complete treatments can be found in Delgado and Delgado (1962), Sidman (1960), and Underwood (1957).

Every student of behavior accepts the basic working assumption that behavior, like other natural events, is not random, but organized in space and time. It has form or structure, and shows orderliness with respect to the frequency with which it occurs and the situations in which it appears. Most behavioral scientists have elected to work with molar patterns, rather than with isolated movements of muscles or glands, and they have tried to use responses that can be registered reliably by any competent observer within the framework of a particular recording system.

Beyond these familiar generalities there is the difficult task of selecting particular aspects of behavior for study, for it is clear that we cannot investigate behavior as a global process, but must focus our attention on specific responses or response patterns. Selection is usually determined by practical as well as theoretical considerations, and responses have been defined and classified in many ways: in terms of their form ("grimace"), their effects on the environment ("lever pressing"), or their relations to some antecedent condition ("displacement reaction" or "learned response"). Many different classifications are possible, even for the same event, and there are no simple criteria for judging a meaningful or useful response. Two types of response classification are of special importance in investigations of primate social behavior; these are the species-typical pattern and the index response. The distinction between them is not absolute, but in practice these responses have been used in quite different ways, and for different purposes. The species-typical pattern is defined by its form and is frequently used in nonexperimental research, whereas the index response is most often defined with reference to a specific apparatus and set of measurement procedures. The time and place of its occurrence is largely determined by the investigator.

Species Typical Patterns

In fieldwork, as a practical necessity, the observer focuses on conspicuous, recurrent motor patterns that are fairly easy to detect and that can be recorded reliably without special equipment. The patterns are frequently complex and component responses vary somewhat with individuals or situations. Although these variations are sometimes described, the investigator's principal aim is to achieve a generalized description of the species' repertoire that is representative of most animals most of the time. Such an account is commonly called a behavioral inventory or ethogram. The behavioral inventory has wide utility in field research because it provides a set of explicit descriptive units ("grimace," "lipsmack," and "eyelid threat") that can be used in both narrative and quantitative treatments of social interaction.

Close, but not perfect, agreement between different observers of the same species lends confidence to the idea that the behavioral inventory is a reliable descriptive instrument (compare, for example, Altmann's with Hinde and

Rowell's ethograms for the rhesus monkey). Even so, the inventory always involves some degree of simplification and abstraction, and the actual definition and number of responses will depend upon the objectives of the research and the capabilities of the recording system. As a rule, smaller descriptive units are preferable and can easily be thrown into larger categories after the fact (Altmann 1965). For some problems, however, particularly those that require simultaneous observations on several animals, it may be necessary to use rather gross response units. Insofar as scoring criteria are explicit, and the various responses included within a single category are carefully described and have similar functions, discrepancies will probably not be serious between gross and refined units with respect to findings or interpretation of results.

The species-typical response obviously has much in common with the ethologists' "fixed action patterns,"[2] and offers some of the same advantages:

Functional relevance.—Many species-typical patterns have fairly direct and obvious effects on the environment, particularly on other individuals. They play a conspicuous part in sexual attraction, mating, and the care of the young. They are significantly involved in relations with competitors and predators, and they figure prominently in intraspecific aggression. In investigations of social behavior under natural conditions species-typical patterns are a major resource for studying causes as well as effects, thus serving in different contexts as either independent or dependent variables.

Organismic relevance.—Species-typical motor patterns can often be viewed as integral parts of broader organismic systems. These systems are the "instincts" of an earlier day, and their existence is inferred from the fact that certain patterns (1) tend to occur together in predictable combinations or sequences, (2) respond in similar fashion to physiological alterations or changes in environmental conditions, or (3) can be arranged into groups or classes on the basis of their relation to common end points or consummatory activities. For example, sexual receptivity in macaque monkeys is associated with rhythmic lip movements, the "sporadic arm reflex," and changes in the frequency of grooming and aggression, as well as with increases in sexual presentation and mounting (Bernstein 1963; Carpenter 1942a; Kaufmann 1965; Rowell 1963; Tokuda 1961). Although authors do not always agree on the reliability and direction of specific changes, laboratory studies indicate that at least some of them can be related to variations in hormone levels or other physiological factors (Ball and Hartman 1935; Freedman and Rosvold 1962; Michael and Herbert 1963).

---

[2]The "fixed action pattern" is a theoretical term applying to behaviors the form of which is genetically determined and varies within rather narrow limits. Many of the patterns appearing in primate behavioral inventories may, in fact, be fixed action patterns, but fieldworkers have been far less concerned with establishing this than with finding patterns that are representative of the species and socially significant.

The nature and number of such systems have not been determined in monkeys and apes. Their analysis may present special difficulties in primates owing to broad evolutionary changes as, for example, in the specificity of eliciting stimuli and in the linkage between physiological factors and behavior (Beach 1947), but there is every reason to expect that it will be feasible and instructive.

Adaptive significance.—Because of the characteristics that we have described as functional and organismic relevance, species-typical patterns often provide a clear suggestion of adaptive benefits for the individual or for the species, as with the "grimace" of macaques, which appears to reduce intragroup strife by providing a distinct signal of subordination that can forestall attack by an animal of superior strength. The question of the adaptive value of a particular pattern adds a useful explanatory dimension in any form of behavioral research, but it occupies a central place in discussions of behavioral evolution. Naturally, questions of adaptive significance are pertinent not only to response patterns, but also to higher descriptive levels, for example, social organization.

Comparative utility.—The value of stereotyped species-typical patterns for phylogenetic comparison has been established in ethological studies, chiefly of birds and fish. Careful analysis of primate postures, facial expressions, vocalizations, and locomotor patterns can be expected to reveal similarities and contrasts between allied groups that are related to other taxonomic characters, and can help to clarify significant evolutionary features (Andrew 1963*b;* van Hooff 1962).

The salient characteristics of species-typical patterns (ease of identification, prominence in social behavior, and biological relevance) are strong reasons for using these responses in experimental research. In fact there are many instances in which they have been used as dependent variables—for example, investigations of reactions to various stimulus conditions such as snakes, novel inanimate objects, or people (Bernstein and Mason 1962; Fletcher and Emlen 1964; Menzel 1964; Rowell and Hinde 1963), and studies of the effects of rearing conditions and of motivational factors on social responsiveness (Hansen 1962; Mason 1960, 1965; Seay 1966). Their use as stimuli or independent variables is more limited because of technical difficulties in controlling the stimulus, a problem that some workers have solved with photographic techniques (Butler 1961; Miller, Murphy, and Mirsky 1959; Sackett 1965).

One of the great benefits of laboratory research utilizing species-typical patterns is the obvious relevance of the findings to behavior in nature. The comparability of descriptive units can serve a most important function in bridging the gap between naturalistic research and experiment. With proper precautions direct quantitative comparisons can be made between data secured in the laboratory and in the field.

The Index Response

In seemingly sharp contrast to experiments recording complex species-typical patterns, are the many investigations in which the primary unit of measurement is a discrete response (for example, lever-pressing, displacing a block of wood, or taking peanuts from a chute). These responses may be quite remote from normal social patterns, and because their relevance to naturalistic research is obscure, the fieldworker often fails to appreciate their significance.

It is obvious that they offer some methodological advantages: They place few demands on the observational skills of the experimenter; they can be recorded easily (often automatically); they are resistant to observer bias; and they yield large amounts of precise quantitative information within a brief span of time. These are useful attributes, but they do not in themselves provide a sufficient justification for the use of such responses. The primary value of the discrete response measure is its utility as an indicator reaction in investigations of abstract processes, traits, abilities, systems, and the like that are not reflected adequately in any single response, but must be inferred from information on how, when, or under what conditions a particular overt reaction occurs.

In most behavioral research the need for hypothetical terms is inescapable. Even field research, in spite of its descriptive emphasis, must occasionally use terms that refer to covert processes or hypothetical traits. A few of these terms are as follows: dominance, leader, aggressiveness, identification (with another), observational learning, tension (of group), cohesiveness, social bond, territoriality, and social structure. Clearly, not one of these terms signifies a specific and identifiable pattern, such as "lipsmacking" or "threat face." The problem of definition is often met in field research by listing the specific attributes that are believed to reflect the trait or process. Estrus is operationally defined by Carpenter (1942a) in terms of ten primary behavioral and physical signs. Schaller (1963) defines leadership in gorillas with reference to morphology and to complex behavioral characteristics that include not only the actions of the leader, but also reactions to him by other group members. Hall (1962b) identifies a number of specific behaviors that reflect "intragroup tension."

This type of extensive definition can be satisfactory for most purposes, but it becomes difficult to use when the process, rather than its manifestations, is of central concern. For example, how does one treat a concept such as "aggressiveness" quantitatively when perhaps a dozen different responses can be regarded as meaningful measures of aggression? Does an increase in the frequency of facial threats bear the same relation to aggressiveness as does an increase in the frequency of chasing or biting? One solution is to arrange responses so that they represent different magnitudes or intensities, as Altmann (1962a) has done for the aggressive repertoire of rhesus monkeys. Presumably, any condition or procedure that increases aggressiveness would result in a shift toward the high end of the scale. Another solution, which has been favored in experimental research, is to select a single response, the quantitative variations of which are thought to be correlated with changes in some covert process. The response becomes an operationally defined measure of the process. Thus, changes in the frequency of chasing might be used to measure levels of aggressiveness, just as the choice of the correct or baited stimulus object at frequencies greater than chance is used in many primate studies as an operationally defined measure of discrimination learning.

Such an operationally defined measure is an indispensable tool in behavioral research, and its power and efficiency have been amply demonstrated— not only in studies of learning, but also in investigations of perception, hunger, maternal "drive," anxiety, curiosity, and social attachment. Because the operational definition is restrictive and unequivocal, it facilitates experimental analysis and the communication of results. Usually, however, a single operational definition does not encompass all the phenomena embraced by the common-sense understanding of a particular process, such as learning, and in this respect it is only a partial definition. More operational definitions can be added, and as their logical and empirical interrelationships are worked out, the operationally defined concept becomes more general. In Harlow's experiments with artificial mothers, for example, the primary measure of strength of attachment was duration of contact with the surrogate (Harlow and Zimmermann 1958). This measure alone, however, would have expressed only a limited aspect of what is usually understood by "attachment." It is not surprising that infant monkeys (or any young mammals) spend more time in contact with a soft, padded object than with one constructed of metal. This difficulty was resolved by a combination of procedures designed to yield a broader assessment of the strength and nature of the filial bond. In special tests, monkeys were deprived of their artificial mothers, exposed to stress in the presence and absence of the device, given the surrogate as an incentive for lever-pressing, and so forth. Although some use was made of species-typical patterns, the majority of measures were of simple responses, each providing, in effect, an operational definition of some aspect of filial attachment.

As a concept is elaborated operationally, it may become more like the common-sense version; but we may also discover in what respects the common-sense version is faulty or ambiguous. Frequently, however, no attempt is made to add new measures, and a single operationally defined response carries almost the entire burden in a lengthy series of investigations. This is particularly likely to occur if the "reference" phenomena have not been described adequately. In the absence of such a description, reliance on a simple and operationally defined response can restrict investigation to a particular set of procedures and variables and lead to results that are tangential to the main problem and of limited theoretical interest, in spite of their precision and objectivity.

This, apparently, is the basis for Hall's indictment of most experimental investigations of primate social behavior (Hall, Chap. 13, 1963*a*, 1963*b*). Evaluation of a scientific technique is based on three factors: the reliability of the data it produces, their generality, and their scientific importance (Sidman 1960). By any reasonable criteria, the reliability and generality of the majority of experimental findings on primate learning and social behavior are securely established, and one must therefore view Hall's criticisms of this research as a judgment on its scientific importance. We may infer that in Hall's judgment scientific importance here can be equated with "understanding the behavior of natural groups." This is only one aspect of the complex question of scientific importance, but it is an aspect of special concern to us here.

REMEDIAL POSSIBILITIES

Broadening Laboratory Experiment

The question of why experimental studies have not offered more of direct relevance to the behavior of natural groups has already been given a partial answer: They have been chiefly concerned with individuals rather than groups. This concern reflects a traditional interest of psychology, but it also reveals a lack of awareness of the primate group as the setting in which most natural behavior occurs, and as a social entity that is an appropriate object of study.

A major factor in creating such awareness is the field study. Dominance was for years defined in experimental research in terms of success in competition for food. The definition was workable and convenient, and as the result of its use we now have information on many variables that influence success (drugs, hormones, brain lesions, food deprivation, caging arrangements, punishment, and previous success). However, as yet the findings have not contributed much in idea or substance toward understanding the nature of social rank in free-ranging troops. The explanation for this has less to do with theory or methodology, than with the amount and kinds of information available.

Early discussions of the behavior of free-ranging primates indicated that success in competition was a prominent and important characteristic of social life (Carpenter 1942*b;* Zuckerman 1932). It is only within the last few years that this view has been modified as the result of more complete descriptions of the range and functions of behaviors associated with social rank in natural groups. Reports such as Altmann's (1962) and Washburn and DeVore's (1961*b*), by providing detailed and explicit descriptions of the behavior of dominant males, have suggested fresh approaches to the experimental investigation of social rank of which Bernstein's work is a notable example (Bernstein 1964*b*, 1964*c*).

It is evident that laboratory research can be responsive to descriptions from the field, particularly when the data are presented in a form that suggests specific variables and testable hypotheses. And it can be argued that the likelihood of obtaining such data will be increased as greater use is made of quantitative methods and experimental procedures in the field.

Qualitative versus Quantitative Description

Naturalistic research on a new species necessarily relies heavily on qualitative description as the most effective means of providing a balanced, comprehensive, and intelligible overview of social behavior and ecology. Nothing is gained from using quantitative methods prematurely in the field, but when such techniques can be introduced without detracting from the major objectives of field research it is obviously desirable to do so. The advantages of quantitative data in precision, convenience, economy of expression, and amenability to statistical treatment are fully sufficient to justify Hall's recommendation that ". . . field observers should be trained to think quantitatively, for this will affect their whole approach to the task and need in no way vitiate accuracy of their qualitative descriptions." 1965*b*:32) Quantitative methods are not new to primate field studies and they have been used in several ways. Probably the most common application is to gross aspects of group phenomena, such as size, composition, range, and activity counts.

There are three additional types of quantitative information that are more relevant to laboratory research and can be looked upon as standing between the qualitative field report and the controlled laboratory experiment. These are the normative study, the correlational study or natural experiment, and the field experiment.

Normative Studies of Social Behavior

As the name implies, the central purpose of the normative study is to provide a representative overview of some aspect of social life. The data may relate to particular classes or types of individuals, to the frequency and direction of various social activities, or to some combination of these. Thus, attention might be directed toward interaction between siblings, grooming behavior, or social development from birth to maturity. Most field studies include some information of this sort, although intensive quantitative studies are usually deferred until a generalized qualitative overview is achieved, and some idea can be formed of the variables that are worth quantifying. For the more thoroughly studied primates (especially the macaques) detailed and topic-oriented normative studies are beginning to appear (Furuya 1965; Kaufmann 1966; Sade 1965; Tokuda 1961). Because they can provide a representative view of social patterns and relationships, indicate the range of normal variation, and suggest influential variables that may not be present in the usual laboratory environment, normative studies in the field can contribute directly to the design of experimental research and to the interpretation of laboratory findings.

Correlational Studies

Quantitative methods have also been used in the field in an effort to establish relationships between different natural events. Although the process of data collection and the events recorded may be the same as in the normative study, this approach is more directly oriented toward the discovery of causal relationships, and consequently has special relevance to experimental research. One of the simplest forms of this approach involves comparison of two conditions, for example, the incidence of fighting during breeding and nonbreeding periods, or the comparison of various behaviors in captive and free-ranging groups (Kummer and Kurt 1965). It may also be concerned with the relation between different levels of one variable and the magnitude of another (for example, the relation between amount of available food and incidence of fighting). Many field reports offer a clear suggestion of such relationships, and some data are sufficient to permit a statistical demonstration. Thus, Hall (1962b) was able to show a significant positive correlation between aggressive behavior by females within a group and the daily frequency of mating by a male. Altmann's (1965) analysis of communicative behavior is the most ambitious and sophisticated example of this general approach applied to primate social interaction. Of course, both variables need not be behavioral, as in Altmann's research; an investigator could equally well use ecological variation, morphological characters, age, or physiological measures.

Field Experiment

Role of field experiment.—In the foregoing examples the investigator attempts to determine causal relationships in a situation that he has had no hand in creating. The correlational study or natural experiment can reveal variables of particular importance to the behavior of free-ranging groups, and it may be the only method possible for studying the effects of radical alterations in such factors as climate, food supply, predation, or disease. Its value is limited, however, when the study situation is encountered infrequently, or is so complex as to preclude any clear statement of causal relationships. Under some circumstances the amount and precision of the data can be increased by arranging special conditions in the field.

Thus far, there have been few systematic attempts at any form of behavioral experiment with primates under field conditions. The field experiment was first suggested as a methodological resource in primate research by Carpenter (1934), who subsequently illustrated its use in a preliminary study of the effects of removal of dominant males on group range (Carpenter 1942b). More recently, Hall (1965b) and Itani (1965) have presented their observations on the acquisition of food habits, which suggest interesting possibilities for experimental investigation in the field. Reactions to strangers have been investigated by Hall (1965b), and in greater detail, by Kummer (in press).

Most of these researches were performed in the course of other ongoing field activities. They were designed to provide the investigator with leads and hypotheses that he would not have had otherwise, and they served this purpose well; but they are only a beginning in the systematic use of experimental methods in the field.

Methodological problems.—Naturally, the primate field experiment will encounter technical and methodological problems. Variables such as climate, predation, food supply, group composition, and individual social experience (which may be extraneous to the purpose of the experiment) often cannot be controlled, although they may have large but undetermined effects on the experimental results. It may be difficult to decide in advance the probable nature and locus of the experimental effect so that appropriate measurement procedures can be designed. What kinds of behavior should be recorded—spatial relations, species-typical patterns, or a discrete index response? Should one focus on a single key animal, on selected individuals or special subgroups, or is the effect more likely to be detected in the group as a whole? What techniques will provide a sensitive measure of the anticipated effect—photography, check lists, frequency counts, narrative description— and will they actually work in the experimental situation? In answering these questions the field investigator's strongest asset is his knowledge of the social organization and response patterns of the subject species and of its behavior in the habitat in which the experiment is to be performed.

The same methodological problems must be met in designing a laboratory experiment, but they are resolved more easily because more variables are under the experimenter's control. In the laboratory the scientist usually has more latitude in selecting subjects; if necessary, he can pretrain them to produce the response he will measure. He also has much more freedom than his colleague in the field in arranging the environment and test conditions to suit his purposes. By placing restrictions and constraints on his subjects the laboratory researcher increases his own flexibility; at the same time he hopes to reduce the amount of uncontrolled variation in his data and to improve his chances of obtaining an interpretable outcome.

Because of practical limitations, the field experiment usually cannot achieve the same level of technical precision that is possible in the laboratory, but it can produce reliable and useful results. To increase the likelihood that this will happen, a few simple criteria are suggested that might serve as helpful guidelines in setting up or evaluating experimental procedures. Fundamentally, the behavioral experiment is concerned with the factors producing a change or modification in behavior; it seeks to clarify a causal relationship between behavior (the dependent variable) and other conditions (the independent variables). The demonstration of such a relationship requires a comparison of behavior under at least two conditions. This can be accomplished by measuring the same subject in the presence or absence of the experimental variable, or at various levels of the experimental condition, or by making use of an independent control group. In addition, the reliability of the effect should be established, and this is usually achieved by some form of replication, by repeated measures on the same subject (whether group or individual), by the use of multiple subjects, or by some combination of these procedures. The primary purpose of the replication is to provide reasonable assurances that the relationship between independent and dependent variables is "real," although the same technique is also used to assess the generality of the effect.

Note that these criteria make no special assumptions about the phenomena studied. The subject unit can be groups or individuals; the response can be as simple as displacing a block of wood, or as complex as the movement of an entire troop; and the behavioral change can be transient (for example, a momentary increase in aggression) or enduring (for example, the acquisition of a new food habit).

Examples.—The range of problems that can be investigated experimentally in the field is vast, and we can only hope here to illustrate a few possibilities. Two recent investigations provide useful examples of how simple experimental methods can be used profitably in the field. The first, by Menzel, is concerned with the factors influencing responsiveness to objects in Japanese monkeys (Menzel 1966). As test stimuli he used common objects such as dolls, toys, and rope, which were presented to the animals on rocks, pathways, or in prepared test areas. Responses were recorded narratively and with a camera equipped with a wide-angle lens that covered an area 10 meters in diameter. The photographs gave a record of the number of animals in the test area and their distance from the stimulus. In some experiments test stimuli were placed in proximity to food to create an element of conflict. Menzel found clear relations between group reactions and such factors as the presence or absence of the test stimulus, its size, and the distance between the stimulus and the food. Of special interest with respect to social behavior are the findings that responsiveness varied between sexes and in different age groups. The results also confirmed earlier work on captive animals, but indicated that the level of overt affective reactions was attenuated under field conditions, probably because of the existence of greater latitude for spatial adjustment.

A different application of experimental technique was used by Kummer (in press) to determine whether observer tolerance (or flight distance) varied with location and activity in baboons. Kummer used the method of limits, a standard technique for establishing thresholds in psychophysical experiments. The observer, who also served as stimulus, slowly approached a seated party of baboons until one of the animals got up and left, whereupon the observer halted. Flight distance was defined as the distance between the person and the animals when the first departure occurred. Kummer found that flight distance was related to location and to the ongoing activity or "mood" of the group. Reactions varied, for example, according to whether the animals were eating, drinking, resting, or preparing to travel. They showed most tolerance of the observer in the evenings when they were settling for the night on the sleeping rock, and least in the morning as they were leaving it.

Labeling experimental effects.—Kummer refers to the phenomenon he studied as "flight distance," whereas Menzel uses "responsiveness" (a more general term) to characterize his results. But it is not essential that we be able to apply a familiar label to the effect, as long as the experimental procedure is described in operational language. Such terms as "curiosity," "fear," and "learning" are useful, but mainly because of what they communicate by drawing upon conventional meanings and connotations. Their virtue is to suggest, in a general way, something about the nature of the experimental effect—the form or "class" of the response, whether the modification is retained—and to give an idea of the conditions preceding the behavioral change, and, possibly, of the situation in which it occurred.

Labeling is thus a matter of achieving a fit between usage and an observed phenomenon. If the fit is a good one it facilitates communication; if not, it will have the opposite effect. But in any case there is no direct relation between the label and either the methodological adequacy of the experiment or its theoretical importance. It is conceivable that one might do an experiment, the outcome of which was completely unequivocal, and still be unable to characterize the effect in conventional terms. The point is obvious, but seems worth emphasizing here because the complexity of variables in the field situation will probably produce many effects that cannot be ascribed to learning, fear, curiosity, or similar covert processes without doing some violence to current scientific usage. The major difficulty is that these terms refer to individuals. To say that a group is fearful or has learned a new response always reduces to a question of which animals (or how many) showed the effect and to what degree. In some studies we may have the data to make such statements, but there will be times when the information is not available or when group reactions are simply more interesting. At the moment, however, we are handicapped in dealing with group phenomena by the lack of an adequate technical vocabulary. We can coin new terms, but there are obvious reasons for restraint here; a flood of neologisms will hardly improve communication, at least until we have enough information to decide which phenomena are important enough or have sufficient generality to deserve special names.

Phenomenon-oriented and process-oriented approaches to labeling.—Until such information is available, there seem to be two common ways of coping with the problem of labeling. One is to suggest a conventional term that appears to identify the most important individual process in the group effect, and to fall back on more controlled small group studies to fill in the details; the other is to use a simple descriptive term that is noncommittal with respect to hypothetical processes. The choice is determined by personal aims and interests, and, as would be expected, the decisions to refer to covert processes or to remain at a descriptive level have different consequences.

We can illustrate these consequences by considering recent treatments of the acquisition and propagation of new feeding patterns. Reports from the Japan Monkey Center first drew attention to the fact that acceptance of certain new foods in free-ranging Japanese monkeys started with a few individuals and gradually spread to other members of the troop (Itani 1965; Kawamura 1963; Kawai 1965; Yamada 1957). Hall (1962a) found evidence of a similar phenomenon in baboons.

Hall saw that the acquisition of new food preferences was dependent on social learning and he believed this was true of many phases of social life. Accordingly, he used his field observations as a starting point for laboratory investigations of the social learning process (Hall and Goswell 1964). Social learning implies that a stimulus (or model) affects the subject in such a way that its behavior is changed, and that the change is retained. In essence, therefore, investigations of social learning are concerned with three questions: (1) What information is transmitted? (2) How is it transmitted? and (3) What determines the efficiency of the transmission process? In operational terms this has meant studies of stimulus functions, of motivation and the mechanisms of reinforcement, and of the retention and generalization of learned responses. One of the important consequences of Hall's field experience was that it gave him a different view of these variables from that found in traditional experimental studies of social learning. For Hall, the major scientific outcome of his findings on the acquisition of a new food habit was the generation of new hypotheses about social learning to be followed up in systematic laboratory research.

The progression from field observations to laboratory investigations of covert processes is a sound research strategy, but others are possible. The Japanese papers, in particular, illustrate an alternate course that is equally worthwhile. In the Japanese research the phenomenon, not the supporting mechanism, is of central concern. The important questions are how do group factors such as habitat, history, size, and structure, affect the acquisition and propagation of a new feeding pattern? Are the pathways over which the habit moves related to age, sex, social status, and to the frequency and quality of the food and on the movment patterns required to obtain it and to prepare it social contacts? Is the rate of spread dependent upon the taste and texture of for eating? Many of these factors could be the subject of a series of experiments in the laboratory, but if one were interested in the acquisition and propagation of feeding patterns as they occur within a natural group, much could be done in the field before the special controls of the laboratory were required. For example, various animals could be captured and then returned to the group after a training regimen designed to establish a new preference or to permit the animal to cope with a new form of food packaging. The individuals so trained could be selected to represent different social classes or age groups. Or it would be possible to examine the reactions of several groups known to differ in the range of foods they take in the natural habitat in order to determine whether being accustomed to a varied diet facilitates acceptance of an entirely new food.

These experiments, which are suggested by the Japanese reports, are directly oriented toward the problem of the acquisition and spread of new food habits. Naturally, they would be complemented by more systematic investigations of specific mechanisms or processes, but they cannot be supplanted by such studies. The distinction between the two strategies is one of emphasis. It is analogous to that between applied and basic research in other fields in the behavioral sciences, and here, as elsewhere, the distinction is relative rather than absolute.

Conclusion.—In spite of the short history of the primate field experiment, we have enough information to know that it is feasible, and to suspect that it will play an important part in any long-range program on the natural behavior of the primates. The fact that most experiments have been conducted in the laboratory by one breed of scientists, whereas those of another persuasion have been most active in the field, is an accident of history. The situation is already changing, and as it does we can be confident that a much broader range of problems will be opened to coordinate study in the laboratory and the field.

SUMMARY

The study of primate social behavior is a new, exciting, and rapidly growing enterprise to which many different disciplines can contribute. It is important to encourage this interdisciplinary character and to prevent any breakdown in communication among the various participating groups.

No such breakdown has yet occurred, but in one area in particular the interchange has not been vigorous or especially fruitful. It is a peculiarity of primate research that naturalistic field studies and experimental laboratory research have developed independently. Other writers have recognized that the two approaches are far apart, but they have not offered a balanced appraisal of the causes, which must be one of the first steps taken in a search for possible remedies.

Inasmuch as both approaches are concerned with the same subject—primate social behavior—and must solve the same methodological questions, they should be closer together. To explain why they are not, historical factors, personality characteristics, and current training arrangements must be taken into account. These factors have been associated with different interests and research objectives. The laboratory experiment, on the one hand, has been mainly concerned with the causal analysis of individual behavior; even in social experiments one animal is treated as "subject," and the other as "stimulus." The field study, on the other hand, has been chiefly concerned with collecting normative information on groups.

How can the two approaches be brought into a closer working relationship? Not by asking either group to abandon its traditional activities, which would be unrealistic as well as unwise, but by exploring new possibilities. We can begin by examining the language that is used to describe social phenomena. The three major dimensions for describing primate behavior are spatial arrangement, enumeration of classes and numbers of individuals, and responses. Time is a fourth dimension that can be combined with the other three to deal with the dynamics of group behavior.

The response dimension holds the greatest immediate promise of bringing about a closer articulation of laboratory and field research. There are many ways of classifying responses, but two classifications are especially important for the relationship between field and laboratory research. These are the species-typical pattern and the index response. Although the difference between them is not absolute, they have been used in different ways and for a different purpose in practice. Species-typical patterns are defined by their form; grooming, lipsmacking, opened-mouth threat, and sexual presentation are familiar examples. They are relatively easy to identify, occupy a prominent place in social interaction, and are often part of broader organismic systems—the instincts of an earlier day. They are used extensively in normative field research, and their use in experimental investigations is growing. In contrast to the species-typical pattern, the index response is usually a simple act, such as pressing a lever. Its major value is found in quantitative investigations of covert processes in which it provides an operational definition of the process. It is a powerful investigative technique, but used uncritically it can lead to results that have no obvious theoretical importance. This has occurred, at least to some degree, in experimental studies of social behavior.

Field research can help correct this situation, especially if findings are presented in a way that suggests specific variables, relationships, and hypotheses for laboratory test. This is most likely to happen when quantitative language is used to (1) describe specific phases or facets of social life (as in the normative study); (2) to point up associations between variables, as in the correlational study; or (3) to suggest cause-and-effect relationships, as in the field experiment.

All behavioral experiments deal with the modification of behavior. To determine whether a behavioral change has occurred, conditions must be arranged to permit a comparison of behavior under at least two conditions. In addition, the experiment is usually repeated in order to make certain that the experimental effect is real. Field experiments can fulfill these conditions, and they do not require elaborate equipment or complicated procedures in order to do so. The field experiment may provide new ideas about the mechanisms or processes underlying behavioral change, which can be followed up in the laboratory where the necessary controls are available, or it may be used to provide more systematic information on the factors influencing a complex social change in which many different mechanisms are involved. In any event, the field experiment can be looked upon as an essential investigative technique in any long-range program on the social behavior of the primates.

15

AGGREGATION AND DISPERSAL:

TWO FUNCTIONS

IN PRIMATE COMMUNICATION[1]

Peter Marler

INTRODUCTION

An appreciation of the pattern of spatial distribution of the members of a species is essential to understanding how the resources of an environment are exploited and what factors place limits on the total population that can live in an area. The requirements of spatial distribution in turn restrict the type of society that can exist and thus influence the pattern of reproduction and many aspects of social behavior. Behavior concerned with social communication is related to patterns of spatial distribution in a particularly intimate way, for the nature of signaling behavior may be profoundly influenced by the distance over which the signal must be transmitted.

Despite their importance, comprehensive pictures of the patterns of distribution of natural populations of animals are rarely presented. One reason for their rarity is the difficulty of collecting the information. Practical considerations often limit the records to some indirect measure such as the distance of the nearest neighbor (Clark and Evans 1954). The predominance of botanical examples in theoretical discussions of distribution is further evidence of the difficulty of describing animal distribution patterns.

[1]The author gratefully acknowledges criticisms of this manuscript by Stuart Altmann, John and Judy Ellefson, Phyllis Jay, Jane Lancaster, Donald Lindburg, Carl Koford, Hans Kummer, Anita Pearson, Thomas Struhsaker, and Nicholas Thompson, as well as many contributions from other participants in the Wenner-Gren symposium on primate social behavior made in discussion.

Large animals that stand out in their natural habitat are among the easiest to study. Some primates come into this category, and their distribution patterns fully warrant the special ecological attention devoted to them (Hall and DeVore 1965; Struhsaker 1965, 1967c, in press).

There is a simple vocabulary for describing the spatial distribution of animals (Hutchinson 1953; Slobodkin 1961). Individuals may be distributed randomly with respect to each other; they may be evenly distributed, more so than would be expected by chance; or they may have a clumped distribution. Where clumping occurs, we can ask whether the clumps are distributed with respect to each other; whether they are evenly spaced; or whether they are arranged in still larger clusters. A complete analysis would also take into account the characteristics of the clumps, the number of clumps, the number of individuals, their sex and age-class distribution, their distribution patterns within clumps, and perhaps their lineages (whether they constitute a family, for example). More than one type of clump may occur (for example, with different sex ratios). The distribution pattern is also likely to change with time, either irregularly or on a daily, seasonal, or some other regular basis.

There is already sufficient information on some primates to permit us to submit them to a rough analysis of this type. Certain prosimians such as *Daubentonia* and *Cheirogaleus* seem to have a nonclustered type of distribution, but they are the exception (Petter 1965). A clumped pattern seems to be the rule in most primates. In some species there is a family group with an adult male and female as the basic unit, as in the white-handed gibbon (Carpenter 1940; Ellefson, this vol.); the New World *Callicebus* (Mason, this vol.), and in some lemurs (Petter 1965). Often the group is larger than a single family, comprising several adults of both sexes, subadults, and infants. The chacma and olive baboons, the rhesus, bonnet, and Japanese macaques, and the vervet are examples of this type of organization (Hall and DeVore 1965; Southwick, Beg, and Siddiqi 1965; Simonds 1965; Yoshiba, this vol.; Struhsaker 1967c; Gartlan and Brain, this vol.). In baboon and Japanese macaque troops, adult females tend to outnumber adult males about two or three to one. This trend goes further in the hamadryas baboon, where the basic and most stable unit for clumping comprises one adult male and as many as four adult females, these units being assembled into larger troops (Kummer and Kurt 1965; Kummer 1957, this vol.). Groups of patas monkeys also have only one adult male and several adult females and young (Hall, Boelkins and Goswell 1965).

Some species have more than one type of group or troop in the same geographical area. Thus howlers have large groups of mixed sexes and small groups of only males (Altmann 1959; Carpenter 1965). Gorillas and the black-and-white colobus also have the same two types of grouping (Marler, in preparation; Koford, in preparation; Schaller 1965). Work on the common langur illustrates a further complication with the finding of variation in distribution patterns in different parts of the species range. In

North India there are groups of both sexes and also all-male groups (Jay 1965*a*). In South India the same two types of groupings occur, but the mixed groups consist of several females and fewer adult males, often only one (Sugiyama 1964; Yoshiba, this vol.).

In all these species the units that form the basis of the clumped pattern of distribution are more or less well defined. In the gorilla, and more especially the chimpanzee, the pattern is less clear. Although individuals are clustered, the units are variable. The size and composition of gorilla groups varies with time and from place to place though a group always contains one old, silver-backed male and several adult females (Schaller 1963, 1965). In chimpanzees the alternative types of groupings include all male groups, mothers with young, groups containing adults of both sexes, and other combinations—a much more variable pattern than has been recorded in any other primate in one geographical area (Goodall 1965; Reynolds 1965; Reynolds and Reynolds 1965).

A clumped distribution is obviously the rule in higher primates. In all species with a relatively orderly pattern of spatial distribution, the arrangement of clumps seems to show some element of even distribution. Sometimes this is only poorly defined and the data are often insufficient for an accurate judgment, but the general trend seems clear.

The distribution of individuals in a population at one instant gives only a limited picture of its organization. Do animals maintain a stable position in space, in the course of time, or do they meander through their environment, constantly invading new terrain? In all the primates studied so far, perhaps even in the chimpanzee, movements are confined to a particular location. Thus there is some element of what Mayr (1963) calls philopatry, the tendency to stay in one place. From a map of the movements of a group over a period of time, say a month or a year, we get a picture of the home range. The home ranges of adjacent groups hardly overlap at all in some species such as *Callicebus,* the black-and-white colobus, vervets, and the white-handed gibbon (Mason, this vol.; Marler, in preparation; Struhsaker 1967*c;* Gartlan and Brain, this vol.; Carpenter 1940; Ellefson, this vol.). In other species there is a degree of overlap; this is sometimes considerable, as in baboons. Often, however, at least part of the home range is rarely penetrated by adjacent troops; this is the condition in howlers, langurs, rhesus and bonnet macaques, and the gorilla (Carpenter 1965; Jay 1965*a;* Southwick *et al.* 1965; Simonds 1965; Schaller 1963, 1965).

SPACING AND COMMUNICATION

Within the general pattern of dispersion of higher primates, individuals are clustered in space in groups of varying size and composition. The groups show some tendency toward philopatry, and their spacing relative to each other tends to be uniform. There are many possible ways by which this dispersion pattern could be maintained. It could be dictated by a similarly patterned distribution of habitats within the environment. No such environmental pattern has been described in any of these primate studies, beyond the obvious correlations between species' range and general habitat type. Often the dispersion pattern seems to exist in a more or less homogeneous habitat. In these primates the uniform spacing of groups almost certainly results from some form of mutual repulsion between the groups. At the same time, there must be a degree of mutual attraction among the group members, together with whatever repulsion is required to maintain spacing within the group.

One of the functions of communication signals is to maintain patterns of spatial distribution. Tinbergen (1959) clarified the function of many of the visual displays of gulls by distinguishing between distance-increasing and distance-reducing signals. A similar approach may conceivably illuminate our understanding of primate communication, particularly if we consider the functions of the signals within the prevailing type of social system.

We can postulate at least four categories of communication signals that might aid in maintaining the typical pattern of primate dispersion. These are:

1. Distance-increasing signals. These would be called into play by deviation from the pattern of even spacing of groups or, on a different scale, the spacing of individuals within groups, if they came too close together. Their effect would be one of mutual repulsion, restoring the spacing characteristic of the species.

2. Distance-maintenance signals. A useful function might be served by another set of signals concerned not so much with increasing the distance between groups or individuals but with maintaining a certain spacing.

3. Distance-reducing signals. Like those in the first category, these signals would facilitate a change in spacing, serving to bring animals or groups into closer proximity.

4. Proximity-maintenance signals. These signals would function in prolonging the proximity that exists between individual members of many primate groups, or between groups.

How far can we go, on the basis of our limited knowledge, in classifying the communication signals of primates in this way and seeking correlations between distinctive properties of the signals and the function they serve? Consider first the use of distance-increasing and distance-maintaining signals in the relationship between groups.

SIGNALS THAT INCREASE DISTANCE
BETWEEN GROUPS

Within the framework of philopatric, uniformly dispersed groups, signals for distance-increase will be provoked in one group if another group comes too close. The outcome will normally be withdrawal of the intruding group.

Thus production of distance-increasing signals will eventually elicit withdrawal. What types of behavior are employed in this context? Already some generalizations are emerging.

In a number of primate species, members of two groups engage in some form of tree- or branch-shaking. Male rhesus macaques in India run along a tree limb and bounce vigorously, apparently as a threatening gesture to members of an adjacent troop (Southwick 1962). Similar behavior in intergroup encounters is recorded among the rhesus introduced on Cayo Santiago.

> An adult male would run to, then bound up a tree or palm. When near the top, he would grasp the trunk with both hands, bounce vigorously against the trunk with the hind legs, thereby shaking the whole tree. (Altmann 1962a:379; cf. Koford 1963a).

If two troops of Japanese macaques meet, adult males may climb up and shake trees. Holding the trunk fast with both hands, each violently shakes the tree and rushes down when he is finished (Imanishi 1957; Itani 1963). Adult male irus macaques also shake branches in intertroop encounters (Shirek-Ellefson, personal communication).

Adult and subadult male vervets shake branches when another group comes close.

> While leaping and running through the trees the males occasionally paused momentarily on a branch and then, in rapid succession, alternately flexed and extended their arms once or twice. The effect of this motion was a very brief but obvious branch shaking. (Struhsaker 1967b; cf. Gartlan and Brain, this vol.)

In the course of repelling another group, an adult male black-and-white colobus shakes branches by violent leaps from one branch to another, landing with so much impact that dead limbs may break off with a loud crack (Marler, in preparation). Under similar circumstances a male white-handed gibbon swings rapidly from branch to branch, sometimes breaking off large branches that go crashing to the forest floor (Ellefson, this vol.). One phase of the spectacular chest-beating display of the adult male mountain gorilla, occasionally provoked by the presence of another group, includes branch shaking and sweeping movements of one arm, shaking and breaking off branches and saplings.

Branch-shaking is one of several signals that commonly serves to increase the distance between groups of primates. A variety of threat gestures that also occur in intragroup interactions may be used including such widespread movements as staring, head flagging or head bobbing, and open-mouthed threat. Physical combat seems to be uncommon, except in some populations of rhesus and irus macaques (Southwick 1962; Southwick *et al.* 1965; Shirek-Ellefson, personal communication). Vocalizations occasionally accompany the visual signals and the sounds of branch shaking, though they are often rare or lacking. One accompaniment in the Japanese macaque is a rapid sequence of from three to seven deep guttural sounds (Itani 1963). Rhesus use a "ho-ho-ho" call in similar circumstances (Altmann 1962*a;* Southwick 1962). In vervets the intergroup chutter is sometimes used (Struhsaker 1965, 1967*a*). On sighting another group, adult male patas monkeys give a bark that seems to have a distance-increasing function (Hall, Boelkins, and Goswell 1965). The only sound regularly used in repelling a neighboring troop in the black-and-white colobus is tongue clicking (Marler, in preparation). In gibbons, sounds play a more prominent role in increasing distance from another troop, particularly the "conflict hoo" (Ellefson, this vol.). Similarly, in South America a *Callicebus* pair will repel another family group by a combination of visual signals—arching the back, stiffening or bowing of the arms, pilo-erection and rushing—with long sequences of an "u-ah" call, increasing rapidly in tempo and loudness (Mason, this vol.). Marking behavior suggests that olfactory signals may also be involved, as is recorded for vervets (Gartlan and Brain, this vol.). The howler monkey is exceptional in that repulsion of another group is achieved by vocal signaling alone (Altmann 1959; Southwick 1962).

In some primate species, groups seem to move apart without any special visual or auditory signaling. When two troops of chacma or olive baboons come close together, their subsequent movements seem to result from a combination of mutual avoidance and their philopatric tendencies (Hall and DeVore 1965). There is no evidence that olfactory marking of the environment occurs in these species. Sometimes the larger of two groups will hold ground or advance while the smaller withdraws, again with little overt signaling. Such behavior is also recorded in rhesus; one group may consistently withdraw from another even if it is not smaller in size (Southwick *et al.* 1965). Bonnet macaque groups avoid each other with a minimum of display (Simonds 1965). Groups of North Indian langurs that come into proximity usually withdraw with little detectable signaling. A smaller group may withdraw in the face of another's advances, again without display (Jay 1965*a*). Mutual withdrawal of groups without signaling occurs also in other species, particularly the mountain gorilla (Schaller 1965).

Conclusions

Visual signals seem to carry the greatest burden in increasing distance between primate groups. This is particularly manifest in branch-shaking, which generates sound as well. Gestural signals that function to increase encounters in some species. Sounds are used mainly as an accompaniment to distance between members of a group may also be used in intergroup visual signals. In the white-handed gibbon and the *Callicebus* sounds seem to be relatively more important, but only in the howler is there a suggestion that one group can repel another with vocal signals alone.

When the distance between groups is increased without exchange of particular signals, vision has obvious importance. Mutual avoidance depends on the two groups' seeing each other. Where a regular dominance relationship exists, so that one troop regularly takes precedence irrespective of troop size differences, visual recognition of individual members seems to be implied. The precedence that large groups take over smaller ones must also be mediated by vision.

SIGNALS THAT MAINTAIN DISTANCE

BETWEEN GROUPS

Signals that increase distance between groups are triggered by approach. The locomotor and signaling behavior, especially when expressed in combat and final withdrawal, involves considerable expenditure of energy. This is presumably justified by the possibility of competitive gain, particularly perhaps in circumstances of unstable environments, high population pressure, and limited resources. Under less competitive conditions, one method of reducing energy expenditure is to announce the presence of a group by signs perceptible to neighboring groups at a considerable distance—at least at the intergroup distance characteristic of the dispersal pattern of the population.

The distances involved are too great for visual signaling to be effective, and there are often physical obstacles. Sound signals are obviously suited to such a situation, and a number of primate species seem to use them. Evidence that sound signals function to maintain a certain spacing is hard to come by; the proposition that they serve to maintain the status quo is hard to prove by observation alone. Nevertheless several observers are convinced that this is the normal function of certain sound signals of primates, and several of their properties seem to be at least consistent with the requirements for such a system of distance maintenance.

A classic example is the howler monkey. Invariably as dawn breaks on Barro Colorado Island the adult males of one group break forth into howls, to be followed by similar roars from adjacent groups. The vocalizations spread from group to group until most troops have howled. Again, about the time when groups first begin progression during the early morning, and again, in the early forenoon, rather general howling occurs. "These vocalizations function, apparently, as stimuli of intergroup stimulation at a distance and signalize the location of the various groups" (Carpenter 1934). Carpenter states his belief that the roars are important in regulating the direction of group progression and the relative distribution of troops. Howler groups rarely come into close proximity (Altmann 1959).

After an encounter between two *Callicebus* groups, when normal spacing has been resumed, there is often a call "sounding from a distance very much like the gobbling of a turkey. Its most interesting feature, however, is not its sound quality, but the fact that it is given simultaneously by several groups. Typically one animal or a single group begins the call and within a fraction of a second it is taken up by other groups and passes rapidly through the forest as a kind of chain reaction" (Mason, this vol.). Again some function in maintaining spacing between groups seems to be implied.

Adult male langurs give a particular call when a group is about to move suddenly or for a long distance; it is a deep resonant "whoop" that carries over a considerable range. Jay (1965*a*) believes this call provides "an effective spacing mechanism that allows groups to determine each other's position. Langur groups seldom come together in the forest or in open fields since groups are separated very effectively by their daily routes and patterns of range use."

A similar situation prevails in another colobine monkey, the black-and-white colobus. Adult males give a long, rapid series of deep rattling sounds that are audible for a mile or more. The sounds are especially common after dawn and in the evening. The calling is contagious, spreading through the forest from group to group (Ullrich 1961; Marler, in preparation). The first male often seems to start calling without any immediate external trigger, much as a male bird will suddenly break into a song. It is hard to avoid the impression that this call aids in maintaining the spacing between groups. Contacts between groups are rare, in spite of the relatively small area that each group occupies.

The "morning calls" of adult male and female gibbons, which play a role in maintaining spacing of the groups, consist of a series of hoots with rising inflection, rising pitch, and increasing tempo with the climax followed by two or three notes of lower pitch (Carpenter 1940). This call is most frequent in the early morning and tends to elicit similar calling in neighboring groups. Its most important function is that of location. "It is at one time, both a proclamation 'here we are' by the callers, and a signal 'there they are' for the hearers" (Ellefson, this vol.).

Although distance maintenance seems to be a prime function of this calling, the issue can become more complicated. Ellefson points out that calling occasionally elicits approach of another group. This response may also be elicited by some of the other distance-maintaining calls we have been discussing, depending in part on the position of the calling group in space. If a neighboring group locates the source of the call outside the area they occupy, they are likely to reply in kind. If they locate it close to the edge of their area, or within it, they may approach the source as a prelude to the use of distance-increasing signals. Thus, exchange of signals such as the gibbon great call can also serve to provide information that the stable pattern of group dispersion has been disrupted and can so lead to distance reduction.

Of the other apes, it is not clear whether the gorilla has any signals that might function to maintain spacing (Schaller 1965). Chimpanzees certainly possess suitable signals that share some properties of the sound signals we have been discussing, such as frequent occurrence in dawn choruses, social contagiousness, and audibility over a wide range (Reynolds and Reynolds 1965; Goodall 1965). However, the dispersion pattern is too complex to fit our present scheme.

Some species seem to lack any mechanism for distance maintenance. No signals have been recorded for rhesus macaques, bonnet macaques, or Japanese macaques that seem to fit this category, although there is a suggestion that branch-shaking may sometimes be given spontaneously, perhaps functioning for distance maintenance as well as for distance increase (Altmann 1962*b;* Itani 1963; Simonds, personal communication). Adult male irus macaques have a roar, the loudest sound in the repertoire, given before and during group movement that may serve to keep groups spaced out (Shirek-Ellefson, personal communication). Chacma and olive baboons have no special signals for this function, although the barking of some forest populations of baboons may serve in this way (Hall 1965*c*). Of all primates, macaques and baboons show the greatest tendency to invade open country. The most terrestrial of the cercopithecine monkeys, vervets and the patas monkey, likewise seem to lack a distance signal that might function to maintain spacing (Hall 1965*c;* Struhsaker 1965). Whatever mechanism these species possess to maintain distance between groups must depend mainly on the groups' seeing one another.

Conclusions

Many species seem to have different sets of signals for maintaining and for increasing the distance between groups; the former are predominantly auditory, the latter visual and auditory. In a pioneering paper on animal communication, Haldane (1954) pointed out that some signals elicit similar behavior in the respondent, whereas others elicit different, often complementary, behavior. The distinction is well illustrated here. For example, on the one hand, distance-increasing signals may at first elicit like behavior, but eventually a complementary response is elicited—namely withdrawal. Distance-maintaining signals, on the other hand, tend to elicit like behavior in the respondent; this is consistent with their function, which is to perpetuate an already established condition.

Several other characteristics of the sounds that maintain intergroup distance seem consistent with their function. Such sounds usually are among the loudest that the species utters, softer sounds usually being used to increase distance. They tend to be more structured than other sounds in the repertoire in the sense that temporal organization is often elaborate. They sometimes have a purer tone than the grunts and barks used in closer range signaling. Thus they are clearly identifiable at a distance, even with a considerable level of background noise. Finally, they differ from many communication signals in their lack of dependence upon particular eliciting circumstances. Often they are given apparently spontaneously, so that several observers have interpreted them as expressions of well being or exuberance. If their function is to maintain the *status quo,* they can have no complete dependence on external triggering situations, such as can exist with distance-increasing signals. The spontaneous calling is often concentrated in the early morning.

The distinction between distance-increasing and distance-maintaining functions is not always clear. We have noted that the great call of gibbons can even elicit the approach of another group, probably depending on the location of the calling group. The same alternatives may exist in *Callicebus.* The hoots of howlers may both maintain and increase distance between groups, again depending on the spatial relationships of the troops. Much may also depend on the history of the relationship between two groups. A stable relationship may lead to reliance upon distance-maintaining signals to perpetuate the pattern of distribution. Factors such as changing relationship, intrusion of a new troop into an area, or restriction of suitable habitat may all disrupt this stability and shift the emphasis to distance-increasing signals.

A final comment on the species that seem to lack special signals for maintaining intergroup distance may be added. Southwick (1962) suggests that intergroup conflicts are more frequent among rhesus macaques than among, for example, howlers. This could be a consequence of the lack of distance signals for avoiding contact. The home ranges of adjacent rhesus groups overlap quite extensively. However, it may also be a manifestation of a different kind of ecology. The capacity of the rhesus and perhaps other open-country primates to invade many types of habitat, some of which may be only temporarily suitable, might be associated with reduced philopatry and a tendency to press constantly at the boundaries of the home range. It may be no accident that those species with the best developed distance-maintaining signals live in the high forest, which is a relatively stable environment. Within that environment they can operate with great efficiency. Lacking the more opportunistic capacities of the macaques, such species may be much more vulnerable to change in the environment.

SPACING WITHIN GROUPS

In his classic field studies of the social behavior of primates, C. R. Carpenter noted the importance of spatial relationships between members of a troop. "The strength of the attachment between two individuals may be judged, or actually measured, by observing for a period of time the average distance which separates the two animals" (Carpenter 1942b). Nevertheless, there has been little systematic study of intragroup spacing.

In macaques and baboons certain pairs of individuals, such as the mother and her juvenile offspring, are often in close proximity. The bond is particularly close with infants but also extends into subadulthood, at least with female offspring. Adult males and females in consortship keep close together, and the "short distance separating the two animals and the continuance of this close association are reliable indicators of estrus in the female" (Carpenter 1942b). Adult females are often more closely spaced than are adult males, which are surrounded by free space much of the time (Chance 1956). On Cayo Santiago the most dominant males in a rhesus group tend to maintain around themselves an area about eight feet in diameter that is devoid of other monkeys (Altmann 1962a). Some pairs of adult males may keep nearer to each other than others, particularly close-ranking males high in the dominance hierarchy (Chance 1956).

The members of a captive hamadryas baboon troop tended to maintain characteristic interindividual distances, averaging 3.1 meters and varying somewhat with ongoing activity (Kummer 1957). Similarly, in the wild the average distance from females to their males was 0.65 meters when resting and about 3 meters when the troop was moving and feeding (Kummer and Kurt 1965). The spacing of any two animals may be affected by their relationship to others, as when two animals cooperate in repelling a third. Altmann (1962a) gives illustrations of how complex such conditions can be in rhesus. Relative proximity to females also affects the spacing of males. Chance and Mead (1953) note varying patterns of spacing of captive male rhesus that correlate with relative proximity to an estrous female as well as with the males' own relative dominance status.

In spite of the limited data it already appears that the spacing of individuals within macaque and baboon groups is no random affair, but is subject to rules that relate to kinship, sex, individual identity, age, reproductive condition, and dominance status. There are differences in these rules between macaque species, such as pigtail and bonnet macaques (Rosenblum, Kaufman, and Stynes 1964). Similar rules with further characteristic spatial relationships may pertain in other species (for example, langurs, Jay 1965b; colobus, Marler in preparation), sometimes complicated by the development within the troop of subgroupings. These are often genealogically related, as in the rhesus and Japanese macaque, for example (Imanishi 1957; Southwick *et al.* 1965; Sade 1965). Communicatory behavior seems to play an important role in maintaining these spatial relationships, and again its function requires that it have both repellent effects, increasing and maintaining distance, and attractive effects, encouraging and maintaining proximity.

SIGNALS THAT INCREASE DISTANCE BETWEEN GROUP MEMBERS

A typical consequence of threat behavior is to increase distance between individuals. Such behavior is often provoked by infraction of the minimum distances characteristic of the stable pattern of intragroup dispersal. Visual gestures figure prominently in this behavior and similar basic patterns recur in many primate groups. Without reviewing them exhaustively, we may mention bristling of the fur, biting, chasing, slapping at the opponent or the ground, head bobbing, or lunging and staring; all occur in one form or another in rhesus and other macaques, baboons, and langurs. Distinctive patterns also occur, such as the formalized neck-biting of bonnet macaques and hamadryas baboons (Simonds 1965; Kummer 1957; Kummer and Kurt 1965).

Another element of behavior to increase distance in many primates is a particular facial expression (Andrew 1963a; van Hooff 1962); this is the open-jawed gesture Altmann describes (1962a), with the lips tense, the corners of the open mouth drawn forward, and the teeth mainly concealed. A stare directed at the opponent may have similar effects; it is often accompanied by movements of the brows, and sometimes by lowered lids and retracted ears. These accessory gestures, which serve to dramatize the expression further, are particularly characteristic of macaques, baboons, and mangabeys (van Hooff 1962), but also occur in vervets (Struhsaker 1967b, 1967d). A variety of sounds may be associated with these displays.

The behavior complementary to that of the animal taking a positive role in restoring spacing is withdrawal by the other participant. It is often accompanied or preceded by special movements that seem to function to avert an increase in the vigor of the opponent's attack. These movements include distinctive postures and another facial expression, the grimace or grin, in which the corners of the mouth are drawn back and the teeth bared (Altmann 1962a; Hinde and Rowell 1962). The posture is sometimes hunched, and often the animal has a shifty gaze, avoiding a direct stare at the opponent (van Hooff 1962; Struhsaker 1967b, 1967d).

In many species interindividual spacing is restored with a minimum of this special signaling. There may be no more than a brief stare by one animal and withdrawal of the other, or even mutual withdrawal. Visual cues to individual identity, sex, and age must play a key role in mediating such exchanges which are especially common when two individuals have a stable dominance relationship.

Conclusions

Visual elements seem to predominate among the signals that serve to increase distance between individuals in a group. The visual signals occur in rich variety and can be varied and combined in many ways to generate compound signals. The sublety of these signals as a means of communication correlates with the short distance over which they are normally received. Like the visual signals, the sounds used to increase distance between individuals also tend to be highly graded in structure (Rowell and Hinde 1962; Rowell 1962; Marler 1965). Such signals, like those used to increase distance between groups, usually elicit complementary reactions in the respondent, although there are occasions of mutual withdrawal and occasions when neither will withdraw, at least for a period of time.

The listing of some signals as increasing distance between individuals should not be taken to imply that this is the only function they serve. For example, neck biting by a male hamadryas baboon repels strange juvenile females, but has the opposite effect when directed at a female in his own group. The adult male maintains the coherence of his harem of females by biting them on the neck if they lag behind or wander off. In response to the neck bite the female will immediately reduce the distance between herself and the male and follow him more closely than before (Kummer 1957; Kummer and Kurt 1965). Thus the effect of the neck bite depends on the context in which it is given. Similarly in rhesus, an animal can use threatening behavior toward an opponent as a means of reducing its distance from a third individual (Altmann 1962a). Here the orientation of the behavior is crucial.

SIGNALS THAT MAINTAIN DISTANCE
WITHIN GROUPS

When a group of monkeys is foraging, there is a chance the spacing pattern may be disrupted by individuals' moving off while others linger. Many species seem to have a characteristic call, given in this circumstance, that aids in the maintenance of the spacing pattern. Generally, it is a repetitive grunt such as that used by gorillas (Schaller 1963, 1965).

Grunting of both chacma and olive baboons in this situation varies in frequency from slow, about one every two seconds, to very rapid, sometimes as a chorus through the group (Hall and DeVore 1965). Rhesus have a deep muffled grunt "hu, hu, hu" that serves to coordinate group movement (Altmann 1962a, 1962b). Japanese macaques use particular sounds when feeding or moving through the forest. "It is certain that they help the individuals know each other's whereabouts when they are dispersed in a bush and are unable to catch sight of each other" (Itani 1963). Often such calls are repeated in chorus by members of the group.

The "progression grunt" of vervets evokes similar calls from all individuals in the immediate vicinity, and apparently helps to hold the group together (Struhsaker 1965, 1967a). Two other species of *Cercopithecus* (*C. ascanius* and *C. mitis*) have similar calls (also contagious) given in this context, and again they seem to function by enabling foraging animals to maintain a certain distance between them (Marler, in preparation). When a male howler initiates a group progression, he gives a series of deep, hoarse clucks which apparently induce others to move, thus maintaining the coherence of the group (Carpenter 1934, 1965).

The black-and-white colobus lacks any such call. Instead, it seems to rely on visual cues for maintaining intragroup spacing during movement. The conspicuous pelage and the habit of keeping high in the tree tops and out of dense cover apparently permit visual coordination of activities. Visual cues, such as a tail raised high while the animal forages in tall grass, must be important in some species.

An individual that is preparing to change location will sometimes give visual cues as well as auditory ones. When a male gorilla stands motionless, facing in a certain direction before moving off, his posture serves to ready other members of the group for locomotion in the same direction (Schaller 1963, 1965). A male colobus will stare fixedly in the line he is going to travel, probably facilitating coherence of group movement (Marler, in preparation). Male hamadryas initiate a group's departure from the sleeping rock by a particular swinging gait (Kummer, this vol.). No doubt other species have visual cues that prelude movement.

The spacing within a group is rarely uniform. The characteristic spacing between two individuals may vary according to their kinship, sex, age, or dominance relationships. Visual cues, such as the visible signs of sex and age, may be important here in maintaining a certain distance. In several species characteristic postures are associated with different levels of the dominance hierarchy. The status indicators in rhesus, Japanese macaques, and baboons include a particular gait and tail position (Altmann 1962a; Kummer 1957; Hall and DeVore 1965). In addition, the particular dominance relationship between two adjacent individuals is repeatedly manifest as unilaterally directed signals, such as mounting of one by the other or glaring by one and looking away by another, perhaps again having repercussions on the distance maintained between them. At any rate, as Altmann (1962a) points out, such exchanges serve a different function from that of threat behavior in the usual sense.

Conclusions

If sounds are to aid in maintaining the spacing pattern of a group, their source should be readily locatable. The repetitive grunts often used in this context are very suitable for auditory localization as a result of the time cues that they provide (Marler 1955). The close range at which they are used minimizes the requirement for species specificity, hence perhaps the simplicity of the structure and temporal organization of these sounds. The repetitive grunts of sympatric species may be very similar, as in *Cercopithecus mitis* and *C. ascanius*. Calling often elicits like calling in others, a further aid in maintaining interindividual distances. Such calls are often a prelude to more or less rapid locomotion. Visual cues can actually forecast the direction to be taken by pointing to the proposed course. Visual factors are also supremely important in maintaining the differential spacing within the group that correlates with sex, age, and dominance status.

SIGNALS THAT REDUCE DISTANCE
WITHIN GROUPS

If an individual gets separated from the group, re-establishment of contact is made possible by any signal that announces the group's position. Special signals may be used in such circumstances (for example, rhesus, Altmann 1962b). Japanese macaques (Itani 1963) use a form of the progression grunt (the A-group of calls), which elicits a reply in kind and so enables contact to be re-established, the lost individual approaching the group after signal exchange. When a lost infant calls, the mother leaves the group and approaches it. The special cries given by the infant in this situation sometimes seem to be individually recognized by the mother (for example, Japanese macaques, Itani 1963; irus macaques, Shirek-Ellefson, personal communication; vervets, Struhsaker 1965, 1967a).

Most of the signals functioning in distance reduction within a group are concerned with the more delicate adjustment of distance between individuals already in sensory contact. Distance reduction in this context requires a lessening of the customary interindividual distance, and thus a suspension of distance-increasing behavior. The main strategy for achieving this end seems to be to elicit an activity that involves proximity, such as mounting or grooming—an activity that is incompatible with distance-increasing behavior and thus encourages peaceful approach.

Invitations to participate in grooming are among the most widespread signals for distance reduction within primate groups. Grooming may be initiated by one animal's approaching another and presenting part of the body for grooming. A widespread prelude to participation in the active role is what is known as lip-smacking. The tongue, jaw, and lips move repeatedly and generate a smacking sound in a movement that is also common during actual grooming in many species (van Hooff 1962; Altmann 1962*b;* Hinde and Rowell 1962; Hall and DeVore 1965; Goodall 1965). Variations include in-and-out movements of the tongue (in howlers, Carpenter 1934; in langurs, Jay 1965*a;* in irus macaques, Shirek-Ellefson, personal communication) and teeth chattering (in baboons and vervets, Struhsaker 1967*a*). These sounds and expressions used during distance reduction may be followed by some activity other than grooming such as copulation or simply by the participants' sitting close together.

Both male and female precopulatory patterns, in normal or modified form, are used in distance reduction. In addition to presentation by an estrous female for copulation, noncopulatory presentation is recorded in baboons, macaques, chimpanzees, langurs, and vervets (Hall and DeVore 1965; Altmann 1962*a;* Goodall 1965; Jay 1965*a;* Struhsaker 1967*b*). It often occurs in female-female and male-male encounters, and sometimes clearly functions in distance reduction (Hall and DeVore 1965). The elicited response may be complete mounting, but is often some fragmentary or modified version such as grasping the hindquarters or simply touching some part of the body.

We have noted that lip-smacking is sometimes divorced from any immediate association with grooming, tending to assume status in its own right as a kind of greeting behavior. Other signals have a similar property of eliciting approach and further signal exchange without providing any direct introduction to what will follow after distance reduction. Although the available data are still limited, some patterns seem to be shared by a number of species.

Reaching out a hand to touch another animal occurs in langurs, vervets, irus macaques, baboons, and chimpanzees. Contact may be made with any part of the body, but often it seems to focus on two areas—the head, including the lips, and the inguinal region, including the groin, thigh, and genitalia. A male is often touched on the scrotum, and an estrous female on her sexual swelling. The contact may be made by the mouth rather than the hand, and is often either mouth-to-mouth or mouth-to-genitalia. More extensive areas of the body may come into contact, as in dorso-ventral or ventro-ventral embraces (Jay 1965*a;* Struhsaker 1967*b;* Hall 1962; Hall and DeVore 1965; Goodall 1965; Shirek-Ellefson, personal communication).

These greetings occur in all types of interindividual contacts among adults or, for example, between adults and infants. Adult male and female baboons will pick up a black infant and either touch or kiss the genital area. Male infant langurs will run to greet an adult male by mounting him, by a ventro-ventral embrace, or by touching the genital area with the hand. The recurrence of sexual elements in situations that are obviously dissociated from copulatory activities is manifest not only in the manual or oral contacts with the genitalia but also in the penile erections that occur when males perform embracing and other greeting gestures.

Conclusions

The distance-reducing function of these signals requires not only the elicitation of activities during which animals must be close together, but also some degree of prohibition of the use of distance-increasing signals. There are several indications that this consideration has guided the evolution of distance-reducing behavior. Grooming and greeting behavior have obvious soothing effects on the participants, reducing their state of arousal below that associated with threat behavior and strong alarm, and to a condition of relaxation. Some of the gestures seem designed to emphasize the absence of distance-increasing signals. The face is often turned away from the companion during presentation for grooming (Furuya 1965). The trend reaches its extreme in the crouched posture of a badly beaten animal, which seems to have a definite inhibitory effect on aggressive behavior in several species. Screaming may have a similar effect.

Some of the strongest stimuli for distance-increasing behavior probably relate to strangeness. Certain of the elements in greeting behavior may serve in part to provide, on the one hand, signals as to individual identity and, on the other, response patterns to acknowledge individual recognition. The mouth and genital areas might provide the active participant with olfactory cues to the passive animal's identity. At the same time, these areas are richly supplied with touch receptors providing the passive participant with a highly sensitive register of the tactile stimuli.

Some signals that typically serve to increase interindividual distance can also reduce distance. Rhesus, for example, can use threat behavior to approach closer to another animal by directing it to a third animal, or even to an empty space (Altmann 1962a; Sade 1965). Similarly, the grimace, often used to evade another animal with a minimum of aggressive arousal, is sometimes used in approaching another individual. Altmann (1962a) records the use of this gesture by a dominant male rhesus in approaching a female. We are reminded again that the response that the signal elicits may vary strikingly according to the context in which it is given (Smith 1965).

SIGNALS THAT MAINTAIN PROXIMITY
WITHIN A GROUP

Although used in combat to increase distance, signals involving physical contact play a dominant role in reducing distance between individuals. They must be equally important in maintaining proximity, although the two functions are hard to separate. Of the three main types of behavior that serve to reduce distance—mounting, greeting actions, and grooming—the contact involved in the first two is only transient. Only grooming involves sustained contact and surely must be the most important in maintaining proximity. The opportunity to groom or to be groomed is known to be rewarding in a learning situation (Falk 1958).

The importance of sexual bonds, proposed by Zuckerman (1932) as underlying the coherence of the primate group, has been de-emphasized by recent investigators. The existence of marked breeding seasons in several primates and the relative brevity of consortships argue against sexual attraction as the main factor maintaining proximity in primate groups (Altmann 1962a; Lancaster and Lee 1965; Washburn, Jay, and Lancaster 1965). Nevertheless, the degree of emancipation of primate sexual behavior from strict control by the underlying hormonal substrates is unusual compared with other animals (Beach 1965). The prominence of actions with sexual overtones in the context of greeting behavior (such as manual or oral contact with the genitalia) occurs in many mammals, but is apparently even further dramatized in these primates. Penile erection and mounting behavior occur, and suggest an alternative social role for sexual bonds. They may be important in achieving a reduction of distance between individuals without necessarily contributing to the attraction that maintains proximity.

A large part of primate sociability may be manifest simply as a preference for having familiar companions in view or nearby (Altmann 1962a). Only males seem ready to separate from the group for long periods of time, and it may be that sexual motives sometimes drive them back. However, proponents of the view that sexual bonds constitute the cement of primate society would have to admit that the attraction that exists between infants and adult monkeys of either sex is just as strong. Of all the discoveries in recent primate studies, none is more striking than the interest that is shown in a newborn infant by adult females other than the mother, adult males, and even subadult animals. Jay estimates, for example, that on the first day of an infant langur's life it may spend several hours being carried by most of the adult females in the group. There is similar interest in other species (Jay 1962, 1965b; Itani 1959; Rowell, Hinde, and Spencer-Booth 1964;

DeVore 1963; Hall and DeVore 1965; Marler, in preparation). The bonds of the infant with the mother are especially durable in young females and provide the basis for some of the subgroupings that occur in a primate troop. Young males often associate more with adults of their own sex.

Thus the signals that maintain proximity in a primate group are complex, with tactile stimuli playing a dominant role from the relations between infant and mother through adulthood. As yet we know little of the stimulus patterns involved or of the functional significance of their variations. Tactile communication is difficult to study. But if we are right in suggesting that it is a primary factor in the cohesion of primate societies, the difficulties are worth overcoming. We may learn something about ourselves in the process.

16

PRIMATE COMMUNICATION SYSTEMS

AND THE EMERGENCE

OF HUMAN LANGUAGE[1]

Jane B. Lancaster

INTRODUCTION

The interest in human evolution and in the origin of human language has distorted the study of the communication systems of the nonhuman primates. These systems are not steps toward language, and have much more in common with the communication systems of other mammals than with human language. In this chapter we shall analyze this major gap that separates language from nonhuman communication, and suggest conditions that might have led to the evolution of language. With this aim in mind we will consider: (1) the nature of primate communication systems, (2) the nature of language, (3) the anatomical basis for language, and (4) a possible evolutionary origin of human language.

Man is so accustomed to sounds having definite, restricted meanings that the first question asked on hearing a monkey sound is, "What does it mean?"

[1]This paper is part of a program on primate behavior supported by the United States Public Health Service (Grant Number MH 8623). I am most grateful for the helpful comments and criticisms on the manuscript from Anne Brower, Phyllis Jay, and Donald Sade. I especially wish to thank S. L. Washburn for his continuing encouragement and criticism throughout the writing of this paper. I am also particularly indebted to both Norman Geschwind and Daniel Slobin for the stimulation I have found from their own research and for opportunities of discussing with them many of the complexities and problems in the study of human language.

In our experience it takes some time for a student to lose this human bias and to understand the sounds in the context of normal monkey behavior. Man expects sounds alone to carry meaning, but in nonhuman communication sounds usually carry only a part of the meaning; facial expressions, gestures, and postures are essential in conveying the full message. The sound may be only for emphasis, and, even in the case of warning cries, the warning may give no indication of the exact nature of the danger. In contrast, human language is essentially a system of names placed in a traditional order. Most of the meaning of the communication is carried by a single sensory modality. In the communication systems of the nonhuman primates there are no names. The most elementary part of the human system is not present, nor is the anatomical basis for this apparently simple act of naming.

Most acts of communication in a social group of primates occur in a context of long-term social relations (DeVore 1965; Washburn, Jay, and Lancaster 1965). Monkey and ape societies are usually composed of animals of both sexes and all ages. Most members of the group have spent their entire lives within the same social context. Even in species in which there may be no encompassing stable group there are still stable subgroups with continuing, long-term social relationships. Communication rarely occurs between strangers, but for the most part is between animals that have known each other as individuals over long periods of time. The context of any communicative act includes a network of social relations that have a considerable history behind them, all relevant to the message and how it is received and responded to.

An understanding of the emergence of human language rests upon a comprehension of the factors that led to the evolution of a system of names. The ability to use names allows man to refer to the environment and to communicate information about his environment as opposed to the ability to express only his own motivational state. Object-naming is the simplest form of environmental reference. It is an ability that is unique to man. In itself it is not language, but without it human language cannot exist. The communication systems of nonhuman primates are important to understand if human language is to be understood, not because they are similar but because they are different; understanding here comes from analyzing contrasts, and not similarities.

PRIMATE COMMUNICATION

Studies of Primate Communication

The study of the communication systems of Old World monkeys and apes is a new and rapidly expanding field. Until recently most studies of communicative gestures and sounds were done either on caged animals in an impoverished social environment or in a group of free-ranging animals as a preliminary part of a larger study of social behavior. Valuable information has come from both kinds of studies. Workers such as Andrew (1962, 1963*a*, 1963*b*, 1963*c*, 1964), Bolwig (1964), and van Hooff (1962) have been able to record a variety of sounds, gestures, and facial expressions of caged monkeys and apes. They have been successful in sampling a wide variety of genera and species and in gaining useful insights into the possible evolutionary history of particular gestures or vocalizations. Many recent fieldworkers have also attempted to describe the communication system of a single species and to show how it relates to the social system of the group under study (Hall and DeVore 1965; Goodall 1965; Kummer and Kurt 1965; Jay 1965*b;* Schaller 1963). These fieldworkers have had to present the communication system as a given; their focus was necessarily on patterns that tended to be of high frequency, and often on those that were least variable. Their interest lay in regularities in social interactions and in social systems—to them understanding the communication system provided a means of entrance into the workings of the social system, but it was not an object of study in itself.

Only a few workers have focused on the communication system itself, recording a large sample of sounds, gestures, and expressions and struggling seriously with the infinite variety of problems of description and analysis. A number of studies have now been made on colonies living in outdoor compounds (Goustard 1963; Hinde and Rowell 1962; Rowell 1962; Rowell and Hinde 1962; Zhinkin 1963), on free-ranging groups that are artificially fed (Altmann 1962*a*, 1965; Itani 1963), and on free-ranging groups living in their natural habitats (Struhsaker, in press). With the single exception of Struhsaker's work on vervets, all these studies have been on either baboons or macaques, two closely related genera of terrestrial Old World monkeys. A second sampling bias has also developed because of the comparative ease of recording and describing the morphology of communicative sounds through the use of electronic recording equipment and the sound spectrograph. Although photographic equipment is easily used, there is no photographic equivalent of the sound spectrograph when it comes to describing and analyzing complex patterns of movement. The result of these two biases in sampling is that we know a fair amount about the nature of the vocalizations of two genera of Old World monkeys, and much less about the communication systems of most of the Old World monkeys and apes.

The Form and Nature of the Signals

Marler (1965) presented a summary and interpretation of the nature of primate communication systems based on field accounts and laboratory studies published before 1963. One of the most significant generalizations, which he found demonstrated over and over again, is that the communication systems of higher primates are extraordinarily complex (when compared with those of a rat or gull, for example) and that they rely heavily on multimodal signals. A vocalization, a gesture, or a facial expression in itself usually does not represent a complete signal, but is only a part of a complex constellation of sound, posture, movement, and facial expression. Parts of such a complex pattern may vary independently, and may help to express changes in intensity or level of motivation. Sometimes olfactory elements are also present in the signal pattern but in monkeys and apes and in man the senses of vision, audition, and touch are important in receiving communicative signals. The complex multimodal signal is eminently suited to the kind of social system typical of monkeys and apes, where groups or at least subgroups are in relatively continuous, long-term contact. Most group members are within sight of the rest of the group most of the time. This close-range, continuous contact with other group members means that complex multimodal signals can be easily received and comprehended. When signals have to pass over greater distances or between animals that may be strangers, multimodal constellations of signal elements become difficult to receive and interpret correctly. In such situations unambiguous signals sent in a single optimal modality are likely to evolve. Furthermore, vocalizations that are often very important in long-distance signals are much less significant in close-range systems. Many field and laboratory workers (Hall and DeVore 1965; Rowell 1962) have emphasized that vocalizations do not carry the major burden of meaning in most social interactions, but function instead either to call visual attention to the signaler or to emphasize or enhance the effect of visual and tactile signals. In other words, a blind monkey would be greatly handicapped in his social interactions whereas a deaf one would probably be able to function almost normally. The notion that a deaf monkey might suffer only a relatively minor social handicap should be investigated experimentally. Placing deaf monkeys in a social group would permit an analysis of the relative roles of sound and gesture in the communication system.

Another important generalization that has emerged from the field studies of higher primates is the major role that context plays in the total meaning of the signal pattern (Altmann 1965; Marler 1965). The receiver of a signal is presented with an extremely complex pattern of stimuli. Not only are the posture, gestures, vocalization, and facial expression of the signaling animal important, but also the total context of that pattern is an essential part of the message. The immediately preceding events, the social context, and the environmental context, all play major roles in the way a signal is received, interpreted, and responded to. A threat display given by a juvenile may be ignored in one context, whereas if the same display is given again when he is near his mother, and if she shows some interest in what he is doing, it may produce an entirely different response in the animal receiving the threat. The major function of context in the total meaning of the signal makes the study of primate communication systems very difficult. Responses to a signal pattern may seem highly variable and erratic until a large number has been sampled and the relevant aspects of the varying contexts of the signal have been taken into account.

Besides being multimodal, primate signals are often graded in form (Marler 1965), that is, variations that reflect differences in meaning occur in a single behavior pattern, such as a threat gesture. In a graded or continuous system of behavior patterns each grade or degree has at least the potential for expressing slight differences in intensity of motivation. The advantage of discrete nongraded signals, of the sort typical of many passerine birds, is that their lack of ambiguity makes them easy to receive and to comprehend. Graded signals place greater demands on the receiver of the signal but they have great value in their ability to express slight shifts in motivation. In a complex, enduring social system in which individuals are obliged to make a continuous series of adjustments and accommodations to each other, it is important to be able to express not just that one is aroused or frightened, but also the degree and direction of changes in motivation. A good documentation of graded signals is found in Rowell and Hinde's description of communication in a colony of rhesus macaques (Hinde and Rowell 1962; Rowell 1962; Rowell and Hinde 1962). In this system many signals were not only graded in form but also intergraded with each other. Rowell and Hinde demonstrated this by making spectrographs of all sounds that occurred in agonistic situations. They found what they thought were nine harsh sounds ranging from a growl to a squeal. After a large number of these had been recorded and analyzed with a sound spectrograph, they discovered that the sounds in fact formed a single intergrading system that seemed to be expressive of the full range of emotions usually associated with agonistic interactions. These agonistic sounds were linked by a continuous series of intermediates and apparently each grade along the continuum potentially expressed a slightly different level of emotion. There was also one example of a multidimensional variation in which the pant-threat graded independently into three other calls. With such a system, a rhesus monkey is able to express quite complex patterns of motivation, but most of the variations in signal form rest on contrasts in intensity of one or more of the components of the motivational state. In concert, this use of intergrading signals and of composites from several sensory modes produces a rich potential for the expression of very slight but significant changes in the intensity and nature of the mood of the signaling animal. Slight shifts or vacillations in arousal can be expressed by slight shifts in the vocalizations and gestures.

Not all primate signals belong to graded systems, and there are undoubtedly species differences in how much use is made of discrete and graded signals. Struhsaker (in press) has described the vocalizations of vervets, which he recorded in their natural free-ranging situation. He found 36 different sounds that were comparatively distinct both to the human ear and when analyzed by a sound spectrograph. The majority of vervet sounds seem to be of the discrete type although there were two groups of sounds that may form graded systems. With more and more study on primates it will probably be shown that their communication systems tend to be of mixed type in which both graded and discrete signal patterns are used depending on the relative efficiency of one or the other form in serving a specific function. In such systems of communication as those of the monkeys and apes, complexity and subtlety of expression are always bought at a sacrifice to clarity and specificity. With complexity comes ambiguity, and greater burdens of reception and interpretation are placed on the nervous system of the receiver of the signal, which in turn places limits on the potential of the communication system.

The Nature of the Messages

It is clear that the communication systems of monkeys and apes are rich in their ability to express the motivational state of the animals. Most of these messages facilitate social interactions. In baboons and macaques motivational information, particularly in relation to dominance and subordinance relationships, constitutes the largest category of messages (Itani 1963; Marler 1965; Rowell 1962). Even greetings and other messages exchanged when one animal approaches another often serve to reassert recognized differences in dominance between two animals. Sometimes the dominant animal will gesture or indicate in some other way the pacific nature of his intentions at the same time that he displays his dominance. Compared to birds or primitive mammals, monkeys and apes have developed very complex signal patterns expressing submission, aggression, anxiety, fear, and other motivational states associated with agonistic situations; in addition, they also use a limited number of signal patterns in mating and mother-infant interactions. There are also signals that keep the group together and coordinate group movement. In most of the primate species these signals are generally only a small part of the total repertoire compared to the part devoted to agonistic communication (Marler 1965).

Nonhuman primates can send complex messages about their motivational states but they communicate almost nothing about the state of their physical environments. Marler (1965:584) in his review of research on primate communication systems concluded:

> Environmental information, present or past, figures very little in the communication systems of these animals, and a major revolution in information content is still required before the development of a variety of

signals signifying certain objects in the environment and a system of grammar to discourse about them can be visualized.

It may not even be accurate to speak about such a simple reference to the environment as a food call. Human beings possess a communication system that is highly evolved in its ability to make environmental references, but this is a distinctively human specialization that should not be taken for granted in monkeys and apes. Marler was unable to find any clear examples of food calls, and it is probable that what have been labeled food calls by many early fieldworkers are really expressions of a general level of excitement, which is often associated with food but which may be given in other circumstances as well. For example, Andrew (1962) reports that in many species of primate the same sounds that are given at the sight of food are also given in greeting a fellow animal. In both instances the animal vocalized upon perceiving a desired object; it was not giving a food call in the sense of making reference to specific items in its environment.

Even in a call warning of a threat of predation on the group, not much specific information about the danger itself is necessarily given. In baboons when an alarm cry is made the other animals try to see what the calling animal is looking at (Hall and DeVore 1965). The cry itself gives no specific information about the form or position of the danger, but only indicates the level of excitement or alarm of the animal that first gave the call. Only by looking does the rest of the group learn what is the cause of the state of alarm in one of its members. Alarm cries of birds and other mammals are just as informative to a baboon as are the alarm cries given by a member of his own social group.

There are a few calls given by nonhuman primates that convey some information about the physical environment. They are rare, and they represent important specializations of the few species that use them. In situations where monkeys are preyed upon by different kinds of predators an elaboration of alarm cries may occur. Struhsaker (in press) describes three high-intensity alarm cries of vervet monkeys that are very different in form and that evoke very different responses: a snake chutter, another call given when an airborne predator is seen, and a chirp that signals a terrestrial predator. There is an appropriate and different response to each of these calls. The snake call evokes a mobbing response similar to owl mobbing by birds. On hearing the call signaling an air-borne predator, vervets seek cover either by running into tall grass or by dropping out of the tree branches into the dense thickets below, depending on where they were when they first heard the alarm. The response to the chirp that warns of a terrestrial predator is exactly the opposite of that elicited by the call that warns of an aerial one; the vervets run to the trees and go out onto the ends of branches, which would be a dangerous place if the predator were airborne (a monkey-eating eagle, for example), but which is safe if the predator, such as a lion, is on the ground.

This kind of specialization in vervets in which some limited but vital information about the environment is communicated has occurred in many different species of animals ranging from chickens to rodents and can be expected when a species is hard pressed by such different kinds of predators as snakes, birds, and large mammals (Collias 1960). This differentiation of high-intensity alarm calls to communicate some information about the environment is a specialization that should not be thought of as pointing toward the kind of major revolution in information content suggested by Marler as a requisite of human language.

Aside from predator alarms, Old World monkeys and apes probably have little ability to communicate about their environment. The ecology of nonhuman primates is such that communication about the environment can be, and is, very restricted, whereas exactly the opposite is true of man and human language. For monkeys and apes events inside the social group are of great importance and their communication systems, therefore, are highly evolved in their capacity to express motivation of individuals and to facilitate social relations. Without this ability to express emotion, monkeys and apes would not be able to engage in the subtle and complex social interactions that are a major feature of their adaptations.

HUMAN LANGUAGE

Introduction

The more that is known about the communication systems of nonhuman primates the more obvious it is that these systems have little relationship with human language, but much with the ways human beings express emotion through gesture, facial expression, and tone of voice. There is no evidence that human displays expressing emotion, such as laughing, smiling, or crying, are any more or less complex than are displays of monkeys and apes or that they differ in form or function (Bastian 1965). It is human language, a highly specialized aspect of the human system of communication, that has no obvious counterpart in the communication systems of man's closest relatives, the Old World monkeys and apes.

In addition to a quite efficient system, possessed in common by all the higher primates that expresses motivation or mood by gesture and vocalization, another system has evolved in man that is admirably suited for making reference to the environment. This unique human system allows one man to communicate to another what the environment is like at any moment, how it has been in the past, and how it will be in the future. The simplest and most primitive aspect of this system, which is now so complex and elaborated, is the ability to understand names. This ability is one of the first aspects of language to appear in the human child and it may well have been the first to emerge in human evolution. Recent work on the comparative anatomy of primate brains and on clinical problems, such as aphasia, suggests that there is an anatomical basis for this ability and that these structures are found only in the brain of man. Geschwind (1964, 1965) has recently synthesized this material, presented below, and has interpreted its significance.

The Cerebral Cortex

The cortex of the brain can be divided into a number of subareas that are differentiated on the basis of both their function and their structure. Geschwind (1965) points to five major areas of the cortex that can be called "primordial zones" because they are the first to myelinate. Myelination, the process by which a nerve fiber acquires a medullary sheath, is simply a convenient index of maturation. For example, myelination in the "primordial zones" is well advanced by the time of birth, whereas in the "terminal zones," the areas last to mature, myelination does not even begin until the second month of life and it continues for several years (Flechsig 1901, 1920, 1927). One of the "primordial zones" is on the medial surface of the temporal lobe (see Figs. 16–1*A* and 16–1*B)*. This temporal region forms a part of the limbic system and is thus closely related to the sensations and activities involved with emotional states.[2] The other early maturing areas of the cortex are the classic motor cortex and the three primary centers where visual, auditory, and somesthetic or tactile sensations are received by the brain. In an animal such as a cat or rabbit these "primordial zones" make up most of the cerebral cortex.

In monkeys and apes, and especially in man, the primordial centers are separated by evolutionarily more recent areas of cortex called association areas. In man there are large regions of association cortex for vision,

---

[2]The "limbic system" refers to the phylogenetically old parts of the cortex and its related nuclei (MacLean 1963; Altman 1966). Most of the cortex of the "lower mammalian brain" is found in the limbic lobe, a large cerebral convolution that surrounds the brain stem. The limbic lobe is common to the brains of all mammals. In contrast to phylogenetically new cortex, the limbic cortex has strong connections with the hypothalamus and midbrain tegmentum, areas that are important in the integrative mechanisms for autonomic activity involved with self-preservation and procreation. Just as the limbic lobe is found as a common denominator in the brains of all mammals, so the categories of behavior that it controls are common to all mammals. This group of activities is characterized by their intimate connection with the basic needs of the organism, self-preservation and reproduction. Stimulation of a part of the limbic system often elicits not only physiological changes, but also emotional sensations that provide the animal with a state of heightened motivation to perform a behavior pattern that is critical in species survival (Hamburg 1963). The limbic system is closely associated with emotions; it makes the animal want to do what it has to do to survive and reproduce.

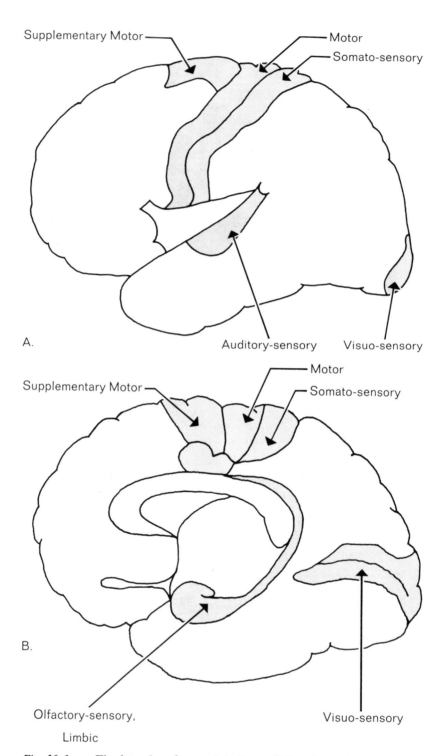

Fig. 16–1.   a. The lateral surface and b. the medial surface of the human brain showing the major areas of early myelination: the classic motor cortex and the sensory centers for vision, olfaction, and somesthesis. (*Simplified after Flechsig 1920*)

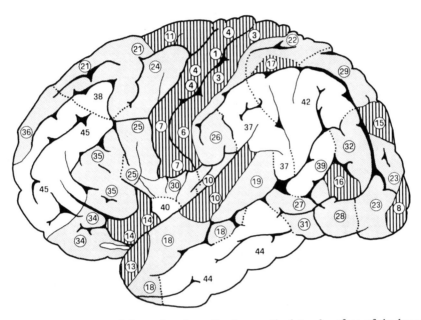

Fig. 16–2. A map of the order of myelination on the lateral surface of the human brain. The darkest areas indicate "primordial" zones which are myelinated at birth. The dotted areas are the "intermediary" zones which myelinate between birth and one month after birth. The white areas are the "terminal" zones, the last area of the cortex to complete myelination. The numbers 1 through 45 represent the order of myelination and should not be confused with the numbers traditionally associated with Brodman's cytoarchitectural fields. (*After Flechsig 1920*)

audition, and somesthesis. The massive development of association cortex in man has crowded most of the somatic sensory and motor areas into the central sulcus, the auditory area into the lateral fissure, and the visual area into the calcarine fissure on the medial side of the occipital lobe (see Fig. 16–2). Each primary center where sensations are received by the brain and the classic motor cortex have special areas of the association cortex closely related to them. In Fig. 16–2 most of the dotted areas represent association cortex; for example, the region numbered 23 is visual association cortex and the region numbered 8 is primary visual cortex. Association cortices are more like each other than they are like the primordial zones to which each is related. All association cortex matures later and is classified as "intermediary" by Flechsig (1901, 1920). Moreover, there is some evidence that they are biochemically distinct; for example, in some cases of premature senility (Alzheimer's disease) the association cortex is severely involved both anatomically and functionally whereas the primary zones show little or no involvement (Geschwind 1965).

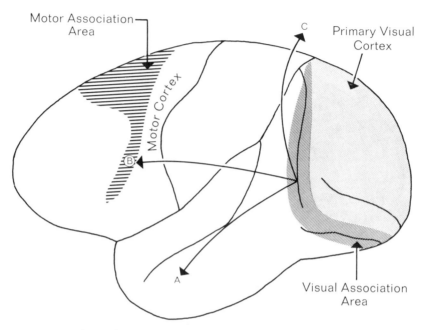

Fig. 16–3. The major connections of visual association cortex of the rhesus
macaque. *a.* The connection to the "association cortex" for the limbic
system on the lateral and basal surfaces of the temporal lobe via the
inferior longitudinal fasciculus; *b.* the connection to motor association
cortex via the superior longitudinal fasciculus; *c.* the connection to the
visual association cortex of the opposite hemisphere via the splenium of
the corpus callosum. (*After von Bonin and Bailey 1961; Crosby* et al.
1962; Geschwind 1965)

Somewhat surprisingly, in monkeys, apes, and man there are no important
cortical-cortical connections between any of the primordial zones. In fact,
the primordial zones have direct cortical-cortical connections only with their
respective adjacent association areas. These association areas in turn have
connections with other parts of the cerebral cortex but not with all parts
equally; there are special large bundles of fibers that connect particular areas.
In Fig. 16–3 this fact is illustrated for the visual association cortex in the
brain of a rhesus monkey. The association area for vision has major
connections with only three other areas of cortex, one via the inferior
longitudinal fasciculus to an area on the lateral and basal surface of the
temporal lobe that probably functions as the association area for the limbic
system, one via the superior longitudinal fasciculus to the association area of
the classic motor cortex, and one via the corpus callosum to its opposite
number in the other half of the brain (Geschwind 1965). Although the
evidence is less clear, partly owing to lack of relevant experiments, the

situation appears to be similar for the association cortices of audition and somesthesis. This suggests that there are no large cortical-cortical connections between the association areas of vision, audition, and somesthesis in the brain of a monkey, ape, or man.

Intermodal Associations and Object Naming

In monkeys, apes, and man there is no significant number of direct connections between the auditory, visual, and somesthetic association areas, nor indeed does there appear to be any cortical area in monkeys and apes that acts primarily as a way station for indirect connections between such areas. Corresponding to this anatomical arrangement one finds that it is easy to train a monkey to form an association between a nonlimbic (visual, auditory, somesthetic) stimulus and a limbic stimulus, but it is very difficult or impossible to train the animal to form associations between the nonlimbic stimuli.[3] For example, a monkey can be taught to choose the form of a circle in preference to that of a square when it is presented to him visually by being rewarded on the sight of the circle or punished on the sight of the square (Ettlinger 1960). The monkey can learn this quickly and can reliably perform a discrimination between the two after very few trials. However, if he is then presented with carved forms of a square and a circle that he can feel but not see, he will not be able to make the discrimination that previously he had learned visually. He has no easy way to relate sensations in the visual association areas to sensations in the tactile association area. If he can learn to do this or a similar task eventually, it is only after exhaustive training, and he is likely to forget it again very easily. It should be strongly emphasized here that ease of learning, and not whether a monkey can or cannot do something if tremendous efforts are made to train him to do so, is the important criterion.

Adult humans have less trouble with the problem just described, and in general, man forms at least certain kinds of associations between sensations received in different sensory modalities. Geschwind believes that this ability provides the basis for understanding names, which in its simplest form most often involves an association between sensations in the visual cortex aroused by the sight of the stimulus and the name of the stimulus, an association which in normal adult humans is localized in a part of the auditory

[3]All learning (that is, the formation of association chains) whether in a monkey or in a man eventually is related to the limbic system. The distinction being made here is between a monkey that can form a nonlimbic-limbic association and a man who can form a stable nonlimbic-nonlimbic-limbic associative chain. Neither a man nor a monkey can learn or function effectively without ultimately relating his sensory experiences to the limbic system.

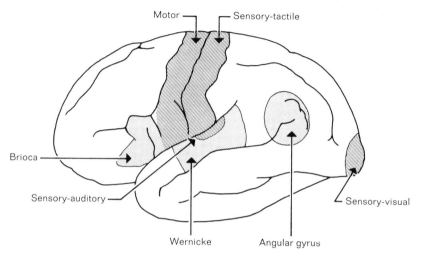

Fig. 16–4. The major areas of the cerebral cortex associated with language and speech. Broca's Area, the part of the supplementary motor cortex controlling speech; Wernicke's Area, the part of the auditory association area most concerned with the sounds of words; and the Angular Gyrus, the waystation for the formation of intermodal associations. (*After Crosby, Humphrey, and Lauer 1962; Penfield and Roberts 1959*)

association area.[4] Geschwind (1965) suggests that the intermodal association involved in learning names is accomplished through cortical-cortical connections within the inferior parietal lobule, and these connections are present in abundance only in man and not in other animals. This region, which includes the angular gyrus, provides the anatomical basis of the ability to understand names (see Fig. 16–4). The area of the angular gyrus lies between the association areas for vision, audition, and somesthesis. It is richly connected to all three by short association fibers and so is structurally situated to mediate between them, in other words, to act as the association area for the sensory association areas. The angular gyrus probably neither receives nor sends long connections to other parts of the cortex as do the sensory association areas, and the angular gyrus has few thalamic afferents, so that there is little likelihood of its serving other functions. This region is one of the last to mature in the brain of man (Flechsig 1901), and it does not stop myelinating until the age of four years, or even later (see Fig. 16–1). It is so large in man compared with its size in other mammals that some authors have asserted that it is almost unique to man.[5]

The ability to name objects provided man with a way to refer to his environment and to communicate information about his environment to other men. If Geschwind is correct that the inferior parietal lobule provides the anatomical basis for this ability, then it is important to stress again that the facilitation of the ability to refer to the environment by using this anatomical structure carried with it a measure of independence of the signal from the limbic system and the direct, unconscious expression of individual emotion. This may form the basis for Andrew's (1964) statement that the emancipation of vocalizations from emotions and the lowering of stimulus threshold for vocalizing are major prerequisites for human language. The rare examples of nonhuman primates' communicating some information about the environment in their high-intensity alarm calls are not relevant to the evolution of a system of object-naming. The similarity between these abilities is only a minor, superficial one, and the underlying mechanisms are entirely different. The contrasting of design features (such as environmental reference) of the communication systems of different species has illuminated major differences in both their form and function (Hockett 1960; Hockett and Ascher 1964; Altmann 1966). However, it is apparent that the ability of the vervet monkey to refer to the environment, a design feature which is superficially similar to man's object-naming but which is in fact based on

---

[5]It will be noticed that no mention has been made of the anatomical mechanisms used in making sounds. This deliberate omission comes from the conviction that no evolution in the mouth, tongue, or larynx was necessary to initiate the origin of human language. The nonhuman primates make a wide variety of sounds. The initial question in the origin of language is why our ancestors started using some of these sounds to name objects, and the particular sounds used are not important. After the beginning of learning object names brought in new selection pressures, there may have been evolutionary changes in the sound-producing structures, especially in the nervous control of lips, tongue, and laryngeal muscles. The argument is essentially the same as that on the relation of tools to the brain and hand. The adaptive success of early tool use changed selection so that the area of the cortex devoted to hand and hand skills greatly increased, and the structure of the hand itself evolved for more efficient grasping. Human language might easily have evolved based on a range of sounds different from those used today. The rudiments of object naming and grammar could not evolve without fundamental evolutionary changes in the structure of the brain. This evolution expresses itself in the ease with which the human child learns naming, grammar, and the whole complex of language, and in the difficulty with which a monkey or ape learns any rudiment of what might conceivably be called language. The ape makes many sounds. It sees much as we do. Its facial expressions are rich in number and meaning. But the structural basis for combining these abilities into meaningful language is lacking.

quite different underlying neurological mechanisms, cannot be suggested as representing a possible step toward language. Object-naming is unique to man because the anatomical basis of the ability is also unique to man.

Child Language

The ability to name objects, even on a very primitive level, would have enormous adaptive significance to a species that was evolving a new way of life, different from that of other primates, that necessitated the communication of information about the environment between different members of the group. Slobin (1965) has suggested that child language may be useful in providing a model for human language at an early, emergent phase of evolution. Child language is not offered here as representing a stage in the evolution of human language in the sense of ontogeny specifically recapitulating phylogeny; rather, it is used as a model for a simpler form of human language than that of adult humans. Child language, in spite of its simplicity, is still very efficient in its function.

There have been only a few naturalistic studies of child language and these have all been on children speaking Western European languages (Bellugi and Brown 1964; Weir 1962). In many of these studies the spontaneous utterances of children have been recorded over a period of months or years. The authors of these studies have been interested in regularities in the patterns of language acquisition by children and how these regularities may be linked to a maturational timetable. We are particularly interested in the early stages of language acquisition, especially the stage of two-word utterances. Children begin making two-word utterances perhaps six months after they begin talking, usually between 18 and 24 months (Braine 1963; Miller and Ervin 1964; Brown and Fraser 1964). These two-word utterances are not random combinations of words, but conform to rules of rudimentary grammar. These rules are neither direct copies nor simple reductions of adult speech, and their regularity suggests that the organization of the two-word utterances is imposed by the child rather than drawn directly from the adult system (Brown and Bellugi 1964). At this early stage there are two classes of words. One is a very large and open class that contains mainly the names of objects or activities important to the life of the particular child, such as cookie, blanket, or pacifier. The second class is much smaller and comprises what are called "pivot-words" by Braine (1963) or "operators" by Miller and Ervin (1964). They are the action words of the utterance even though, according to adult usage, they may be classified as prepositions or object names. For example, a child will say things like: "bandage on," "blanket on," "fix on," and "take on" (Slobin 1965). The word "on" is a pivot word—it always remains in the same position and it can be combined with words drawn from the large open class of object names.

The class of pivot words is small but contains words of high frequency and membership in this class is stable. Pivot words as a class may be either in the first or second position in the two word utterance but a particular pivot word has a relatively fixed position. As Slobin (1965) has noted, these two classes (pivot words and names of objects) are similar to the distinction made in adult speech between function words and content words. The child uses these two word utterances largely in naming objects and describing actions. This system of two-word utterances rapidly expands and within a year or so, depending on the individual, the major features of adult language are correctly applied by the child.

It is significant that it is not until a much later stage, at the age of three years or more, that the child makes any consistent attempts to express his emotions using language, although certainly emotion is communicated by tone of voice and other attributes of speech (Brown and Bellugi 1964; Slobin 1965). Often it is as late as two years after the first two-word utterances that a child consistently expresses disappointment, anger, or fear verbally. Language is used to describe the world and to tell people what to do but not to express emotion. One might think that "baby mad" would be as easy and frequent an utterance as "baby blanket," but in fact it is not. The expression of emotion using language is a very rare type of utterance in young children, and when it does occur it is usually not in the appropriate context. During these years it is probably easier and certainly more efficient to use what are really typical primate displays to express emotion such as crying, weeping, and temper tantrums. It is only adult human beings who are effective in their attempts to express emotion verbally, and even for adults the display system continues to function and to be very important in the expression of motivation, especially at the higher intensities of emotional excitement. It is commonly recognized that humans often become speechless with the excitement of high levels of emotional intensity regardless of the kind of emotion aroused.

In summary, language for young children serves a special function in social communication—one of reference to the environment—and it is not for a year or more after the beginning of language use that children are able to express their moods or emotions with language. The early stage represents an efficient system, which is highly developed before other functions or uses begin to appear. This stage provides a model for reconstructing the emergence of human language. Early in the evolution of man, when small-brained, bipedal forms were using simple pebble tools, a proto or emergent language may have begun to develop. It is a safe assumption that the display system of these early hominids was just as highly evolved and useful as those of any modern monkey, ape, or man. A rudimentary language would not have added much to the display system if it were used only to express emotion and to facilitate social interactions. But it is easy to imagine that an emergent language that provided the most limited ability to name objects would be highly adaptive even at the simplest level of its development because it served a new function not met by the primitive primate display system of communication.

The Evolution of Environmental Reference

Ability to name objects, even on a very primitive level, would have had great adaptive value to the species evolving a new way of life different from that of other primates, a way of life that required communication of information about the environment among members of the group. Even a very small vocabulary of object names (which might have been combined in simple utterances of only a word or two) could have been very effective. A few pivot words suggesting major activities such as hunting and a few others indicating relative nearness in space and time, in combination with a small vocabulary of object names, could have had enormous adaptive significance.

The ability would have greatly facilitated hunting and gathering with the use of tools. The way man uses tools is an activity just as uniquely human as is language (Lancaster, in preparation). This is probably no coincidence. It is worth considering whether the one unique ability, tool use, might not be closely related to the other, language,—and especially environmental reference. Tool use in itself tends to focus attention on objects in the environment so that a stone or stick that has no significance or meaning in the life of a monkey, or at least none that need be communicated to others, may have great importance to the maker of primitive pebble tools. Understanding names means that simple but highly significant communications can be made in which raw materials or tools can be referred to, and animals and plants named.

The ability to make environmental reference can greatly alter the way in which a group can exploit its home range. If a social group can split up into subunits that forage separately during the day or for a few days and then join again, they can much more efficiently utilize the food resources of a large home range. The chances of locating rare, dispersed, and seasonal food sources is greatly increased. But such an ability presupposes a place to meet where food can be shared with those who were not successful or were not gathering. A permanent home base would limit the potential size of the home range, but if a group had a way to designate a future meeting place a home range of hundreds of square miles could be utilized effectively. Even on the rudimentary level of a simple place name, the naming of objects could have had great selective advantage to a form that was moving into a way of life based on tool use, hunting and gathering, and food sharing.

This ability for environmental reference both reflects and permits a different sort of relationship between the species and its environment from that which is usual for other primates. The emergence of language is related to changes in the ecology of the evolving species. According to this view, the evolution of the abilities to use tools and to name objects are closely linked. These abilities form an important and very early human specialization which, even on its earliest and most rudimentary level of development, could have had great adaptive significance.

17

AGGRESSIVE BEHAVIOR

IN OLD WORLD

MONKEYS AND APES[1]

S. L. Washburn and D. A. Hamburg

In this essay we hope to use the problem of aggression as an example of evolutionary perspective as a scientific tool. We are interested in the way the behavior of the nonhuman primates may be useful in increasing our understanding of man. Study of the forces and situations that produced man is one way of attempting to understand human nature, of seeing ourselves in evolutionary perspective. Because the use of man's closest relatives in the laboratory is the nearest approach to experimenting on man himself, the use of primates as laboratory animals is increasing rapidly. As in so much of science, there is no boundary between the pure and the applied, and the answers to our questions lie in the domain of many different disciplines. Since no one could possibly master all the relevant information, we wish to clarify our objectives before proceeding to the main topic of the paper. In discussions at the conference a series of general questions emerged, many of which we have encountered before—since the beginning of our collaboration at the Center for Advanced Study in the Behavioral Sciences in 1957. We propose to deal with these recurrent, general questions first.

Field studies in a comparative evolutionary framework do not permit the

[1]This paper is part of a program on primate behavior supported by the United States Public Health Service (Grant No. MH 08623) and aided by a Research Professorship in the Miller Institute for Basic Research in Science at the University of California at Berkeley. We particularly want to thank Dr. Jack Barchas, Dr. Phyllis C. Jay, Dr. Donald Lunde, and Mrs. Jane B. Lancaster for advice and help in the preparation of this paper.

manipulation of variables and the precision of measurement that are possible in laboratory experiments. They are, however, likely to give new perspectives which suggest fruitful directions for experiments and for deeper analysis of problems of living organisms. Field studies do not replace other methods of investigation, nor do studies on animals substitute for the direct study of man. For example, Prechtl (1965) has pointed out that much of the behavior of the human newborn is understandable only in phylogenetic perspective. This does not mean that comparison is the only way to approach the study of behavior in the newborn but only that inclusion of some comparison enriches the understanding of what is being observed. In advocating the use of the evolutionary approach, we are not suggesting that it is the only method or that it is always relevant. We are suggesting, however, that the comparative, evolutionary study of behavior offers many insights that are unlikely to come from other sources. We believe that the combination of the evolutionary perspective with experimental science provides a powerful approach to biological problems including those of behavior, and we echo Simpson's 1964 statement "100 years without Darwin are enough."

A central problem in the study of the evolution of behavior is that contemporary monkeys and apes are not the equivalents of human ancestors. To what extent their behaviors may be used as indicators of the behaviors of long-extinct fossil forms is debatable. Obviously this is not a simple question, and the possibility of reconstruction differs with each particular behavior. Each answer is a matter of probability, and there is great variation in the adequacy of evidence bearing on different questions. For example, in all the nonhuman primates females have brief, clearly limited periods of estrus. Since this state is universal and highly adaptive, it is virtually certain that this condition was present in our ancestors. Although the time of the loss of estrus cannot be dated, the comparison calls attention to the significance of the loss. The physiology of human females is quite different from that of any other primate, and many specifically human customs and problems are directly related to continuing receptivity in the human female. The human family is based upon a female physiology different from that of any other primate, and the physiology may well be the result of selection for stable male-female relations. The close similarity in much reproductive physiology permitted the use of the rhesus monkey as the most important laboratory animal in working out the human female's reproductive cycle (Corner 1942), but the behavioral approach emphasizes the significance of the differences. Our understanding benefits from seeing the nature of both the similarity and the difference. The problems of reconstructing behavior are discussed more fully in Washburn and Jay (1965).[2]

[2]After this paper was in nearly final form we received *Adaptation et Agressivité* (1965), edited by Kourilsky, Soulairac, and Grapin, and *On Aggression* (1966), by Konrad Lorenz. *Conflict in Society* (de Reuck 1966) also appeared, although we had access to part of that data in prepublication. We find ourselves in general agreement

Estrus has been used as an example of a problem of the reconstruction of behavior when there is no direct fossil evidence. The same kind of logical reconstruction from indirect evidence can be applied to many other behaviors. We have indirect evidence, for example, that our remote ancestors probably matured more rapidly than we do, lived in small areas, were very aggressive, and hunted little, if any. Let us consider this first statement: If the infant is to cling to the mother, as does the infant monkey and ape, then the infant must be born able to cling. A human infant born with this ability would need far too large a brain at the time of birth, and the adaptation of the mother's holding the immature infant may be looked on as an adaptation to the evolution of the brain. Monkeys are born with more highly developed nervous and motor capabilities than those of apes at birth. A gorilla mother must help her baby for approxomately six weeks before it can cling entirely unaided (Schaller 1963). In *Homo erectus* (Java man, Pekin man, and comparable forms) the brain was approximately twice the size of a gorilla, and the infant's behavior must have been much more like that of modern man than like that of an ape.

The implication of the clinging of the nonhuman primate infant can be generalized that biology guarantees the infant monkey or ape a far greater chance of appropriate treatment than it does the human infant. So far as early experience is important in determining later performance, man should show by far the greatest variability of all primates. The study of comparative behavior calls attention to the uniqueness of the human condition, the importance of early events, and of the human mother's need to acquire complex skills of child care.

In addition to the reconstruction of behavior, another problem that has arisen repeatedly in discussions of the comparison of behavior is the extent to which behaviors in different groups of animals are comparable. The issue is whether behaviors labeled, for example, "aggression" or "play" are comparable enough so that comparisons are useful, or whether these are simply subjective human words used to symbolize collection of noncomparable behaviors. There are four important considerations.

The first is that the words are least likely to be misleading when animals, whose behaviors are being compared, are closely related. For example, we think there would be little disagreement as to which behaviors should be called "play" or "aggression" in Old World monkeys and apes, but the problem is very different if the behaviors of monkeys and birds are to be compared.

---

with these new sources, and only wish that we had had them a year ago. We have found J. Altman's *Organic Foundations of Animal Behavior* (1966) exceedingly valuable, and it too would have been very useful if it had been available earlier. None of these references would have led us to different conclusions, and we hope that the point of view presented in the introduction to this paper may help to bridge the gap between the thinking of the students of animal behavior and the social scientists.

The second point is that in the observation of the behavior we are not limited to the view of a single animal or to one occasion. An observer sees repeated interactions of animals in the social group or groups. The judgment that an action is threatening, for example, is based on the repeated specifiable response of the other animals. The response to biting in play and in aggression is very different, and the difference is unmistakable in the response of the bitten animals, although it would often be hard for the human observer to perceive the difference in the actual bite.

The third point is that in classifying and labeling behavior we are not limited to the external view of the actions. For example, Delgado (1963) has shown that stimulation of certain brain areas elicits threat behavior in rhesus monkeys. Although present evidence is limited, we think it likely that the same brain areas are concerned with rage in man. If it can be shown that the behaviors that are classified together are mediated by comparable structures, then the classification is much more likely to be useful. This is best exemplified by the category "sexual," in which the interrelations of behaviors, nervous system, hormones, and experience have been thoroughly investigated (Beach 1965b). This takes us back to our first point: One reason that labeling categories of behavior is less likely to be misleading when the animals are closely related is that the internal biological mechanisms on which these actions are based are more likely to be similar.

The fourth point is that the human observer is most likely to detect relevant cues when observing the behavior of animals closely related to himself. We do not underestimate the formidable problems of observation and the need for experimental clarification of what is being observed in the behavior of monkeys and apes, but at least the special senses and central nervous system of the observer are highly similar to those of the animals being observed. Even within the primates the interpretation of observations becomes much more difficult with the prosimians. Since the sense of smell is important in prosimians and the animals have special tactile hairs that we lack, in many situations there is no assurance that the human observer has access to information of importance to the animal being observed. The human can see a dog in the act of smelling, but simple observation gives no knowledge of the information received by the dog. Viewed in this way, the human observer is more likely to be able to see and record the actions that are important in the analysis of behavior when studying monkeys and apes than he is when watching any other animal.

This does not mean that observations are necessarily easy or correct, but it does mean that man is potentially able to see, describe, and interpret actions made by a close relative, especially in a mode that approximates the judgments the animals themselves are making. The more distantly the animal is related to man, the less the human perception of the situation is likely to correspond to that of the animal's. For example, a human observer can learn the facial expressions, gestures, and sounds that express threat in a species of

Fig. 17–1. Baboon threatening through car window in response to human mimicking of baboon threat. (*Photograph by Sherwood Washburn*)

monkey, with some assurance that the signals are seen in the same way a monkey sees them. It is possible to play back their recorded sound to monkeys and most sounds without gestures produce no response. Some monkey gestures can be learned by man, and the human face is sufficiently similar that a monkey interprets certain human expressions as threats and responds with appropriate actions. Without experiment a human observer would hardly have expected that a male turkey would display to the isolated head of a female (Schein and Hale 1959; reprinted in McGill 1965). Even when a bird and a mammal are responding to the same sense, vision, in this case, the internal organization of perception is so different that comparison can be made only on the basis of experiments. In monkey, ape, and man the internal organizations are highly similar, and the use of a word such as aggression carries far more comparable meaning than when the same word is used to describe a category of behavior in vertebrates in general. We are not belittling the importance of the study of behavior in a wide variety of animals, but we are emphasizing that the problems of comparison in such studies are more complex than they are in these comparing a very few of man's closest relatives.

We are writing on aggression in certain monkeys and apes because we think that there is enough information to make such an essay useful. The word "aggression" only indicates the area of our interest and our use of it does not mean that we think the area is fully understood or precisely defined. Accurate definition often comes at the end of research; initially, definitions serve only to clarify the general nature of the subject to be explored. For the purpose of opening the area for exploration and discussion we find that the definition of Carthy and Ebling (1964:1) is useful. They state that "An animal acts aggressively when it inflicts, attempts to inflict, or threatens to inflict damage on another animal. The act is accompanied by recognizable behavioral symptoms and definable physiological changes." Carthy and Ebling recognize the displacement of aggression against self or an inanimate object, but rule out predation as a form of aggression. For our analysis, it is not useful to accept this limitation; if one is concerned with aggressive behavior in man, the degree to which human carnivorous and predatory activity is related to human aggressiveness should be kept open for investigation and not ruled out by definition.

In discussing aggression it is important to consider both the individual actor and the social system in which he is participating. In the social systems of monkeys and apes evolution has produced a close correlation between the nature of the social system and the nature of the actors in the system. Societies of gibbons, langurs, and macaques represent different sociobiological adaptations, and, as will be developed later, the form and function of aggressive behaviors are different in these groups (Jay 1965a). Through selection, evolution has produced a fit between social system and the biology of the actors in the system. Aggression is between individuals or very small groups, and individual animals must be able to make the appropriate decisions and fight or flee. Rapoport (1966), in particular, has argued that war between modern nations has nothing to do with the aggressiveness of individuals, but rather is a question of culture, of human institutions. Although agreeing that it is very important to understand the cultural factors in war, we think that it is important to understand the human actors too. It is still individuals who make decisions, and it is our belief that the limitations and peculiarities of human biology play an important part in these decisions. We will return to this issue later; at this point we only want to emphasize that it is necessary, particularly in the case of man, to think both of the social system and the actors. It was not long ago that human war was carried out on a person-to-person basis, and our present customs go back to those times.

Finally, we return to a point of view which we have discussed elsewhere (Washburn and Hamburg 1965a), but which needs emphasis and clarification particularly in the context of aggression. The result of evolution is that behaviors that have been adaptive in the past history of the species, which led to reproductive success, are easy to learn and hard to extinguish. As Hinde and Tinbergen have put it: "This exemplifies a principle of great importance: many of the differences between species do not lie in the first instance in stereotyped behavior sequences but consist in the possession of a propensity to learn" (1958:255, reprinted in McGill 1965). It is particularly important to consider ease of learning, or the propensity to learn, when we are discussing monkeys and apes. These forms mature slowly and there is strong reason to suppose that the main function of this period of protected youth is to allow learning and hence adaptation to a wide variety of local situations.

There is a feedback relation between structure and function starting in the early embryo. Structure sets limits and gives opportunities. Apes cannot learn to talk because they lack the neurological base. Man can easily learn to be aggressive because the biological base is present, is always used to some degree, and is frequently reinforced by individual success and major social reward. The biological nature of man, now far more amenable to scientific analysis than ever before, is thus relevant to aggressive behavior in ways that include learning and social interaction.

THE BIOLOGICAL BASIS OF AGGRESSION

Collias (1944) in a major review of aggressive behavior in vertebrates concluded that the function of the behavior was control of food and reproduction through the control of territory and the maintenance of hierarchy and that males were responsible for most of the aggressive behavior. Scott (1958, 1962) supported these main conclusions, and emphasized the importance of learning in the development of aggressive behavior. Breeds of dogs differ greatly in aggressiveness, but the expression of these differences is greatly modified by learning and the social situation. Recently, Wynne-Edwards (1965) has stressed the role of social behavior in control of territory, hierarchy, and reproduction as mechanisms of species dispersion and population control. In general, the biological studies indicate that aggression is one of the principal adaptive mechanisms, that it has been of major importance in the evolution of the vertebrates (Lorenz 1966).

We think that these major conclusions will apply to the primates, although adequate data are available on only a few forms and these will be discussed later. Order within most primate groups is maintained by a hierarchy, which depends ultimately primarily on the power of the males. Groups are separated by habit and conflict. Aggressive individuals are essential actors in the social system and competition between groups is necessary for species dispersal and control of local populations. In view of the wide distribution of these behaviors and their fundamental importance to the evolutionary process, it is not surprising to discover that the biological basis for aggressive behavior is similar in a wide variety of vertebrates. As presently understood, the essential structures are in the phylogenetically oldest parts of the brain, and the principal male sex hormone testosterone is significant for aggression. In general, motivational-emotional patterns essential to survival and reproductive success in mammals find their main structural base in the older parts of the brain, particularly in hypothalamus and limbic system. In the higher primates this mammalian "common denominator" is linked to a remarkable development of newer parts of the brain. These are mainly concerned with increasing storage (learning), more complex discrimination, and motor skills; they function in a complex feedback relationship with the older parts (Noback and Moskowitz 1963; MacLean 1963). This interrelation of the older and newer parts of the brain is especially important to remember when monkeys and apes are considered because the expression of the brain-hormone-behavior paradigm may be greatly modified by learning in a social environment. A simple release of a complicated emotion-motor pattern in aggression is not to be expected in such species.

The recognition of a biological factor in aggressive behavior long antedates modern science; stock breeders certainly recognized differences in individuals, in breeds, and in the effects of castration. Comparison of the behaviors of ox and bull, as well as experiments such as those of Beeman (1947) on mice, show that a part of the difference in aggressive behavior between males and females is due to the sex hormones. Testosterone makes it easier to stimulate animals to fight, and aggressive behavior in males tends to be more frequent, more intense, and of longer duration than in females. Experimental studies fully support the conclusions of Collias' (1944) survey of vertebrate behavior, and are in agreement with the field studies of primate behavior. It would be extremely interesting to trap a male baboon from a troop that had been carefully studied, castrate him, and release him back into the same troop. The effects of the operation could then be studied relative to hierarchy, predators, and participation in troop life in general.

However, the relation of the hormone to the behavior is not simple, for androgen stimulates protein anabolism in many animals (Nalbandov 1964), and this is one of the factors accounting for the greater size of males. Skeletal muscles of castrated males and females grow less rapidly than those of intact animals, and androgen administration increases the number and thickness of fibers. The sex hormones affect the growth of the brain, and appear to act in an inductive way to organize certain circuits into male and female patterns (Harris 1964; Levine and Mullins 1966). This effect is comparable to that on the undifferentiated genital tract. There is then an interplay, a feedback, among hormones, structure, and behavior, and the nature of this relation changes during development. Testosterone is first a factor in influencing the structure of the brain (especially the hypothalamus) and of the genitals. Later it is a factor in influencing both muscle size and the more aggressive play of males. Finally, it is important in influencing both aggressive and sexual behavior in adults. We stress the complex interplay between hormones, structures, and behavior throughout the life of the individual. It can be seen at once that the concept of a system of coadapted genes is so important because such a developmental and functional pattern depends on the interaction of many different biological entities; variation in any of these may affect the final result. It is probably the primary methodological difficulty in the science of behavior genetics that even apparently simple behaviors are often built from very complex biological bases.

Two groups of experiments yield what seems to be particularly important information regarding factors influencing male aggression. Harris and Levine have studied the sexual behavior patterns in female rats that had received early androgen treatment; treatment of newborn rats with testosterone results in abolition of estrous behavior combined with an exaggeration of male patterns, particularly in the aggressive sphere. Young, Goy, and Phoenix (1964) and Goy (personal communication) gave testosterone to pregnant rhesus monkeys during approximately the second quarter of gestation. In addition to producing pseudohermaphroditic females, the behavior of the prenatally treated females was modified in the male direction. Rosenblum (1961) has shown that there are marked sexual differences in the play of infant rhesus monkeys. The masculinized females were allowed to play for 20 minutes per day, five days a week, from the age of two months; this continued for more than two years (at the time of writing). They threatened, initiated play, and engaged in rough play more than did the controls. Like the males studied by Rosenblum, the masculinized females withdrew less often than did untreated females from initiations, threats, and approaches of other animals. They also showed a greater tendency to mounting; evidently there is a general tendency toward male behavioral repertoire. Treatment changed the whole brain-hormone-behavior complex, and the results of the prenatal treatment persisted into the third year of life.

However, it should be stressed that the expression of the pattern depended on social learning. The infant monkeys were allowed to play, and Harlow and Harlow (1965) have shown that gross behavioral deficits in behavior result from early social isolation. It is also important to remember that these testosterone-treated monkeys were protected. In a free-ranging troop of rhesus, subject to human harassment, predation, intertroop conflict, and intratroop aggression (Jay, personal communication; Southwick *et al.* 1965), such an animal would probably be punished for inappropriate behavior. The experimentally masculinized female does not have the large canine teeth, jaw muscles, or body size to be successfully aggressive against males under natural conditions. A similar point is well illustrated in an experiment by Delgado (1963). A monkey in whose brain an electrode had been implanted so that threat behavior could be stimulated at the experimenter's will, was put in a cage with four other monkeys. In the test where the experimental animal was dominant over the other four, stimulation led him to threaten and immediately attack. But when the experimental animal was subordinate to all four of the other monkeys, stimulation led to his being attacked and cowering. Even when there is a restricted biological base for a behavior, the expression of the behavior will be affected by socio-environmental factors.

This brings us to a closer examination of the brain in relation to aggressive behavior. Perhaps, the most thorough work has been done on cats and this is summarized by Brown and Hunsperger (1965). Their experiments show several areas in which electrical stimulation will elicit threat and escape behavior. They have been able to elicit such behavior by stimulation in portions of the midbrain, hypothalamus, and amygdala. Although, just as in monkeys, threat can be elicited from only a very small part of the brain, it is not a single or simple area. The threat behaviors are multiple and it is especially interesting that escape is closely related to threat. Brown and Hunsperger relate the anatomical facts to the behavioral fact that following threat an animal may either attack or escape. Certainly this is frequently seen in monkeys; whether threat ends in attack or flight depends on the participating animal's appraisal of the situation. In the laboratory, the direction and intensity of the attack resulting from stimulation of the brain depends on what is available for attack, and may be changed by offering the cat a dummy or a real rat.

In man the same parts of the brain are believed to be involved in rage reactions. Obviously, the same kind of detailed stimulation cannot be undertaken on man, but clinical evidence including neurological studies suggests that the limbic system and hypothalamus are very important in mediation of emotional experiences, positive and negative, including anger.

AGGRESSION IN FREE-RANGING APES
AND MONKEYS

Just as the biological basis of aggression that we have been discussing can only be seen and analyzed in the laboratory, so the functions and frequencies of aggressive behaviors can only be determined by field studies. The field studies have recently been reviewed by Hall (1964) and Washburn (1966), and here we will call attention only to a few of the major points of interest from an evolutionary point of view.

Conflict between different species is infrequent, even when the species are competing for the same food. Places where the general situation can be most easily observed are at water holes in the large African game reserves. Particularly at the end of the dry season, hundreds of animals of many species may be seen in close proximity in South Africa, Rhodesia, or Tanzania. The Ngorongoro crater affords magnificent views over vast

Fig. 17–2. Typical scene at water hole at Amboseli Game Reserve. Baboons, warthogs, and zebras mingle and feed without interaction. (*Photograph by Sherwood Washburn*)

numbers of animals, and from this vantage point it becomes clear that the human notion of "wild," that is, that animals normally flee, is the result of human hunting. In Amboseli it is not uncommon to see various combinations of baboons, vervet monkeys, warthogs, impala, gazelle of two species, zebra, wildebeest (gnu), giraffe, elephant, and rhinoceros around one water hole. Even carnivores, when they are not hunting, attract surprisingly little attention. When elephants walk through a troop of baboons the monkeys move out of the way in a leisurely manner at the last second, and the same indifference was observed when impala males were fighting among the baboons or when a rhinoceros ran through the troop. On one occasion two baboons chased a giraffe, but, except where hunting carnivores are concerned, interspecies aggression is rare. Most animals under most conditions do not show interest in animals of other species, even when eating the same food—warthogs and baboons frequently eat side by side. The whole notion of escape distance is predicted on the presence of a hunter.

Although the general situation seems to be great tolerance for other species (Hall 1964), there are exceptions. Gibbons usually drive monkeys from fruit trees (Ellefson, this vol.). Goodall has shown remarkable motion pictures of baboons and chimpanzees in aggressive encounters. Baboons have been seen trying to drive vervets (*Cercopithecus aethiops*) from fruit trees in which the baboons had been feeding. There is some deliberate hunting by monkeys and apes. DeVore (personal communication) and Struhsaker (1965) have seen baboons catch and eat vervets. Goodall (1965) records chimpanzees' hunting and eating red colobus monkeys. Nestling birds and eggs are probably eaten by most monkeys, but the majority of interspecific encounters among the primates appear to be neutral, causing little or no reaction among the species.

Monkeys and apes certainly take aggressive action against predators, and this has been particularly well described by Struhsaker (1965) for vervets. Vervet alarm calls distinguish among snakes, ground predators, and birds, and the monkeys respond with different appropriate actions. Baboons have been seen to chase cheetahs and dogs. Monkeys and apes make agonistic displays against predators, including man, and these behaviors have been reviewed by Hall (1964; this vol.) and Washburn (1966). The amount of this agonistic behavior leads us to think that predation and interspecies conflict may have been underestimated in the field studies so far available. The problem is that although the primates may have become conditioned to the observer's presence, he is likely to disturb the predator. A fuller picture of interspecies conflict requires field studies of a nonprimate species involved in conflict with primates.

Relations among groups of the same species range from avoidance to agonistic display and actual fighting. In marked contrast to the normally neutral relations with other species, animals of the same species evoke interest and action. This can be seen when strange animals of the same species are artificially introduced (Gartlan and Brain, this vol.; Kummer, this vol.; Hall 1964; Washburn 1966), on the occasions when an animal changes troops, and when troops meet. We think these behaviors suggest that intertroop conflict is an important mechanism for species spacing. The spacing represents a part of the adjustments of the species to the local food supply. The quantity of food is a very important factor in determining the density of primate populations. It has been shown in both Japan and a small island off Puerto Rico where rhesus monkeys were introduced that population expands at a rate of more than 15 percent per year if food is supplied ad libitum (Koford 1966). Intertroop aggression either leads to one group's having the resources of an area at its exclusive disposal, or at least creates a situation in which one group is much more likely to obtain the food in one area. The clearest description of extreme territorial defense is Ellefson's account (Chap. 6) of gibbons. The relation of food supply to population size is considered by Hall (this vol.). A very clear case of the relation of food supply to territorial defense is given by Gartlan and Brain (Chap. 10): Where food was abundant and there was a high density of vervets, the monkeys showed territorial marking and defense. These behaviors were absent in an area of poor food supply and low population density. From this and other examples (rhesus, langurs) it is clear that one cannot describe a primate species as "territorial" in the same sense the word has been used for species of birds. In monkeys and apes the behavior of a part of a species will depend both on biology (perhaps best shown by the gibbon) and on the local conditions. The intertroop fighting of city rhesus monkeys appears to depend both on high density and on the great overlap of living areas that is a product of the city environment (Southwick *et al.* 1965). The intertroop conflict of langurs described by Yoshiba (this vol.) also occurred in an area in which the population is estimated at possibly more than 300 langurs per square mile.

It is our belief that intertroop aggression in primates has been greatly underestimated. No field study has yet been undertaken with this problem as a focus, and no effort has been made to study situations in which conflict is likely to be frequent. More important, the groups of a species are normally spaced well apart, and the observer sees the long-term results of aggression and avoidance, not the events causing it. (In this regard, as in so many others, gibbons are exceptional.) A further complication is that the groups of monkeys which are likely to meet have seen each other before. The relations among groups has been established in previous encounters, and one is exceedingly unlikely to see strange troops meet or some major event change the relative strength of the troops. Carpenter (1964), particularly, has called attention to the importance of sounds in species spacing, and, in species in which this mechanism is important, group avoidance does not even require that the animals see each other. The importance of both sounds and gestures in intertroop relations is discussed by Marler (this vol.). Lorenz (1964, 1966) has stressed the ritualistic nature of the vast majority of aggressive encounters.

In evaluating the amount of intertroop aggression in Old World monkeys and apes, it is important to keep in mind that the data have increased very rapidly. In Scott's (1962) review on aggression in animals the only major sources of information on primates were Carpenter's studies of the howling monkey (1934) and of the gibbon (1940). In Hall's review of aggression in primate society (this vol.) the data are chiefly from publications in 1962 or later. We stress the frequency and importance of aggressive behavior more than Hall does, in part because of our greater emphasis on the biological importance of aggression in species spacing, but more importantly because there is much more information available in recent accounts. Aggression in langurs is described by Ripley (1965) and Yoshiba (this vol.). Many more observations of aggressive encounters in rhesus, including intertroop fighting in forest troops, are now available (Jay, personal communication). Shirek (personal communication) has observed a complex pattern of intertroop fighting in *Macaca irus*. Ellefson (this vol.) has given a much more complete account of intertroop encounters, including actual fighting, in gibbons. For vervets, Gartlan and Brain (this vol.) and Struhsaker (1965) have provided descriptions of intertroop encounters and of the settings that increase their frequency.

AGGRESSION WITHIN THE LOCAL GROUP

Conflict between individuals within the local group or aggregation is far more frequent than intergroup or interspecies conflicts. It is impossible to watch monkeys and apes for any long period without seeing conflict over food or in interpersonal relations. Scott (1962) has emphasized the importance of learning in the development of aggressive behaviors and Hall (this vol.) has shown that most learning in monkeys takes place in a group and is appropriate to the group's social structure, individual biology, and ecology. In the societies of nonhuman primates aggression is constantly rewarded. In baboons (DeVore and Hall 1965; Hall and DeVore 1965) the most dominant male can do what he wants (within the limits of the traditions of the troop), and he takes precedence in social situations. As DeVore first emphasized, the dominant male is attractive to the other members of the troop. When he sits in the shade, others come to him to sit beside him and groom him. When the troop moves, it is the behavior of the dominant males in the center of the troop that ultimately decides the direction the troop will follow. The whole social structure of the troop rewards the dominant animal, or animals, and when a dominant animal is sick or injured and loses position the change can be seen in the behavior of the other animals. No longer is precedence granted to him for social position, grooming, food, sex, or leadership. Thus, monkeys not only have the biological basis for aggressive behavior, but also use this equipment frequently, and success is highly rewarded.

There are marked species differences in aggressive behavior and in the dominance hierarchies that result from it. Baboons and macaques are probably the most aggressive of the monkeys, but even here there are species differences. *M. radiata* is far less aggressive than *M. mulatta* (Simonds 1965). The behavior of *Papio hamadryas* is certainly different from that of other baboons (Kummer, this vol.). But *interindividual conflict is important in all species described so far*. Even in chimpanzees with their very open social organization (Goodall 1965; Reynolds and Reynolds 1965) some males are dominant. Goodall had to make elaborate arrangements to prevent a few large males from taking all the food when bananas were provided.

The position of the individual animal relative to other animals in the group is learned, and this process starts with the mother and her support of her

Fig. 17–3. Female baboon grooming wound that was the result of a fight for dominance. (*Photograph by Sherwood Washburn*)

infant in aggressive encounters (Yamada 1963; Sade 1965, 1966). Sons of dominant females are more likely to be dominant. The passing of the infant langur from one female to another may be one of the factors in the lack of development of clearly defined dominance hierarchies in this species (Jay 1965).

Since the animals in a local group know one another, the dominance order is understood, is normally maintained by threat, and usually serves to preserve a relatively peaceful situation. For example, a small group of crab-eating macaques *(M. irus)* kept in a runway (16 by 75 feet) at Berkeley was dominated by one male. For more than two years there had not been a single serious bite by any member of the group. When the dominant animal was removed, no change occurred for two weeks; the social habits continued.

Then the formerly number two animal asserted his power, and four adult animals received deep canine bites. (These bites are quite different from incisor nipping, which hurts the other animal but does not do serious damage. Incisor nipping is the normal mode of biting when an animal gives mild punishment.) Two infants were killed in the encounters. This incident clearly shows the role of dominance in preventing fighting. It also shows another characteristic of dominance behavior in macaques. In the runway all animals had access to ample food; they had comfortable social position including opportunities for grooming; and the dominant animal, although he copulated more than the others, did not prevent them from access to females. Being dominant appears to be its own reward—to be highly satisfying and to be sought, regardless of whether it is accompanied by advantage in food, sex, or grooming. In the long run, position guarantees reward, but in the short run, position itself is the reward, as this monkey's actions suggest; satisfaction apparently comes from others being unable to challenge effectively, as well as from more tangible rewards.

Evolution of Conflict

The aggressive behaviors that are the basis of dominance within the group, that are a factor in spacing groups, and that may result in some predation are rooted in the biology of the species and are learned in the social group. As noted earlier, the biological roots of these behaviors are complex, and the individual animal, which carries out the threat or other aggressive action, must have the necessary structure, physiology, and temperament. For example, males tend to be more aggressive than females, and this difference depends on testosterone and is altered by castration of the male or prenatal treatment of the female. The aggressive actions are practiced and brought to a high level of skill in play. Then, as the male monkey becomes fully adult, the canine teeth erupt. Notice that the whole practiced, skillful, aggressive complex is present before the canine teeth erupt. The really dangerous weapon is not present until the male monkey is a fully adult, experienced member of the social group. As the canine teeth erupt, the temporal muscles more than double in size, and the male changes from a roughly playing juvenile to an adult that can inflict a very serious wound, even death, with a single bite.

All the parts of this aggressive complex evolve, and this is best shown by the differences between species. The differences between baboons and patas monkeys give an example of very different ways of adapting to savanna life (Hall, this vol.; DeVore and Hall 1965; Hall and DeVore 1965). Differences between *Cercopithecus aethiops* and *C. mitis* are noted by Gartlan and Brain (this vol.). Since selection is for reproductive success, it is clear that there must be a balance between all the different structural and physiological factors that make aggressive actions adaptive; although the biological elements seem remarkably similar in primates, the pattern and degree of development may be very different in various species. It is no accident that the differences between male and female monkeys are in body size, tooth form, neck muscles, hormones, brain, play patterns, and adult behavior, and this whole pattern of sexual differentiation may result in sex difference that is extreme (as in baboons and macaques) or very minor (as in *Presbytis rubicunda* or *Cercopithecus nictitans*). But as these species have evolved, the process has been slow enough so that selection has modified the whole complex of the adapting aggressive behaviors and their biological base. In man, however, the whole technical-social scene has changed so rapidly that human biological evolution has had no opportunity to keep pace. Throughout most of human history societies have depended on young adult males to hunt, to fight, and to maintain the social order with violence. Even when the individual was cooperating, his social role could be executed only by extremely aggressive action that was learned in play, was socially approved, and was personally gratifying.

In the remainder of this paper we wish to consider human aggression, and the problems created by the nature of man.

As Lorenz (1964, 1966) has stressed, most conflict between animals is ritualized. Gestures and sounds convey threats and greatly reduce the amount of actual fighting. This is certainly true for the primates, and many structures are understandable only as the basis for displays. Dramatic structures of this kind, such as the laryngeal sac of the siamang gibbon, have long been recognized, but many less noticeable (from a human point of view) should be included—for example, the pads of connective tissue on the head of the male gorilla or those of the male orangutan's cheeks. Motions of the ears, scalp, eyelids, are important in gesture. The posture, or the position of the tail, may signal social status. Hair, particularly on the shoulders and neck, erects, signaling aggressive intent, and the manes of many male primates probably are to be interpreted as structural adaptations for agonistic display. Man lacks the kind of structures that the other primates use in threat and agonistic display. Although the structures used in display may differ to some extent from species to species, it is remarkable that man has none—no erecting hair, colored skin, callosities, or dramatic actions of ears or scalp. The kinds of gesture that communicate threat in the nonhuman primates have been shifted to the hand (freed by bipedalism and made important by tools) and to language. The evolution of language as a more efficient method of social communication, including the communication of threat, changed the pressures on a wide variety of other structures that must have functioned in agonistic display, unless it is postulated that our ancestors were unique among mammals and lacked all such adaptations. For example, only about one-half of the behavioral items that Brown and Hunsperger (1965) list as indicating agnostic behavior are anatomically possible in man. It is

Fig. 17–4. Lioness threatening baboons who have escaped into a tree at Nairobi Park. (Photograph by Sherwood Washburn)

particularly the kind of structures that signal threat at a distance that have been lost. But even the structures that serve in close, face-to-face social communication may have been simplified. Human facial muscles have been described as more complex than those of the apes, making more elaborate expressions possible, but this is surely a misreading of the anatomical evidence and there is no evidence that the facial muscles of a chimpanzee are less complicated than those of man. Certainly the chimpanzee's mouth is more mobile and expressive, and a much wider variety of mouth expressions are possible in an ape than in man.

If we read the evidence correctly, in man language replaces the agonistic displays of nonhuman primates, and it opens the way to the existence of a social system in which aggressive behavior is not constantly rewarded. As noted earlier, in the societies of monkeys and apes dominance is the key to social order. Even if the dominance system of a group is not a rigid one, individuals in protecting young, gaining access to food, sex, grooming, or social position often threaten, and the threat—or, rarely, actual aggression—is rewarded with the acquisition of the desired goal. Agonistic behavior is an essential element in the day-to-day behavior of monkeys and apes, and language removes the necessity of rewarding this kind of aggressive behavior.

Just as the changed selection that came with tools led to increase in the parts of the brain controlling manual skills and to reduction in the whole tooth-fighting complex, so the origin of language led to changes in parts of the brain (Lancaster, this vol.) and to a reduction or loss of most structures concerned with displays. In this sense the human body is in part a product of language and of the complex social life that language made possible. Similarly, the emotions of man have evolved in a way that permits him to participate in complex social life (Hamburg 1963). We think it is probable that individuals with uncontrollable rage reactions were killed and that, over many thousands of years, there was selection for temperaments compatible with moderately complex social situations. This process may have been somewhat like the early stages of domestication that involved the removal of socially impossible individuals, rather than the breeding of animals according to any plan. It is a fact that the human adrenals are relatively small compared to those of nonhuman primates and in this way man differs from the ape as domestic rats do from wild rats.

The expression of the emotions in man is more complex than in nonhuman primates, and, although emphasizing the continuity of the biological nature of aggressive behavior, we do not forget the remarkable differences. Compared with the ape or monkey, all the association areas of the human brain have undergone a three-fold increase in size. These are the areas particularly concerned with the ability to remember, to plan, and to inhibit inappropriate action. The increase in these areas is probably the result of new selection pressures that came with the evolution of more complex forms of social life, and is probably highly related to the evolution of language which made the new ways of life possible. Taken together the new parts of the association areas and the parts of the brain making language possible might be thought of as the "social brain"—the parts of the brain that (from an evolutionary point of view) evolved in response to social pressures and the parts that today mediate appropriate social action. This concept is consistent with the fact that degeneration in these parts leads to senile dementia, the inability of some old people to continue normal social life—to remember, to plan, and to keep actions appropriate to time and place. However, the social world in which the human brain and emotions evolved was very different from the present one.

Throughout most of human history (at least 600,000 years, if by "man" we mean the genus *Homo,* large-brained creatures who made complex tools, hunted big animals, and at least some of whom used fire), our ancestors lived in small groups, and (as evidenced by the ethnographic literature, archeology, and the behavior of the nonhuman primates) males were expected to hunt and to fight, and to find these activities pleasurable. Freeman (1964) has given us an anthropological perspective on aggression; the record of war, torture, and planned destruction is exceedingly impressive.

Most of the behaviors are so repugnant to our present beliefs and values that people do not want to consider them; in spite of the vast number of courses offered in the modern university, usually there is none on war, and aggression is treated only incidentally in a few courses. As ordinarily taught, history is expurgated, and the historian considers the treaties that were never kept rather than the actual experiences of war.

The situation relative to human aggression can be briefly stated under three headings. First, man has been a predator for a long time and his nature is such that he easily learns to enjoy killing other animals. Hunting is still considered a sport, and millions of dollars are spent annually to provide birds, mammals, and fish to be killed for the amusement of sportsmen. In many cultures animals are killed for the amusement of human observers (in bullfighting, cockfighting, bear baiting, and so forth). Second, man easily learns to enjoy torturing and killing other human beings. Whether one considers the Roman arena, public tortures and executions, or the sport of boxing, it is clear that humans have developed means to enjoy the sight of others being subjected to punishment. Third, war has been regarded as glorious and, whether one considers recent data from tribes in New Guinea or the behavior of the most civilized nations, until very recently war was a normal instrument of national policy and there was no revulsion from the events of victorious warfare, no matter how destructive. Aggression between man and animals, between man and man and between groups of men has been encouraged by custom, learned in play, and rewarded by society. Man's nature evolved under those conditions, and many men still seek personal dominance and national territory through aggression.

The consequence of this evolutionary history is that large-scale human destruction may appear at any time social controls break down; recent examples are Nazi Germany, Algeria, the Congo, Vietnam. Further, it must be remembered that the customs governing our lives evolved in the era when killing animals for fun, the brutal torture of human beings, and war were opposed by few. It is not only our bodies that are primitive, but also our customs, which are not adapted to the crowded and technical world that is dominated by a fantastic acceleration of scientific knowledge. Traditional customs nurtured aggression and frequently continue to do so.

The view that man is aggressive because of his evolutionary past, because of his biological nature, seems pessimistic to some, but we agree with Freeman that if aggression is to be controlled in a way compatible with survival and the realities of the new world of science, "it is only by facing the realities of man's nature and of our extraordinary history as a genus that we shall be able to evolve methods likely, in some measure, to succeed." (1964:116)

The situation might be compared to that of a bank. It is desirable to have employees who are honest people who will abide by the bank's customs. But no bank would rely solely on the honesty of its employees. The best auditing and accounting devices are used to make it virtually impossible for the human element to disrupt the functions of the institution. But on the international scene no comparable institutions for accounting and auditing exist, and reliance is still placed on the judgment of leaders and the customs of states. But these states have used war as a normal instrument of policy, their customs have glorified war, and all history shows that nothing in the human leader will necessarily restrain him from war if he sees success as probable. There is a fundamental difficulty in the fact that contemporary human groups are led by primates whose evolutionary history dictates, through both biological and social transmission, a strong dominance orientation. Attempts to build interindividual relations, or international relations, on the wishful basis that people will not be aggressive is as futile as it would be to try to build the institution of banking with no auditing on the basis that all employees will be honest.

In summary, in Old World monkeys and apes aggression is an essential adaptive mechanism. It is an important factor in determining interindividual relations; it is frequent; and successful aggression is highly rewarded. It is a major factor in intergroup relations, and the importance of aggression as a species-spacing mechanism means that aggression is most frequent between groups of the same species. Both within groups and between groups aggression is an integral part of dominance, feeding, and reproduction. The biological basis of aggressive behaviors is complex, including parts of the brain, hormones, muscles-teeth-jaws, and structures of display; successful aggression has been a major factor in primate evolution.

Man inherits the biological base, modified by the great development of the social brain and language. Aggression may be increased by early experience, play, and the rewards of the social system. The individual's aggressive actions are determined by biology and experience. But an aggressive species living by prescientific customs in a scientifically advanced world will play a tremendous price in interindividual conflict and international war.

18

ETHOLOGICAL PERSPECTIVES

ON PRIMATE STUDIES

Irenäus Eibl-Eibesfeldt

Behavior patterns are adapted to fit specific features of the environment. Such adaptation can be the result of individual learning, or it can come about by phylogenetic processes, and this latter aspect of behavior will be emphasized here. In learning, the information is stored in the central nervous system of the individual, whereas in phylogenetic adaptation it is stored in the genoma of the species and decoded during the ontogeny of the individual. This decoding takes place with some environmental interaction, but the essential fact is that the adaptation develops in the absence of any information about the specific environmental situation. The deprivation experiments establishing this are discussed in detail by K. Lorenz (1961, 1965).

Such experiments show that phylogenetic adaptations can determine the behavior of animals in a variety of ways. On the motor side they exist as fixed action patterns (instinctive movements); animals show innate skills. On the receptor side they may be described as a sort of "innate knowledge" of certain stimuli; that is, animals react to certun stimulus situations, prior to any experience of them, with a specific motor pattern. Phylogenetic adaptations exist also in the form of dispositions to specific learning and in the form of special motivating mechanisms.

Inborn motor patterns have been found in every animal species so far examined, including man. Some are present at hatching or at birth (for example, the motor pattern of sucking in neonates), whereas others mature in much the same way as organs grow and mature in the course of the development of the individual. Some birds, for example, develop their song, or the species-specific call notes, even if deprived of an opportunity to hear other conspecifics sing (Sauer 1954), and some achieve this even when deafened (Konishi 1963). Red squirrels show a highly adaptive sequence of movements that serve to hide nuts; they tamp the nut down with rapid blows of the snout and cover the hole with the previously dug-up earth, using sweeping movements of the paws, finally packing down the earth with pressing movements. A squirrel that has been raised in a cage without any opportunity to dig and that has been fed only a liquid diet will nevertheless demonstrate this same sequence of movements if it is given its first nuts as an adult. These patterns are part of a genetically based program of motor events that run successively, once triggered by a specific stimulus, and they will take place even though the environment makes them inappropriate.

With time and opportunity the animals learn where and how best to hide nuts. If the performance of the hoarding acts leaves the nut still visible, the squirrel will often take it and hide it in another place; thus it eventually learns to dig in the earth. Similarly, if an inexperienced animal has left the nut visible because it has covered the nut while turning away to run, it will learn to perform the covering movement adequately by readjusting its orientation. The animal perfects this behavioral sequence by the learned improvement of an orientation component in an otherwise innate behavior pattern; in the same way polecats learn the right orientation of the killing bite, as well as of the neck grip necessary for successful copulation (Eibl-Eibesfeldt 1963).

Learning is also involved in the perfection of adaptive behavior by animals endowed with a number of innate action patterns which they must learn to link in the most efficient way. For example, inexperienced rats perform all the basic nest-building movements, but not in the perfect functional order they learn with experience (Eibl-Eibesfeldt 1963). Another example is the nut-opening technique of the squirrel; gnawing and splitting, which are involved in this technique, are fixed movements that are innate in squirrels, like ready-made tools, but they must be integrated into a functional pattern by learning.

Animals often have to learn the usefulness of an inborn behavior pattern. This is true of rats in nest-building and appears also to be true of the woodpecker finch of the Galapagos Islands, which at first uses twigs and spines to poke into cracks and holes at random and only later learns to use these tools to probe for insects and to collect them.

In mammals, many of these final adjustments of phylogenetically adapted behavior patterns are learned in the juvenile phase, which is characterized by play behavior. This type of behavior seems to serve the function of learning. Playing animals are engaged in an experimental dialogue with the environment, experimenting with the abilities of their own bodies as well as investigating and learning the characteristics of the environment. For this "purpose" they are endowed with a specific motivational mechanism, which has not yet been studied in detail. We do know, however, that "curiosity" plays an important role. By curiosity, I mean the experimentally demonstrable fact that animals actively seek new stimuli-situations to explore, the opportunity to do so acting as a reward in learning situations.

Furthermore, we observe that playing animals perform acts which belong to different functional cycles (hunting, sexual behavior, fighting, nest-building, and so forth) and which normally cannot occur in combination. Some special mechanisms must have been developed to make behavior patterns available in this way for experimentation and for combination in novel ways. The argument that play may simply be immature behavior does not hold, since the animals are often already capable of serious fighting or other mature activity. In play, however, the behavior looks completely different. Fighting dogs snarl and bite each other severely, and their fighting ends with submission or flight by the loser. Play fighting observed in the same animals looks completely different. The animals wag their tails, even when otherwise behaving as if they were in earnest; they do not break the skin in biting; and they repeatedly change the roles of pursuer and pursued. Such behavior can continue for a long time, interrupted by or combined with other activities, such as hunting or sexual behavior.

It has sometimes been argued that play is not a special category of behavior, but the characteristics mentioned above indicate that it is. We should therefore study its functional and its physiological aspects in more detail. Studies on polecats show that in playful wrestling males learn the right orientation of the copulation grip on the nape of the female's neck. Males that had been isolated after a period of two months of play with litter mates, later grasped females in the right way, whereas isolates without any play experience did not. In spite of their interest in the females, these males had to adjust by *learning* in order to copulate successfully. The descriptions by H. F. Harlow and M. K. Harlow (1962), W. A. Mason (1965), and others, of the sexual behavior of *Rhesus* isolates indicate that deprivation caused similar disturbance in behavior in this species. The male isolates tried to copulate with females in estrus, but did not mount with the right orientation. A study should be made of the way in which play behavior contributes to the normal ontogeny of sexual behavior.

To learn about the adaptedness of behavior patterns, we must study animals in their natural environment. In this way we obtain a catalog of behavior patterns—the ethogram. Apart from individual idiosyncrasies, we find a number of behavior patterns occurring in each individual of the same species, sex, and age; these are characterized by the same pattern of muscle contractions and show variation mainly in the degree of intensity and almost not at all in the specificity of the patterning—they are, in short, constant in form. If we compare this catalog of behavior patterns with that of closely related species, we often find great similarities in the behavioral repertoires. This was first observed by the zoologist and taxonomist O. Heinroth (1911), who, in looking for criteria useful for taxonomic purposes, studied the phylogenetic relationship within the family Anatidae. K. Lorenz (1941) and many other zoologists have since treated behavior patterns as morphological criteria for the study of phylogenetic relationships of different animal groups. The criteria of homology are the same as those used in morphology—similarity in form, similarity in topography, similarity in ontogeny, and linkage by intermediating forms (for details see W. Wickler 1961; G. P. Baerends 1958). If animals of different taxonomic groups living in the same environment show similar behavior patterns, we must be careful with our interpretation, since analogies are very probable.

In order to make phylogenetic comparisons, the observed behavior patterns should be described with the greatest care and they should be named. However, even the most detailed physical description is already an interpretation, since every describer describes only what he considers significant. A slight wiggling of the tail may escape his attention, and exactly this may be of great interest to another observer, as a possible rudimentary behavior pattern. For this reason, every behavior student should film the behavior patterns, publish the films in addition to his publications, and preserve a duplicate of his negative in a large official film library. The films are then preserved just as type specimens are preserved.[1]

I would like to comment on an apparent omission in studies of human behavior. In the pursuit of our interest in the evolution of human expressive movements, Hans Hass and I went through the film archives looking for unstaged examples of human facial expressions and gestures. We wanted to compare people of different cultures and races, filmed without their knowledge, expressing fear, anger, and affection—laughing, smiling, and so forth—in order to discover the invariables that occur independently of culture in the expression of the human being. To our great surprise, the only available films showed the way different tribes construct huts, build boats, form pots, and carry on all sorts of cultural activities (all staged, by the way), and none dealt with our basic behavioral repertory. This whole field of most important behavior has been neglected in documentation, although the cross-cultural comparison of these behavior patterns could tell us the extent to which phylogenetic adaptation on the motor side determines human

---

[1]There is an international organization in Göttingen (Institut für den Wissenschaftlichen Film), the aim of which is to publish such film strips in the "Encyclopaedia cinematorgraphica" (ed. G. Wolf). Films showing locomotion, grooming behavior, feeding, predation, courtship, nest-building, and the like, are published by activity according to species; this allows comparison of the same activity in different species. Several copies of each film are made and constitute a film library for research. Accompanying each film is a short detailed report by the author, and published in the journal, *Publikationen zu Wissenschaftlichen Filmen*. In addition, a duplicate negative is stored. This is of special importance for the scientist carrying out primate research in the field, since he is studying vanishing species in their natural environment, and thus obtains most important documents which by all means should be preserved for the future. For example, Baron and Baroness Van Lawick-Goodall's excellent films should be pubished in this way, as should Irven DeVore's baboon studies.

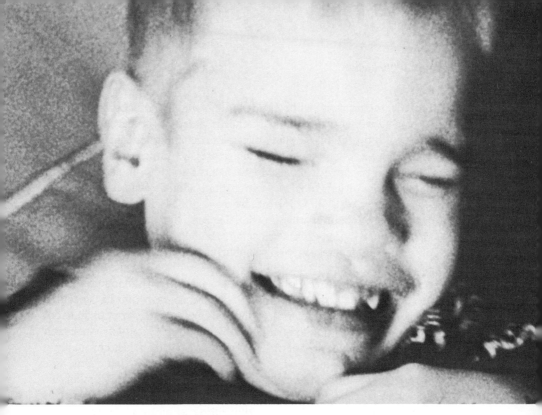

Fig. 18–1. The laughing response of a deaf and blind boy, five years of age (Contergan case). (*Taken from a 16mm film. Photograph: I. Eibleibesfeldt.*)

behavior. The cross-cultural comparison is our most important source of information, since chance deprivation experiments, such as children born blind and deaf provide, are rare. D. G. Freedman (1964) described the smiling response of such children, which is not basically different from that of normal ones, and therefore certainly a fixed action pattern (Figs. 18–1, 18–2, and 18–3). In starting to fill the gap, H. Hass and I are engaged in a cross-cultural study of facial expressions and gestures. Using special mirror lenses, we film people without their knowledge. We collect "natural" documents, which we evaluate by situational analysis; we do not interpret the picture from the single frame, but by the event that occurred before, while, and after we filmed the subject. We have already uncovered surprising similarities in the expressive movements of people of different racial and cultural backgrounds. Basic similarities have been found in greeting, flirting, and praying rituals (Eibl-Eibesfeldt 1966). For example, complex flirting behavior can be reduced to a few variables that occur in human females of very different cultural backgrounds. We have filmstrips of Samoan, French, Nilohamitic (Turkana), and Japanese girls. In all the films, the subject first turns toward the male, smiles, and raises the eyebrows in a rapid "flash," a behavior that also occurs in very friendly greeting. Then, however, a more ritualized turning away of the head or even the whole body occurs, the head often being lowered, and in very naïve subjects sometimes hidden shamefully with one hand. Giggling may occur as approach and withdrawal alternate in conflict. Some of the human expressive movements seem to be of quite ancient origin. K. Lorenz (1941) has already pointed out that in rage we contract our hair-erector muscles along shoulder and back, producing a "shudder" (thus fluffing fur that we have already lost), and by rolling the shoulders inward we assume a posture exactly like a threatening chimp. Darwin mentioned that in extreme rage the canine teeth are displayed in man. N. Kohts (1935) mentioned basic similarities in the facial expression of chimps and man.

Much of our gestural repertoire has been inherited from our ancestors (Van Lawick-Goodall, this vol.). Chimps embrace each other in greeting; they reassure by touching each other; they seek reassurance by stretching out the hands, palm up, waiting to be touched by the other's hand—very like our own touching of hands in greeting. Chimps greet with a kiss, probably a ritualized form of offering food.

Film documents of such events in man and other primates are of the greatest importance for a comparative analysis of the species-specific behavior patterns. They will help in our efforts to find out in which ways phylogenetic adaptations on the motor side govern even our behavior.

Thus far this chapter has dealt with motor patterns. We now turn to other phylogenetically acquired mechanisms that determine behavior. Phylogenetic adaptations on the receptor side are well known to students of behavior. Animals react predictably and in a highly specific way to certain stimuli. A young toad, immediately after metamorphoses, flaps its tongue toward every moving object—artificially moved pebbles or leaves as well as insects—but motionless insects are ignored. This simple reaction to certain sign stimuli is an efficient mechanism for the toad, since normally small moving objects indicate prey. If by chance it snaps at something unpalatable it will spit it out and to a certain extent will learn to avoid undesirable objects in the future (I. Eibl-Eibesfeldt 1951).

In red-breasted robins, the male's aggressive behavior is released by the red feathers on the chests of other robins. A stuffed male without red feathers, mounted within the territory of a male, will be ignored, but a bushel of red feathers will be attacked as if it were a rival (D. Lack 1943). Experiments with decoys have shown similar behavior in stickleback males (Tinbergen 1951). Other stimuli release other specific responses, for example, courtship or fertilization.

In order for such selective responses to occur in specific stimuli situations, we must assume special mechanisms that give way to specific muscle impulses on the receipt of certain stimuli. These mechanisms, acting as filters for the incoming stimuli, are called innate releasing mechanisms. The stimuli can be auditory, olfactory, visual, or tactile, and very often several act in combination. For example, the gaping response of young birds can be released visually, acoustically, and tactilely by touching the nest; each stimulus adds to the total releasing mechanism. In the male stickleback the red belly is one releasing stimulus for aggressive behavior, and the head-down threatening posture is another. Either stimulus alone triggers an aggressive response, which is intensified in combination. Here the stimulus situation becomes a configurational one.

For intraspecific and interspecific communication (for example, in symbiotic relationships), special signals have been developed fitting special innate releasing mechanisms of the receiver. The signals may be bodily structures to which the animals respond visually (the red-feather patch of the red-breasted robin, the red belly of the stickleback), they may be chemical ("Duftstoffe"), they may be sounds, or they may be the multitude of movements and postures that we label "expressive movements." Since all these different signals serve the function of communication, we call them social releasers ("Auslöser").

Although primate experiments with decoys are still rare, we know that these releasers serve an important function in primate behavior, because primates (including man) often react to very crude imitations of natural releasing situations, and, in addition, their manner of response is automatic. It is well known that many primates react to the distress call of young with a blind attack, even upon a caretaker with whom they are on friendly social terms at other times (R. M. Yerkes 1943; S. Zuckerman 1932). Infants of a number of primates (baboons, for example) have a conspicuously different color from that of adults, and this seems to protect them from the aggression of adults, although experiments confirming this are lacking. In man, certain features of a baby constitute what we consider "cute." K. Lorenz mentions the roundness, the short extremities, the round cheeks, the small face with the large eyes, and the dominating front skull. In a similar way, we react to very crude dummies of facial expressions. A sad face can be drawn with only a few lines, and can be changed into a friendly smiling face by just turning up the down-curved mouth, as we all know from cartoons.

W. Wickler (1965) recently made a comparative investigation of the pattern of the swellings around the anogenital region of female primates, which primarily serve to release sexual responses when presented to a male. These swellings are signals, which by eliciting sexual responses at the same time inhibit aggression of the males. Behavior with this same function has been adaptive in some groups for the males as well. In submission, baboons present to the opponent, often releasing a mounting response. In some species the males even exhibit the swelling pattern of the females, for example in the young males of the olive Colobus (*Procolobus*); the pattern is strikingly similar to that of the females, although the structures involved are not homologous (W. Wickler 1966).

Phylogenetic adaptations are also found in the form of special learning dispositions. We know that an animal does not learn all things at all times with equal ease. There are, for example, periods of special sensitivity in which the animals learn very specific things (for example, feeding habits). One of these learning dispositions is known as imprinting (K. Lorenz 1935; E. H. Hess 1959). The newly hatched chicks of some altricial birds are inclined to follow almost every moving object, and once a chick has followed a specific object it continues to do so. A goose that has followed a man, for example, will never accept his goose mother; its following reaction is irreversibly imprinted to man, and this imprinting takes place only during a short period. Such an object-fixation by learning can occur even before the reaction that is fixated to the object has matured. Jackdaws raised by man will leave him to fly with conspecifics as soon as they can fly, but when sexually mature they do not mate with conspecifics, but return to man and court him. This preference lasts, even if one brings them to accept a conspecific as a mate; such a mate acts as a substitute object only; if given a choice, the jackdaw will choose the imprinting object (Schutz 1965).

Finally, phylogenetic adaptations are found in the form of specific motivating mechanisms. An animal does not passively wait for a stimulus to impinge upon it, but actively seeks specific stimuli situations. This behavior we call "appetitive behavior." We know that animals are not always in the same "mood," but can be variously motivated (for example, by hunger or by sex), and we also have some knowledge of the arousing mechanisms, such as hormones, signals coming from internal receptors and the spontaneous activity of the central nervous system (for detailed discussion see I. Eibl-Eibesfeldt 1966). These factors urge an animal to perform activities if they have not been performed for a given length of time. It seems as though a central excitation is somehow stored up during rest, and is consumed by activity. From von Holst's study on the locomotion of fishes, we know that such processes indeed occur. This spontaneity of behavior needs to be studied in more detail.

In summary we may say that phylogenetic adaptations determine the behavior of animals through fixed action patterns, innate releasing mechanisms, innate learning dispositions, and innate motivating mechanisms. The higher primates, because of their close relation to man, are most important research tools. Exploring their behavior using ethological concepts will help us to understand the extent to which our own behavior is governed and determined by phylogenetic adaptations.

19

PRIMATE FIELD STUDIES

AND HUMAN EVOLUTION

Phyllis Jay

INTRODUCTION

In the preceding chapters the authors of this book have presented and evaluated new data on primate behavior. The importance of our practical understanding of the primates and the use of primates in biomedical research is fully documented by the references in *Index Medicus*. Here the concern is with the more philosophical questions of seeking to understand the origins of human nature, of seeing how we differ from nonhuman primates, and of speculating on the causes and history of some of these differences.

This inquiry into human evolution is tentative, and it touches only a very few facets of behavior. In the following pages most of the suggested history of development for specific behavior patterns has to be acknowledged either as only a partial appraisal—a glimpse into what may have occurred—or as reconstructed history that must be stated in terms of probability. Selection is for whole patterns of successful behavior, but, unfortunately for the investigator, many activities vitally important in the way of life of a species are not reflected in the fossils. A great deal can be learned from the bones that comprise our fossil record, but the life of ancestral primates comprised much more than the obvious functions of these bony parts. For example, a certain kind of roughened surface on a fossilized ischium indicates merely that the primate had ischial callosities. But by looking at how living primates with these callosities behave, it is possible to infer that in all likelihood the ancient animal slept sitting up rather than on its side or in a nest (Washburn 1957).

This may seem trivial, but when many such clues to behavior are gathered and collated, the total picture of an animal's way of life fills out to a closer approximation of what it must have been.

Knowledge of the comparative anatomy, physiology, and behavior of living primates, including man, is added to the study of the sequence of fossils and the tools associated with them. Modern human behavior is the result of thousands of generations of change, and today's patterns are the most recent in a long sequence of successful behaviors. Our ancestors were not the same as living primates, but the rich variability of behavior of modern monkeys and apes makes it possible to reconstruct the most probable patterns of behavior of related forms in the past.

The reconstruction of some behavior patterns (aggression, language and the brain) has already been discussed in the preceding chapters (see also, Washburn 1963). Here we consider several other complexes of behavior that leave no marks on fossils—the use of space or land by a social group, female sexual receptivity (estrus among monkey and ape females), and primate tool use. Several closely related aspects of behavior that are very important to normal primate life (for example, play) are mentioned briefly.

DIFFICULTIES AND POTENTIALITIES OF
RECONSTRUCTIONS

Animals' use of space and female sexual receptivity are very different kinds of behaviors, and are examples of widely dissimilar problems in the reconstruction of behavior history. It is not possible to reconstruct behavior in general, but only with respect to very clearly defined specific problems. If a behavior varies greatly among the living monkeys and apes, then reconstructing the ancestral behavior is extremely difficult. Group size is an example of an aspect of life that is exceedingly unamenable to reconstruction for very early stages of human evolution. Information about living nonhuman primates is far more useful in answering questions about the use of land and female sexual receptivity than for supporting speculations about the composition and organization of groups of early man. Evidence from living hunting and gathering societies suggests that the size of early man's groups was small. Because group organization is very different among chimpanzees, gorillas, and gibbons, the problem of relating these patterns to those of early man is correspondingly difficult. The generalization emerges that all monkeys and apes are social, as is man, and this fundamental aspect of human behavior must be deeply rooted in our primate past. (The importance of this has been discussed by Hamburg 1963.)

There are exceptions, then, to the immediate usefulness of reconstructing behavior patterns, but the method is still of great value if it is possible to demonstrate reasons for the exceptions. Consider the question of whether our ancestors slept in trees or on the ground. A great majority of monkeys and apes sleep in trees, and many species spend most of their days in trees. Some gorillas sleep on the ground and can do so with relative impunity because they are tremendously strong and large (Schaller 1963). Whether or not they could continue to sleep on the ground if there were lions in the same area is another question that cannot be answered yet. If our ancestors were larger than gorillas they may have slept on the ground, but this "if" is contraindicated by the fossil record. It is much more probable that until our ancestors were protected by weapons they slept in trees. Some baboons sleep on the ground or on rocks, but only in areas where there are few or no trees (Chap. 11). Kummer discusses the adaptation of hamadryas baboons to such desert conditions, but this is a very special case that does not modify speculation about the savanna- and forest-living ancestors of man. The behaviors of the gorilla and the hamadryas baboon have no direct implications for reconstructing conditions of human evolution since there is no evidence that our ancestors were either giants (pace Weidenreich!) or desert adapted.

There is a simple logic for the reconstruction of behavior of our ancestors, and it can be stated briefly. First, there are behavior patterns that distinguish man from the nonhuman primates. Some of these behaviors that are not present in man are universal among the nonhuman primates living in natural conditions, and because of their presence among monkeys and apes there is every reason to suppose that these behaviors were characteristic of our ancestors. Where human behavior patterns differ from those of nonhuman primates, if the reason for changes from the probable ancestral condition can be shown, then this supports the likelihood that the reconstructed condition is accurate. If the condition is variable and is characteristic of only a few kinds of nonhuman primates, the exceptions must be shown to fit into situations that have no place in human evolution. If this is possible, then even these variable behavior patterns may be of use in reconstruction, as contrasts are themselves reconstructable. New data from field studies, more archeological information, additional fossils, and more accurate dates for past events will make it possible to analyze other behavior categories and to reconstruct much more of our ancestors' ways of life. If our purpose is to understand events leading to the differentiation of man and ape, this kind of information is absolutely necessary.

Behavior reconstruction is not limited to probing into man's past. There are studies of the behavior of related macaque species, and it should soon be possible to ask questions about the evolution of behavior patterns of some of these closely related species. Eventually this should be possible for species of the genus *Papio,* if it remains a separate genus from *Macaca,* or of still more *Macaca* species if the two genera are combined. However, any analysis of the phylogeny of behavior patterns is not practical until the limits of variability in these patterns, and more of the causes or determinates of variation are known.

SPECIFIC PROBLEMS IN RECONSTRUCTION

One of the most important factors in primate life is the relationship of a social group to the area in which it lives. However this area is designated— as territory or as home range (see introduction to Part Three of this volume) —it is correlated with food, water, sleeping locations, and escape routes, all of which are necessary to the daily life and the secure world of the individual. The very nature of this area is a powerful factor in determining group size, frequency of contact among groups, and the relationship of the primate group to other species. The total amount of land one group occupies varies from a few acres as for gibbons (Chap. 6) and the *Callicebus* monkey (Chap. 7) to an intermediate few square miles for chimpanzees (Goodall 1965) and gorillas (Schaller 1965), to more than 15 square miles for savanna-living baboons (Hall and DeVore 1965). It is not always quite this simple to generalize for an entire genus, and it may be somewhat misleading in several instances. For example, troops of primarily forest-living baboons occupy smaller areas than do those in the open plains (Rowell 1966). But in general larger areas tend to be characteristic of large ground-living forms, and it appears that the smaller the primate and the more arboreal its way of life, the more likely it is that the area it uses will be correspondingly small. There are exceptions, but in general there is a high positive correlation between spending most of the time on the ground in open areas and having the largest space for group life.

As long as our ancestors were arboreal apes, they probably lived in small ranges, as do all the contemporary arboreal primates. When our ancestors came to the ground their range may have been considerably extended, but perhaps to no larger a space than that used by modern chimpanzees and gorillas. These apes utilize very small areas when compared with human hunters who require something on the order of 100 times the area per individual that is required by an ape. This great difference appears to be purely human, a product of the human way of life, and it is not even suggested in the behaviors of the nonhuman primates.

If Washburn and Lancaster are correct in suggesting that the causes for the change from the "usual" primate pattern to the human pattern of territorial behavior are tool use, carrying, and hunting, then the change can be dated.

Men of the Middle Pleistocene time hunted large animals; the tools they used were made from selected kinds of stone that do not occur in all areas. This indicates that social groups of early man must have occupied large areas, since evidence on contemporary hunters and gatherers demonstrates that small areas will not support hunters of large game (Lee 1965). It is a great deal more difficult to reconstruct the behavior of Early Pleistocene *Australopithecus* (*Australopithecus* in a general sense). Some stones found in deposits with these fossils appear to have been brought from considerable distances, but this has not yet been determined exactly (Brain, personal communication). Nor has the controversy been resolved as to whether the *Australopithecus* were responsible for bringing to their living sites the bones that evidence consumption of large animals. Studying the effect of predators on bone remains of their kills and then comparing the results with bones found with early man would make it possible to determine whether it is likely that man at this time hunted large animals for food. If he did, it indicates that, like more recent hunters of large animals, he required large areas where he could hunt freely.

Man's exceptional behavior in his occupation of large areas, this variation from an apparently basic primate way of life, is a pattern of behavior that evolved late in human history. What has been reconstructed has important implications. Monkeys and apes have special senses very similar to those of humans, and this indicates that they are at least able to perceive similar aspects of the environment. Monkeys can easily outrun a man on the ground for short distances, but, nevertheless, nonhuman primate groups limit their activities to highly selected portions within relatively small areas of land. Barring catastrophe or some lesser but still disruptive event, the nonhuman social group lives its entire life in a small area. It is not that they cannot, but that they do not leave the area to investigate the surrounding world. Their world view does not incorporate even the exploration of preferred fruit trees that may be in full view beyond the habitual area of use. There may be reasons for this failure to explore actively; these adjacent areas may be occupied by larger, stronger, or more dominant groups that are hostile to encroachment on their land, but even when no danger appears to threaten, exploratory behavior is strictly limited. The fact remains that living in a small space limits the experience of the environment and the social contacts, and also affects the patterns of interaction among groups. This has substantial effects upon the spread of pathogens, adaptation, and populations genetics, each of which depends upon the numbers of individuals that do change from one group to another.

It is a remarkable aspect of human nature that man's attitude toward his environment is so different from that of his ancestors. The study of contemporary primates makes it possible to see how unique man is, and in turn allows the reconstruction of the most probable ancestral condition.

ESTRUS

A second example of reconstructing a behavior that cannot be observed directly in the fossil record is female sexual receptivity. Reproductive patterns have not been described for all species of nonhuman primates, but in species observed living under natural conditions the female is sexually receptive only during relatively brief periods of time. In many species (of genera such as *Papio, Macaca, Cercocebus,* and *Pan*), coincident with sexual receptivity, females are subject to physical changes in coloration and/or swelling of the area around the anal and vaginal regions. Other species, such as the Indian langur (*Presbytis entellus*), lack obvious physical signs of receptivity, and the female signals her willingness to copulate by specific gestures or sounds. In most kinds of monkeys adult males seldom, if ever, copulate with a female unless she is in estrus. When additional species are observed some variation from this pattern of clear receptivity or nonreceptivity may be found, especially among the genus *Cercopithecus.* It is also possible that in some species copulations may occur during a longer period of the female's estrous cycle than the few days prior to, during, and immediately after ovulation, or in the first or second month of pregnancy as has been observed for rhesus monkeys in north India (Lindburg, personal communication). Copulations have been observed at different times in a female's cycle in many other-than-normal situations (in cages or colonies), but the references here are only to free-ranging monkeys and apes.

Not all monkey or ape females are sexually receptive for the same amount of time, but when compared with the human, the nonhuman female primate is sexually receptive for a very small part of her adult life, and her periods of receptivity are hormonally rather than directly socially determined. There is undoubtedly a relationship between social stress and the suppression of normal estrous cycles, and it is possible that females may be facilitated in displaying estrous periods when placed with other females in estrus. There are apt to be striking changes in a female's behavior during estrous periods. She is more active and aggressive, and seeks the attentions of adult males, often including the ones she may have avoided when she was not sexually active. Not only are some social relationships at least temporarily altered by the stresses of increased activity, but when many adult females in a group are receptive at the same time there also may be substantial changes in the behavior of the group as a whole (DeVore 1962; Jay 1965*a*). Some of these changes are alterations in the frequency of grooming, in patterns of foraging, and in intensity as well as frequency of aggressiveness within the group.

The chimpanzee, so like man in many respects, is very dissimilar with regard to female sexual behavior. Goodall (1965) describes as many as twenty males consorting with a single female chimpanzee when she is in estrus. There is no mistaking when a chimpanzee female is sexually receptive because she usually has a swelling, sometimes immense and very bright pink, around the perianal region. Goodall suggests that an obvious function of a large sexual swelling is to signal males, near and far, that the female is in estrus (Van Lawick-Goodall 1966). When a female is in estrus she is surrounded by a much noisier and more boisterous group than when she is not receptive. Males congregate in her vicinity and follow her closer than at any other time, sometimes threatening if she tries to move away without them.

On the basis of our present knowledge of living nonhuman primates it appears that periodic sexual behavior is associated with an estrous cycle, and is characteristic of females living under natural conditions (Lancaster and Lee 1965). Because this cycle is typical of the living nonhuman primates it is most likely that our female ancestors had a similar sexual pattern, and the intriguing question remains as to why natural selection favored the loss of estrus from our behavior. A great advantage of this loss might have been the furthering of a consistent and orderly social system in which there were no sudden periodic increases in tension and aggressiveness because of sexual activity among group adults. At least, this may have been an advantage as far as human evolution is concerned. Loss of estrus may also have had significant effects on mother-infant relationships; it is possible that with fewer potentially traumatic aggressive interactions when the mother consorted with adult males, the infant experiences a calmer period of early development. The evolution of human society depended on the evolution of a physiology that permitted order (loss of estrus, reduction of rage, and the control of many behaviors) coupled with adaptive social customs that depended on the order. The advantages of controlling rage and sex are apparent when the behavior of the nonhuman primates is observed.

Speculations about the development of the human family all presuppose that estrous behavior disappeared and that females of whatever time level is under consideration had a physiology very similar to that of modern females. This assumption is in spite of general basic similarities of reproductive physiology among primate females. It has been suggested that it would have been difficult for early man to maintain a small family group if the adult female's sexual behavior was based on an estrous cycle. However, the gibbon family or group is composed of an adult male, an adult female, and young (Chap. 6), and yet adult female gibbons have estrous cycles. Thus the gibbon might seem an exception that disproves the generalization that estrus is incompatible with the small group, but there are reasons for the gibbon's ability to live this way. Adult gibbons are very apt to be hostile to each other, especially to others of the same sex, and as the young mature they are gradually forced out of the small social group in which they are born. Sexual behavior is infrequent, and it is certainly possible, even likely, that the sex drive among gibbons is far less strong than among monkeys, and it is definitely much less than among chimpanzees. The gibbon has developed a small-group social organization in which the adult female's sexual behavior is regulated by an estrous cycle of receptivity and nonreceptivity, and the male is probably much less sexually active than most other apes and the monkeys. The complex of gibbon behavior that allows small groups is very unlike man's most probable ancestral behavior.

Field observations indicate that estrous behavior can cause problems even in a group composed of many animals, but these problems are less serious if the intensity of estrous behavior is reduced, or, in addition, if the sexual drive of the males is reduced at least during part of the year. Estrus as a set of behaviors cannot be considered apart from the context that includes the organization of male behavior. There are alternative solutions to the problem of estrus in the small group, but the observation of the apparent exceptional sexual pattern in the gibbon has stimulated investigation that may lead to a better comprehension of the role of estrus in human evolution by a closer look at the possible similarities and differences between the types of small group that characterized both primates.

The female primate and her offspring form an enduring social group (Sade 1965; Goodall 1965) that is important in the daily life of each individual member as reflected by preferred grooming patterns and spatial arrangements. The origin of the human family required only the addition of a male, with cooperation and the division of labor between the male and the female. It appears that the female-young nucleus is far older and more fundamental than what we know as a human family.

TOOL USE

Few topics are more interesting to the anthropologist than the evolution of man's uniquely skillful ability to make and to use tools. In his paper, "Tool-using Performances as Indicators of Behavioral Adaptability," (this vol.), Hall effectively interpreted information on use of tools and object manipulation by monkeys and apes to gain insights into the development of human tool-using efficiency. It is a clear statement on an aspect of nonhuman primate behavior that has stimulated a great deal of speculation and generated many theories (Lancaster, in press; Washburn and Jay, in press). Very restricted object use has been described for a variety of animals from insects to mammals, and as one might expect there are some kinds of nonhuman primates in this growing list. Recent observation by the Van Lawicks (1967) of Egyptian vultures' throwing stones to break open ostrich eggs suggests that we still may not have completed the roster of animals capable of manipulating objects, for whatever reason. It is notable, however, that if a species uses tools, it is usually only one kind of tool, such as the cactus spines that a particular kind of finch uses for getting grubs from underneath bark.

Almost all tool use by vertebrates (with the exception of man) has to do with different aspects of either feeding behavior or nest preparation. With rare exceptions, such as elephants' using sticks to rub themselves, the use of sticks, leaves, or other objects in self-grooming is virtually absent in animals (with the exception of the chimpanzee). Aggressive displays during which objects are handled, thrown, or manipulated in some way are observed only among monkeys, apes, and man.

One of Hall's major points is essential to the understanding of tool use by animals: an animal that uses objects as tools is not necessarily especially intelligent. In the example given earlier, a species of finch that uses a cactus spine to spear grubs otherwise out of reach is not necessarily any more intelligent than another kind of finch; it has merely evolved a behavior pattern rather than a morphological structure to increase feeding efficiency and the variety of its foods. This interpretation is of special importance to an understanding of the relationship of tools to intelligence and brain size in man's history.

It is crucial in evaluating an item as a tool to know exactly what the animal does with the object. One stricture Hall followed in his collection of examples of tool-using was to consider as data only those incidents observed under natural conditions. Anyone who has watched a monkey or ape in a zoo or circus knows that it is relatively simple to encourage several species to handle objects, and with training many can be made to perform quite complicated tasks. Equally familiar are the anecdotes and stories of tool use by animals told by travelers and natives which either they or others have observed. The fanciful and fantastic are quickly sorted from the more plausible, but sources must be reliable and the situations in which the actions occurred must be natural if adaptive actions are to be distinguished from activity produced under atypical and unnatural conditions. It is crucial to be able to make these distinctions because monkeys, and apes especially, are capable of many behaviors not representative of their normal patterns of behavior. Learning certain kinds of tasks, such as the use of objects, is easier for some types of monkeys than others, and it is almost inevitable for chimpanzees. A long list of what monkeys and apes do under all conditions shows only that some kinds of nonhuman primates can and do learn manipulative patterns easily. What such a list does not tell us is the relationship of this ability to the biology and survival of the species, except to suggest that it is doubtlessly useful.

According to Hall, observational learning among nonhuman primates is much less common than one would imagine, and, predictably, is highly variable. Whether a monkey or ape does learn by observing others perform depends to a large degree on the particular action or behavior and on the situation in which learning occurs. The normal context for observational learning, the one in which these abilities must have been organized, is the social group. This is the environment of maximum security and close association, in which individuals are surrounded by familiar animals and close emotional ties. Besides differences in habitats and social tradition, other factors are relevant to variation in the ability of primates to learn to use tools. The most important may be a basic biological limitation of the ability to learn, and this probably varies from one species to another, as suggested by the tremendous differences in abilities and tendencies to manipulate objects. As mentioned earlier, part of this variation in ability is probably an artifact of species specializations, rather than a mirror of actual differences in intelligence among different kinds of animals.

The human observer's interest and concern with his own evolution and his awareness of the way in which modern man uses tools has biased descriptions and interpretations of monkey and ape behavior that appears similar to that of man. Of all tool use investigators (for example, Kortlandt 1962; Kortlandt and Kooij 1963), Hall was the first to recognize, on the basis of the evidence available to him, that object manipulation by monkeys was limited to agonistic displays. Such displays are rare in other animals. It was only with more observations, following those that Hall knew, that we discovered additional examples of monkey tool use for getting food.

The most elaborate and frequent use of objects as tools by any nonhuman primate has been reported for the chimpanzee (Goodall 1965; Van Lawick-Goodall, personal communication). Not only do chimpanzees termite with grass stems and twigs, but they also wipe themselves with leaves, chew leaves to use as sponges, pry with sticks, throw stones; and they will undoubtedly be observed to use objects in yet other ways.

It is possible that long-term studies of chimpanzee groups living elsewhere than in the Gombe Reserve will reveal significant variations in the range of chimpanzee tool behavior. Eventually we will understand the ontogeny of these abilities. All chimpanzees may not use the same tools, or even any one type of tool in the same way, since differences in habitat could influence the choice of sticks, grasses, and other objects. Variations in chimpanzee tool-using behavior among different populations, is unknown because Van Lawick-Goodall's analysis is the only long study on habituated animals in which this kind of information could be gathered. Other chimpanzee studies are under way and will surely provide much needed comparative information (particularly the Japan Monkey Centre's research in Tanzania and Uganda; Shigeru and Toyoshima 1961, 1962; and Itani and Kawamura, personal communication).

Of the reliably described displays by chimpanzees (Goodall 1965), by gorillas (Schaller 1963, 1966), and by orangutans (Harrisson 1962), surely the most dramatic and impressive display with the use of objects is that of the chimpanzee. When the animals, especially adult males with fur erect, dash from one place to another, jumping and running, hooting and screaming, flinging branches, and even rolling huge rocks. Only slightly less impressive, at least to the observer, is the gorilla's display when the ape runs, calls, gestures, and, sometimes, pulls grass or other plants and throws them as he runs (Schaller 1963). Many species of monkeys when excited during agonistic interactions with other monkeys or toward a human will shake branches vigorously by jumping up and down on them (for example, the red spider monkey, Carpenter 1935; baboons, Hall 1962*b;* Hall and DeVore 1965; rhesus, Hinde and Rowell 1962).

There are some striking features common to these examples. In each, the animal is very effective in making itself appear as large, fierce, and noisy as possible by erecting its hair, gesturing, and calling. When the animal jumps on a branch or throws it (and in rarer instances when a stone is thrown), the display is just that much more effective and impressive to the beholder. This is especially true if the object happens to fall nearby or hits the observer, as when the missile is excrement.

In a recent field study of the South American cebus monkey in Colombia, Thorington (personal communication) watched these animals manipulate twigs by breaking them off and peeling away the bark, and then use them to pick out small insects below the bark of larger trees. Object manipulation is part of their biology and a normal part of their lives in the wild. It is not surprising that these monkeys are well known for their manipulative abilities in captivity, but it is manipulation for obtaining food and not for making or using tools agonistically as in the sense of weapons.

A most important point emerges from Hall's paper, and is touched upon by Washburn and Hamburg (this vol.). Our confusion of the nonhuman primates' object-in-display type of behavior with man's tool use in the sense of weaponry has impaired our thinking about monkey and ape tool use in general. This had to be made explicit before it was possible to analyze display behaviors and to understand their relevance to the interpretation of the evolution of human tool use.

If using objects in agonistic display is looked at as a behavioral category we may be closer to answering two questions that have been asked over and over in primate research. First, why didn't efficient and persistent tool use evolve in other primates besides man, and, second, what were the important factors in human evolution that produced man's unique complex use of tools? To humans, tool use has such tremendous advantages in enhancing life that we tend to assume it is so highly adaptive that it would have been selected for whatever and whenever it occurred.

First consider the apparent lack of tool use among living nonhuman primates. Hall recognized that most of the monkey and ape behavior that had been called tool use was either an artifact of captive conditions (where animals lived in greatly impoverished social and physical environments and then were given objects to handle), or an example drawn from natural conditions in which animals were using objects in display. Anyone who has seen a monkey or ape, and particularly a chimpanzee, use a stick or stone in display knows how much more effective the display is than when the animal does not use objects. In most nonhuman primate displays, if the object is thrown rather than merely shaken, it usually does not seem to be accurately aimed. Because the goal does not seem to be to hit the person or animal toward whom the display is directed, this strongly suggests that there has been a lack of natural selection for effective tools and skills; that is, for the ability to choose more suitable branches or for more accurate aiming. There is excellent evidence indicating a high percentage of aimed throwing among chimpanzees (Goodall 1964; Van Lawick-Goodall, personal communication), which is consistent with the chimpanzee's great adeptness in tool using in general in contrast to other nonhuman primates.

Human tools may have developed from several sources, including the use of objects in economic activities and the use of objects in display (Washburn 1965). It is easy to see that the use of objects to increase food-getting efficiency would have been strongly advantageous in the course of human evolution. Similarly, if an opponent or assailant was actually hit with a stone or stick that had been hurtled or swung in display, and this situation occurred many thousands of times over a long period of time, there would have been that many discoveries that actually hitting with an object was much more effective than mere display. It is not difficult to imagine that these might have been the routes via which man evolved efficient tool use for economic purposes and for weaponry.

Additional fossil discoveries (L.S.B. and M.D. Leakey), new methods of dating (Fleischer, Leakey, Price and Walker 1965), and results of primate field studies have changed our thinking on the evolution of man's tool use. New radiogenic dates for the duration of the Pleistocene indicate a long span of time with little change in the biology of the tool-makers. Now the estimate is of approximately two million years of tool use prior to the time when hand-axe cultures developed and *Homo erectus* was present over a large area of the Old World. This means that small-brained man used pebble tools for at least four times as many years as in all the subsequent stages during which culture developed relatively rapidly and man's present biology evolved.

There are still unanswered questions as to why more effective tool use did not develop among some monkeys and apes during the millions of years when man's precursors were developing their skills. At least one aspect of the biological basis for the evolution of skillful object use is apparent among living primates. Species that throw and handle objects in the same way do so because they are similar in the anatomical structure of the arm and trunk (Grand 1964). The actions that are easiest and most natural for men and apes are difficult or impossible for monkeys. To the apes, which walk on their knuckles, underhand grasping and throwing are easy movements—quite similar to those of walking. For a baboon or a macaque, animals that normally walk on all fours, it is very difficult and most inefficient to pick up an object by hand and throw it. To toss or throw, a quadrupedal animal places his hand with the palm down on the object, and then trys to propel it forward with the same motion he uses when he walks. This is awkward and exceedingly inefficient. However, the differences between a chimpanzee and a baboon in manipulating items by hand are functions not only of very different forelimb structure, but also of differences in the brain itself, with consequently dissimilar aptitudes or abilities to learn to manipulate objects in different ways. Some evidence suggests that specific motor patterns important in using objects as tools may be determined by the genetic heredity of a species (Schiller 1957; Chance 1960).

In summary, the outstanding difference between nonhuman and human manufacture and use of tools is *skill* (Oakley 1954), and the biology that makes skill possible. Many primates use tools, usually in the context of feeding, whereas only a few species use tools or objects in agonistic displays and these are limited almost exclusively to apes and men. Tool use per se does not indicate intelligence, as evidenced by man's history when for a long time his ancestors had small brains and yet used tools as part of their way of life. It was not until late in the Pleistocene that there were large-brained hominids and complex tool traditions, and it was at this time that the transition to skillful use of tools occurred.

If Lancaster (this vol.) and Geschwind (1964) are correct in their estimates of the amount of brain necessary for language, the use of tools long preceded the emergence of human language. Among the other questions that may be raised relating to populations of early Pleistocene hominids (the *Australopithecus,* in a general sense) and the tools that have been found with them is that perhaps not all fossil populations of early man used tools in the same manner or abundance and maybe not all populations had tools. Variability in early hominid patterns of culture has not been determined. Comparative information is lacking, but it is possible that there are substantial differences in the use of tools by modern chimpanzee populations.

The incomplete fossil record has given rise to many controversies as to the taxonomic position and importance of certain isolated fossils from early stages of man's development. The discovery of fragments from the Miocene (Leakey 1967), again emphasizes the question of when tools became associated with man's ancestors. The frustration of having only vague notions of the relationships of different major fossil forms is increased by the dearth of finds in the same locations. Awareness of the dimensions of the range of morphological and behavioral differences among and within species of living primates should help in the assessment of the taxonomic status of certain fossils in the human record. More information on closely related species and subspecies living together in the same or adjacent areas, and on their relationships may suggest adaptations of populations in the past.

Washburn and Hamburg (this vol.) have discussed some of the implications of tool development on changing selection pressures—for increase in some parts of the brain, decrease in the tooth-fighting complex, and likely new patterns of behavior. With the origin of human language there was probably a reduction in aggressive behavior and displays in general, as complex and especially long-distance signals were developed. After initial behavioral changes, the biological basis and physical structures of early hominids must have changed, or the social and behavioral aspects of these changes would not have continued. Indeed, it is artificial to separate the interaction of structure and behavior through a long and complicated history of development.

In contrast to our interest in tool use, the importance of some other categories of behavior is not always apparent, particularly those activities not considered especially significant in human life. Willingness to recognize important categories of behavior different from those that have concerned traditional anthropology should stimulate innovation in the analysis of human behavior. Appreciating the significance of an activity to monkeys and apes should enable a more accurate assessment of its possible importance to man, and although present ideas of human categories of activity will not be replaced, certain behaviors will be given greater emphasis.

It is not difficult to recognize general categories of behavior for a species of nonhuman primate, even after a relatively short period of observation if the observer is familiar with the behavior of related species. With longer study the list of categories increases in length, and, presumably, in accuracy. The rhesus monkey (*Macaca mulatta*) is one example of a species that has been studied under a variety of conditions, free-ranging and captive, and for which there are relatively complete inventories of behavioral repertoire (Hinde and Rowell 1962; Rowell and Hinde 1962; and Altmann 1962a). The pig-tail monkey *(M. nemestrina)* and bonnet macaques *(M. radiata)* have been described by Kaufman and Rosenblum (1966). It is one thing to recognize and describe units of behavior, but quite another to estimate their importance. Until behaviors are observed in a natural situation it is not always clear just what problems most warrant investigation. Field studies offer the great advantages of opportunities to discern relationships of biology to social behavior and to see the meaning of the interrelationship of description and experiment.

Play is one of the most important activities of young primates; it is an activity that is easily recognized, but it has received less than due attention. The significance of play among humans has been overlooked, although it must be a category of overwhelming importance in the behavior of our young. The age-graded behaviors of nonhuman primates develop in a maturational sequence that appears to be adjusted to the particular species. This sequence of events is an obvious part of the process of acquiring adaptation or organization of behavior in the life span of the individual. The importance to the individual of a peer group continues into adult life when patterns of social dominance established years earlier may influence his eventual status and status changes. Play as motivation for learning has yet to be investigated systematically, but field studies leave no doubt that this will be very fruitful.

The size of play groups varies among species according to total group size. In those species in which the social group consists of only a pair of adults, as among the gibbons and *Callicebus,* the young peer group is almost, if not completely, nonexistent. In contrast, in the macaque group, which is usually much larger, there are at least several young born each year and group play is almost assured for each individual.

The play behavior of chimpanzee and man is remarkably more complex than that of monkey, with man being the most manipulative and object oriented of all primates in his play. Surely it is more than a coincidence that the nonhuman primate taxonomically closest to man according to many investigators (Goodman 1963; Klinger *et al.* 1963; Sarich and Wilson 1966; Simpson 1966) is also the most manipulative, exploratory, and similar to man in play. The range of variation in play form and games among chimpanzees is second only to man.

Diversity of object use by adults could be predicted by watching the play and investigation of young chimpanzees. Object manipulation is an important part of investigating the environment, and sticks and twigs are frequently used to poke and pry, long before any ability to termite appears. That an animal practices in play the skills and activities he needs when grown is of tremendous evolutionary importance. Infant and juvenile stages of development last much longer in the chimpanzee than similar phases do in monkeys, and it is reasonable to suppose that the chimpanzee has correspondingly more to learn. This supposition is supported by the richness of adult chimpanzee social behavior when compared with that of any monkey, and, for that matter, to that of the other apes, although a great deal more is known about several species of monkeys than about any ape other than the chimpanzee.

Comparison of chimpanzee and baboon play would be very revealing, especially comparison of the amount and kinds of attention paid to manipulatable items of the environment. Most, if not all, young primates spend a great deal of time playing, and a comparative study of the patterns and duration of play should be highly correlated with adult behaviors. Infancy is the period during which a young animal can "afford" to make mistakes because he is tolerated to an extent that he never again enjoys. He is protected by his elders and led by the group, and during those early weeks or months his life is sheltered by generally permissive adults. This is a crucial period for the development of social skills, and laboratory experiment has demonstrated that if certain experiences are not part of the animal's early life, the damage may be irreparable or very difficult to correct later in life (Harlow 1962; Harlow and Harlow 1962; Mason 1961*a*, 1961*b*, 1961*c*, 1963; Mason and Green 1962).

When contrasted with chimpanzee play, in which object manipulation is a major feature, monkey play involves predominantly locomotor patterns such as wrestling and chasing with other young. The infant is soon adept at moving quickly and accurately, responding to the cues of adults and especially to those cues that signal threat or danger. Little, if any, attention is directed to play with objects or to manipulation of many items in the environment. Elements of adult gesture and vocalization appear gradually in the repertoire of the infant and juvenile, and with practice they are displayed appropriately and skillfully.

The monkey or ape appears free to experiment and express itself in many ways during play, and, with the exception of preventing the young from disturbing the peace and repose of the adults, and protecting them from harm by predators or other stronger young, the adult nonhuman primate appears to allow the young free rein. Play is of such great importance to the development of monkeys and apes that it is necessary to ask how appropriate it is for us to shape and control the play activities of our young.

CONCLUSION

The analysis of modern monkey and ape behavior has made it possible to reconstruct some of the early stages of human development. The later phases of man's development may require a different approach. Several authors have assumed that social evolution has progressed too rapidly in recent time for biological evolution to keep pace (Hamburg 1963; Washburn and Hamburg, this vol.). If this is true, the phases of man's nature that seem unadaptive today should give us clues to the social systems of times past.

Our ancestors lived in small hunting and gathering societies for many thousands of generations, and the risks and problems of survival must have been quite different from those that confront us today. The life span was much shorter and conditions of survival were more critical and challenging than they are now. It was under those early conditions of life that human nature evolved to meet the rigorous physical demands of daily existence. Patterns of behavior were fitted to these circumstances, and not to the conditions of the crowded, technical society that we live in today.

Man has evolved to think in terms of short intervals of time, short distances, and very small numbers of people. At earlier stages the individual had relatively few social and emotional bonds in comparison with the extent of commitment to others that society attempts to create in us today. It will help if there is an understanding of our apparent lack of concern with the problems of today's world, and our great lack of capacity to be moved by events and conditions that are a long distance away, that happened in the past, or that lie years in the future. This obviously has created and perpetuates problems of relationships in a world where most populations are potentially interacting, in which great distances are traveled quickly and frequently, and in which technology is capable of effecting drastic and irreversible change. The face-to-face group is becoming a large portion of the world as transportation and communication improve, and thus reduce distances. Lack of concern with other peoples may prove to be a lethal deficiency, but to interpret our behavior it is necessary to be aware of its probable evolutionary background. Our deep-rooted preoccupation with the *now* may help us to understand our heedless destruction of natural resources, the pollution of air, and the apparent difficulty of combining ecological and esthetic senses in our pursuit of an expanding technology and ecology. Profound changes in our lives and surroundings have been, for the first time perhaps, rapid enough for one generation to be aware of them. In efforts to increase communication and concern among peoples of widely distant lands, and in attempts to control the potentially destructive tendencies of modern man we must recognize his biological and social heritage that disposes him to be concerned with relatively few people and to be aggressive. With this knowledge we can be more realistic in our efforts to live together in peace.

In summary, the theory of natural selection requires that evolution be understood in terms of successful behaviors. Since behavior does not fossilize, human evolution can best be appreciated through imaginative reconstruction of the long sequence of behavior patterns that separates man from his ape ancestors. To reconstruct patterns of the past requires both a fossil record and field studies of contemporary primates. Since man differs from all living monkeys and apes in many ways, these studies provide the basis not only for reconstructing changes that have taken place in the evolution of modern ways of behavior, but also for an understanding of the apparent exceptions to the general patterns for primates.

This chapter has had to remain tentative and suggestive. It will be some time before we can write with authority on the details of the development of man's behavior, but that time will arrive sooner if we appreciate fully the usefulness of nonhuman primate behavior in gaining insight into our present lives.

BIBLIOGRAPHY

Allee, W. C., A. E. Emerson, O. Park, and K. P. Schmidt, 1949, *Principles of Animal Ecology*. Philadelphia: W. B. Saunders Company.

Altman, J., 1966, *Organic Foundations of Animal Behavior*. New York: Holt, Rinehart and Winston, Inc.

Altmann, S. A., 1959, "Field Observations on a Howling Monkey Society," *J. Mammal.*, 40:317–330.

———, 1962a, "A Field Study of the Sociobiology of Rhesus Monkeys, *Macaca mulatta*," *Ann. N.Y. Acad. Sci.*, 102 (2):338–435.

———, 1962b, "The Social Behavior of Anthropoid Primates: An Analysis of Some Recent Concepts," *The Roots Of Behavior*, E. L. Bliss, ed. New York: Harper and Row, pp. 277–285.

———, 1965, "Sociobiology of Rhesus Monkeys. II. Stochastics of Social Communication," *J. Theoret. Biol.*, 8:490–522.

———, 1967, "The Structure of Primate Social Communication," *Social Communication among Primates*, S. A. Altmann, ed. Chicago: University of Chicago Press, pp. 325–362.

Andrew, R. J., 1962, "The Situations that Evoke Vocalization in Primates," *Ann. N.Y. Acad. Sci.*, 102:296–315.

———, 1963a, "Evolution of Facial Expression," *Science*, 142:1034–1041.

———, 1963b, "The Origin and Evolution of the Calls and Facial Expressions of the Primates," *Behaviour*, 20:1–109.

———, 1963c, "Trends Apparent in the Evolution of Vocalization in the Old World Monkeys and Apes," *Symp. Zool. Soc. London*, 10:89–101.

———, 1964, "The Displays of Primates," *Evolutionary and Genetic Biology of Primates*, Vol. II, J. Buettner-Janusch, ed. New York: Academic Press, pp. 227–309.

Asami, C., 1964, "Comparative Psychology of Personality, (1): Behavioral Development of Japanese Monkey Infants," *Jinbun-Kagaku-Kiyo*, 17.

Azrin, N. H., R. R. Hutchinson, and D. F. Hake, 1963, "Pain-induced Fighting in the Squirrel Monkey," *J. Exp. Anal. Behav.*, 6:620.

———, ———, and R. McLaughlin, 1965, "The Opportunity for Aggression as an Operant Reinforcer during Aversive Stimulation," *J. Exp. Anal. Behav.*, 8:171–180.

Baerands, G. P., 1958, "Comparative Methods and the Concept of Homology in the Study of Behaviour," *Arch. Neerl. Zool.*, 13:401–417.

Ball, J., and C. G. Hartman, 1935, "Sexual Excitability as Related to the Menstrual Cycle in the Monkey," *Amer. J. Obstet. and Gynecol.*, 29:117–119.

Bandura, A., and R. H. Walters, 1963, *Social Learning and Personality Development*. New York: Holt, Rinehart and Winston, Inc.

Bastian, J. R., 1965, "Primate Signaling Systems and Human Languages," *Primate Behavior: Field Studies of Monkeys and Apes,* I. DeVore, ed. New York: Holt, Rinehart and Winston, Inc., pp. 585–606.

Beach, F. A., 1947, "Evolutionary Changes in the Physiological Control of Mating Behavior in Mammals," *Psychol. Rev.,* 54:297–315.

―――, 1960, "Experimental Investigations of Species-specific Behavior," *Amer. Psychol.* 15:1–18.

―――, 1965a, "Biological Bases for Reproductive Behavior," *Social Behavior and Organization Among Vertebrates,* W. Etkin, ed. Chicago: University of Chicago Press, pp. 117–142.

―――, 1965b, *Sex and Behavior.* New York: Wiley.

Bellugi, U., and R. Brown, eds., 1964, "The Acquisition of Language," *Monogr. Soc. Res. Child Devel.,* 29.

Berkson, G., W. A. Mason, and S. V. Saxon, 1963, "Situations and Stimulus Effects on Stereotyped Behaviors of Chimpanzees," *J. Comp. Physiol. Psychol.,* 56(4):786–792.

Berlyne, D. E., 1960, *Conflict, Arousal, and Curiosity.* New York: McGraw-Hill.

Bernstein, I. S., 1963, "Social Activities Related to Rhesus Monkey Consort Behavior," *Psychol. Rep.,* 13:375–379.

――― 1964a, "A Field Study of the Activities of Howler Monkeys," *Anim. Behav.,* 12:92–97.

―――, 1964b, "Group Social Patterns as Influenced by Removal and Later Reintroduction of the Dominant Male Rhesus," *Psychol. Rep.,* 14:3–10.

―――, 1964c, "The Role of the Dominant Male Rhesus Monkey in Response to External Challenges to the Group," *J. Comp. Physiol. Psychol.,* 57:404–406.

―――, and W. A. Mason, 1962, "The Effects of Age and Stimulus Conditions on the Emotional Responses of Rhesus Monkeys: Responses to Complex Stimuli," *J. Genet. Psychol.,* 101:279–298.

Bishop, W. W., and M. Posnansky, 1960, "Pleistocene Environments and Early Man in Uganda," *Uganda J.,* 24:44–61.

Bolwig, N., 1964, "Facial Expression in Primates with Remarks on a Parallel Development in Certain Carnivores," *Behaviour,* 22:167–193.

Bonin, G. von, and P. Bailey, 1961, "Pattern of the Cerebral Isocortex," *Primatologia* II (2):1–42.

Brain, C. K., 1958, "The Transvaal Ape-Man-Bearing Cave Deposits," *Tvl. Mus. Mem.,* 11:1–131.

――― (in press), "Observations on the Behaviour of Vervet Monkeys, *Cercopithecus aethiops,*" *Proc. Zool. Soc. S. Africa Symp. on African Mammals.*

Braine, M. D. S., 1963, "The Ontogeny of English Phrase Structure: The First Phase," *Language,* 39:1–13.

Brown, J. L., and R. W. Hunsperger, 1965, "Neuroethology and the Motivation of Agonistic Behavior," *Readings in Animal Behavior,* T. E. McGill, ed. New York: Holt, Rinehart and Winston, Inc., pp. 148–161.

Brown, R., and U. Bellugi, 1964, "Three Processes in the Child's Acquisition of Syntax," *New Directions in the Study of Language,* E. H. Lenneberg, ed. Cambridge, Mass.: M. I. T Press., pp. 131–162.

————, and C. Fraser, 1964, "The Acquisition of Syntax," *Monogr. Soc. Res. Child Devel.,* 29:43–79.

Burt, W. H., 1940, "Territorial Behavior and Populations of Some Small Mammals in Southern Michigan," *Mus. Zool. Univ. Mich., Misc. Pub.,* 45:1–58.

————, 1943, "Territoriality and Home Range Concepts as Applied to Mammals," *J. Mammal.,* 24:346–352.

Butler, R. A., 1961, "The Responsiveness of Rhesus Monkeys to Motion Pictures," *J. Genet. Psychol.,* 98:239–245.

Carpenter, C. R., 1934, "A Field Study of the Behavior and Social Relations of Howling Monkeys *(Alouatta palliata),*" *Comp. Psychol. Monogr.,* 10(2):1–168.

————, 1935, "Behavior of Red Spider Monkeys in Panama," *J. Mammal.,* 16:171–180.

————, 1940, "A Field Study in Siam of the Behavior and Social Relations of the Gibbon *(Hylobates lar),*" *Comp. Psychol. Monogr.,* 16(5):1–212.

————, 1942a, "Sexual Behavior of Free-ranging Rhesus Monkeys *(Macaca mulatta).* I. Specimens, Procedures and Behavioral Characteristics of Estrus," *J. Comp. Psychol.,* 33:113–142.

————, 1942b, "Societies of Monkeys and Apes," *Biol. Symp.,* 8:177–204.

————, 1950, "General Plans and Methodology for Field Studies of the Naturalistic Behavior of Animals," *Ann. N. Y. Acad. Sci.,* 51:1006–1008.

————, 1952, "Social Behavior of Nonhuman Primates," *Colloq. Int. Cent. Nat. Rech. Sci. (Paris),* 34:227–246.

————, 1954, "Tentative Generalizations on the Grouping Behavior of Nonhuman Primates," *Human Biol.,* 26:269–276.

————, 1958, "Territoriality: A Review of Concepts and Problems," *Behavior and Evolution,* A. Roe and G. G. Simpson, eds. New Haven: Yale University Press, pp. 224–250.

————, 1964, *Naturalistic Behavior of Nonhuman Primates.* University Park, Pa.: Pennsylvania State University Press.

————, 1965, "The Howlers of Barro Colorado Island," *Primate Behavior: Field Studies Of Monkeys and Apes,* I. DeVore, ed. New York: Holt, Rinehart and Winston, Inc., pp. 250–291.

Carthy, J. D., and F. J. Ebling, eds., 1964, *The Natural History of Aggression.* New York: Academic Press.

Chance, M. R. A., 1956, "Social Structure at a Colony of *Macaca mulatta,*" *Brit. J. Anim. Behav.,* 4:1–13.

————, 1960, "Köhler's Chimpanzees—How Did They Perform?" *Man,* 60:130–135.

————, and A. P. Mead, 1953, "Social Behavior and Primate Evolution," *Symp. Soc. Exp. Biol.,* 7:395–439.

Clark P. J., and F. C. Evans, 1954, "Distance to Nearest Neighbor as a Measure of Spatial Relationships in Populations," *Ecology,* 34(4):445–453.

Collies, N. E., 1944, "Aggressive Behavior among Vertebrate Animals," *Physio. Zool.,* 17:83–123.

————, 1960, "An Ecological and Functional Classification of Animal Sounds," *Animal Sounds and Communication,* W. E. L. Lanyon and W. N. Tavolga, eds. Washington, D. C.: American Inst. of Bio. Sciences, pp. 368–391.

————, and C. H. Southwick, 1952, "A Field Study of Population Density and Social Organization in Howling Monkeys," *Proc. Amer. Phil. Soc.,* 96:143–156.

Corner, G. W., 1942, *The Hormones in Human Reproduction.* Princeton, N. J.: Princeton University Press.

Crawford, M. P., 1937, "The Cooperative Solving of Problems by Young Chimpanzees," *Comp. Psychol. Monogr.,* 14(2):1–88.

Crook, J. H., 1966, "Gelada Baboon Herd Structure and Movement: A Comparative Report, *Symp. Zool. Soc. London,* 18:237–258.

————, and J. S. Gartlan, 1966, "The Evolution of Primate Societies," *Nature* (London) 210:1200–1203.

Crosby, E. C., T. Humphrey, and K. W. Lauer, 1962, *Correlative Anatomy of the Nervous System.* New York: Macmillan.

Dandelot, P., 1959, "Note sur la Classification des Cercopithèques du Groupe *aethiops,*" *Mammalia,* 23:357–368.

————, Delgado, J. M. R., 1963, "Cerebral Heterostimulation in a Monkey Colony," *Science,* 141:161–163.

————, 1965, "Cerebral Heterostimulation in a Monkey Colony," *Readings in Animal Behavior,* T. E. McGill, ed. New York: Holt, Rinehart and Winston, Inc., pp. 161–165.

Delgado, J. M. R., 1963, "Cerebral Heterostimulation in a Monkey Colony," *Science,* 141:161–163.

de Reuck, A., and J. Knight, eds., 1966, *Conflict in Society.* Boston: Little, Brown.

DeVore, I., 1962, "The Social Behavior and Organization of Baboon Troops," unpublished Ph.D. thesis, University of Chicago.

————, 1963a, "Comparative Ecology and Behavior of Monkeys and Apes," *Classification and Human Evolution,* S. L. Washburn, ed. Viking Fund Pub. No. 37, New York: Wenner-Gren Foundation, pp. 301–319.

————, 1963b, "Mother–Infant Relations in Free-ranging Baboons," *Maternal Behavior in Mammals,* H. Rheingold, ed. New York: Wiley, pp. 305–335.

————, ed, 1965, *Primate Behavior: Field Studies of Monkeys and Apes.* New York: Holt, Rinehart and Winston, Inc.

————, and K. R. L. Hall, 1965, "Baboon Ecology," *Primate Behavior: Field Studies of Monkeys and Apes,* I. DeVore, ed. New York: Holt, Rinehart and Winston, Inc., pp. 20–52.

————, and S. L. Washburn, 1963, "Baboon Ecology and Human Evolution," *African Ecology and Human Evolution,* F. C. Howell, and F. Bourlière, eds. New York: Viking Fund Publication No. 36, pp. 335–367.

Eibl-Eibesfeldt, I, 1951, "Nahrungserwerk und Beuteschema der Erdkröte *(Bufo bufo L.),*" *Behaviour,* 4:1–35.

————, 1963, "Angehorenes und Erworbenes im Verhalten einiger Sauger," *Zeits. f. Tierpsychol.,* 20:705–754.

————, 1966, "Ethologie, die Biologie des Verhaltens," *Handbk. d. Biologie* 6, F. Gessner, ed. Frankfurt: Akad. Verlagsges.

Emlen, J. T., 1962, "The Display of the Gorilla." *Proc. Amer. Phil. Soc.,* 106:516–619.

Etkin, W., 1964, "Theories of Socialization and Communication," *Social Behavior and Organization among Vertebrates,* W. Etkin, ed. Chicago: University of Chicago Press, pp. 167–205.

Ettlinger, G., 1960, "Cross-modal Transfer of Training in Monkeys," *Behaviour,* 16:56–64.

Falk, J. L., 1958, "The Grooming Behavior of the Chimpanzee as a Reinforcer, *J. Exp. Anal. Behav.,* 1:83–85.

Flechsig, P., 1901, "Developmental (Melogenetic) Localisation of the Cerebral Cortex in the Human Subject," *Lancet,* 2:1027–1029.

————, 1920, *Anatomie des Menschlichen Gehirns und Rückenmarks auf Myelogenetischer Grundlage.* Leipsig:Thieme.

————, 1927, *Meine Myelogenetische Hirnlehre.* Berlin:Springer.

Fleischer, R. L., L. S. B. Leakey, P. B. Price, and R. M. Walker, 1965, "Fission Track Dating of Bed I, Olduvai Gorge," *Science,* 148:72–74.

Fletcher, J. J., and J. Emlen, 1964, "A Comparison of the Responses to Snakes of Lab- and Wild-Reared Rhesus Monkeys," *Anim. Behav.,* 12:348–352.

Ford, E. B., 1940, "Genetic Research in the Lepidoptera," *Ann. Eug.,* 10:227–252.

Frank, L. K., 1958, "Tactile Communication," ETC: A Review of General Semantics, San Francisco: Autumn.

Freedman, D. G., 1964, "Smiling in Blind Infants and the Issue of Innate versus Acquired," *J. Child Psychol. Psychiat.,* 5:171–184.

Freedman, L., 1957, "The Fossil Cercopithecoidea of South Africa," *Ann. Tvl. Mus.* 23(2):121–262.

Freedman, L. Z., and H. E. Rosvold, 1962, "Sexual, Aggressive and Anxious Behavior in the Laboratory Macaque," *J. Nerv. Ment. Disease,* 134:18–27.

Freeman, D., 1964, "Human Aggression in Anthropological Perspective," *The Natural History of Aggression,* J. D. Carthy and F. J. Ebling, eds. New York: Academic Press, pp. 109–119.

Frisch, J., 1959, "Research on Primate Behavior in Japan," *Amer. Anthrop.,* 61:584–596.

————, 1963a, "Japan's Contribution to Modern Anthropology," *Studies in Japanese Culture,* J. Roggendorf, ed. Tokyo: Sophia University, pp. 225–244.

————, 1963b, "Sex Differences in the Canines of the Gibbon, *(Hylobates lar),*" *Primates,* 4:1–10.

Furuya, Y., 1965, "Grooming Behavior in Wild Japanese Monkeys," *Japanese Monkeys,* K. Imanishi and S. A. Altmann, eds. Edmonton: University of Alberta Press, pp. 1–29.

————, (ms. no date), "Some Aspects of Behaviour and Ecology in Monkeys of the Group *Cercopithecus aethiops.*"

Geschwind, N., 1964, "The Development of the Brain and the Evolution of Language," *Monogr. Ser. on Language and Linguistics,* 17:155–169.

————, 1965, "Disconnection Syndromes in Animals and Man," *Brain,* 88:237–294, 585–644.

Goodall, J., 1962, "Nest Building Behavior in the Free-ranging Chimpanzee," *Ann. N. Y. Acad. Sci.,* 102:455–467.

————, 1963, "Feeding Behaviour of Wild Chimpanzees: A Preliminary Report," *Symp. Zool. Soc. London,* 10:39–47.

————, 1964, Tool-using and Aimed Throwing in a Community of Free-living Chimpanzees," *Nature,* 201:1264–1266.

————, 1965, "Chimpanzees of the Gombe Stream Reserve," *Primate Behavior: Field Studies of Monkeys and Apes,* I. DeVore, ed. New York: Holt, Rinehart and Winston, Inc., pp. 425–473.

Goodenough, F. L., 1932, "Expression of the Emotions in a Blind–Deaf Child," *J. Abnorm. Soc. Psychol.,* 27:328–333.

Goodman, M., 1963, "Serological Analysis of the Phyletic Relationships of Recent Hominoids," *Human Biology,* 35:377–436.

Goustard, M., 1963, "Introduction a l'étude de la Communication Vocale chez *Macaca irus," Ann. Sci. Nat. Zool. et Biol. Anim.,* 12ᵉ, Serie, Tome 5, Fasc. 4.

Grand, T. I., 1964, "The Functional Anatomy of the Shoulder of the Chimpanzee," unpublished Ph.D. thesis, University of California.

Haddow, A. J., 1952, "Field and Laboratory Studies on an African Monkey, *Cercopithecus ascanius schmidti* Matchie," *Proc. Zool. Soc. London,* 122:297–394.

——, 1956, "The Blue Monkey Group in Uganda," *Uganda Wild Life and Sport,* 1:22–26.

Haldane, J. B. S., 1954, "La Signalisation Animale," *Ann. Biol.,* 30:89–98.

Hall, K. R. L., 1962(*a*), "Numerical Data, Maintenance Activities, and Locomotion of the Wild Chacma Baboon, *Papio ursinus," Proc. Zool. Soc. London,* 139:181–220.

——, 1962*b*, "The Sexual, Agonistic, and Derived Social Behaviour Patterns of the Wild Chacma Baboon, *Papio ursinus," Proc. Zool. Soc. London,* 139:283–327.

——, 1963*a*, "Observational Learning in Monkeys and Apes," *Brit. J. Psychol.,* 54:201–226.

——, 1963*b*, "Some Problems in the Analysis and Comparison of Monkey and Ape Behavior," *Classification and Human Evolution,* S. L. Washburn, ed. Viking Fund Pub. No. 37, New York: Wenner-Gren Foundation, pp. 273–300.

——, 1963*c*, "Variations in the Ecology of the Chacma Baboon, *Papio ursinus," Symp. Zool. Soc. London,* 10:1–28.

——, 1964, "Aggression in Monkey and Ape Societies," *The Natural History of Aggression,* J. D. Carthy and F. J. Ebling, eds. New York: Academic Press, pp. 51–64.

——,1965*a*, "Behaviour and Ecology of the Wild Patas Monkeys, *Erythrocebus patas,* in Uganda," *J. Zool. Soc. London,* 148:15–87.

——, 1965*b*, "Experiment and Quantification in the Study of Baboon Behavior in its Natural Habitat," *The Baboon in Medical Research,* H. Vagtborg, ed. Austin: University of Texas Press, pp. 29–42.

——, 1965*c*, "Social Organisation of the Old World Monkeys and Apes," *Symp. Zool. Soc. London,* 14:265–289.

——, R. C. Boelkins, and M. J. Goswell, 1965, "Behaviour of Patas Monkeys, *Erythrocebus patas,* in Captivity, with Notes on the Natural Habitat," *Folia Primat.,* 3:22–49.

——, and I. DeVore, 1965, "Baboon Social Behavior," *Primate Behavior: Field Studies of Monkeys and Apes,* I. DeVore, ed. New York: Holt, Rinehart and Winston, Inc., pp. 53–110.

——, and J. S. Gartlan, 1965, "Ecology and Behaviour of the Vervet Monkey, *Cercopithecus aethiops,* Lolui Island, Lake Victoria," *Proc. Zool. Soc. London,* 145:37–56.

——, and M. J. Goswell, 1964, "Aspects of Social Learning in Captive Patas Monkeys," *Primates,* 5(3-4):59–70.

——, and B. Mayer, 1967, "Social Interactions in a Group of Captive Patas Monkeys (*Erythrocebus patas*)," *Folia Primat.,* 5:213–236.

Hamburg, D. A., 1963, "Emotion in the Perspective of Human Evolution," *Expression of the Emotions in Man,* P. Knapp, ed. New York: International Universities, pp. 300–317.

Hansen, E. W., 1962, "The Development of Maternal and Infant Behavior in the Rhesus Monkey," unpublished Ph.D. thesis, University of Wisconsin.

———, and W. A. Mason, 1962, "Socially Mediated Changes in Lever-responding of Rhesus Monkeys," *Psychol. Rep.,* 11:647–654.

Harlow, H. F., 1948, "Studying Animal Behavior," *Methods of Psychology,* T. Andrews, ed. New York: Wiley, pp. 319–347.

———, 1959, "Basic Social Capacity of Primates," *The Evolution of Man's Capacity for Culture,* J. N. Spuhler, ed. Detroit: Wayne State University Press, pp. 40–52.

———, 1960, "Primary Affectional Patterns in Primates," *Amer. J. Ortho-Psychiat.,* 30:676–684.

———, 1962, "The Development of Affectional Patterns in Infant Monkeys," *Determinants of Infant Behavior,* B. M. Foss, ed. New York: Wiley, pp. 75–97.

———, and M. K. Harlow, 1962, "Social Deprivation in Monkeys," *Sci Amer.,* 207:137–146.

———, and ———, 1965, "The Affectional Systems," *Behavior of Nonhuman Primates,* Vol. II, A. M. Schrier, H. F. Harlow, and F. Stollnitz, eds. New York: Academic Press, pp. 287–334.

———, and R. R. Zimmerman, 1958, "The Development of Affectional Responses in Infant Monkeys," *Proc. Amer. Phil. Soc.,* 5:501–509.

Harris, G., 1964, "Sex Hormones, Brain Development and Brain Function," *Endocrin.,* 75:627–648.

Harrison, J. L., 1955, "Apes and Monkeys of Malaya (Including the Slow Loris)," *Malayan Mus. Pam.,* 9.

Harrisson, B., 1962, *Orangutan,* London: Collins.

Hazama, N., 1964, "Weighing Wild Japanese Monkeys in Arashiyama," *Primates,* 5(3-4):81–104.

Hediger, H., 1964, *Wild Animals in Captivity.* New York: Dover.

Heinroth, O., 1911, "Beiträge zur Biologie, Namentlich Ethologie und Psychologie der Anaiden," *Inst. Ornith. Kongr., Berlin,* 5:589–702.

Hershkovitz, P., 1963, "A Systematic and Zoogeographic Account of the Monkeys of the Genus *Callicebus* (Cebidae) of the Amazonas and Orinoco River Basins," *Mammalia,* 27:1–79.

Hess, E. H., 1959, "Imprinting. An Effect of Early Experience," *Science,* 130:133–141.

Hinde, R. A., and T. E. Rowell, 1962, "Communication by Postures and Facial Expressions in the Rhesus Monkey (*Macaca mulatta*)," *Proc. Zool. Soc. London,* 138:1–21.

Hinde, R. A., and N. Tinbergen, 1958, "The Comparative Study of Species-Specific Behavior," *Behavior and Evolution,* A. Roe and G. G. Simpson, eds. New Haven: Yale University Press, pp. 251–268.

Hingston, R. W. G., 1920, *A Naturalist in Himalaya.* London: Witherby.

Hockett, C. F., 1960, "Logical Considerations in the Study of Animal Communication," *Animal Sounds and Communication,* W. E. Lanyon and W. N. Tavolga, eds. Washington, D.C.: Amer. Inst. Biol. Sci., pp. 392–430.

———, and R. Ascher, 1964, "The Human Revolution," *Cur. Anthro.,* 5:135–147.

Hückstedt, B., 1965, "Experimentelle Untersuchungen zum 'Kindehenschema'," *Z. exp. u. angen. Psychol.,* 12:421–450.

Hutchinson, G. E., 1953, "The Concept of Pattern in Ecology," *Proc. Nat. Acad. Sci.,* 105:1–12.

Imanishi, K., 1957, "Social Behavior in Japanese Monkeys, *Macaca fuscata,*" *Psychologia,* 1:47–54.

———, 1960, "Social Organization of Subhuman Primates in Their Natural Habitat," *Cur. Anthro.,* 1:393–407.

Itani, J., 1958, "On the Acquisition and Propagation of a New Food Habit in the Troop of Japanese Monkeys at Takasakiyama," *Primates,* 1(2):84–98.

———, 1959, "Paternal Care in the Wild Japanese Monkey, *Macaca fuscata fuscata,*" *Primates,* 2:61–93.

———, 1963, "Vocal Communication of the Wild Japanese Monkey," *Primates,* 4(2):11–66.

———, 1965, "On the acquisition and Propagation of a New Food Habit in the Troop of Japanese Monkeys at Takasakiyama," *Japanese Monkeys,* K. Imanishi and S. A. Altmann, eds. Edmonton: University of Alberta Press, pp. 52–65.

———, K. Tokuda, Y. Furuya, K. Kano, and Y. Shin, 1963, "The Social Construction of Natural Troops of Japanese Monkeys in Takasakiyama," *Primates,* 4(3):1–42.

Jackson, G., and J. S. Gartlan, 1965, "The Flora and Fauna of Lolui Island, Lake Victoria, Uganda," *J. Ecology,* 53(3):573–598.

Jay, P., 1962, "Aspects of Maternal Behavior Among Langurs," *Ann. N.Y. Acad. Sci.,* 102:468–476.

———, 1963a, "Mother–Infant Relations in Langurs," *Maternal Behavior in Mammals,* H. Rheingold, ed. New York: Wiley, pp. 282–304.

———, 1963b, "The Indian Langur Monkey (*Presbytis entellus*)," *Primate Social Behavior,* C. H. Southwick, ed. Princeton, N.J.: Van Nostrand, pp. 114–123.

———, 1965a, "Field Studies," *Behavior of Nonhuman Primates,* A. M. Schrier, H. F. Harlow, and F. Stollnitz, eds. New York: Academic Press, pp. 525–591.

———, 1965b, "The Common Langur of North India," *Primate Behavior: Field Studies of Monkeys and Apes,* I. DeVore, ed. New York: Holt, Rinehart and Winston, Inc., pp. 197–249.

Jolly, C. J., 1963, "A Suggested Case of Evolution by Sexual Selection in Primates," *Man,* 63:177–178.

———, 1964, *The Origins and Specializations of the Long-faced Cercopithecoidea,* unpublished Ph.D. thesis, University of London.

Kaufman, I. C., and L. A. Rosenblum, 1966, "A Behavioral Taxonomy for *Macaca nemestrina* and *Macaca radiata:* Based on Longitudinal Observation of Family Groups in the Laboratory," *Primates,* 7(2):205–258.

Kaufmann, J. H., 1962, "Ecology and Social Behavior of the Coati, *Nasua narica,* on Barro Colorado Island, Panama," *Univ. Calif. Pub. Zool.,* 60(3):95–222.

———, 1965, "A Three-year Study of Mating Behavior in a Free-ranging Band of Rhesus Monkeys," *Ecology,* 46:500–512.

———, 1966, "Behavior of Infant Rhesus Monkeys and Their Mothers in a Free-ranging Band," *Zoologica,* 51(1):17–28.

Kawai, M., 1958, "On the Rank System in a Natural Group of Japanese Monkeys," *Primates,* 1(2):84–98.

————, 1960, "A Field Experiment on the Process of Group Formation in the Japanese Monkey (*Macaca fuscata*), and the Releasing of the group at Ohirayama," *Primates,* 2(2):181–255.

————, 1964, *The Ecology of Japanese Monkeys.* Tokyo: Kawade-Shoko.

————, 1965, "Newly-Acquired Precultural Behavior of the Natural Troops of Japanese Monkeys on Koshima Islet," Primates, 6(1):1–30.

Kawamura, S., 1959, "The Process of Subculture Propagation among Japanese Macaques," *Primates,* 2(1):43–60.

————, 1965, "Subculture among Japanese Macaques," *Monkeys and Apes,* S. Kawamura and J. Itani, eds. Tokyo: Chuohoron-sha, pp. 239–292.

Kettlewell, H. B. D., 1957, "The Contribution of Industrial Melanism in the Lepidoptera to Our Knowledge of Evolution," *Brit. Assoc. Adv. Sci.,* 52:245–252.

Klinger, H. P., J. L. Hamerton, D. Mutton, and E. M. Lang, 1963, "The Chromosomes of the Homonoidea," *Classification and Human Evolution,* S. L. Washburn, ed. Viking Fund Publ. in Anthropology No. 37, New York: Wenner-Gren Foundation, pp. 235–242.

Koford, C., 1963*a*, "Group Relations in an Island Colony of Rhesus Monkeys," *Primate Social Behavior,* C. H. Southwick, ed. Princeton, N.J.: Van Nostrand, pp. 136–152.

————, 1963*b*, "Rank of Mothers and Sons in Bands of Rhesus Monkeys," *Science,* 141:356–357.

————, 1966, "Population Changes in Rhesus Monkeys, 1960–1965," *Tul. Studies in Zool.,* 13:1–7.

Köhler, W., 1925, *The Mentality of Apes.* New York: Harcourt.

Kohts, N., 1935, "Infant Ape and Human Child (Instincts, Emotions, Play, Habits)," *Sci. Mem. Mus. Darwinianum,* 3:586.

————, (in press), "Socio–Sexual Signals and Their Imitation Among Primates," *Primate Ethology,* D. Morris, ed.

Konishi, M., 1963, "The Role of Auditory Feedback in the Vocal Behavior in the Domestic Fowl," *Zeits. f. Tierpsychol.,* 20:349–367.

Kortlandt, A., 1962, "Observing Chimpanzees in the Wild," *Sci. Amer.,* 206(5):128–138.

————, and M. Kooij, 1963, "Protohominid Behaviour in Primates," *Symp. Zool. Soc. London,* 10:61–88.

Kourilsky, R., A. Soulairac, and P. Grapin, 1965, *Adaptation et Agressivité.* Paris: Presses Universitaires de France.

Kummer, H., 1957, "Soziales Verhalten einer Mantelpavian-Gruppe," *Schweiz-Zeits. Psychol.,* 33:91 pp.

————, 1967, "Tripartite Relations in Hamadryas Baboons," *Social Communication Among Primates,* S. A. Altmann, ed. Chicago: University of Chicago Press, pp. 63–71.

————, (in press), *Social Organization of Hamadryas Baboons: A Field Study.*

————, (in press), "Two Basic Variations in the Social Organization of the Genus *Papio.*"

————, and F. Kurt, 1963, "Social Units of a Free-living Population of Hamadryas Baboons," *Folia Primat.,* 1:4–19.

————, and ————, 1965, "A Comparison of Social Behavior in Captive and Wild Hamadryas Baboons," *The Baboon in Medical Research,* H. Vagtborg, ed. Austin: University of Texas Press, pp. 65–80.

Lack, D., 1943, *The Life of the Robin,* London: H. F. and G. Witherby, Ltd.

Lancaster, J. B., (n.d.) "The Evolution of Tool-Using Behavior: Primate Field Studies, Fossil Apes and the Archeological Record."

————, and R. Lee, 1965, "The Annual Reproductive Cycle in Monkeys and Apes," *Primate Behavior: Field Studies of Monkeys and Apes,* I. DeVore, ed. New York: Holt, Rinehart and Winston, Inc., pp. 486–513.

Leakey, L. S. B., 1967, "An Early Miocene Member of the Hominidae," *Nature,* 213:155–163.

Leakey, M. D., 1966, "A Review of the Oldowan Culture From Olduvai Gorge, Tanzania," *Nature,* 210:462–466.

Lee, R. B., 1965, "Subsistence Ecology of Kung Bushman," unpublished Ph.D. thesis, University of California.

Leuba, C., 1955, "Toward Some Integration of Learning Theories: The Concept of Optimal Stimulation," *Psychol. Rep.,* 1:27–33.

Levine, S., and R. F. Mullins, Jr., 1966, "Hormonal Influences on Brain Organization in Infant Rats," *Science,* 152:1585–1592.

Lewin, K., 1935, *A Dynamic Theory of Personality: Selected Papers.* New York: McGraw-Hill.

Lorenz, K. Z., 1935, "Der Kumpan in der Umwelt des Vogels," *J. Ornithol.,* 83:137–213, 289–413.

————, 1941, "Vergleichende Bewegungsstudien an Anatiden," *J. Ornithol.,* 89:194–293.

————, 1961, "Phylogenetische Anpassung und Adaptive Modifikation des Verhaltens," *Zeits. f. Tierpsychol.,* 18:139–187.

————, 1964, "Ritualized Fighting," *The Natural History of Aggression,* J. D. Carthy and F. J. Ebling, eds. New York: Academic Press, pp. 39–50.

————, 1965, *Evolution and Modification of Behavior.* Chicago: University of Chicago Press.

————, 1966, *On Aggression.* New York: Harcourt.

Lundholm, B. G., 1950, "Mammals Collected During the Carp Expedition to S. Rhodesia and Mocambique, 1950," *M. Tvl. Mus.*

MacLean, P. D., 1963, "Phylogenesis," *Expression of the Emotions in Man,* P. Knapp, ed. New York: International Universities,, pp. 16–35.

Marler, P., 1955, "The Characteristics of Some Animal Calls," *Nature,* 176:6–8.

————, 1965, "Communication in Monkeys and Apes," *Primate Behavior: Field Studies of Monkeys and Apes,* I. DeVore, ed. New York: Holt, Rineheart and Winston, Inc., pp. 544–584.

Mason, W. A., 1960*a,* "Socially Mediated Reduction in Emotional Responses of Young Rhesus Monkeys," *J. Abnorm. Soc. Psychol.,* 60:100–104.

————, 1960*b,* "The Effects of Social Restriction on the Behavior of Rhesus Monkeys: I. Free Social Behavior," *J. Comp. Physiol. Psychol.,* 53:582–589.

————, 1961*a,* "The Effects of Social Restriction on the Behavior of Rhesus Monkeys: II. Tests of Gregariousness," *J. Comp. Physiol. Psychol.,* 54:287–290.

————, 1961*b,* "Effects of Age and Stimulus Characteristics on Manipulatory Responsiveness of Monkeys Raised in a Restricted Environment," *J. Genet. Psychol.,* 99:301–308.

————, 1961*c,* "The Effects of Social Restriction on the Behavior of Rhesus Monkeys; III. Dominance Tests," *J. Comp. Physiol. Psychol.,* 54:694–699.

————, 1963, "Social Development of Rhesus Monkeys with Restricted Social Experience," *Percept. Mot. Skills,* 16:263–270.

————, 1964, "Sociability and Social Organization in Monkeys and Apes," *Recent Advances in Experimental Psychology,* L. Berkowitz, ed. 1:277–305.

————, 1965, "Determinants of Social Behavior in Young Chimpanzees," *Behavior of Nonhuman Primates,* Vol. II, A. M. Schrier, H. F. Harlow, and F. Stollnitz, eds. New York: Academic Press, pp. 335–364.

————, 1966, "Social Organization of the South American Monkey, *Callicebus mollock:* A Preliminary Report," *Tul. Studies in Zool.,* 13:23–28.

————, and P. C. Green, 1962, "The Effects of Social Restriction on the Behavior of Rhesus Monkeys: IV. Repsonses to a Novel Environment and to an Alien Species," *J. Comp. physiol. Psychol.,* 55:363–368.

Mayr, E., 1963, *Animal Species and Evolution.* Cambridge, Mass.: Harvard University Press.

McGill, T. E., ed., 1965, *Readings in Animal Behavior.* New York: Holt, Rinehart and Winston, Inc.

Meester, J., D. H. S. Davis, and C. G. Cootsee, 1964, "An Interim Classification of Southern African Mammals," duplicated report.

Menzel, E. W. Jr., 1964, "Patterns of Responsiveness in Chimpanzees Reared through Infancy under Conditions of Environmental Restriction," *Psychol. Forsch.,* 27:337–365.

————, 1966, "Responsiveness to Objects in Free-ranging Japanese Monkeys," *Behaviour,* 26:130–150.

Michael, R. P., and J. Herbert, 1963, "Menstrual Cycle Influences Grooming Behavior and Sexual Activity in Rhesus Monkey," *Science,* 140:500–501.

Miller, R. E., J. V. Murphy, and I. A. Mirsky, 1959, "Relevance of Facial Expression and Posture as Cues in Communication of Affect between Monkeys," *Arch. Gen. Psychiat.,* 1:480–488.

Miller, W., and S. Ervin, 1964, "The Development of Grammar in Child Language," *Monog. Soc. Res. Child Devel.,* 29:9–33.

Miminoshvili, D. I., G. O. Magakian, and G. I. Kokaia, 1960, "Attempts to obtain a Model of Hypertension and Coronary Insufficiency in Monkeys," *Theoretical and Practical Problems of Medicine and Biology in Experiments on Monkeys,* I. A. Utkin, ed. New York: Pergamon Press, pp. 103–121.

Mirsky, I. A., R. E. Miller, and J. V. Murphy, 1958, "The Communication of Affect in Rhesus Monkeys," *J. Amer. Psychoanal. Assoc.,* 6:433–441.

Miyadi, D., 1964, "Social Life of Japanese Monkeys," *Science,* 143:783–786.

Monod, T., 1963, "The Late Tertiary and Pleistocene in the Sahara and Adjacent Southerly Regions, with Implications for Primate and Human Distributions," *African Ecology and Human Evolution,* F. C. Howell, and F. Bourlière, eds. New York: Viking Fund Pub. in Anthropology No. 36, pp. 117–229.

Mowrer, O. H., 1960, *Learning Theory and the Symbolic Process.* New York: Wiley.

Murphy, J. V., R. E. Miller, and I. A. Mirsky, 1955, "Interanimal Conditioning in the Monkey," *J. Comp. physiol. Psychol.,* 48:211–214.

Nalbandov, A. V., 1964, *Reproductive Physiology.* San Francisco: W. H. Freeman.

Nice, M. M., 1933, "The Theory of Territorialism and Its Development," *Fifty Years Progress of American Ornithology,* Lancaster, Pa: A.O.U. 89–100.

————, 1941, "The Role of Territory in Bird Life," *Am. Midland Naturalist,* 26:441–487.

Nicolai, J., 1956, "Zur Biologie und Ethologie des Gimpels (*Pyrrhula pyrrhula L.*)," *Zeits. f. Tierpsychol.,* 13:93–132.

————, 1959, "Familientradition in der Gesangsentwicklung des Gimpels (*Pyrrhula pyrrhula L.*)," *J. f. Ornithol.,* 100:39–46.

Noback, C. R., and N. Moskowitz, 1963, "The Primate Nervous System: Functional and Structural Aspects in Phylogeny," *Evolutionary and Genetic Biology of Primates* Vol. I, J. Buettner-Janusch, ed. New York: Academic Press, pp. 131–177.

Noble, G. K., 1939, "The Role of Dominance in the Social Life of Birds," *The Auk,* 56:263–273.

Oakley, K. P., 1954, "Skill as a Human Possession," *A History of Technolgy,* Vol. I, C. Singer, E. J. Holmyard, and A. R. Hall, eds. Oxford: Clarendon Press, pp. 1–37.

Odum, E. P., and E. J. Kuenzler, 1955, "Measurement of Territory and Home Range Size in Birds," *The Auk,* 72:128–137.

Osborn, R., 1963, "Observations on the Behaviour of the Mountain Gorilla," *Symp. Zool. Soc. London,* 10: 29–37.

Penfield, W., and L. Roberts, 1959, *Speech and Brain Mechanisms.* Princeton, N.J.: Princeton University Press.

Petter, J., 1965, "The Lemurs of Madagascar," *Primate Behavior: Field Studies of Monkeys and Apes,* I. DeVore, ed. New York: Holt, Rinehart and Winston, Inc., pp. 292–319.

Pitman, C. R. S., 1954, "The Influence of the Belgian Congo on the Distribution of Uganda's Primates and Some of Their Characteristics," *Ann. Mus. Congo.* Tervuren in -4⁰, *Zool.,* 1.

Prechtl, H. F. R., 1965, "Problems of Behavioral Studies in the Newborn Infant," *Advances in the Study of Behavior,* D. S. Lehrman, R. A. Hinde, and E. Shaw, eds. New York: Academic Press, pp. 75–98.

Puri, G. C., 1960, *Indian Forest Ecology.* New Delhi: Oxford Book.

Rapoport, A., 1966, "Models of Conflict: Cataclysmic and Strategic," *Conflict in Society,* A. de Reuck and J. Knight, eds. Boston: Little, Brown, pp. 259–287.

Reynolds, V., 1965, "Some Behavioral Comparisons Between the Chimpanzee and the Mountain Gorilla in the Wild," *Amer. Anthrop.,* 67:691–706.

————, and F. Reynolds, 1965, "Chimpanzees in the Budongo Forest, *Primate Behavior: Field Studies of Monkey sand Apes,* I. DeVore, ed. New York: Holt, Rinehart and Winston, Inc., pp. 368–424.

Richards, P. W., 1952, *The Tropical Rain Forest: An Ecological Study.* Chicago: University of Chicago Press.

Ripley, S., 1965, "The Ecology and Social Behavior of the Ceylon Gray Langur," unpublished Ph.D. thesis, University of California.

Robinson, J. T., 1963, "Adaptive Radiation in the Australopithecines and the Origin of Man," *African Ecology and Human Evolution,* F. C. Howell and F. Bourlière, eds. New York: Viking Fund Pub. in Anthrop. No. 36, pp. 385–416.

Rosenblum, L. A., 1961, "The Development of Social Behavior in the Rhesus Monkey," unpublished doctoral thesis, University of Wisconsin.

————, I. C. Kaufman, and A. J. Stynes, 1964, "Individual Distance in Two Species of Macaque," *Anim. Behav.,* 12:338–342.

Rowell, T. E., 1962, "Agonistic Noises of the Rhesus Monkey (Macaca mulatta)," *Symp. Zool. Soc. London,* 8:91–96.

———, 1963, "Behaviour and Female Reproductive Cycles of Rhesus Macaques," *J. Reprod. Fertil.,* 6:193–203.

———, 1966, "Forest Living Baboons in Uganda," *J. Zool. London,* 149:344–364.

———, and R. A. Hinde, 1962, "Vocal Communication by the Rhesus Monkey (*Macaca mulatta*)," *Proc. Zool. Soc. London,* 138:279–294.

———, and ———, 1963, "Responses of Rhesus Monkeys to Mildly Stressful Situations," *Anim. Behav.,* 11:235–243.

———, ———, and Y. Spencer Booth, 1964, "Aunt–Infant Interaction in Captive Rhesus Monkeys," *Anim. Behav.,* 12:219–226.

Sackett, G. P., 1965, "Response of Rhesus Monkeys to Social Stimulation Presented by Means of Colored Slides," *Percept. Mot. Skills,* 20:1027–1028.

Sade, D. S., 1965, "Some Aspects of Parent-Offspring and Sibling Relations in a Group of Rhesus Monkeys, with a Discussion of Grooming," *Amer. J. Phys. Anthrop.,* 23:1–17.

———, 1966, "Ontogeny of Social Relations in a Free-ranging Group of Rhesus Monkeys," unpublished Ph.D. thesis, University of California, Berkeley.

Sarich, V. M., and A. C. Wilson, 1967, "Quantitative Immunochemistry and the Evolution of Primate Albumins: Microcomplement Fixation," *Science,* 154:1561–5.

Sauer, F., 1954, "Die Entwicklung der LautäuBerungen vom Ei ab schalldicht gehaltener Dorngrasmücken (*Sylvia c. communis* Latham) im Vergleich mit später isolierten und mit wildlekenden Artgenossen," *Zeits. f. Tierpschol.,* 11:10–93.

Schaller, G. B., 1961, "The Orangutan in Sarawak," *Zoologica,* 46(2):73–82.

———, 1963, *The Mountain Gorilla: Ecology and Behavior.* Chicago: University of Chicago Press.

———, 1964, *The Year of the Gorilla.* Chicago: University of Chicago Press.

———, 1965, "The Behavior of the Mountain Gorilla," *Primate Behavior: Field Studies of Monkeys and Apes,* I. DeVore, ed. New York: Holt, Rinehart and Winston, Inc., pp. 324–367.

Schein, M. W., and E. B. Hale, 1965, "The Effect of Early Social Experience on Male Sexual Behaviour of Androgen Injected Turkeys," *Readings in Animal Behavior,* T. E. McGill, ed. New York: Holt, Rinehart and Winston, Inc., pp. 314–329.

Schiller, P. H., 1957, "Innate Motor Action as a Basis of Learning," *Instinctive Behavior,* C. H. Schiller, ed. New York: International Universities Press, pp. 264–287.

Schneirla, T. C., 1946, "Problems in the Biopsychology of Social Organization," *J. Abnorm. Soc. Psychol.,* 41:385–402.

———, 1952, "A Consideration of Some Conceptual Trends in Comparative Psychology," *Psychol. Bull.,* 49:559–597.

Schutz, F., 1965, "Sexuelle Prägung bei Anatiden," *Zeits. f. Tierpsychol.,* 22:50–102.

Scott, J. P., 1958, *Aggression.* Chicago: University of Chicago Press.

———, 1962, "Hostility and Aggression in Animals," *Roots of Behavior,* E. L. Bliss, ed. New York: Harper, pp. 167–178.

Seay, B., 1966, "Maternal Behavior in Primiparous and Multiparous Rhesus Monkeys," *Folia Primat.,* 4:146–168.

Shigeru, A., and A. Toyoshima, 1961–1962, "Progress Report of the Survey of Chimpanzees in Their Natural Habitat, Kabongo Point Area, Tanganyika," *Primates,* 3(2):61–70.

Sidman, M., 1960, *Tactics of Scientific Research.* New York: Basic Books.

Simonds, P. E., 1965, "The Bonnet Macaque in South India," *Primate Behavior: Field Studies of Monkeys and Apes,* I. DeVore, ed. New York: Holt, Rinehart and Winston, Inc., pp. 175–196.

Simons, E. L., 1964, "The Early Relatives of Man," *Sci Amer.,* 211(1):50–62.

——, 1965, "New Fossil Apes from Egypt and the Initial Differentiation of the Homnoidea," *Nature,* 205:136–139.

Simpson, G. G., 1964, *This View of Life,* New York: Harcourt.

——, 1966, "The Biological Nature of Man," *Science,* 152:472–478.

Slobin, D., 1965, "Language and Communication," paper presented at the Wenner-Gren Conference on *The Origin of Man,* April 2–4, 1965, University of Chicago.

Slobodkin, L. B., 1961, *Growth and Regulation of Animal Populations.* New York: Holt, Rinehart and Winston, Inc.

Smith, W. J., 1965, "Message, Meaning and Content in Ethology," *Amer. Nat.,* 99:405–409.

——, and E. B. Hale, 1959, "Modification of Social Rank in the Domestic Fowl," *J. Comp. physiol. Psychol.,* 52:373–375.

Southwick, C. H., 1962, "Patterns of Intergroup Social Behavior in Primates, with Special Reference to Rhesus and Howling Monkeys," *Ann. N. Y. Acad. Sci.,* 102:436–454.

——, M. A. Beg, and M. R. Siddiqi, 1965, "Rhesus Monkeys in North India," *Primate Behavior: Field Studies of Monkeys and Apes,* I. DeVore, ed., New York: Holt, Rinehart and Winston, Inc., pp. 111–159.

Starck, D., and H. Frick, 1958, "Beobachtungen an äthiopischen Primaten," *Zool. Jahr.,* 86:41–70.

Struhsaker, T., 1967a, "Auditory Communications among Vervet Monkeys (*Cercopithecus aethiops*)," *Social Communication Among Primates,* S. A. Altmann, ed., Chicago: University of Chicago Press, pp. 281–324.

——, 1967b, "Behavior of Vervet Monkeys (*Cercopithecus aethiops*)," Univ. Calif. Publ. Zool. 82:1–74.

——, 1967c, "Social Structure among Vervet Monkeys (*Cercopithecus aethiops*)," *Behaviour,* 29:6–121.

——, 1967d, "Behavior of Vervet Monkeys and Other Cercopithecines," *Science* 156:1197–1203.

——, in press, "Ecology of Vervet Monkeys (*Cercopithecus aethiops*) in the Masai-Amboseli Game Reserve, Kenya," *Ecology.*

Sugiyama, Y., 1964, "Group Composition, Population Density, and Some Sociological Observations of Hanuman Langurs (*Presbytis entellus*)," *Primates,* 5(3-4):7–38.

——, 1965, "Behavioral Development and Social Structure in the Two Troops of Hanuman Langurs (*Presbytis entellus*)," *Primates,* 6(2):213–247.

——, K. Yoshiba, and M. D. Parthasarathy, 1965, "Home Range, Mating Season, Male Group, and Intertroop Relations in Hanuman Langurs (*Presbytis entellus*)," *Primates,* 6(1):73–106.

Takeda, R., 1961, "Development of Vocal Communication during Babyhood of Japanese Monkeys," *Primates,* 3(1):76–77.

Tappen, N. C., 1960, "Problems of Distribution and Adaptation of the African Monkeys," *Cur. Anthrop.,* 1(2):91–120.

Thorpe, W. H., 1958*a,* "Further Studies on the Process of Song-learning in the Chaffinch (*Fringilla coelebs gengleri*)," *Nature,* 182:554–557.

———, 1958*b,* "The Learning of Song Patterns by Birds, with Special Reference to the Song of the Chaffinch, *Fringilla coelebs,*" *Ibis,* 100:535–570.

———, 1963, "Antiphonal Singing in Birds as Evidence for Avian Auditory Reaction Time," *Nature,* 197:774-776.

Tinbergen, N., 1951, *The Study of Instinct.* London: Clarendon Press.

———, 1959, "Comparative Studies of the Behaviour of Gulls (Laridae): A Progress Report," *Behaviour,* 15:1–70.

Tokuda, K., 1961–1962, "A Study on the Sexual Behavior in the Japanese Monkey Troop," *Primates,* 3(2):1–40.

Ullrich, W., 1961, "Zur Biologie und Soziologie der Colobusaffen (*Colobus guereza caudasus* Thomas 1885)," *Der Zool. Garten,* 25(6):305–368.

Underwood, B. J., 1957, *Psychological Research.* New York: Appleton-Century-Crofts.

van Hooff, J. A. R. A. M., 1962, "Facial Expressions in Higher Primates," *Symp. Zool. Soc. London,* 8:97–125.

Van Lawick-Goodall, J., 1966, *Chimpanzee Social Behavior,* unpublished Ph.D. Thesis, University library, Cambridge England.

Van Lawick-Goodall, J. (in press), "Mother–Offspring Relationships in Free-ranging Chimpanzees," *Primate Ethology,* Desmond Morris, ed.

Washburn, S. L., 1957, "Ischial Callosities as Sleeping Adaptations," *Amer. J. Phys. Anthrop.,* 15(2):269–276.

———, 1963, "Behavior and Human Evolution," *Classification and Human Evolution,* S. L. Washburn, ed. Viking Fund Pub. in Anthropology No. 37., New York: Wenner-Gren Foundation, pp. 190–203.

———, 1966, "Conflict in Primate Society," *Conflict in Society,* A. de Reuck and J. Knight, eds. Boston: Little, Brown, pp. 3–15.

———, and I. DeVore, 1961*a,* "Social Behavior of Baboons and Early Man," *Social Life of Early Man,* S. L. Washburn, ed. Chicago: Aldine, pp. 91–105.

———, and ———, 1961*b,* "Social Life of Baboons," *Sci. Amer.,* 204:62–71.

———, and D. A. Hamburg, 1965*a,* "The Implications of Primate Research," *Primate Behavior: Field Studies of Monkeys and Apes,* I. DeVore, ed. New York: Holt, Rinehart and Winston, Inc., pp. 607–622.

———, and———, 1965*b,* "The Study of Primate Behavior," *Primate Behavior: Field Studies of Monkeys and Apes,* I. DeVore, ed. New York: Holt, Rinehart and Winston, Inc., pp. 1–13.

———, and P. Jay, 1965, "The Evolution of Human Nature," unpub. paper presented at the Amer. Anthrop. Assoc. Meeting, Denver, Nov. 19, 1965.

———, and ———, (in press) "More on Tool Use in Primates," *Current Anthro.*

———, ———, and J. B. Lancaster, 1965, "Field Studies of Old World Monkeys and Apes," *Science,* 150:1541–1547.

———, and C. S. Lancaster (N.D.), "The Evolution of Hunting."

———, and J. Shirek (in press), "Human Evolution," *Behavior Genetics,* E. W. Caspari, ed.

Weir, R. H., 1962, *Language in the Crib.* The Hague: Mouton.

Wickler, W., 1960, "Belegexemplare zu Ethogrammen," *Zeits, f. Tierpsychol.,* 17:141–142.

———, 1961, "Okologie und Stammesgeschichte von Verhaltensweisen," *Fortschr. der Zool.,* 13:303–365.

———, 1965, "Die äuseren Genitalien als soziale Signale bei einigen Primaten," *Die Naturwissenschaften,* 52:269–270.

———, 1966, "Ursprung und biologische Deutung des Genitalpräsentierens männlicher Primaten," *Zeits. f. Tierpsychol.,* 23:422–437.

Wynne-Edwards, V. C., 1962, *Animal Dispersion in Relation to Social Behavior.* New York: Hafner.

———, 1965, "Selfregulating Systems in Poulations of Animals," *Science,* 147:1543–1548.

Yamada, M., 1957, "A Case of Acculturation in a Subhuman Society of Japanese Monkeys," *Primates,* 1(1):30–46.

———, 1963, "A Study of Blood-Relationship in the Natural Society of the Japanese Macaque," *Primates,* 4:43–65.

Yerkes, R. M., 1943, *Chimpanzees: A Laboratory Colony.* New Haven: Yale University Press.

———, and A. W. Yerkes, 1929, *The Great Apes.* New Haven: Yale University Press.

Yoshiba, K. (in press), "A Case of New Troop Formation and Social Organization in Hanuman Langurs," *Primates,* 7(3).

Young, W., R. Goy, and C. Phoenix, 1964, "Hormones and Sexual Behavior," *Science,* 143:212–218.

Zhinkin, N. I., 1963, "An Application of the Theory of Algorithms to the Study of Animal Speech: Methods of Vocal Intercommunication between Monkeys," *Acoustic Behavior of Animals,* R. G. Busnel, ed. Amsterdam: Elsevier, pp. 132–180.

Zuckerman, S., 1932, *The Social Life of Monkeys and Apes.* London: Routledge and Kegan Paul.

Name Index

Allee, W. C., 182
Altman, J., 447, 460
Altmann, S. A., 8, 9, 11, 17, 125, 126, 155, 181, 183, 209, 293, 297, 301, 303, 310, 332, 342, 405, 406, 409, 410, 412, 421, 422, 425, 427, 428, 430, 431, 432, 433, 434, 435, 436, 437, 441, 442, 453, 500
Andrew, R. J., 11, 322, 334, 407, 431, 441, 445, 453
Asami, C., 244
Ascher, R., 453
Azrin, N. H., 399

Baerends, G. P., 482
Bailey, P., 450
Ball, J., 406
Bandura, A., 384
Bastian, J. R., 446
Beach, F. A., 402, 407, 437, 461
Beatty, H., 142
Beeman, E. A., 465
Beg, M. A., 421
Bellugi, U., 454, 455
Bere, R. M., 48
Berkson, G., 330
Berlyne, D. E., 396
Bernstein, I. S., 11, 61, 209, 406, 407, 411
Bierens de Haan, J. A., 143
Bigourdan, J., 38, 48, 77
Bingham, H. C., 7, 11
Birch, H. G., 143
Bishop, A., 40
Bishop, W. W., 261
Boelkins, R. C., 11, 12, 80, 150, 157, 421, 425
Bolwig, N., 9, 11, 101, 143, 151, 441
Bonin, G. von, 450
Booth, A. H., 9, 21, 34, 35, 74
Booth, C., 11
Boulenger, E. G., 136
Bourlière, F., 9, 11, 25
Bowman, R. I., 140
Brain, C. K., 253–292, 421, 422, 424, 425, 469, 471, 473, 491
Braine, M. D. S., 454
Brehm, A. E., 136
Brown, J. L., 467, 474
Brown, R., 454, 455
Buettner-Janusch, J., 37
Burt, W. H., 182, 201
Butler, R. A., 407

Calhoun, J. B., 124
Carpenter, C. R., 7, 8, 9, 11, 12, 25, 125, 134, 135, 136, 159, 180, 181, 184, 194, 209, 213, 214, 216, 329, 331, 394, 401, 404, 406, 408, 410, 413, 421, 422, 427, 430, 433, 435, 470, 497
Carthy, J. D., 463
Chance, M. R. A., 11, 430, 499
Chisholm, A. H., 133
Clark, P. J., 420
Collias, N. E., 9, 183, 446, 464, 465
Cooper, L. R., 138
Corner, G. W., 459
Crawford, M. P., 399
Crook, J. H., 259, 281
Crosby, E. C., 450, 452

Dandelot, P., 254
Dart, R. A., 151, 161
Dekeyser, P. L., 35, 38, 39, 40
Delgado, J. M. R., 404, 461, 466
Delgado, R. R., 404
de Reuck, A., 459
De Vore, I., 8, 10, 12, 13, 14, 16, 17, 18, 19, 22, 23, 25, 27, 33, 39, 48, 49, 58, 67, 69, 81, 101, 104, 106, 113, 116, 120, 121, 123, 125, 127, 134, 143, 150, 151, 152, 153, 154, 155, 160, 173, 176, 177, 201, 209, 223, 287, 293, 301, 303, 308, 309, 329, 330, 331, 332, 350, 357, 360, 374, 377, 411, 421, 425, 433, 435, 438, 440, 441, 442, 445, 469, 471, 473, 482, 490, 492, 497
Duerden, J. E., 134

Ebling, F. J., 463
Eibl-Eibesfeldt, I., 381, 479–486
Ellefson, J. O., 180–199, 216, 421, 422, 424, 425, 427, 469, 471
Emlen, J. T., 407
Ervin, S., 454
Etkin, W., 384
Ettlinger, G., 451
Evans, F. C., 420

Falk, J. L., 437
Fisher, E. M., 141
Flechsig, P., 447, 448, 449, 453
Fleischer, R. L., 498
Fletcher, J. J., 407
Frank, L. K., 352, 360, 371
Fraser, C., 454

521

Subject Index

HIGH SCHOOL MUSICAL

ISBN 978-1-4234-5752-7

Walt Disney Music Company

DISTRIBUTED BY

HAL•LEONARD®
CORPORATION

7777 W. BLUEMOUND RD. P.O. BOX 13819 MILWAUKEE, WI 53213

In Australia Contact:
Hal Leonard Australia Pty. Ltd.
4 Lentara Court
Cheltenham, Victoria, 3192 Australia
Email: ausadmin@halleonard.com.au

Visit Hal Leonard Online at
www.halleonard.com

CONTENTS

NOW OR NEVER

Words and Music by MATTHEW GERRARD
and ROBBIE NEVIL

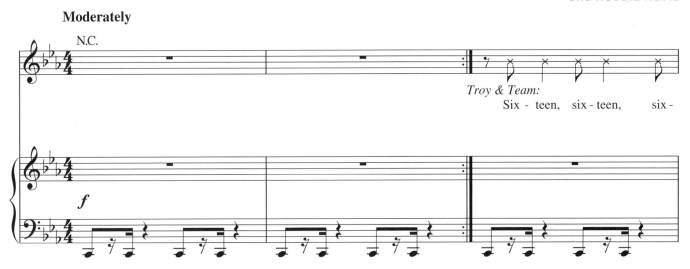

Yeah! Hey. We're the best. Gon-na win.

Troy: Got-ta show'em how we do it. (Game on!) All:

Cm   Cm/B♭

Troy: This is the last __ time to get it right. This is the last __ chance to make it our night.

Am7♭5   A♭   B♭(add4)

We got-ta show __ what we're all a - bout, work __ to - geth - er.

RIGHT HERE RIGHT NOW

Words and Music by
JAMIE HOUSTON

Troy: Can you i - mag - ine what would hap - pen if we could have an - y dream?

I'd wish this mo - ment was ours to own _ it, and that it would nev - er leave. Then I would thank _

I WANT IT ALL

Words and Music by MATTHEW GERRARD
and ROBBIE NEVIL

Sharpay: I -
mag-ine hav-ing ev-'ry-thing we ev-er dreamed. Don't you want it? May-be. Can't you see

Ryan: *Sharpay:*

Recorded a half step lower.

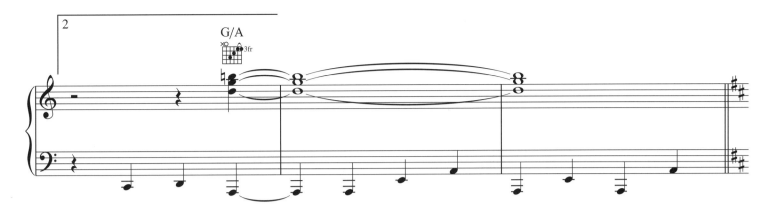

Tempo I

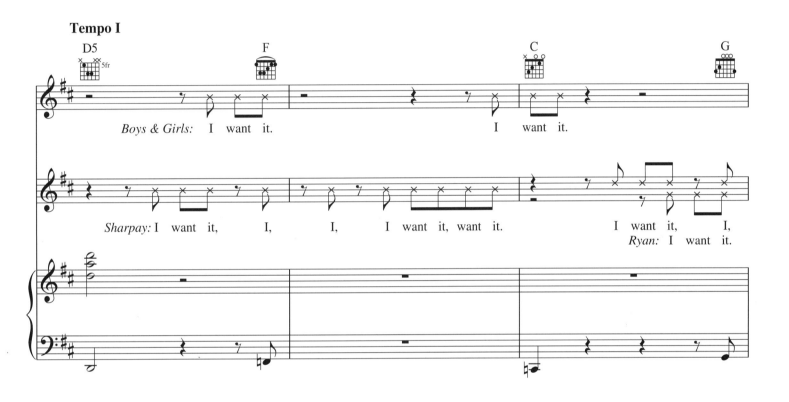

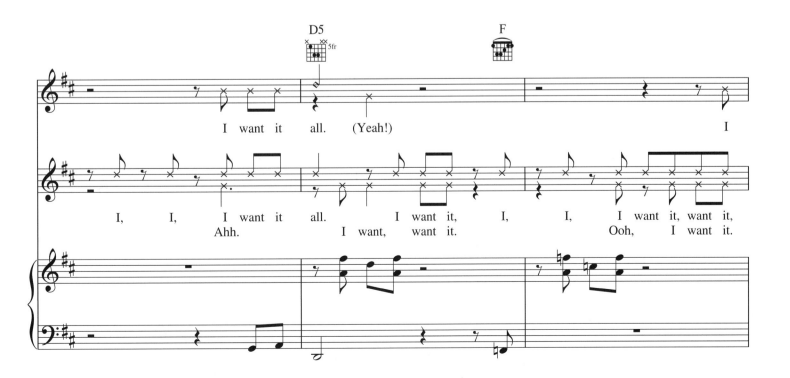

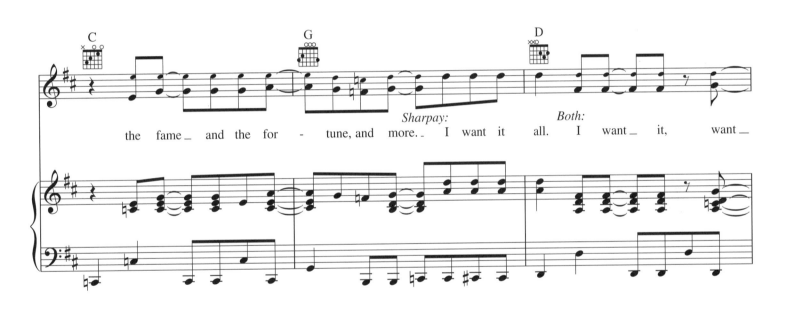

CAN I HAVE THIS DANCE

Words and Music by ADAM ANDERS
and NIKKI HASSMAN

JUST WANNA BE WITH YOU

Words and Music by ANDY DODD
and ADAM WATTS

A NIGHT TO REMEMBER

Words and Music by MATTHEW GERRARD
and ROBBIE NEVIL

THE BOYS ARE BACK

Words and Music by MATTHEW GERRARD
and ROBBIE NEVIL

72

The boys   are back.

WALK AWAY

Words and Music by
JAMIE HOUSTON

SCREAM

Words and Music by
JAMIE HOUSTON

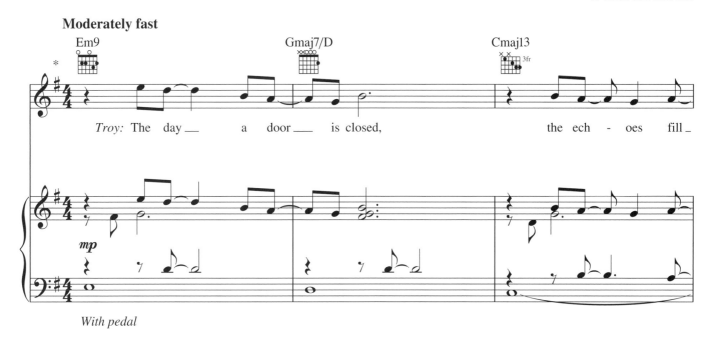

Troy: The day __ a door __ is closed, the ech - oes fill __

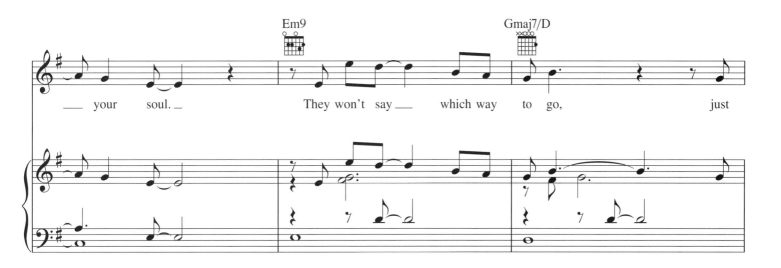

__ your soul. __ They won't say __ which way to go, just

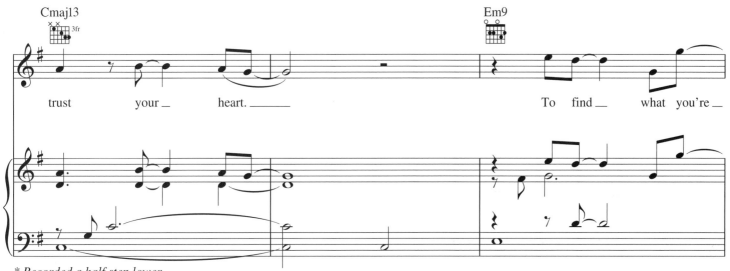

trust your __ heart. __ To find __ what you're __

* Recorded a half step lower.

search - in', search - in', can't find the... (way that I should turn.)

If I _____

_____ should turn, right or left, it's, it's like noth - ing works _____

_____ with - out you. I don't know where to

go! What's the right team? I want my own thing

WE'RE ALL IN THIS TOGETHER
(Graduation Version)

Words and Music by MATTHEW GERRARD
and ROBBIE NEVIL

Females: To-geth - er, to-geth - er,

to-geth - er, ev-'ry - one. To-geth - er, to-geth - er,

come on ___ let's have some fun.

Males: Here and now, it's
Males: We're all here, and

*Recorded a half step lower.

100

HIGH SCHOOL MUSICAL

Words and Music by MATTHEW GERRARD
and ROBBIE NEVIL

Fast Rock

Male: Look- in' for-ward from cen- ter stage to grad-u-a - tion day, time to get____ the fu-ture start - ed.____

G F G C
Both:
- ten it, Male: and now we have a chance to. Female: But some - day we'll be look -
(8vb)
G C G F
D.S. al Coda
Female: Both:
- ing back. Mem - o - ries we'll have of the songs that we lived through.
(8vb)
CODA
F C
Both: Now we fi - nal - ly re -
G D F
- al - ize Female: who we are. It just took some time.

It's the best part we've ev - er known; __ step in - to the fu - ture, __ but hold on to high school mu - si - cal. __ Let's cel - e - brate __ where we __ come from, __ the friends who've been __ there all __ a - long, __ oh yeah. __

1- 866-809-6695

ref#: 15530106

$4.32 (Aluminum)

(0262666346)

$3,000   , 4,000

$ 2013.07

(987.)

31